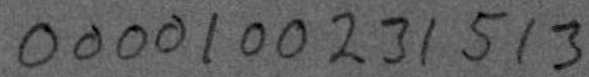

ATLAS OF AMERICAN HISTORY
CSS

ADVISORY COUNCIL

ATLAS OF
AMERICAN HISTORY

ATLAS OF AMERICAN HISTORY

Revised Edition

KENNETH T. JACKSON

EDITOR

JAMES TRUSLOW ADAMS

EDITOR IN CHIEF, ORIGINAL EDITION

CHARLES SCRIBNER'S SONS / NEW YORK

1 3 5 7 9 11 13 15 17 19 V/C 20 18 16 14 12 10 8 6 4 2

PRINTED IN THE UNITED STATES OF AMERICA

Library of Congress Catalog Card Number 77-76851

ISBN 0-684-15052-2

CONTENTS

CONTENTS

VII THE CIVIL WAR AND RECONSTRUCTION / *147*

VIII THE END OF THE FRONTIER / *167*

CONTENTS

INTRODUCTION TO THE REVISED EDITION

JAMES TRUSLOW ADAMS died in 1949, just six years after the *Atlas of American History* first appeared. Although he was noted for many books which achieved both critical and commercial success, Adams took special pride in this volume because of the great care with which it was produced. Coordinating the efforts of many talented individuals, Adams operated on the premise that a map should be easily understandable and should not require a half hour of concentration in order for the information to come across. To this end, he chose a narrow focus for most of the maps and adopted the uncluttered format with which users of this volume have become familiar. Adams' second passion was accuracy, and he was adamant in his insistence that the user see the area exactly as it was during the period under consideration. Thus, no locations appear that were not there at the time.

Because of *Atlas of American History* has earned a well-deserved reputation for scholarship and usefulness, we have retained every map that originally appeared in the first edition. We have, however, added fifty-one maps to the 147 which made up the 1943 volume. The heavy emphasis of that edition was on the frontier—broadly considered. The Atlas was particularly strong on boundary disputes during the colonial period, on battles of the American Revolution and the Civil War, on early routes to the West, and on the American Indian. Only occasionally have we seen fit to add to these distinguished series. For example, we have added maps on Indian Tribal Groups, Indian Wars Before 1690, and Indian reservations, none of which appeared in the first edition. In addition, we have added maps on Commercially Navigable Waterways, Railroad Passenger Lines, and the Interstate Highway System to the earlier coverage of transportation.

Most of the new maps deal with twentieth-century developments or with other subjects that were considered only slightly or not at all by Adams and his co-workers. Under the broad category of human rights, we have added maps on Major Utopian Experiments Before 1860, Universal Male Suffrage, Woman's Suffrage, the Abolition of Slavery, and Major Race Riots. For general economic developments, we have added maps showing Major Industrial Centers Before 1860, Leading Industrial States in 1850 and 1973, Labor Strife, and the contemporary economic development of some of the significant growth states of modern America—Texas, Florida, California, Hawaii, and Alaska. A third of the new maps are essentially demographic in nature; they show sources of immigration, percentage of foreign born by state at various times, black migration to cities, population density in 1970, changes in farm population, the country's largest cities at different periods, and the change in the nation's center of population. We have also introduced a series of maps depicting areas of settlement in 1700, 1800, 1850, and 1890. Finally, whereas none of the maps in the first edition dealt with areas outside the continental United States, we have added maps showing America as a world power and tracing overseas conflicts from the Spanish-American War to the Vietnam War. Less dramatic interventions, as in the case of various Pacific territories, the Panama Canal Zone, and the Caribbean, are also depicted in special maps, as are the locations of contemporary American military installations, both domestic and foreign.

The essentially chronological organization of the maps adopted in the first edition has been retained. We have added a Table of Contents, that was missing from the earlier work, and have revised and expanded the Index.

The cartographic work for the revised edition was done with care and resourcefulness by David Lunn. In addition, I wish to thank Aaron Berman, Amy Helaine Mittleman, and Mark L. Kenchelian, all of Columbia University, for their assistance with research, documentation, and proof-reading. At Charles Scribner's Sons, Hope Hockenberry and Christiane Deschamps became valued co-workers on the enterprise. Finally, Norman Kotker, the editor of Pictorial Books at Scribners, gave himself to this project with great generosity. I am grateful to him for the initial conception of the book, for his precise and imaginative probing of historical materials, for his assistance in solving more than a dozen problems, and for the drive and inspiration which he provided for the *Atlas of American History*.

I accept full responsibility for any errors.

KENNETH T. JACKSON
Columbia University
November, 1977

FOREWORD

DISCOVERY, exploration, frontier posts, settlement, territorial organization, extension of communication—this, repeated time after time, has, to a large degree, been the history of the United States.

Thus, much of our history is concerned with places; and to understand *what* happened, we must also know *where* it happened.

Yet, to locate many places commonly mentioned in our factual histories has heretofore called for reference to scores of widely separated books, atlases or original maps, often difficult of access and seldom at hand when needed, clumsy to handle—and generally not available in the average library.

The preparation and publication of the *Dictionary of American History* pointed the need for a concise, easy to use, carefully thought out, authoritative atlas of American history. The editors and scholars associated with the production of the earlier work accordingly set themselves the task of making an atlas which would present our geographical history as completely and as readily as the *Dictionary of American History* presents our written history.

The plan and scope of the work received long and careful editorial consideration. It was the judgment of the editors that the need was for maps that would interpret our history through the location of places as they actually existed and exactly where they existed at a given time. Graphs, diagrams and other non-exact pictorial interpretations were, in general, to be avoided as having no place in this Atlas.

That the maps should proceed chronologically was obvious. That the areas and periods dealt with in each map should be entities was desirable. That each map should gear in with the preceding and succeeding maps was important. The intent was to so arrange the maps that, as the pages turned, the development of the country would become more clear and take on a new meaning and significance.

The decision as to what places to show on each map was arrived at by a number of approaches. The standard histories and source materials were indexed. Contemporary maps were examined. Partly on the basis of frequency of reference to a place, and partly on the basis of whether a place was sufficiently important historically to be shown, the locations were made on rough drafts—subject to criticism and revisions.

Then the supervision of each map was assigned to an historian or group of historians familiar with the period and area involved. The supervisor added or eliminated or criticized, and thus the map progressed. But no map was finished until it had been considered in connection with the related maps—to the end that each should supplement the other. From the rough drafts—often worn to tatters by revision—the finished drawings were made.

Every map in this work has been drawn in our editorial offices, under the direct supervision of the editors for factual presentation, and of Mr. Appleton for cartographic presentation—and in every case subject to the final approval of the supervisors.

In general the maps are based upon the best and latest government surveys, but with adjustments to earlier maps in case physical changes have occurred, such as rivers cutting new channels or reefs forming where formerly no reefs existed.

Sixty-four historians actively supervised the drawing of the 147 plates which appear in this Atlas. Many others advised and assisted. Thus, the exact location of Fort Ross was directed by Prof. E. O. Essig of the University of California. Stella Drumm, of the Missouri Historical Society, advised regarding locations on the Missouri River. Prof. R. L. Meriwether, of the University of South Carolina, aided in locations relating to Kings Mountain. Painstaking research, sometimes on the ground, went into the location of many places.

To enable the user of the Atlas to find, easily and quickly, the place which he is looking for, a place index has been made a part of the volume. Where was Kaskaskia? Logstown? Fallen Timbers? South Pass? or any one of the hundreds of other historically important places now lost from our maps or buried under a mass of other names? The index carries the reader instantly to the map or maps where these places are shown. There he sees not only the location of the place, but its relation to other historically important places of the same time.

For those who wish to trace a particular subject from period to period and from area to area, the chronological arrangement of the maps, together with the index, will prove helpful. For example, suppose the reader is interested in following the advance of the frontier: Through the Index, and from map to map, he will see the falling back of the Indians, the establishment of trading posts, the growth of settlements, the formation of territories and the organization of states.

An illustration of the importance of geographical knowledge in our history may be found in so well known a story as that of Boone's blazing the trail to Kentucky. Every schoolchild thinks he knows it. But does he know it? Boone started from the Sycamore Shoals of the Watauga. (Only the local historians now know the spot, yet, there, in 1775, was held a great treaty by which the Cherokee Indians ceded to the Transylvania Company the vast territories of Kentucky and part of Tennessee.) Boone went across the Long Island of Holston. (That location is not readily found on present-day maps, yet it was a landmark in the history of the early southwest.) He passed through Moccasin Gap. (This appears only on the most detailed maps.) He went over Clinch River and Powell Mountain to Cumberland Gap and on into Kentucky. Some of these places are shown on several maps in the Atlas, and all are shown with the route indicated on Plate 62. To see not only the route, but its relation to other routes (shown on other maps) coming down from Virginia and up from Carolina enables one to understand the importance of what Boone did, and why he did it when he did it.

The organization and admittance of states is treated as a part of our western development, yet every territory is brought into being in its proper area and proper period and every new state is admitted, with the dates given in each case, and with the changes in area of each territory or state clearly shown.

In the making of this Atlas, as in the making of all works of this sort, the question of where to stop has been a problem. Many more maps could have been made—and there was often the wish to make them. Many places could have been shown which are not shown, and there was often the inclination to show them. The editors can only hope that they have shown, and have shown in their proper relationship, those places having importance in our history in so far as that history had significance in our national development. Strictly local history, if one can say what is local history as differentiated from national history, had to be passed by. That a question may be raised as to why one place is shown and another not, the editors recognize full well and can only say that they have made the best decisions they could.

Throughout, the intent has been to provide a sufficient number of maps to avoid overcrowding any area. Where a relatively congested area has appeared in an otherwise general map, that area has been treated in broad outline on the general map and then given a separate map in which the details are shown without crowding. The test which the editors themselves applied was whether every location could readily be found without resort to guides on the margins of the maps. Accordingly, it is the belief of the editors that the grid (cross-section) method of indexing has properly been omitted.

As our task nears completion, we wish to express our appreciation of the contribution made by the members of the Advisory Council, who have given most generously of their time and knowledge in helping to plan the work as a whole.

To the Supervisors we are deeply indebted not only for advice and criticism in connection with the drawing of their particular maps, but also for their patience and understanding as the work progressed and each map had to be revised time after time in order to bring it into proper relationship with other maps dealing in part with related periods and areas.

We also desire to express special appreciation of the service of LeRoy H. Appleton, the Chief Cartographer, for his skillful and beautiful presentation of the subject matter of each map, either as drawn by his own pen or as a result of his direction of others. The drawing of maps is an art, to an extent not often realized. It is our belief that Mr. Appleton has set a new standard for maps as drawn in America —in their clarity, their balance of letter and line, and their artistic quality.

Back of each map and back of the work as a whole, lies an immense amount of careful, patient work. To those who, through the two years in which the Atlas was being prepared, faithfully worked out the details, we wish to extend our thanks: To Thomas Robson Hay, Associate Editor, for his constant oversight and particularly for his help on the Civil War maps; to Arthur S. Bryant, Assistant Cartographer, whose sure and experienced hand appears in almost every map; to E. Graham Platt, who was associated with the work throughout; to Marion G. Barnes, whose careful checking, from the making of the rough drafts of the maps to the completion of the Index, has saved us from many a possible error.

Finally, as Editor in Chief, I wish to express my personal and deep indebtedness to R. V. Coleman, Managing Editor. Not only has he supervised the entire work and seen that threads did not become tangled in what became an increasingly complex task, but he did much more. His knowledge of American history, not merely in its broad outlines but in its local details in all sections, has been of immense help in enabling us so to plan the maps and their relations to one another that instead of a series of disjointed plates they form an articulated whole which, in its unity, tells the story of the growth of the nation.

It is the earnest hope, as it has been the

constant effort, of all those who have shared in the preparation of this work, that it may prove to be a genuinely useful aid to the better understanding and more correct interpretation of our national story. In scope and plan we have endeavored not only to provide the professional scholar with a new and accurate tool for his research, but also to help the students and readers in high schools, colleges and the home to gain access to that geographical material relating to our history, which is so essential but which hitherto has been difficult or impossible for them to obtain. We can only trust that we have in part, at least, succeeded in accomplishing the task to which we set ourselves.

Feb. 8, 1943

JAMES TRUSLOW ADAMS

ADVISORY COUNCIL

Randolph G. Adams
Director, William L. Clements Library of American History, University of Michigan

Paul M. Angle
Librarian, Illinois State Historical Library

Julian P. Boyd
Librarian, Princeton University

Lloyd Arnold Brown
Librarian, Peabody Institute Library

Solon J. Buck
Director of Publications, The National Archives

Dan E. Clark
Head, Department of History, University of Oregon

E. Merton Coulter
Professor of History, University of Georgia

Douglas Southall Freeman
Editor, The Richmond News Leader; President, Southern Historical Society

LeRoy R. Hafen
Historian and Curator, Colorado State Historical Society

Louise Phelps Kellogg
Research Associate, Wisconsin State Historical Society

Lawrence Martin
Chief, Division of Maps, Library of Congress

Walter Prichard
Head, Department of History, Louisiana State University

Milo M. Quaife
Secretary-Editor, The Burton Historical Collection of the Detroit Public Library

Charles W. Ramsdell
Professor of American History, University of Texas

John K. Wright
Director, American Geographical Society

LeRoy H. Appleton
Cartographer

I AMERICA AT THE TIME OF DISCOVERY

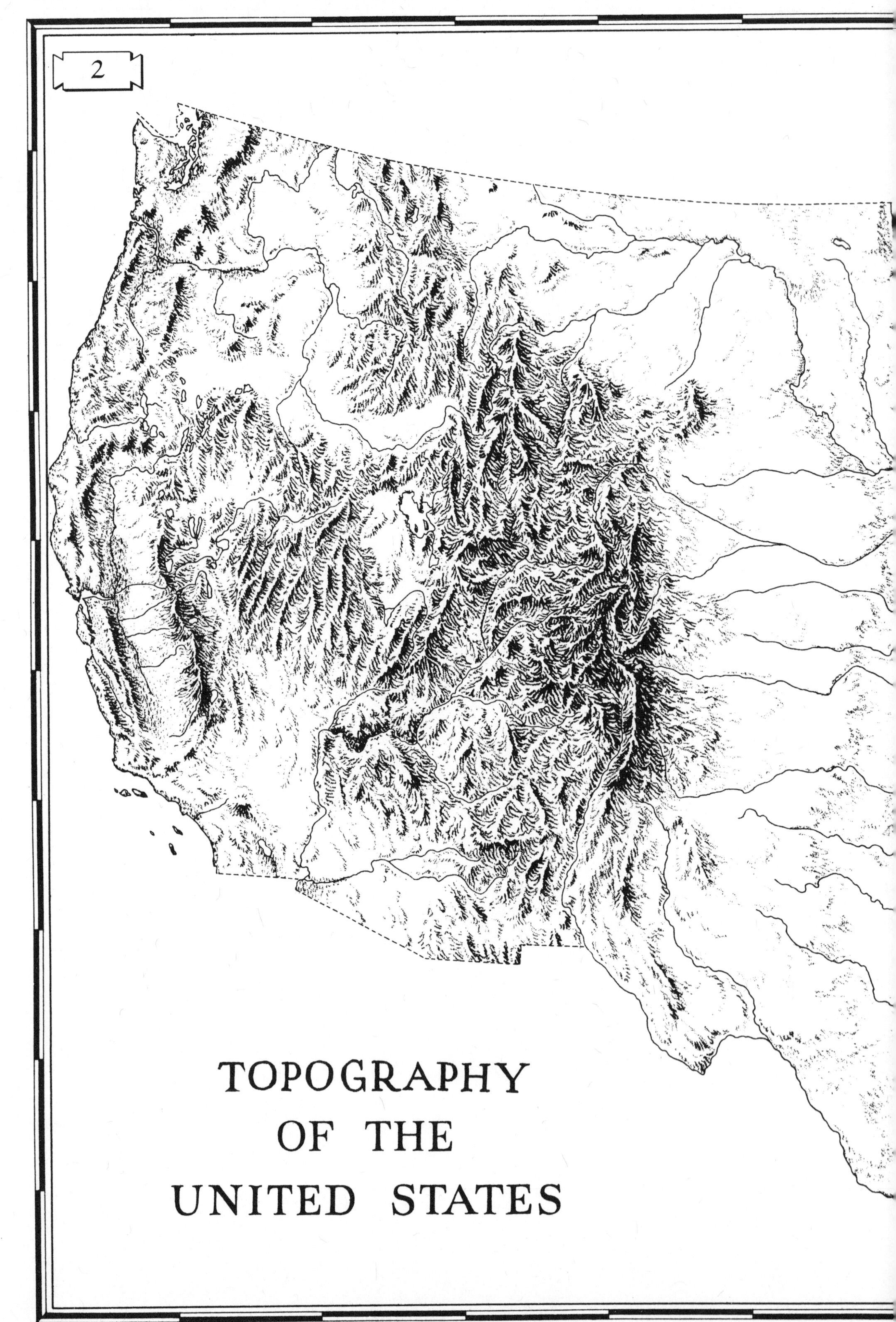
2
TOPOGRAPHY
OF THE
UNITED STATES

Drawn under the supervision of LLOYD A. BROWN

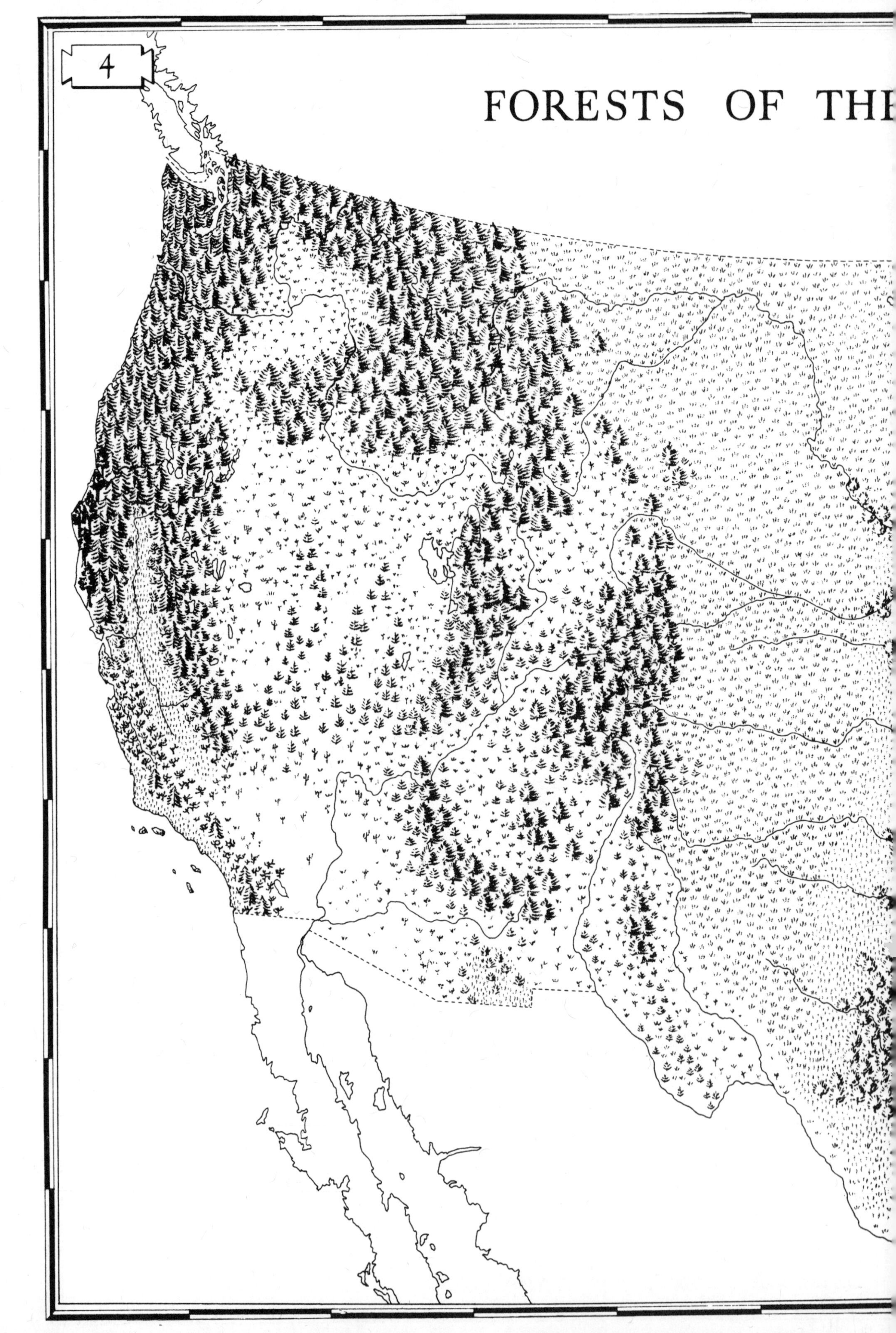

4
FORESTS OF THE

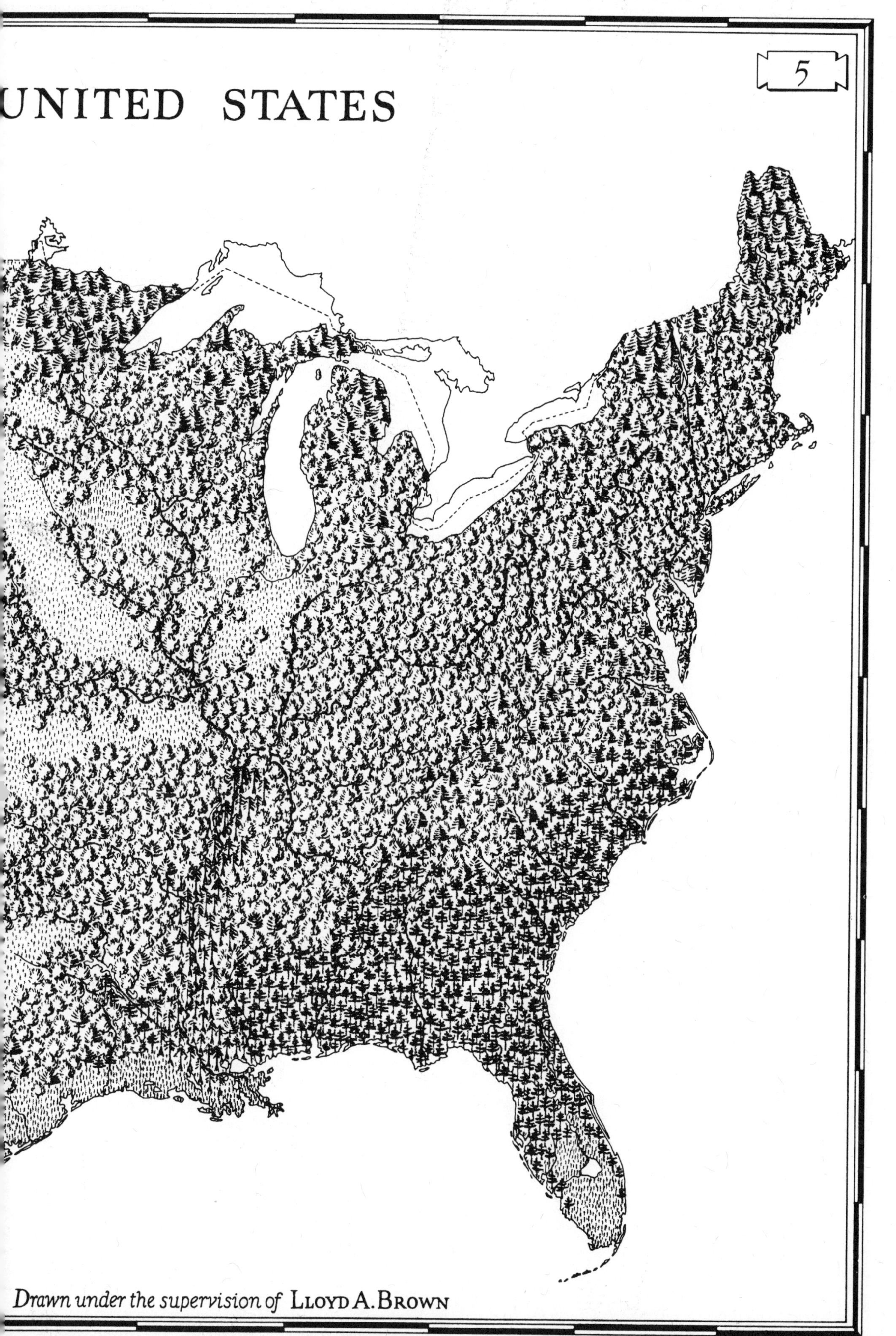
5
UNITED STATES
Drawn under the supervision of LLOYD A. BROWN

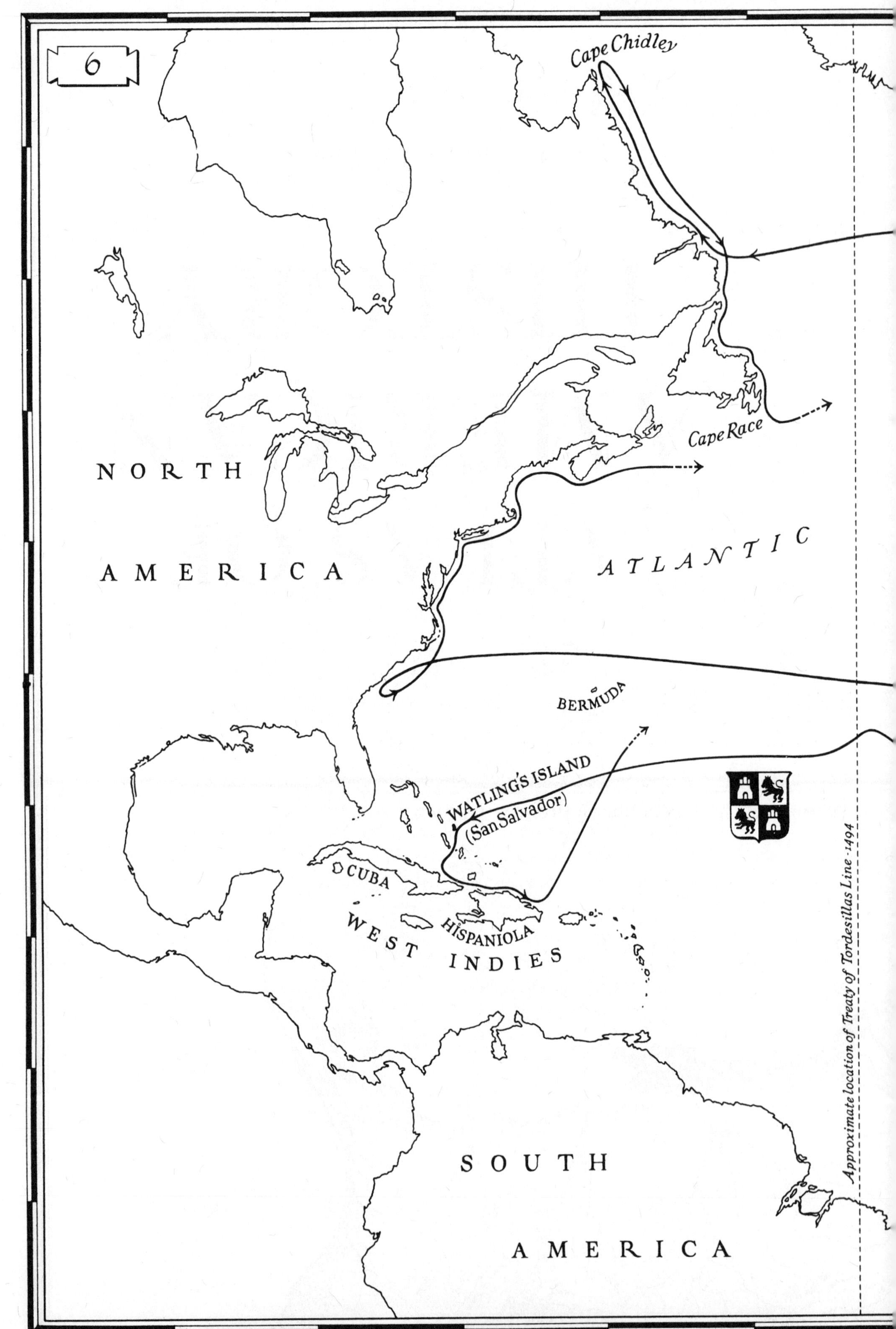
6
Cape Chidley
Cape Race
NORTH
AMERICA
ATLANTIC
BERMUDA
WATLING'S ISLAND
(San Salvador)
CUBA
HISPANIOLA
WEST INDIES
SOUTH
AMERICA
Approximate location of Treaty of Tordesillas Line · 1494

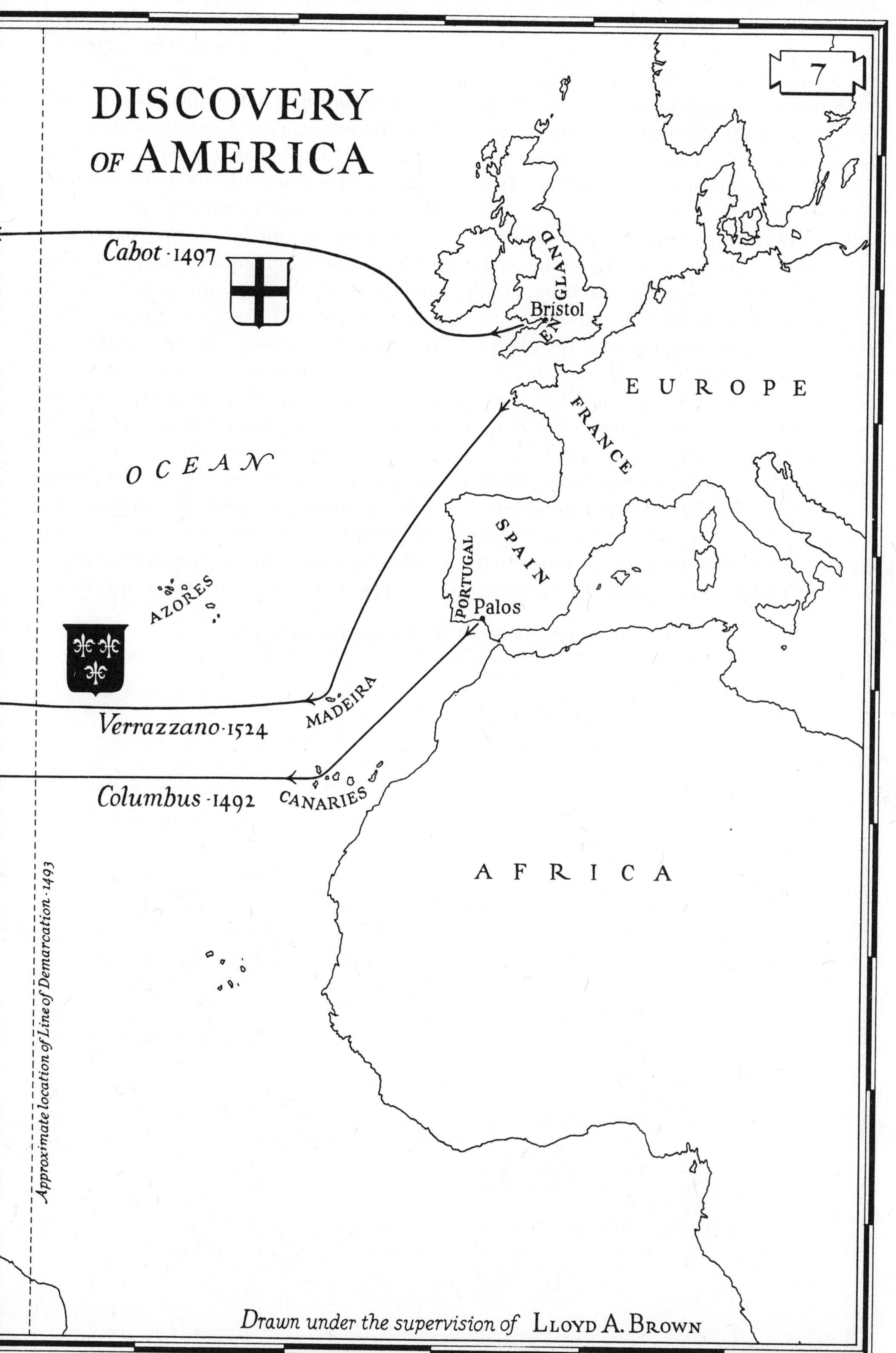
7
DISCOVERY
OF AMERICA
Cabot · 1497
ENGLAND
Bristol
EUROPE
FRANCE
OCEAN
SPAIN
PORTUGAL
Palos
AZORES
MADEIRA
Verrazzano · 1524
Columbus · 1492
CANARIES
AFRICA
Approximate location of Line of Demarcation · 1493
Drawn under the supervision of LLOYD A. BROWN

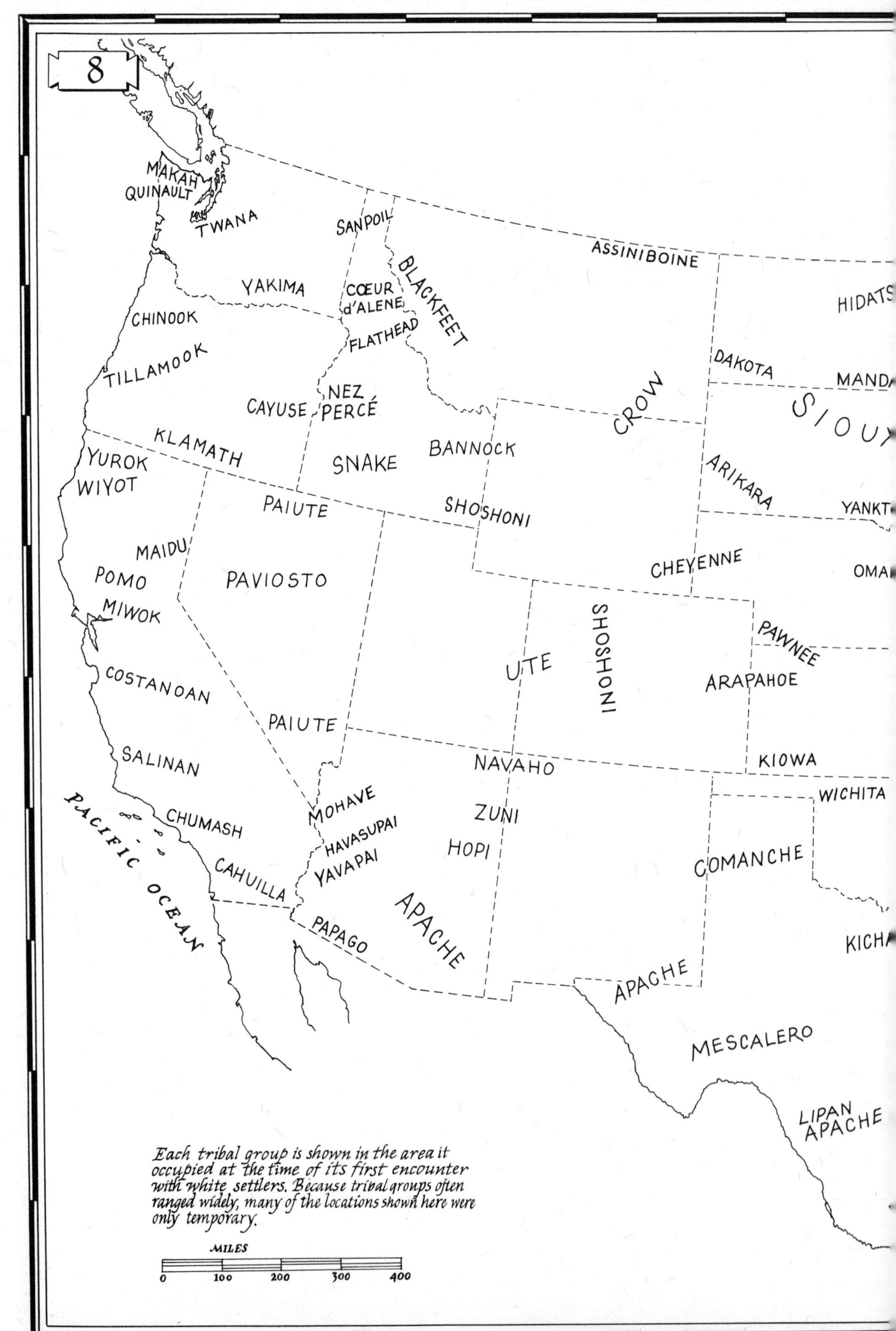

Each tribal group is shown in the area it occupied at the time of its first encounter with white settlers. Because tribal groups often ranged widely, many of the locations shown here were only temporary.

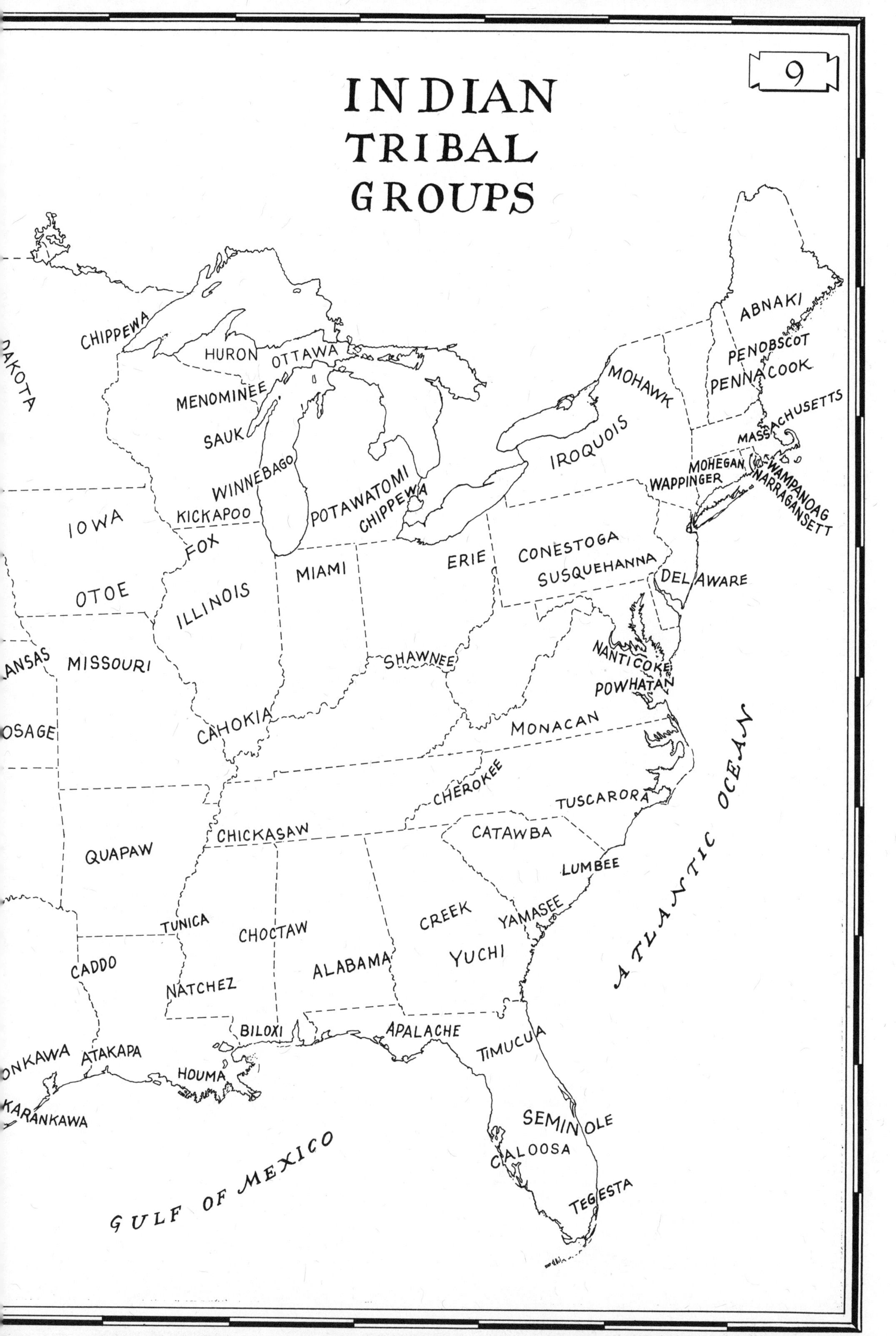
9
INDIAN
TRIBAL
GROUPS
CHIPPEWA
HURON
OTTAWA
MENOMINEE
SAUK
WINNEBAGO
POTAWATOMI
CHIPPEWA
KICKAPOO
IOWA
FOX
OTOE
ILLINOIS
MIAMI
ERIE
MISSOURI
SHAWNEE
CAHOKIA
OSAGE
ABNAKI
PENOBSCOT
PENNACOOK
MOHAWK
MASSACHUSETTS
IROQUOIS
MOHEGAN
WAPPINGER
WAMPANOAG
NARRAGANSETT
CONESTOGA
SUSQUEHANNA
DELAWARE
NANTICOKE
POWHATAN
MONACAN
CHEROKEE
TUSCARORA
CHICKASAW
CATAWBA
QUAPAW
LUMBEE
TUNICA
CHOCTAW
CREEK
YAMASEE
CADDO
ALABAMA
YUCHI
NATCHEZ
BILOXI
APALACHE
TIMUCUA
ATAKAPA
HOUMA
KARANKAWA
SEMINOLE
CALOOSA
TEGESTA
ATLANTIC OCEAN
GULF OF MEXICO

II FRENCH AND SPANISH EXPLORATION AND SETTLEMENT

12

SIXTEENTH CENTURY

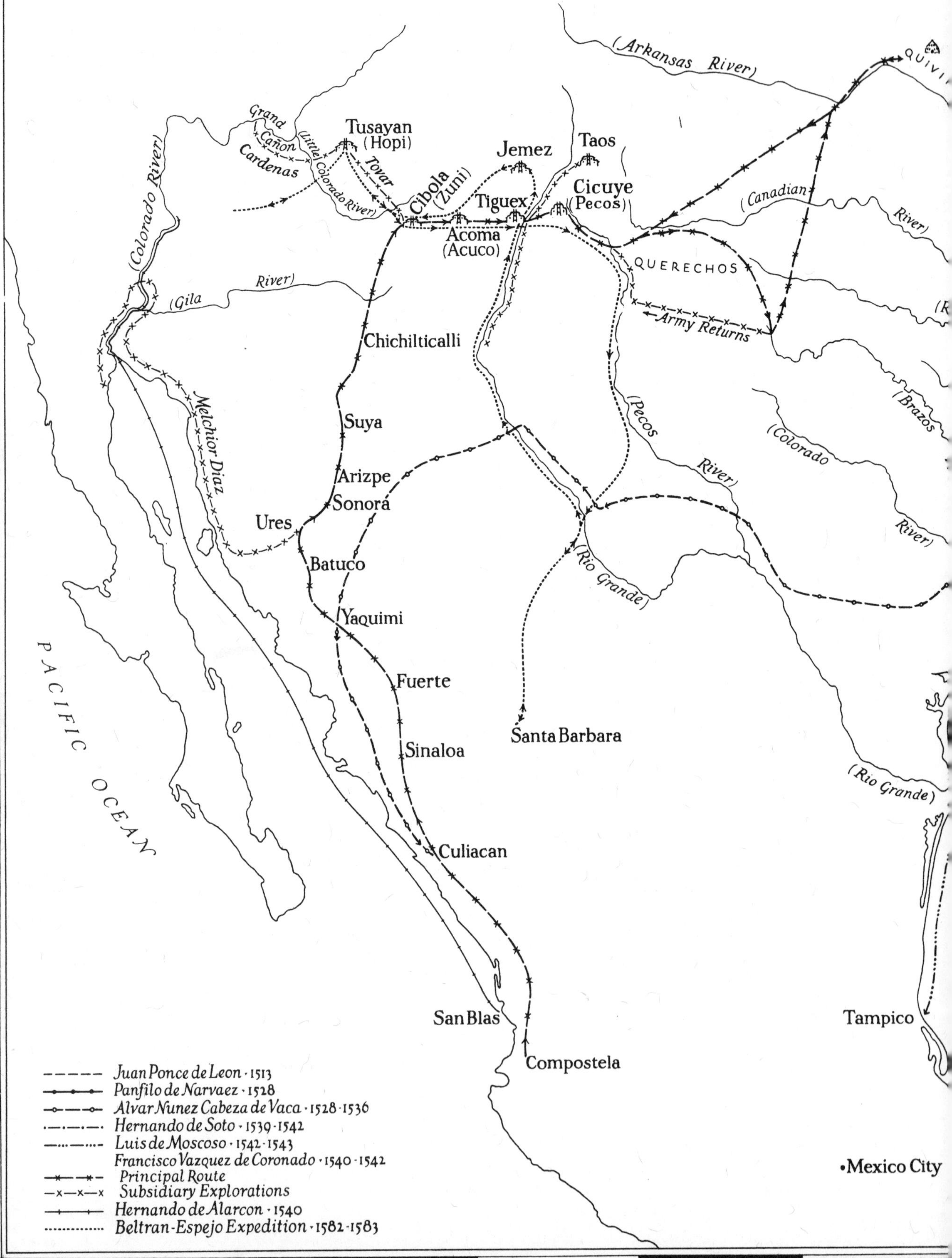

(Arkansas River)
QUIVI
Grand Cañon
Cardenas
(Little) Colorado River)
Tusayan (Hopi)
Tovar
Jemez
Taos
Cibola (Zuni)
Tiguex
Cicuye (Pecos)
Acoma (Acuco)
(Canadian
River)
QUERECHOS
Army Returns
(Colorado River)
(Gila River)
Chichilticalli
Suya
Melchior Diaz
Arizpe
Sonora
Ures
Batuco
Yaquimi
Fuerte
Sinaloa
Santa Barbara
Culiacan
San Blas
Compostela
(Pecos River)
(Brazos
(Colorado River)
(Rio Grande)
PACIFIC OCEAN
Tampico
•Mexico City

Juan Ponce de Leon · 1513
Panfilo de Narvaez · 1528
Alvar Nunez Cabeza de Vaca · 1528-1536
Hernando de Soto · 1539-1542
Luis de Moscoso · 1542-1543
Francisco Vazquez de Coronado · 1540-1542
Principal Route
Subsidiary Explorations
Hernando de Alarcon · 1540
Beltran-Espejo Expedition · 1582-1583

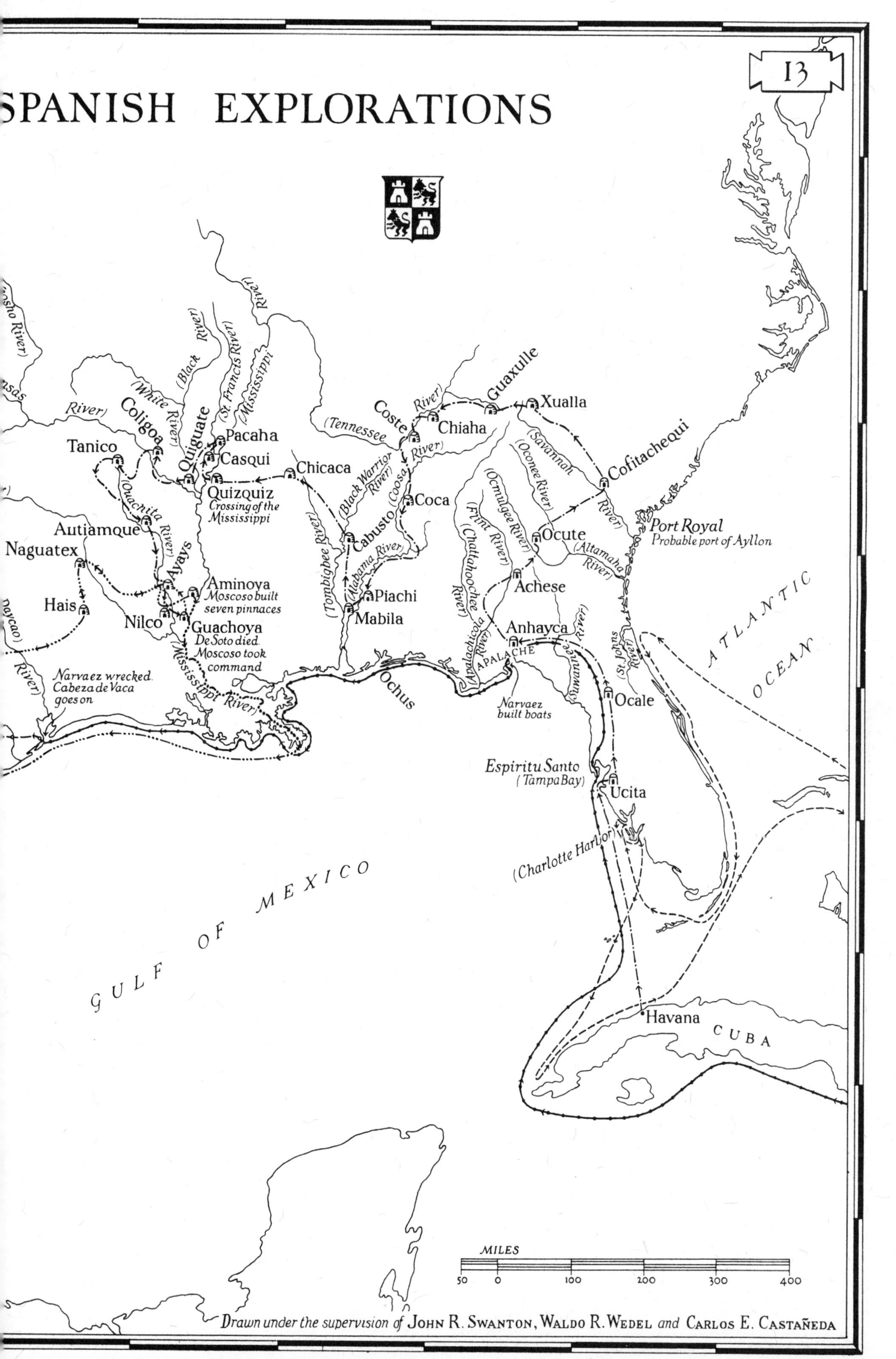

13
SPANISH EXPLORATIONS
GULF OF MEXICO
ATLANTIC OCEAN
CUBA
Havana
Espiritu Santo
(Tampa Bay)
Ucita
(Charlotte Harbor)
Ocale
Narvaez built boats
Anhayca
APALACHE
Achese
Ocute
Cofitachequi
Port Royal
Probable port of Ayllon
Xualla
Guaxulle
Chiaha
Coste
Coca
Cabusto
Piachi
Mabila
Ochus
Chicaca
Pacaha
Casqui
Quiguate
Coligoa
Tanico
Quizquiz
Crossing of the Mississippi
Autiamque
Naguatex
Hais
Ayays
Aminoya
Moscoso built seven pinnaces
Nilco
Guachoya
De Soto died. Moscoso took command
Narvaez wrecked. Cabeza de Vaca goes on
(Mississippi River)
(St. Francis River)
(Black River)
(White River)
(Ouachita River)
(Tennessee River)
(Black Warrior River)
(Coosa River)
(Alabama River)
(Tombigbee River)
(Apalachicola River)
(Chattahoochee River)
(Flint River)
(Ocmulgee River)
(Oconee River)
(Savannah River)
(Altamaha River)
(Suwannee River)
(St. Johns River)
MILES
50 0 100 200 300 400
Drawn under the supervision of John R. Swanton, Waldo R. Wedel and Carlos E. Castañeda

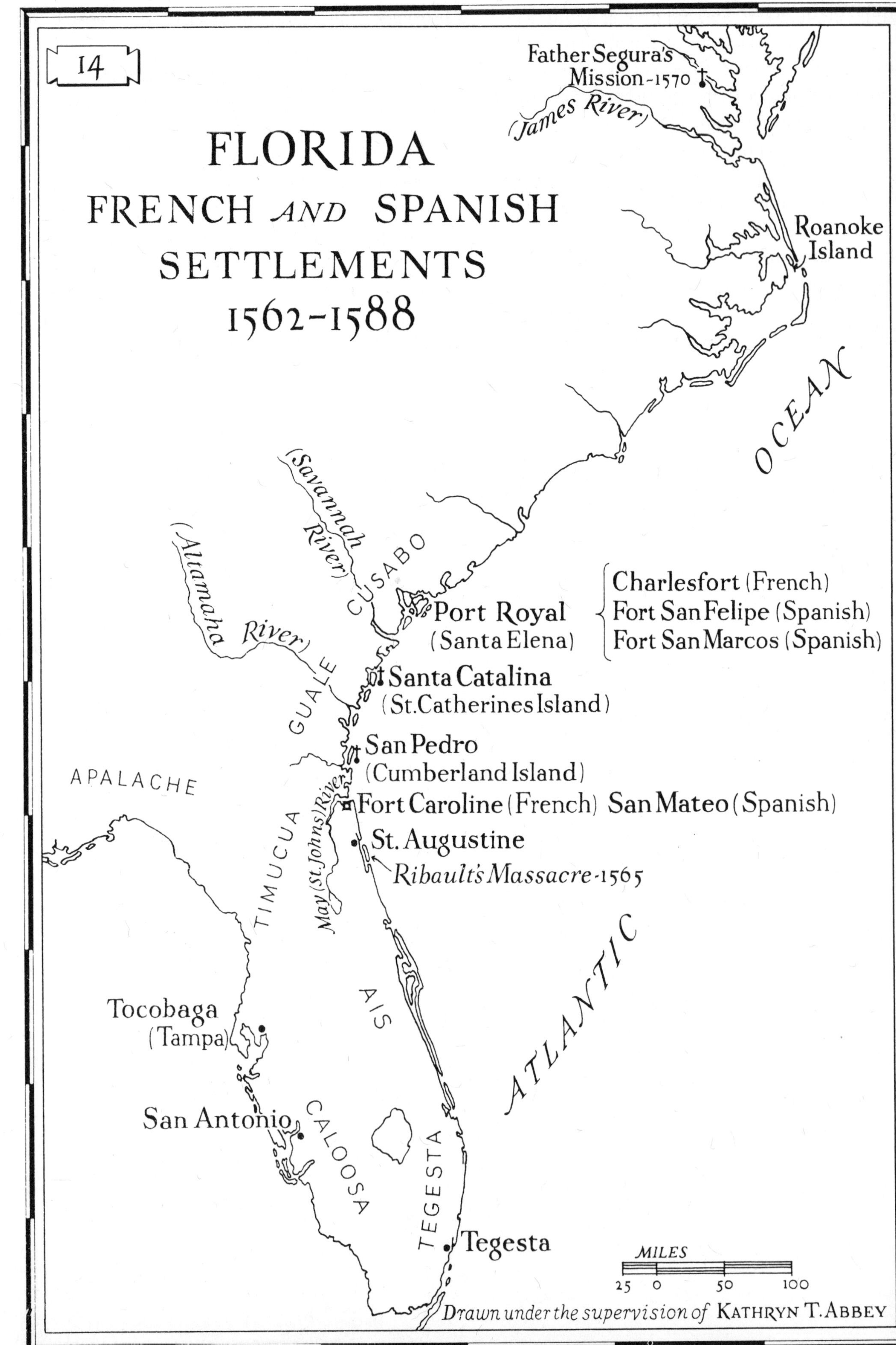
14
FLORIDA
FRENCH AND SPANISH
SETTLEMENTS
1562-1588
Father Segura's
Mission-1570
(James River)
Roanoke
Island
OCEAN
(Savannah
River)
(Altamaha
River)
CUSABO
Port Royal
(Santa Elena)
Charlesfort (French)
Fort San Felipe (Spanish)
Fort San Marcos (Spanish)
GUALE
Santa Catalina
(St.Catherines Island)
San Pedro
(Cumberland Island)
APALACHE
May (St.Johns) River
Fort Caroline (French)
San Mateo (Spanish)
TIMUCUA
St. Augustine
Ribault's Massacre-1565
ATLANTIC
AIS
Tocobaga
(Tampa)
San Antonio
CALOOSA
TEGESTA
Tegesta
MILES
25
0
50
100
Drawn under the supervision of KATHRYN T. ABBEY

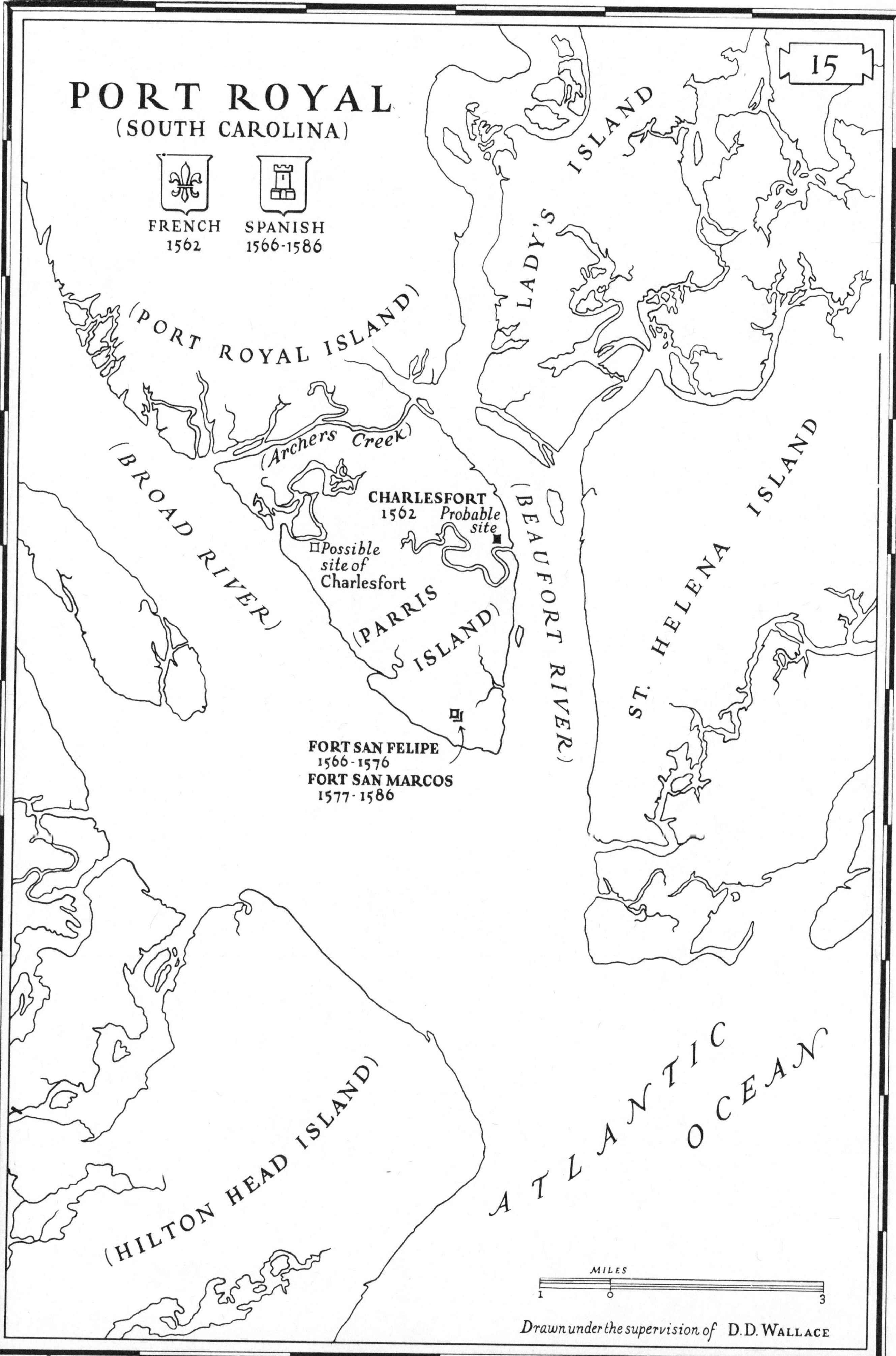
15
PORT ROYAL
(SOUTH CAROLINA)
FRENCH
1562
SPANISH
1566-1586
(PORT ROYAL ISLAND)
LADY'S ISLAND
(Archers Creek)
(BROAD RIVER)
CHARLESFORT
1562
Probable site
Possible site of Charlesfort
(PARRIS ISLAND)
(BEAUFORT RIVER)
ST. HELENA ISLAND
FORT SAN FELIPE
1566-1576
FORT SAN MARCOS
1577-1586
(HILTON HEAD ISLAND)
ATLANTIC OCEAN
MILES
1 0 3
Drawn under the supervision of D. D. WALLACE

16
Lac Superieur
Sault Ste. Marie
St. Mary's River
St. Ignace
Mission du St. Esprit
Michilimackinac
Lac Huron
MENOMINEE
Baye des Puans
WINNEBAGO
FOX
SAUK
Marquette died (1675)
Mississippi River
River
Fox River
St. François Xavier
MASCOUTEN
MIAMI
KICKAPOO
Wisconsin
Portage
Lac des Ilinois (Michigan)
Des Plaines River
St. Joseph River
Lac Erie
Kaskaskia Village
Portage
Kankakee River
Illinois River
Illinois Village
PIASA
(Missouri River)
(Ohio River)
DISCOVERY OF THE MISSISSIPPI
JOLLIET and MARQUETTE
1673
Mississippi River
(Arkansas River)
Arkansas Village
MILES
50 0 100
Drawn under the supervision of JEAN DELANGLEZ

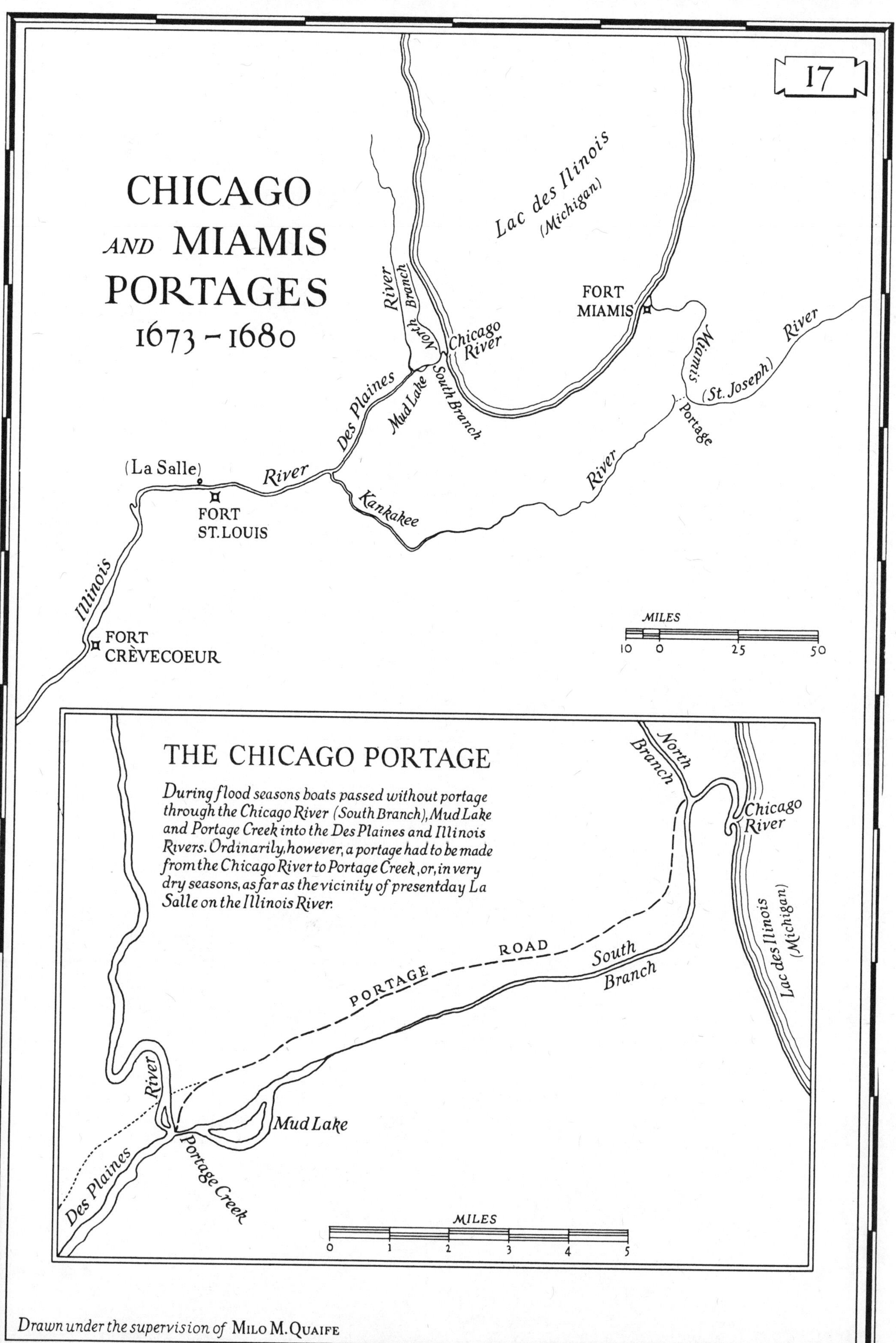
17
CHICAGO AND MIAMIS PORTAGES 1673–1680
Lac des Ilinois (Michigan)
FORT MIAMIS
North Branch
River
Chicago River
Miamis
(St. Joseph) River
Portage
Mud Lake
South Branch
Des Plaines
(La Salle)
River
FORT ST. LOUIS
Kankakee
River
Illinois
FORT CRÈVECOEUR
MILES
10 0 25 50
THE CHICAGO PORTAGE
During flood seasons boats passed without portage through the Chicago River (South Branch), Mud Lake and Portage Creek into the Des Plaines and Illinois Rivers. Ordinarily, however, a portage had to be made from the Chicago River to Portage Creek, or, in very dry seasons, as far as the vicinity of presentday La Salle on the Illinois River.
North Branch
Chicago River
Lac des Ilinois (Michigan)
PORTAGE ROAD
South Branch
River
Mud Lake
Des Plaines
Portage Creek
MILES
0 1 2 3 4 5
Drawn under the supervision of MILO M. QUAIFE

NEW FRANCE
TO 1673

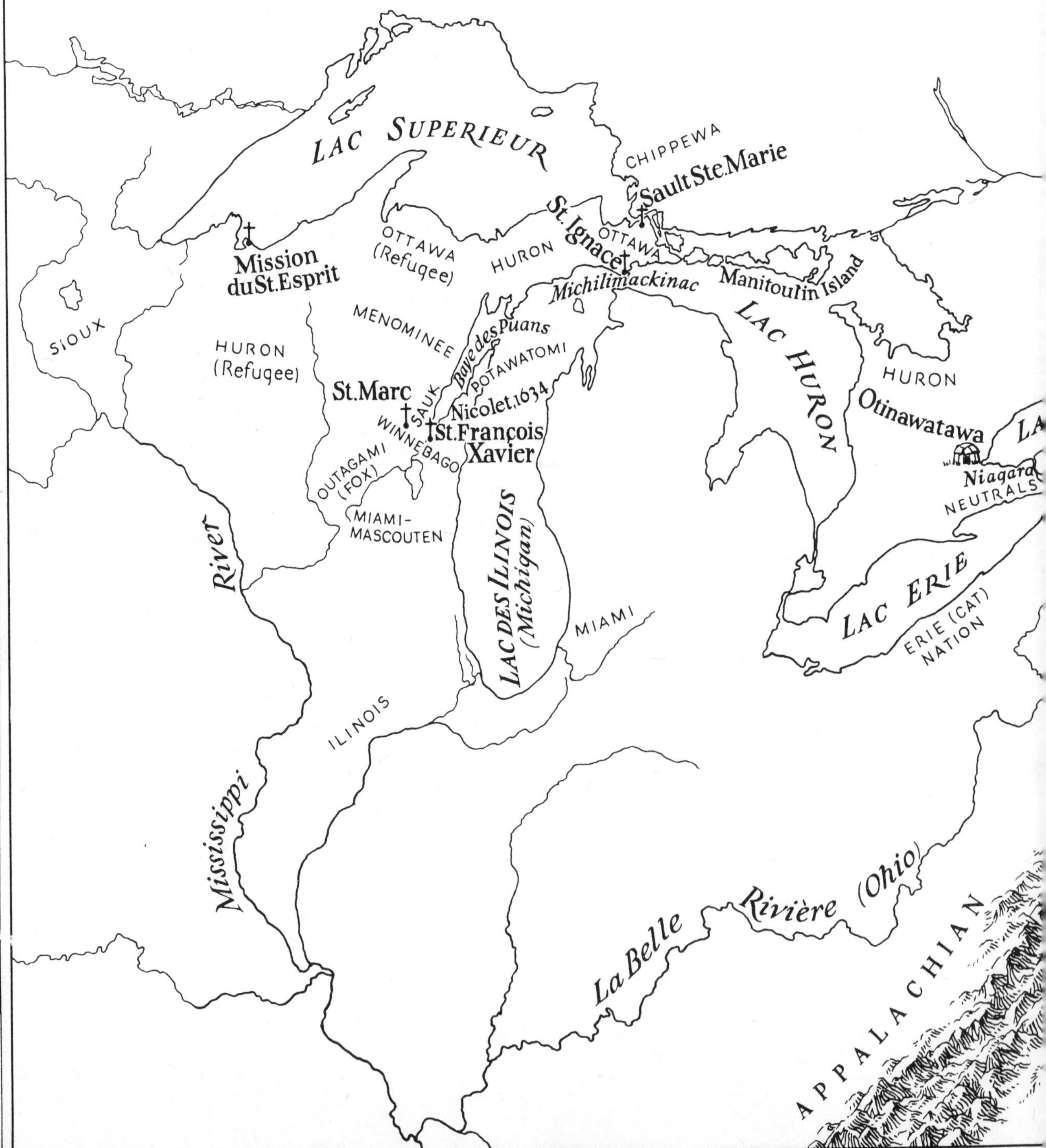

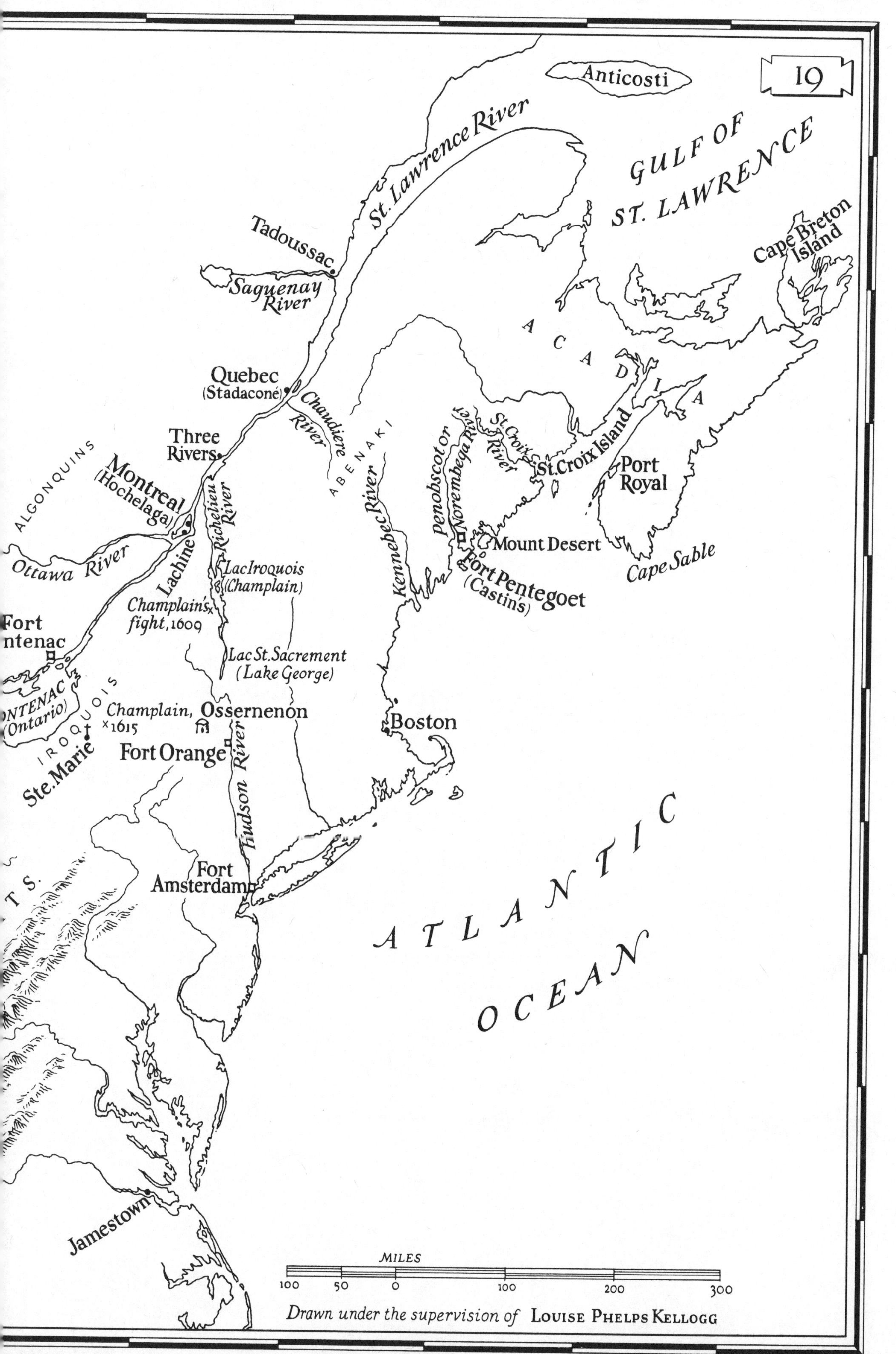
19
Anticosti
GULF OF ST. LAWRENCE
St. Lawrence River
Tadoussac
Saguenay River
Cape Breton Island
ACADIA
Quebec
(Stadaconé)
Chaudière River
ABENAKI
Three Rivers
ALGONQUINS
Montreal
(Hochelaga)
Richelieu River
Kennebec River
Penobscot or Norembega River
St. Croix River
St. Croix Island
Port Royal
Mount Desert
Fort Pentegoet
(Castin's)
Cape Sable
Ottawa River
Lachine
Lac Iroquois
(Champlain)
Champlain's fight, 1609
Fort
ntenac
Lac St. Sacrement
(Lake George)
NTENAC
(Ontario)
IROQUOIS
Champlain, 1615
Ossernenon
Boston
Ste. Marie
Fort Orange
Hudson River
Fort Amsterdam
ATLANTIC OCEAN
Jamestown
MILES
100 50 0 100 200 300
Drawn under the supervision of LOUISE PHELPS KELLOGG

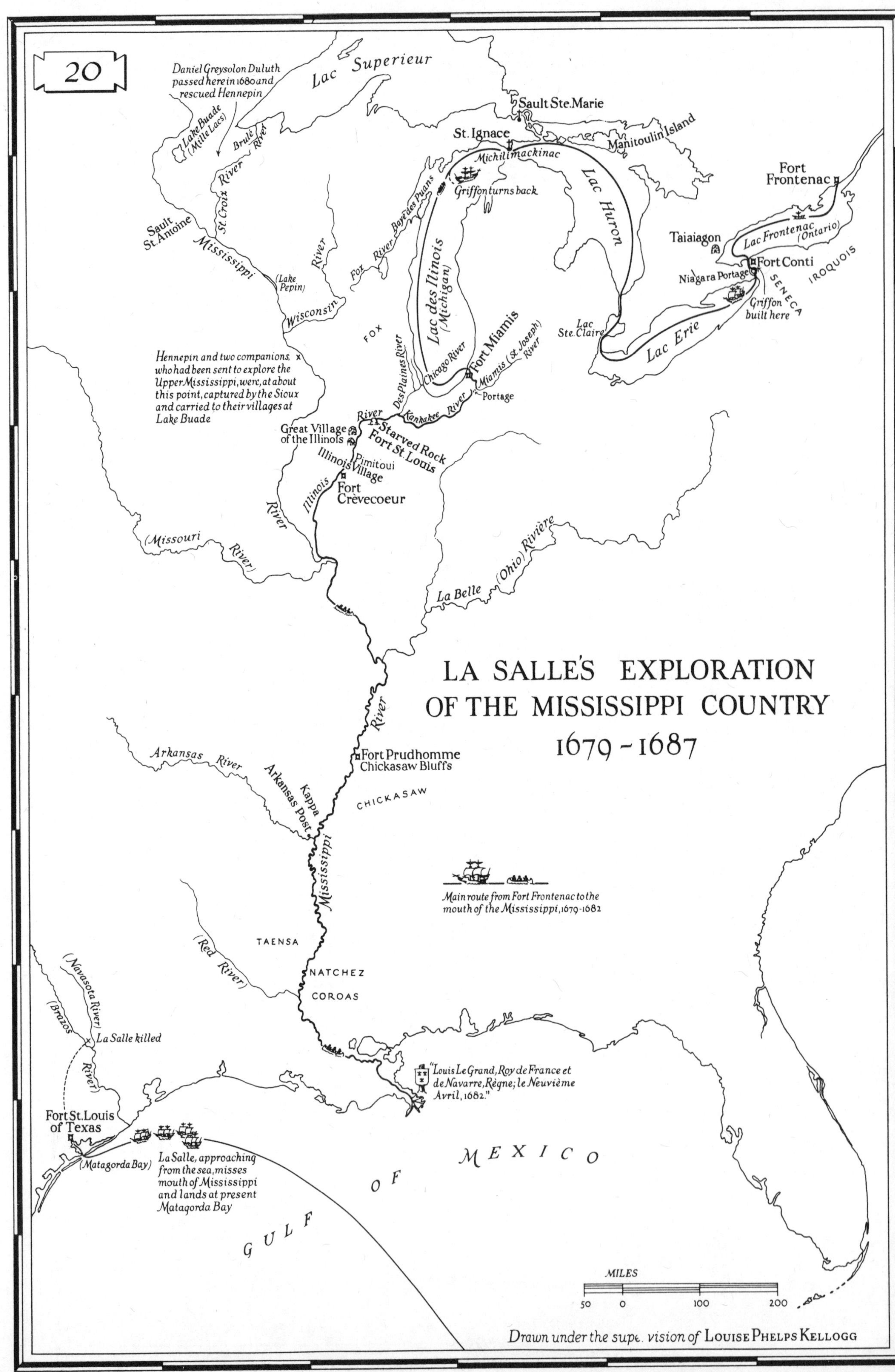

20
LA SALLE'S EXPLORATION OF THE MISSISSIPPI COUNTRY 1679 - 1687
Lac Superieur
Daniel Greysolon Duluth passed here in 1680 and rescued Hennepin
Lake Buade (Mille Lacs)
Brulé River
St. Croix River
Sault St. Antoine
Mississippi
(Lake Pepin)
Wisconsin
Fox River
Baye des Puans
FOX
Sault Ste. Marie
St. Ignace
Michillimackinac
Manitoulin Island
Griffon turns back
Lac Huron
Lac des Ilinois (Michigan)
Fort Frontenac
Lac Frontenac (Ontario)
Taiaiagon
Fort Conti
Niagara Portage
SENECA
IROQUOIS
Griffon built here
Lac Ste. Claire
Lac Erie
Hennepin and two companions, who had been sent to explore the Upper Mississippi, were, at about this point, captured by the Sioux and carried to their villages at Lake Buade
Des Plaines River
Chicago River
Fort Miamis
Miamis (St. Joseph) River
Portage
Kankakee River
Great Village of the Illinois
Starved Rock
Fort St. Louis
Pimitoui
Illinois Village
Illinois River
Fort Crèvecoeur
(Missouri River)
La Belle (Ohio) Rivière
Mississippi River
Fort Prudhomme
Chickasaw Bluffs
Arkansas River
Kappa
Arkansas Post
CHICKASAW
Main route from Fort Frontenac to the mouth of the Mississippi, 1679-1682
TAENSA
(Red River)
NATCHEZ
COROAS
(Navasota River)
(Brazos River)
La Salle killed
Fort St. Louis of Texas
(Matagorda Bay)
La Salle, approaching from the sea, misses mouth of Mississippi and lands at present Matagorda Bay
"Louis Le Grand, Roy de France et de Navarre, Règne; le Neuvième Avril, 1682."
GULF OF MEXICO
MILES
50 0 100 200
Drawn under the supervision of Louise Phelps Kellogg

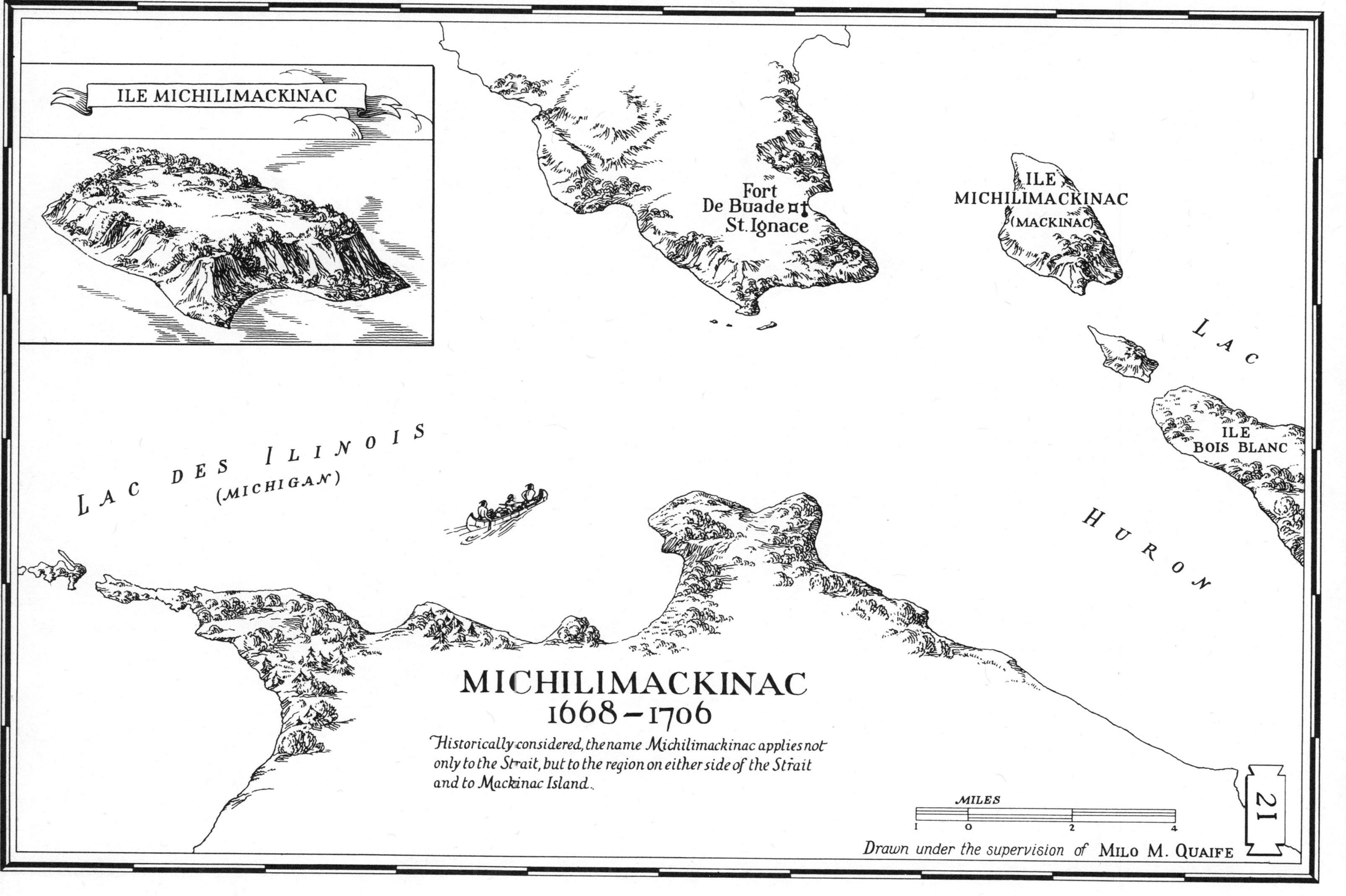
ILE MICHILIMACKINAC
Fort
De Buade
St. Ignace
ILE
MICHILIMACKINAC
(MACKINAC)
LAC
ILE
BOIS BLANC
HURON
LAC DES ILINOIS
(MICHIGAN)
MICHILIMACKINAC
1668–1706
Historically considered, the name Michilimackinac applies not only to the Strait, but to the region on either side of the Strait and to Mackinac Island.
MILES
1 0 2 4
21
Drawn under the supervision of MILO M. QUAIFE

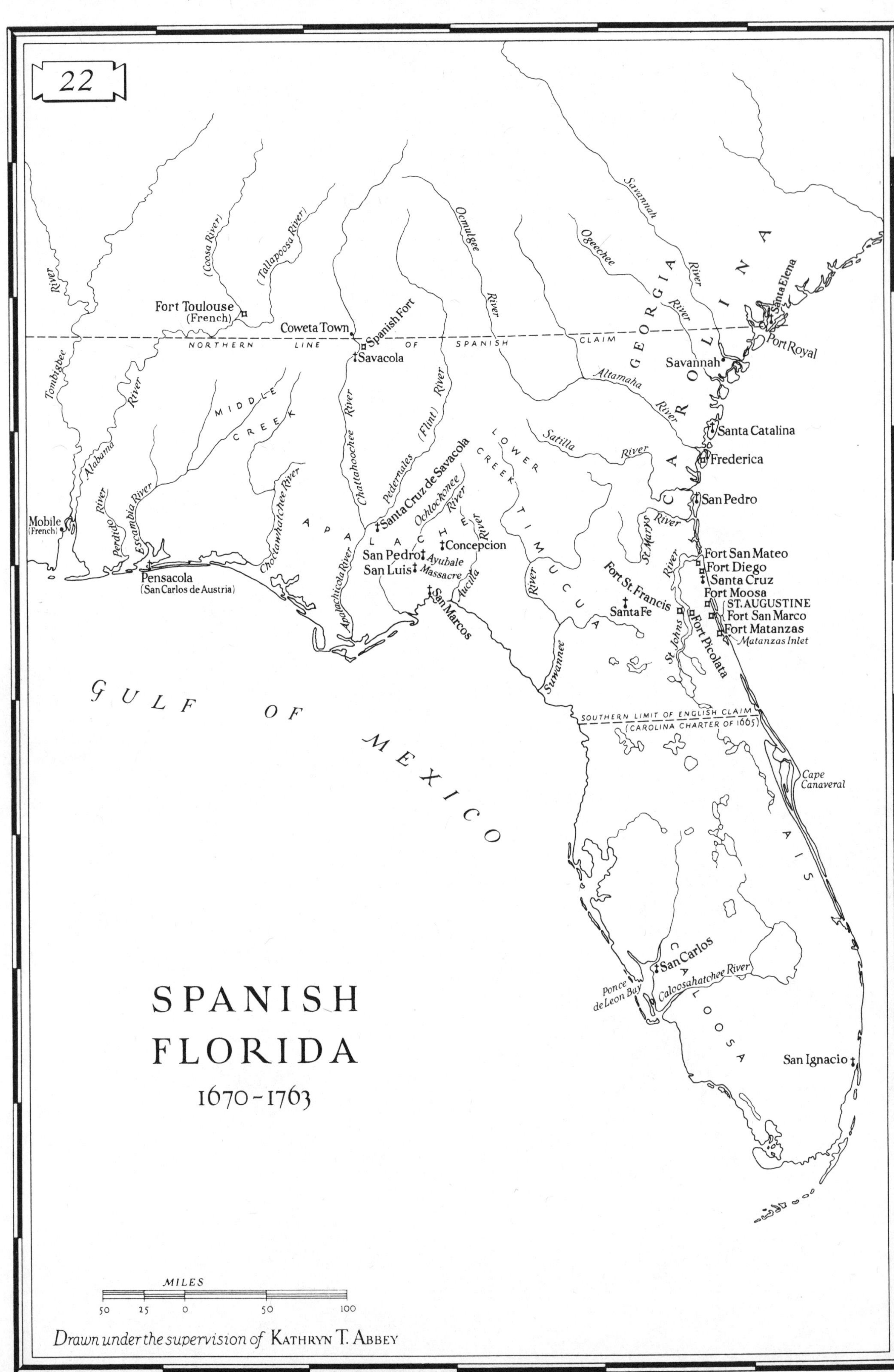
22
SPANISH FLORIDA
1670-1763
Drawn under the supervision of Kathryn T. Abbey
MILES
50 25 0 50 100
Fort Toulouse (French)
Coweta Town
Spanish Fort
Savacola
NORTHERN LINE OF SPANISH CLAIM
Mobile (French)
Pensacola (San Carlos de Austria)
Santa Cruz de Savacola
San Pedro
San Luis
Ayubale Massacre
Concepcion
San Marcos
Santa Fe
Fort St. Francis
Fort Picolata
Fort San Mateo
Fort Diego
Santa Cruz
Fort Moosa
ST. AUGUSTINE
Fort San Marco
Fort Matanzas
Matanzas Inlet
San Pedro
Frederica
Santa Catalina
Savannah
Port Royal
Santa Elena
SOUTHERN LIMIT OF ENGLISH CLAIM (CAROLINA CHARTER OF 1665)
Cape Canaveral
San Carlos
Ponce de Leon Bay
Caloosahatchee River
San Ignacio
GULF OF MEXICO
GEORGIA
CAROLINA
MIDDLE CREEK
LOWER CREEK
APALACHE
TIMUCUA
AIS
CALOOSA
Tombigbee River
Alabama River
Coosa River
Tallapoosa River
Perdido River
Escambia River
Choctawhatchee River
Apalachicola River
Chattahoochee River
Pedernales
Flint River
Ochlockonee River
Aucilla River
Suwannee River
Ocmulgee River
Oconee River
Altamaha River
Satilla River
St. Marys River
St. Johns River
Ogeechee River
Savannah River

TRANS-MISSISSIPPI - FRENCH & SPANISH
1600 – 1750

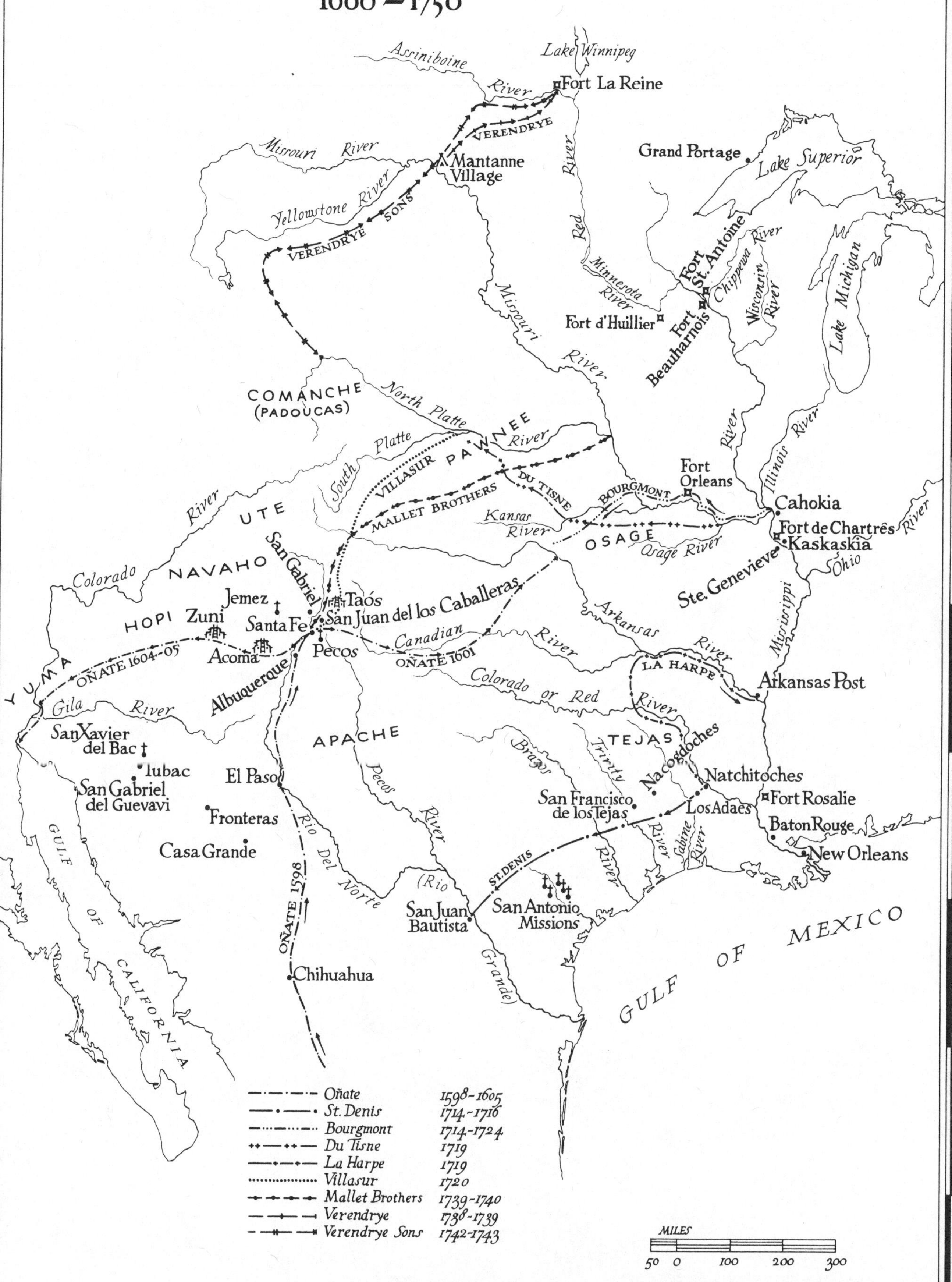

Drawn under the supervision of WALTER PRICHARD & CARLOS E. CASTAÑEDA
The Verendrye routes drawn under the supervision of O. G. LIBBY

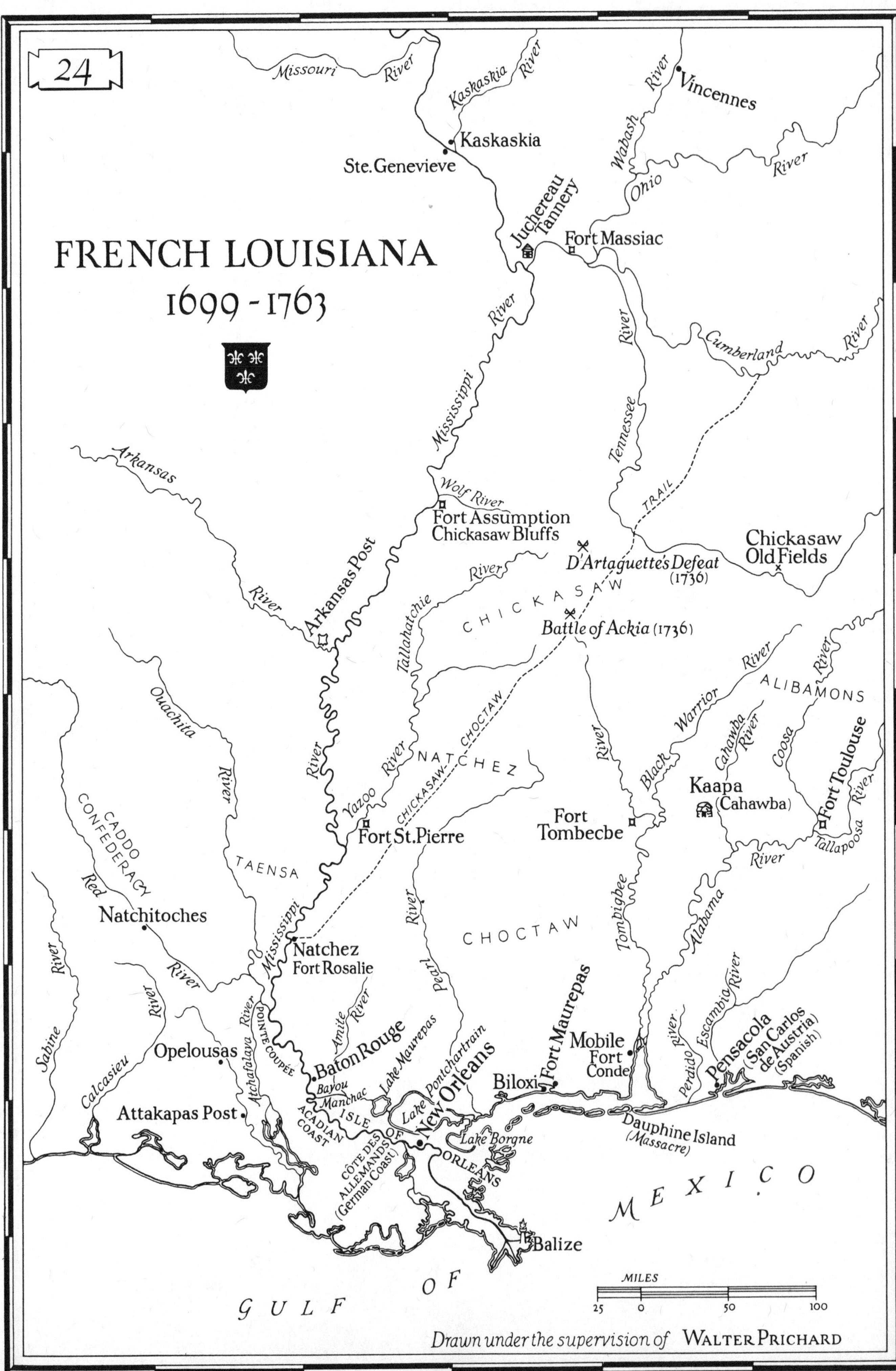

24
FRENCH LOUISIANA
1699-1763
Missouri River
Kaskaskia River
Kaskaskia
Ste. Genevieve
Vincennes
Wabash River
Ohio River
Juchereau Tannery
Fort Massiac
Mississippi River
Tennessee River
Cumberland River
Arkansas River
Wolf River
Fort Assumption
Chickasaw Bluffs
TRAIL
Chickasaw Old Fields
D'Artaguette's Defeat (1736)
Arkansas Post
Tallahatchie River
CHICKASAW
Battle of Ackia (1736)
Ouachita River
Yazoo River
NATCHEZ
CHICKASAW-CHOCTAW
Black Warrior River
ALIBAMONS
Cahawba River
Coosa River
Kaapa (Cahawba)
Fort Toulouse
Fort Tombecbe
Tallapoosa River
CADDO CONFEDERACY
Fort St. Pierre
TAENSA
Red River
Natchitoches
Mississippi
Natchez
Fort Rosalie
Pearl River
CHOCTAW
Tombigbee River
Alabama River
Sabine River
Calcasieu River
Atchafalaya River
POINTE COUPÉE
Amite River
Opelousas
Baton Rouge
Lake Maurepas
Bayou Manchac
Lake Pontchartrain
New Orleans
Fort Maurepas
Biloxi
Mobile
Fort Conde
Perdido River
Escambia River
Pensacola (San Carlos de Austria) (Spanish)
Attakapas Post
ACADIAN COAST
ISLE OF ORLEANS
CÔTE DES ALLEMANDS (German Coast)
Lake Borgne
Dauphine Island (Massacre)
MEXICO
Balize
GULF OF
MILES
25 0 50 100
Drawn under the supervision of WALTER PRICHARD

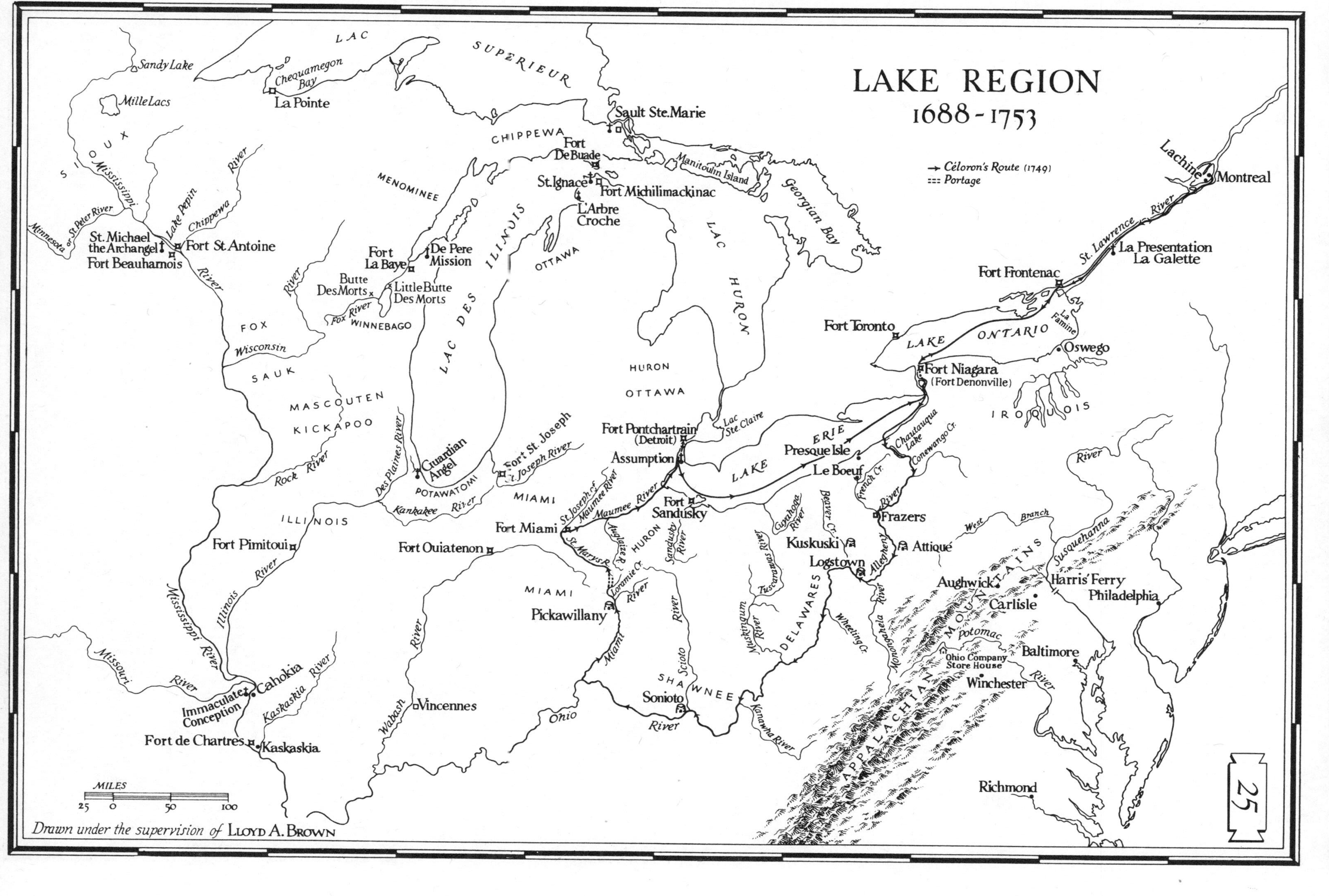
LAKE REGION
1688 - 1753
Céloron's Route (1749)
Portage
25
LAC SUPERIEUR
Sandy Lake
Mille Lacs
Chequamegon Bay
La Pointe
Sault Ste. Marie
CHIPPEWA
Fort DeBuade
St. Ignace
Fort Michilimackinac
L'Arbre Croche
Manitoulin Island
Georgian Bay
LAC HURON
Lachine
Montreal
St. Lawrence River
La Presentation
La Galette
Fort Frontenac
La Famine
Oswego
LAKE ONTARIO
Fort Toronto
Fort Niagara
(Fort Denonville)
IROQUOIS
SIOUX
Mississippi
St. Peter River
Minnesota
Lake Pepin
Chippewa
River
St. Michael the Archangel
Fort St. Antoine
Fort Beauharnois
MENOMINEE
Fort La Baye
De Pere Mission
Butte Des Morts
Little Butte Des Morts
Fox River
WINNEBAGO
FOX
Wisconsin
SAUK
MASCOUTEN
KICKAPOO
Rock River
Des Plaines River
LAC DES ILLINOIS
OTTAWA
Guardian Angel
POTAWATOMI
Kankakee River
Fort St. Joseph
St. Joseph River
HURON
OTTAWA
Lac Ste. Claire
Fort Pontchartrain
(Detroit)
Assumption
LAKE ERIE
Presque Isle
Le Boeuf
Chautauqua Lake
Conewango Cr.
French Cr.
Frazers
MIAMI
St. Joseph of Maumee River
Maumee River
Fort Sandusky
Fort Miami
St. Marys R.
Auglaize R.
HURON
Sandusky River
Cuyahoga River
Beaver Cr.
Kuskuski
Logstown
Allegheny
Attiqué
Tuscarawas River
Muskingum River
DELAWARES
Wheeling Cr.
Monongahela River
ILLINOIS
Fort Pimitoui
Illinois River
Fort Ouiatenon
Loramie Cr.
MIAMI
Pickawillany
Miami River
Scioto River
SHAWNEE
Sonioto
River
Ohio
Kanawha River
Mississippi River
Missouri River
Cahokia
Immaculate Conception
Kaskaskia River
Fort de Chartres
Kaskaskia
Wabash River
Vincennes
West Branch
Susquehanna
APPALACHIAN MOUNTAINS
River
Aughwick
Harris' Ferry
Philadelphia
Carlisle
Potomac
Ohio Company Store House
Winchester
River
Baltimore
Richmond
MILES
25 0 50 100
Drawn under the supervision of LLOYD A. BROWN

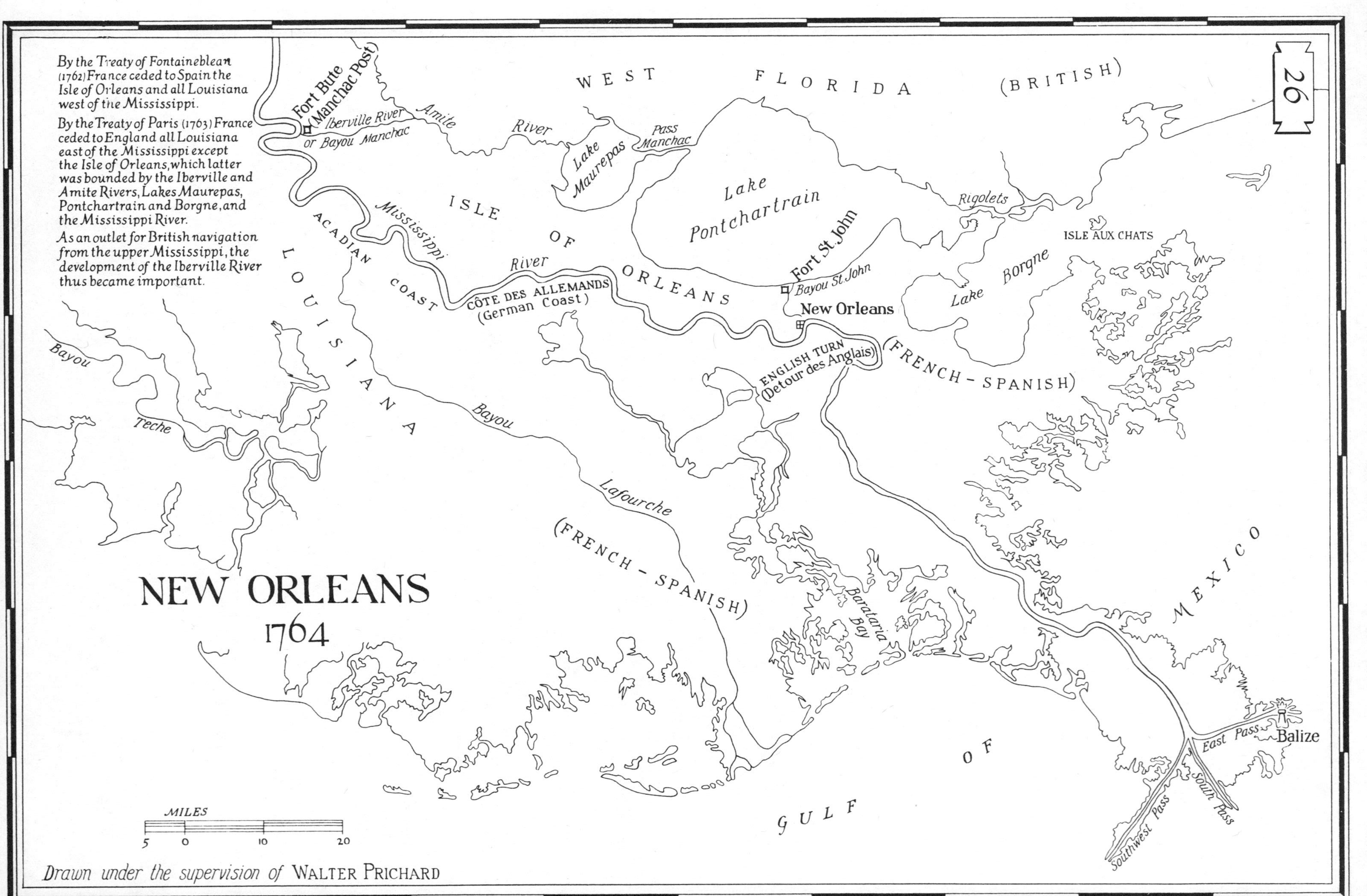
26
By the Treaty of Fontainebleau (1762) France ceded to Spain the Isle of Orleans and all Louisiana west of the Mississippi.
By the Treaty of Paris (1763) France ceded to England all Louisiana east of the Mississippi except the Isle of Orleans, which latter was bounded by the Iberville and Amite Rivers, Lakes Maurepas, Pontchartrain and Borgne, and the Mississippi River.
As an outlet for British navigation from the upper Mississippi, the development of the Iberville River thus became important.
NEW ORLEANS
1764
WEST FLORIDA (BRITISH)
Fort Bute (Manchac Post)
Iberville River
or Bayou Manchac
Amite River
Lake Maurepas
Pass Manchac
Lake Pontchartrain
Rigolets
ISLE AUX CHATS
Lake Borgne
ISLE OF ORLEANS
Mississippi River
Fort St. John
Bayou St. John
New Orleans
ENGLISH TURN
(Detour des Anglais)
(FRENCH - SPANISH)
ACADIAN COAST
CÔTE DES ALLEMANDS
(German Coast)
LOUISIANA
Bayou Teche
Bayou Lafourche
(FRENCH - SPANISH)
Barataria Bay
GULF OF MEXICO
East Pass
Balize
South Pass
Southwest Pass
MILES
5 0 10 20
Drawn under the supervision of WALTER PRICHARD

27
ILLINOIS COUNTRY
1700 - 1763
Lake Michigan
Guardian Angel
Chicago Portage
Des Plaines River
Rock River
Starved Rock
Kankakee River
Illinois River
Fort Pimitoui
Mississippi
Cahokia Mounds
Cahokia
Missouri River
Des Peres
St. Philippe
Michigamea
Fort de Chartres
Prairie du Rocher
Kaskaskia
Ste. Genevieve
River
Kaskaskia River
Wabash River
Vincennes
Ohio River
Juchereau Tannery
Fort Massiac
MILES
25
0
50
Drawn under the supervision of PAUL M ANGLE

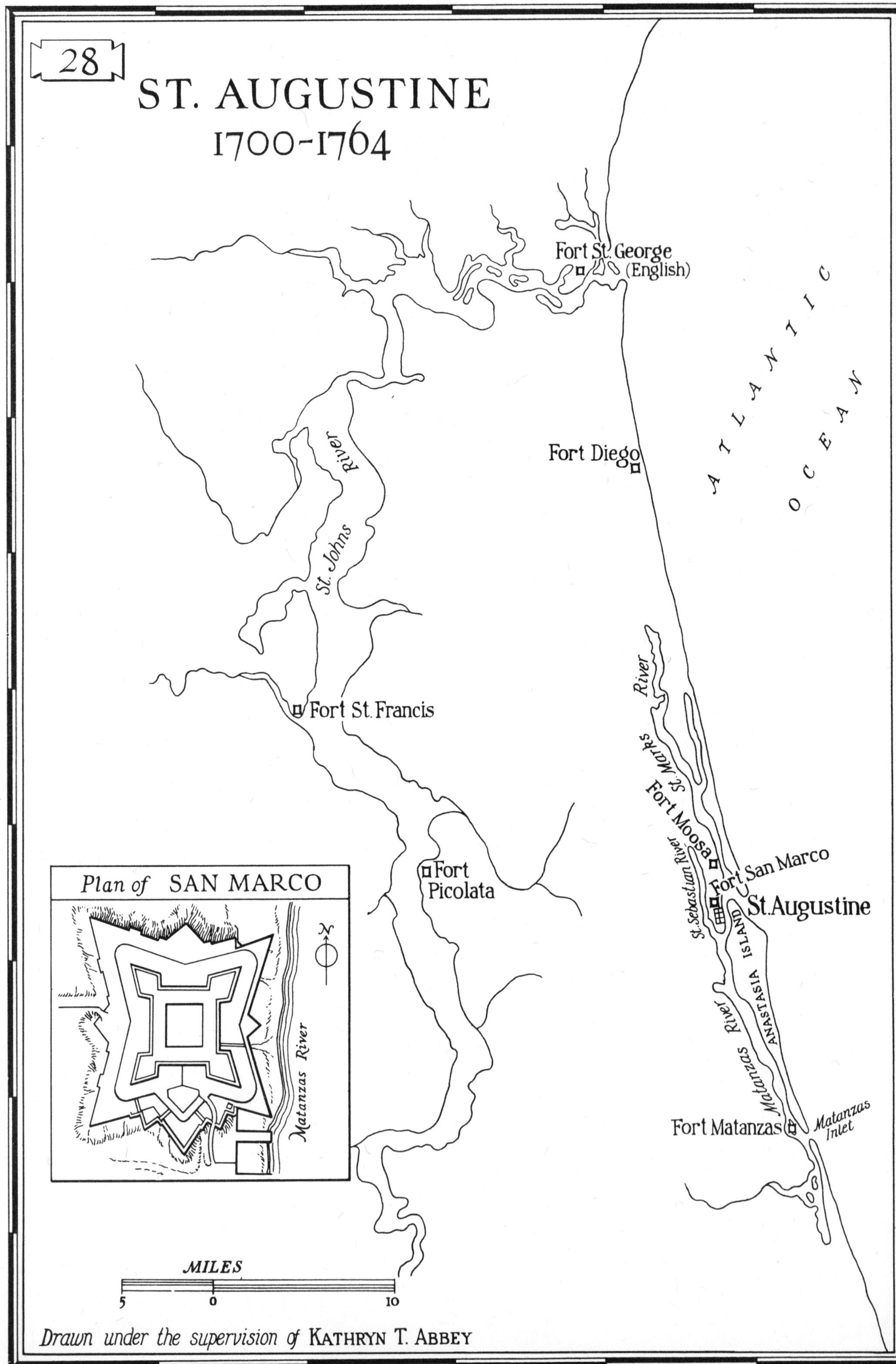
28
ST. AUGUSTINE
1700-1764
Fort St. George
(English)
ATLANTIC
OCEAN
Fort Diego
St. Johns River
Fort St. Francis
St. Marks River
Fort Moosa
Fort San Marco
St. Augustine
St. Sebastian River
ANASTASIA ISLAND
Fort Picolata
Matanzas River
Fort Matanzas
Matanzas Inlet
Plan of SAN MARCO
Matanzas River
MILES
5
0
10
Drawn under the supervision of KATHRYN T. ABBEY

III LAND GRANTS AND SETTLEMENT OF THE THIRTEEN COLONIES

30
ROANOKE ISLAND COLONIES 1584-1591
(Chowan River)
CHAWANOAC
WEAPEMEOC
(ALBEMARLE SOUND)
MORATUC
Moratuc (Roanoke) River
ROANOKE ISLAND
English Settlement
HATORASCK
DASAMONQUEPEUC
SECOTAN
(Pamlico River)
AQUASEOGOC
CROATOAN
(PAMLICO SOUND)
WOCOCON
ATLANTIC OCEAN
(Neuse River)
MILES
5 0 10 20
Drawn under the supervision of C. C. Crittenden

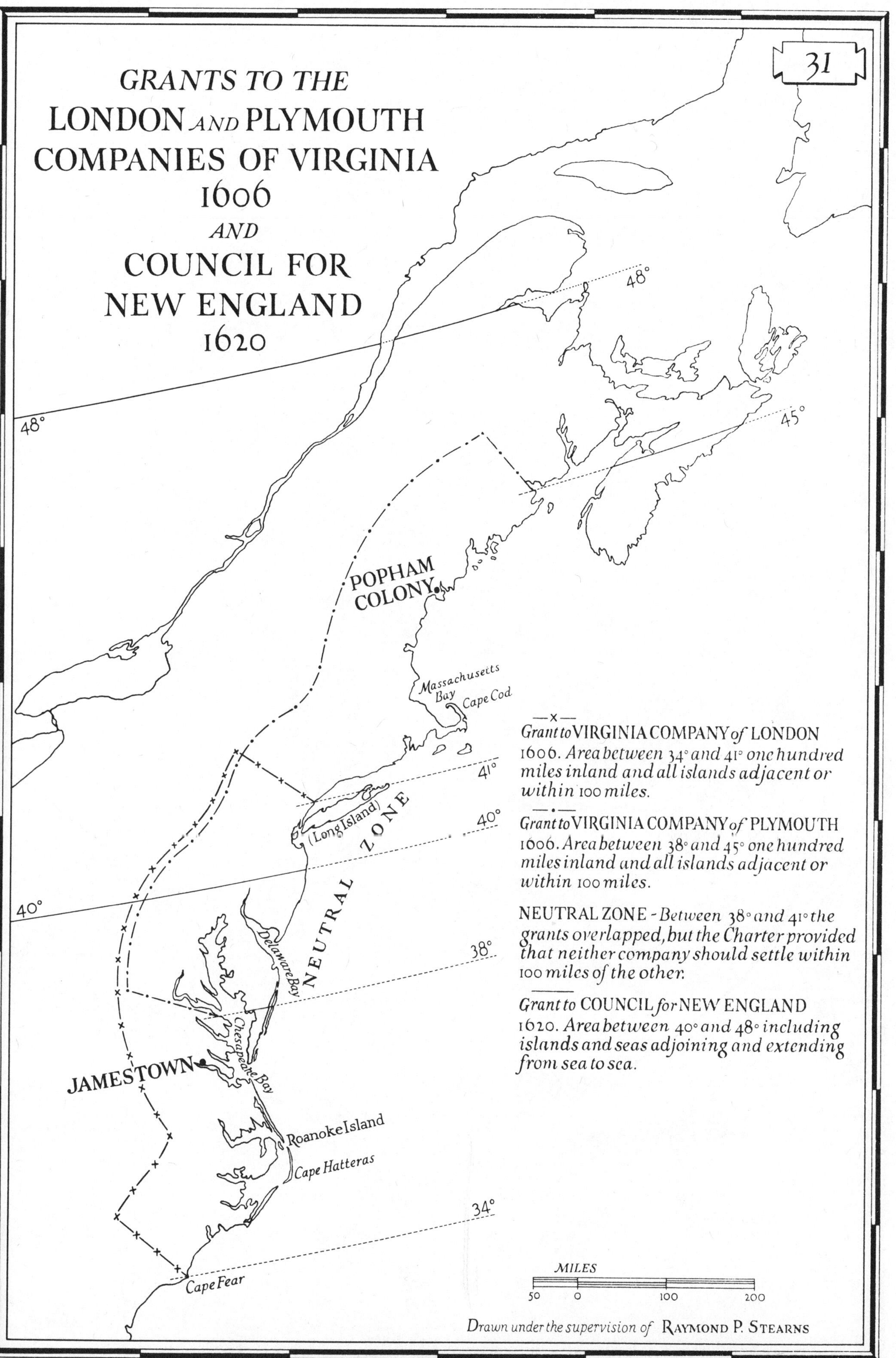
31
GRANTS TO THE
LONDON AND PLYMOUTH
COMPANIES OF VIRGINIA
1606
AND
COUNCIL FOR
NEW ENGLAND
1620
48°
48°
45°
POPHAM COLONY
Massachusetts Bay
Cape Cod
41°
(Long Island)
40°
40°
NEUTRAL ZONE
Delaware Bay
38°
Chesapeake Bay
JAMESTOWN
Roanoke Island
Cape Hatteras
34°
Cape Fear
Grant to VIRGINIA COMPANY of LONDON 1606. Area between 34° and 41° one hundred miles inland and all islands adjacent or within 100 miles.
Grant to VIRGINIA COMPANY of PLYMOUTH 1606. Area between 38° and 45° one hundred miles inland and all islands adjacent or within 100 miles.
NEUTRAL ZONE - Between 38° and 41° the grants overlapped, but the Charter provided that neither company should settle within 100 miles of the other.
Grant to COUNCIL for NEW ENGLAND 1620. Area between 40° and 48° including islands and seas adjoining and extending from sea to sea.
MILES
50 0 100 200
Drawn under the supervision of RAYMOND P. STEARNS

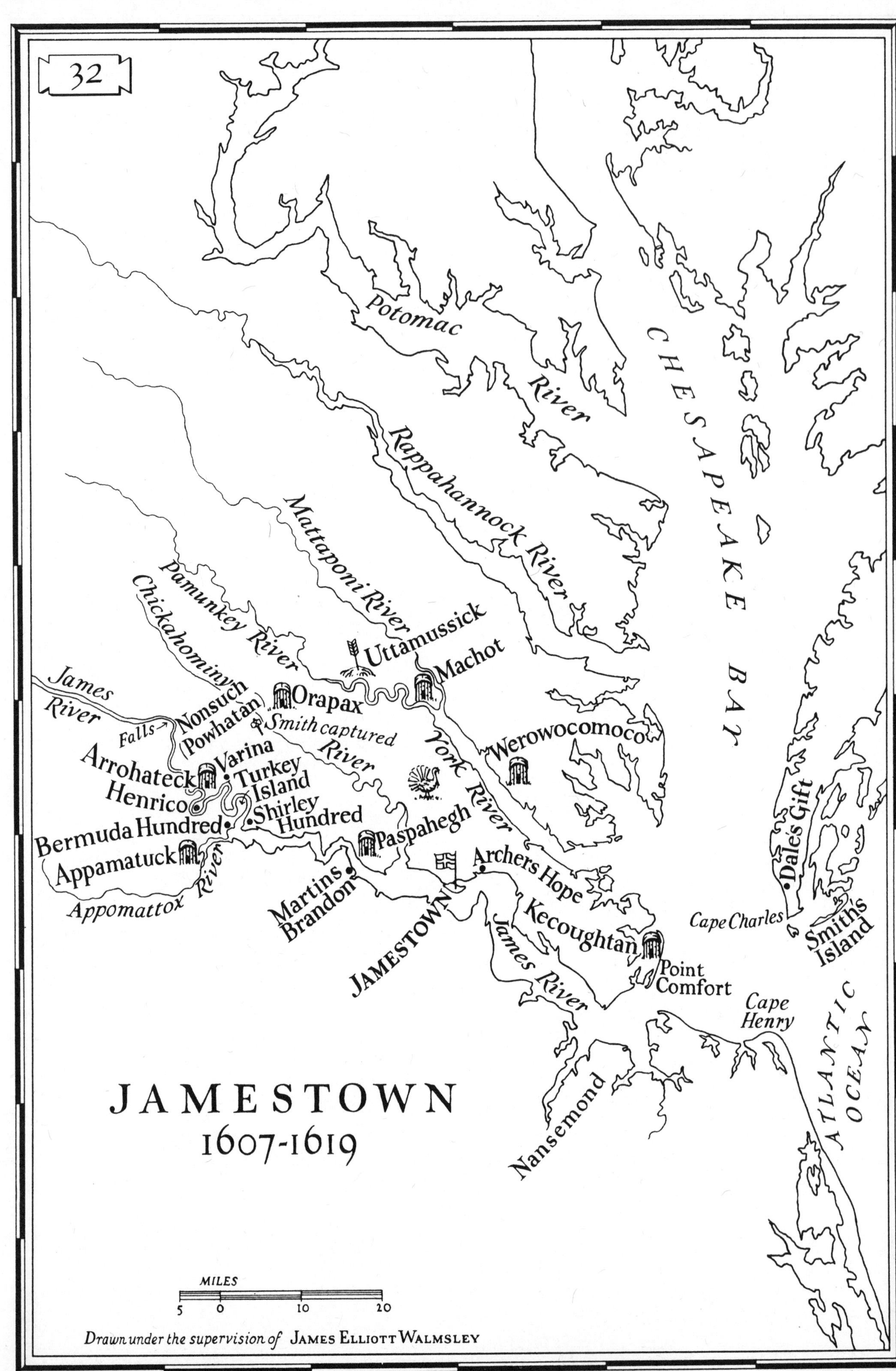
32
Potomac
River
Rappahannock River
Mattaponi River
Pamunkey River
Chickahominy
James
River
Falls
Nonsuch
(Powhatan)
Uttamussick
Machot
Orapax
Smith captured
River
York River
Werowocomoco
CHESAPEAKE BAY
Arrohateck
Varina
Turkey
Island
Henrico
Shirley
Hundred
Bermuda Hundred
Paspahegh
Appamatuck
Appomattox River
Archers Hope
Martins
Brandon
JAMESTOWN
Kecoughtan
James River
Point
Comfort
Dale's Gift
Cape Charles
Smith's
Island
Cape
Henry
ATLANTIC
OCEAN
Nansemond
JAMESTOWN
1607-1619
MILES
5 0 10 20
Drawn under the supervision of JAMES ELLIOTT WALMSLEY

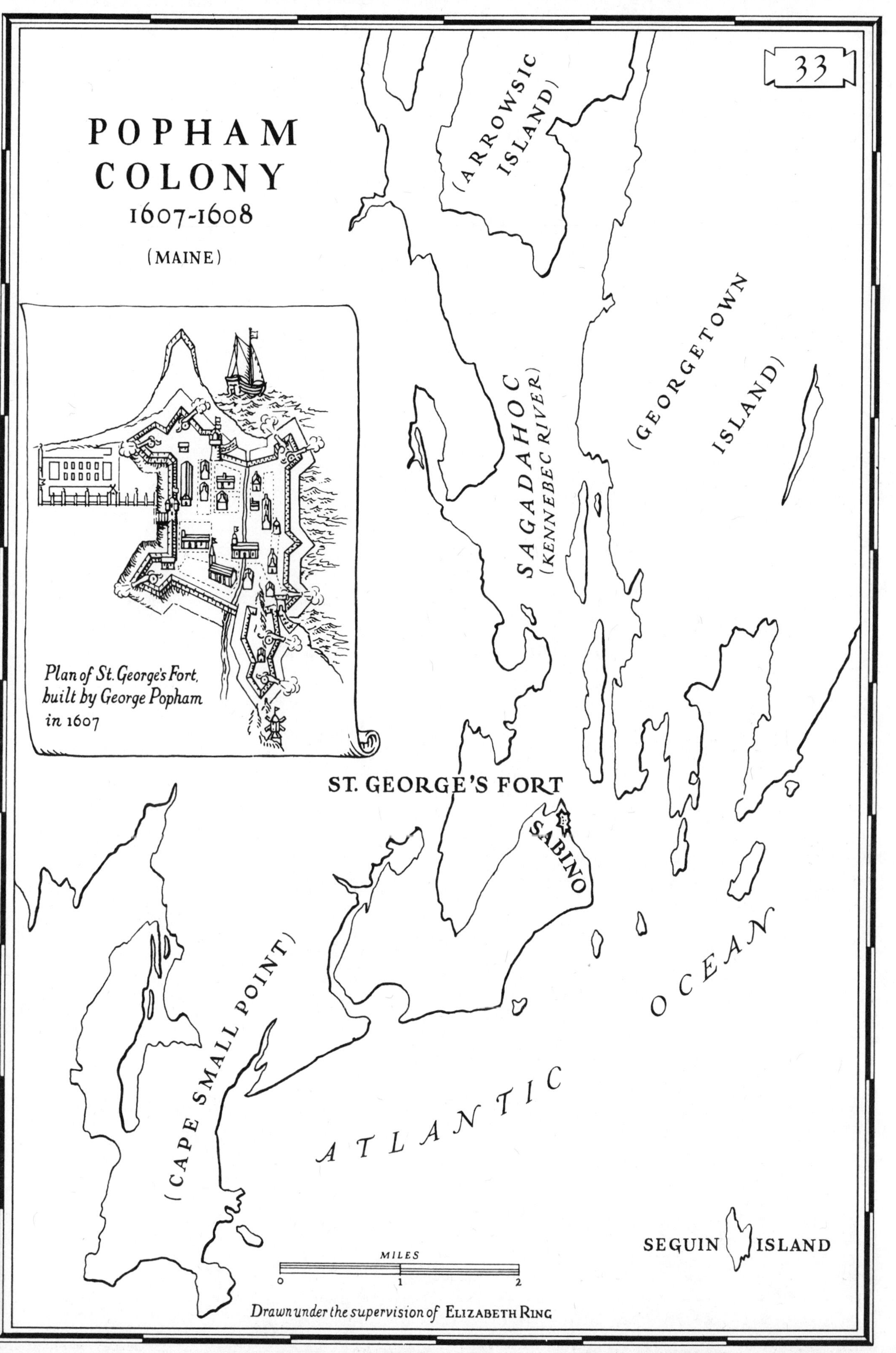
33
POPHAM
COLONY
1607-1608
(MAINE)
Plan of St. George's Fort, built by George Popham in 1607
(ARROWSIC ISLAND)
(GEORGETOWN ISLAND)
SAGADAHOC
(KENNEBEC RIVER)
ST. GEORGE'S FORT
SABINO
(CAPE SMALL POINT)
ATLANTIC OCEAN
SEGUIN ISLAND
MILES
0
1
2
Drawn under the supervision of ELIZABETH RING

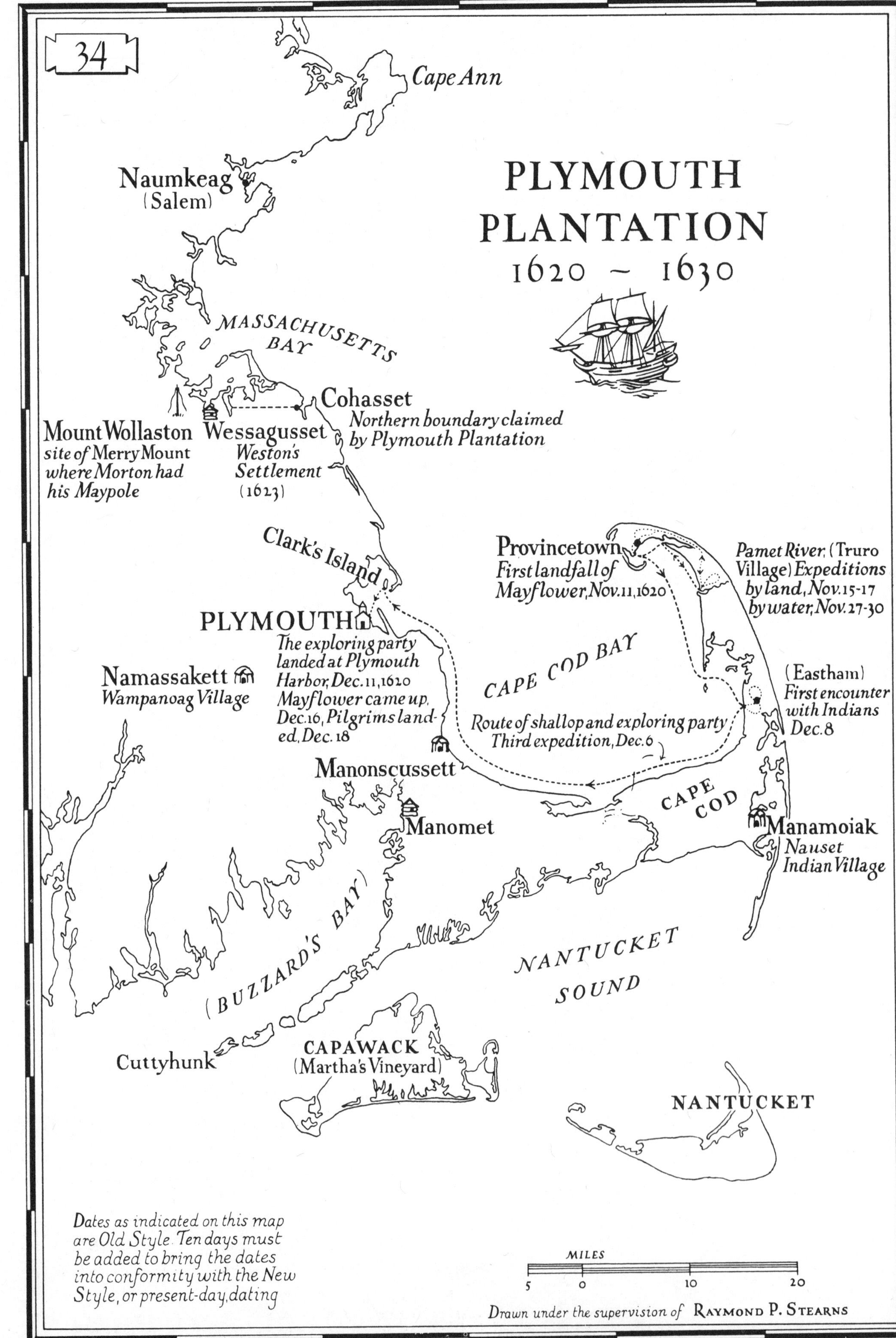
34
Cape Ann
PLYMOUTH
PLANTATION
1620 ~ 1630
Naumkeag
(Salem)
MASSACHUSETTS
BAY
Cohasset
Northern boundary claimed
by Plymouth Plantation
Mount Wollaston
site of Merry Mount
where Morton had
his Maypole
Wessagusset
Weston's
Settlement
(1623)
Clark's Island
Provincetown
First landfall of
Mayflower, Nov. 11, 1620
Pamet River, (Truro
Village) Expeditions
by land, Nov. 15-17
by water, Nov. 27-30
PLYMOUTH
The exploring party
landed at Plymouth
Harbor, Dec. 11, 1620
Mayflower came up,
Dec. 16, Pilgrims land-
ed, Dec. 18
CAPE COD BAY
(Eastham)
First encounter
with Indians
Dec. 8
Namassakett
Wampanoag Village
Route of shallop and exploring party
Third expedition, Dec. 6
Manonscussett
CAPE
COD
Manomet
Manamoiak
Nauset
Indian Village
(BUZZARD'S BAY)
NANTUCKET
SOUND
CAPAWACK
(Martha's Vineyard)
Cuttyhunk
NANTUCKET
Dates as indicated on this map
are Old Style. Ten days must
be added to bring the dates
into conformity with the New
Style, or present-day, dating
MILES
5 0 10 20
Drawn under the supervision of Raymond P. Stearns

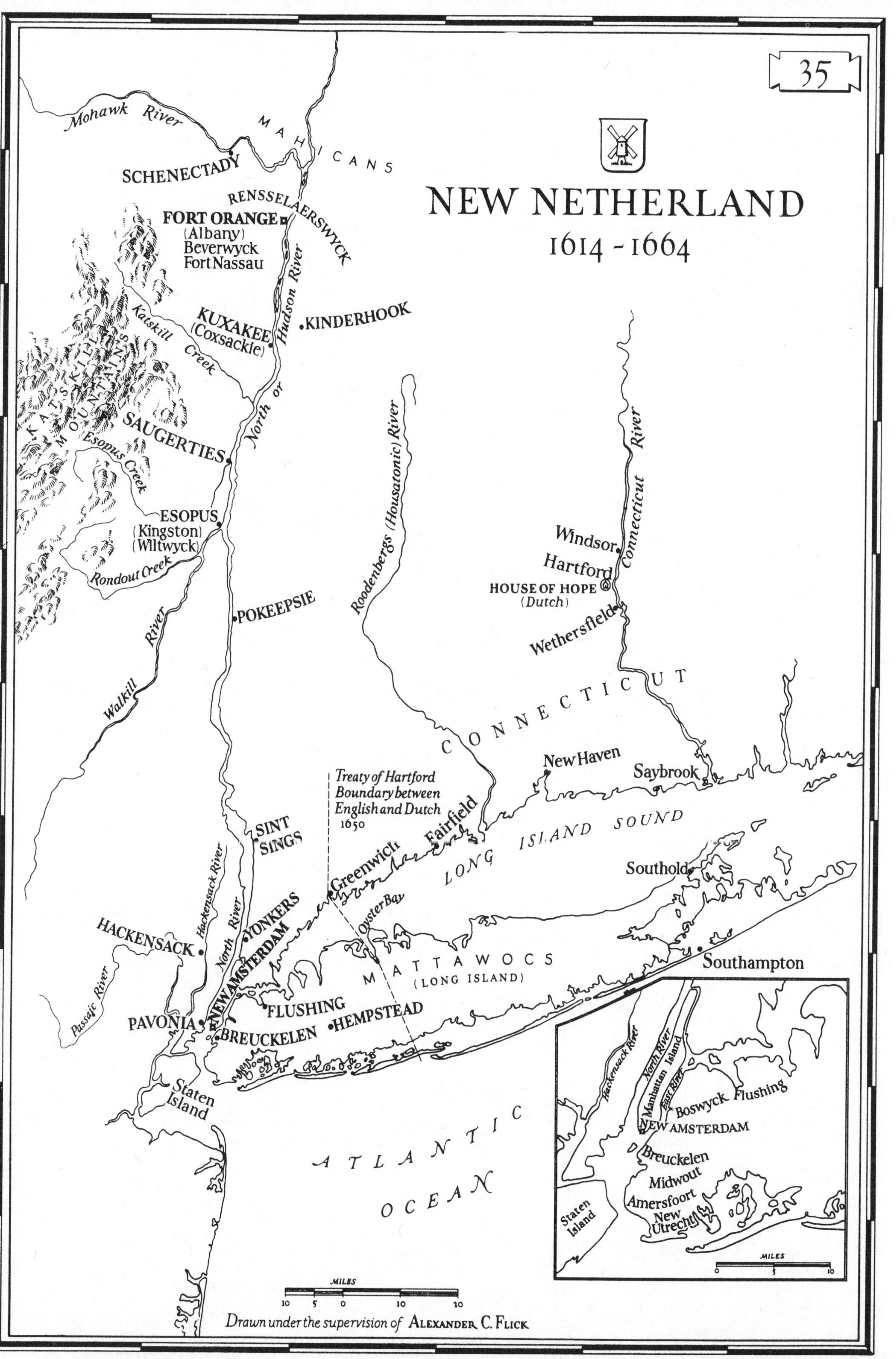
35
NEW NETHERLAND
1614 - 1664
Mohawk River
MAHICANS
SCHENECTADY
RENSSELAERSWYCK
FORT ORANGE
(Albany)
Beverwyck
Fort Nassau
Hudson River
North or
KINDERHOOK
KUXAKEE
(Coxsackie)
Katskill Creek
KATSKILL MOUNTAINS
SAUGERTIES
Esopus Creek
ESOPUS
(Kingston)
(Wiltwyck)
Rondout Creek
POKEEPSIE
Walkill River
Roodenbergs (Housatonic) River
Connecticut River
Windsor
Hartford
HOUSE OF HOPE
(Dutch)
Wethersfield
CONNECTICUT
New Haven
Saybrook
Treaty of Hartford
Boundary between
English and Dutch
1650
SINT SINGS
Fairfield
LONG ISLAND SOUND
Greenwich
Southold
Oyster Bay
YONKERS
Hackensack River
North River
HACKENSACK
NEW AMSTERDAM
MATTAWOCS
(LONG ISLAND)
Southampton
Passaic River
FLUSHING
HEMPSTEAD
PAVONIA
NEW AMSTERDAM
BREUCKELEN
Staten Island
ATLANTIC OCEAN
Hackensack River
North River
Manhattan Island
East River
Boswyck
Flushing
NEW AMSTERDAM
Breuckelen
Midwout
Amersfoort
New Utrecht
Staten Island
MILES
0 5 10
MILES
10 5 0 10 20
Drawn under the supervision of Alexander C. Flick

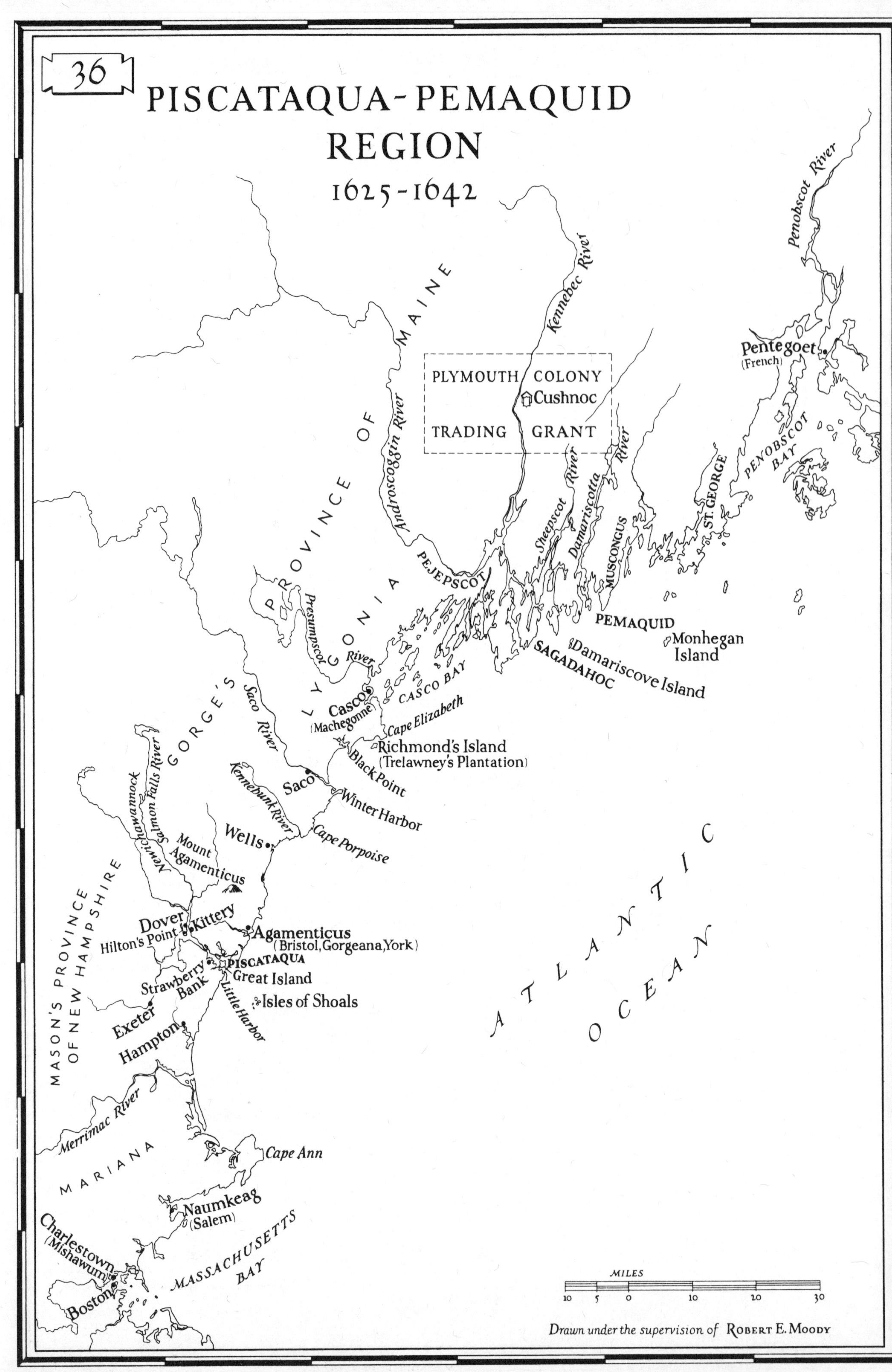
36
PISCATAQUA-PEMAQUID REGION
1625-1642
Penobscot River
Kennebec River
PROVINCE OF MAINE
Pentegoet
(French)
PLYMOUTH COLONY
Cushnoc
TRADING GRANT
Androscoggin River
Sheepscot River
Damariscotta River
MUSCONGUS
ST. GEORGE
PENOBSCOT BAY
PEJEPSCOT
PROVINCE OF LYGONIA
Presumpscot River
PEMAQUID
Monhegan Island
Damariscove Island
SAGADAHOC
CASCO BAY
Casco
(Machegonne)
Cape Elizabeth
Richmond's Island
(Trelawney's Plantation)
Black Point
GORGE'S
Saco River
Saco
Winter Harbor
Kennebunk River
Wells
Cape Porpoise
Newichawannock
Salmon Falls River
Mount Agamenticus
MASON'S PROVINCE OF NEW HAMPSHIRE
Dover
Hilton's Point
Kittery
Agamenticus
(Bristol, Gorgeana, York)
PISCATAQUA
Great Island
Strawberry Bank
Isles of Shoals
Little Harbor
Exeter
Hampton
ATLANTIC OCEAN
Merrimac River
MARIANA
Cape Ann
Naumkeag
(Salem)
Charlestown
(Mishawum)
Boston
MASSACHUSETTS BAY
MILES
10 5 0 10 20 30
Drawn under the supervision of Robert E. Moody

MASSACHUSETTS BAY 1630-1642

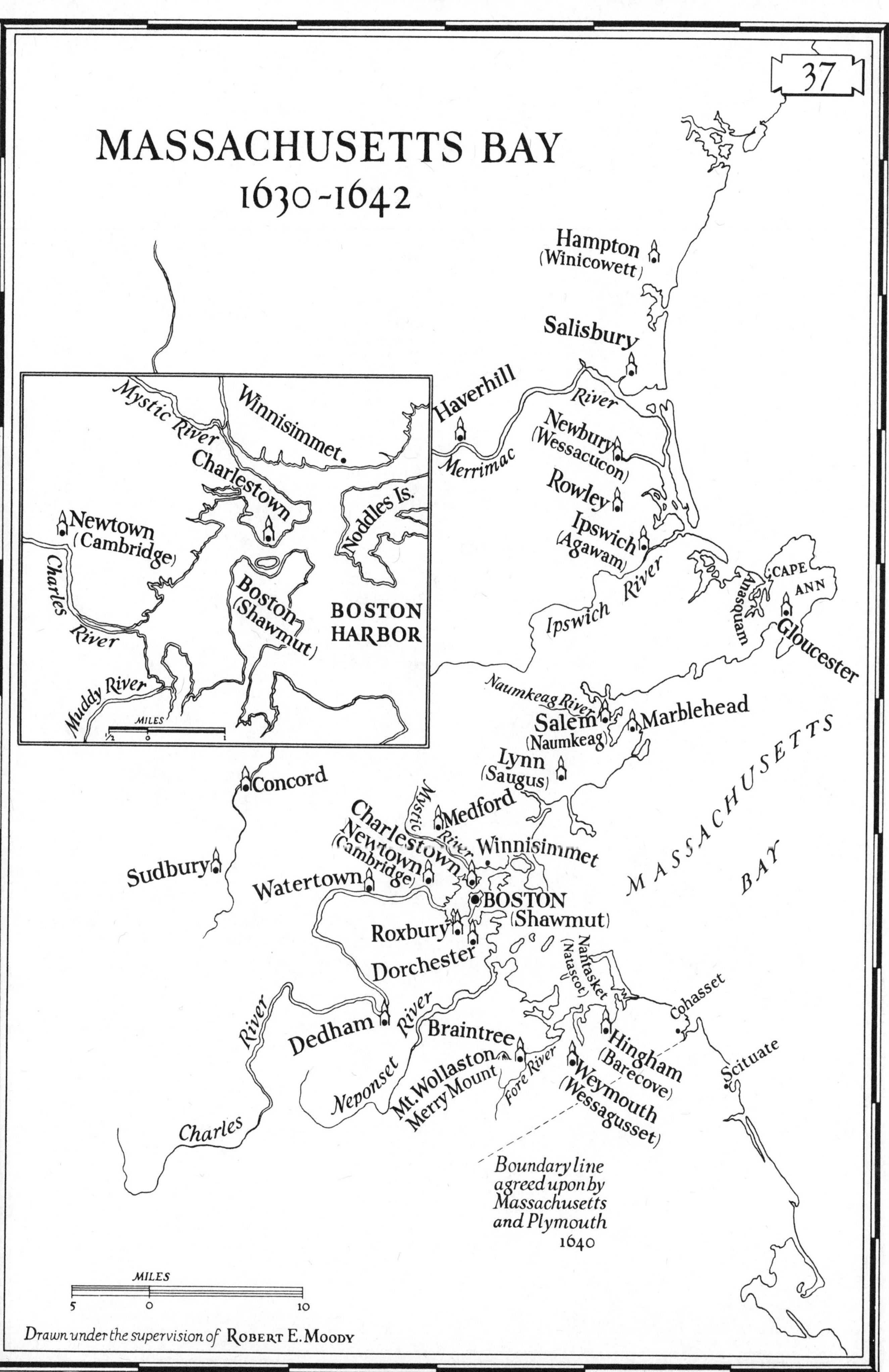

Hampton
(Winicowett)
Salisbury
Haverhill
River
Merrimac
Newbury
(Wessacucon)
Rowley
Ipswich
(Agawam)
Ipswich River
CAPE ANN
Annisquam
Gloucester
Naumkeag River
Salem
(Naumkeag)
Marblehead
Lynn
(Saugus)
Concord
Mystic River
Medford
Charlestown
Newtown
(Cambridge)
Winnisimmet
Sudbury
Watertown
BOSTON
(Shawmut)
Roxbury
Dorchester
Nantasket
(Natascot)
Cohasset
Dedham
Neponset River
Braintree
Mt. Wollaston
Merry Mount
Fore River
Hingham
(Barecove)
Weymouth
(Wessagusset)
Scituate
Charles River
MASSACHUSETTS BAY
Boundary line agreed upon by Massachusetts and Plymouth 1640
MILES
5 0 10
Mystic River
Winnisimmet.
Charlestown
Noddles Is.
Newtown
(Cambridge)
Charles River
Boston
(Shawmut)
BOSTON HARBOR
Muddy River
MILES
1/2 0 1

Drawn under the supervision of Robert E. Moody

38

CONNECTICUT AND NEW HAVEN COLONIES 1635–1660

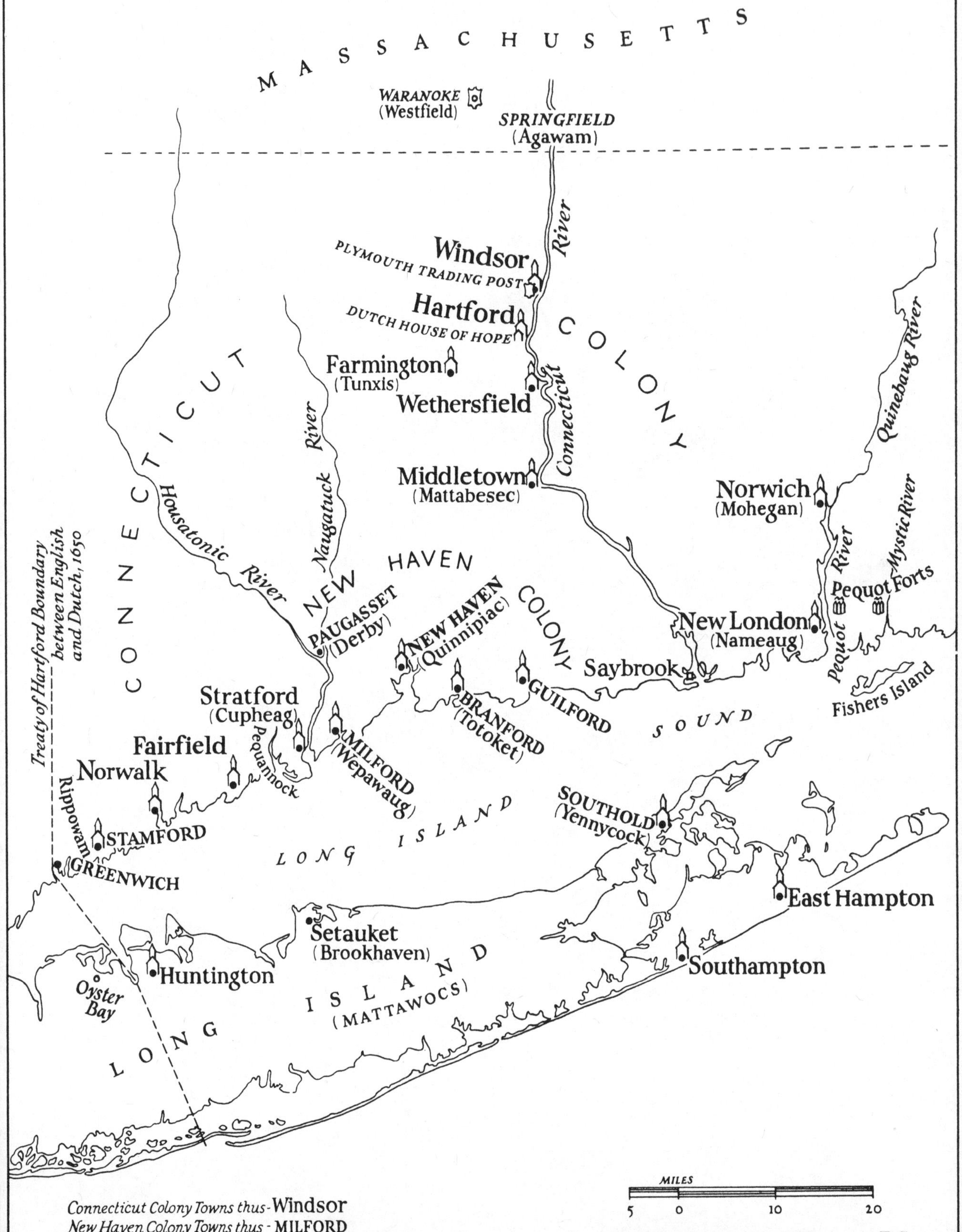

MASSACHUSETTS
WARANOKE (Westfield)
SPRINGFIELD (Agawam)
Connecticut River
Windsor
PLYMOUTH TRADING POST
Hartford
DUTCH HOUSE OF HOPE
Farmington (Tunxis)
Wethersfield
Middletown (Mattabesec)
CONNECTICUT COLONY
Naugatuck River
Housatonic River
Quinebaug River
Norwich (Mohegan)
Mystic River
Pequot River
Pequot Forts
New London (Nameaug)
Saybrook
Fishers Island
NEW HAVEN COLONY
PAUGASSET (Derby)
NEW HAVEN (Quinnipiac)
BRANFORD (Totoket)
GUILFORD
Stratford (Cupheag)
MILFORD (Wepawaug)
Pequannock
Fairfield
Norwalk
Rippowam
STAMFORD
GREENWICH
Treaty of Hartford Boundary between English and Dutch, 1650
LONG ISLAND SOUND
SOUTHOLD (Yennycock)
East Hampton
Southampton
Setauket (Brookhaven)
Huntington
Oyster Bay
LONG ISLAND (MATTAWOCS)

MILES
5 0 10 20

Connecticut Colony Towns thus - Windsor
New Haven Colony Towns thus - MILFORD

Drawn under the supervision of MARJORIE E. CASE

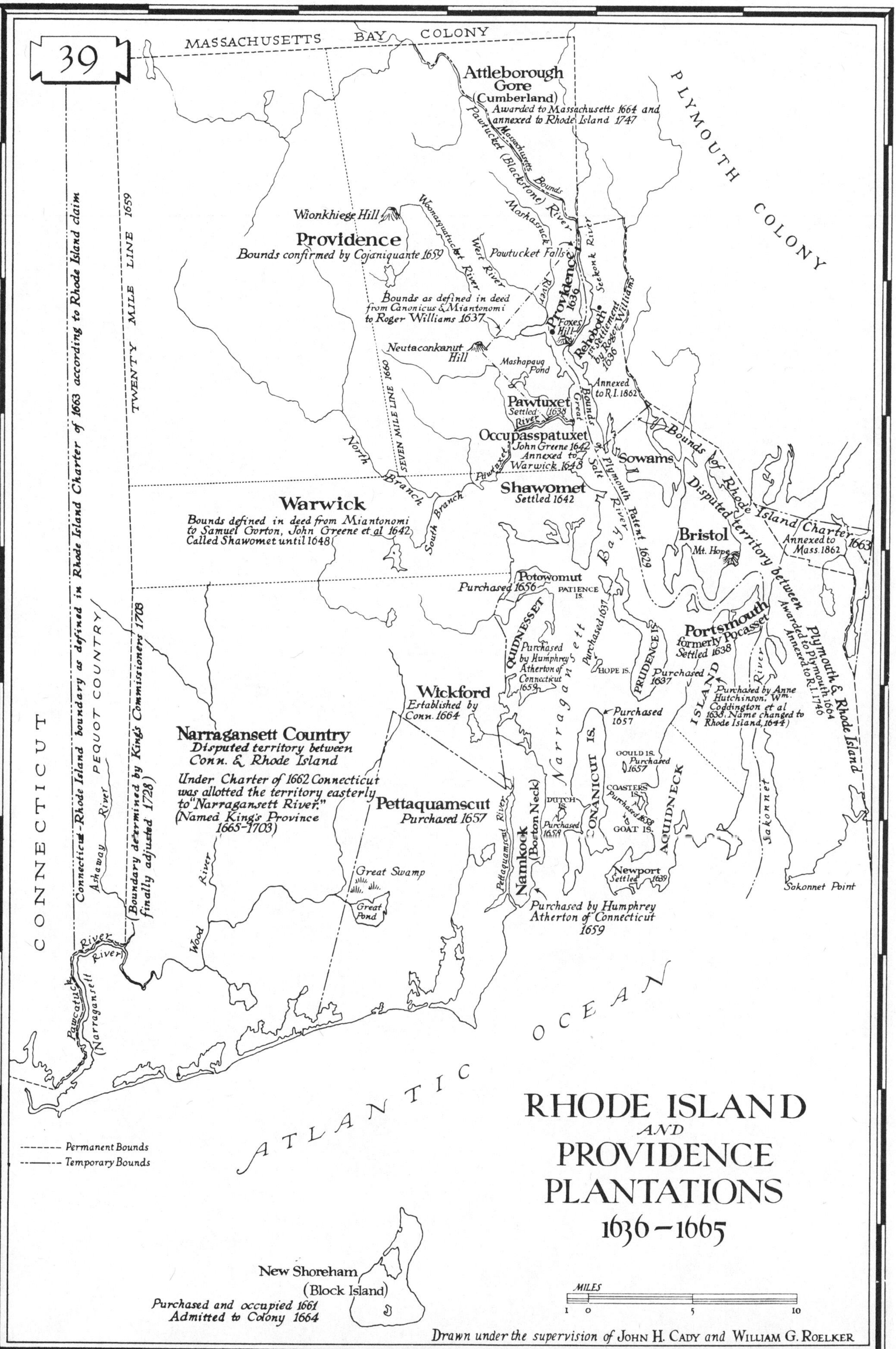

39
MASSACHUSETTS BAY COLONY
PLYMOUTH COLONY
Attleborough Gore (Cumberland)
Awarded to Massachusetts 1664 and annexed to Rhode Island 1747
Pawtucket (Blackstone) River
Providence
Bounds confirmed by Cojaniquante 1659
Bounds as defined in deed from Canonicus & Miantonomi to Roger Williams 1637
Providence 1636
Rehoboth 1st Settlement by Roger Williams 1636
Annexed to R.I. 1862
Pawtuxet
Settled 1638
Occupasspatuxet
John Greene 1642 Annexed to Warwick 1648
Sowams
Shawomet
Settled 1642
Warwick
Bounds defined in deed from Miantonomi to Samuel Gorton, John Greene et al 1642 Called Shawomet until 1648
Bristol
Annexed to Mass. 1862
Bounds of Rhode Island Charter 1663
Disputed territory between Plymouth & Rhode Island
Potowomut
Purchased 1656
Portsmouth formerly Pocasset Settled 1638
Wickford
Established by Conn. 1664
Narragansett Country
Disputed territory between Conn. & Rhode Island
Under Charter of 1662 Connecticut was allotted the territory easterly to "Narragansett River." (Named King's Province 1665-1703)
Pettaquamscut
Purchased 1657
Newport
Settled 1639
Purchased by Humphrey Atherton of Connecticut 1659
Connecticut-Rhode Island boundary as defined in Rhode Island Charter of 1663 according to Rhode Island claim
(Boundary determined by King's Commissioners 1703 finally adjusted 1728)
TWENTY MILE LINE 1659
SEVEN MILE LINE 1660
CONNECTICUT
PEQUOT COUNTRY
ATLANTIC OCEAN
New Shoreham (Block Island)
Purchased and occupied 1661 Admitted to Colony 1664
Permanent Bounds
Temporary Bounds
RHODE ISLAND AND PROVIDENCE PLANTATIONS 1636–1665
MILES
Drawn under the supervision of JOHN H. CADY and WILLIAM G. ROELKER

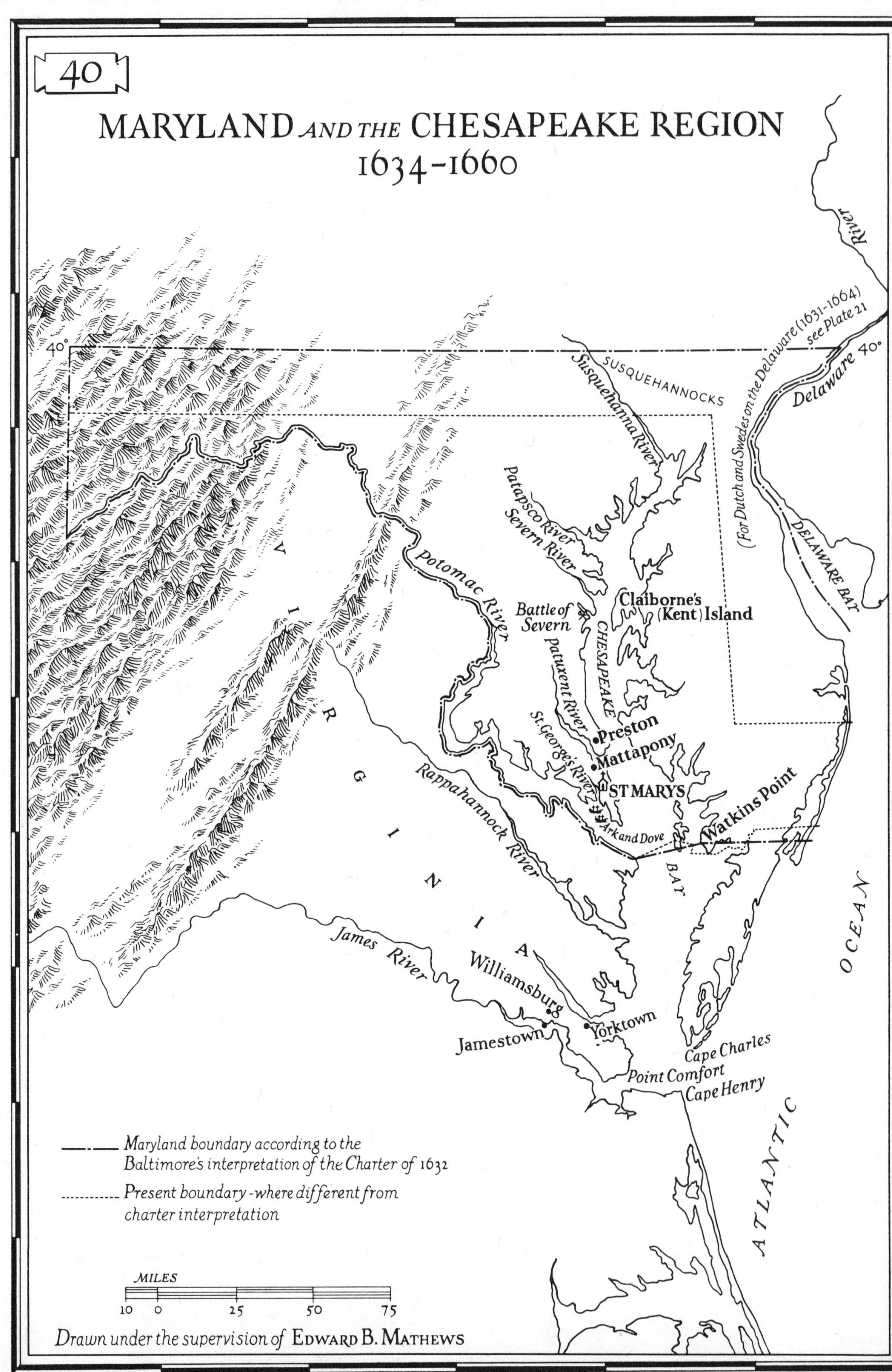
40
MARYLAND AND THE CHESAPEAKE REGION
1634-1660
40°
SUSQUEHANNOCKS
Susquehanna River
(For Dutch and Swedes on the Delaware (1631-1664) see Plate 21
Delaware 40°
River
DELAWARE BAY
Patapsco River
Severn River
Potomac River
Battle of Severn
Claiborne's (Kent) Island
Patuxent River
CHESAPEAKE
BAY
St. George's River
Preston
Mattapony
ST MARYS
Ark and Dove
Watkins Point
V I R G I N I A
Rappahannock River
James River
Williamsburg
Yorktown
Jamestown
Cape Charles
Point Comfort
Cape Henry
ATLANTIC
OCEAN
Maryland boundary according to the Baltimore's interpretation of the Charter of 1632
Present boundary - where different from charter interpretation
MILES
10 0 25 50 75
Drawn under the supervision of Edward B. Mathews

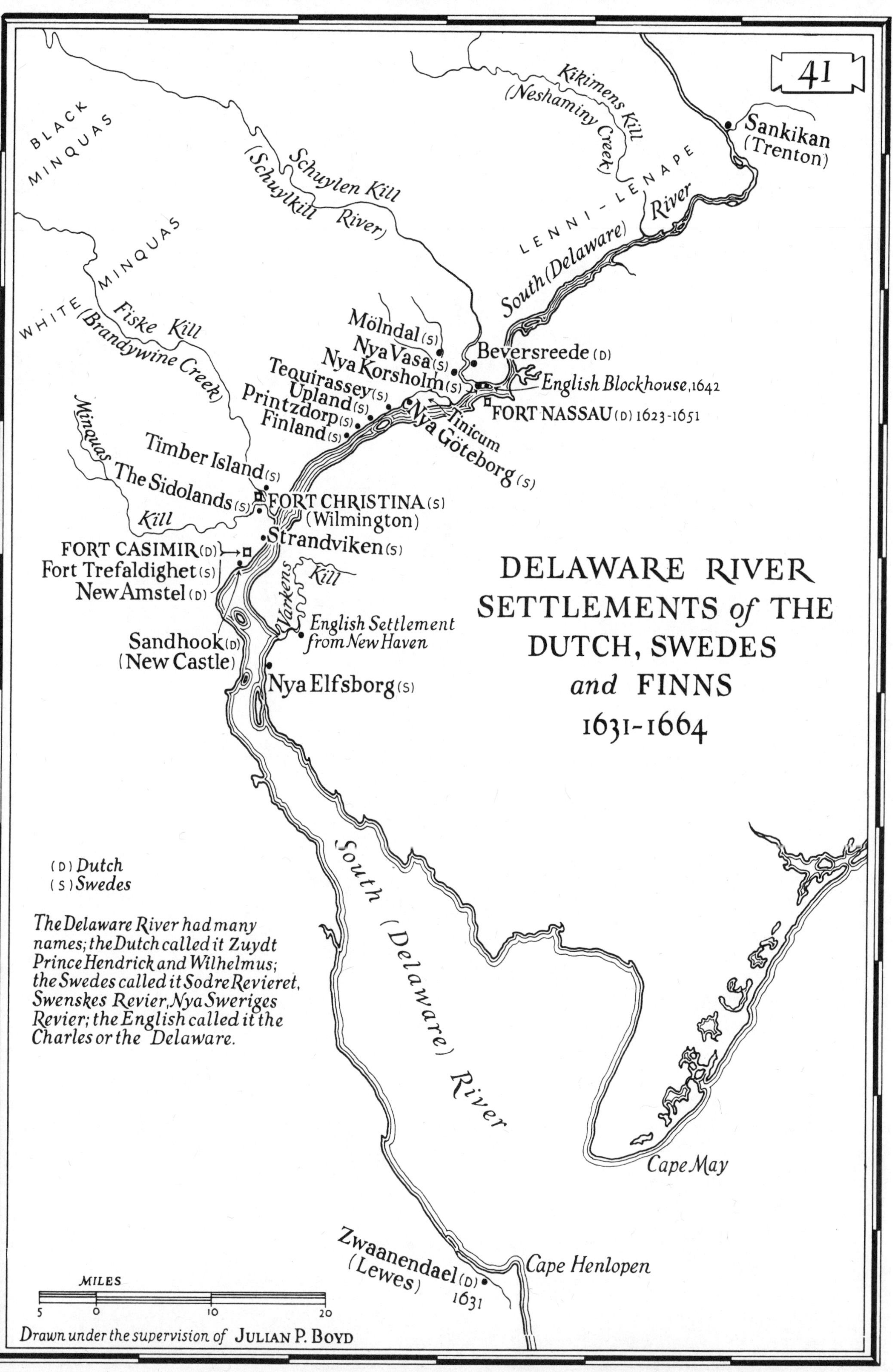
41
DELAWARE RIVER SETTLEMENTS of THE DUTCH, SWEDES and FINNS 1631-1664
BLACK MINQUAS
WHITE MINQUAS
LENNI-LENAPE
Kikimens Kill (Neshaminy Creek)
Sankikan (Trenton)
Schuylen Kill (Schuylkill River)
South (Delaware) River
Fiske Kill (Brandywine Creek)
Minquas Kill
Möndal (S)
Nya Vasa (S)
Nya Korsholm (S)
Beversreede (D)
English Blockhouse, 1642
Tequirassey (S)
Upland (S)
Printzdorp (S)
Finland (S)
Tinicum
FORT NASSAU (D) 1623-1651
Nya Göteborg (S)
Timber Island (S)
The Sidolands (S)
FORT CHRISTINA (S) (Wilmington)
Strandviken (S)
FORT CASIMIR (D)
Fort Trefaldighet (S)
New Amstel (D)
Varkens Kill
English Settlement from New Haven
Sandhook (D) (New Castle)
Nya Elfsborg (S)
South (Delaware) River
Cape May
Cape Henlopen
Zwaanendael (D) (Lewes) 1631
(D) Dutch
(S) Swedes
The Delaware River had many names; the Dutch called it Zuydt Prince Hendrick and Wilhelmus; the Swedes called it Sodre Revieret, Swenskes Revier, Nya Sweriges Revier; the English called it the Charles or the Delaware.
MILES
5 0 10 20
Drawn under the supervision of JULIAN P. BOYD

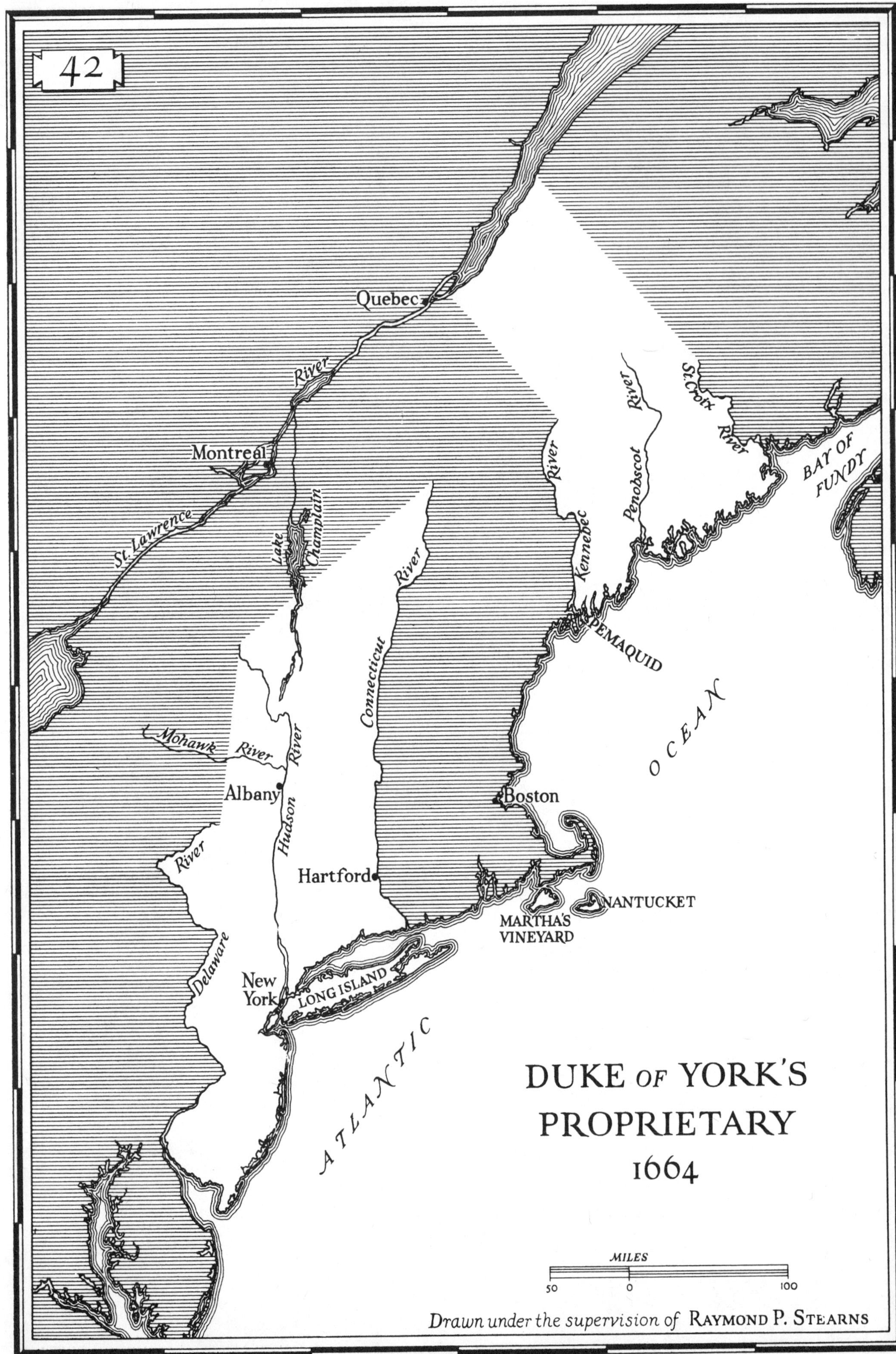
42
Quebec
River
St. Croix
River
River
Penobscot
River
Montreal
BAY OF FUNDY
St. Lawrence
Lake
Champlain
River
Kennebec
PEMAQUID
Connecticut
OCEAN
Mohawk
River
River
Albany
Hudson
Boston
River
Hartford
NANTUCKET
MARTHA'S VINEYARD
Delaware
New York
LONG ISLAND
ATLANTIC
DUKE OF YORK'S
PROPRIETARY
1664
MILES
50
0
100
Drawn under the supervision of RAYMOND P. STEARNS

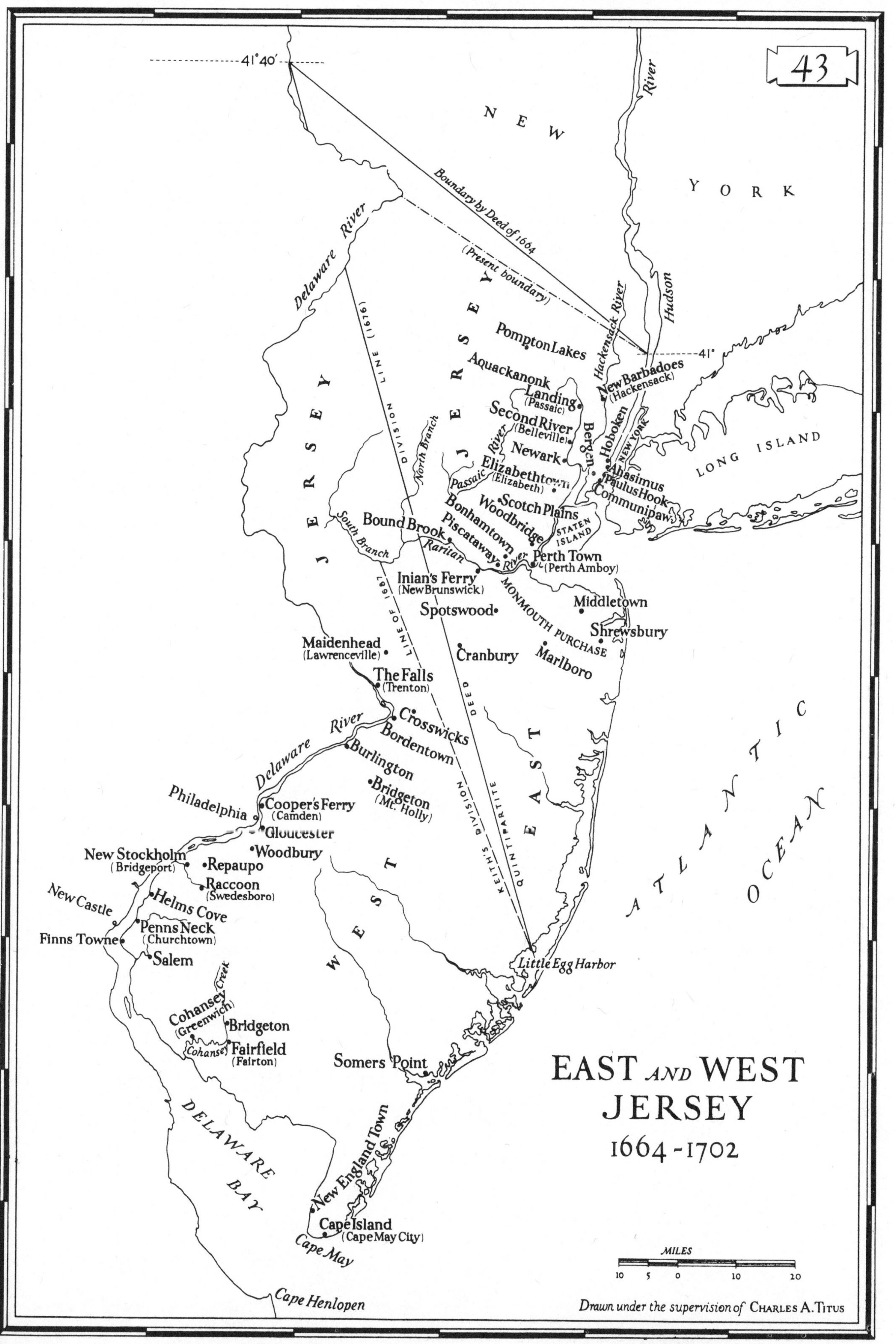
41°40′
NEW YORK
Boundary by Deed of 1664
(Present boundary)
Delaware River
River
Hudson
Hackensack River
41°
Pompton Lakes
Aquackanonk Landing
(Passaic)
New Barbadoes
(Hackensack)
Second River
(Belleville)
Bergen
Hoboken
NEW YORK
LONG ISLAND
Newark
Passaic River
North Branch
Elizabethtown
(Elizabeth)
Ahasimus
Paulus Hook
Communipaw
Scotch Plains
Woodbridge
STATEN ISLAND
Bonhamtown
Piscataway
Bound Brook
South Branch
Raritan River
Perth Town
(Perth Amboy)
Inian's Ferry
(New Brunswick)
DIVISION LINE (1676)
EAST JERSEY
WEST JERSEY
Middletown
Spotswood
Shrewsbury
MONMOUTH PURCHASE
Maidenhead
(Lawrenceville)
LINE OF 1687
Cranbury
Marlboro
The Falls
(Trenton)
Crosswicks
Bordentown
Burlington
Bridgeton
(Mt. Holly)
Delaware River
Philadelphia
Cooper's Ferry
(Camden)
Gloucester
Woodbury
KEITH'S DIVISION
QUINTIPARTITE DEED
ATLANTIC OCEAN
New Stockholm
(Bridgeport)
Repaupo
Raccoon
(Swedesboro)
New Castle
Helms Cove
Penns Neck
(Churchtown)
Finns Towne
Salem
Little Egg Harbor
Cohansey Creek
Cohansey
(Greenwich)
Bridgeton
Cohansey
Fairfield
(Fairton)
Somers Point
DELAWARE BAY
New England Town
Cape Island
(Cape May City)
Cape May
Cape Henlopen
MILES
10 5 0 10 20
Drawn under the supervision of CHARLES A. TITUS

EAST AND WEST JERSEY 1664-1702

44
CAROLINAS AND VIRGINIA 1663-1729
Drawn under the supervision of E. Merton Coulter
MILES
25 0 50 100
WEST JERSEY
Cape May
LOWER COUNTIES OF DELAWARE
MARYLAND
VIRGINIA
Potomac River
FAIRFAX PROPRIETARY (Northern Neck)
Western boundary of the Fairfax Proprietary
Germanna
Rappahannock River
Route of Spotswood's Expedition
Shenandoah
WILLIAMSBURG
James River
Fort Henry
Yorktown
Norfolk
Northern Boundary of Carolina under Charter of 1665
36° 30'
Currituck
Northern Boundary of Carolina under Charter of 1663
36°
35° 34'
Roanoke River
Chowan River
ALBEMARLE
Edenton
(GRANVILLE GRANT)
NORTH CAROLINA
Neuse River
Fort Nohoroco
Pamlico Sound
New Berne
TUSCARORA
Cape Fear River
CLARENDON
Brunswick
Cape Fear
CHEROKEE
CATAWBA
Broad River
Wateree River
Saluda River
Peedee River
SOUTH CAROLINA
Santee River
Jamestown
ST. JOHN'S BERKELEY
The Orange Quarter
Cooper R.
Ashley R.
CHARLESTON
Edisto River
Savannah River
YAMASEE
Beaufort
Stuart's Town
Port Royal
Ogeechee River
Oconee River
Ocmulgee River
Altamaha River
CREEK
Coweta Town
Savacola (Spanish)
Chattahoochee River
Flint River
Fort King George
Southern Boundary of Carolina under Charter of 1663 31°
St. Marys River
Santa Cruz de Savacola (Spanish)
AYUBALE
San Luis (Spanish)
APALACHE
Apalachicola River
Ochlockonee River
St. Johns River
St. Augustine (Spanish)
Southern Boundary of Carolina under Charter of 1665
29°

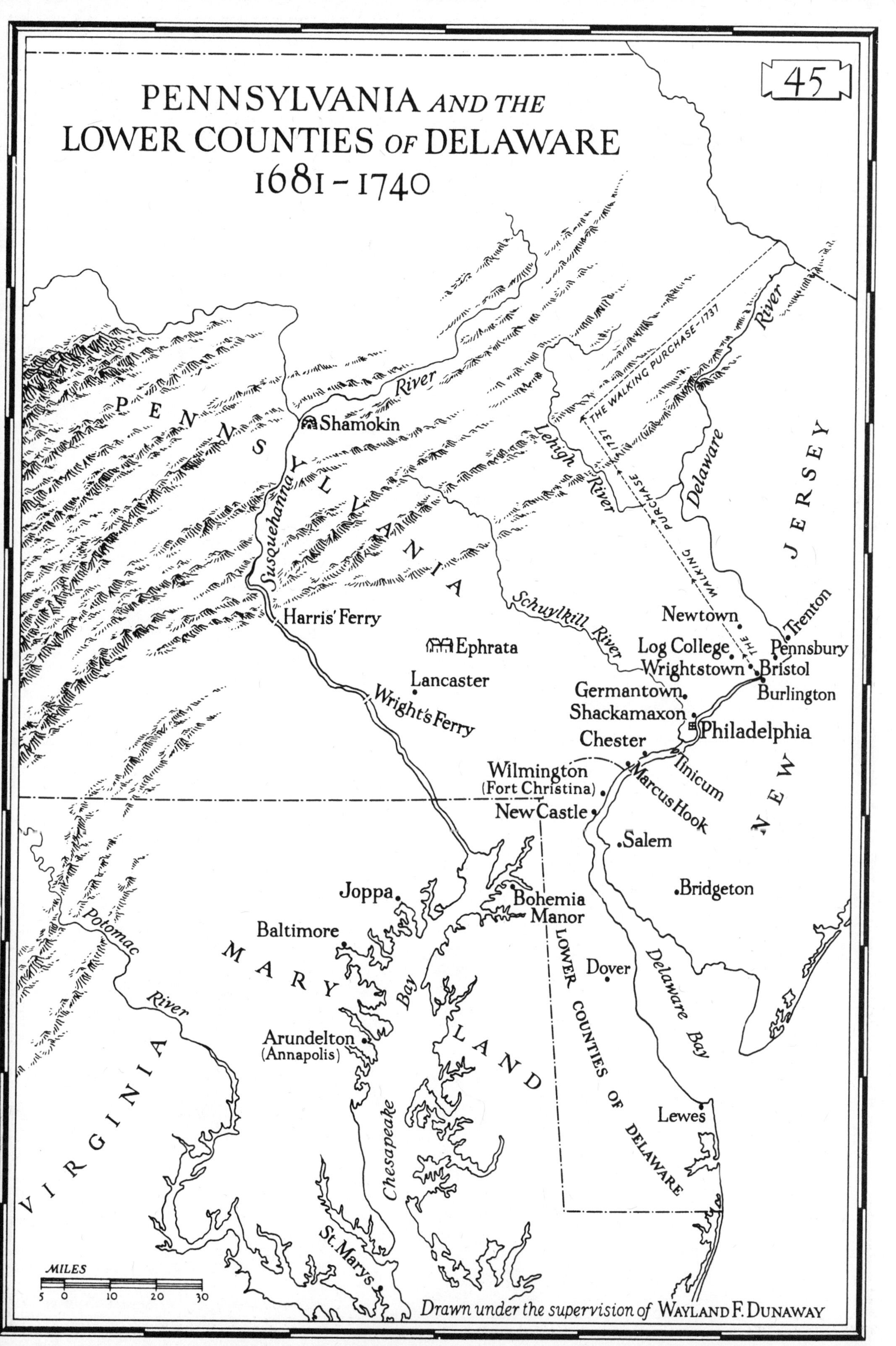

45
PENNSYLVANIA AND THE LOWER COUNTIES OF DELAWARE 1681-1740
PENNSYLVANIA
Shamokin
River
Susquehanna
Lehigh River
THE WALKING PURCHASE-1737
THE WALKING PURCHASE 1737
Delaware River
NEW JERSEY
Harris' Ferry
Ephrata
Lancaster
Wright's Ferry
Schuylkill River
Newtown
Trenton
Log College
Pennsbury
Wrightstown
Bristol
Burlington
Germantown
Shackamaxon
Philadelphia
Chester
Tinicum
Wilmington (Fort Christina)
Marcus Hook
New Castle
Salem
Bridgeton
Joppa
Bohemia Manor
Baltimore
Potomac River
MARYLAND
Chesapeake Bay
Dover
Delaware Bay
Arundelton (Annapolis)
LOWER COUNTIES OF DELAWARE
Lewes
VIRGINIA
St. Marys
MILES
5 0 10 20 30
Drawn under the supervision of WAYLAND F. DUNAWAY

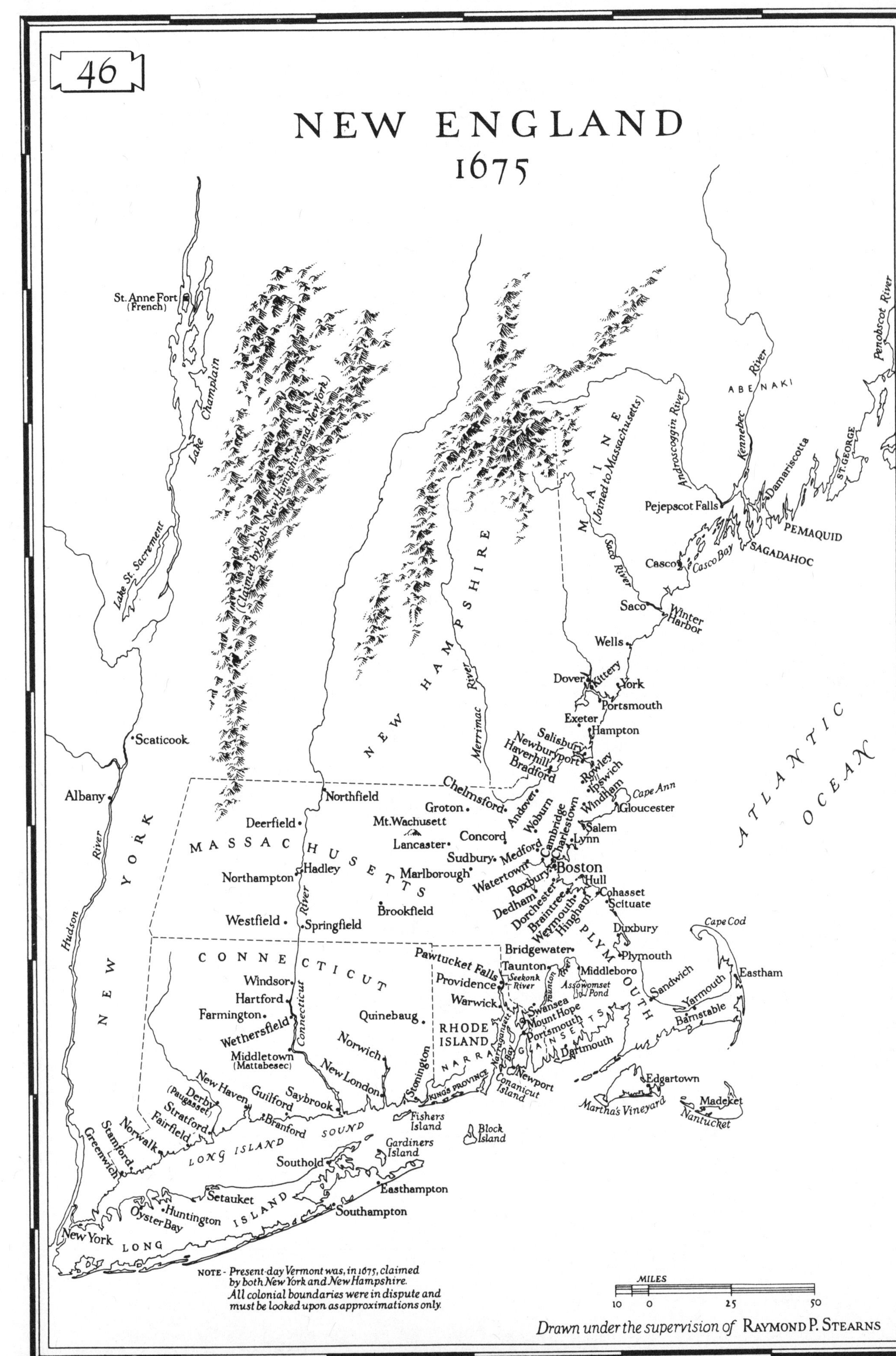
46
NEW ENGLAND
1675
St. Anne Fort (French)
Lake Champlain
Lake St. Sacrement
(Claimed by both New Hampshire and New York)
NEW HAMPSHIRE
MAINE
(Joined to Massachusetts)
ABENAKI
Androscoggin River
Kennebec River
Penobscot River
ST. GEORGE
Damariscotta
Pejepscot Falls
PEMAQUID
SAGADAHOC
Casco
Casco Bay
Saco River
Saco
Winter Harbor
Wells
Dover
Kittery
York
Portsmouth
Exeter
Hampton
Merrimac River
Salisbury
Newburyport
Haverhill
Bradford
Rowley
Ipswich
Cape Ann
Gloucester
Windham
Salem
Lynn
Chelmsford
Andover
Groton
Woburn
Cambridge
Charlestown
Medford
Concord
Mt. Wachusett
Lancaster
Sudbury
Watertown
Marlborough
Roxbury
Boston
Hull
Cohasset
Scituate
Dedham
Dorchester
Braintree
Weymouth
Hingham
Duxbury
PLYMOUTH
Plymouth
Cape Cod
Eastham
Sandwich
Yarmouth
Barnstable
ATLANTIC OCEAN
Scaticook
Albany
Hudson River
NEW YORK
MASSACHUSETTS
Northfield
Deerfield
Hadley
Northampton
Brookfield
Westfield
Springfield
Connecticut River
CONNECTICUT
Windsor
Hartford
Farmington
Wethersfield
Middletown (Mattabesec)
Quinebaug
Norwich
New London
Stonington
Pawtucket Falls
Providence
Seekonk River
Warwick
Bridgewater
Taunton
Taunton River
Middleboro
Assowomset Pond
Swansea
Mount Hope
Portsmouth
RHODE ISLAND
NARRAGANSETTS
Narragansett Bay
KING'S PROVINCE
Conanicut Island
Newport
Dartmouth
Edgartown
Martha's Vineyard
Madeket
Nantucket
New Haven
Derby (Paugasset)
Guilford
Saybrook
Stratford
Branford
Fairfield
Norwalk
Stamford
Greenwich
Fishers Island
Block Island
Gardiners Island
LONG ISLAND SOUND
Southold
Easthampton
Setauket
Huntington
Oyster Bay
Southampton
New York
LONG ISLAND
NOTE - Present-day Vermont was, in 1675, claimed by both New York and New Hampshire. All colonial boundaries were in dispute and must be looked upon as approximations only.
MILES
10 0 25 50
Drawn under the supervision of RAYMOND P. STEARNS

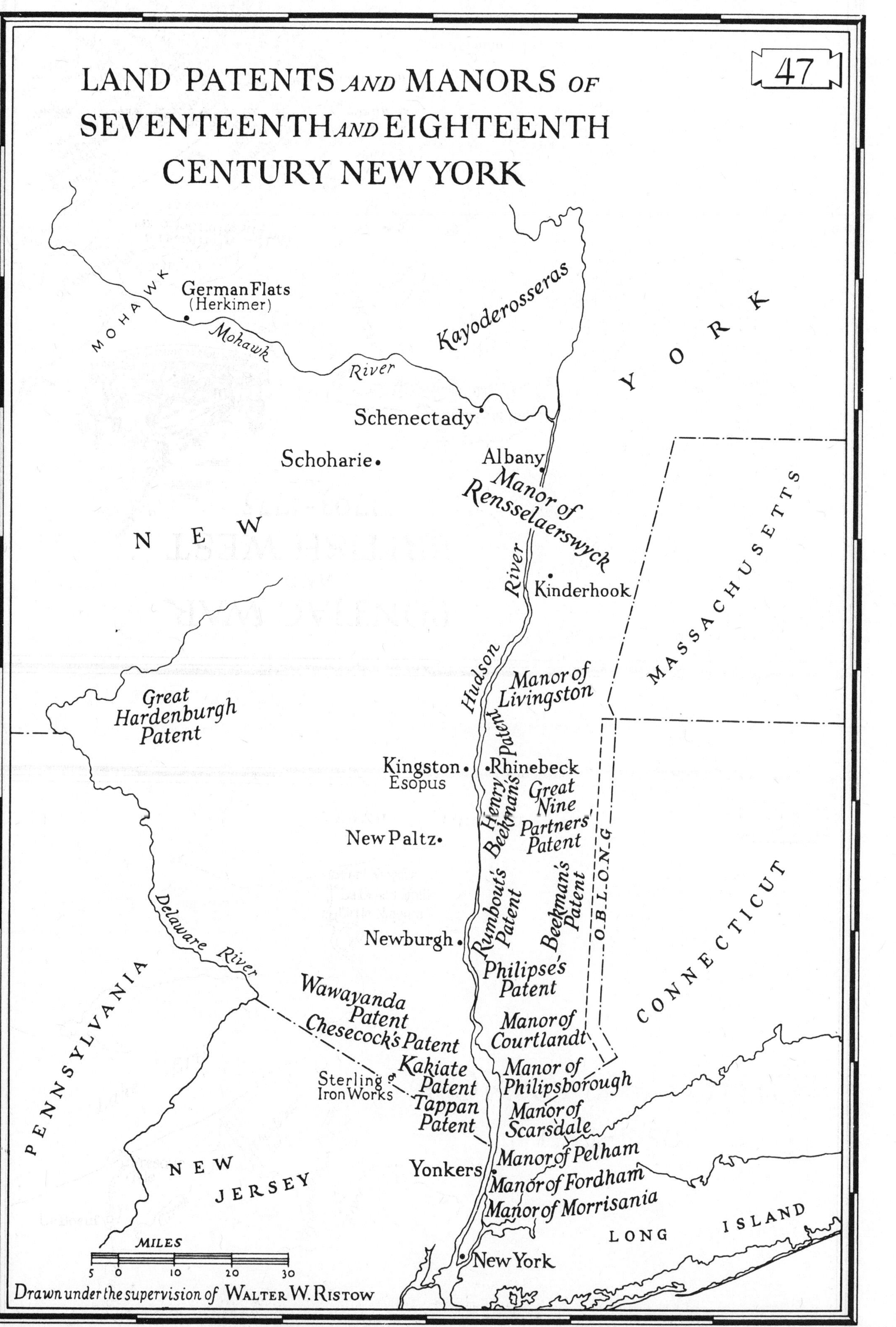

47
LAND PATENTS AND MANORS OF SEVENTEENTH AND EIGHTEENTH CENTURY NEW YORK
NEW YORK
MOHAWK
German Flats
(Herkimer)
Mohawk River
Kayoderosseras
Schenectady
Schoharie
Albany
Manor of Rensselaerswyck
Kinderhook
Hudson River
MASSACHUSETTS
Great Hardenburgh Patent
Manor of Livingston
Henry Beekman's Patent
Kingston
Esopus
Rhinebeck
Great Nine Partners' Patent
New Paltz
Rumbout's Patent
Beekman's Patent
OBLONG
CONNECTICUT
Newburgh
Delaware River
Philipse's Patent
PENNSYLVANIA
Wawayanda Patent
Chesecock's Patent
Manor of Courtlandt
Kakiate Patent
Sterling Iron Works
Manor of Philipsborough
Tappan Patent
Manor of Scarsdale
Manor of Pelham
Yonkers
Manor of Fordham
Manor of Morrisania
NEW JERSEY
LONG ISLAND
New York
MILES
5 0 10 20 30
Drawn under the supervision of WALTER W. RISTOW

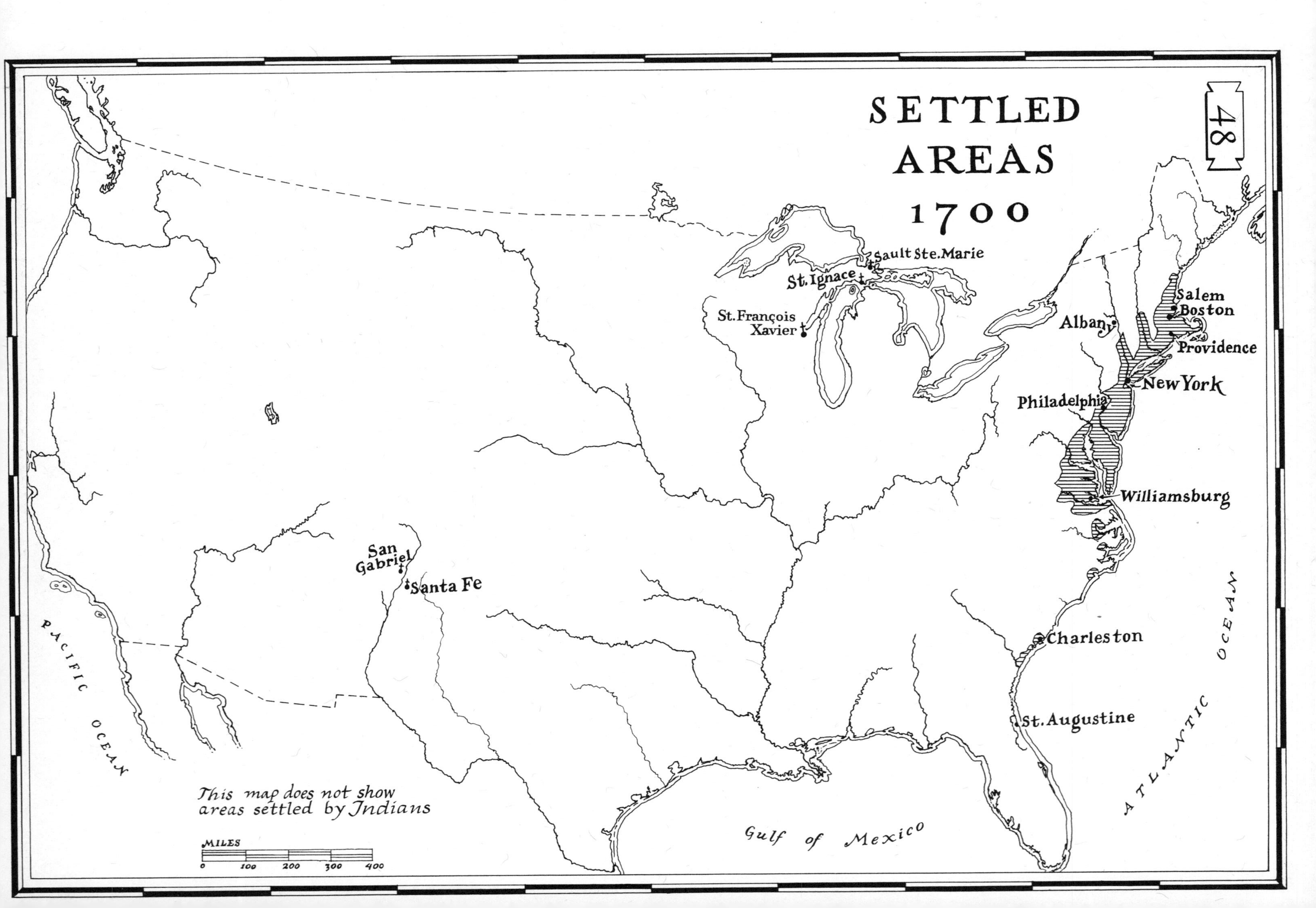
48
SETTLED
AREAS
1700
Sault Ste. Marie
St. Ignace
St. François
Xavier
Salem
Boston
Albany
Providence
New York
Philadelphia
Williamsburg
San
Gabriel
Santa Fe
Charleston
St. Augustine
PACIFIC OCEAN
ATLANTIC OCEAN
Gulf of Mexico
This map does not show
areas settled by Indians
MILES
0
100
200
300
400

49
GEORGIA
1732-1755
FORT AUGUSTA
Savannah River
Ogeechee River
Beaufort
Ebenezer
Purrysburg
Abercorn
Josephs Town
SAVANNAH
Port Royal
FORT ARGYLE
Tybee Island
Altamaha River
YAMACRAWS
MIDWAY DISTRICT
St. Catherines Island
CREEK
DARIEN
Sapelo Island
New Inverness
FREDERICA
St. Simons Island
Bloody Marsh
FORT ST. SIMONS
Satilla River
Jekyl Island
ST. ANDREWS FORT
Cumberland Island
St. Marys River
FORT WILLIAM
Okefenokee Swamp
Amelia Island
Suwannee River
FORT ST. GEORGE
St. Johns River
ATLANTIC OCEAN
ST. AUGUSTINE
MILES
25 0 50
Drawn under the supervision of E. Merton Coulter

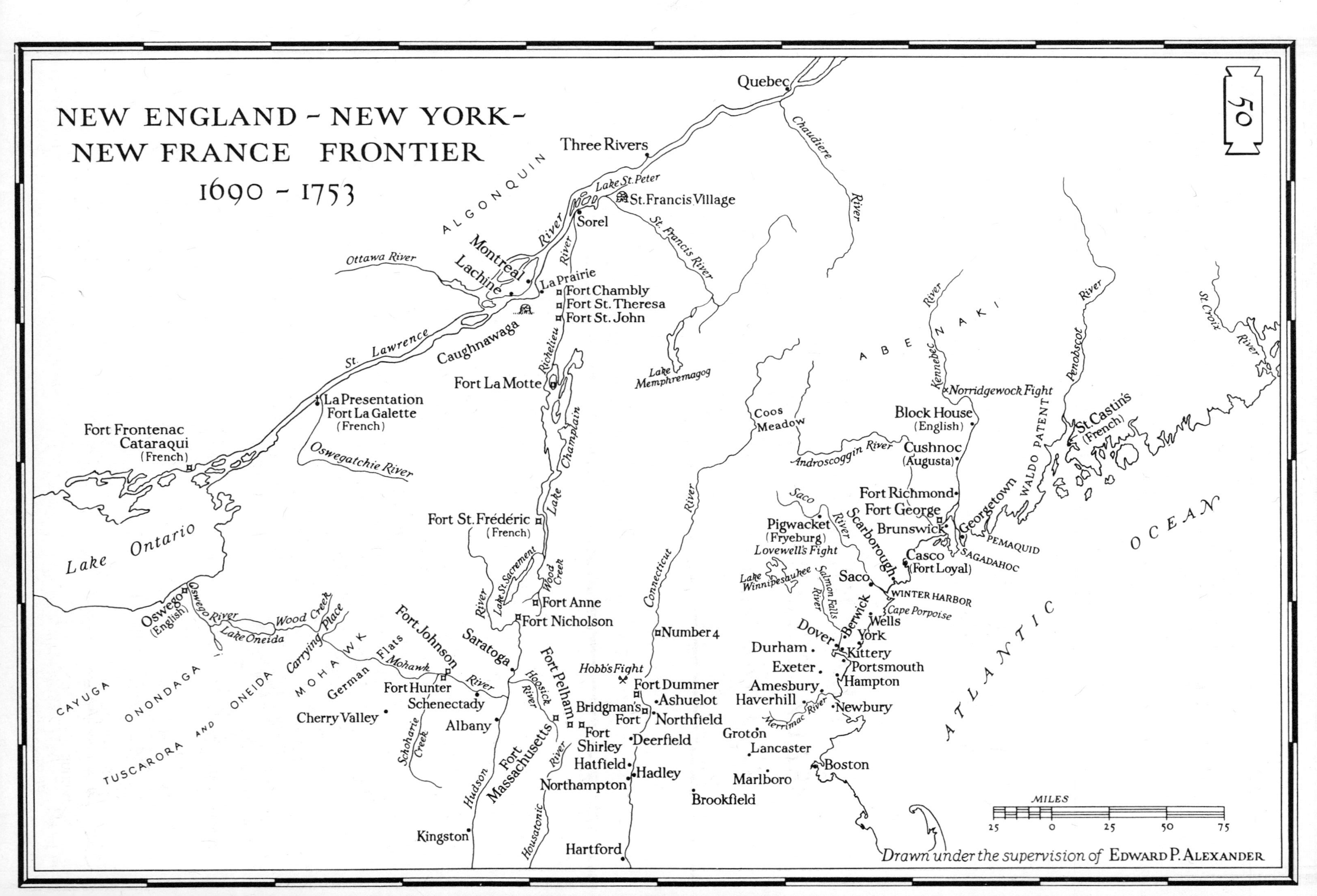
50
NEW ENGLAND - NEW YORK -
NEW FRANCE FRONTIER
1690 - 1753
Quebec
Chaudiere River
Three Rivers
Lake St. Peter
St. Francis Village
Sorel
St. Francis River
ALGONQUIN
River
Montreal
Lachine
La Prairie
Ottawa River
Fort Chambly
Fort St. Theresa
Fort St. John
Caughnawaga
St. Lawrence
Richelieu
Fort La Motte
Lake Memphremagog
La Presentation
Fort La Galette
(French)
Oswegatchie River
Fort Frontenac
Cataraqui
(French)
Lake Ontario
Lake Champlain
Fort St. Frédéric
(French)
Lake St. Sacrement
Wood Creek
Fort Anne
Fort Nicholson
Oswego
(English)
Oswego River
Lake Oneida
Wood Creek
Carrying Place
MOHAWK
German Flats
Mohawk River
Fort Johnson
Saratoga
Fort Hunter
Schenectady
Albany
Cherry Valley
Schoharie Creek
Hudson
Kingston
CAYUGA
ONONDAGA
ONEIDA
TUSCARORA AND
Fort Pelham
Hoosick River
Fort Massachusetts
Housatonic River
Northampton
Hartford
Connecticut River
Number 4
Hobb's Fight
Fort Dummer
Ashuelot
Bridgman's Fort
Northfield
Fort Shirley
Deerfield
Hatfield
Hadley
Brookfield
Coos Meadow
ABENAKI
Kennebec River
Norridgewock Fight
Block House
(English)
Androscoggin River
Cushnoc
(Augusta)
Penobscot River
WALDO PATENT
St. Castin's
(French)
St. Croix River
Fort Richmond
Fort George
Brunswick
Georgetown
PEMAQUID
SAGADAHOC
Saco River
Pigwacket
(Fryeburg)
Lovewell's Fight
Scarborough
Casco
(Fort Loyal)
Lake Winnipesaukee
Salmon Falls River
Saco
WINTER HARBOR
Cape Porpoise
Wells
Berwick
York
Dover
Kittery
Durham
Portsmouth
Exeter
Hampton
Amesbury
Haverhill
Merrimac River
Newbury
Groton
Lancaster
Marlboro
Boston
ATLANTIC
OCEAN
MILES
25
0
25
50
75
Drawn under the supervision of EDWARD P. ALEXANDER

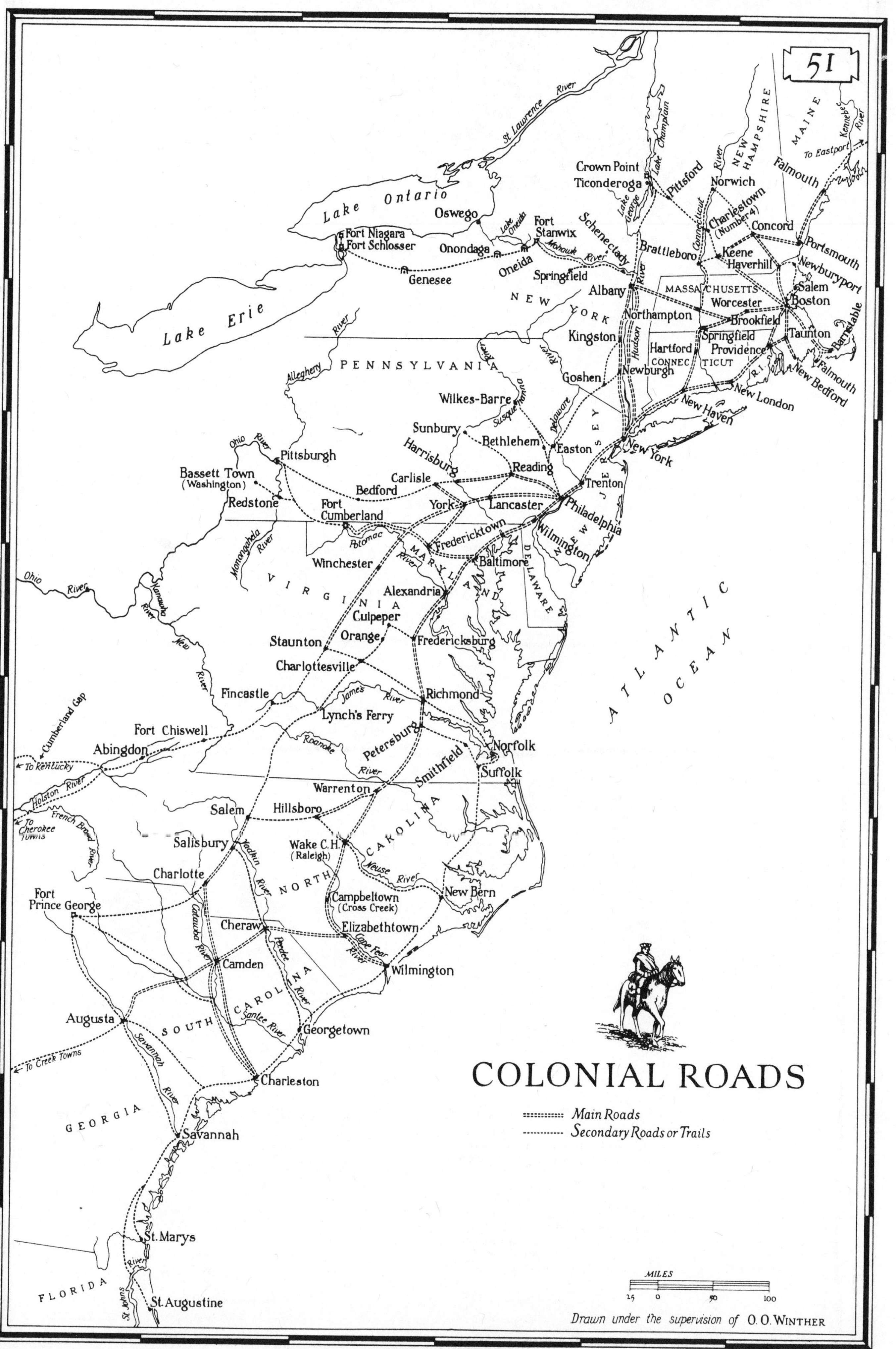
51
COLONIAL ROADS
Main Roads
Secondary Roads or Trails
Drawn under the supervision of O. O. Winther
MILES
25
0
50
100
St. Lawrence River
Lake Champlain
Lake Ontario
Lake Erie
Lake George
Lake Oneida
Crown Point
Ticonderoga
Pittsford
Oswego
Fort Niagara
Fort Schlosser
Fort Stanwix
Onondaga
Oneida
Genesee
Mohawk River
Schenectady
Springfield
Albany
NEW YORK
Brattleboro
Connecticut River
Norwich
NEW HAMPSHIRE
MAINE
Kennebec River
To Eastport
Falmouth
Charlestown (Number 4)
Concord
Keene
Haverhill
Portsmouth
Newburyport
Salem
Boston
MASSACHUSETTS
Worcester
Northampton
Brookfield
Springfield
Taunton
Barnstable
Hartford
Providence
CONNECTICUT
R.I.
Falmouth
New Bedford
Kingston
Hudson River
Newburgh
Goshen
New London
New Haven
New York
Allegheny River
PENNSYLVANIA
Delaware River
Susquehanna River
Wilkes-Barre
Sunbury
Bethlehem
Easton
NEW JERSEY
Harrisburg
Reading
Trenton
Ohio River
Pittsburgh
Bassett Town (Washington)
Redstone
Carlisle
Bedford
York
Lancaster
Philadelphia
Fort Cumberland
Potomac
Fredericktown
Wilmington
Monongahela River
Winchester
MARYLAND
Baltimore
DELAWARE
Ohio River
Kanawha River
VIRGINIA
Alexandria
Culpeper
Orange
Fredericksburg
Staunton
New River
Charlottesville
ATLANTIC OCEAN
Fincastle
James River
Richmond
Lynch's Ferry
Cumberland Gap
Fort Chiswell
Abingdon
To Kentucky
Holston River
Roanoke River
Petersburg
Norfolk
Smithfield
Suffolk
Warrenton
To Cherokee Towns
French Broad River
Salem
Hillsboro
Salisbury
Yadkin River
Wake C.H. (Raleigh)
NORTH CAROLINA
Neuse River
Charlotte
New Bern
Fort Prince George
Campbeltown (Cross Creek)
Cheraw
Elizabethtown
Catawba River
Pedee River
Cape Fear River
Camden
Wilmington
SOUTH CAROLINA
Santee River
Augusta
Georgetown
To Creek Towns
Savannah River
Charleston
GEORGIA
Savannah
St. Marys
River
FLORIDA
St. Johns
St. Augustine

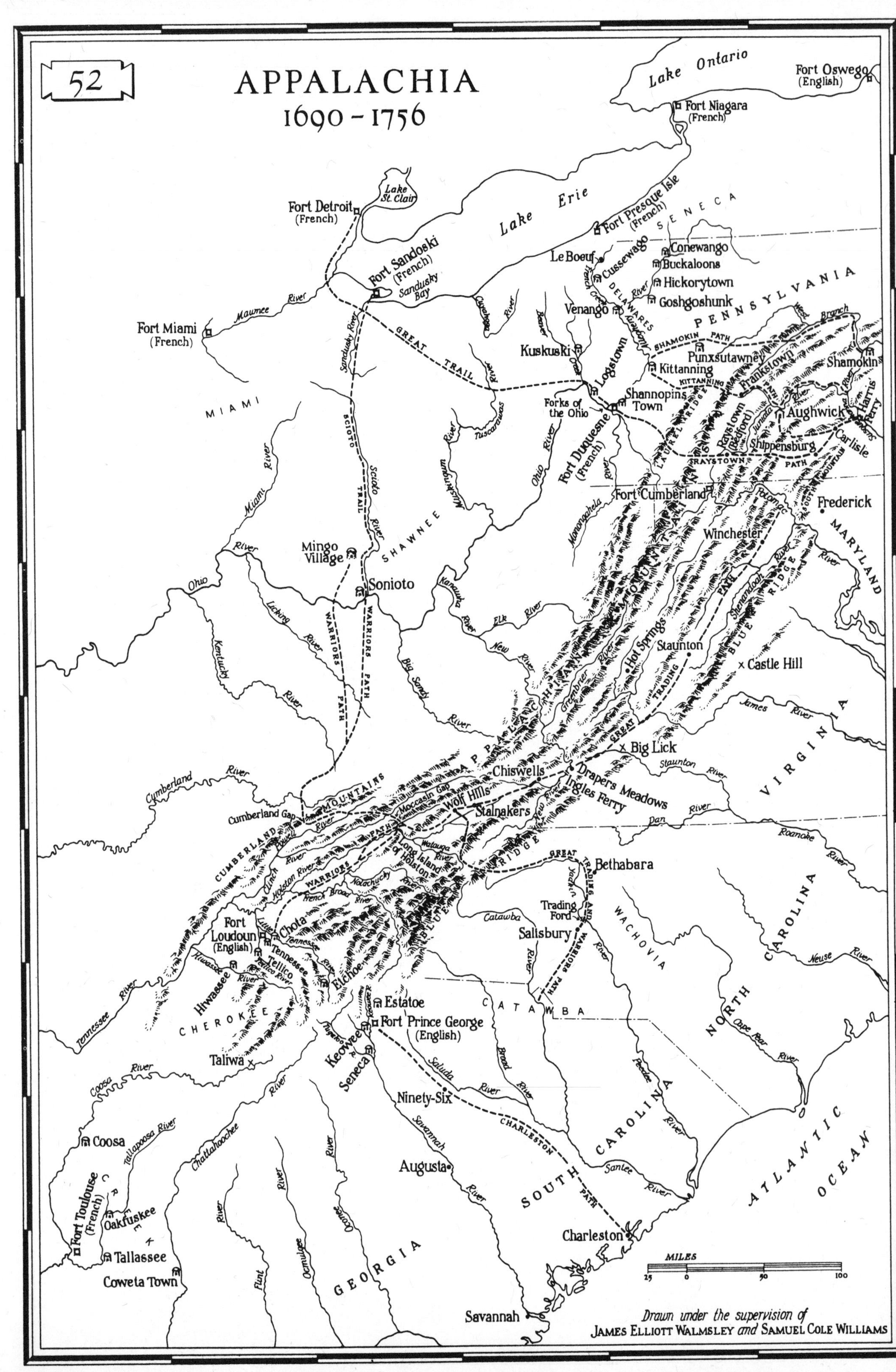

52
APPALACHIA
1690 - 1756
Lake Ontario
Fort Oswego (English)
Fort Niagara (French)
Lake St. Clair
Fort Detroit (French)
Lake Erie
Fort Presque Isle (French)
SENECA
Le Boeuf
Cussewago
Conewango
Buckaloons
Hickorytown
Goshgoshunk
Fort Sandoski (French)
Sandusky Bay
Fort Miami (French)
Maumee River
GREAT TRAIL
Venango
DELAWARES
PENNSYLVANIA
SHAMOKIN PATH
Punxsutawney
Shamokin
Kuskuski
Kittanning
KITTANNING
Frankstown
Logstown
Shannopins Town
Forks of the Ohio
Fort Duquesne (French)
Aughwick
Harris Ferry
Carlisle
Shippensburg
Raystown
Bedford
RAYSTOWN PATH
MIAMI
SCIOTO TRAIL
Scioto River
Muskingum River
Tuscarawas
Ohio River
Miami River
Fort Cumberland
Frederick
MARYLAND
Winchester
Potomac
Monongahela
SHAWNEE
Mingo Village
Sonioto
Ohio River
Kanawha River
Elk River
New River
Licking River
WARRIORS PATH
Kentucky River
Big Sandy River
Hot Springs
Staunton
Castle Hill
BLUE RIDGE
Shenandoah River
GREAT TRADING PATH
James River
VIRGINIA
APPALACHIAN MOUNTAINS
Greenbrier River
Big Lick
Staunton River
Chiswells
Drapers Meadows
Ingles Ferry
Wolf Hills
Stalnakers
Dan River
Roanoke River
Cumberland River
Cumberland Gap
MOUNTAINS
Moccasin Gap
CUMBERLAND
Powell River
Clinch River
Holston River
Long Island of Holston
Watauga River
WARRIORS PATH
Nolachucky River
French Broad River
Bethabara
GREAT TRADING AND WARRIORS PATH
Trading Ford
Salisbury
Catawba
Yadkin
WACHOVIA
NORTH CAROLINA
Neuse River
Fort Loudoun (English)
Chota
Tennessee
Tellico
Tellico River
Hiwassee
Hiwassee River
Echoe
Tennessee River
CHEROKEE
Estatoe
Fort Prince George (English)
Keowee
Seneca
Taliwa
CATAWBA
Cape Fear River
Saluda River
Broad River
Pedee River
Ninety-Six
CHARLESTON PATH
SOUTH CAROLINA
Santee River
Coosa River
Coosa
Tallapoosa River
Chattahoochee
Fort Toulouse (French)
CREEK
Oakfuskee
Tallassee
Coweta Town
Savannah River
Augusta
Oconee
Ocmulgee
Flint
GEORGIA
Charleston
Savannah
ATLANTIC OCEAN
MILES
25 0 50 100
Drawn under the supervision of JAMES ELLIOTT WALMSLEY and SAMUEL COLE WILLIAMS

53
MARYLAND
VIRGINIA
Fort Cumberland
Wills Creek
Oldtown (Cresaps)
Potomac River
Cacapon River
Black Creek
Packhorse Ford
Shepherdstown (Mecklinborough Town)
Harpers Ferry (Shenandoah Falls)
Vestal Gap
North Branch
Potomac River
Patterson Creek
River
South Branch Potomac
SOUTHWESTERN BOUNDARY OF FAIRFAX PROPRIETARY
Winchester (Frederick Town)
Fort Loudoun
Opequon
Battletown (Berryville)
Greenway Court
Shenandoah River
Strasburg
Woodstock
Powells Fort
North Fork
South Fork
South Fork
North Fork
South Branch
Fort Seybert
Upper Tract
New Market
Harrisonburg
Port Republic
Fort Defiance
Jennings Gap
Buffalo Gap
Old Stone Church
Staunton
Tinkling Spring
Betsy Bell
Mary Gray
Cowpasture River
Calfpasture River
Rapidan River
Spotswood Expedition, 1716
Swift Run Gap
Charlottesville
Rockfish Gap
Rockfish River
James River
Timber Ridge
Lexington
North River
Natural Bridge
James River
MASSANUTTEN MOUNTAIN
BLUE RIDGE MOUNTAINS
SHENANDOAH MOUNTAINS
SHENANDOAH VALLEY 1716-1780
MILES
5 0 10 20 30
Drawn under the supervision of JAMES ELLIOTT WALMSLEY

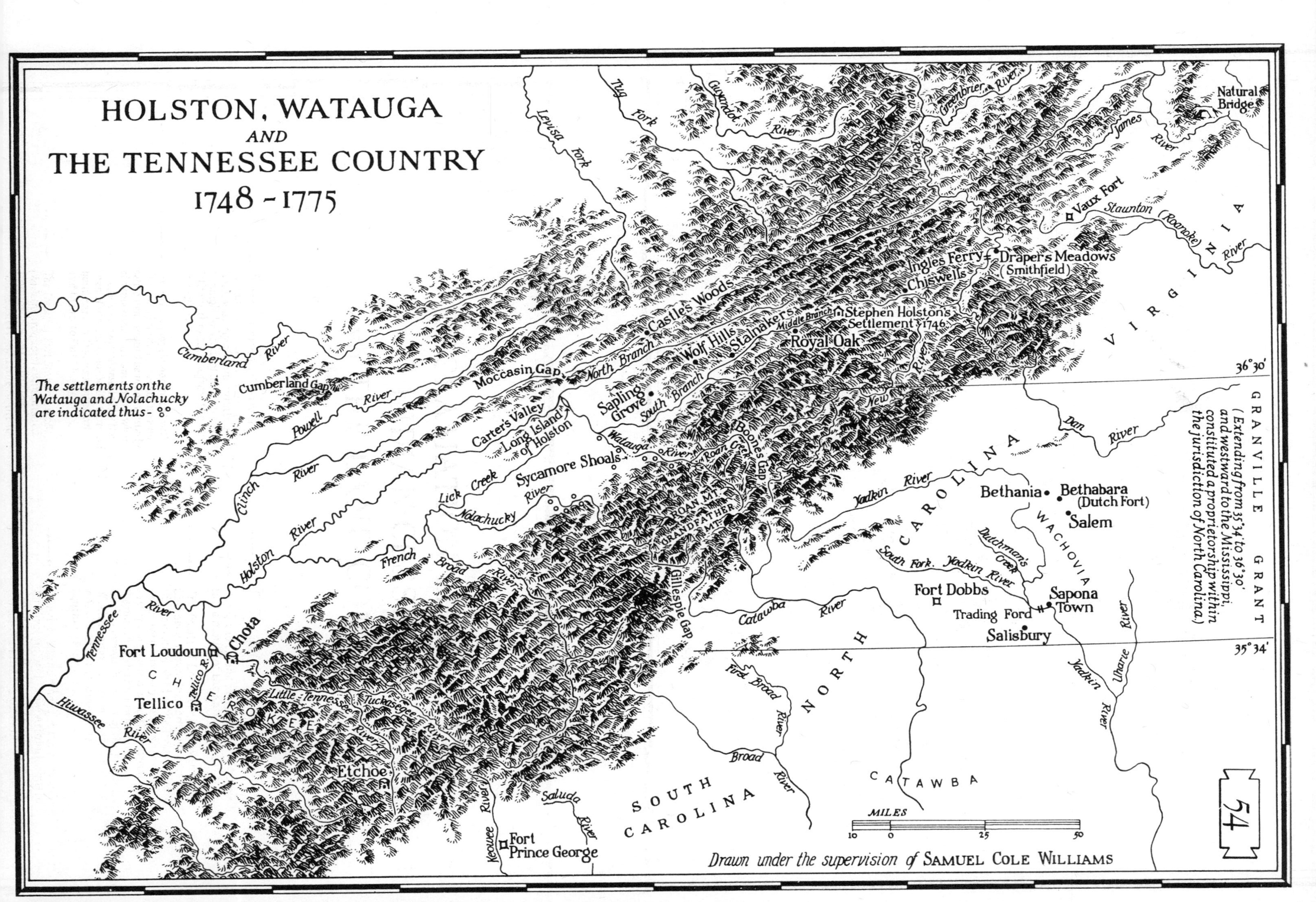
HOLSTON, WATAUGA
AND
THE TENNESSEE COUNTRY
1748 - 1775
54
The settlements on the Watauga and Nolachucky are indicated thus -
GRANVILLE GRANT
(Extending from 35°34' to 36°30' and westward to the Mississippi, constituted a proprietorship within the jurisdiction of North Carolina.)
36°30'
35°34'
VIRGINIA
NORTH CAROLINA
SOUTH CAROLINA
CATAWBA
CHEROKEE
WACHOVIA
Natural Bridge
Vaux Fort
Draper's Meadows
(Smithfield)
Ingles Ferry
Chiswells
Stephen Holston's Settlement 1746
Royal Oak
Stalnakers
Wolf Hills
Castle's Woods
Sapling Grove
Moccasin Gap
Cumberland Gap
Carter's Valley
Long Island of Holston
Sycamore Shoals
Boones Gap
Roan Mt.
Grandfather Mt.
Gillespie Gap
Bethania
Bethabara
(Dutch Fort)
Salem
Sapona Town
Trading Ford
Salisbury
Fort Dobbs
Fort Loudoun
Chota
Tellico
Etchoe
Fort Prince George
Greenbrier River
Guyandot River
Tug Fork
Levisa Fork
James River
Staunton (Roanoke) River
New River
Middle Branch
North Branch
South Branch
Cumberland River
Powell River
Clinch River
Holston River
Watauga River
Roan Creek
Lick Creek
Nolachucky River
French Broad River
Tennessee River
Tellico R.
Little Tennessee
Tuckasegee River
Hiwassee River
Keowee River
Saluda River
Dan River
Yadkin River
South Fork Yadkin River
Dutchman's Creek
Catawba River
First Broad River
Broad River
Uharie River
MILES
10 0 25 50
Drawn under the supervision of Samuel Cole Williams

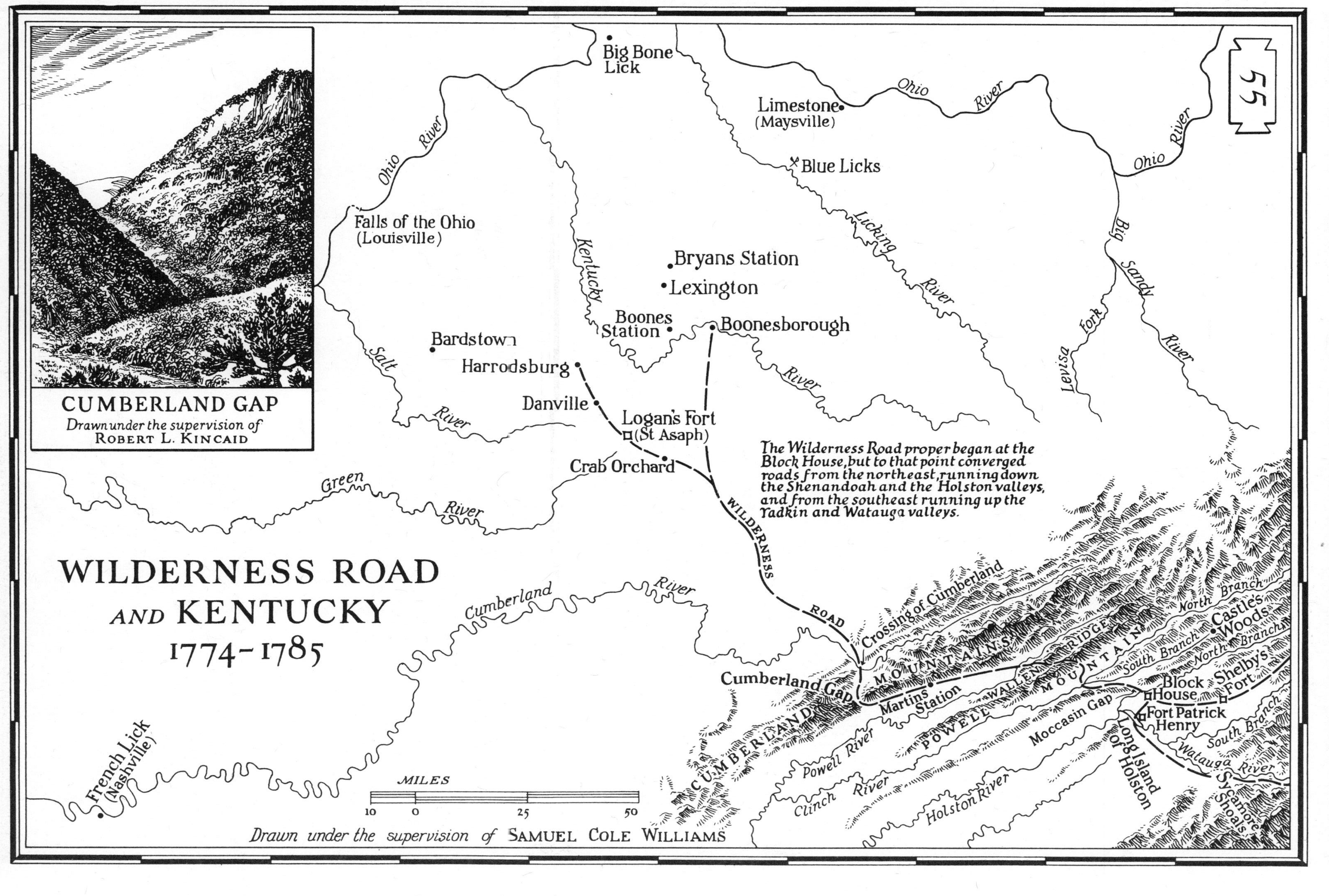
55
WILDERNESS ROAD
AND KENTUCKY
1774-1785
CUMBERLAND GAP
Drawn under the supervision of
ROBERT L. KINCAID
The Wilderness Road proper began at the Block House, but to that point converged roads from the northeast, running down the Shenandoah and the Holston valleys, and from the southeast running up the Yadkin and Watauga valleys.
Big Bone Lick
Limestone (Maysville)
Blue Licks
Ohio River
Falls of the Ohio (Louisville)
Kentucky
Licking River
Big Sandy River
Levisa Fork
Bryans Station
Lexington
Boones Station
Boonesborough
Bardstown
Harrodsburg
Danville
Logan's Fort (St Asaph)
Crab Orchard
Salt River
Green River
Cumberland River
WILDERNESS ROAD
Crossing of Cumberland
Cumberland Gap
Martins Station
CUMBERLAND MOUNTAINS
WALLEN RIDGE
POWELL MOUNTAIN
Powell River
Clinch River
Holston River
Moccasin Gap
Long Island of Holston
Block House
Shelby's Fort
Fort Patrick Henry
Castles Woods
North Branch
South Branch
Watauga River
Sycamore Shoals
French Lick (Nashville)
MILES
10 0 25 50
Drawn under the supervision of SAMUEL COLE WILLIAMS

IV COLONIAL WARS OF THE INDIANS, FRENCH AND BRITISH

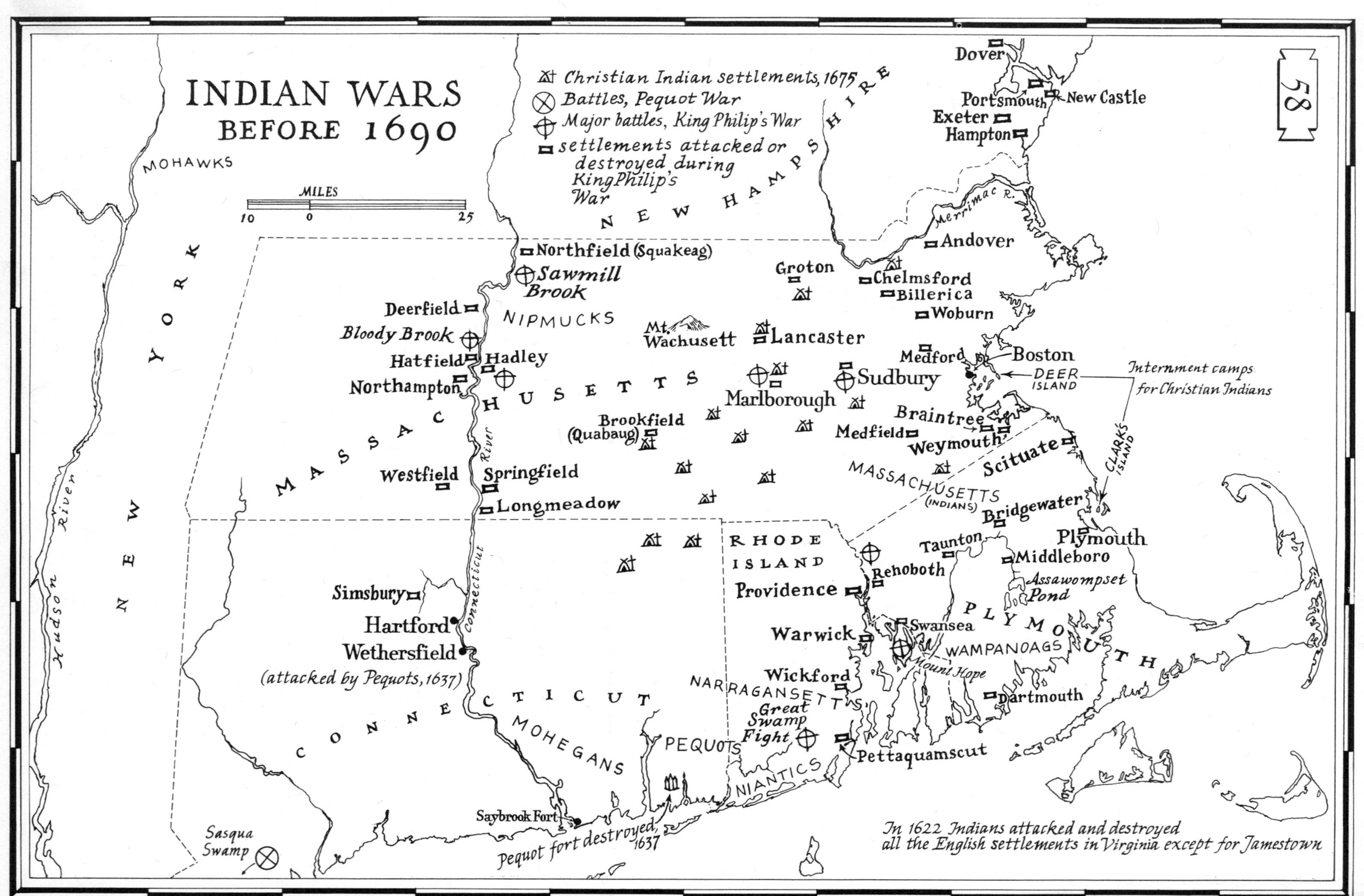
58
INDIAN WARS
BEFORE 1690
Christian Indian settlements, 1675
Battles, Pequot War
Major battles, King Philip's War
settlements attacked or destroyed during King Philip's War
MILES
10
0
25
MOHAWKS
NEW YORK
NEW HAMPSHIRE
MASSACHUSETTS
CONNECTICUT
RHODE ISLAND
PLYMOUTH
Hudson River
Connecticut River
Merrimac R.
Dover
Portsmouth
New Castle
Exeter
Hampton
Andover
Northfield (Squakeag)
Sawmill Brook
Groton
Chelmsford
Billerica
Woburn
Deerfield
NIPMUCKS
Mt. Wachusett
Lancaster
Bloody Brook
Hatfield
Hadley
Medford
Boston
Northampton
Sudbury
DEER ISLAND
Internment camps for Christian Indians
Marlborough
Braintree
Brookfield (Quabaug)
Medfield
Weymouth
CLARK'S ISLAND
Scituate
Westfield
Springfield
Longmeadow
MASSACHUSETTS (INDIANS)
Bridgewater
Plymouth
Taunton
Middleboro
Rehoboth
Assawompset Pond
Simsbury
Providence
Hartford
Swansea
Warwick
Wethersfield
(attacked by Pequots, 1637)
WAMPANOAGS
Mount Hope
Wickford
NARRAGANSETTS
Dartmouth
Great Swamp Fight
MOHEGANS
PEQUOTS
Pettaquamscut
NIANTICS
Saybrook Fort
Sasqua Swamp
Pequot fort destroyed, 1637
In 1622 Indians attacked and destroyed all the English settlements in Virginia except for Jamestown

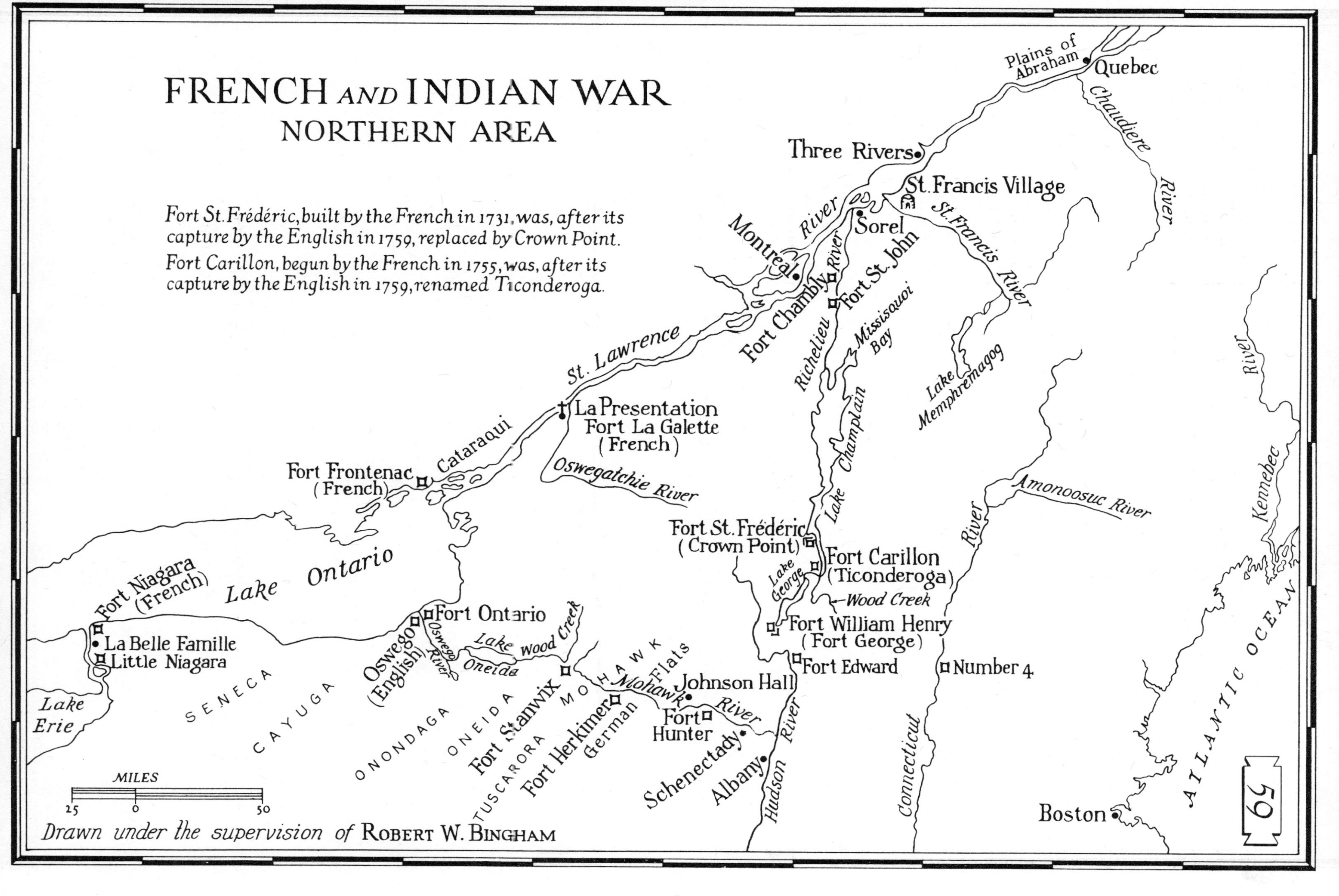
FRENCH AND INDIAN WAR
NORTHERN AREA
Fort St. Frédéric, built by the French in 1731, was, after its capture by the English in 1759, replaced by Crown Point.
Fort Carillon, begun by the French in 1755, was, after its capture by the English in 1759, renamed Ticonderoga.
59
Plains of Abraham
Quebec
Chaudiere River
Three Rivers
St. Francis Village
St. Francis River
Sorel
Montreal
River
Richelieu River
Fort Chambly
Fort St. John
Missisquoi Bay
Lake Memphremagog
Lake Champlain
St. Lawrence
La Presentation
Fort La Galette
(French)
Oswegatchie River
Cataraqui
Fort Frontenac
(French)
Fort St. Frédéric
(Crown Point)
Fort Carillon
(Ticonderoga)
Lake George
Wood Creek
Fort William Henry
(Fort George)
Fort Edward
Number 4
Amonoosuc River
River
Connecticut
Kennebec
River
ATLANTIC OCEAN
Boston
Lake Ontario
Fort Niagara
(French)
La Belle Famille
Little Niagara
Lake Erie
Fort Ontario
Oswego
(English)
Oswego River
Lake Oneida
Wood Creek
Fort Stanwix
MOHAWK Flats
Mohawk River
Johnson Hall
Fort Hunter
Fort Herkimer
German
Schenectady
Albany
Hudson River
SENECA
CAYUGA
ONONDAGA
ONEIDA
TUSCARORA
MILES
25
0
50
Drawn under the supervision of ROBERT W. BINGHAM

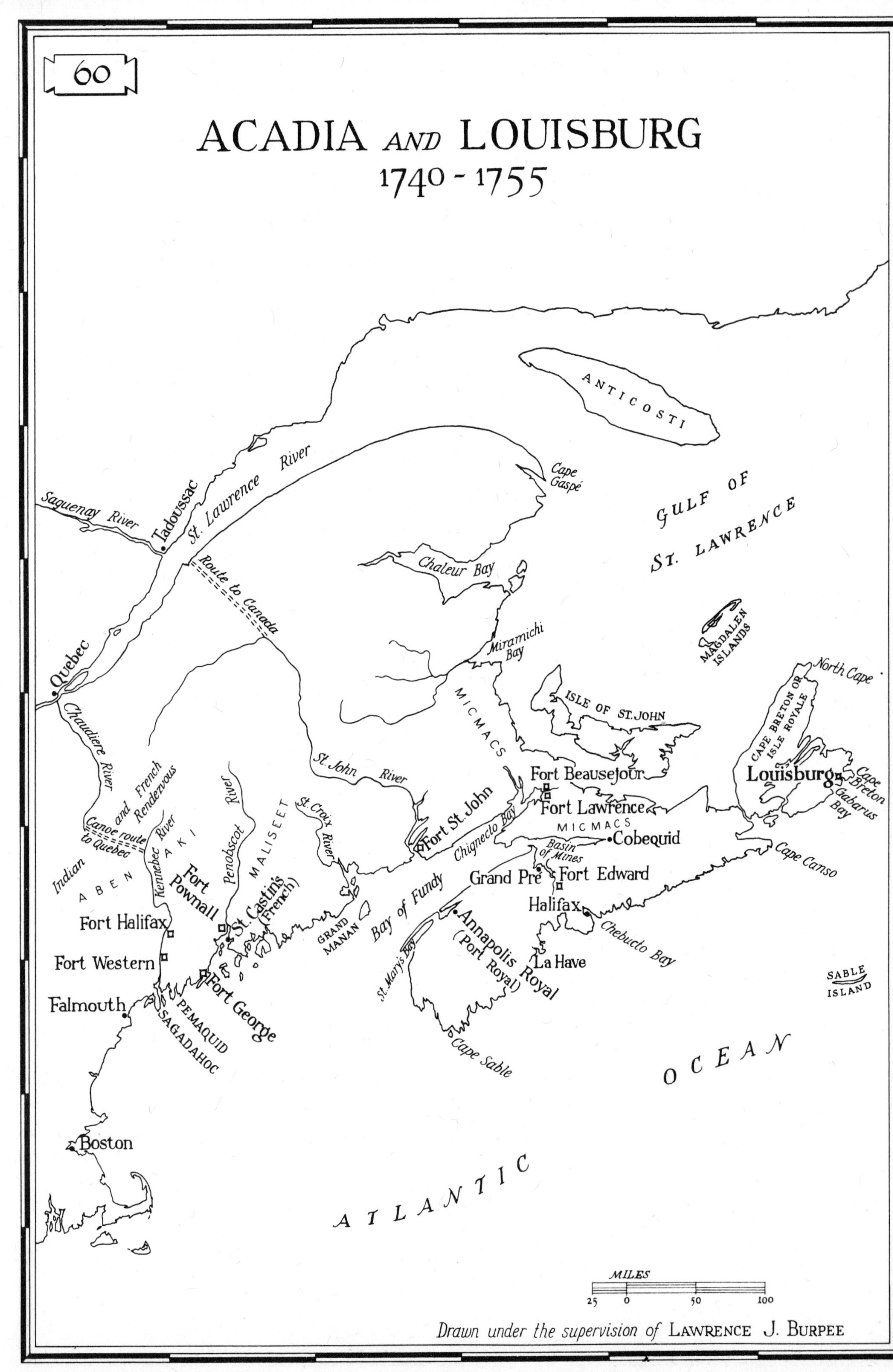

60
ACADIA AND LOUISBURG
1740 - 1755
ANTICOSTI
Cape Gaspé
GULF OF ST. LAWRENCE
Saguenay River
Tadoussac
St. Lawrence River
Route to Canada
Chaleur Bay
Quebec
Miramichi Bay
MAGDALEN ISLANDS
North Cape
ISLE OF ST. JOHN
CAPE BRETON OR ISLE ROYALE
MICMACS
Chaudiere River
St. John River
Fort Beausejour
Louisburg
Cape Breton
Gabarus Bay
Indian and French Rendezvous
Canoe route to Quebec
Kennebec River
Penobscot River
MALISEET
St. Croix River
Fort St. John
Chignecto Bay
Fort Lawrence
MICMACS
Cobequid
Basin of Mines
Cape Canso
ABEN AKI
Fort Pownall
St. Castin's (French)
GRAND MANAN
Bay of Fundy
Grand Pre
Fort Edward
Halifax
Fort Halifax
Annapolis Royal (Port Royal)
Chebucto Bay
Fort Western
St. Mary's Bay
La Have
Fort George
SABLE ISLAND
Falmouth
PEMAQUID
SAGADAHOC
Cape Sable
OCEAN
Boston
ATLANTIC
MILES
25 0 50 100
Drawn under the supervision of LAWRENCE J. BURPEE

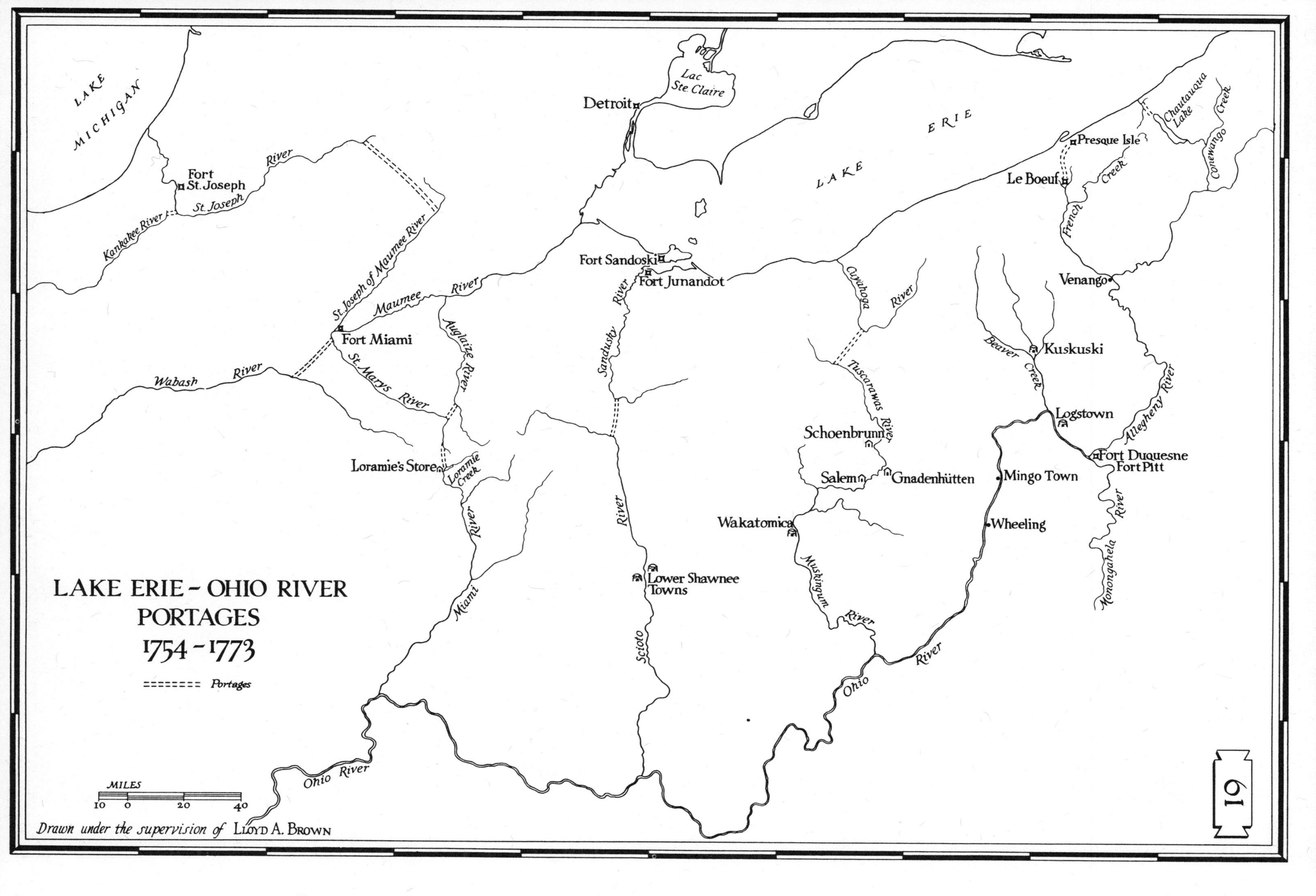
19
LAKE ERIE - OHIO RIVER
PORTAGES
1754 - 1773
Portages
MILES
10 0 20 40
Drawn under the supervision of Lloyd A. Brown
LAKE MICHIGAN
LAKE ERIE
Lac Ste. Claire
Detroit
Fort St. Joseph
St. Joseph River
Kankakee River
St. Joseph of Maumee River
Maumee River
Fort Miami
St. Marys River
Wabash River
Auglaize River
Loramie's Store
Loramie Creek
Miami River
Fort Sandoski
Fort Junandot
Sandusky River
Scioto River
Lower Shawnee Towns
Cuyahoga River
Tuscarawas River
Schoenbrunn
Salem
Gnadenhütten
Wakatomica
Muskingum River
Ohio River
Mingo Town
Wheeling
Logstown
Fort Duquesne
Fort Pitt
Monongahela River
Allegheny River
Kuskuski
Beaver Creek
Venango
French Creek
Le Boeuf
Presque Isle
Chautauqua Lake
Conewango Creek

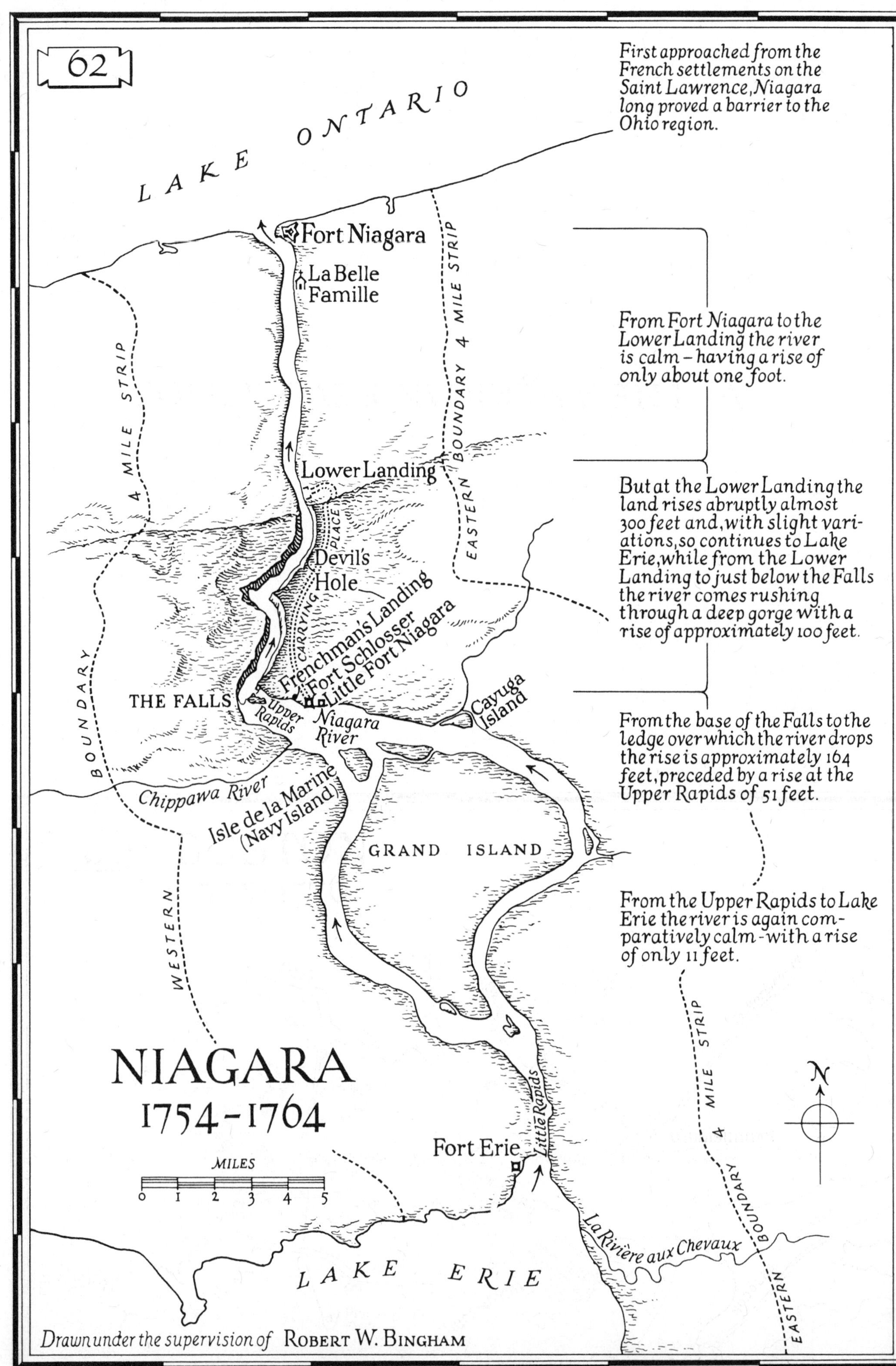
First approached from the French settlements on the Saint Lawrence, Niagara long proved a barrier to the Ohio region.
LAKE ONTARIO
Fort Niagara
La Belle Famille
EASTERN BOUNDARY 4 MILE STRIP
WESTERN BOUNDARY 4 MILE STRIP
From Fort Niagara to the Lower Landing the river is calm – having a rise of only about one foot.
Lower Landing
But at the Lower Landing the land rises abruptly almost 300 feet and, with slight variations, so continues to Lake Erie, while from the Lower Landing to just below the Falls the river comes rushing through a deep gorge with a rise of approximately 100 feet.
CARRYING PLACE
Devil's Hole
Frenchman's Landing
Fort Schlosser
Little Fort Niagara
THE FALLS
Upper Rapids
Niagara River
Cayuga Island
From the base of the Falls to the ledge over which the river drops the rise is approximately 164 feet, preceded by a rise at the Upper Rapids of 51 feet.
Chippawa River
Isle de la Marine (Navy Island)
GRAND ISLAND
From the Upper Rapids to Lake Erie the river is again comparatively calm - with a rise of only 11 feet.
NIAGARA
1754-1764
MILES
0 1 2 3 4 5
Fort Erie
Little Rapids
N
La Rivière aux Chevaux
LAKE ERIE
Drawn under the supervision of ROBERT W. BINGHAM

63
FORKS OF THE OHIO
1754-1759
Lake Ontario
Fort Niagara
La Belle Famille
Little Niagara
SENECA
Lake Erie
Presque Isle
Le Boeuf
Creek
Chautauqua Lake
Conewango Creek
River
French
Allegheny
DELAWARES
Venango
Fort Machault
SHAWNEE
Kuskuski
Murthering Town
Beaver Creek
Connoquenessing Creek
Kittanning
Sawcunk
Ohio River
Logstown
Allegheny River
Kiskiminetas River
Fort Duquesne (Fort Pitt)
Braddock's Defeat
Turtle Cr.
Loyalhanna Creek
Conemaugh River
FORBES ROAD
Loyal Hannon (Ligonier)
Catfish Camp (Washington)
Redstone Old Fort
Fort Burd
Gist's
Fort Necessity
GREAT MEADOWS
Monongahela
Youghiogheny River
CHESTNUT RIDGE
LAUREL RIDGE
ALLEGHENY MOUNTAINS
WILLS MOUNTAIN
Wills Creek
Fort Cumberland
BRADDOCK'S ROAD
Oldtown (Cresaps)
Potomac River
Raystown (Bedford)
TUSSEY MOUNTAIN
Raystown Branch
Little Juniata
Juniata River
Fort Littleton
TUSCARORA MOUNTAIN
Aughwick
Fort Shirley
SIDELING MOUNTAIN
Fort Loudon
Shippensburg
Carlisle
Harris' Ferry
York
SOUTH MOUNTAIN
West Branch
DELAWARES
River
Fort Augusta
Penn Creek
Penn Creek Massacre
Susquehanna
Potomac River
Winchester
Baltimore
MILES
10 5 0 25 50
Drawn under the supervision of ALFRED P. JAMES

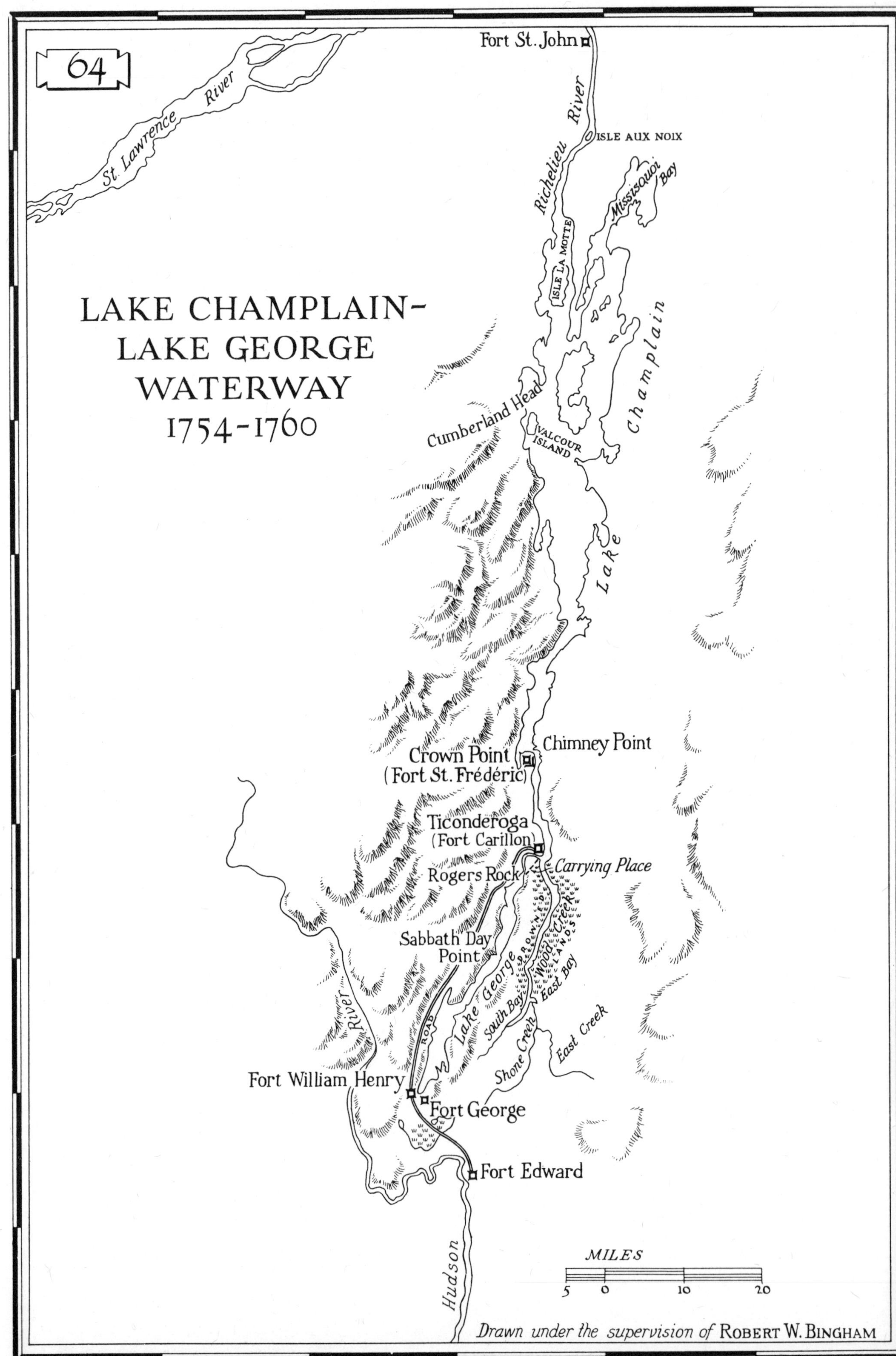
64
LAKE CHAMPLAIN-
LAKE GEORGE
WATERWAY
1754-1760
Fort St. John
St. Lawrence River
Richelieu River
ISLE AUX NOIX
Missisquoi Bay
ISLE LA MOTTE
Lake Champlain
Cumberland Head
VALCOUR ISLAND
Chimney Point
Crown Point
(Fort St. Frédéric)
Ticonderoga
(Fort Carillon)
Carrying Place
Rogers Rock
Sabbath Day
Point
DROWNED LANDS
Wood Creek
East Bay
South Bay
Lake George
ROAD
River
Shone Creek
East Creek
Fort William Henry
Fort George
Fort Edward
Hudson
MILES
5
0
10
20
Drawn under the supervision of ROBERT W. BINGHAM

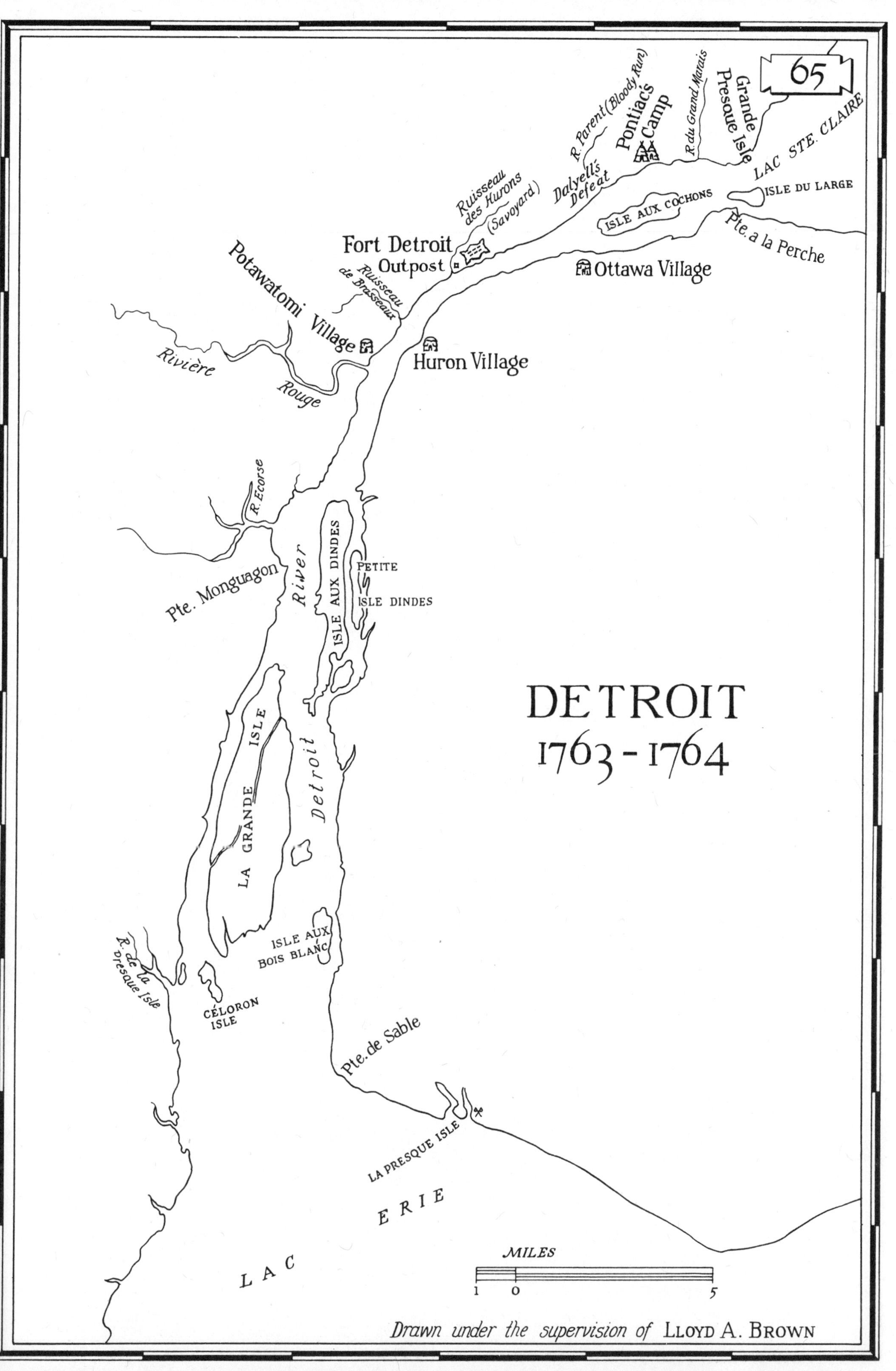
65
DETROIT
1763 - 1764
Fort Detroit
Outpost
Pontiac's Camp
Grande Presque Isle
R. Parent (Bloody Run)
R. du Grand Marais
Dalyell's Defeat
Ruisseau des Hurons (Savoyard)
LAC STE. CLAIRE
ISLE DU LARGE
ISLE AUX COCHONS
Pte. a la Perche
Ottawa Village
Potawatomi Village
Ruisseau de Brasseaux
Huron Village
Rivière Rouge
R. Ecorse
Pte. Monguagon
River
Detroit
ISLE AUX DINDES
PETITE
ISLE DINDES
LA GRANDE ISLE
ISLE AUX BOIS BLANC
R. de la Presque Isle
CÉLORON ISLE
Pte. de Sable
LA PRESQUE ISLE
LAC ERIE
MILES
1 0 5
Drawn under the supervision of LLOYD A. BROWN

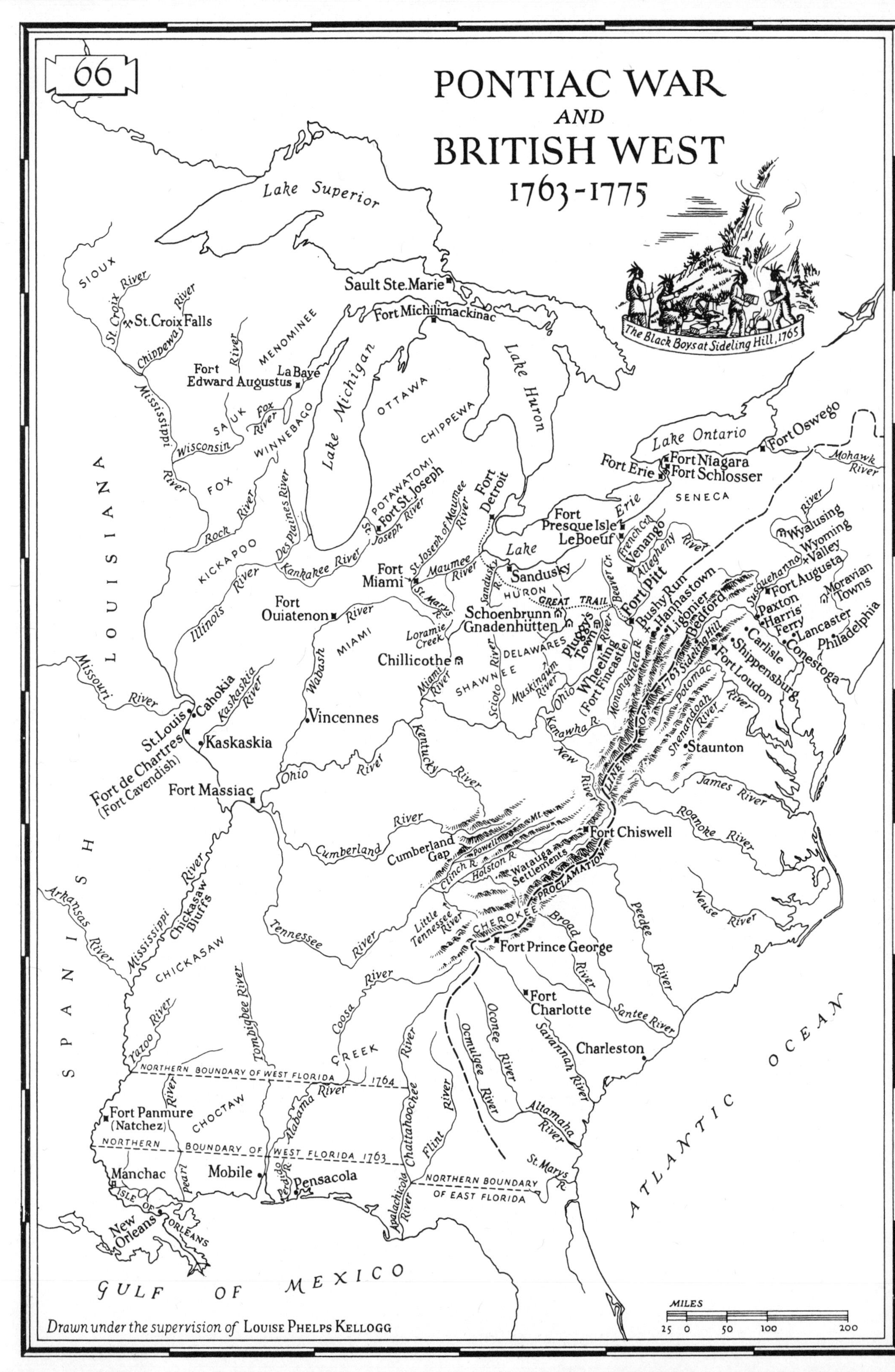
66
PONTIAC WAR AND BRITISH WEST 1763-1775
The Black Boys at Sideling Hill, 1765
Lake Superior
Sault Ste. Marie
Fort Michilimackinac
Lake Huron
Lake Michigan
Lake Ontario
Lake Erie
SIOUX
St. Croix River
St. Croix Falls
Chippewa River
MENOMINEE
Fort Edward Augustus
La Baye
OTTAWA
CHIPPEWA
SAUK
Fox River
WINNEBAGO
Wisconsin
Mississippi River
FOX
Rock River
Des Plaines River
POTAWATOMI
Fort St. Joseph
St. Joseph River
St. Joseph of Maumee River
Fort Detroit
Fort Oswego
Fort Niagara
Fort Erie
Fort Schlosser
Mohawk River
SENECA
Fort Presque Isle
Le Boeuf
French Cr.
Venango
Allegheny River
Wyalusing
Wyoming Valley
Susquehanna River
Fort Augusta
Moravian Towns
Paxton
Harris' Ferry
Lancaster
Philadelphia
Conestoga
Carlisle
Shippensburg
Fort Loudon
Bedford
Ligonier
Hannastown
Bushy Run
Fort Pitt
Beaver Cr.
Sandusky
Sandusky R.
HURON
GREAT TRAIL
Schoenbrunn
Gnadenhutten
Pluggy's Town
DELAWARES
Maumee River
Fort Miami
St. Marys R.
KICKAPOO
Kankakee River
Illinois River
Fort Ouiatenon
Wabash River
MIAMI
Loramie Creek
Chillicothe
SHAWNEE
Scioto River
Muskingum River
Ohio River
Wheeling (Fort Fincastle)
Monongahela R.
Sideling Hill
Potomac River
Shenandoah River
Staunton
Kanawha R.
New River
LINE OF 1763
LOUISIANA
Missouri River
Cahokia
Kaskaskia River
St. Louis
Kaskaskia
Fort de Chartres (Fort Cavendish)
Vincennes
Miami River
Kentucky River
Ohio River
Fort Massiac
Cumberland River
Cumberland Gap
Powell Mt.
Clinch R.
Holston R.
Watauga Settlements
Fort Chiswell
PROCLAMATION
James River
Roanoke River
Neuse River
CHEROKEE
Little Tennessee River
Tennessee River
Fort Prince George
Broad River
Peedee River
Santee River
Fort Charlotte
Charleston
Savannah River
Oconee River
Ocmulgee River
Altamaha River
St. Marys R.
SPANISH
Arkansas River
Mississippi River
Chickasaw Bluffs
CHICKASAW
Yazoo River
Tombigbee River
Coosa River
CREEK
NORTHERN BOUNDARY OF WEST FLORIDA 1764
Fort Panmure (Natchez)
CHOCTAW
Alabama River
Chattahoochee River
Flint River
NORTHERN BOUNDARY OF WEST FLORIDA 1763
Manchac
Pearl River
Mobile
Perdido R.
Pensacola
Apalachicola River
NORTHERN BOUNDARY OF EAST FLORIDA
ISLE OF ORLEANS
New Orleans
ATLANTIC OCEAN
GULF OF MEXICO
MILES
25 0 50 100 200
Drawn under the supervision of Louise Phelps Kellogg

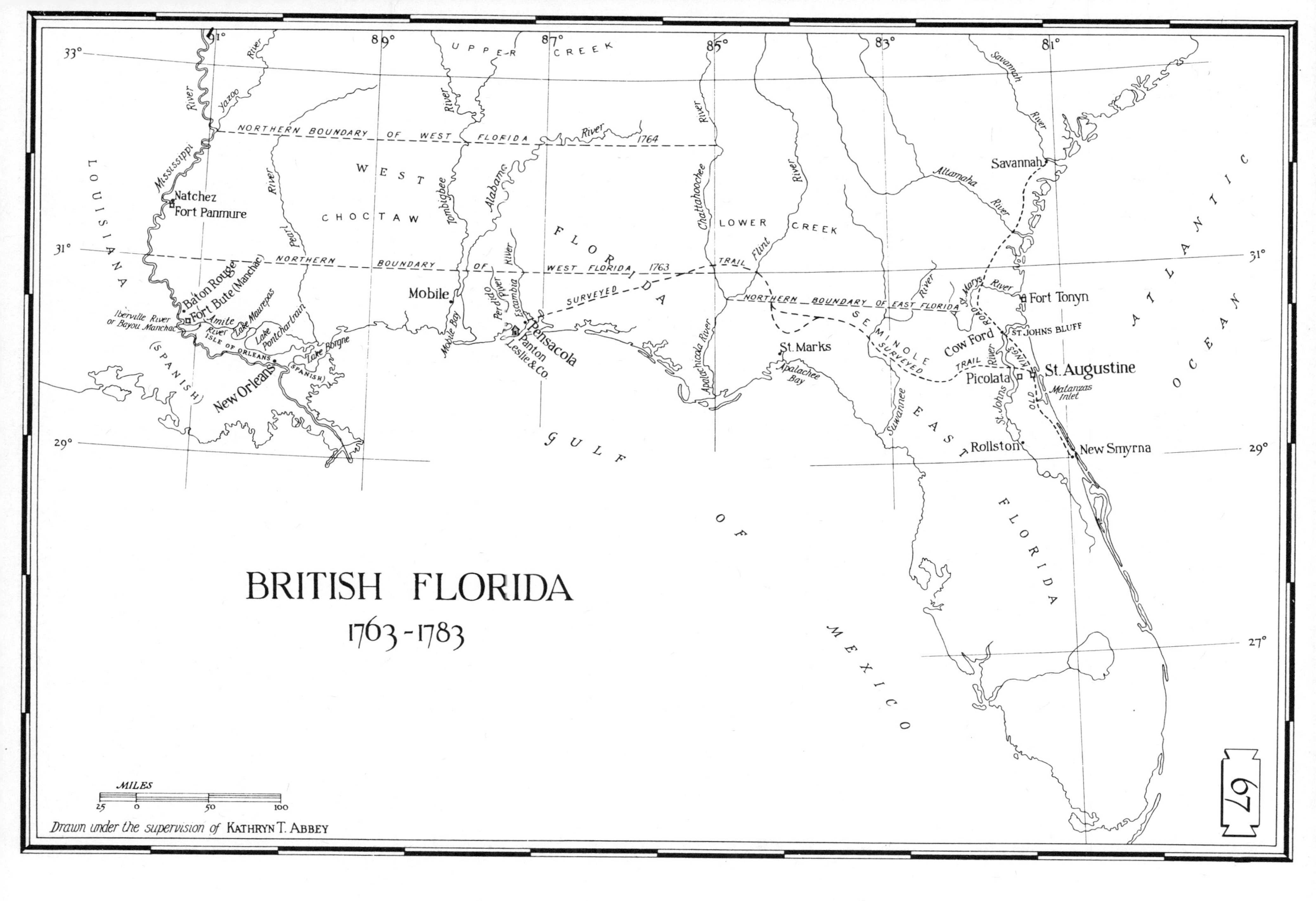

67
BRITISH FLORIDA
1763-1783
MILES
25 0 50 100
Drawn under the supervision of KATHRYN T. ABBEY
LOUISIANA
(SPANISH)
WEST FLORIDA
EAST FLORIDA
UPPER CREEK
LOWER CREEK
CHOCTAW
SEMINOLE
ATLANTIC OCEAN
GULF OF MEXICO
NORTHERN BOUNDARY OF WEST FLORIDA 1764
NORTHERN BOUNDARY OF WEST FLORIDA 1763
NORTHERN BOUNDARY OF EAST FLORIDA
SURVEYED
TRAIL
KINGS ROAD
OLD
Natchez
Fort Panmure
Baton Rouge
Fort Bute (Manchac)
Iberville River or Bayou Manchac
Amite River
Lake Maurepas
Lake Pontchartrain
Lake Borgne
ISLE OF ORLEANS
New Orleans
Mobile
Mobile Bay
Pensacola
Panton Leslie & Co.
Perdido River
Escambia River
St. Marks
Apalachee Bay
Cow Ford
ST. JOHNS BLUFF
Fort Tonyn
St. Augustine
Picolata
Matanzas Inlet
Rollston
New Smyrna
Savannah
Mississippi River
Yazoo River
Pearl River
Tombigbee River
Alabama River
Chattahoochee River
Apalachicola River
Flint River
Altamaha River
Savannah River
St. Marys River
St. Johns River
Suwannee
33°
31°
29°
27°
91°
89°
87°
85°
83°
81°

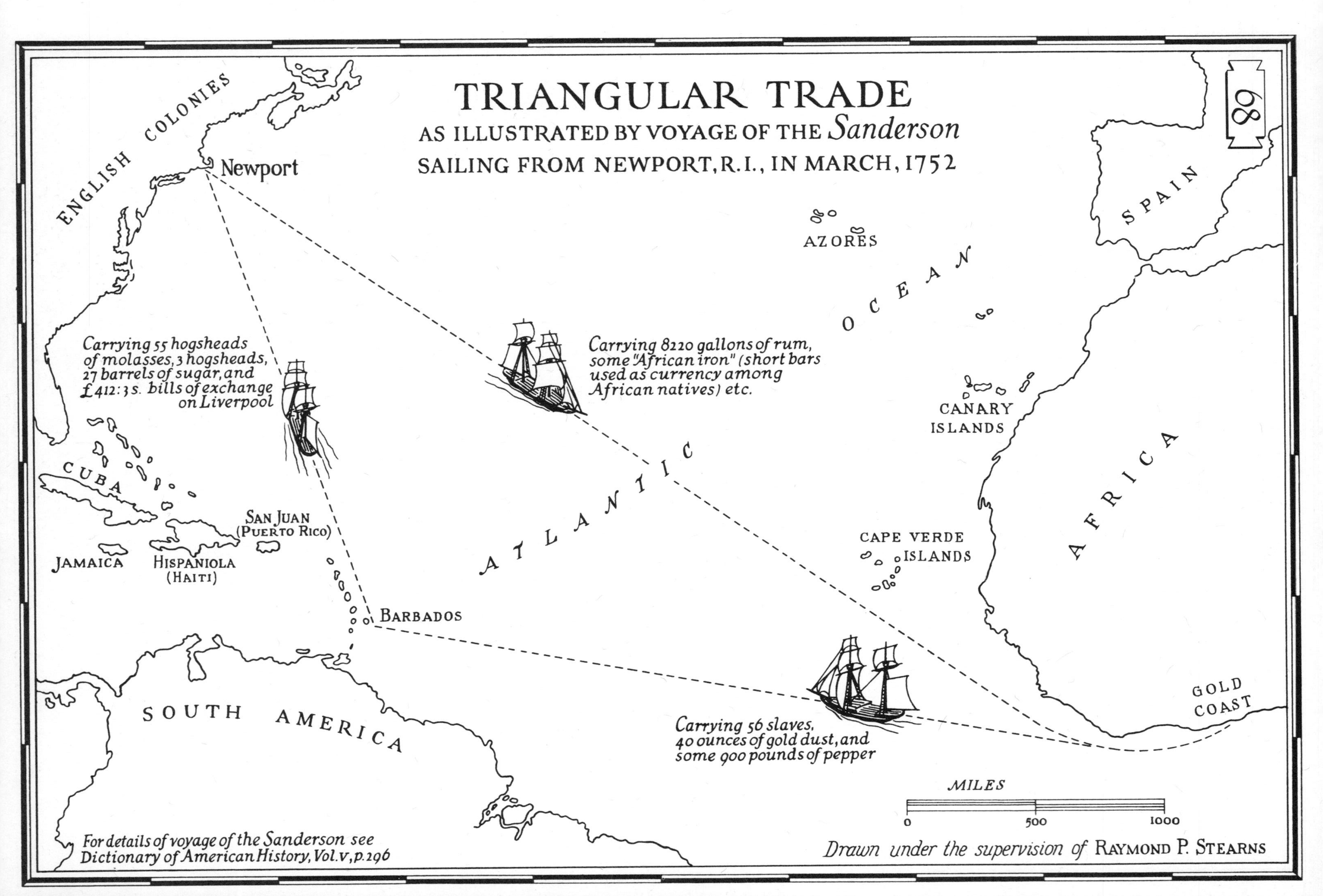

68
TRIANGULAR TRADE
AS ILLUSTRATED BY VOYAGE OF THE *Sanderson*
SAILING FROM NEWPORT, R.I., IN MARCH, 1752
ENGLISH COLONIES
Newport
SPAIN
AZORES
ATLANTIC OCEAN
CANARY ISLANDS
AFRICA
CAPE VERDE ISLANDS
GOLD COAST
Carrying 55 hogsheads of molasses, 3 hogsheads, 27 barrels of sugar, and £412:3s. bills of exchange on Liverpool
Carrying 8220 gallons of rum, some "African iron" (short bars used as currency among African natives) etc.
Carrying 56 slaves, 40 ounces of gold dust, and some 900 pounds of pepper
CUBA
JAMAICA
HISPANIOLA (HAITI)
SAN JUAN (PUERTO RICO)
BARBADOS
SOUTH AMERICA
MILES
0
500
1000
For details of voyage of the Sanderson see Dictionary of American History, Vol. v, p. 296
Drawn under the supervision of RAYMOND P. STEARNS

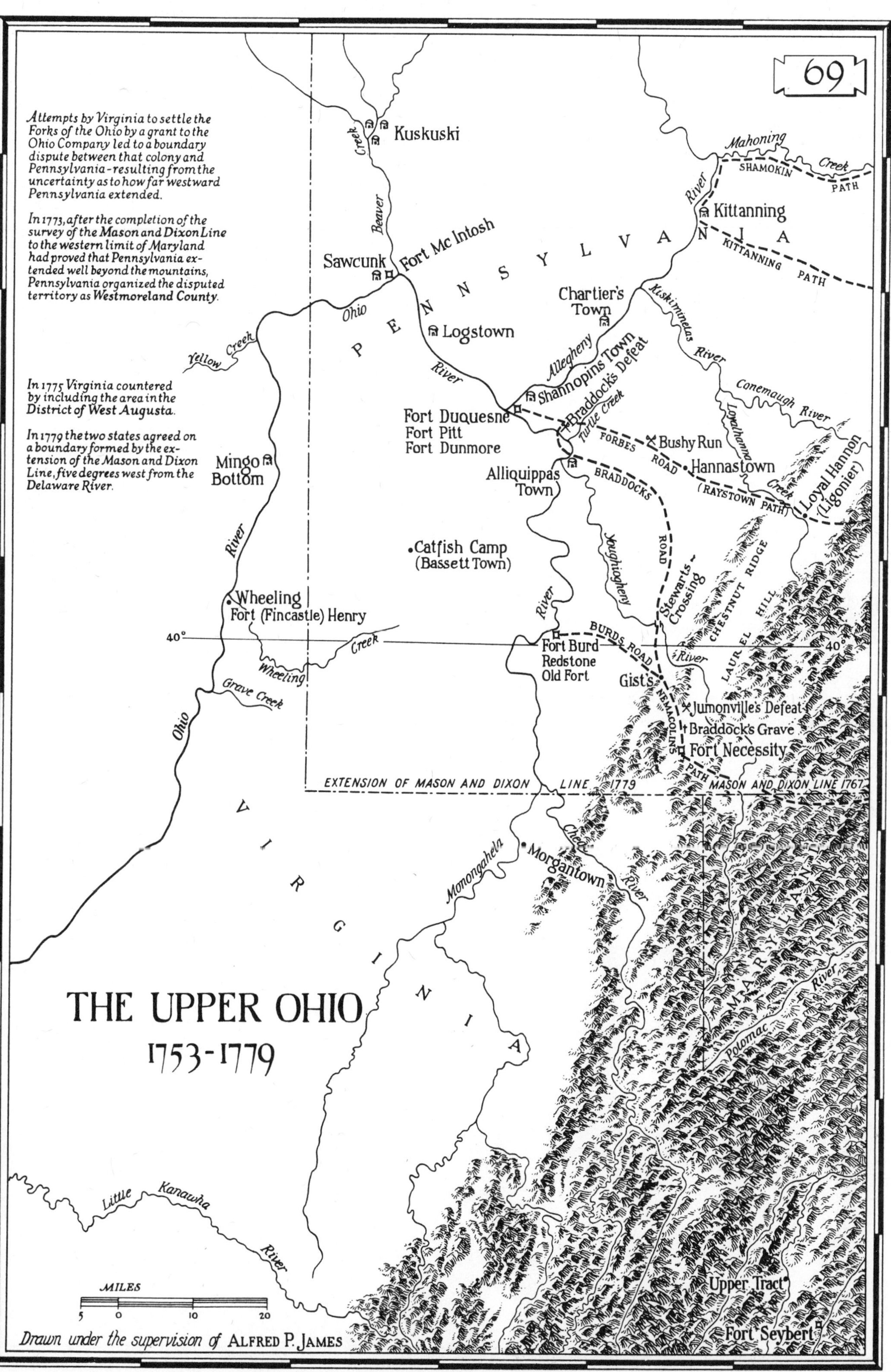
Attempts by Virginia to settle the Forks of the Ohio by a grant to the Ohio Company led to a boundary dispute between that colony and Pennsylvania-resulting from the uncertainty as to how far westward Pennsylvania extended.
In 1773, after the completion of the survey of the Mason and Dixon Line to the western limit of Maryland had proved that Pennsylvania extended well beyond the mountains, Pennsylvania organized the disputed territory as Westmoreland County.
In 1775 Virginia countered by including the area in the District of West Augusta.
In 1779 the two states agreed on a boundary formed by the extension of the Mason and Dixon Line, five degrees west from the Delaware River.
Kuskuski
Beaver Creek
Fort Mc Intosh
Sawcunk
PENNSYLVANIA
Mahoning Creek
SHAMOKIN PATH
Kittanning
KITTANNING PATH
Chartier's Town
Logstown
Ohio River
Allegheny River
Shannopins Town
Braddock's Defeat
Kiskiminetas River
Conemaugh River
Turtle Creek
Fort Duquesne
Fort Pitt
Fort Dunmore
FORBES ROAD
Bushy Run
Hannastown
(RAYSTOWN PATH)
Loyalhanna Creek
Loyal Hannon (Ligonier)
Alliquippas Town
BRADDOCKS ROAD
Yellow Creek
Mingo Bottom
Catfish Camp
(Bassett Town)
Youghiogheny
Stewarts Crossing
CHESTNUT RIDGE
LAUREL HILL
Wheeling
Fort (Fincastle) Henry
40°
Wheeling Creek
Fort Burd
Redstone Old Fort
BURDS ROAD
Gist's
NEMACOLINS PATH
Jumonville's Defeat
Braddock's Grave
Fort Necessity
Grave Creek
EXTENSION OF MASON AND DIXON LINE 1779
MASON AND DIXON LINE 1767
VIRGINIA
Monongahela
Morgantown
Cheat River
MARYLAND
Potomac River
Little Kanawha River
Upper Tract
Fort Seybert
MILES
5 0 10 20

THE UPPER OHIO
1753-1779

Drawn under the supervision of ALFRED P. JAMES

PROCLAMATION LINE *of* 1763 INDIAN CESSIONS *and* THE LAND COMPANIES

— — — *The Proclamation of 1763 forbade the purchase or settlement of Indian lands westerly of a line running through the heads of the rivers which fell into the Atlantic from the west or northwest.*

—x—x— *Tryon's Line, 1767, (by agreement with the Cherokee) directed that no white settlement should be made westerly of a line running from a point where Reedy River was intersected by the then North Carolina-South Carolina boundary, to Tryon's Mountain and thence to Fort Chiswell.*

—+—+— *The Treaty of Fort Stanwix, 1768, (with the Iroquois) extinguished Iroquois claims to the lands southeasterly of a line running from Fort Stanwix to Fort Pitt, and thence along the southern bank of the Ohio to the mouth of the Tennessee (Cherokee) River.*

—o—o— *The Treaty of Hard Labor, 1768, (with the Cherokee) confirmed Tryon's Line*
—x—x— *of 1767 and extended it from Fort Chiswell to the mouth of the Kanawha River.*

—•—•— *The Treaty of Lochaber, 1770, (with the Cherokee) moved the northern part of the line established at the Treaty of Hard Labor westerly to run from six miles east of Long Island of Holston directly to the mouth of the Kanawha River. Lochaber was the name of the plantation of Alexander Cameron, Assistant Commissioner of Indian Affairs for the Southern Provinces.*

—••—••— *Donelson's Line. When Col. Donelson acting for Virginia, and Chief Attakullakulla and Alex. Cameron, acting for the Cherokee, came to run the Lochaber Line, some agreement was entered into by which it was turned westward and made to run with the Kentucky (Louisa) River.*

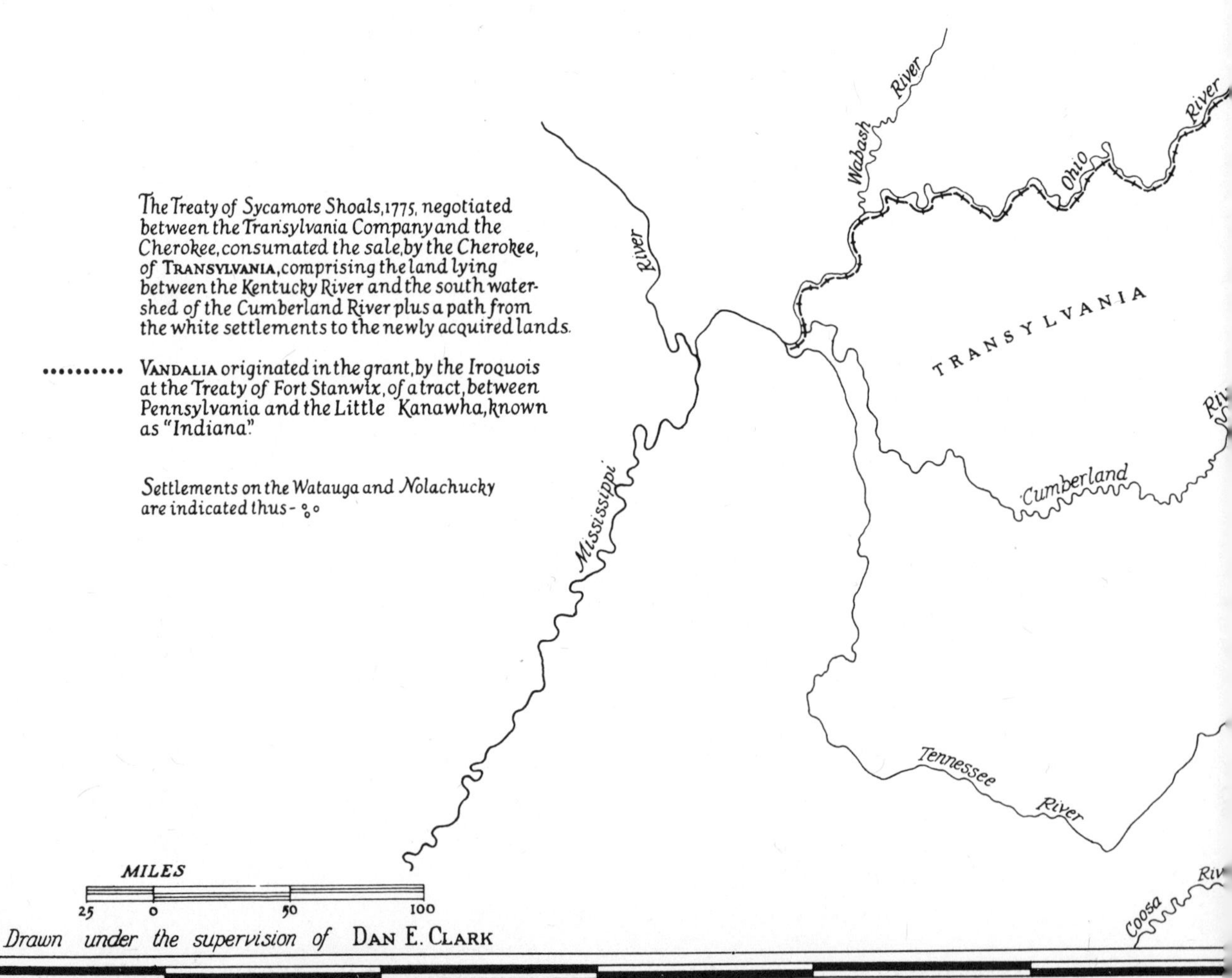
The Treaty of Sycamore Shoals, 1775, negotiated between the Transylvania Company and the Cherokee, consumated the sale, by the Cherokee, of TRANSYLVANIA, comprising the land lying between the Kentucky River and the south watershed of the Cumberland River plus a path from the white settlements to the newly acquired lands.
•••••••••• VANDALIA originated in the grant, by the Iroquois at the Treaty of Fort Stanwix, of a tract, between Pennsylvania and the Little Kanawha, known as "Indiana."
Settlements on the Watauga and Nolachucky are indicated thus - °o
Wabash River
Ohio River
River
Mississippi
TRANSYLVANIA
Cumberland
Tennessee River
Coosa
MILES
25 0 50 100
Drawn under the supervision of DAN E. CLARK

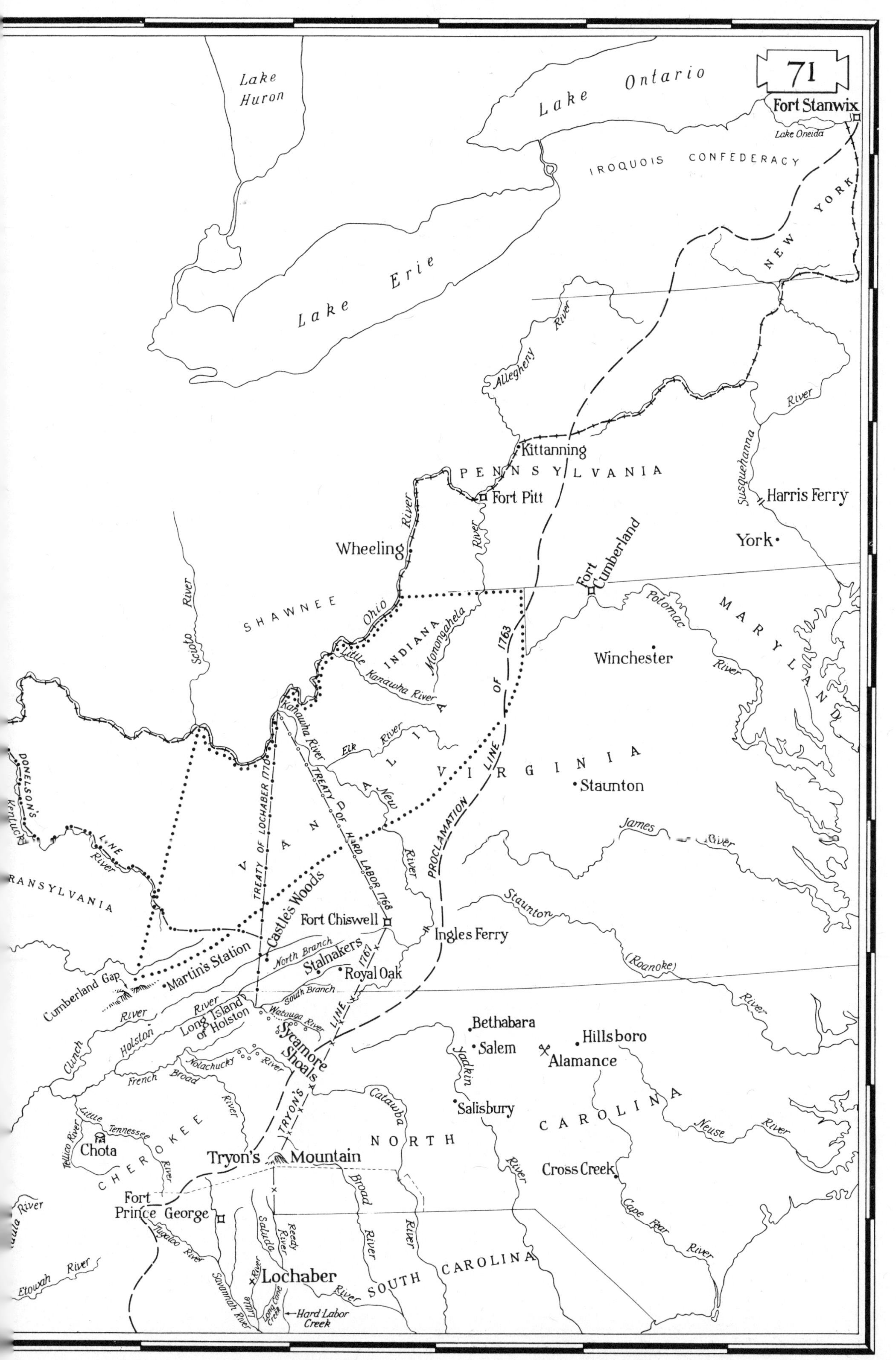
71
Lake Huron
Lake Ontario
Fort Stanwix
Lake Oneida
IROQUOIS CONFEDERACY
NEW YORK
Lake Erie
Allegheny River
Susquehanna River
Kittanning
PENNSYLVANIA
Fort Pitt
Harris Ferry
York
Wheeling
Ohio River
Fort Cumberland
SHAWNEE
Scioto River
INDIANA
Monongahela
Little Kanawha River
MARYLAND
Potomac River
Winchester
PROCLAMATION LINE OF 1763
Kanawha River
Elk River
New River
VANDALIA
VIRGINIA
Staunton
DONELSON'S LINE
Kentucky River
TRANSYLVANIA
TREATY OF LOCHABER 1770
TREATY OF HARD LABOR 1768
James River
Castle's Woods
Fort Chiswell
Ingles Ferry
Staunton
(Roanoke) River
Martin's Station
North Branch
Stalnakers
Royal Oak
LINE 1767
Cumberland Gap
South Branch
Clinch River
Holston River
Long Island of Holston
Watauga River
Sycamore Shoals
Bethabara
Salem
Hillsboro
Alamance
Yadkin
Nolachucky River
French Broad River
TRYON'S LINE
Catawba
Salisbury
NORTH CAROLINA
Neuse River
Little Tennessee River
Tellico River
Chota
CHEROKEE
Tryon's Mountain
Cross Creek
Fort Prince George
Tugaloo River
Saluda River
Reedy River
Broad River
Cape Fear River
Etowah River
Savannah River
Little River
Lochaber
Long Cane Creek
Hard Labor Creek
SOUTH CAROLINA

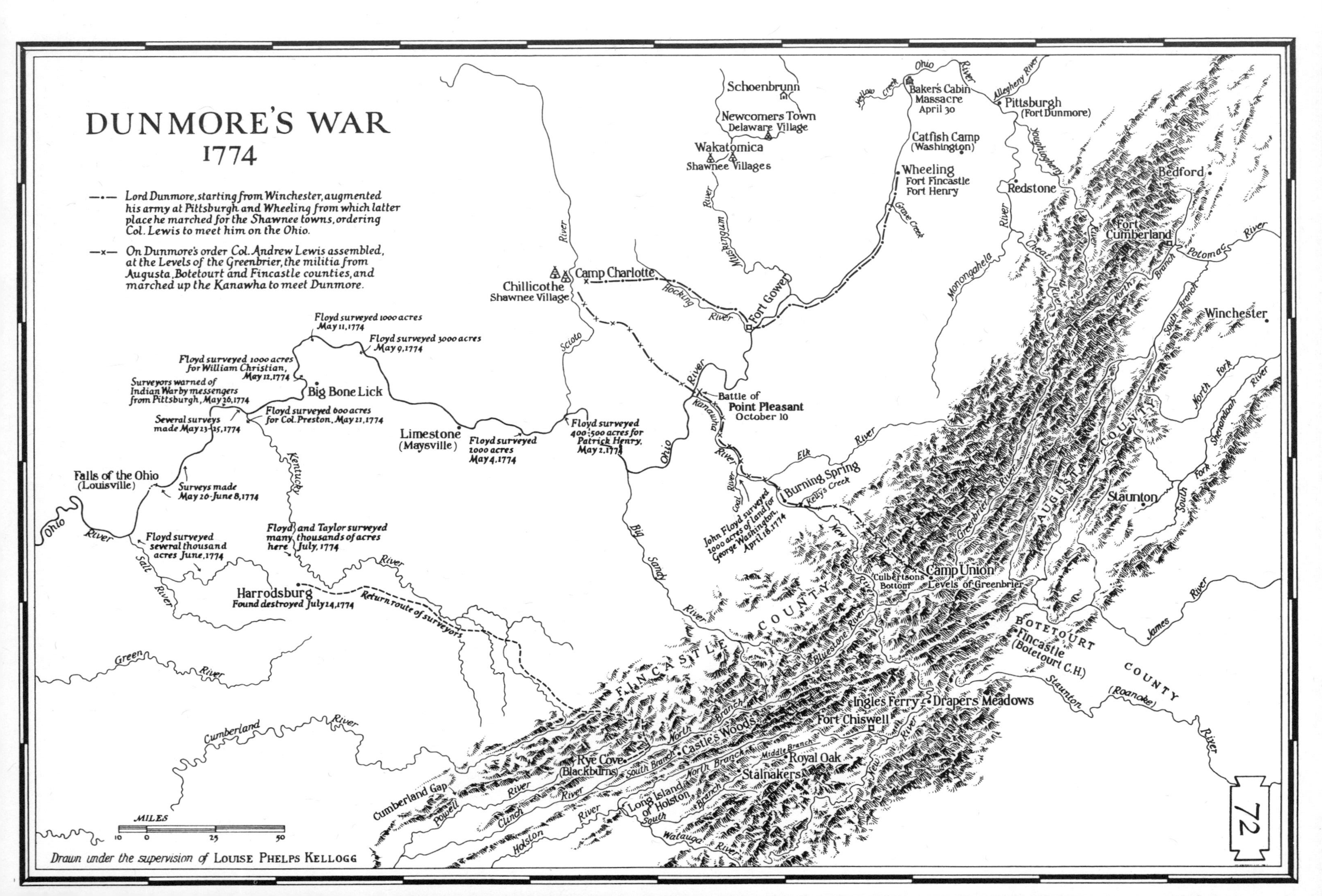

DUNMORE'S WAR
1774
Lord Dunmore, starting from Winchester, augmented his army at Pittsburgh and Wheeling from which latter place he marched for the Shawnee towns, ordering Col. Lewis to meet him on the Ohio.
On Dunmore's order Col. Andrew Lewis assembled, at the Levels of the Greenbrier, the militia from Augusta, Botetourt and Fincastle counties, and marched up the Kanawha to meet Dunmore.
Schoenbrunn
Newcomers Town
Delaware Village
Wakatomica
Shawnee Villages
Baker's Cabin
Massacre
April 30
Pittsburgh
(Fort Dunmore)
Catfish Camp
(Washington)
Wheeling
Fort Fincastle
Fort Henry
Redstone
Bedford
Fort Cumberland
Winchester
Camp Charlotte
Chillicothe
Shawnee Village
Fort Gower
Battle of
Point Pleasant
October 10
Floyd surveyed 1000 acres
May 11, 1774
Floyd surveyed 3000 acres
May 9, 1774
Floyd surveyed 1000 acres
for William Christian,
May 12, 1774
Surveyors warned of
Indian War by messengers
from Pittsburgh, May 26, 1774
Big Bone Lick
Several surveys
made May 23-25, 1774
Floyd surveyed 600 acres
for Col. Preston, May 21, 1774
Limestone
(Maysville)
Floyd surveyed
2000 acres
May 4, 1774
Floyd surveyed
400-500 acres for
Patrick Henry,
May 2, 1774
Falls of the Ohio
(Louisville)
Surveys made
May 20-June 8, 1774
Floyd surveyed
several thousand
acres June, 1774
Floyd and Taylor surveyed
many thousands of acres
here July, 1774
Harrodsburg
Found destroyed July 24, 1774
Return route of surveyors
Burning Spring
Kellys Creek
John Floyd surveyed
1000 acres of land for
George Washington,
April 18, 1774
Camp Union
Culbertsons
Bottom
Levels of Greenbrier
Staunton
AUGUSTA COUNTY
BOTETOURT COUNTY
Fincastle
(Botetourt C.H.)
(Roanoke)
FINCASTLE COUNTY
Ingles Ferry
Drapers Meadows
Fort Chiswell
Castle's Woods
Royal Oak
Rye Cove
(Blackburns)
Stalnakers
Long Island
of Holston
Cumberland Gap
Ohio River
Allegheny River
Youghiogheny
Monongahela River
Cheat River
Potomac River
North Branch
South Branch
North Fork
South Fork
Shenandoah
James River
Staunton River
Yellow Creek
Grave Creek
Muskingum River
Hocking River
Scioto River
Kanawha River
Elk River
Coal River
New River
Greenbrier River
Bluestone River
Big Sandy River
Kentucky River
Salt River
Green River
Cumberland River
Powell River
Clinch River
Holston River
Middle Branch
Watauga River
MILES
10 0 25 50
Drawn under the supervision of LOUISE PHELPS KELLOGG
72

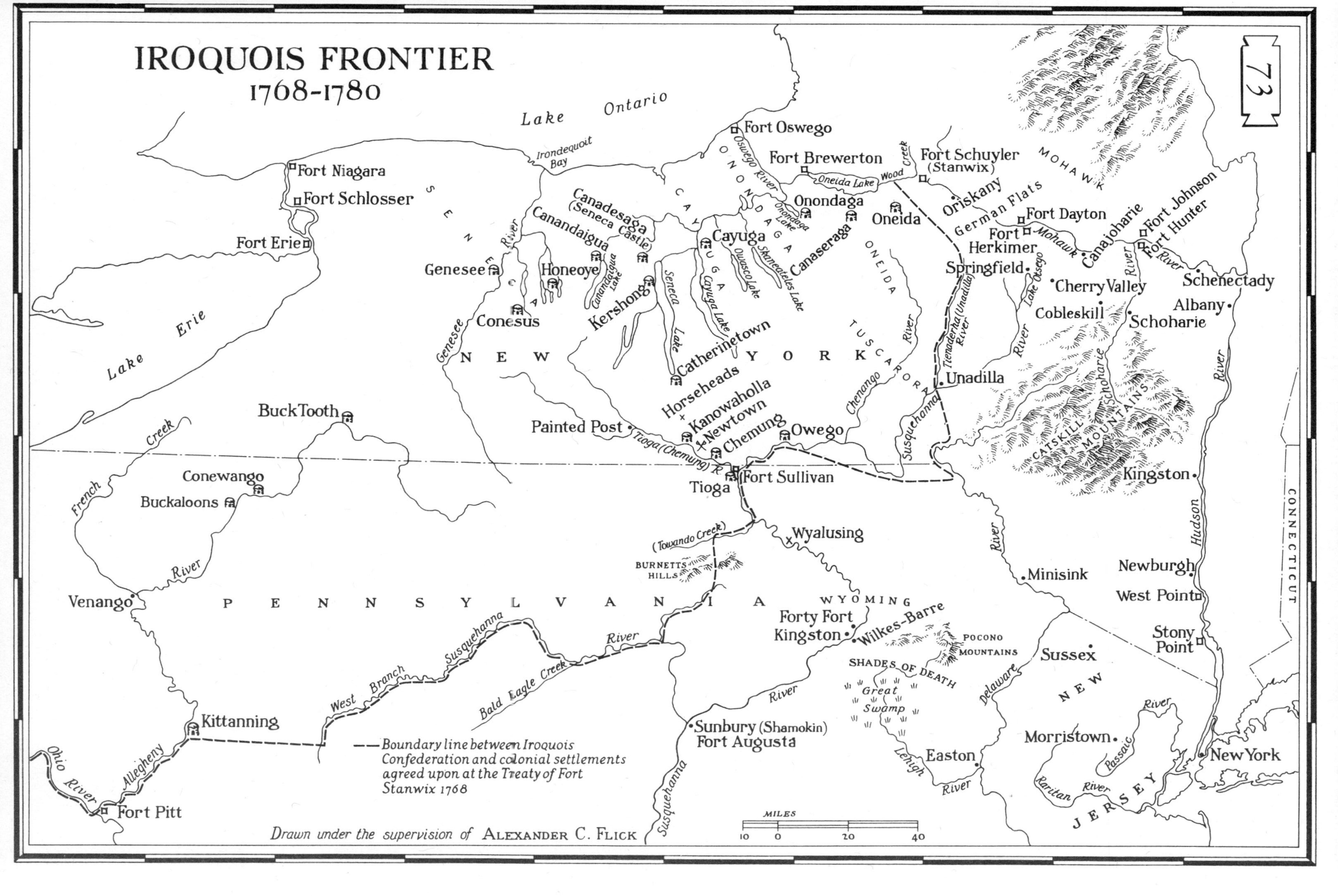

73
IROQUOIS FRONTIER
1768-1780
Lake Ontario
Lake Erie
Irondequoit Bay
Fort Niagara
Fort Schlosser
Fort Erie
Fort Oswego
Fort Brewerton
Fort Schuyler (Stanwix)
Oneida Lake
Wood Creek
Oswego River
Onondaga Lake
Skaneateles Lake
Owasco Lake
Cayuga Lake
Seneca Lake
Canandaigua Lake
Genesee River
SENECA
CAYUGA
ONONDAGA
ONEIDA
TUSCARORA
MOHAWK
NEW YORK
PENNSYLVANIA
NEW JERSEY
CONNECTICUT
WYOMING
Canadesaga (Seneca Castle)
Canandaigua
Genesee
Honeoye
Conesus
Kershong
Catherinetown
Horseheads
Kanowaholla
Newtown
Chemung
Painted Post
Tioga (Chemung) R.
Tioga
Fort Sullivan
Owego
Cayuga
Onondaga
Canaseraga
Oneida
Oriskany
German Flats
Fort Dayton
Fort Herkimer
Mohawk River
Canajoharie
Fort Johnson
Fort Hunter
Schenectady
Albany
Schoharie
Cobleskill
Cherry Valley
Springfield
Lake Otsego
Tienaderha (Unadilla) River
Unadilla
Chenango River
Susquehanna
Schoharie
CATSKILL MOUNTAINS
Kingston
Hudson River
Newburgh
West Point
Stony Point
New York
Minisink
Delaware River
Sussex
Morristown
Passaic River
Raritan River
Easton
Lehigh River
POCONO MOUNTAINS
SHADES OF DEATH
Great Swamp
Wilkes-Barre
Forty Fort
Kingston
Wyalusing
(Towando Creek)
BURNETTS HILLS
Sunbury (Shamokin)
Fort Augusta
Susquehanna River
West Branch
Bald Eagle Creek
Buck Tooth
Conewango
Buckaloons
French Creek
River
Venango
Kittanning
Allegheny
Ohio River
Fort Pitt
Boundary line between Iroquois Confederation and colonial settlements agreed upon at the Treaty of Fort Stanwix 1768
MILES
10 0 20 40
Drawn under the supervision of ALEXANDER C. FLICK

V THE AMERICAN REVOLUTION

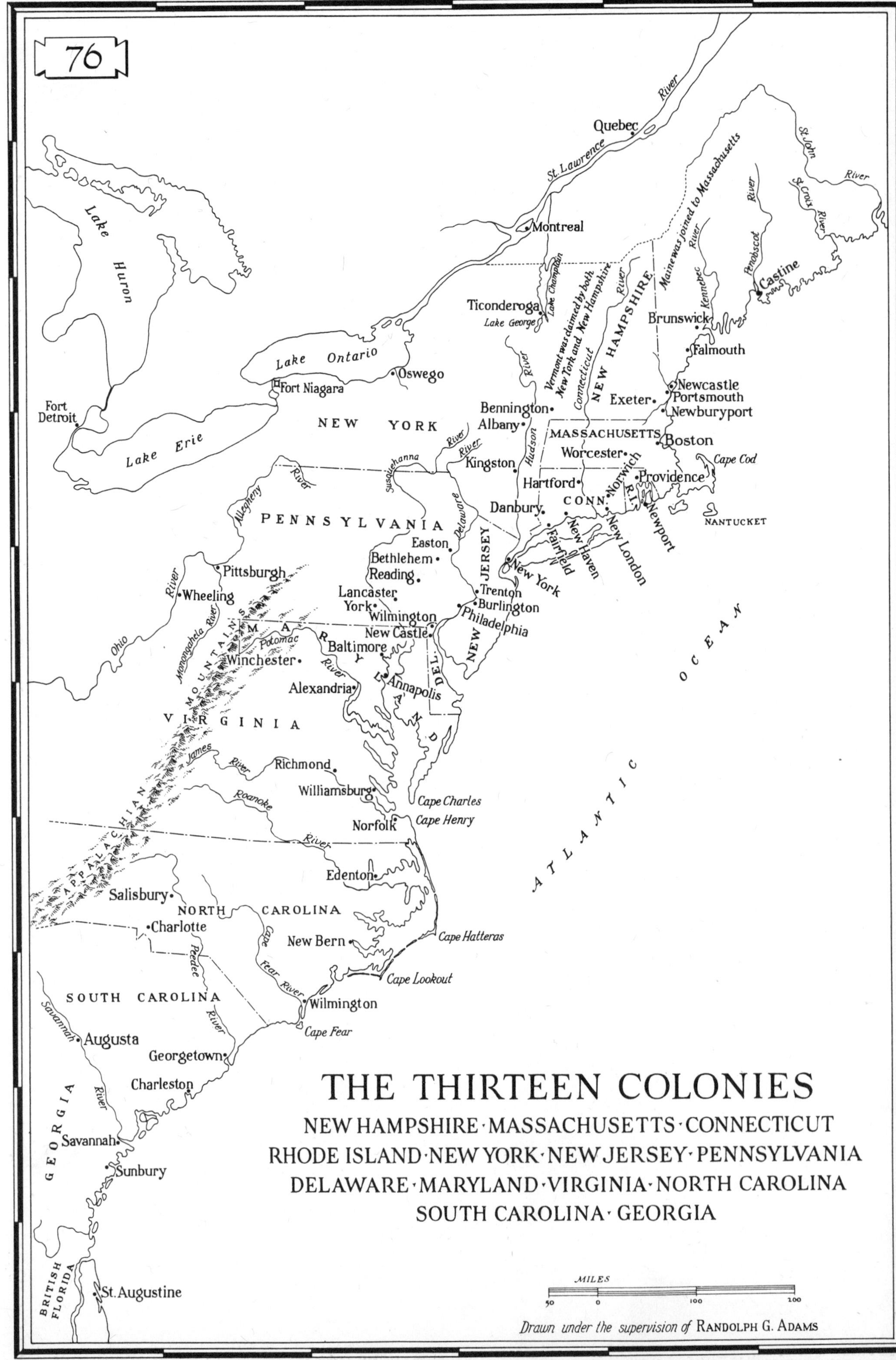
76
THE THIRTEEN COLONIES
NEW HAMPSHIRE · MASSACHUSETTS · CONNECTICUT
RHODE ISLAND · NEW YORK · NEW JERSEY · PENNSYLVANIA
DELAWARE · MARYLAND · VIRGINIA · NORTH CAROLINA
SOUTH CAROLINA · GEORGIA
Quebec
St. Lawrence River
Montreal
Lake Huron
Lake Ontario
Lake Erie
Fort Niagara
Oswego
Fort Detroit
Ticonderoga
Lake George
Lake Champlain
Vermont was claimed by both New York and New Hampshire
Connecticut River
NEW HAMPSHIRE
Maine was joined to Massachusetts
St. John River
St. Croix River
Penobscot
Kennebec
River
Castine
Brunswick
Falmouth
Newcastle
Portsmouth
Newburyport
Exeter
Bennington
Albany
NEW YORK
Hudson River
MASSACHUSETTS
Boston
Worcester
Cape Cod
Providence
Norwich
R.I.
Newport
NANTUCKET
Kingston
Hartford
CONN.
Danbury
Fairfield
New Haven
New London
New York
PENNSYLVANIA
Allegheny River
Susquehanna River
Delaware
Easton
Bethlehem
Reading
Lancaster
York
Pittsburgh
Wheeling
Ohio River
Monongahela River
NEW JERSEY
Trenton
Burlington
Philadelphia
Wilmington
New Castle
DEL.
MARYLAND
Baltimore
Annapolis
Potomac River
Winchester
Alexandria
VIRGINIA
APPALACHIAN MOUNTAINS
James River
Richmond
Williamsburg
Roanoke River
Norfolk
Cape Charles
Cape Henry
Edenton
Salisbury
NORTH CAROLINA
Charlotte
New Bern
Cape Hatteras
Cape Lookout
Cape Fear River
Pedee River
Wilmington
Cape Fear
SOUTH CAROLINA
Savannah River
Augusta
Georgetown
Charleston
GEORGIA
Savannah
Sunbury
BRITISH FLORIDA
St. Augustine
ATLANTIC OCEAN
MILES
50 0 100 200
Drawn under the supervision of RANDOLPH G. ADAMS

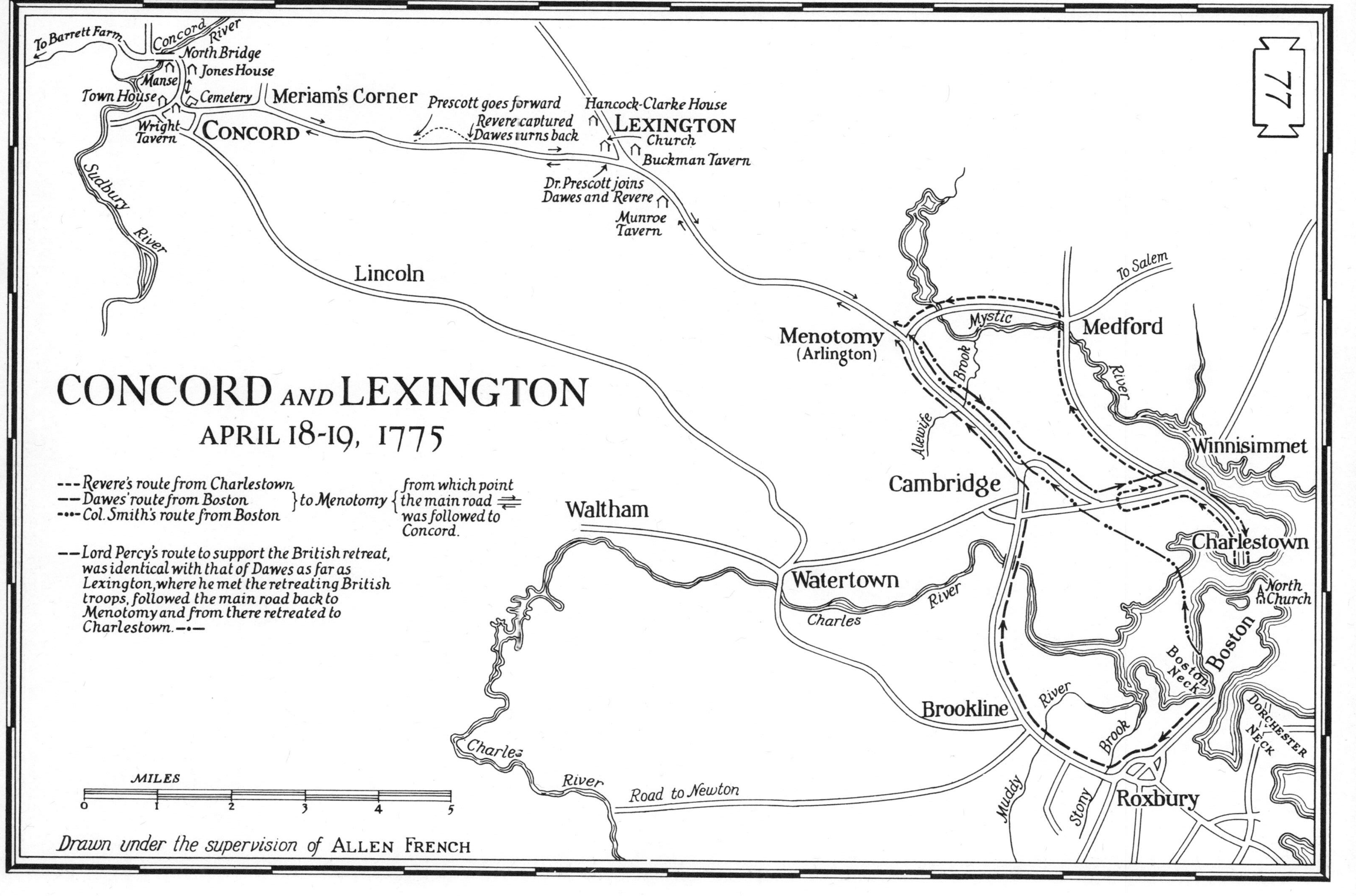
77
CONCORD AND LEXINGTON
APRIL 18-19, 1775
---Revere's route from Charlestown
——Dawes' route from Boston
-•••-Col. Smith's route from Boston
} to Menotomy { from which point the main road ⇄ was followed to Concord.
——Lord Percy's route to support the British retreat, was identical with that of Dawes as far as Lexington, where he met the retreating British troops, followed the main road back to Menotomy and from there retreated to Charlestown. —•—
To Barrett Farm
Concord River
North Bridge
Jones House
Manse
Town House
Cemetery
Wright Tavern
CONCORD
Meriam's Corner
Prescott goes forward
Revere captured
Dawes turns back
Hancock-Clarke House
LEXINGTON
Church
Buckman Tavern
Dr. Prescott joins Dawes and Revere
Munroe Tavern
Sudbury River
Lincoln
Menotomy
(Arlington)
Mystic River
Brook
Alewife
To Salem
Medford
Winnisimmet
Cambridge
Charlestown
North Church
Boston
Boston Neck
Dorchester Neck
Waltham
Watertown
Charles River
Brookline
River
Brook
Muddy
Stony
Roxbury
Road to Newton
Charles River
MILES
0 1 2 3 4 5
Drawn under the supervision of ALLEN FRENCH

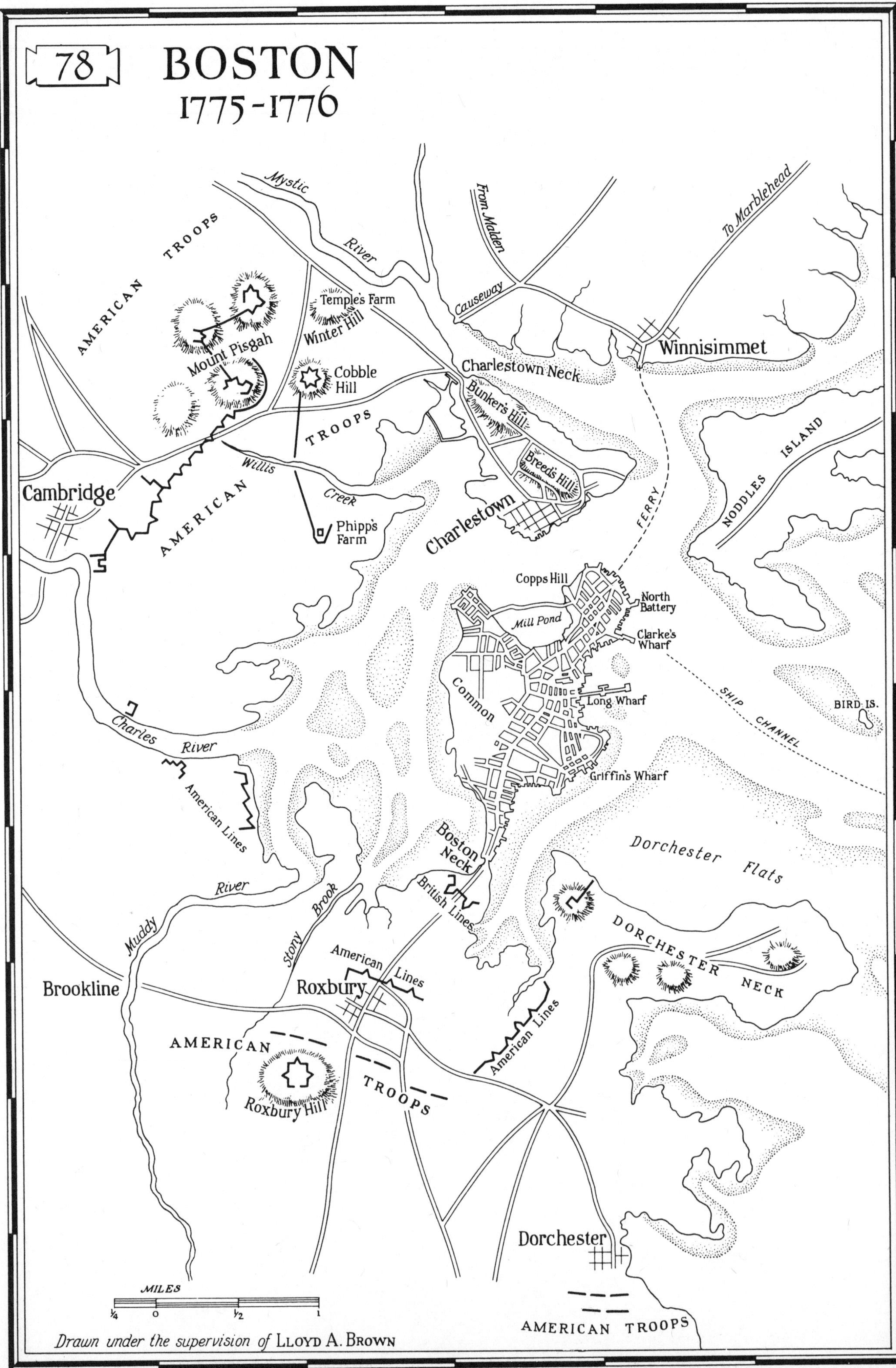
78
BOSTON
1775-1776
Mystic
River
From Malden
To Marblehead
Causeway
AMERICAN TROOPS
Temple's Farm
Winter Hill
Mount Pisgah
Cobble Hill
Charlestown Neck
Winnisimmet
Bunker's Hill
Breed's Hill
TROOPS
Willis
Creek
AMERICAN
Cambridge
Phipp's Farm
Charlestown
FERRY
NODDLES ISLAND
Copps Hill
North Battery
Mill Pond
Clarke's Wharf
Common
Long Wharf
SHIP CHANNEL
BIRD IS.
Charles River
Griffin's Wharf
American Lines
Boston Neck
Dorchester Flats
British Lines
River
Muddy
Stony Brook
DORCHESTER NECK
American Lines
Brookline
Roxbury
American Lines
AMERICAN TROOPS
Roxbury Hill
Dorchester
MILES
¼ 0 ½ 1
AMERICAN TROOPS
Drawn under the supervision of LLOYD A. BROWN

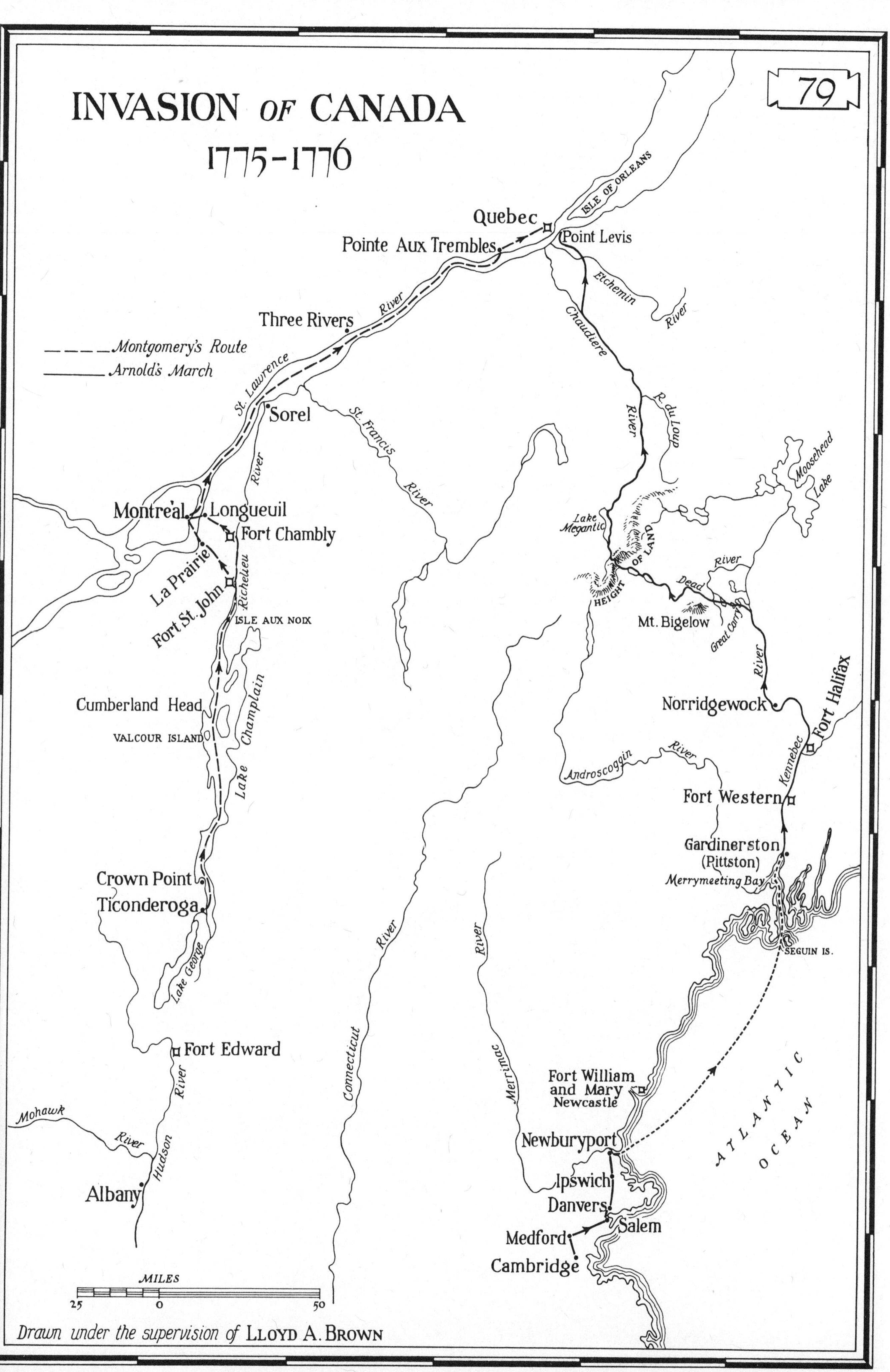

INVASION OF CANADA
1775-1776
79
Montgomery's Route
Arnold's March
Quebec
Isle of Orleans
Point Levis
Pointe Aux Trembles
Three Rivers
St. Lawrence River
Sorel
St. Francis River
Montreal
Longueuil
Fort Chambly
La Prairie
Fort St. John
Richelieu River
Isle aux Noix
Cumberland Head
Valcour Island
Lake Champlain
Crown Point
Ticonderoga
Lake George
Fort Edward
Hudson River
Mohawk River
Albany
Connecticut River
Merrimac River
Chaudiere River
Etchemin River
R. du Loup
Lake Megantic
Height of Land
Dead River
Mt. Bigelow
Great Carry
Moosehead Lake
Norridgewock
Fort Halifax
Androscoggin River
Kennebec
Fort Western
Gardinerston (Pittston)
Merrymeeting Bay
Seguin Is.
Fort William and Mary
Newcastle
Newburyport
Ipswich
Danvers
Salem
Medford
Cambridge
Atlantic Ocean
Miles
25 0 50
Drawn under the supervision of Lloyd A. Brown

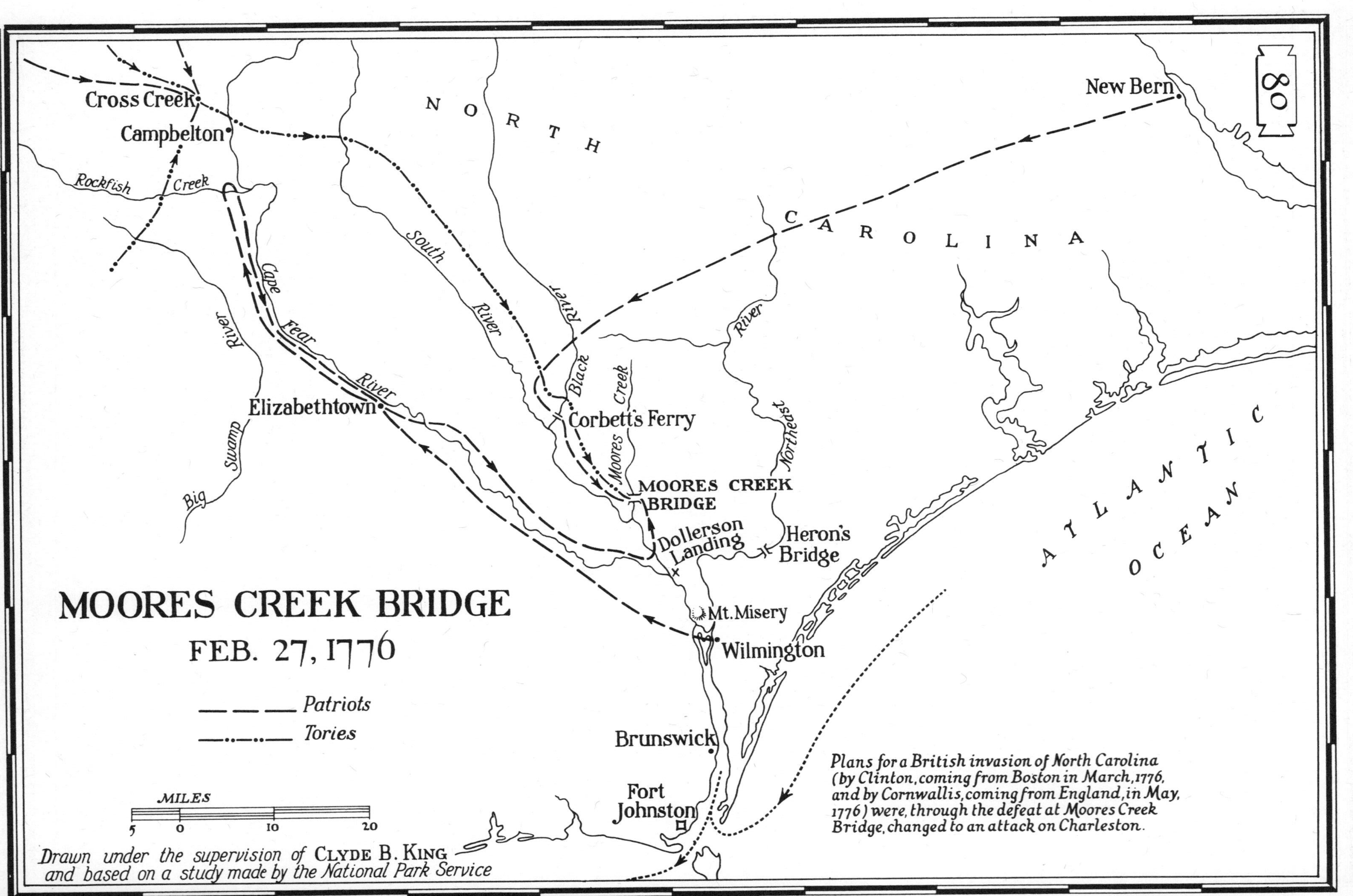
80
Cross Creek
Campbelton
Rockfish Creek
NORTH CAROLINA
New Bern
South River
Black River
Cape Fear River
Big Swamp River
Elizabethtown
Corbett's Ferry
Moores Creek
Northeast River
MOORES CREEK BRIDGE
Dollerson Landing
Heron's Bridge
Mt. Misery
Wilmington
Brunswick
Fort Johnston
ATLANTIC OCEAN
Patriots
Tories
MILES
5 0 10 20
Plans for a British invasion of North Carolina (by Clinton, coming from Boston in March, 1776, and by Cornwallis, coming from England, in May, 1776) were, through the defeat at Moores Creek Bridge, changed to an attack on Charleston.
Drawn under the supervision of Clyde B. King and based on a study made by the National Park Service

MOORES CREEK BRIDGE
FEB. 27, 1776

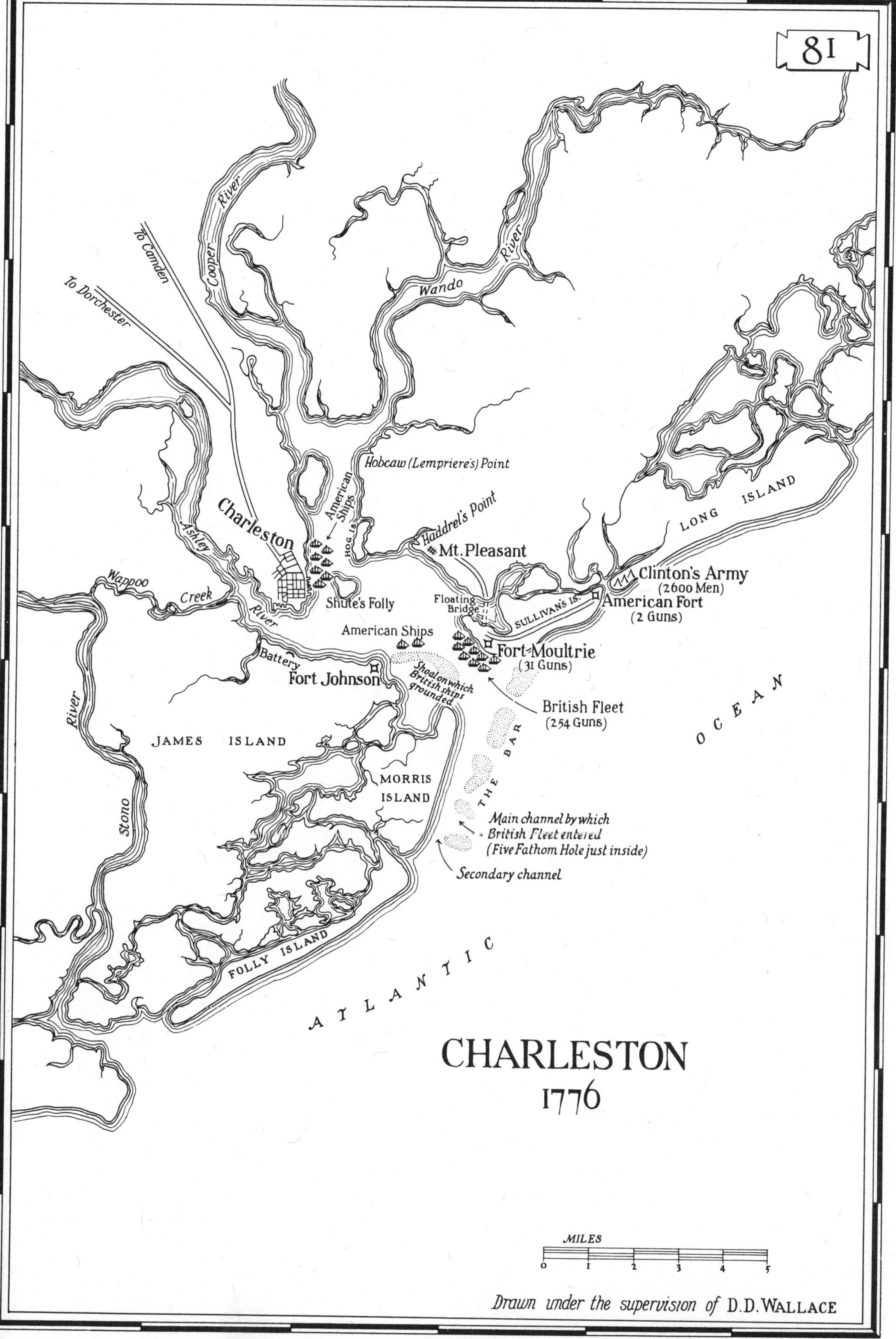
81
To Camden
To Dorchester
Cooper River
Wando River
Hobcaw (Lempriere's) Point
American Ships
Charleston
Ashley River
HOG IS.
Haddrel's Point
Mt. Pleasant
Wappoo Creek
Shute's Folly
Floating Bridge
Clinton's Army
(2600 Men)
American Fort
(2 Guns)
SULLIVAN'S IS.
LONG ISLAND
American Ships
Fort Moultrie
(31 Guns)
Battery
Fort Johnson
Shoal on which British ships grounded
British Fleet
(254 Guns)
OCEAN
JAMES ISLAND
Stono River
THE BAR
MORRIS ISLAND
Main channel by which
British Fleet entered
(Five Fathom Hole just inside)
Secondary channel
FOLLY ISLAND
ATLANTIC
CHARLESTON
1776
MILES
0 1 2 3 4 5
Drawn under the supervision of D.D. WALLACE

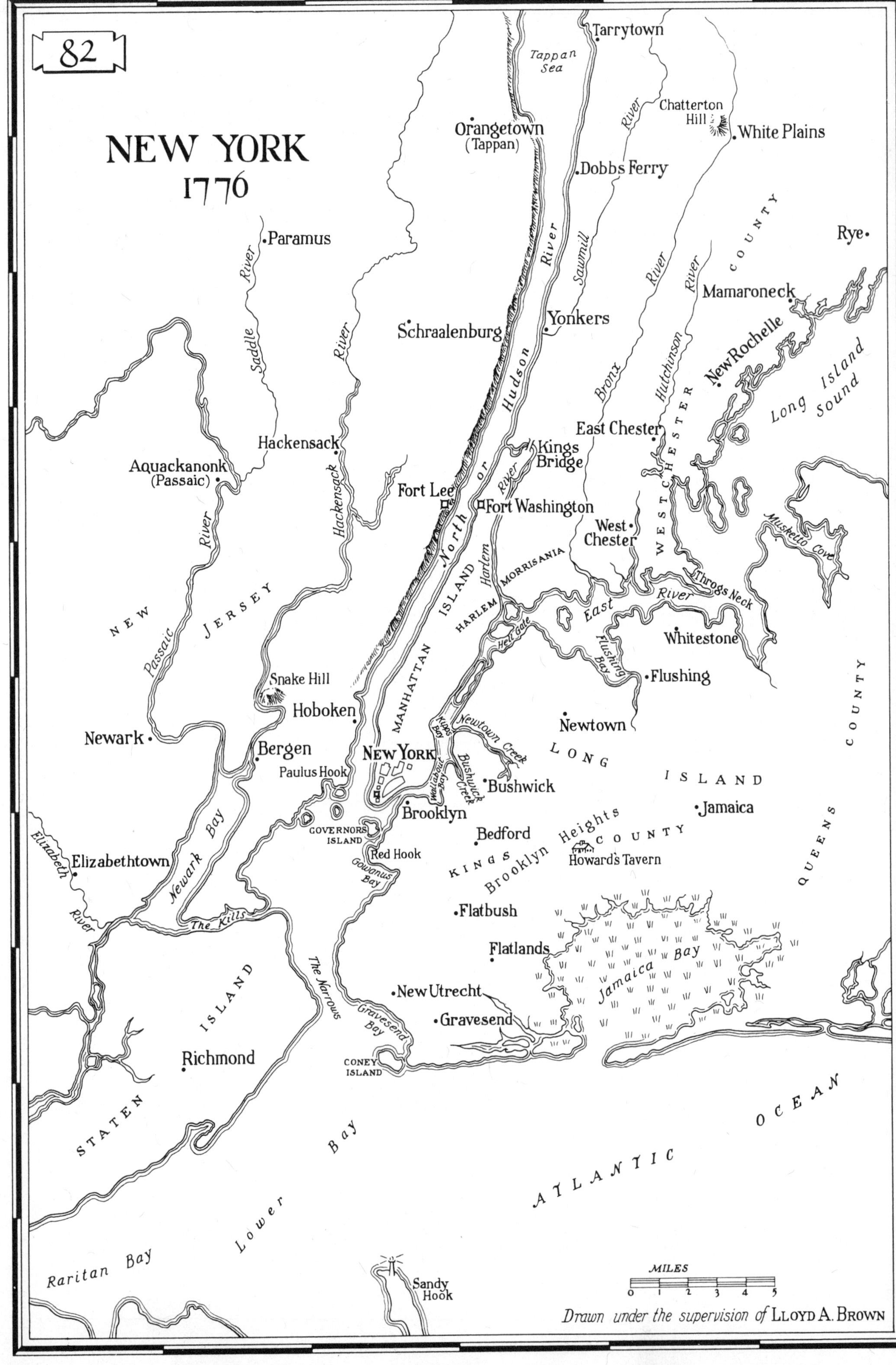
82
NEW YORK
1776
Tarrytown
Tappan Sea
Chatterton Hill
White Plains
Orangetown
(Tappan)
Dobbs Ferry
River
Paramus
Saddle River
Rye
Sawmill River
Bronx River
Hutchinson River
WESTCHESTER COUNTY
Mamaroneck
Schraalenburg
Yonkers
New Rochelle
Long Island Sound
North or Hudson River
Hackensack River
Hackensack
East Chester
Kings Bridge
Aquackanonk
(Passaic)
Fort Lee
Fort Washington
Harlem River
West Chester
Musketto Cove
MORRISANIA
HARLEM
Throgs Neck
East River
Hell Gate
NEW JERSEY
Passaic River
Whitestone
Flushing Bay
Flushing
MANHATTAN ISLAND
Snake Hill
Hoboken
Newtown
Newark
Bergen
NEW YORK
Kips Bay
Newtown Creek
LONG ISLAND
Paulus Hook
Bushwick Creek
Wallabout Bay
Bushwick
Jamaica
Brooklyn
GOVERNORS ISLAND
Bedford
Brooklyn Heights
KINGS COUNTY
Howard's Tavern
QUEENS COUNTY
Red Hook
Gowanus Bay
Elizabethtown
Elizabeth River
Newark Bay
Flatbush
The Kills
Flatlands
Jamaica Bay
The Narrows
New Utrecht
Gravesend
Gravesend Bay
STATEN ISLAND
Richmond
CONEY ISLAND
ATLANTIC OCEAN
Lower Bay
Raritan Bay
Sandy Hook
MILES
0 1 2 3 4 5
Drawn under the supervision of LLOYD A. BROWN

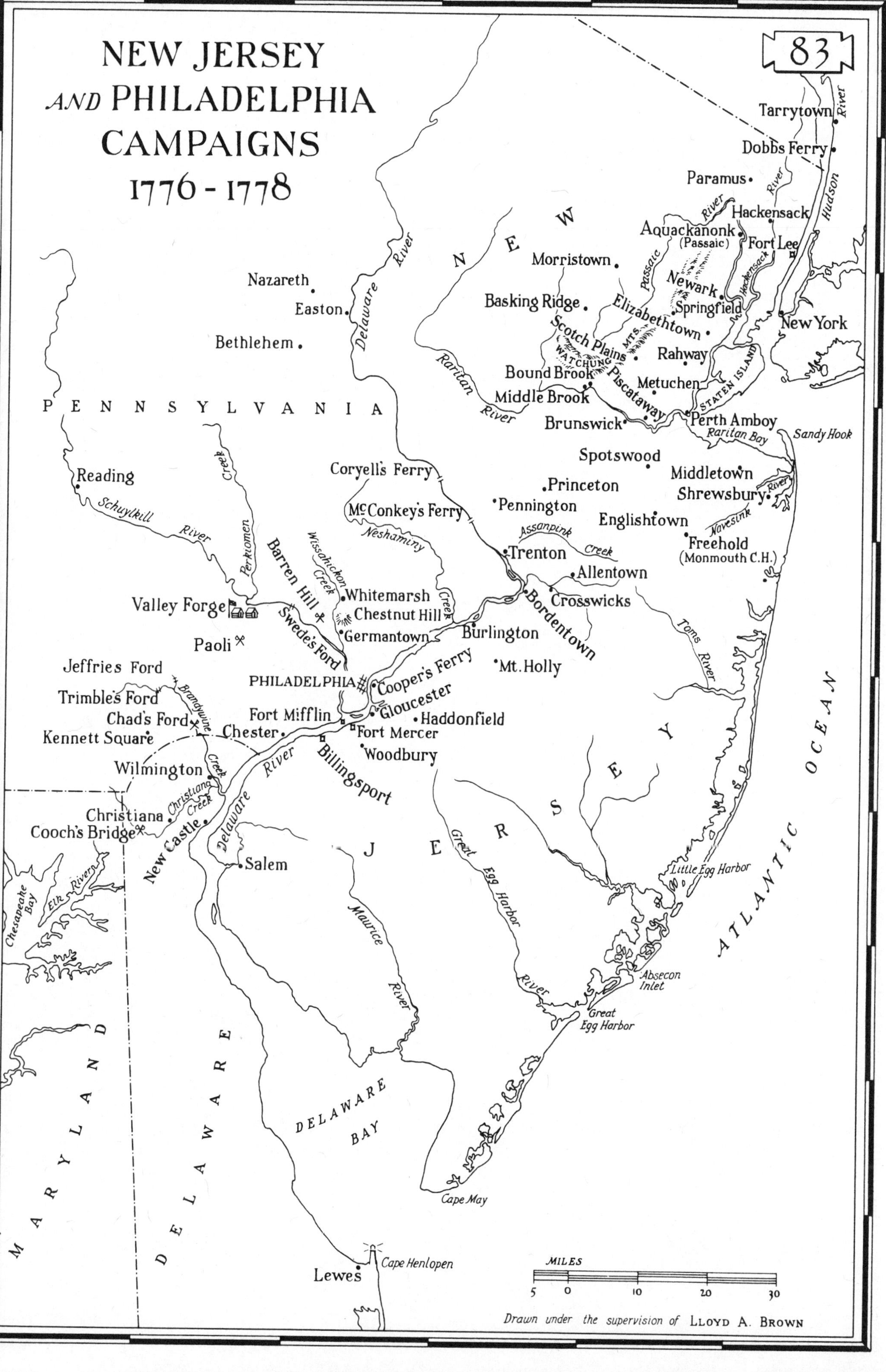

NEW JERSEY AND PHILADELPHIA CAMPAIGNS 1776 - 1778
83
Tarrytown
Dobbs Ferry
Paramus
Hackensack
Aquackanonk (Passaic)
Fort Lee
Hudson
River
Morristown
Newark
Springfield
Basking Ridge
Elizabethtown
New York
Scotch Plains
Watchung Mts.
Rahway
Bound Brook
Middle Brook
Metuchen
Piscataway
Staten Island
Brunswick
Perth Amboy
Raritan Bay
Sandy Hook
Raritan River
Spotswood
Middletown
Shrewsbury
Princeton
Pennington
Englishtown
Navesink
Freehold (Monmouth C.H.)
Assanpink Creek
Trenton
Allentown
Crosswicks
Bordentown
Burlington
Mt. Holly
Toms River
Nazareth
Easton
Bethlehem
Delaware River
PENNSYLVANIA
NEW JERSEY
Reading
Schuylkill River
Perkiomen Creek
Coryell's Ferry
McConkey's Ferry
Neshaminy Creek
Wissahickon Creek
Barren Hill
Whitemarsh
Chestnut Hill
Valley Forge
Swede's Ford
Germantown
Paoli
Jeffries Ford
Trimble's Ford
Brandywine
Chad's Ford
Kennett Square
PHILADELPHIA
Cooper's Ferry
Gloucester
Fort Mifflin
Haddonfield
Chester
Fort Mercer
Woodbury
Billingsport
Wilmington
Christiana Creek
Christiana
Cooch's Bridge
New Castle
Salem
Maurice River
Great Egg Harbor River
Little Egg Harbor
Absecon Inlet
Great Egg Harbor
ATLANTIC OCEAN
Chesapeake Bay
Elk River
MARYLAND
DELAWARE
DELAWARE BAY
Cape May
Cape Henlopen
Lewes
MILES
5 0 10 20 30
Drawn under the supervision of Lloyd A. Brown

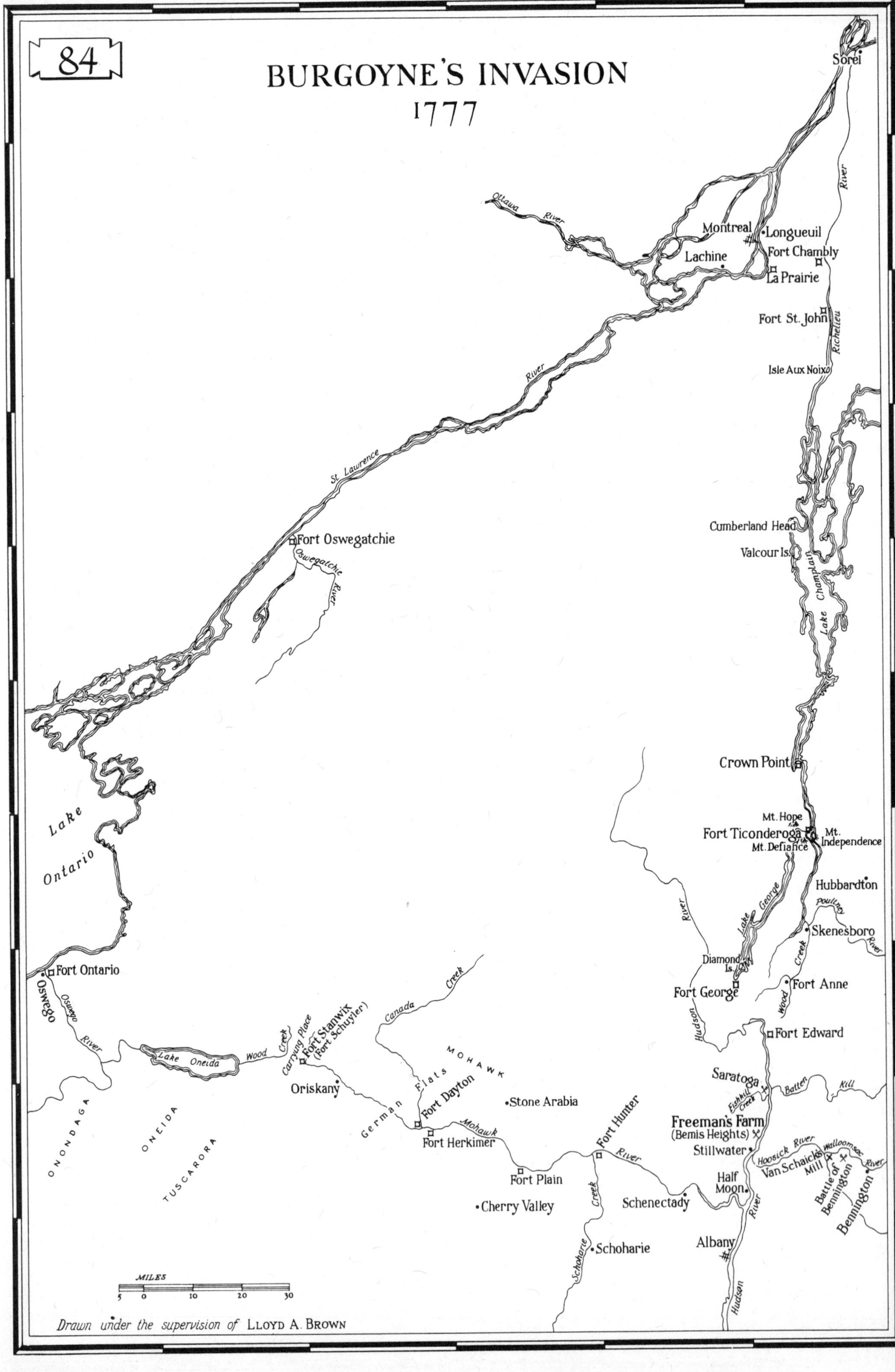
84
BURGOYNE'S INVASION
1777
Sorel
River
Ottawa River
Montreal
Longueuil
Lachine
Fort Chambly
La Prairie
Fort St. John
Richelieu
Isle Aux Noix
River
St. Lawrence
Fort Oswegatchie
Oswegatchie River
Cumberland Head
Valcour Is.
Lake Champlain
Crown Point
Mt. Hope
Fort Ticonderoga
Mt. Independence
Mt. Defiance
Hubbardton
Lake George
Poultney River
Skenesboro
Diamond Is.
Fort George
Wood Creek
Fort Anne
Fort Edward
Lake Ontario
Fort Ontario
Oswego
Oswego River
Lake Oneida
Wood Creek
Carrying Place
Fort Stanwix (Fort Schuyler)
Canada Creek
MOHAWK
German Flats
Oriskany
Fort Dayton
Stone Arabia
Fort Herkimer
Mohawk River
Fort Hunter
Fort Plain
Cherry Valley
Schoharie Creek
Schoharie
Schenectady
ONONDAGA
ONEIDA
TUSCARORA
Hudson River
Saratoga
Fishkill Creek
Batten Kill
Freeman's Farm (Bemis Heights)
Stillwater
Hoosick River
Walloomsac River
Van Schaick's Mill
Battle of Bennington
Bennington
Half Moon
Albany
MILES
5 0 10 20 30
Drawn under the supervision of LLOYD A. BROWN

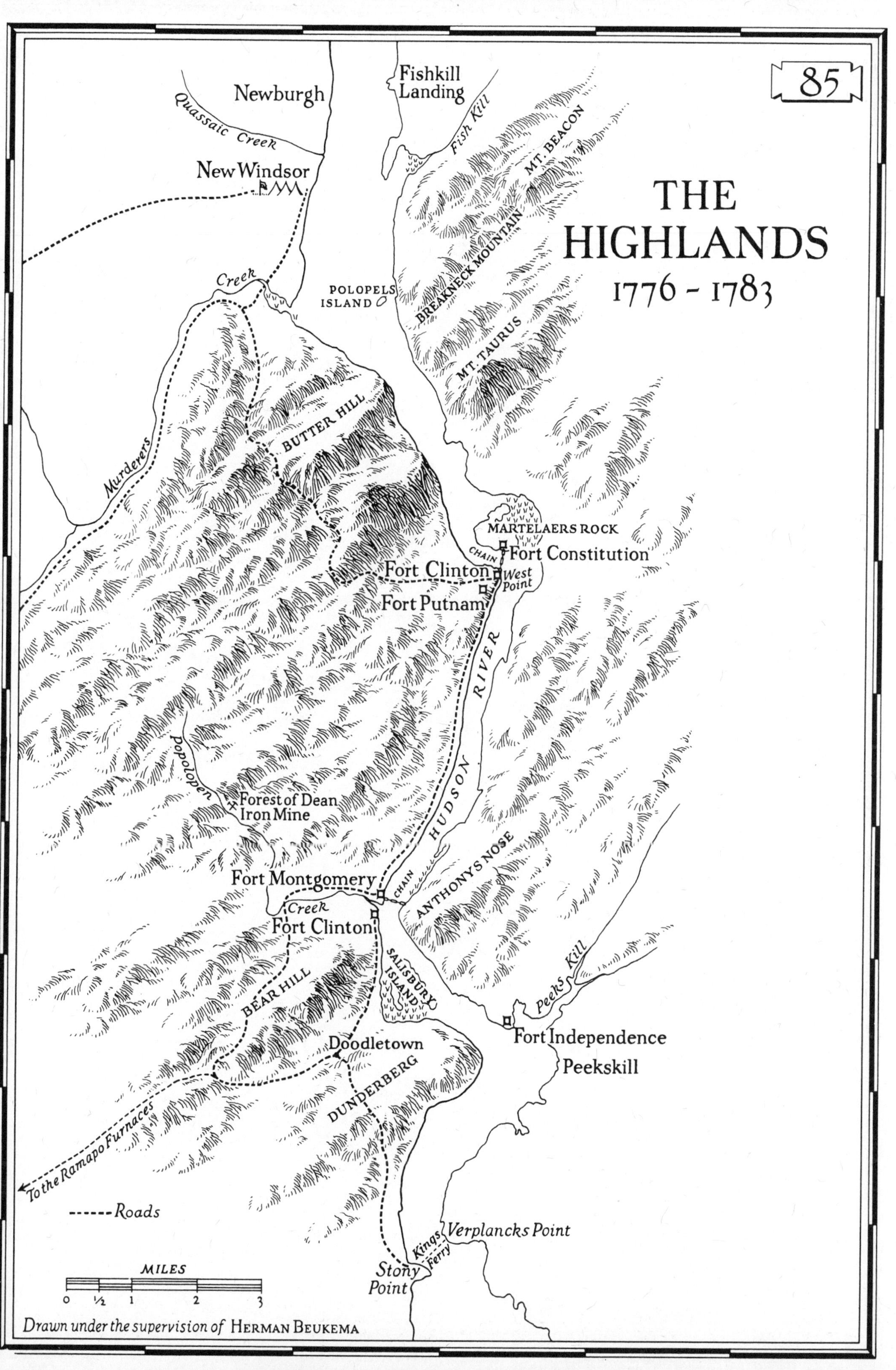
85
THE HIGHLANDS
1776 - 1783
Newburgh
Fishkill Landing
Quassaic Creek
Fish Kill
New Windsor
MT. BEACON
BREAKNECK MOUNTAIN
Creek
POLOPELS ISLAND
MT. TAURUS
BUTTER HILL
Murderers
MARTELAERS ROCK
CHAIN
Fort Constitution
Fort Clinton
West Point
Fort Putnam
RIVER
HUDSON
Popolopen
Forest of Dean Iron Mine
ANTHONYS NOSE
Fort Montgomery
CHAIN
Creek
Fort Clinton
SALISBURY ISLAND
BEAR HILL
Peeks Kill
Fort Independence
Peekskill
Doodletown
DUNDERBERG
To the Ramapo Furnaces
Roads
Verplancks Point
Kings Ferry
Stony Point
MILES
0 ½ 1 2 3
Drawn under the supervision of HERMAN BEUKEMA

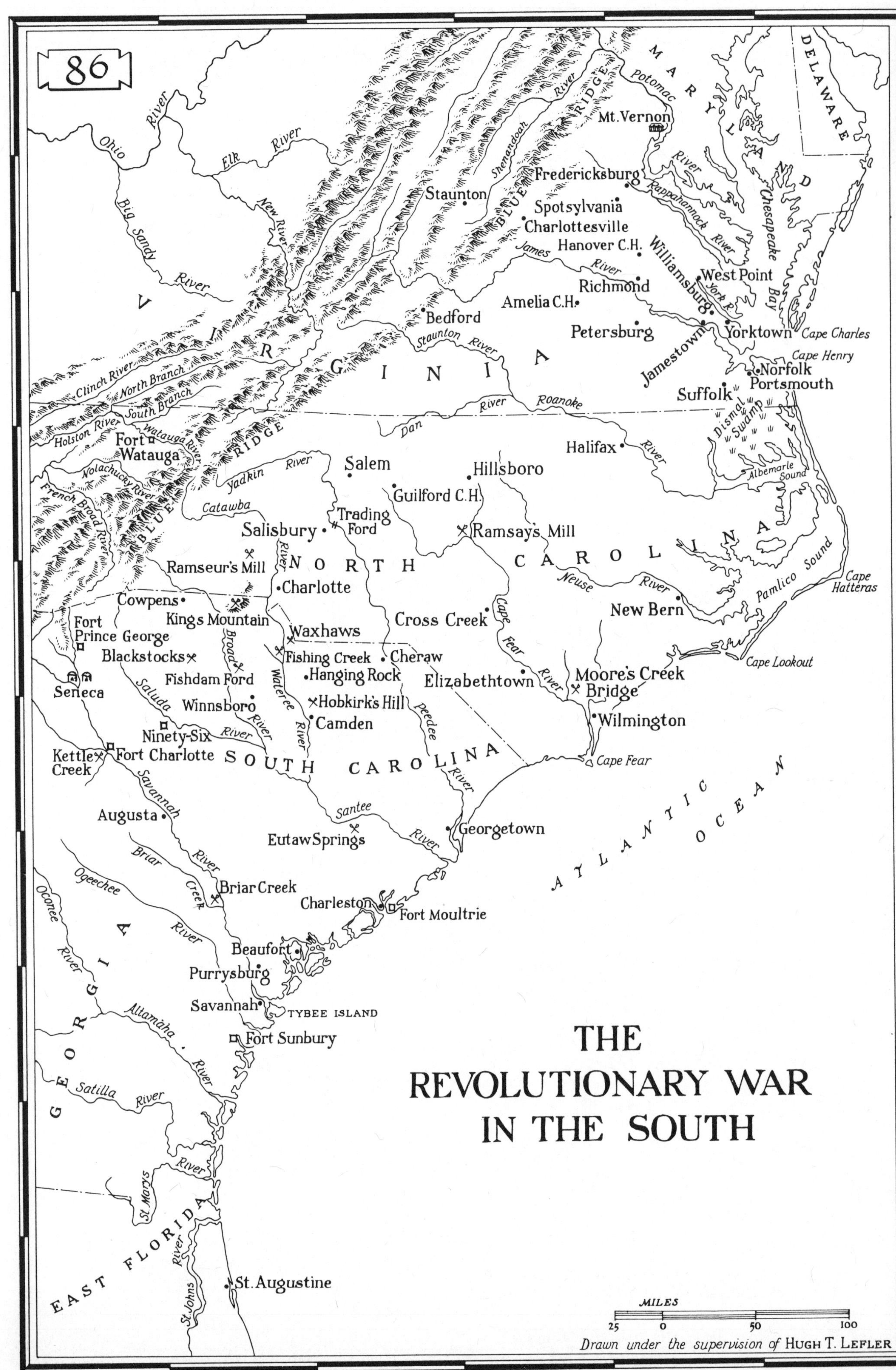
86
THE REVOLUTIONARY WAR IN THE SOUTH
MARYLAND
DELAWARE
VIRGINIA
NORTH CAROLINA
SOUTH CAROLINA
GEORGIA
EAST FLORIDA
ATLANTIC OCEAN
BLUE RIDGE
Ohio River
Elk River
New River
Big Sandy River
Shenandoah River
Potomac River
Rappahannock River
Chesapeake Bay
James River
York R.
Staunton River
Clinch River
North Branch
South Branch
Holston River
Watauga River
Nolachucky River
French Broad River
Dan River
Roanoke River
Yadkin River
Catawba River
Neuse River
Cape Fear River
Broad River
Wateree River
Saluda River
Peedee River
Santee River
Savannah River
Briar Creek
Ogeechee River
Oconee River
Altamaha River
Satilla River
St. Marys River
St. Johns River
Dismal Swamp
Albemarle Sound
Pamlico Sound
Mt. Vernon
Fredericksburg
Staunton
Spotsylvania
Charlottesville
Hanover C.H.
Williamsburg
West Point
Richmond
Amelia C.H.
Bedford
Petersburg
Jamestown
Yorktown
Cape Charles
Cape Henry
Norfolk
Portsmouth
Suffolk
Fort Watauga
Halifax
Salem
Hillsboro
Guilford C.H.
Trading Ford
Salisbury
Ramsay's Mill
Ramseur's Mill
Charlotte
Cowpens
Kings Mountain
Fort Prince George
Waxhaws
Cross Creek
New Bern
Cape Hatteras
Blackstocks
Fishing Creek
Cheraw
Cape Lookout
Fishdam Ford
Hanging Rock
Elizabethtown
Moore's Creek Bridge
Seneca
Winnsboro
Hobkirk's Hill
Camden
Wilmington
Ninety-Six
Kettle Creek
Fort Charlotte
Cape Fear
Augusta
Eutaw Springs
Georgetown
Briar Creek
Charleston
Fort Moultrie
Beaufort
Purrysburg
Savannah
TYBEE ISLAND
Fort Sunbury
St. Augustine
MILES
25 0 50 100
Drawn under the supervision of HUGH T. LEFLER

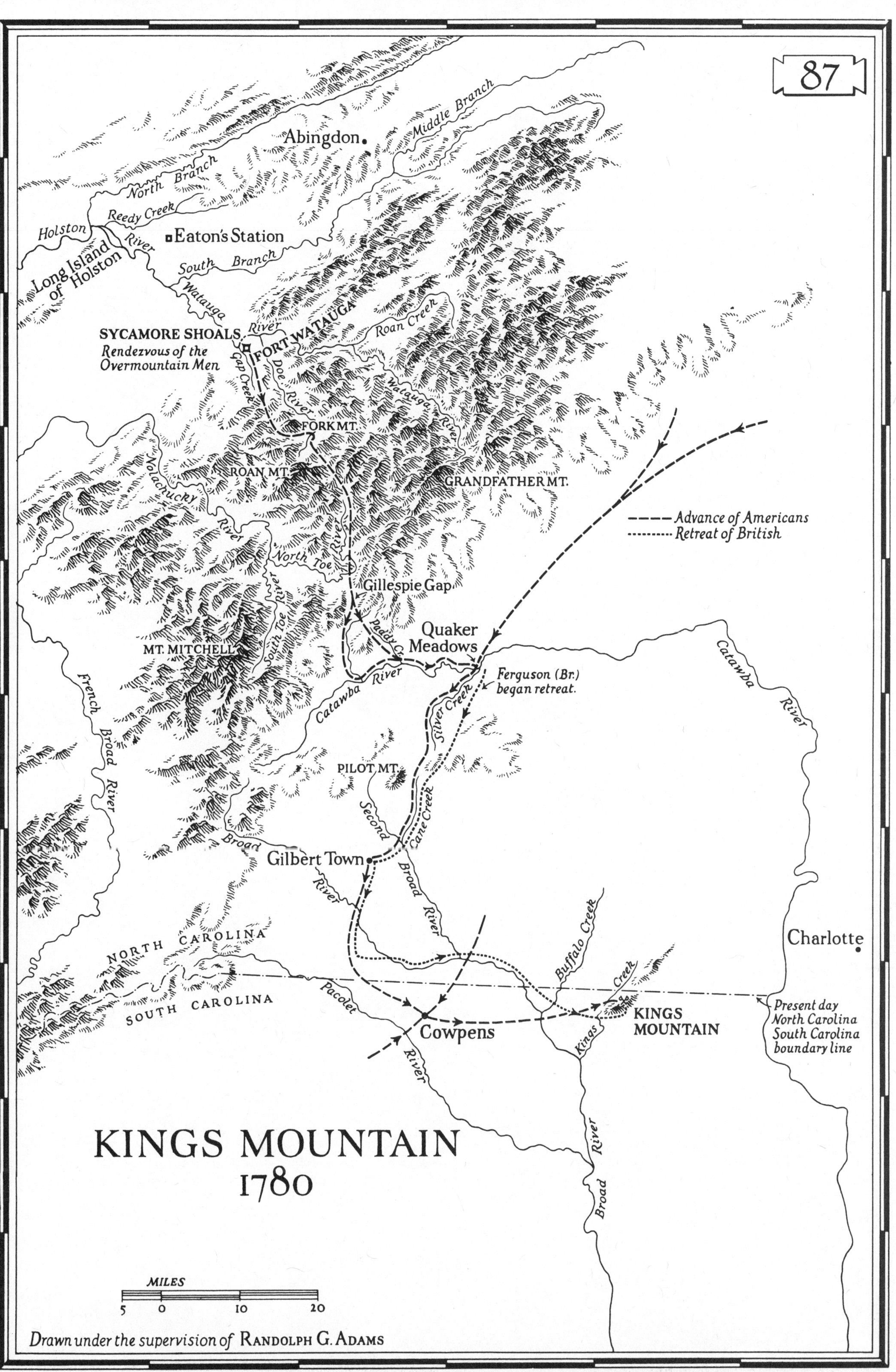
87
Abingdon
Middle Branch
North Branch
Reedy Creek
Holston
River
Eaton's Station
Long Island of Holston
South Branch
Watauga
River
SYCAMORE SHOALS
Rendezvous of the Overmountain Men
FORT WATAUGA
Roan Creek
Gap Creek
Doe River
Watauga River
FORK MT.
ROAN MT.
GRANDFATHER MT.
Nolachucky
River
North Toe
River
Gillespie Gap
South Toe River
MT. MITCHELL
Paddy Cr.
Quaker Meadows
Advance of Americans
Retreat of British
Catawba River
Ferguson (Br.) began retreat.
Silver Creek
French Broad River
PILOT MT.
Second
Cane Creek
Broad
Gilbert Town
River
Broad River
Buffalo Creek
NORTH CAROLINA
SOUTH CAROLINA
Pacolet
River
Cowpens
Kings Creek
KINGS MOUNTAIN
Charlotte
Present day North Carolina South Carolina boundary line
Catawba River
Broad River
KINGS MOUNTAIN 1780
MILES
5 0 10 20
Drawn under the supervision of Randolph G. Adams

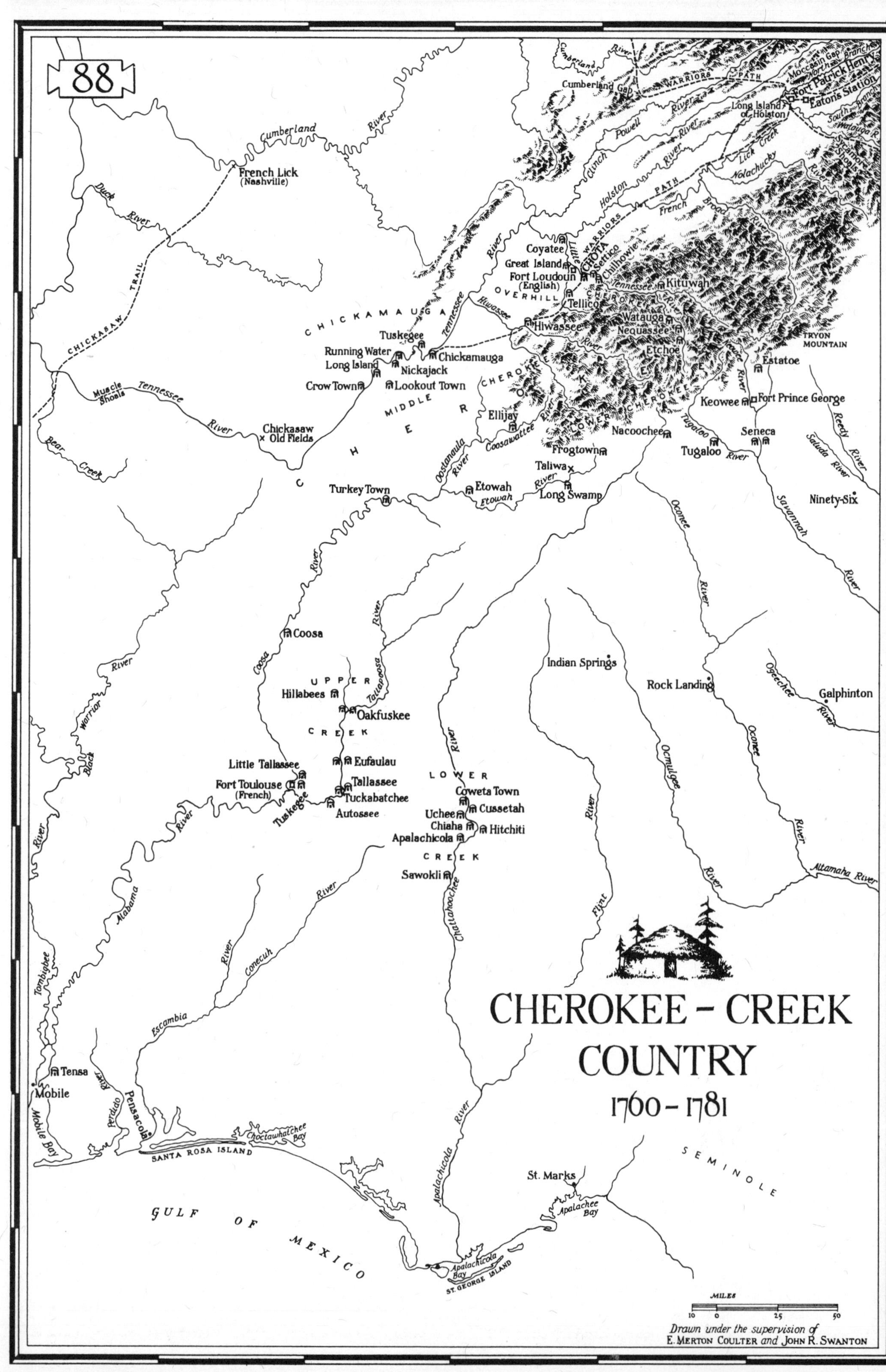
88
CHEROKEE – CREEK COUNTRY 1760–1781
Drawn under the supervision of E. Merton Coulter and John R. Swanton
MILES
10 0 25 50
Cumberland Gap
Fort Patrick Henry
Eaton's Station
Long Island of Holston
Moccasin Gap
Tryon Mountain
French Lick (Nashville)
Chickasaw Trail
Warriors Path
Chickamauga
Overhill
Middle Cherokee
Lower Cherokee
Coyatee
Great Island
Chota
Settico
Chilhowie
Fort Loudoun (English)
Tellico
Kituwah
Hiwassee
Wataugа
Nequassee
Etchoe
Estatoe
Keowee
Fort Prince George
Seneca
Tugaloo
Ninety-Six
Tuskegee
Running Water
Long Island
Nickajack
Chickamauga
Crow Town
Lookout Town
Chickasaw Old Fields
Muscle Shoals
Ellijay
Nacoochee
Frogtown
Taliwa
Etowah
Long Swamp
Turkey Town
Coosa
Upper Creek
Hillabees
Oakfuskee
Eufaulau
Little Tallassee
Fort Toulouse (French)
Tallassee
Tuckabatchee
Tuskegee
Autossee
Lower Creek
Coweta Town
Cussetah
Uchee
Chiaha
Hitchiti
Apalachicola
Sawokli
Indian Springs
Rock Landing
Galphinton
Tensa
Mobile
Pensacola
Santa Rosa Island
Choctawhatchee Bay
St. Marks
Apalachee Bay
Apalachicola Bay
St. George Island
Seminole
Gulf of Mexico

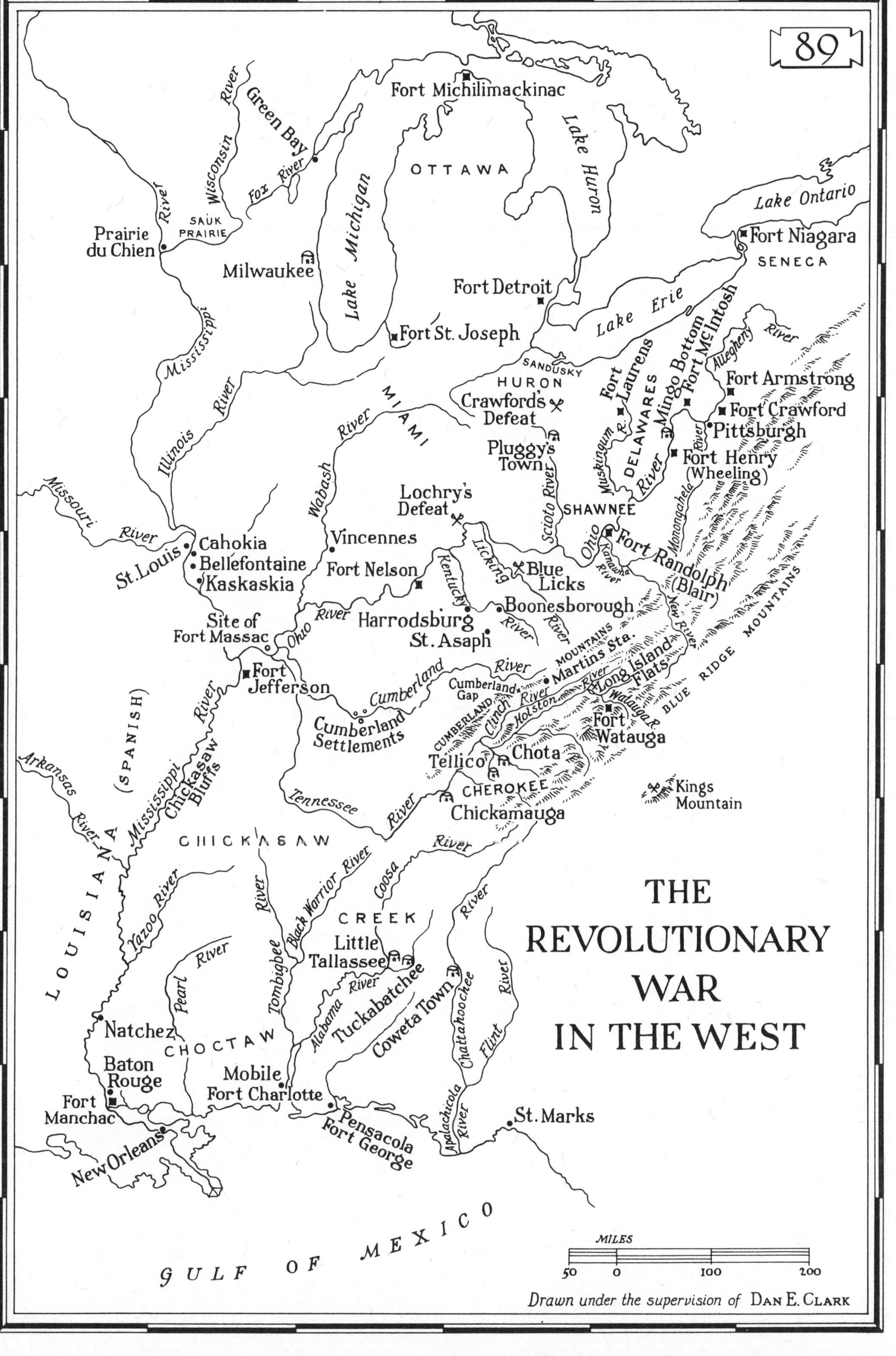
Fort Michilimackinac
Green Bay
Wisconsin River
Fox River
OTTAWA
Lake Michigan
Lake Huron
Lake Ontario
Fort Niagara
SENECA
Prairie du Chien
SAUK PRAIRIE
Milwaukee
Fort Detroit
Lake Erie
Fort St. Joseph
Mississippi River
SANDUSKY
HURON
Crawford's Defeat
Fort Laurens
DELAWARES
Mingo Bottom
Fort McIntosh
Allegheny River
Fort Armstrong
Fort Crawford
Pittsburgh
Fort Henry (Wheeling)
Illinois River
MIAMI
Wabash River
Pluggy's Town
Scioto River
Muskingum R.
Monongahela River
Missouri River
Lochry's Defeat
SHAWNEE
Ohio
Fort Randolph (Blair)
Kanawha River
St. Louis
Cahokia
Bellefontaine
Kaskaskia
Vincennes
Fort Nelson
Kentucky River
Licking River
Blue Licks
Boonesborough
Site of Fort Massac
Ohio River
Harrodsburg
St. Asaph
New River
MOUNTAINS
Martins Sta.
Long Island Flats
Fort Jefferson
Cumberland River
Cumberland Gap
Clinch River
Holston River
Watauga R.
BLUE RIDGE MOUNTAINS
CUMBERLAND
Fort Watauga
(SPANISH)
Cumberland Settlements
Chota
Tellico
CHEROKEE
Kings Mountain
Arkansas River
Mississippi River
Chickasaw Bluffs
Tennessee River
Chickamauga
LOUISIANA
CHICKASAW
Black Warrior River
Coosa River
Yazoo River
River
CREEK
Little Tallassee
Pearl River
Tombigbee
Alabama River
Tuckabatchee
Coweta Town
Chattahoochee
Flint River
Natchez
CHOCTAW
Baton Rouge
Mobile
Fort Charlotte
Fort Manchac
New Orleans
Pensacola
Fort George
Apalachicola River
St. Marks
GULF OF MEXICO
MILES
50
0
100
200
THE REVOLUTIONARY WAR IN THE WEST
Drawn under the supervision of Dan E. Clark

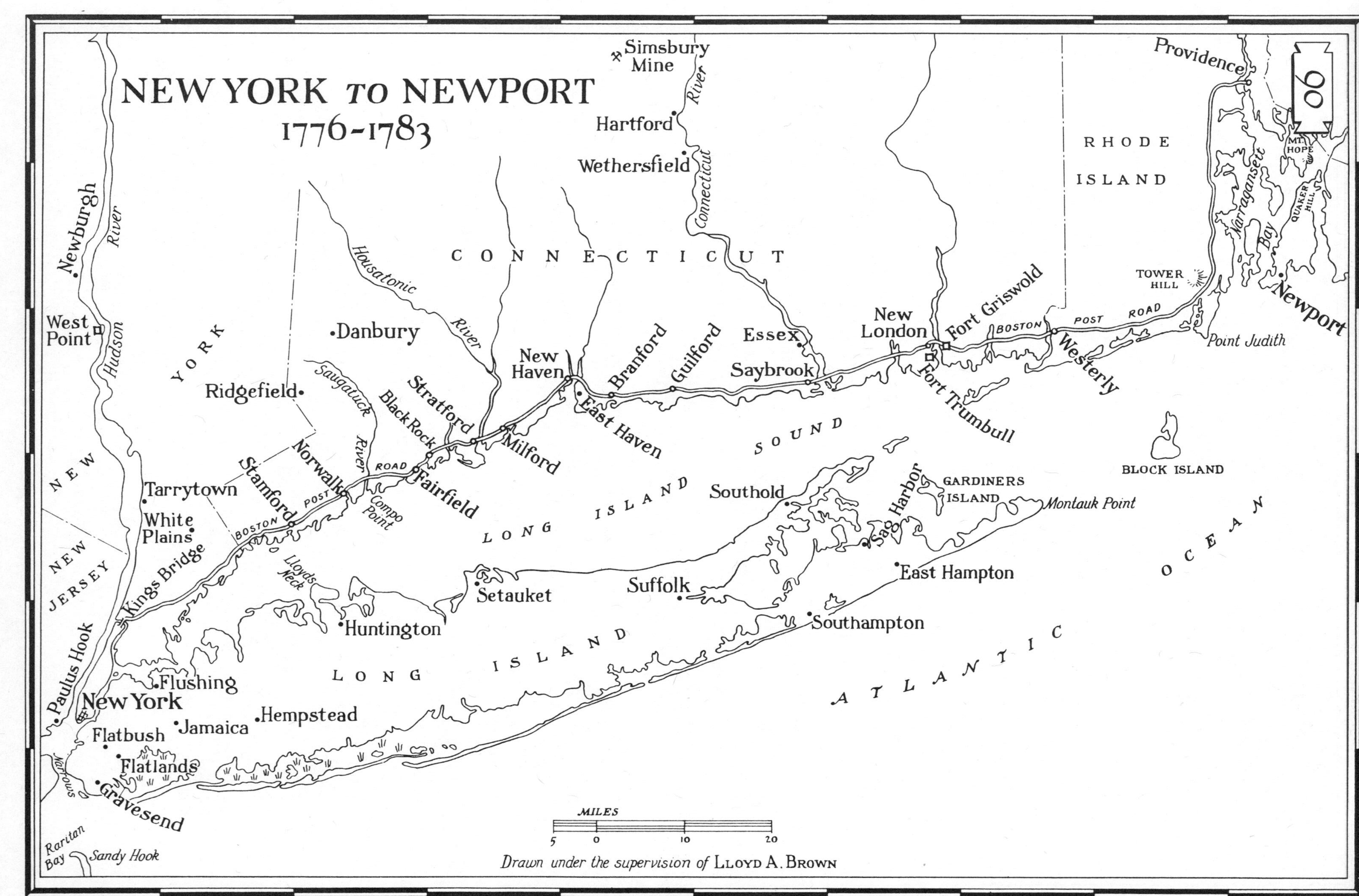
90
NEW YORK TO NEWPORT
1776-1783
Simsbury Mine
Hartford
Wethersfield
Connecticut River
CONNECTICUT
RHODE ISLAND
Providence
Mt. Hope
Quaker Hill
Narragansett Bay
Newport
Tower Hill
Point Judith
Post Road
Boston
Westerly
Fort Griswold
New London
Fort Trumbull
Essex
Saybrook
Guilford
Branford
New Haven
East Haven
Milford
Stratford
Black Rock
Fairfield
Compo Point
Road
Post
Norwalk
Stamford
Housatonic River
Saugatuck River
Danbury
Ridgefield
YORK
Newburgh
Hudson River
West Point
NEW
NEW JERSEY
Tarrytown
White Plains
Kings Bridge
Paulus Hook
New York
Flushing
Jamaica
Hempstead
Flatbush
Flatlands
Gravesend
Narrows
Raritan Bay
Sandy Hook
Lloyds Neck
Huntington
Setauket
Suffolk
Southold
Sag Harbor
Gardiners Island
Montauk Point
East Hampton
Southampton
LONG ISLAND SOUND
LONG ISLAND
BLOCK ISLAND
ATLANTIC OCEAN
MILES
5 0 10 20
Drawn under the supervision of Lloyd A. Brown

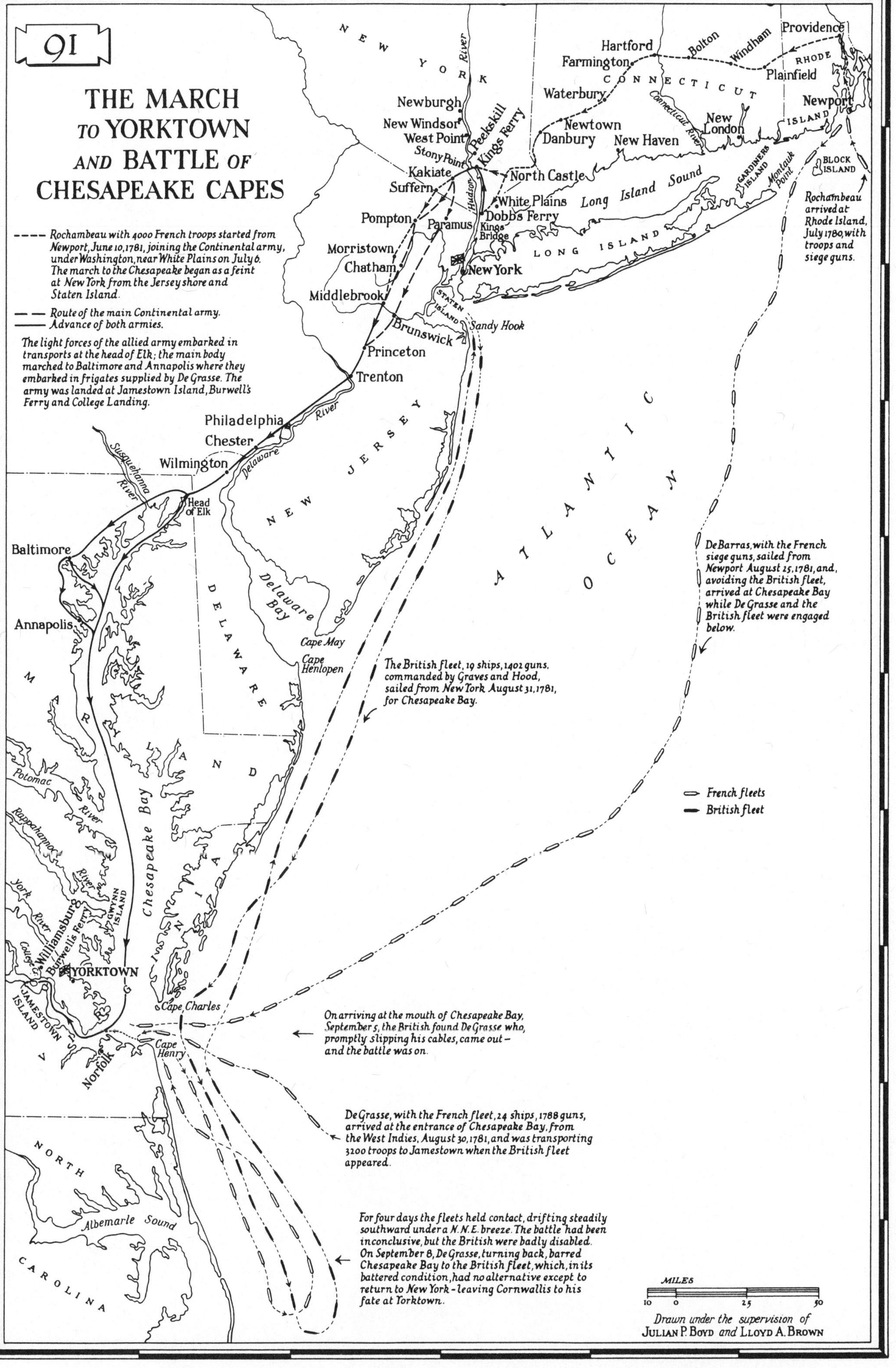
91
THE MARCH TO YORKTOWN AND BATTLE OF CHESAPEAKE CAPES
Rochambeau with 4000 French troops started from Newport, June 10, 1781, joining the Continental army, under Washington, near White Plains on July 6. The march to the Chesapeake began as a feint at New York from the Jersey shore and Staten Island.
Route of the main Continental army.
Advance of both armies.
The light forces of the allied army embarked in transports at the head of Elk; the main body marched to Baltimore and Annapolis where they embarked in frigates supplied by De Grasse. The army was landed at Jamestown Island, Burwell's Ferry and College Landing.
NEW YORK
River
Hudson
Newburgh
New Windsor
West Point
Peekskill
Kings Ferry
Stony Point
Kakiate
Suffern
North Castle
White Plains
Dobbs Ferry
Kings Bridge
Pompton
Paramus
Morristown
Chatham
New York
Middlebrook
STATEN ISLAND
Sandy Hook
Brunswick
Princeton
Trenton
Philadelphia
Chester
Wilmington
Delaware River
Susquehanna River
Head of Elk
Baltimore
Annapolis
Hartford
Farmington
Bolton
Windham
Providence
RHODE ISLAND
Plainfield
CONNECTICUT
Waterbury
Connecticut River
Newport
Newtown
Danbury
New Haven
New London
Long Island Sound
LONG ISLAND
GARDINERS ISLAND
Montauk Point
BLOCK ISLAND
Rochambeau arrived at Rhode Island, July 1780, with troops and siege guns.
NEW JERSEY
ATLANTIC OCEAN
Delaware Bay
Cape May
Cape Henlopen
DELAWARE
MARYLAND
VIRGINIA
Potomac River
Rappahannock River
York River
Chesapeake Bay
GWYNN ISLAND
Williamsburg
Burwells Ferry
College Cr.
YORKTOWN
JAMESTOWN ISLAND
Cape Charles
Cape Henry
Norfolk
NORTH CAROLINA
Albemarle Sound
De Barras, with the French siege guns, sailed from Newport August 25, 1781, and, avoiding the British fleet, arrived at Chesapeake Bay while De Grasse and the British fleet were engaged below.
The British fleet, 19 ships, 1402 guns, commanded by Graves and Hood, sailed from New York August 31, 1781, for Chesapeake Bay.
French fleets
British fleet
On arriving at the mouth of Chesapeake Bay, September 5, the British found De Grasse who, promptly slipping his cables, came out – and the battle was on.
De Grasse, with the French fleet, 24 ships, 1788 guns, arrived at the entrance of Chesapeake Bay, from the West Indies, August 30, 1781, and was transporting 3200 troops to Jamestown when the British fleet appeared.
For four days the fleets held contact, drifting steadily southward under a N.N.E. breeze. The battle had been inconclusive, but the British were badly disabled. On September 8, De Grasse, turning back, barred Chesapeake Bay to the British fleet, which, in its battered condition, had no alternative except to return to New York – leaving Cornwallis to his fate at Yorktown.
MILES
10 0 25 50
Drawn under the supervision of JULIAN P. BOYD and LLOYD A. BROWN

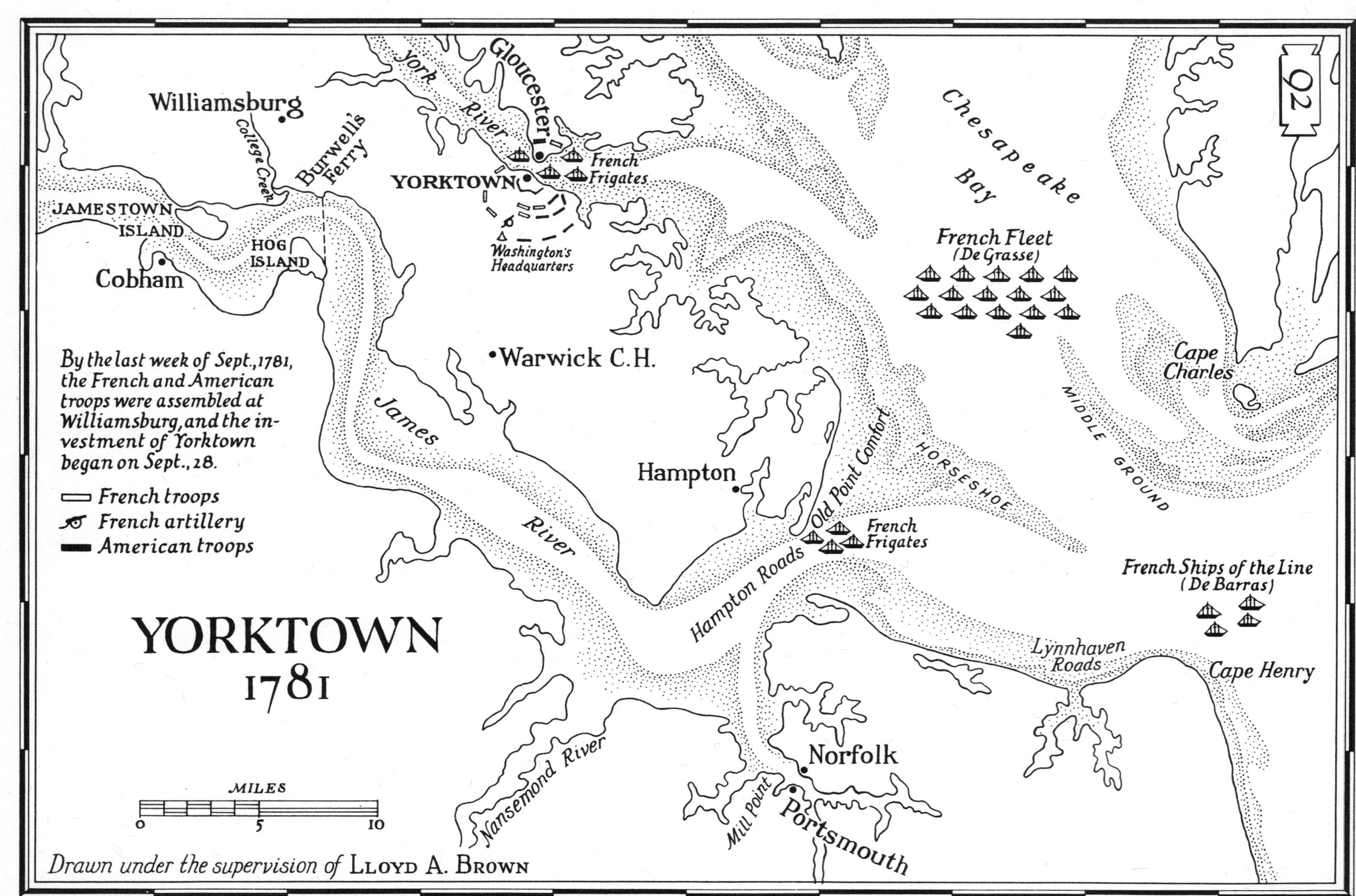
92
Williamsburg
College Creek
Burwell's Ferry
JAMESTOWN ISLAND
HOG ISLAND
Cobham
York River
Gloucester
YORKTOWN
French Frigates
Washington's Headquarters
Chesapeake Bay
French Fleet (De Grasse)
Cape Charles
MIDDLE GROUND
HORSESHOE
Warwick C.H.
Hampton
Old Point Comfort
French Frigates
Hampton Roads
James River
French Ships of the Line (De Barras)
Lynnhaven Roads
Cape Henry
Nansemond River
Mill Point
Norfolk
Portsmouth
By the last week of Sept., 1781, the French and American troops were assembled at Williamsburg, and the investment of Yorktown began on Sept., 28.
French troops
French artillery
American troops
YORKTOWN
1781
MILES
0
5
10
Drawn under the supervision of Lloyd A. Brown

VI THE NEW NATION

94
THE UNITED STATES, 1783-1802
Lake of the Woods
INDEFINITE BOUNDARY
Grand Portage
Lake Superior
CANADA
Fort Michilimackinac
Mississippi River
NORTHWEST
INDIANA
Green Bay
Lake Michigan
NORTHWEST TERRITORY
DIVISION LINE OF 1800
Lake Huron
St. Lawrence River
INDEFINITE BOUNDARY
St. John River
St. Croix River
MAINE (Joined to Mass.)
Pte. au Fer
Oswegatchie
Fort Haldimand
VT. (Admitted 1791)
Montpelier
Connecticut River
NEW HAMPSHIRE
Portland
Lake Ontario
Fort Ontario
Oswego
Fort Niagara
NEW YORK
Albany
Hudson River
Concord
MASS.
Boston
Providence
R.I.
Detroit
Fort Miamis
Lake Erie
Maumee River
TERRITORY 1800
TERRITORY 1787
TERRITORY 1800
Fort Recovery
Wabash
Miami River
Muskingum River
Ohio River
Allegheny
Pittsburgh
PENNSYLVANIA
Philadelphia
Hartford
CONN.
New Haven
NEW JERSEY
New York
Trenton
Susquehanna
Delaware
Baltimore
Wilmington
LOUISIANA
Cahokia
Kaskaskia
Vincennes
Cincinnati
Marietta
Potomac River
MARYLAND
D.C.
Washington
Annapolis
DEL.
Ohio River
Kentucky River
KENTUCKY (Admitted 1792)
SOUTH OF THE RIVER OHIO
VIRGINIA
James River
Richmond
Cumberland River
Nashville
TERRITORY
TENNESSEE (Admitted 1796)
Roanoke River
Raleigh
Fort San Fernando (Spanish)
Tennessee River
NORTH CAROLINA
ATLANTIC OCEAN
Mississippi
Yazoo River
Fort Nogales (Spanish)
Tombigbee River
GEORGIA
Coosa River
River
SOUTH CAROLINA
Columbia
Savannah River
NORTHERN SPANISH CLAIM UNTIL 1795
MISSISSIPPI TERRITORY (1798)
Natchez
Pearl
Fort Adams
Alabama River
Chattahoochee
Flint River
Savannah
SPANISH
SPANISH
St. Marys River
FLORIDA
GULF OF MEXICO
The Northwest Territory of 1787 was formed from Western Lands claimed by NEW YORK, through questionable Indian cessions (ceded to the U.S. in 1782); by VIRGINIA, through the Charter of 1609, giving limits from "sea to sea, west and northwest," and through conquest (ceded to the U.S. in 1784, with the exception of the Virginia Military District, see Plate 85); by MASSACHUSETTS, through the Charter of 1629, giving limits from sea to sea (ceded to the U.S. in 1785); by CONNECTICUT, through the Charter of 1662, giving limits from sea to sea (ceded to the U.S. in 1786, with the exception of the Western Reserve, see Plate 85).
KENTUCKY was a part of Virginia until admitted as a separate state in 1792 (see Plate 84). West Virginia did not exist.
TENNESSEE was a part of North Carolina until admitted as a state in 1796 (see Plate 84).
For the Western Land claims of South Carolina and Georgia, see Plates 88-89.
MILES
50 0 100 200 300
Drawn under the supervision of O. M. Dickerson and Francis P. Weisenburger

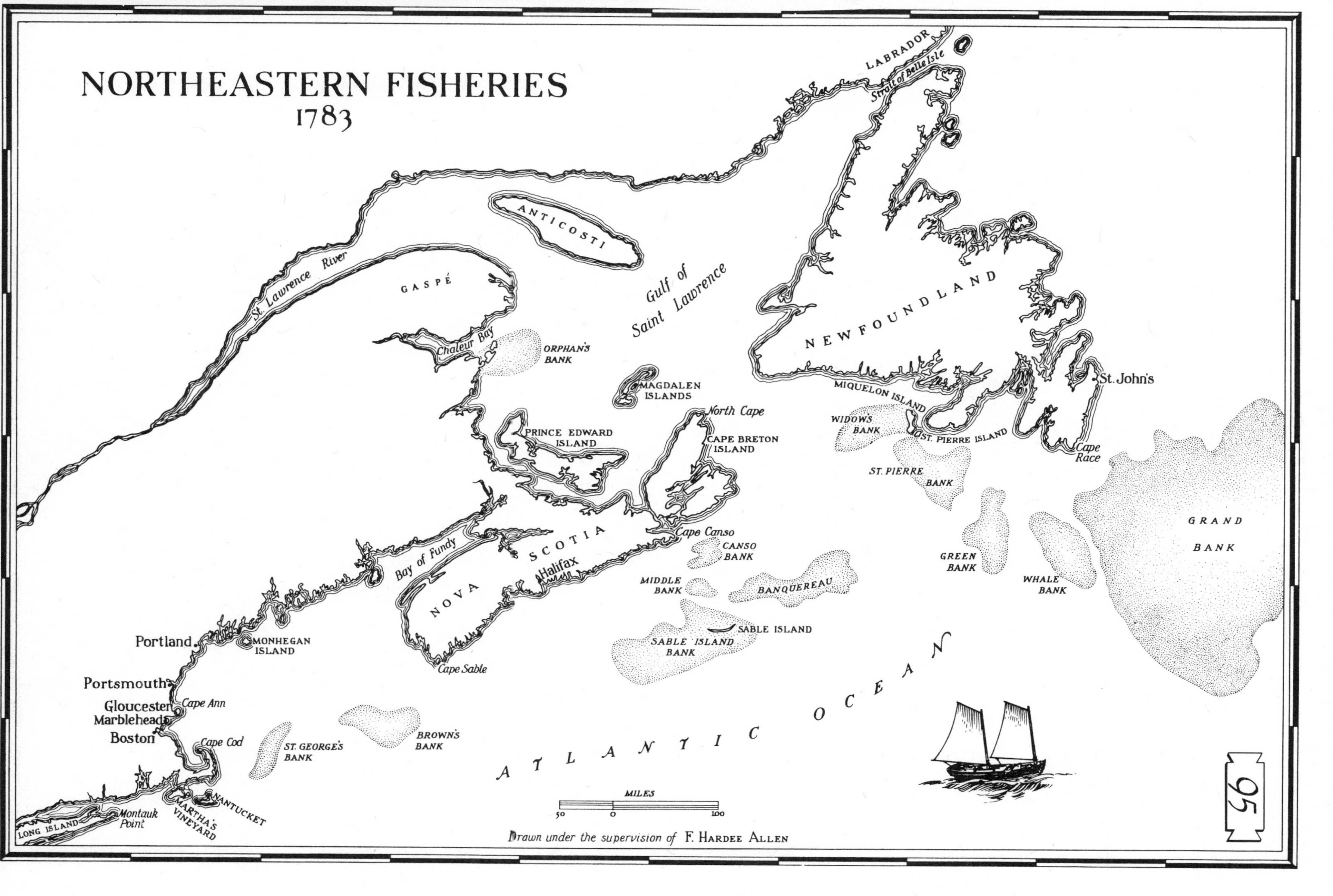
NORTHEASTERN FISHERIES
1783
95
LABRADOR
Strait of Belle Isle
ANTICOSTI
St. Lawrence River
GASPÉ
Gulf of Saint Lawrence
NEWFOUNDLAND
Chaleur Bay
ORPHAN'S BANK
MAGDALEN ISLANDS
St. John's
MIQUELON ISLAND
North Cape
WIDOWS BANK
PRINCE EDWARD ISLAND
CAPE BRETON ISLAND
ST. PIERRE ISLAND
Cape Race
ST. PIERRE BANK
Cape Canso
NOVA SCOTIA
Halifax
Bay of Fundy
CANSO BANK
MIDDLE BANK
BANQUEREAU
GREEN BANK
WHALE BANK
GRAND BANK
SABLE ISLAND
SABLE ISLAND BANK
Portland
MONHEGAN ISLAND
Cape Sable
Portsmouth
Cape Ann
Gloucester
Marblehead
Boston
Cape Cod
ST. GEORGE'S BANK
BROWN'S BANK
ATLANTIC OCEAN
NANTUCKET
MARTHA'S VINEYARD
Montauk Point
LONG ISLAND
MILES
50 0 100
Drawn under the supervision of F. Hardee Allen

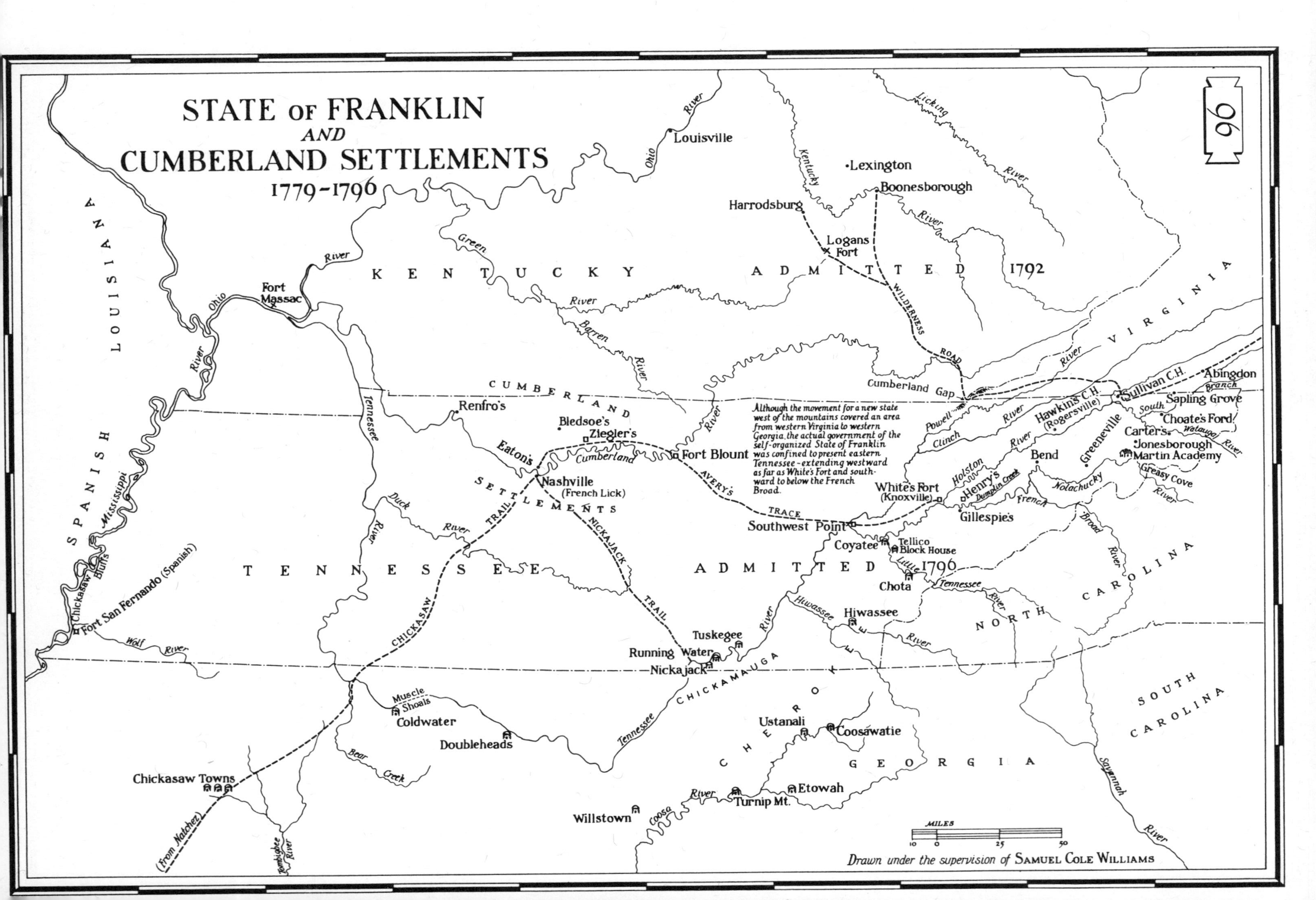
96
STATE of FRANKLIN
AND
CUMBERLAND SETTLEMENTS
1779-1796
Although the movement for a new state west of the mountains covered an area from western Virginia to western Georgia, the actual government of the self-organized State of Franklin was confined to present eastern Tennessee - extending westward as far as White's Fort and southward to below the French Broad.
KENTUCKY ADMITTED 1792
TENNESSEE ADMITTED 1796
VIRGINIA
NORTH CAROLINA
SOUTH CAROLINA
GEORGIA
SPANISH LOUISIANA
CUMBERLAND SETTLEMENTS
CHEROKEE
CHICKAMAUGA
Louisville
Lexington
Boonesborough
Harrodsburg
Logans Fort
Fort Massac
WILDERNESS ROAD
Cumberland Gap
Renfro's
Bledsoe's
Ziegler's
Eaton's
Nashville
(French Lick)
Fort Blount
AVERY'S TRACE
NICKAJACK TRAIL
CHICKASAW TRAIL
Southwest Point
White's Fort
(Knoxville)
Henry's
Gillespie's
Bend
Greeneville
Hawkins C.H.
(Rogersville)
Sullivan C.H.
Abingdon
Sapling Grove
Choate's Ford
Carter's
Jonesborough
Martin Academy
Greasy Cove
Coyatee
Tellico
Block House
Chota
Hiwassee
Tuskegee
Running Water
Nickajack
Muscle Shoals
Coldwater
Doubleheads
Ustanali
Coosawatie
Etowah
Turnip Mt.
Willstown
Chickasaw Towns
(from Natchez)
Chickasaw Bluffs
Fort San Fernando (Spanish)
Ohio River
Mississippi
Tennessee
Cumberland
Green
Barren River
Kentucky
Licking River
Duck River
Wolf River
Bear Creek
Tombigbee River
Coosa River
Hiwassee
Little Tennessee River
French Broad River
Nolachucky
Holston River
Dumplin Creek
Clinch River
Powell River
South Branch
Watauga River
Savannah River
MILES
10 0 25 50
Drawn under the supervision of SAMUEL COLE WILLIAMS

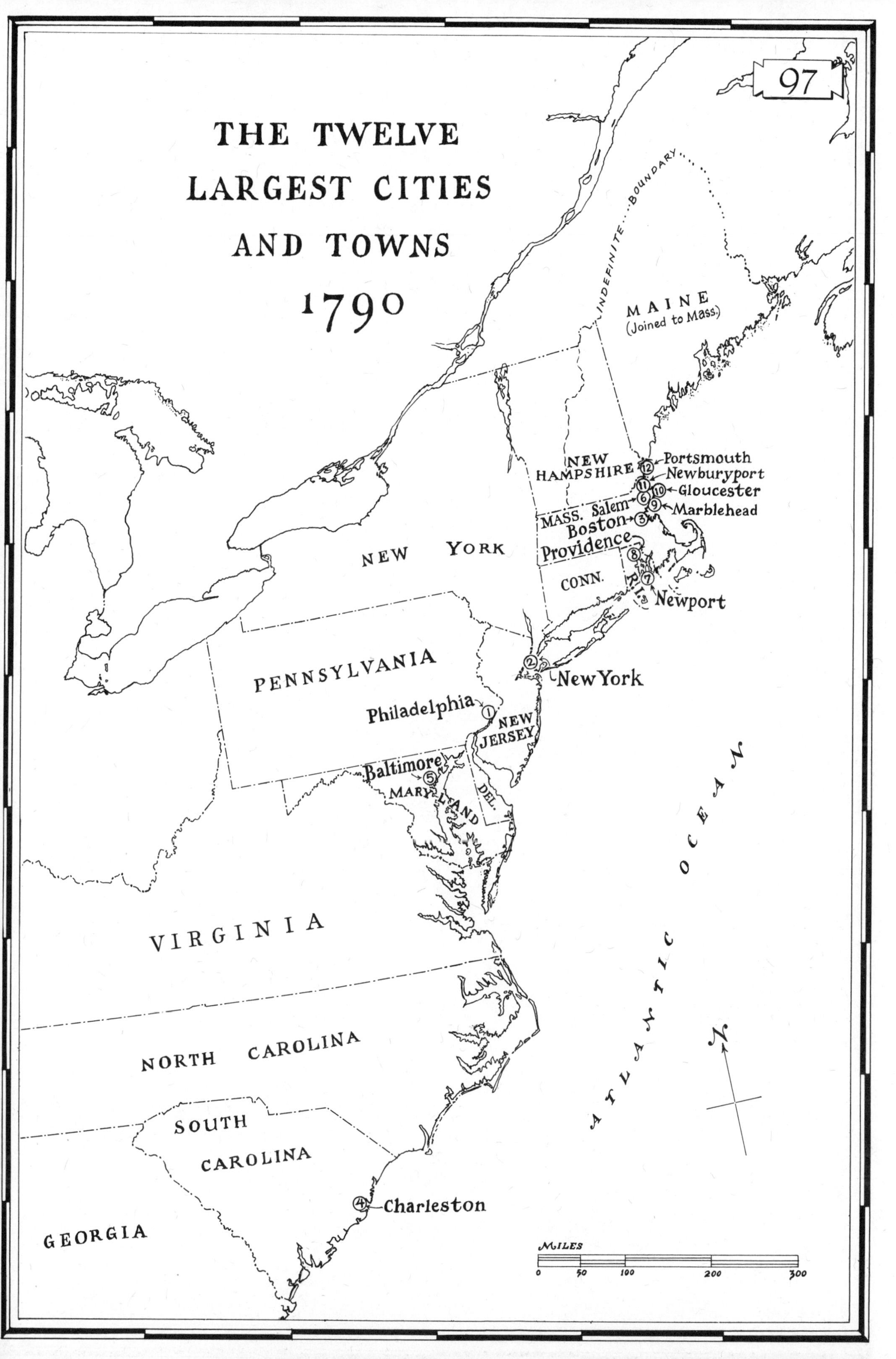
97
THE TWELVE LARGEST CITIES AND TOWNS 1790
INDEFINITE ... BOUNDARY
MAINE
(Joined to Mass.)
NEW HAMPSHIRE
MASS.
CONN.
R.I.
NEW YORK
PENNSYLVANIA
NEW JERSEY
MARYLAND
DEL.
VIRGINIA
NORTH CAROLINA
SOUTH CAROLINA
GEORGIA
ATLANTIC OCEAN
N
1 Philadelphia
2 New York
3 Boston
4 Charleston
5 Baltimore
6 Salem
7 Newport
8 Providence
9 Marblehead
10 Gloucester
11 Newburyport
12 Portsmouth
MILES
0
50
100
200
300

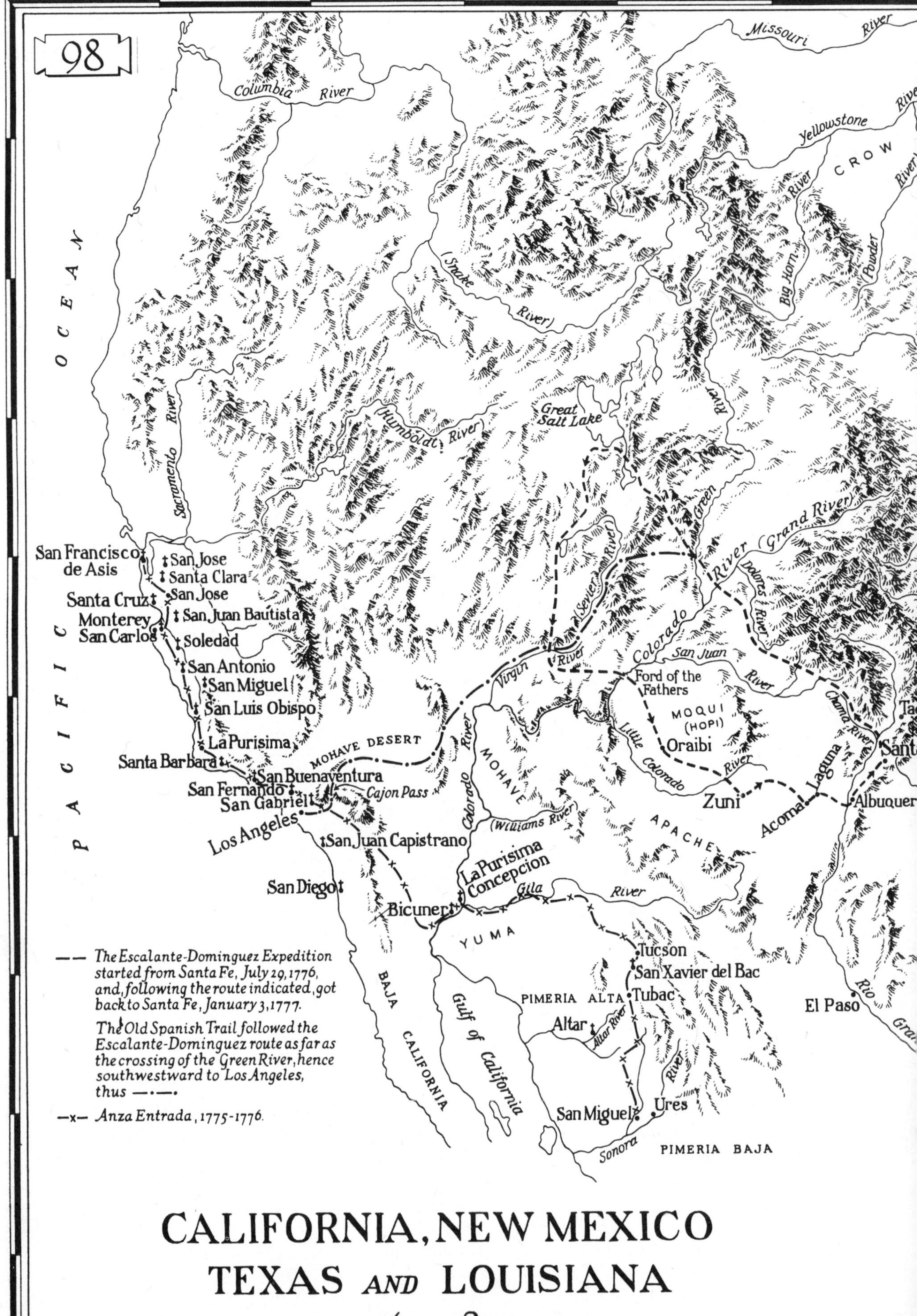

PACIFIC OCEAN
Columbia River
Missouri River
Yellowstone River
CROW
Big Horn River
Powder River
Snake River
Sacramento River
Humboldt River
Great Salt Lake
Green River
Colorado River (Grand River)
Dolores River
Sevier River
Virgin River
San Juan River
Chama River
Ford of the Fathers
MOQUI (HOPI)
Oraibi
Little Colorado River
Zuni
Acoma
Laguna
Albuquer
Santa
San Francisco de Asis
San Jose
Santa Clara
Santa Cruz
San Jose
Monterey
San Carlos
San Juan Bautista
Soledad
San Antonio
San Miguel
San Luis Obispo
La Purisima
Santa Barbara
San Buenaventura
San Fernando
San Gabriel
Cajon Pass
MOHAVE DESERT
MOHAVE
Los Angeles
San Juan Capistrano
Colorado River
(Williams River)
APACHE
La Purisima Concepcion
San Diego
Bicuner
Gila River
YUMA
Tucson
San Xavier del Bac
PIMERIA ALTA
Tubac
Altar
Altar River
BAJA CALIFORNIA
Gulf of California
San Miguel
Ures
Sonora
PIMERIA BAJA
El Paso
Rio Grande
The Escalante-Dominguez Expedition started from Santa Fe, July 29, 1776, and, following the route indicated, got back to Santa Fe, January 3, 1777.
The Old Spanish Trail followed the Escalante-Dominguez route as far as the crossing of the Green River, hence southwestward to Los Angeles, thus
Anza Entrada, 1775-1776.

CALIFORNIA, NEW MEXICO TEXAS AND LOUISIANA 1763-1802

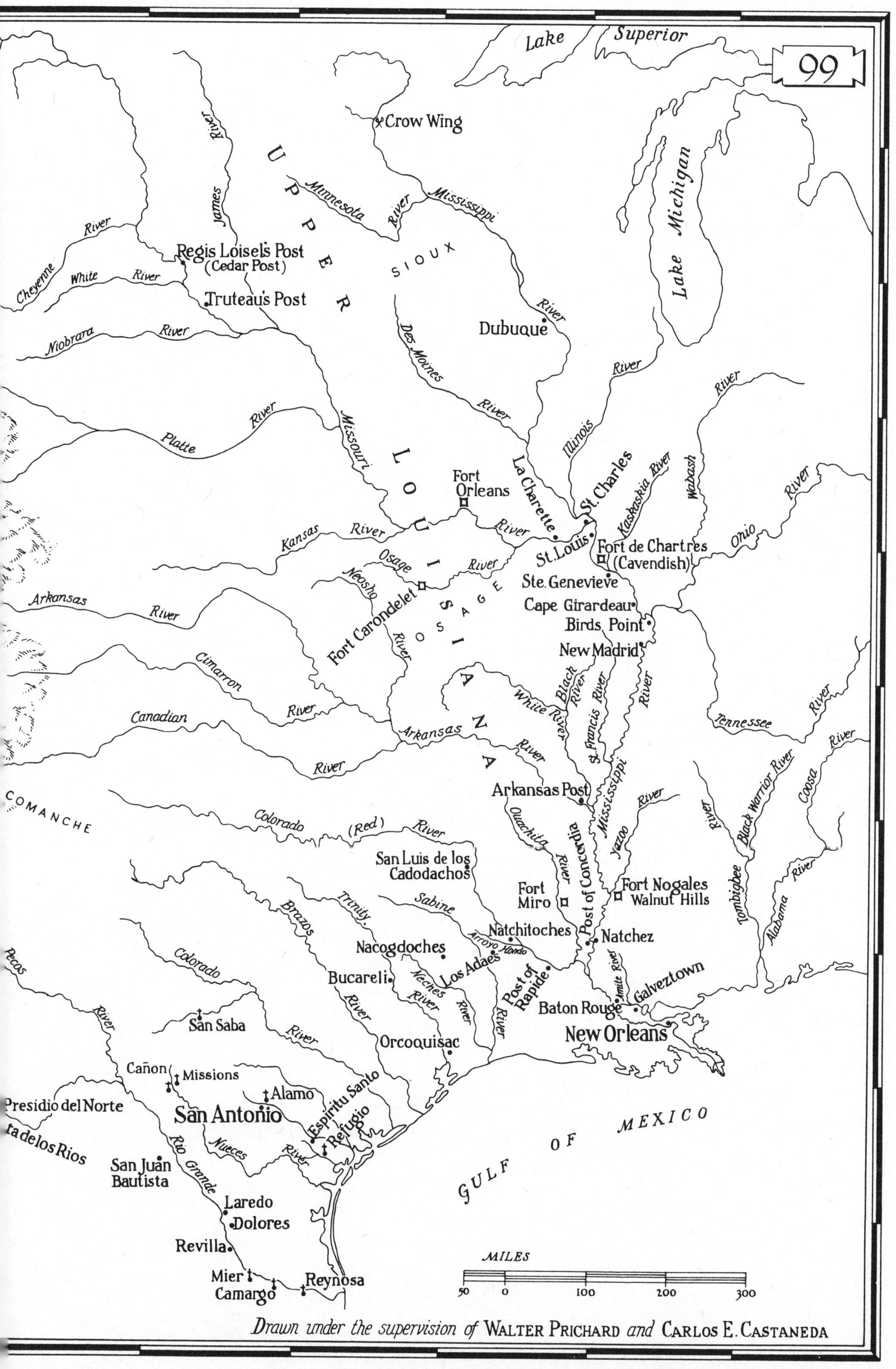
99
Lake Superior
Crow Wing
UPPER LOUISIANA
SIOUX
OSAGE
COMANCHE
James River
Minnesota River
Mississippi
Lake Michigan
Cheyenne River
White River
Regis Loisel's Post (Cedar Post)
Truteau's Post
Niobrara River
Dubuque
River
Des Moines River
River
Illinois
Platte River
Missouri
Fort Orleans
La Charette
St. Charles
Kaskaskia River
Wabash
River
Kansas River
River
St. Louis
Fort de Chartres (Cavendish)
Ohio
Osage River
Neosho
Ste. Genevieve
Arkansas River
Fort Carondelet
Cape Girardeau
Birds Point
River
New Madrid
Cimarron River
Black River
White River
St. Francis River
River
Canadian River
Arkansas River
Tennessee River
Arkansas Post
Mississippi
Coosa River
Black Warrior River
River
Colorado (Red) River
Ouachita River
Yazoo River
Post of Concordia
San Luis de los Cadodachos
Fort Miro
Fort Nogales
Walnut Hills
Tombigbee
Alabama River
Trinity
Sabine
Brazos
Natchitoches
Arroyo Hondo
Natchez
Nacogdoches
Pecos River
Colorado River
Bucareli
Los Adaes
Neches River
Post of Rapide
Amite River
Galveztown
Baton Rouge
River
River
San Saba
Orcoquisac
New Orleans
Cañon
Missions
Alamo
Presidio del Norte
San Antonio
Espiritu Santo
Refugio
GULF OF MEXICO
tadelosRios
Nueces River
San Juan Bautista
Rio Grande
Laredo
Dolores
Revilla
Mier
Camargo
Reynosa
MILES
50 0 100 200 300
Drawn under the supervision of WALTER PRICHARD and CARLOS E. CASTANEDA

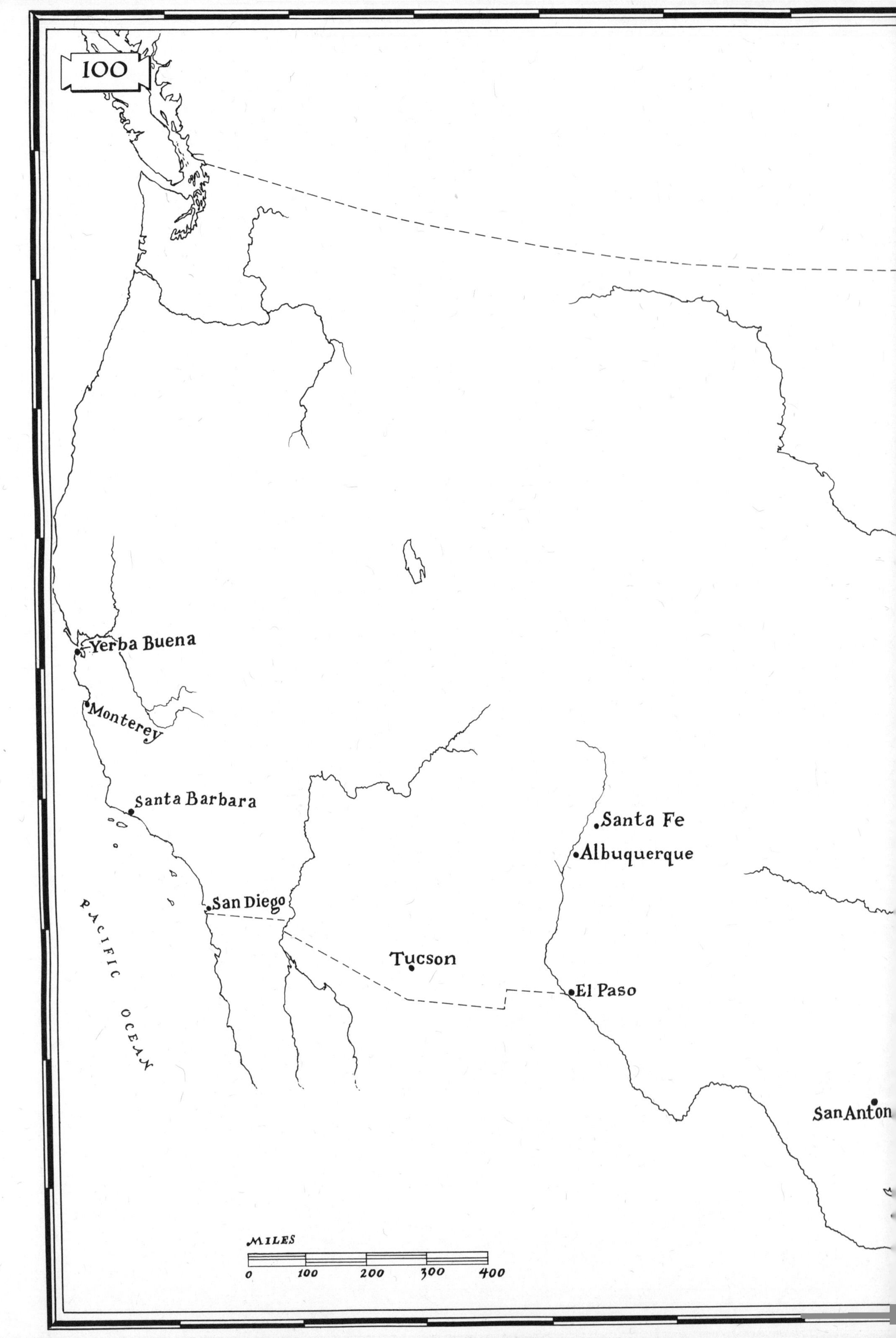
100
Yerba Buena
Monterey
Santa Barbara
San Diego
PACIFIC OCEAN
Santa Fe
Albuquerque
Tucson
El Paso
San Anton
MILES
0
100
200
300
400

SETTLED AREAS 1800

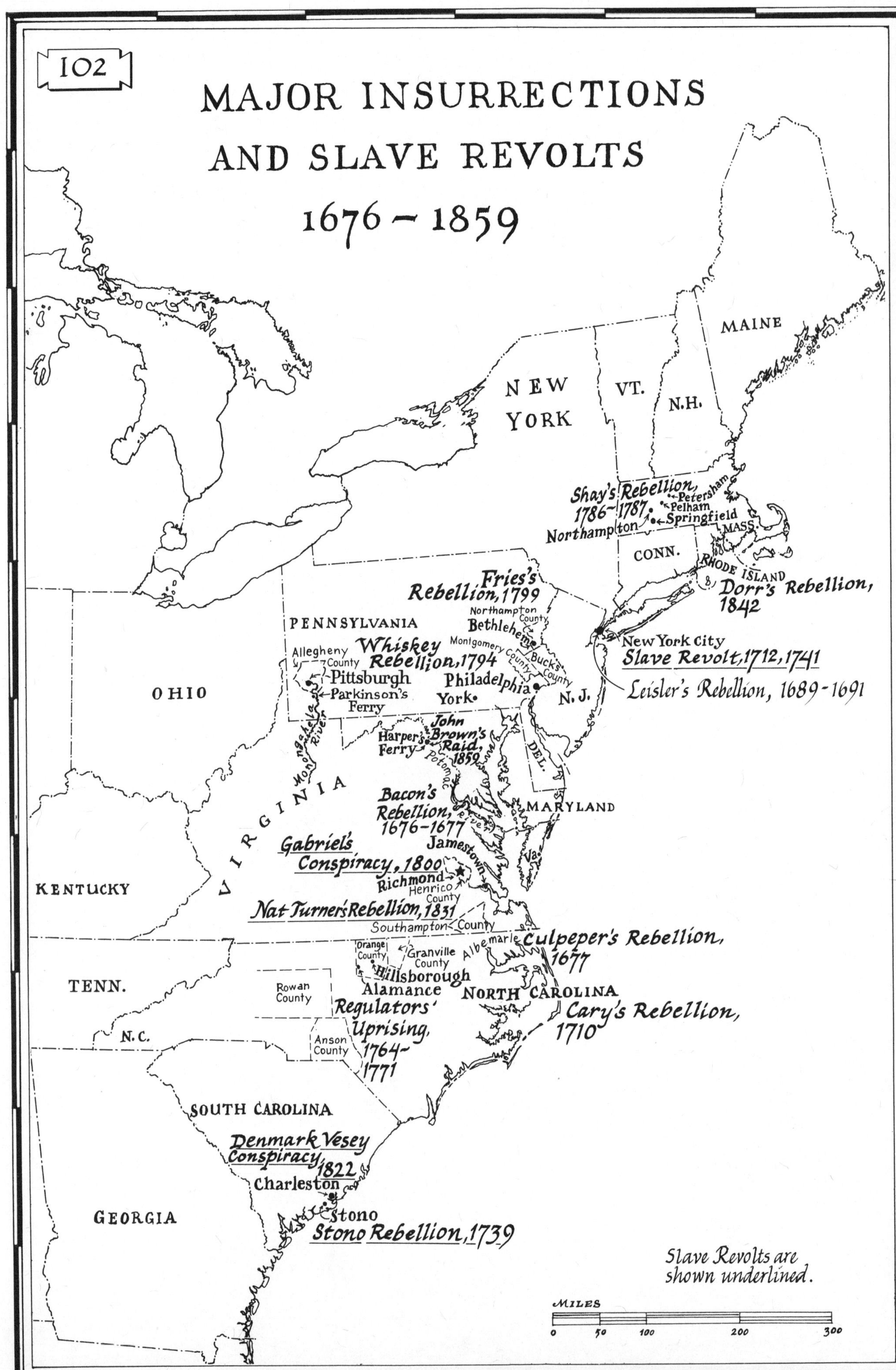
102
MAJOR INSURRECTIONS
AND SLAVE REVOLTS
1676 – 1859
MAINE
NEW YORK
VT.
N.H.
Shay's Rebellion, 1786-1787
Petersham
Pelham
Springfield
Northampton
MASS.
CONN.
RHODE ISLAND
Dorr's Rebellion, 1842
Fries's Rebellion, 1799
Northampton County
Bethlehem
PENNSYLVANIA
Allegheny County
Whiskey Rebellion, 1794
Montgomery County
Bucks County
New York City
Slave Revolt, 1712, 1741
Leisler's Rebellion, 1689-1691
OHIO
Pittsburgh
Parkinson's Ferry
Philadelphia
York
N.J.
Monongahela River
John Brown's Raid, 1859
Harper's Ferry
Potomac
DEL.
VIRGINIA
Bacon's Rebellion, 1676-1677
MARYLAND
Jamestown
Gabriel's Conspiracy, 1800
Richmond
Henrico County
KENTUCKY
Nat Turner's Rebellion, 1831
Southampton County
Orange County
Granville County
Albemarle
Culpeper's Rebellion, 1677
Hillsborough
Alamance
TENN.
Rowan County
NORTH CAROLINA
Regulators' Uprising, 1764-1771
Cary's Rebellion, 1710
N.C.
Anson County
SOUTH CAROLINA
Denmark Vesey Conspiracy, 1822
Charleston
Stono
Stono Rebellion, 1739
GEORGIA
Slave Revolts are shown underlined.
MILES
0
50
100
200
300

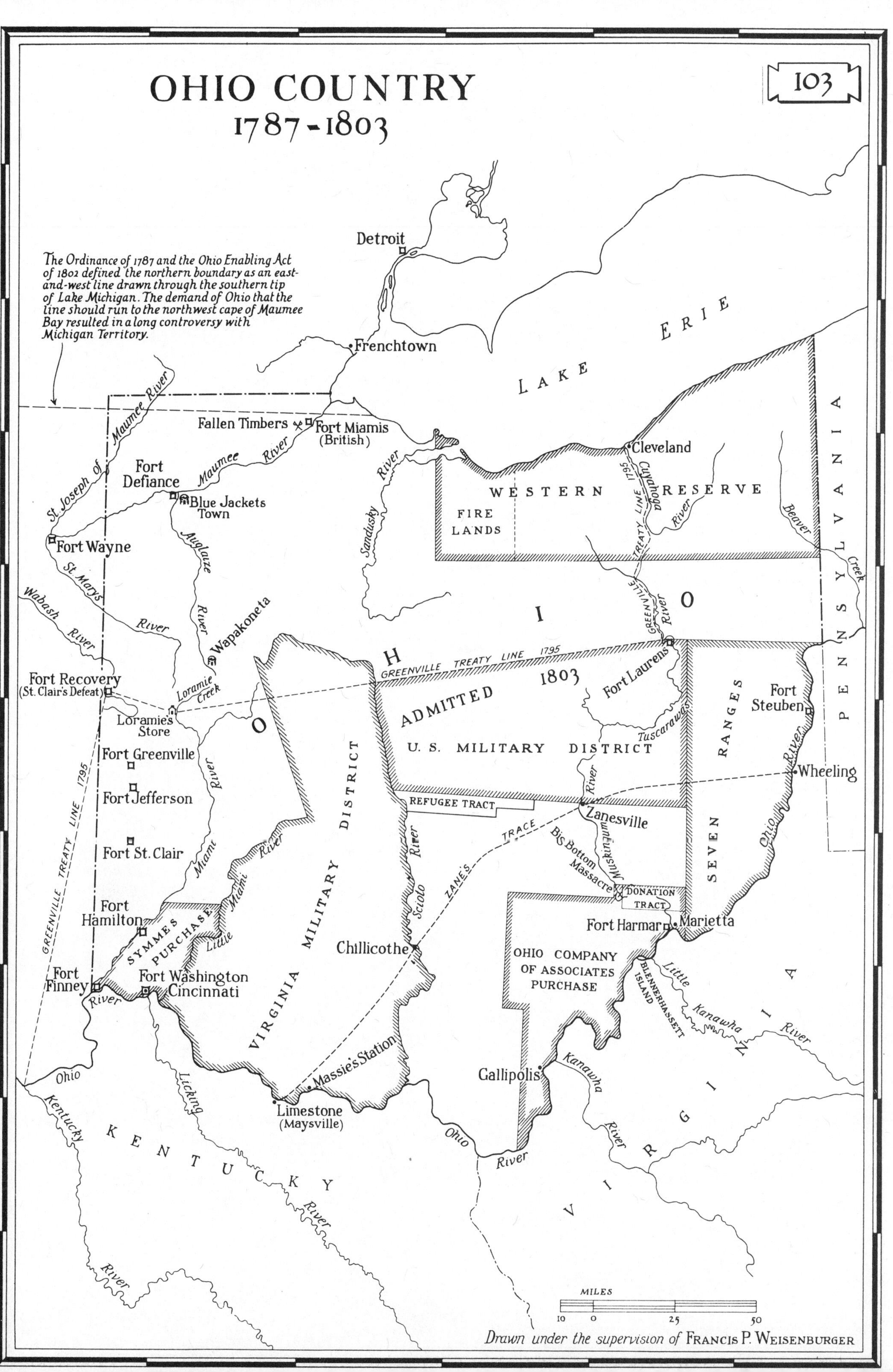

OHIO COUNTRY
1787-1803
103
The Ordinance of 1787 and the Ohio Enabling Act of 1802 defined the northern boundary as an east-and-west line drawn through the southern tip of Lake Michigan. The demand of Ohio that the line should run to the northwest cape of Maumee Bay resulted in a long controversy with Michigan Territory.
Detroit
Frenchtown
LAKE ERIE
Fallen Timbers
Fort Miamis (British)
Cleveland
WESTERN RESERVE
FIRE LANDS
Fort Defiance
Blue Jackets Town
Fort Wayne
St. Joseph of Maumee River
Maumee River
Sandusky River
Cuyahoga River
Beaver Creek
PENNSYLVANIA
Auglaize River
St. Marys River
Wabash River
Wapakoneta
OHIO
GREENVILLE TREATY LINE 1795
ADMITTED 1803
Fort Recovery (St. Clair's Defeat)
Loramie Creek
Loramie's Store
Fort Greenville
Fort Jefferson
Fort St. Clair
Miami River
Fort Laurens
Tuscarawas
U. S. MILITARY DISTRICT
SEVEN RANGES
Fort Steuben
Wheeling
REFUGEE TRACT
Zanesville
ZANE'S TRACE
Big Bottom Massacre
Muskingum
DONATION TRACT
Fort Harmar
Marietta
Ohio River
VIRGINIA MILITARY DISTRICT
Scioto River
Chillicothe
Fort Hamilton
SYMMES PURCHASE
Little Miami
Fort Finney
Fort Washington
Cincinnati
OHIO COMPANY OF ASSOCIATES PURCHASE
BLENNERHASSETT ISLAND
Little Kanawha River
Massie's Station
Gallipolis
Kanawha River
Limestone (Maysville)
Licking River
Kentucky River
KENTUCKY
VIRGINIA
MILES
10 0 25 50
Drawn under the supervision of FRANCIS P. WEISENBURGER

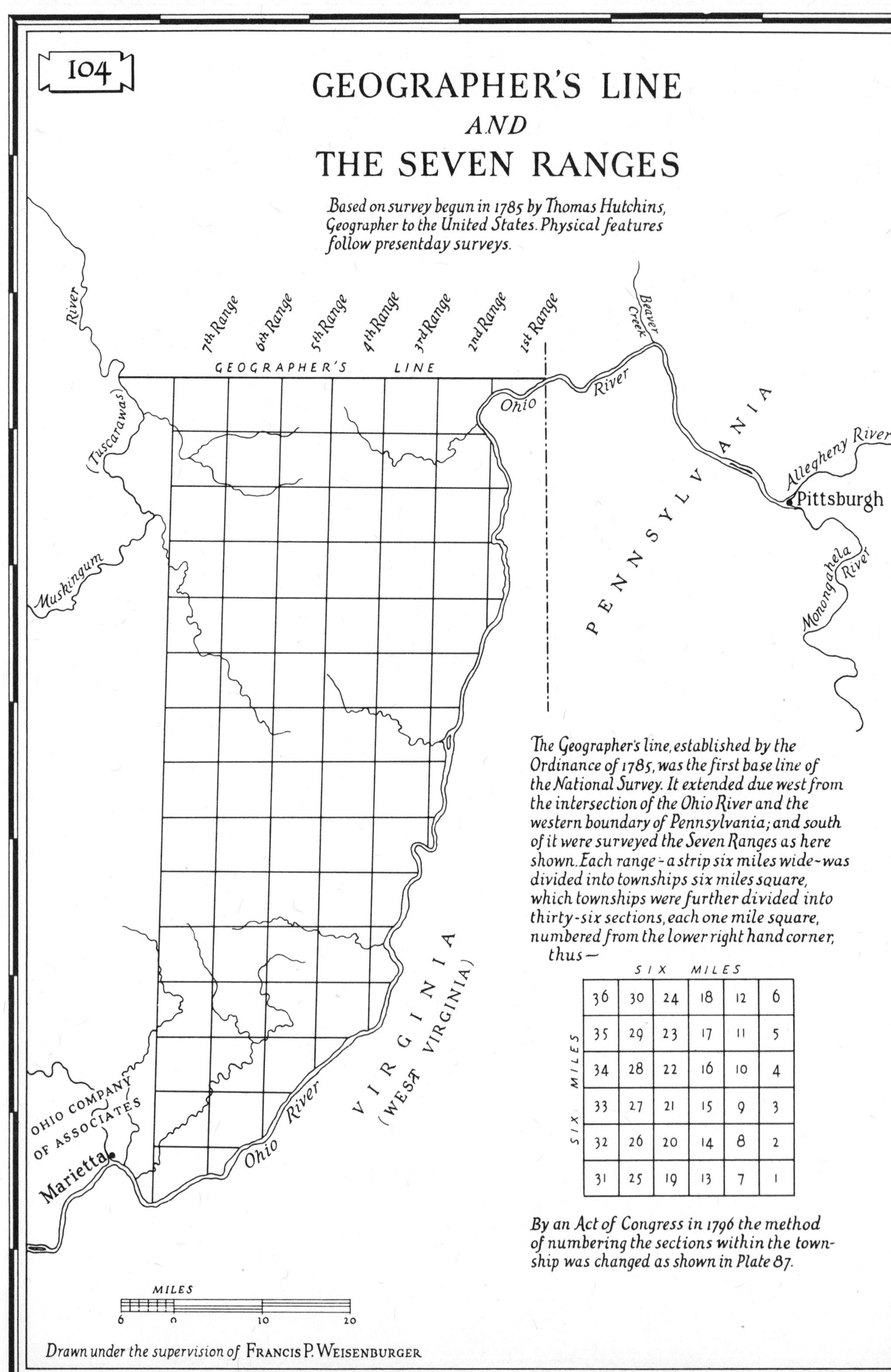
104
GEOGRAPHER'S LINE
AND
THE SEVEN RANGES
Based on survey begun in 1785 by Thomas Hutchins, Geographer to the United States. Physical features follow presentday surveys.
River
7th Range
6th Range
5th Range
4th Range
3rd Range
2nd Range
1st Range
Beaver Creek
GEOGRAPHER'S LINE
Ohio
River
(Tuscarawas)
PENNSYLVANIA
Allegheny River
Pittsburgh
Muskingum
Monongahela River
The Geographer's line, established by the Ordinance of 1785, was the first base line of the National Survey. It extended due west from the intersection of the Ohio River and the western boundary of Pennsylvania; and south of it were surveyed the Seven Ranges as here shown. Each range - a strip six miles wide - was divided into townships six miles square, which townships were further divided into thirty-six sections, each one mile square, numbered from the lower right hand corner, thus —
SIX MILES
SIX MILES
36 30 24 18 12 6
35 29 23 17 11 5
34 28 22 16 10 4
33 27 21 15 9 3
32 26 20 14 8 2
31 25 19 13 7 1
VIRGINIA
(WEST VIRGINIA)
Ohio River
OHIO COMPANY OF ASSOCIATES
Marietta
By an Act of Congress in 1796 the method of numbering the sections within the township was changed as shown in Plate 87.
MILES
6 0 10 20
Drawn under the supervision of FRANCIS P. WEISENBURGER

THE SURVEY *of the* PUBLIC DOMAIN

is based upon the Ordinance of 1785. Beginning with the Seven Ranges (see Plate 86), this survey was continued across the country, although there still remains, in the mountainous sections of the Far West, over one hundred million acres of unsurveyed land. However, with a few local exceptions, the survey applies in every state in the Union, except in the Thirteen Colonies and in Maine, Vermont, Kentucky, Tennessee, West Virginia, and Texas. From arbitrarily selected east-and-west Base Lines and north-and-south Meridians, the land is surveyed into Ranges of Townships, lying north and south of the Base Lines, and east and west of the Meridians. The Ranges are numbered east and west from the Meridians. The Townships, each six miles square, are numbered north and south from the Base Lines. The diagrams below illustrate the actual survey east of the Sixth Principal Meridian and south of a Base Line located on 40° north latitude.

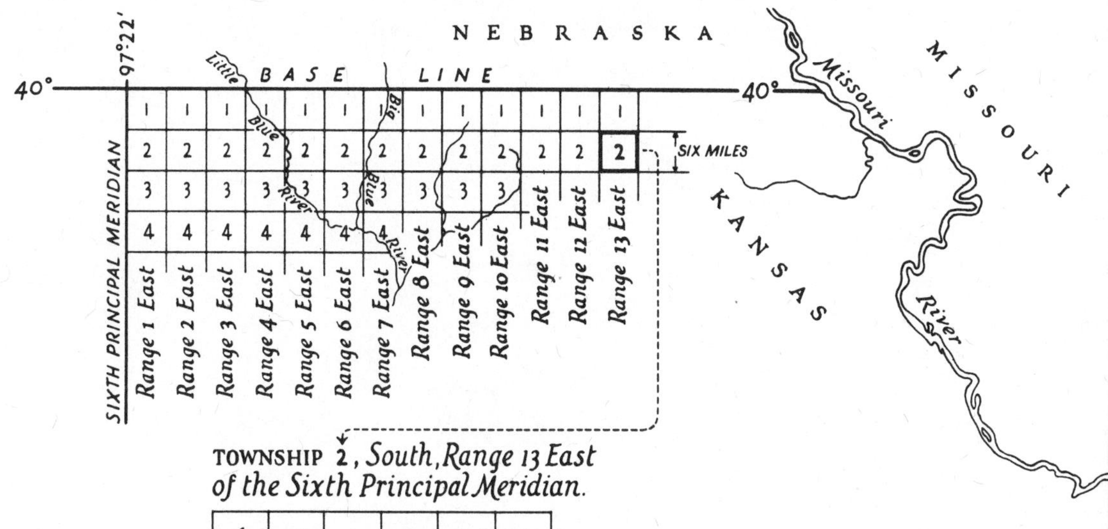

TOWNSHIP 2, *South, Range 13 East of the Sixth Principal Meridian.*

6	5	4	3	2	1
7	8	9	10	11	12
18	17	16	15	14	13
19	20	21	22	23	24
30	29	28	27	26	**25**
31	32	33	34	35	36

SIX MILES — SIX MILES

In 1796 Congress directed that the method of numbering the sections should be as here shown, thus discarding the method followed in the Seven Ranges, (see Plate 86). This method of numbering has prevailed in all surveys subsequent to that date.

SECTION 25, *Township 2, South, Range 13 East of the Sixth Principal Meridian.*

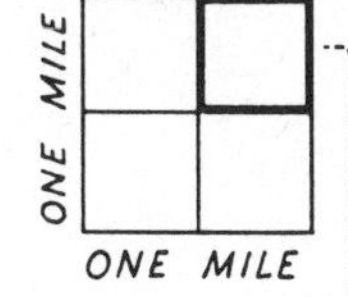

A Section contains 640 acres

NORTHEAST ONE-FOURTH *of Section 25, Township 2, South, Range 13 East of the Sixth Principal Meridian,*

½ MILE — ½ MILE

A Quarter Section contains 160 acres

which, by this description, can be instantly located as lying in an exact place in northeastern Kansas.

Drawn under the supervision of
PAUL WALLACE GATES

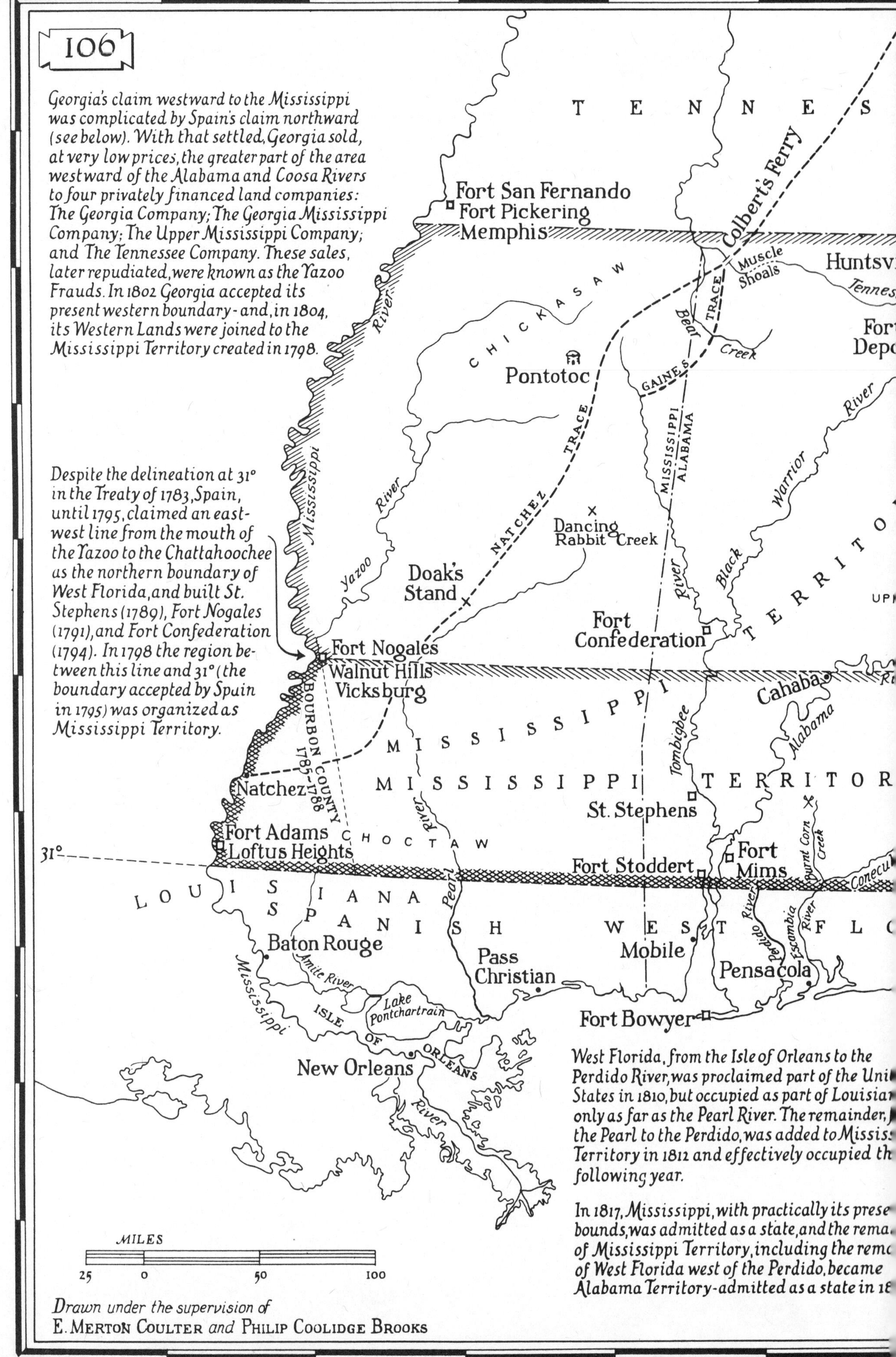
106
Georgia's claim westward to the Mississippi was complicated by Spain's claim northward (see below). With that settled, Georgia sold, at very low prices, the greater part of the area westward of the Alabama and Coosa Rivers to four privately financed land companies: The Georgia Company; The Georgia Mississippi Company; The Upper Mississippi Company; and The Tennessee Company. These sales, later repudiated, were known as the Yazoo Frauds. In 1802 Georgia accepted its present western boundary - and, in 1804, its Western Lands were joined to the Mississippi Territory created in 1798.
Despite the delineation at 31° in the Treaty of 1783, Spain, until 1795, claimed an east-west line from the mouth of the Yazoo to the Chattahoochee as the northern boundary of West Florida, and built St. Stephens (1789), Fort Nogales (1791), and Fort Confederation (1794). In 1798 the region between this line and 31° (the boundary accepted by Spain in 1795) was organized as Mississippi Territory.
West Florida, from the Isle of Orleans to the Perdido River, was proclaimed part of the Uni States in 1810, but occupied as part of Louisia only as far as the Pearl River. The remainder, the Pearl to the Perdido, was added to Missis Territory in 1812 and effectively occupied th following year.
In 1817, Mississippi, with practically its prese bounds, was admitted as a state, and the rema of Mississippi Territory, including the remo of West Florida west of the Perdido, became Alabama Territory-admitted as a state in 18
TENNES
Colbert's Ferry
Fort San Fernando
Fort Pickering
Memphis
Muscle Shoals
Huntsvi
Tennes
CHICKASAW
TRACE
Bear Creek
Fort Depo
Pontotoc
GAINES
MISSISSIPPI
ALABAMA
River
Mississippi River
NATCHEZ TRACE
Yazoo River
Warrior
Dancing Rabbit Creek
Doak's Stand
Black
TERRITO
UPP
Fort Confederation
Fort Nogales
Walnut Hills
Vicksburg
MISSISSIPPI
Cahaba
Alabama
BOURBON COUNTY 1785-1788
MISSISSIPPI TERRITOR
Tombigbee
Natchez
St. Stephens
Fort Adams
Loftus Heights
CHOCTAW
31°
Fort Stoddert
Fort Mims
Burnt Corn Creek
Conecu
LOUISIANA
SPANISH WEST FLO
Pearl
Baton Rouge
Perdido
Escambia River
Pass Christian
Mobile
Pensacola
Amite River
Lake Pontchartrain
ISLE OF ORLEANS
Fort Bowyer
New Orleans
River
MILES
25 0 50 100
Drawn under the supervision of
E. Merton Coulter and Philip Coolidge Brooks

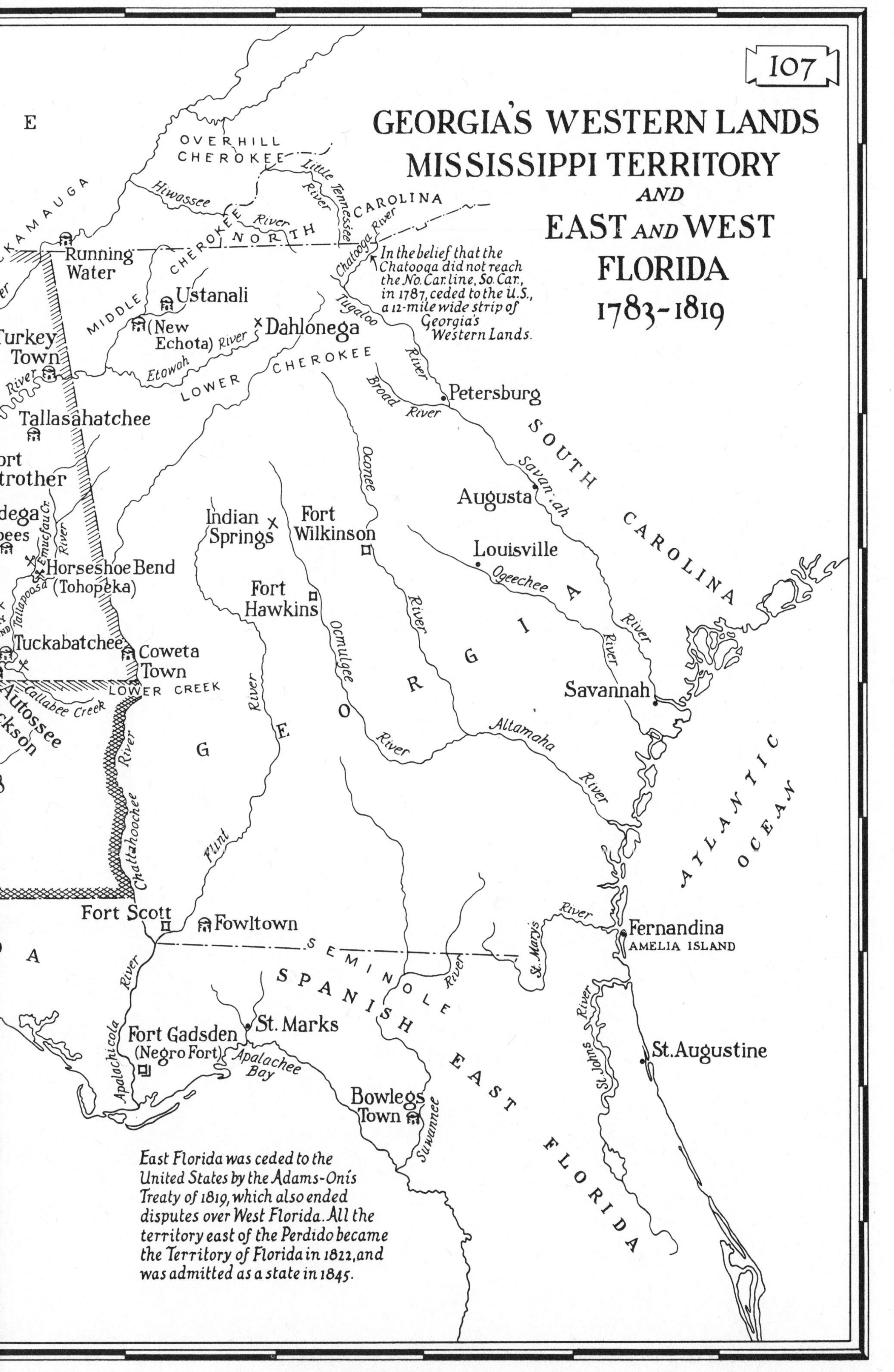
GEORGIA'S WESTERN LANDS
MISSISSIPPI TERRITORY
AND
EAST AND WEST
FLORIDA
1783-1819
In the belief that the Chatooga did not reach the No. Car. line, So. Car., in 1787, ceded to the U.S., a 12-mile wide strip of Georgia's Western Lands.
East Florida was ceded to the United States by the Adams-Onís Treaty of 1819, which also ended disputes over West Florida. All the territory east of the Perdido became the Territory of Florida in 1822, and was admitted as a state in 1845.
OVERHILL CHEROKEE
NORTH CAROLINA
Hiwassee River
Little Tennessee River
Chatooga River
Running Water
MIDDLE CHEROKEE
Ustanali
(New Echota)
Dahlonega
Etowah River
Turkey Town
LOWER CHEROKEE
Tugaloo River
Petersburg
Broad River
Tallasahatchee
SOUTH CAROLINA
Savannah River
Augusta
Oconee River
Indian Springs
Fort Wilkinson
Louisville
Ogeechee River
Horseshoe Bend (Tohopeka)
Emucfau Cr.
Tallapoosa
Fort Hawkins
Ocmulgee River
Tuckabatchee
Coweta Town
LOWER CREEK
Callabee Creek
Savannah
Altamaha River
GEORGIA
Flint River
Chattahoochee River
ATLANTIC OCEAN
Fort Scott
Fowltown
SEMINOLE
St. Marys River
Fernandina
AMELIA ISLAND
SPANISH EAST FLORIDA
Apalachicola River
Fort Gadsden (Negro Fort)
St. Marks
Apalachee Bay
Bowlegs Town
Suwannee
St. Johns River
St. Augustine

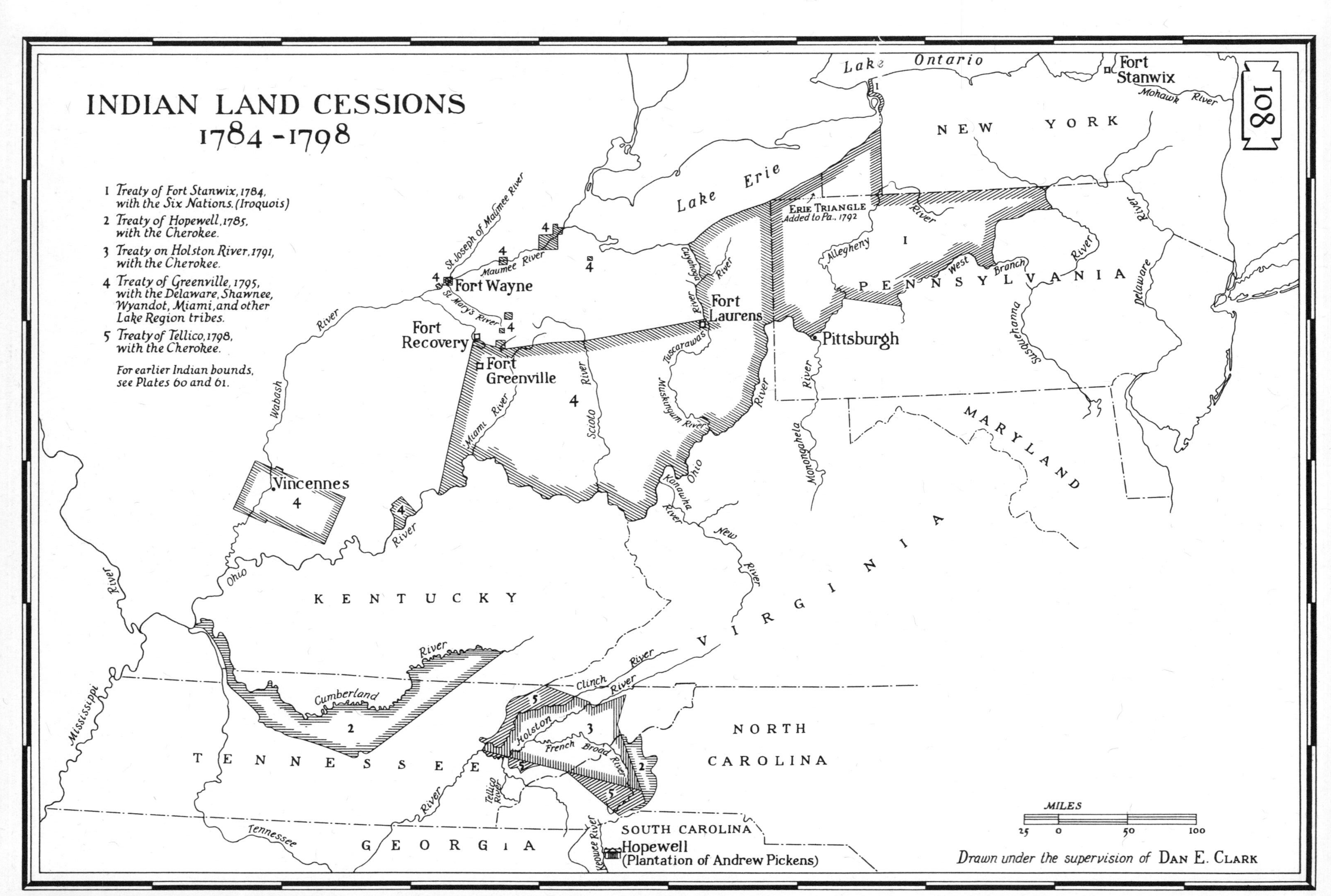

INDIAN LAND CESSIONS
1784-1798
1 Treaty of Fort Stanwix, 1784, with the Six Nations. (Iroquois)
2 Treaty of Hopewell, 1785, with the Cherokee.
3 Treaty on Holston River, 1791, with the Cherokee.
4 Treaty of Greenville, 1795, with the Delaware, Shawnee, Wyandot, Miami, and other Lake Region tribes.
5 Treaty of Tellico, 1798, with the Cherokee.
For earlier Indian bounds, see Plates 60 and 61.
Lake Ontario
Fort Stanwix
Mohawk River
NEW YORK
Lake Erie
ERIE TRIANGLE Added to Pa., 1792
Allegheny River
West Branch
PENNSYLVANIA
Susquehanna River
Delaware River
Pittsburgh
Monongahela River
MARYLAND
Fort Laurens
Cuyahoga River
Tuscarawas River
Muskingum River
Ohio River
Kanawha River
New River
VIRGINIA
St. Joseph of Maumee River
Maumee River
Fort Wayne
St. Mary's River
Fort Recovery
Fort Greenville
Miami River
Scioto River
Wabash River
Vincennes
KENTUCKY
Cumberland River
Mississippi River
TENNESSEE
Clinch River
Holston River
French Broad River
Tellico River
Tennessee River
NORTH CAROLINA
SOUTH CAROLINA
Hopewell (Plantation of Andrew Pickens)
Keowee River
GEORGIA
MILES
25 0 50 100
Drawn under the supervision of DAN E. CLARK

NEW YORK LAND PURCHASES, 1786-1793

By virtue of the Charter of 1629, Massachusetts claimed territorial rights to the land between the Mohawk River settlements of New York (see Plate 78) and the Western Lands ceded to the Federal Government (see Plate 82).

In 1786 New York and Massachusetts reached an agreement by which, in Boston Ten Townships and in the area west of a north-south line 82 miles west of the intersection of the New York-Pennsylvania boundary by the Delaware River (the Pre-emption Line), the jurisdictional rights were vested in New York and the right of ownership (purchase or sale) was vested in Massachusetts.

In both cases the pre-emption rights were promptly sold by Massachusetts, the area west of the Pre-emption Line being first acquired by Phelps and Gorham.

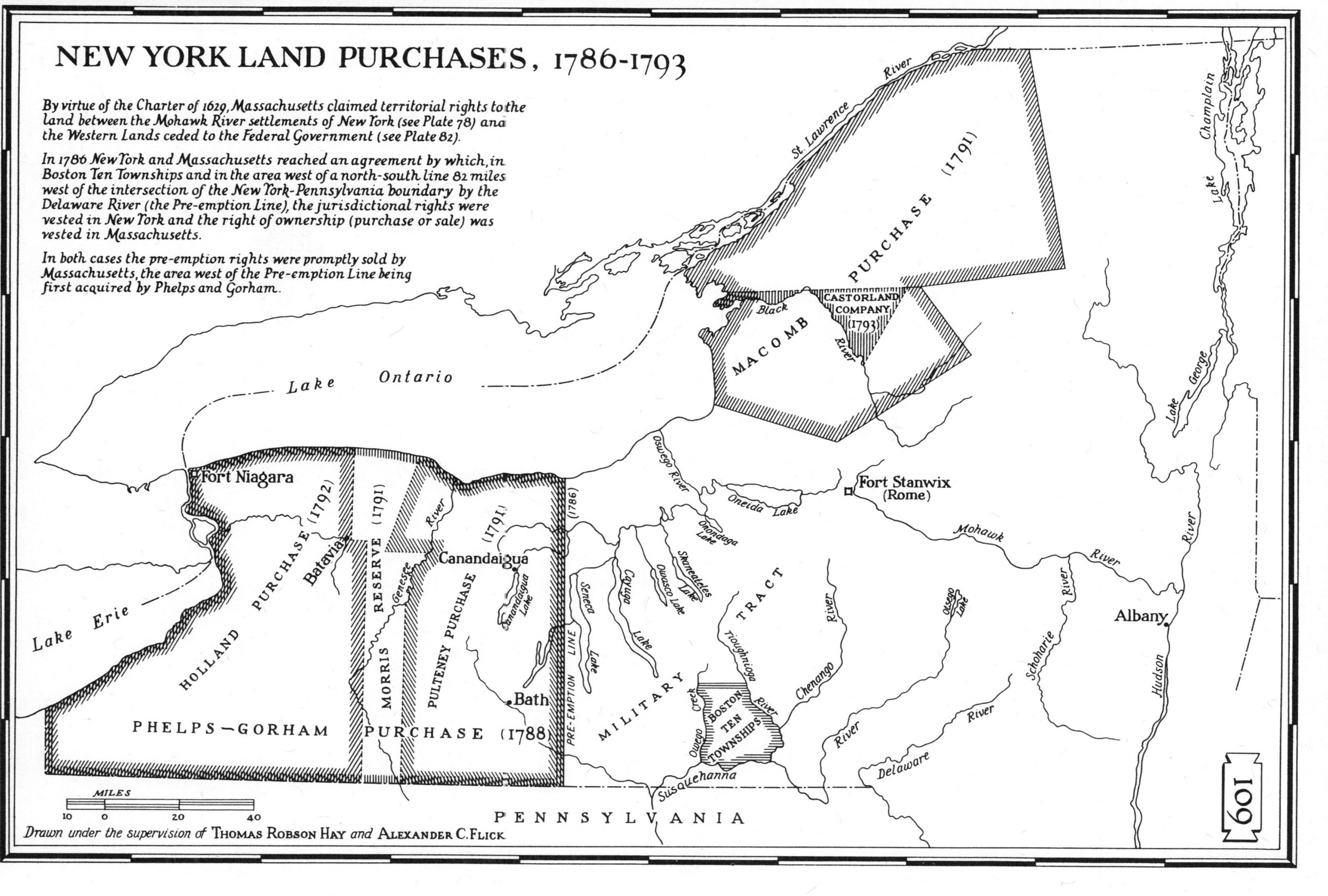

Drawn under the supervision of Thomas Robson Hay and Alexander C. Flick

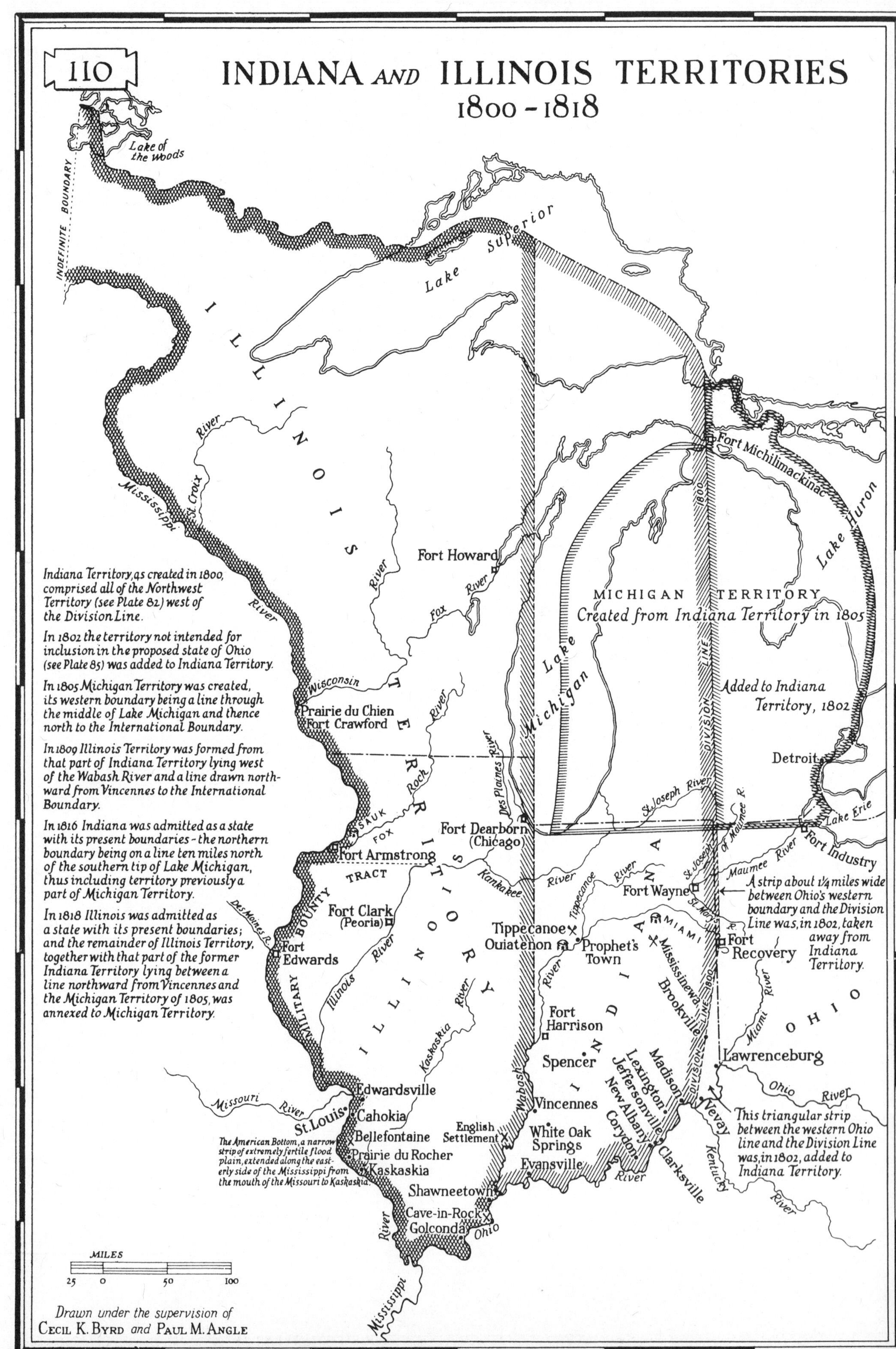

Indiana Territory, as created in 1800, comprised all of the Northwest Territory (see Plate 82) west of the Division Line.

In 1802 the territory not intended for inclusion in the proposed state of Ohio (see Plate 85) was added to Indiana Territory.

In 1805 Michigan Territory was created, its western boundary being a line through the middle of Lake Michigan and thence north to the International Boundary.

In 1809 Illinois Territory was formed from that part of Indiana Territory lying west of the Wabash River and a line drawn northward from Vincennes to the International Boundary.

In 1816 Indiana was admitted as a state with its present boundaries - the northern boundary being on a line ten miles north of the southern tip of Lake Michigan, thus including territory previously a part of Michigan Territory.

In 1818 Illinois was admitted as a state with its present boundaries; and the remainder of Illinois Territory, together with that part of the former Indiana Territory lying between a line northward from Vincennes and the Michigan Territory of 1805, was annexed to Michigan Territory.

Drawn under the supervision of CECIL K. BYRD and PAUL M. ANGLE

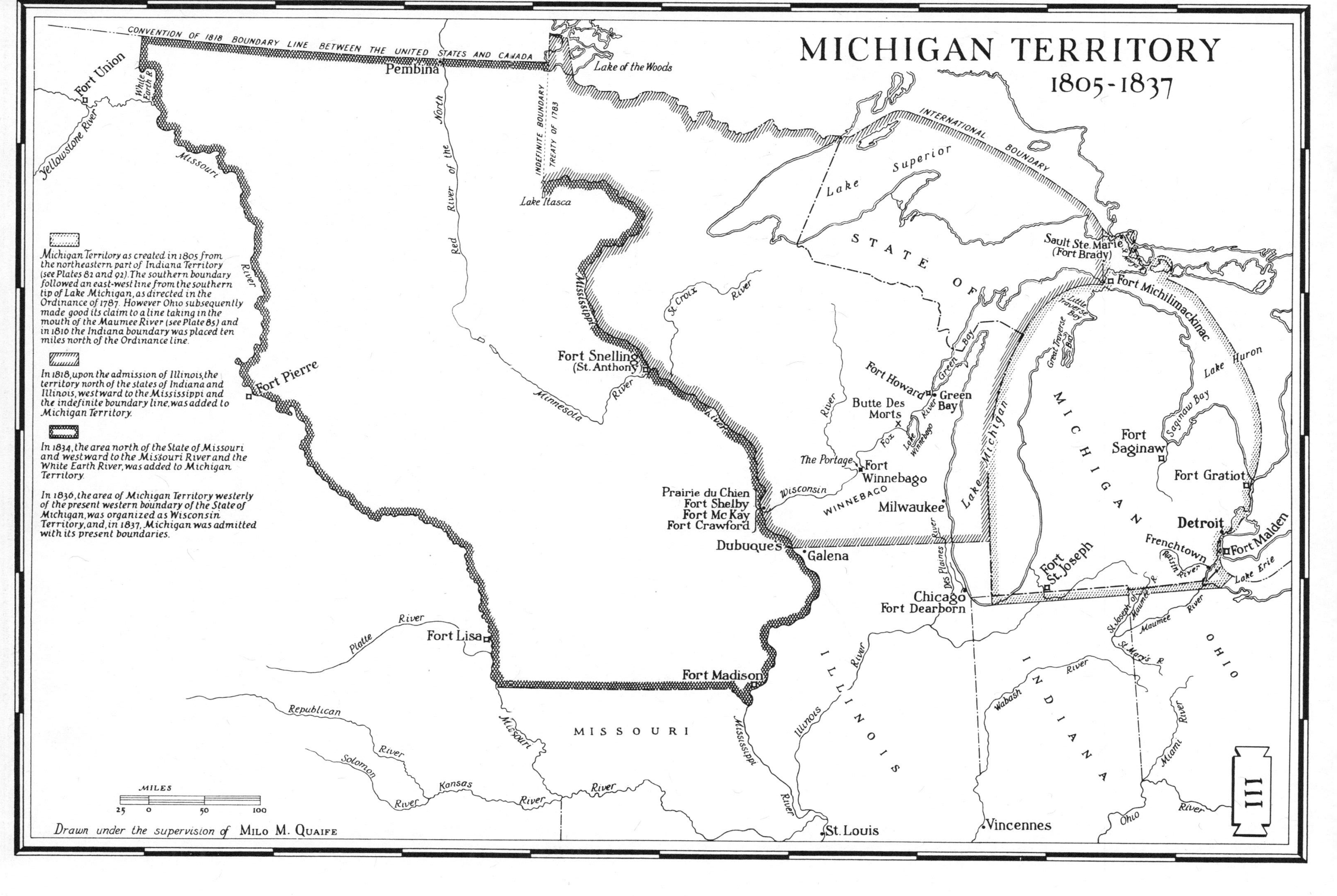

MICHIGAN TERRITORY
1805-1837
III
CONVENTION OF 1818 BOUNDARY LINE BETWEEN THE UNITED STATES AND CANADA
INDEFINITE BOUNDARY
TREATY OF 1783
INTERNATIONAL BOUNDARY
Michigan Territory as created in 1805 from the northeastern part of Indiana Territory (see Plates 82 and 92). The southern boundary followed an east-west line from the southern tip of Lake Michigan, as directed in the Ordinance of 1787. However Ohio subsequently made good its claim to a line taking in the mouth of the Maumee River (see Plate 85) and in 1816 the Indiana boundary was placed ten miles north of the Ordinance line.
In 1818, upon the admission of Illinois, the territory north of the states of Indiana and Illinois, westward to the Mississippi and the indefinite boundary line, was added to Michigan Territory.
In 1834, the area north of the State of Missouri and westward to the Missouri River and the White Earth River, was added to Michigan Territory.
In 1836, the area of Michigan Territory westerly of the present western boundary of the State of Michigan, was organized as Wisconsin Territory, and, in 1837, Michigan was admitted with its present boundaries.
Fort Union
Yellowstone River
White Earth R.
Missouri River
Pembina
Red River of the North
Lake of the Woods
Lake Itasca
Fort Pierre
Minnesota
Fort Snelling
(St. Anthony)
Mississippi River
St. Croix River
Lake Superior
STATE OF MICHIGAN
Sault Ste. Marie
(Fort Brady)
Fort Michilimackinac
Little Traverse Bay
Great Traverse Bay
Lake Huron
Saginaw Bay
Fort Saginaw
Fort Gratiot
Detroit
Fort Malden
Frenchtown
Raisin River
Lake Erie
Fort St. Joseph
Lake Michigan
Green Bay
Fort Howard
Green Bay
Butte Des Morts
Fox River
Lake Winnebago
The Portage
Fort Winnebago
WINNEBAGO
Wisconsin
Milwaukee
Prairie du Chien
Fort Shelby
Fort Mc Kay
Fort Crawford
Dubuque's
Galena
Des Plaines River
Chicago
Fort Dearborn
Platte River
Fort Lisa
Fort Madison
Republican River
Solomon River
Kansas River
Missouri River
MISSOURI
Mississippi River
ILLINOIS
Illinois River
INDIANA
Wabash River
Vincennes
St. Louis
OHIO
Maumee River
St. Joseph R.
Maumee R.
St. Mary's R.
Miami River
Ohio River
MILES
25 0 50 100
Drawn under the supervision of Milo M. Quaife

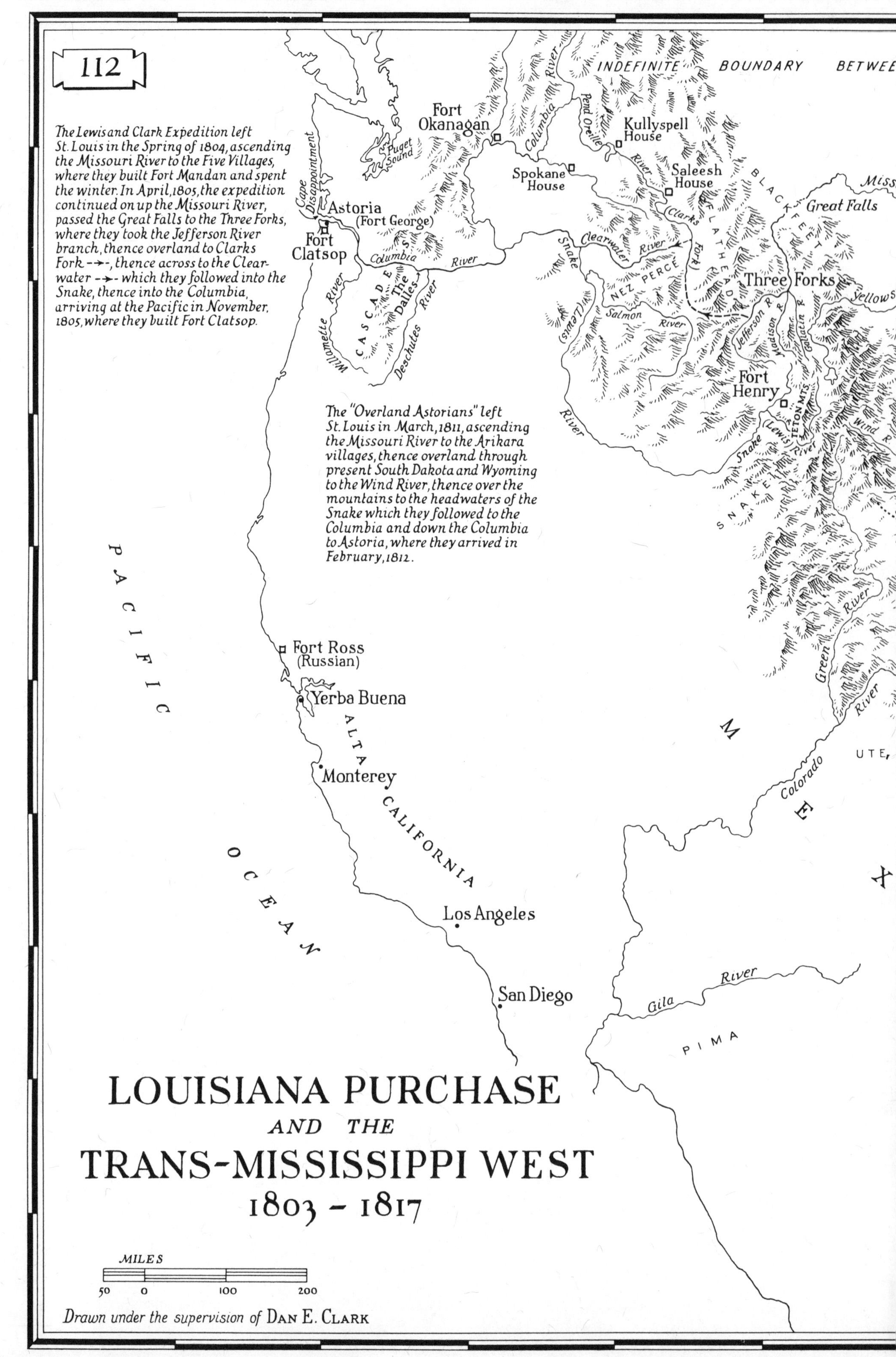
112
The Lewis and Clark Expedition left St. Louis in the Spring of 1804, ascending the Missouri River to the Five Villages, where they built Fort Mandan and spent the winter. In April, 1805, the expedition continued on up the Missouri River, passed the Great Falls to the Three Forks, where they took the Jefferson River branch, thence overland to Clarks Fork --→--, thence across to the Clearwater --→-- which they followed into the Snake, thence into the Columbia, arriving at the Pacific in November, 1805, where they built Fort Clatsop.
The "Overland Astorians" left St. Louis in March, 1811, ascending the Missouri River to the Arikara villages, thence overland through present South Dakota and Wyoming to the Wind River, thence over the mountains to the headwaters of the Snake which they followed to the Columbia and down the Columbia to Astoria, where they arrived in February, 1812.
INDEFINITE BOUNDARY BETWEEN
Fort Okanagan
Kullyspell House
Spokane House
Saleesh House
Puget Sound
Cape Disappointment
Astoria (Fort George)
Fort Clatsop
Columbia River
Pend Oreille
Clarks Fork
Clearwater River
Snake
NEZ PERCE
FLATHEAD
BLACKFEET
Great Falls
Missou
Three Forks
Yellowsto
Salmon River
Jefferson R.
Madison R.
Gallatin R.
Fort Henry
TETON MTS.
Snake (Lewis) River
Wind R.
SNAKE
Willamette River
CASCADES
The Dalles
Deschutes River
PACIFIC OCEAN
Fort Ross (Russian)
Yerba Buena
ALTA CALIFORNIA
Monterey
Los Angeles
San Diego
Green River
Colorado
UTE
MEX
Gila River
PIMA
LOUISIANA PURCHASE AND THE TRANS-MISSISSIPPI WEST 1803 - 1817
MILES
50 0 100 200
Drawn under the supervision of DAN E. CLARK

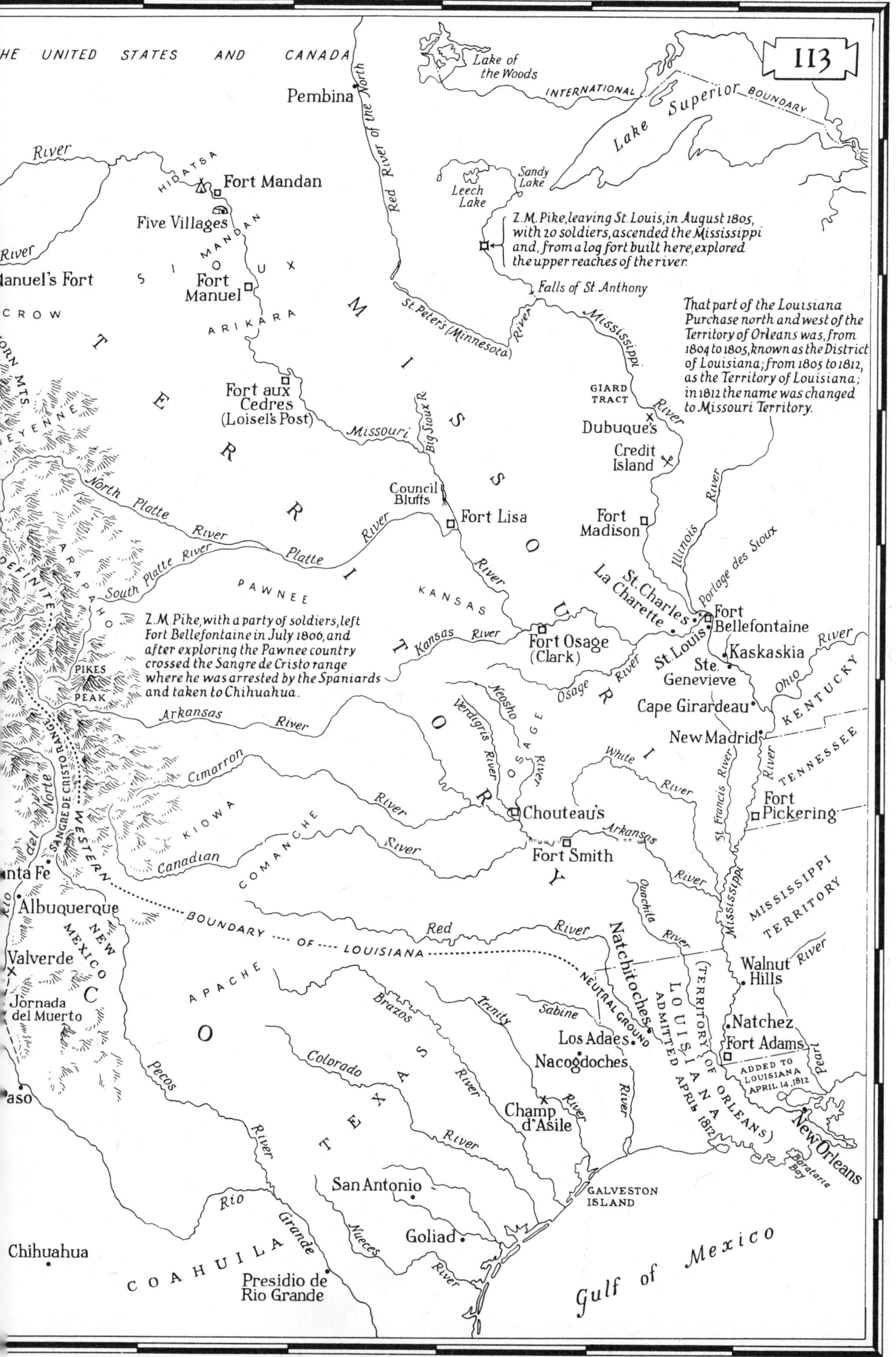
THE UNITED STATES AND CANADA
Lake of the Woods
INTERNATIONAL BOUNDARY
Lake Superior
Pembina
Red River of the North
Fort Mandan
HIDATSA
Five Villages
MANDAN
SIOUX
Fort Manuel
Manuel's Fort
CROW
ARIKARA
Sandy Lake
Leech Lake
Z. M. Pike, leaving St. Louis, in August 1805, with 20 soldiers, ascended the Mississippi and, from a log fort built here, explored the upper reaches of the river.
Falls of St. Anthony
St. Peter's (Minnesota) River
Mississippi River
That part of the Louisiana Purchase north and west of the Territory of Orleans was, from 1804 to 1805, known as the District of Louisiana; from 1805 to 1812, as the Territory of Louisiana; in 1812 the name was changed to Missouri Territory.
MISSOURI TERRITORY
Fort aux Cedres (Loisel's Post)
Missouri
Big Sioux R.
GIARD TRACT
Dubuque's
Credit Island
Council Bluffs
Fort Lisa
Fort Madison
Illinois River
Portage des Sioux
North Platte River
South Platte River
Platte River
PAWNEE
KANSAS
St. Charles
La Charette
Fort Bellefontaine
St. Louis
Z. M. Pike, with a party of soldiers, left Fort Bellefontaine in July 1806, and after exploring the Pawnee country crossed the Sangre de Cristo range where he was arrested by the Spaniards and taken to Chihuahua.
Kansas River
Fort Osage (Clark)
Osage River
Ste. Genevieve
Kaskaskia
Ohio River
KENTUCKY
Cape Girardeau
New Madrid
TENNESSEE
PIKES PEAK
ARAPAHO
CHEYENNE
Arkansas River
Verdigris River
Neosho River
OSAGE
White River
St. Francis River
Fort Pickering
Cimarron River
KIOWA
COMANCHE
Chouteau's
Arkansas River
Fort Smith
Canadian River
SANGRE DE CRISTO RANGE
Rio del Norte
WESTERN BOUNDARY OF LOUISIANA
Santa Fe
Albuquerque
NEW MEXICO
Valverde
Jornada del Muerto
Red River
Ouachita River
Mississippi
MISSISSIPPI TERRITORY
Walnut Hills
Natchitoches
NEUTRAL GROUND
LOUISIANA ADMITTED APRIL 1812
(TERRITORY OF ORLEANS)
APACHE
MEXICO
Brazos
Trinity
Sabine
Los Adaes
Nacogdoches
Natchez
Fort Adams
ADDED TO LOUISIANA APRIL 14, 1812
Pearl
Pecos River
Colorado River
TEXAS
Champ d'Asile
New Orleans
Barataria Bay
El Paso
San Antonio
GALVESTON ISLAND
Rio Grande
Goliad
Nueces River
Chihuahua
COAHUILA
Presidio de Rio Grande
Gulf of Mexico

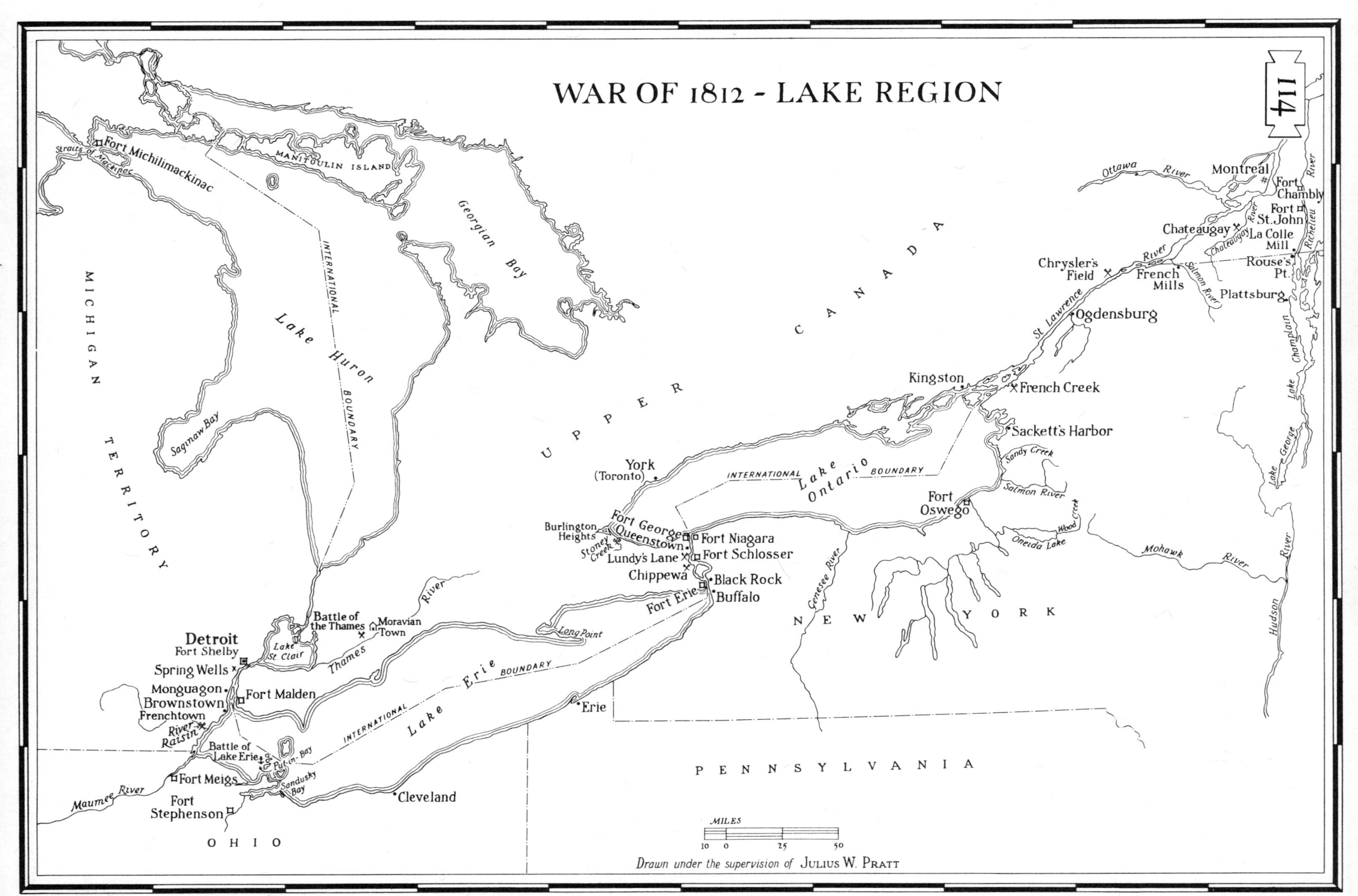
114
WAR OF 1812 - LAKE REGION
Fort Michilimackinac
Straits of Mackinac
MANITOULIN ISLAND
Georgian Bay
Lake Huron
INTERNATIONAL BOUNDARY
MICHIGAN TERRITORY
Saginaw Bay
UPPER CANADA
Ottawa River
Montreal
Fort Chambly
Fort St. John
Richelieu River
Chateaugay
Chateaugay River
La Colle Mill
Rouse's Pt.
Plattsburg
Chrysler's Field
French Mills
Salmon River
St. Lawrence River
Ogdensburg
Lake Champlain
Lake George
Kingston
French Creek
Sackett's Harbor
Sandy Creek
Salmon River
Wood Creek
Oneida Lake
Mohawk River
Hudson River
York (Toronto)
Lake Ontario
Fort Oswego
Burlington Heights
Stoney Creek
Fort George
Queenstown
Fort Niagara
Fort Schlosser
Lundy's Lane
Chippewa
Black Rock
Buffalo
Fort Erie
Genesee River
NEW YORK
Long Point
Battle of the Thames
Moravian Town
River
Thames
Detroit
Fort Shelby
Lake St. Clair
Spring Wells
Monguagon
Brownstown
Frenchtown
Fort Malden
River Raisin
Lake Erie
Erie
Battle of Lake Erie
Put-in-Bay
Sandusky Bay
Fort Meigs
Maumee River
Fort Stephenson
Cleveland
PENNSYLVANIA
OHIO
MILES
10 0 25 50
Drawn under the supervision of Julius W. Pratt

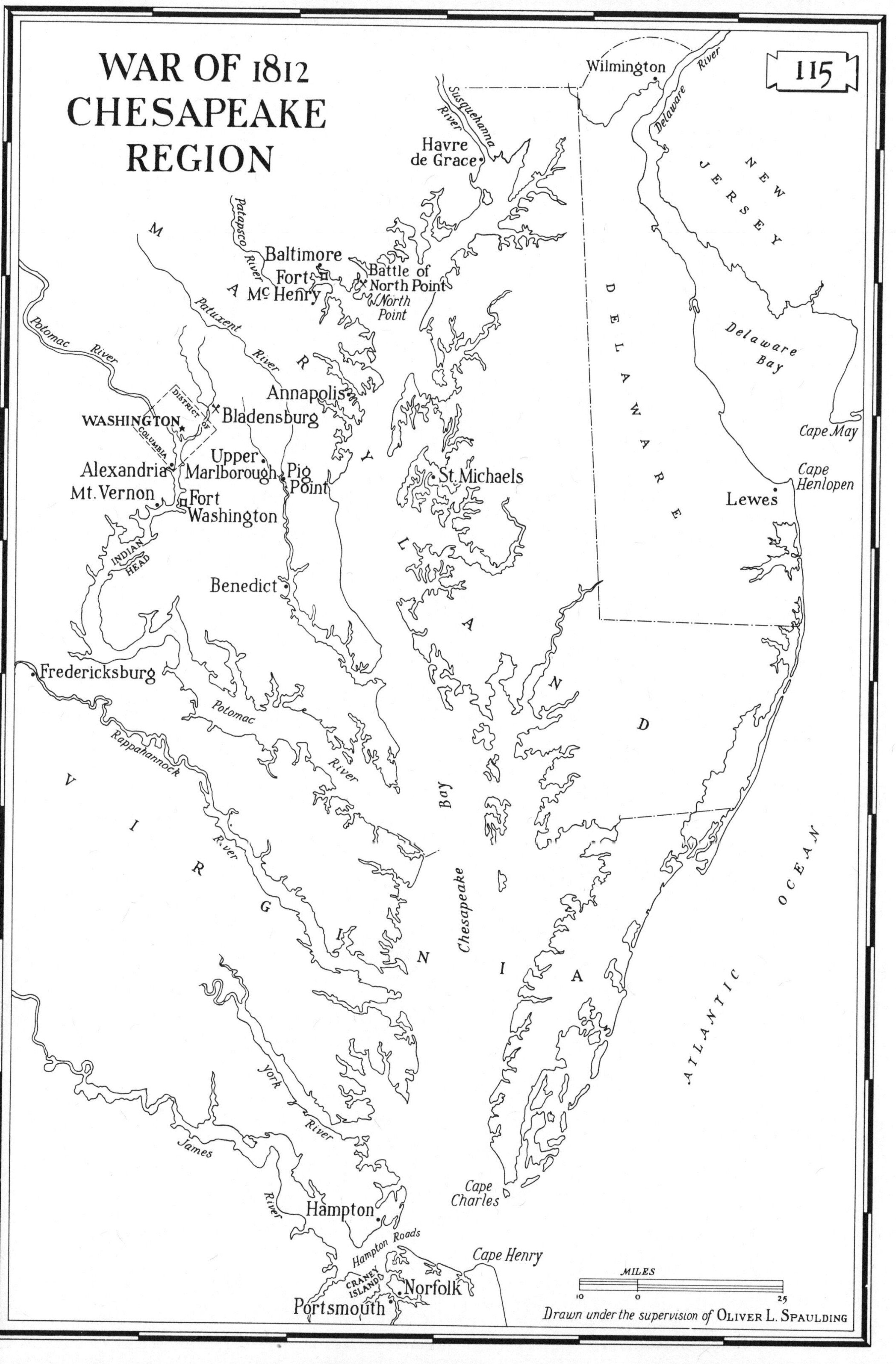
WAR OF 1812
CHESAPEAKE
REGION
115
Wilmington
Delaware River
Susquehanna River
Havre de Grace
NEW JERSEY
Patapsco River
Baltimore
Fort McHenry
Battle of North Point
North Point
MARYLAND
Potomac River
Patuxent River
Annapolis
DISTRICT OF COLUMBIA
WASHINGTON
Bladensburg
Upper Marlborough
Pig Point
Alexandria
Mt. Vernon
Fort Washington
St. Michaels
DELAWARE
Delaware Bay
Cape May
Cape Henlopen
Lewes
INDIAN HEAD
Benedict
Fredericksburg
Potomac River
Rappahannock River
VIRGINIA
Chesapeake Bay
ATLANTIC OCEAN
York River
James River
Hampton
Cape Charles
Hampton Roads
Cape Henry
CRANEY ISLAND
Norfolk
Portsmouth
MILES
10 0 25
Drawn under the supervision of OLIVER L. SPAULDING

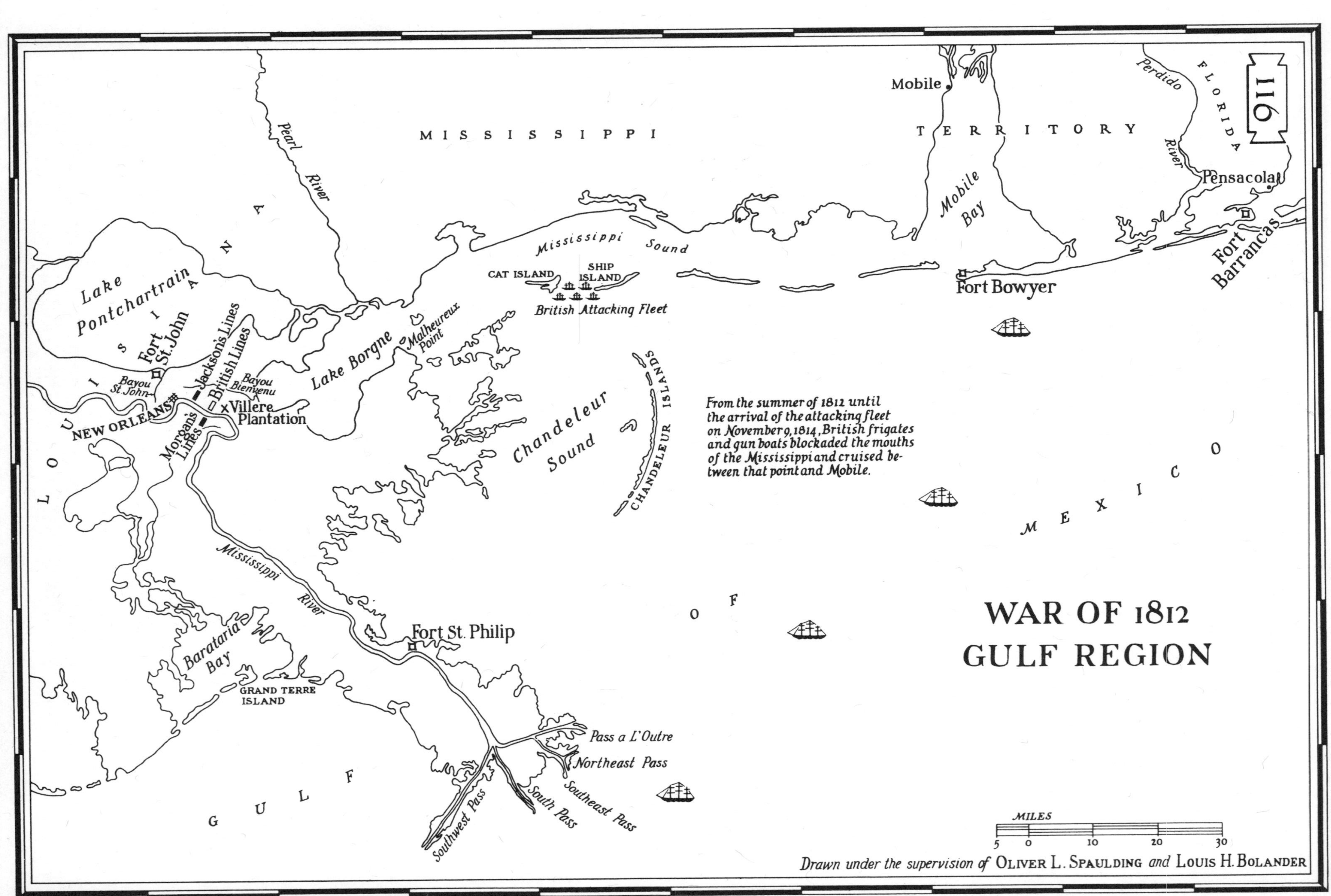
116
WAR OF 1812
GULF REGION
From the summer of 1812 until the arrival of the attacking fleet on November 9, 1814, British frigates and gun boats blockaded the mouths of the Mississippi and cruised between that point and Mobile.
MISSISSIPPI
TERRITORY
FLORIDA
LOUISIANA
GULF OF MEXICO
Mobile
Mobile Bay
Perdido River
Pensacola
Fort Barrancas
Fort Bowyer
Pearl River
Mississippi Sound
CAT ISLAND
SHIP ISLAND
British Attacking Fleet
CHANDELEUR ISLANDS
Chandeleur Sound
Lake Pontchartrain
Fort St. John
Bayou St. John
NEW ORLEANS
Jackson's Lines
British Lines
Morgan's Lines
Bayou Bienvenu
Villere Plantation
Lake Borgne
Malheureux Point
Mississippi River
Fort St. Philip
Barataria Bay
GRAND TERRE ISLAND
Pass a L'Outre
Northeast Pass
Southeast Pass
South Pass
Southwest Pass
MILES
5 0 10 20 30
Drawn under the supervision of Oliver L. Spaulding and Louis H. Bolander

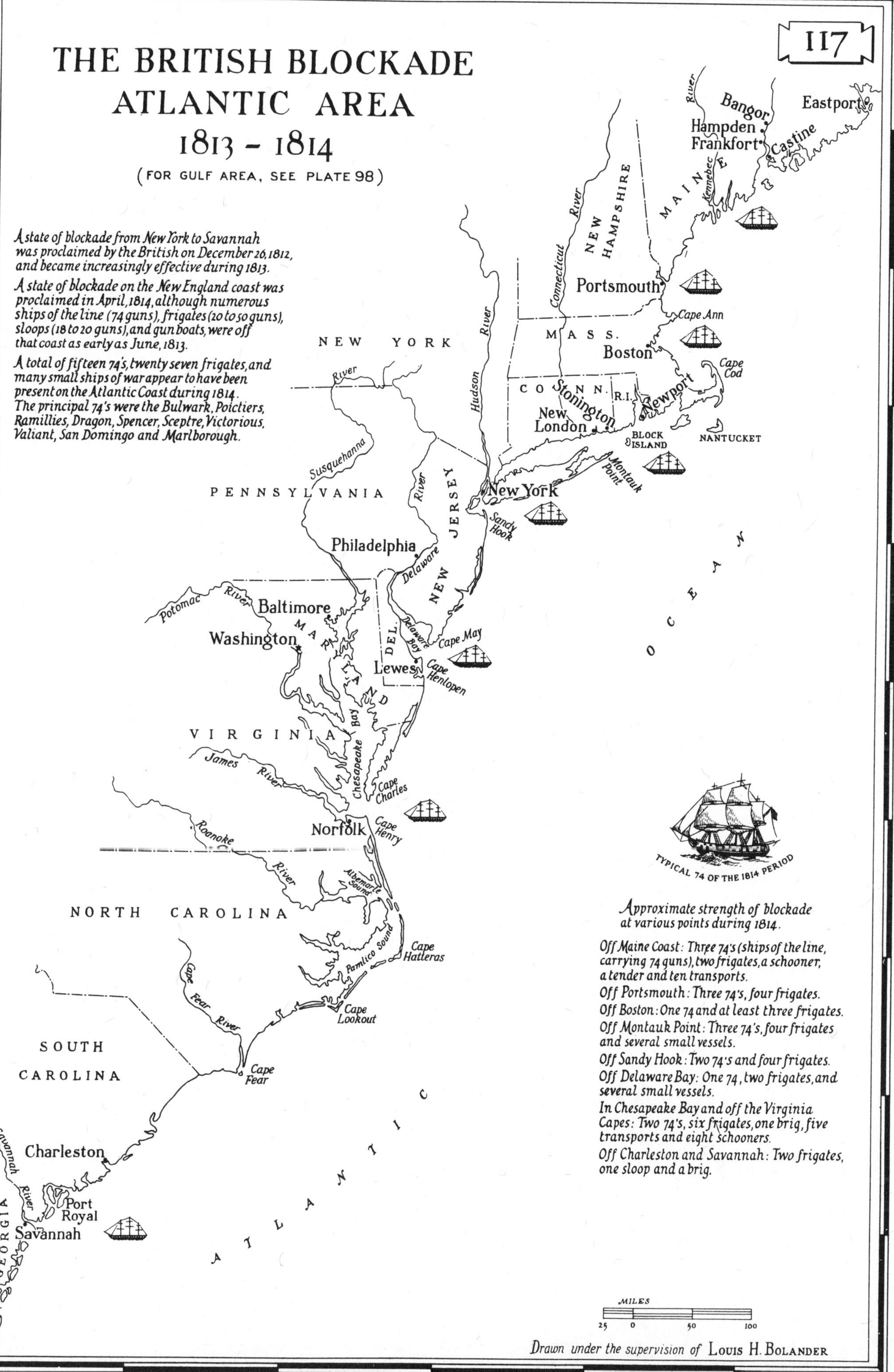
117
THE BRITISH BLOCKADE
ATLANTIC AREA
1813 – 1814
(FOR GULF AREA, SEE PLATE 98)
A state of blockade from New York to Savannah was proclaimed by the British on December 26, 1812, and became increasingly effective during 1813.
A state of blockade on the New England coast was proclaimed in April, 1814, although numerous ships of the line (74 guns), frigates (20 to 50 guns), sloops (18 to 20 guns), and gun boats, were off that coast as early as June, 1813.
A total of fifteen 74's, twenty seven frigates, and many small ships of war appear to have been present on the Atlantic Coast during 1814.
The principal 74's were the Bulwark, Poictiers, Ramillies, Dragon, Spencer, Sceptre, Victorious, Valiant, San Domingo and Marlborough.
Eastport
Bangor
Hampden
Frankfort
Castine
River
Kennebec
MAINE
NEW HAMPSHIRE
Connecticut
River
Portsmouth
Cape Ann
MASS.
Boston
Cape Cod
CONN.
R.I.
Stonington
Newport
New London
BLOCK ISLAND
NANTUCKET
Montauk Point
NEW YORK
River
Hudson
River
Susquehanna
PENNSYLVANIA
River
NEW JERSEY
New York
Sandy Hook
Philadelphia
Delaware
Potomac
River
Baltimore
Washington
MARYLAND
DEL.
Delaware Bay
Cape May
Lewes
Cape Henlopen
OCEAN
VIRGINIA
Chesapeake Bay
James
River
Cape Charles
Norfolk
Cape Henry
Roanoke
River
Albemarle Sound
NORTH CAROLINA
Pamlico Sound
Cape Hatteras
Cape Fear
River
Cape Lookout
SOUTH CAROLINA
Cape Fear
Charleston
Savannah
River
Port Royal
Savannah
GEORGIA
ATLANTIC
TYPICAL 74 OF THE 1814 PERIOD
Approximate strength of blockade at various points during 1814.
Off Maine Coast: Three 74's (ships of the line, carrying 74 guns), two frigates, a schooner, a tender and ten transports.
Off Portsmouth: Three 74's, four frigates.
Off Boston: One 74 and at least three frigates.
Off Montauk Point: Three 74's, four frigates and several small vessels.
Off Sandy Hook: Two 74's and four frigates.
Off Delaware Bay: One 74, two frigates, and several small vessels.
In Chesapeake Bay and off the Virginia Capes: Two 74's, six frigates, one brig, five transports and eight schooners.
Off Charleston and Savannah: Two frigates, one sloop and a brig.
MILES
25 0 50 100
Drawn under the supervision of LOUIS H. BOLANDER

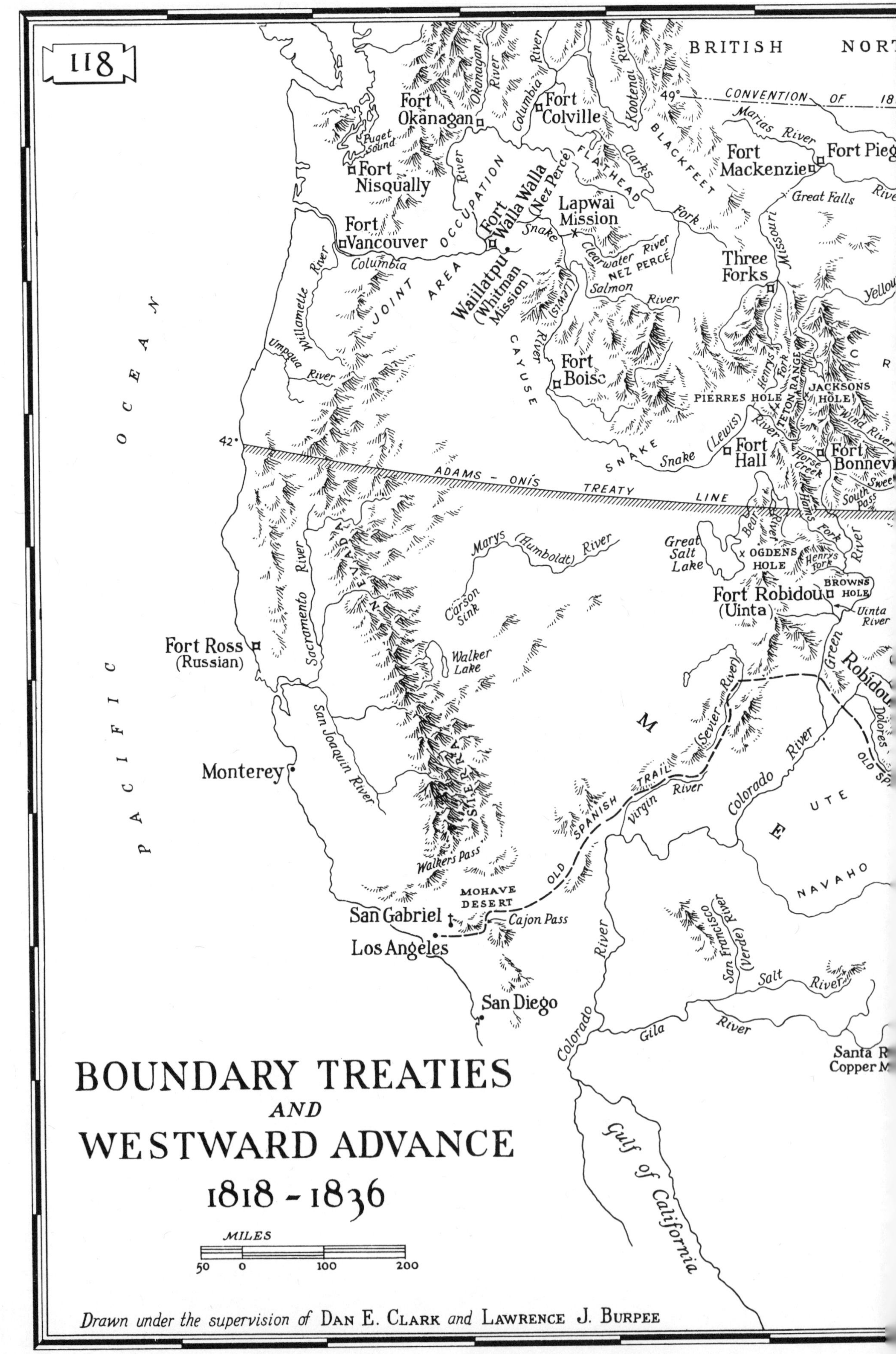

BOUNDARY TREATIES *AND* WESTWARD ADVANCE 1818 - 1836

Drawn under the supervision of DAN E. CLARK *and* LAWRENCE J. BURPEE

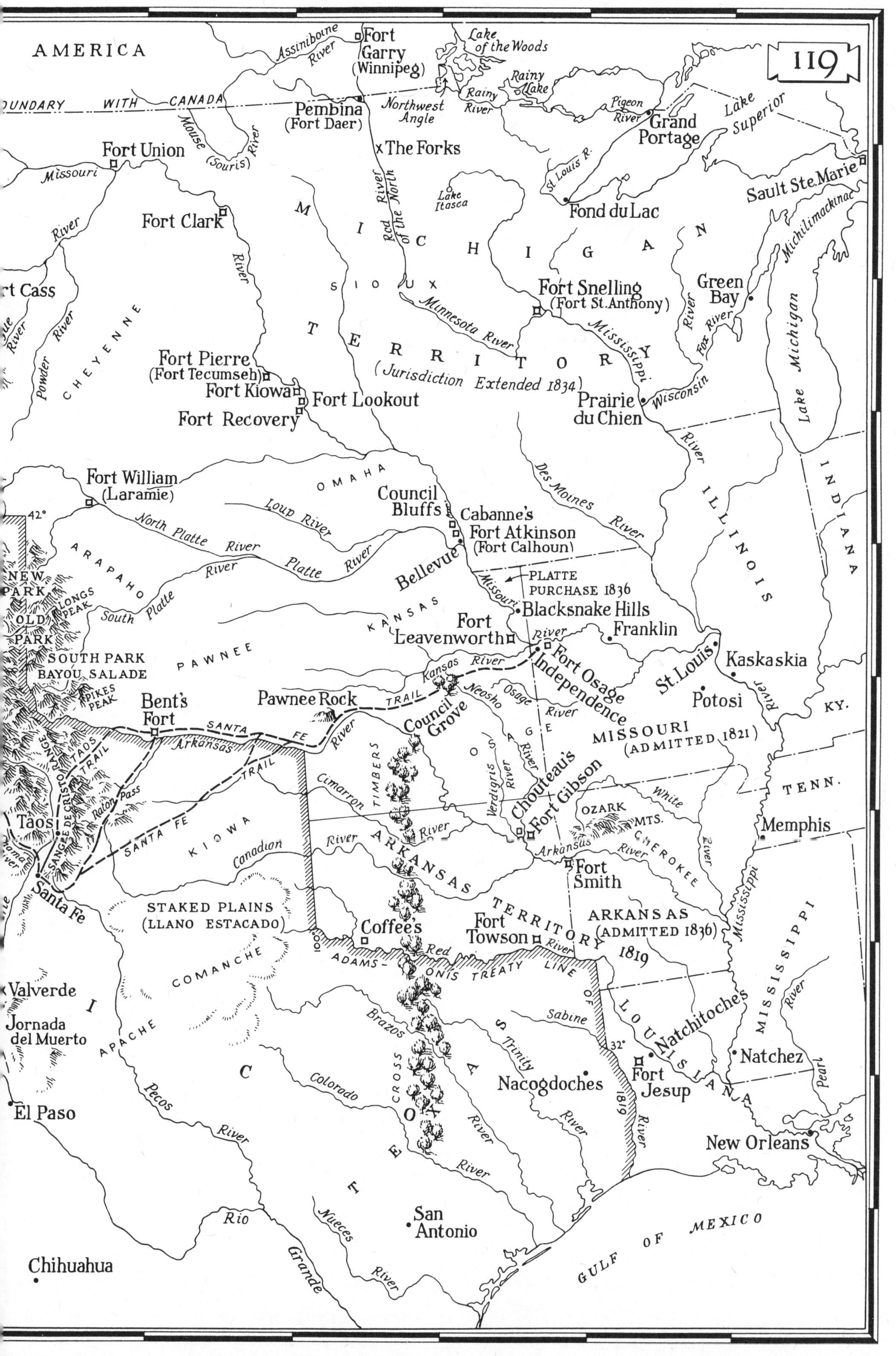
AMERICA
BOUNDARY WITH CANADA
Assiniboine River
Fort Garry (Winnipeg)
Lake of the Woods
Rainy Lake
Rainy River
Northwest Angle
Pembina (Fort Daer)
Pigeon River
Grand Portage
Lake Superior
Mouse (Souris) River
Fort Union
Missouri
The Forks
St. Louis R.
Fond du Lac
Sault Ste. Marie
Michilimackinac
Lake Itasca
Red River of the North
Fort Clark
River
M I C H I G A N
S I O U X
Fort Snelling (Fort St. Anthony)
Green Bay
Fox River
River
Minnesota River
Mississippi
Lake Michigan
Fort Cass
Powder River
CHEYENNE
T E R R I T O R Y
(Jurisdiction Extended 1834)
Fort Pierre (Fort Tecumseh)
Fort Kiowa
Fort Lookout
Fort Recovery
Prairie du Chien
Wisconsin
River
Fort William (Laramie)
OMAHA
Council Bluffs
Cabanne's
Fort Atkinson (Fort Calhoun)
Loup River
North Platte River
Platte River
Des Moines River
INDIANA
ILLINOIS
42°
ARAPAHO
NEW PARK
LONGS PEAK
OLD PARK
South Platte
River
Bellevue
PLATTE PURCHASE 1836
Missouri
Blacksnake Hills
KANSAS
Fort Leavenworth
River
Franklin
PAWNEE
SOUTH PARK
BAYOU SALADE
PIKES PEAK
Kansas River
Fort Osage
Independence
St. Louis
Kaskaskia
Potosi
Bent's Fort
Pawnee Rock
SANTA FE TRAIL
Neosho
Osage
River
Council Grove
MISSOURI (ADMITTED 1821)
KY.
Arkansas
River
TAOS TRAIL
SANGRE DE CRISTO RANGE
Raton Pass
Cimarron
TIMBERS
O S A G E
Verdigris River
River
Chouteau's
Fort Gibson
White
TENN.
Taos
SANTA FE TRAIL
KIOWA
River
OZARK MTS.
CHEROKEE
River
Memphis
Canadian
River
ARKANSAS
Arkansas
River
Fort Smith
Santa Fe
STAKED PLAINS (LLANO ESTACADO)
TERRITORY
ARKANSAS (ADMITTED 1836)
1819
Coffee's
Fort Towson
Red River
Mississippi
MISSISSIPPI
100°
ADAMS-ONIS TREATY LINE OF 1819
COMANCHE
Valverde
Jornada del Muerto
APACHE
Brazos
Sabine
LOUISIANA
Natchitoches
River
Natchez
CROSS TIMBERS
Trinity
32°
Fort Jesup
Pearl
Nacogdoches
Colorado
River
River
Pecos River
El Paso
T E X A S
M E X I C O
River
New Orleans
San Antonio
Rio Grande
Nueces River
GULF OF MEXICO
Chihuahua

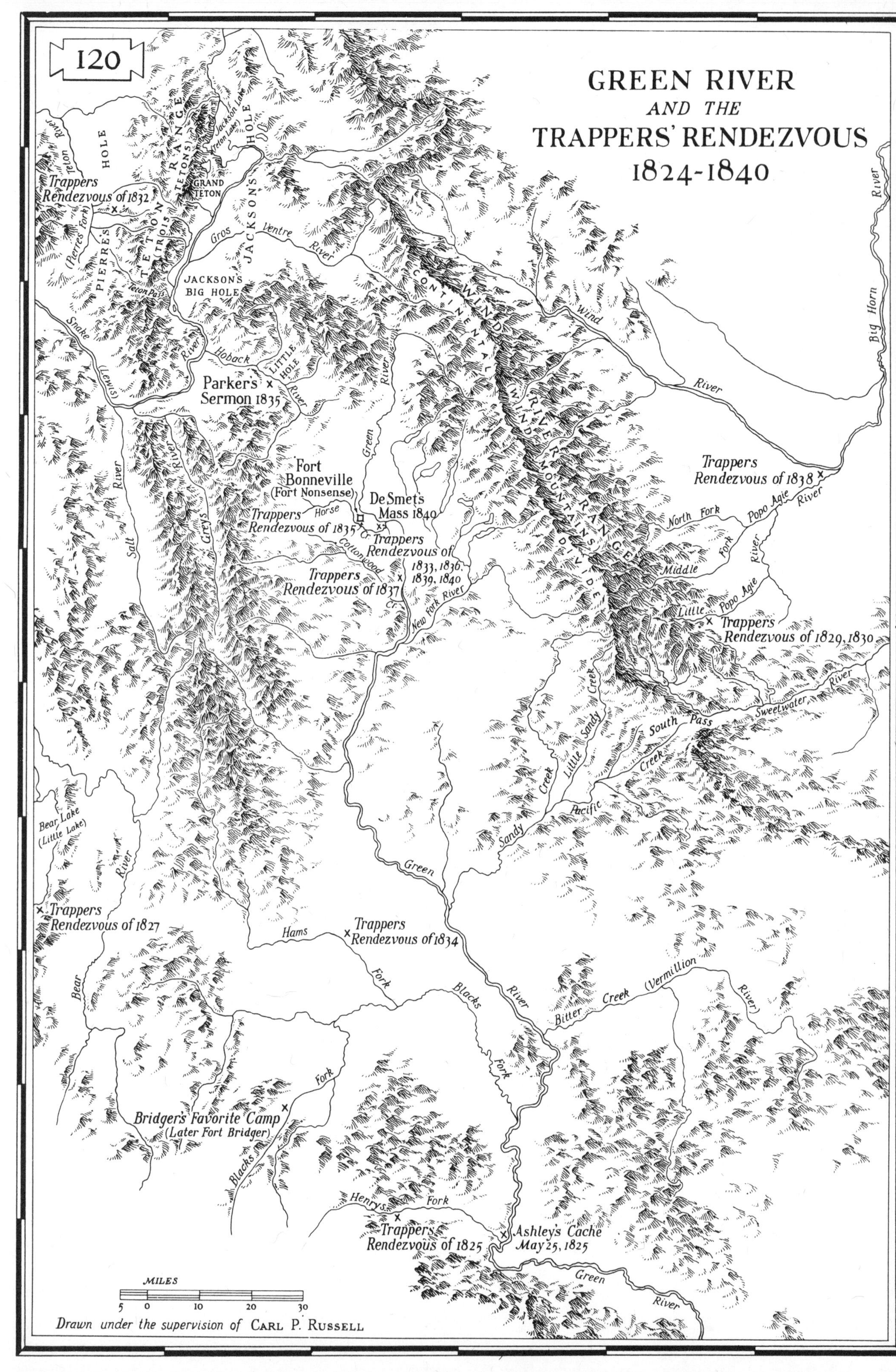

120
GREEN RIVER
AND THE
TRAPPERS' RENDEZVOUS
1824-1840
Trappers Rendezvous of 1832
Parker's Sermon 1835
Fort Bonneville (Fort Nonsense)
De Smet's Mass 1840
Trappers Rendezvous of 1835
Trappers Rendezvous of 1833, 1836, 1839, 1840
Trappers Rendezvous of 1837
Trappers Rendezvous of 1838
Trappers Rendezvous of 1829, 1830
Trappers Rendezvous of 1827
Trappers Rendezvous of 1834
Bridger's Favorite Camp (Later Fort Bridger)
Trappers Rendezvous of 1825
Ashley's Cache May 25, 1825
JACKSON'S BIG HOLE
GRAND TETON
Teton Pass
South Pass
MILES
5 0 10 20 30
Drawn under the supervision of Carl P. Russell

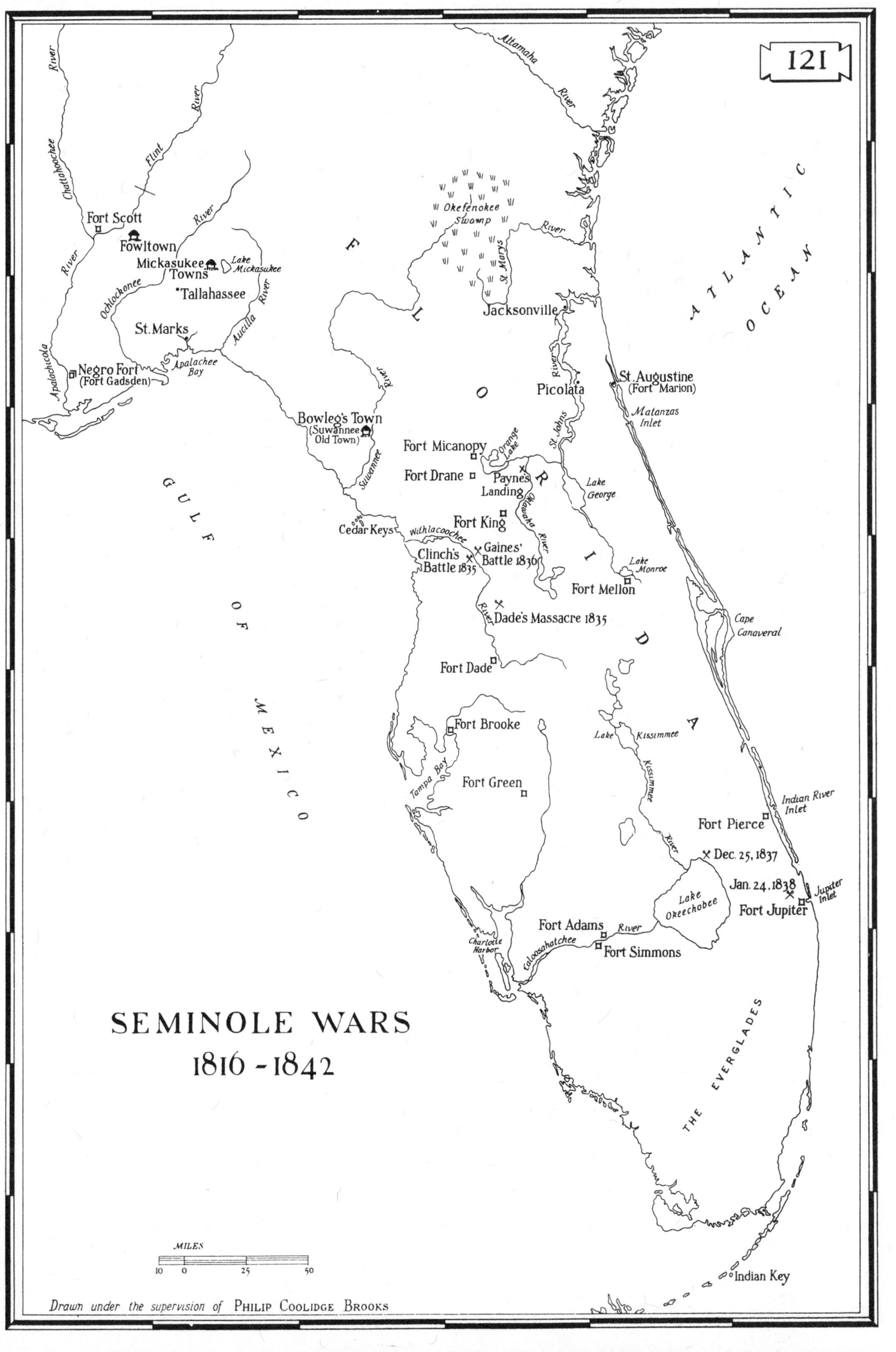
SEMINOLE WARS
1816 - 1842
Fort Scott
Fowltown
Mickasukee Towns
Lake Mickasukee
Tallahassee
St. Marks
Apalachee Bay
Negro Fort (Fort Gadsden)
Apalachicola
Chattahoochee River
Flint River
Ochlockonee River
Aucilla River
Altamaha River
Okefenokee Swamp
St. Marys River
Jacksonville
St. Augustine (Fort Marion)
Matanzas Inlet
Picolata
St. Johns River
ATLANTIC OCEAN
FLORIDA
Bowleg's Town (Suwannee Old Town)
Suwannee River
Fort Micanopy
Orange Lake
Fort Drane
Payne's Landing
Ocklawaha River
Lake George
Fort King
Cedar Keys
Withlacoochee River
Gaines' Battle 1836
Clinch's Battle 1835
Lake Monroe
Fort Mellon
Dade's Massacre 1835
Cape Canaveral
Fort Dade
GULF OF MEXICO
Fort Brooke
Tampa Bay
Fort Green
Lake Kissimmee
Kissimmee River
Indian River Inlet
Fort Pierce
Dec. 25, 1837
Jan. 24, 1838
Jupiter Inlet
Fort Jupiter
Lake Okeechobee
Fort Adams
Caloosahatchee River
Fort Simmons
Charlotte Harbor
THE EVERGLADES
Indian Key
MILES
10 0 25 50
Drawn under the supervision of PHILIP COOLIDGE BROOKS

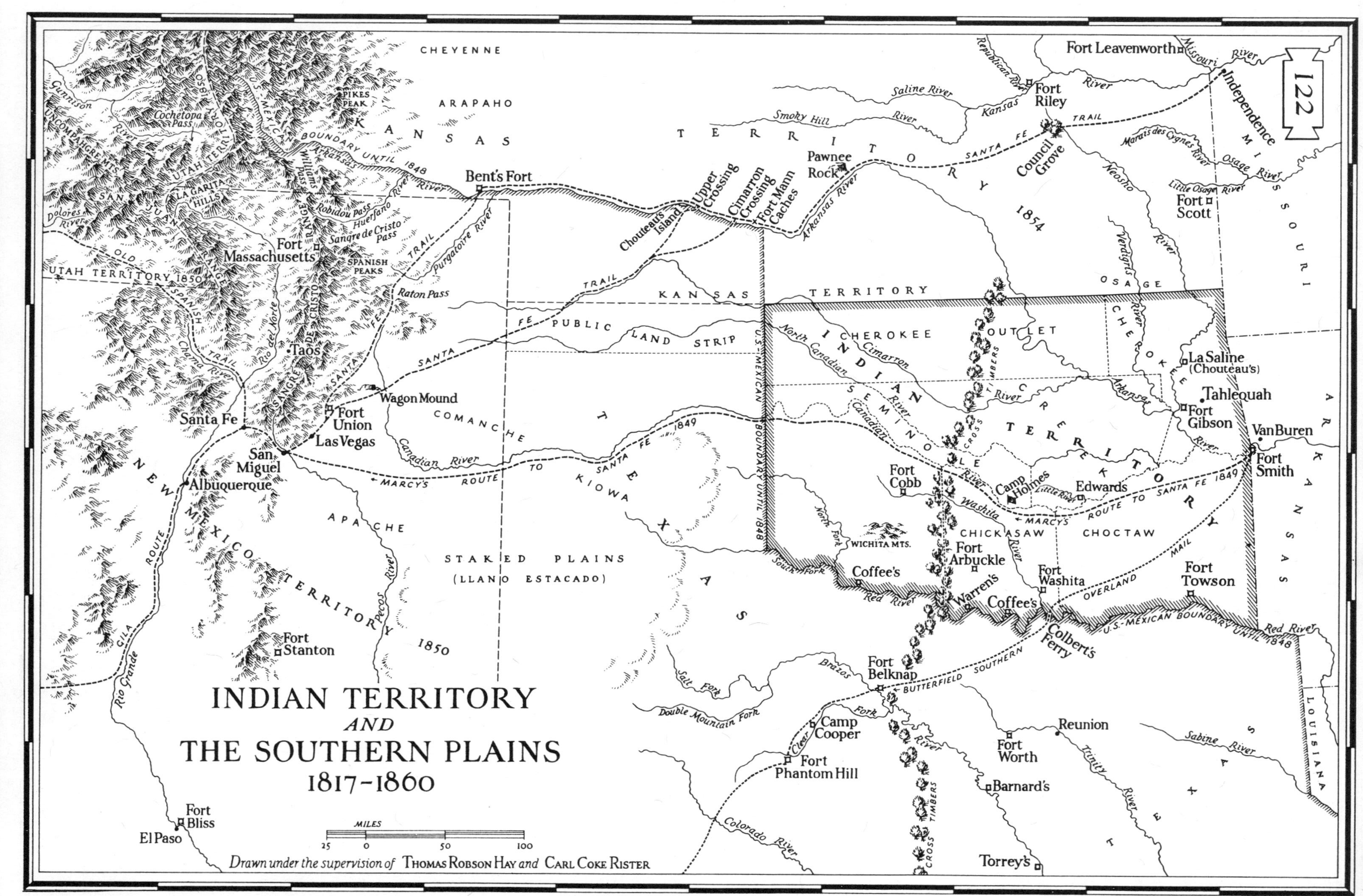

122
INDIAN TERRITORY AND THE SOUTHERN PLAINS 1817-1860
Drawn under the supervision of Thomas Robson Hay and Carl Coke Rister
MILES
25
0
50
100
CHEYENNE
ARAPAHO
KANSAS
KANSAS TERRITORY 1854
MISSOURI
ARKANSAS
LOUISIANA
TEXAS
NEW MEXICO TERRITORY 1850
UTAH TERRITORY 1850
INDIAN TERRITORY
CHEROKEE OUTLET
CHEROKEE
CREEK
SEMINOLE
CHICKASAW
CHOCTAW
OSAGE
COMANCHE
KIOWA
APACHE
PUBLIC LAND STRIP
STAKED PLAINS (LLANO ESTACADO)
U.S.-MEXICAN BOUNDARY UNTIL 1848
SANTA FE TRAIL
OLD SPANISH TRAIL
MARCY'S ROUTE TO SANTA FE 1849
BUTTERFIELD SOUTHERN OVERLAND MAIL
GILA ROUTE
CROSS TIMBERS
Fort Leavenworth
Independence
Fort Riley
Council Grove
Fort Scott
Pawnee Rock
Upper Crossing
Cimarron Crossing
Fort Mann
Caches
Chouteau's Island
Bent's Fort
PIKES PEAK
SPANISH PEAKS
Cochetopa Pass
Williams Pass
Robidou Pass
Huerfano
Sangre de Cristo Pass
Raton Pass
LA GARITA HILLS
SAN JUAN
SANGRE DE CRISTO RANGE
UNCOMPAHGRE MTS.
Fort Massachusetts
Taos
Wagon Mound
Fort Union
Las Vegas
Santa Fe
San Miguel
Albuquerque
Fort Stanton
Fort Bliss
El Paso
La Saline (Chouteau's)
Tahlequah
Fort Gibson
Van Buren
Fort Smith
Fort Cobb
Camp Holmes
Edwards
WICHITA MTS.
Fort Arbuckle
Coffee's
Warren's
Fort Washita
Fort Towson
Colbert's Ferry
Fort Belknap
Camp Cooper
Fort Phantom Hill
Fort Worth
Reunion
Barnard's
Torrey's
Missouri River
Kansas River
Republican River
Saline River
Smoky Hill River
Arkansas River
Neosho River
Marais des Cygnes River
Osage River
Little Osage River
Verdigris River
Purgatoire River
Gunnison River
Dolores River
Rio del Norte
Chama River
Rio Grande
Pecos River
Canadian River
North Canadian
Cimarron River
Washita
Little River
North Fork
South Fork
Red River
Salt Fork
Double Mountain Fork
Brazos
Clear Fork
Colorado River
Trinity River
Sabine River

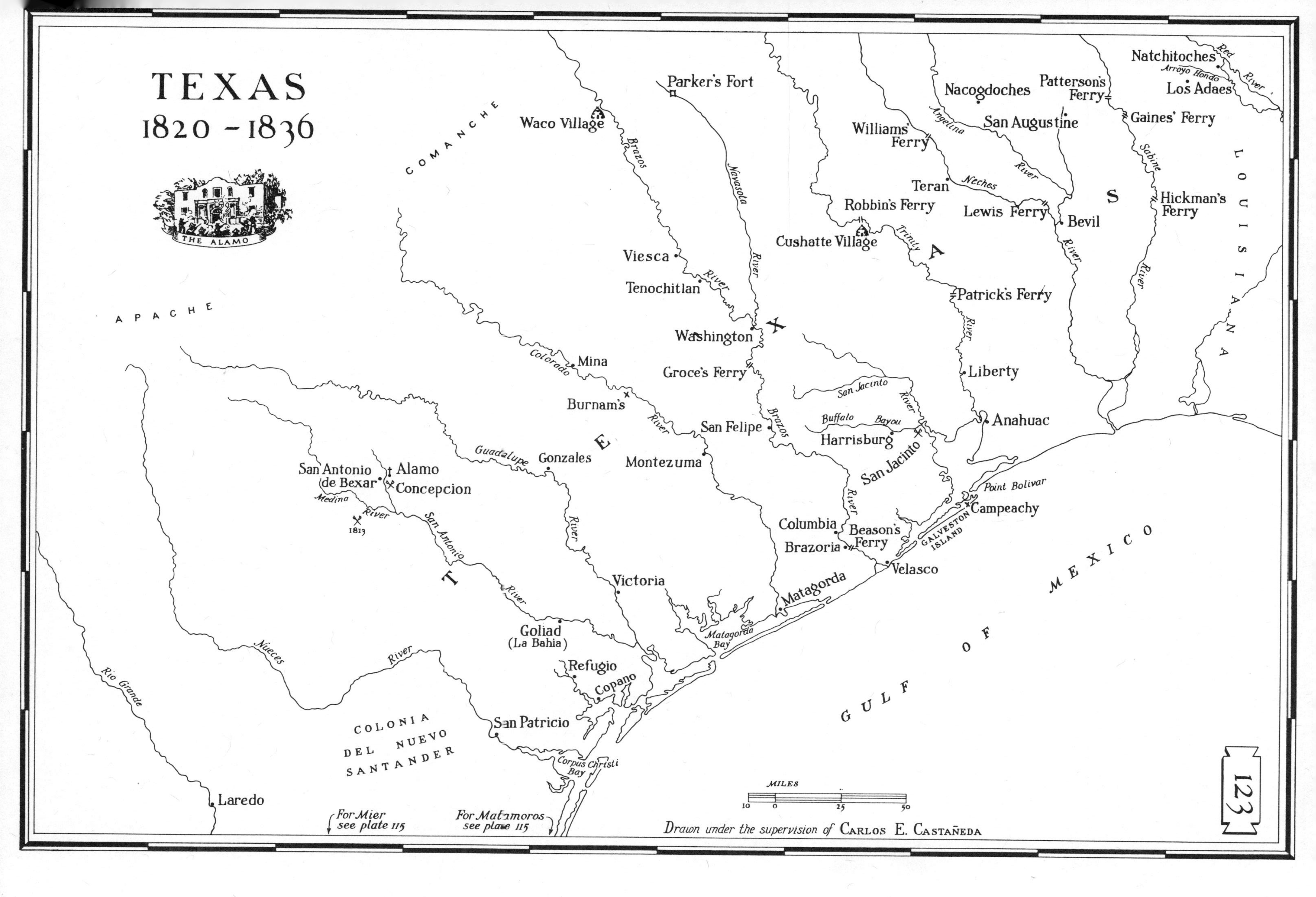
TEXAS
1820 - 1836
THE ALAMO
123
COMANCHE
APACHE
LOUISIANA
TEXAS
GULF OF MEXICO
COLONIA DEL NUEVO SANTANDER
Natchitoches
Red River
Arroyo Hondo
Los Adaes
Nacogdoches
Patterson's Ferry
Gaines' Ferry
San Augustine
Williams' Ferry
Angelina
Sabine
River
Hickman's Ferry
Teran
Neches
River
Robbin's Ferry
Lewis Ferry
Bevil
Cushatte Village
Trinity
River
Patrick's Ferry
River
Liberty
Anahuac
Parker's Fort
Waco Village
Brazos
Navasota
River
Viesca
Tenochitlan
River
Washington
Groce's Ferry
San Jacinto
River
Buffalo
Bayou
Harrisburg
San Jacinto
Brazos
San Felipe
Mina
Colorado
Burnam's
River
Montezuma
Gonzales
Guadalupe
River
San Antonio de Bexar
Alamo
Concepcion
Medina
River
1813
San Antonio
River
Victoria
Columbia
Beason's Ferry
Brazoria
River
Point Bolivar
Campeachy
GALVESTON ISLAND
Velasco
Matagorda
Matagorda Bay
Goliad
(La Bahia)
Refugio
Copano
San Patricio
Corpus Christi Bay
Nueces
River
Rio Grande
Laredo
For Mier see plate 115
For Matamoros see plate 115
MILES
10 0 25 50
Drawn under the supervision of CARLOS E. CASTAÑEDA

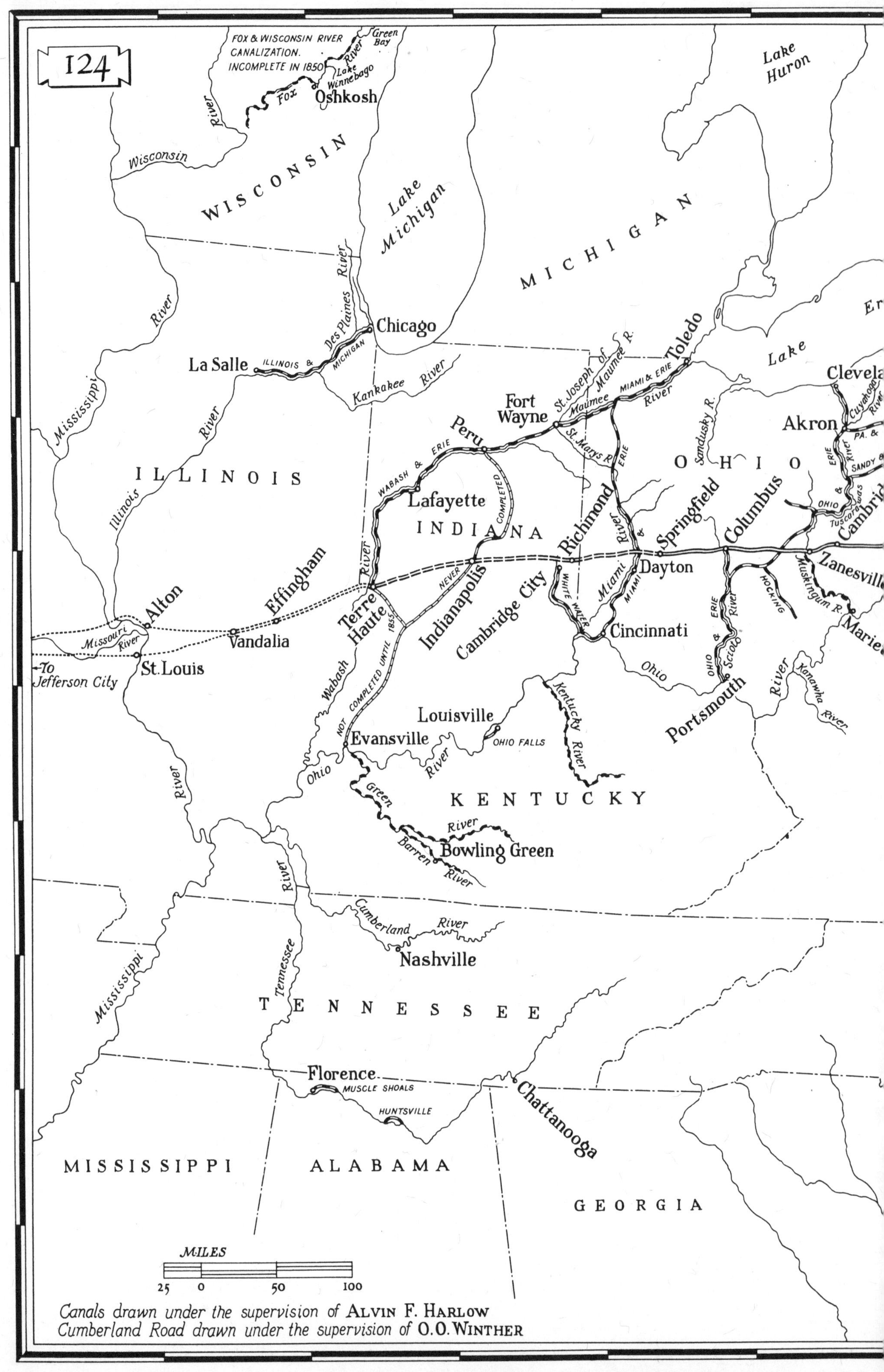
124
FOX & WISCONSIN RIVER CANALIZATION. INCOMPLETE IN 1850
Green Bay
Lake Winnebago
Oshkosh
Fox River
Wisconsin
WISCONSIN
Lake Michigan
Lake Huron
MICHIGAN
Chicago
Des Plaines River
La Salle
ILLINOIS & MICHIGAN
Kankakee River
Mississippi River
Illinois River
ILLINOIS
Fort Wayne
St. Joseph of Maumee R.
Maumee River
MIAMI & ERIE
Toledo
Lake Erie
Cleveland
Cuyahoga River
Akron
Peru
WABASH & ERIE
St. Marys R.
Sandusky R.
OHIO
Lafayette
INDIANA
COMPLETED
NEVER
Richmond
Springfield
Columbus
Tuscarawas
Cambridge
Zanesville
Muskingum R.
Dayton
Miami River
MIAMI
HOCKING
OHIO & ERIE
Scioto River
Alton
Missouri River
Vandalia
Effingham
Terre Haute
Indianapolis
Cambridge City
WHITE WATER
Cincinnati
St. Louis
To Jefferson City
Wabash
NOT COMPLETED UNTIL 1855
Ohio
Portsmouth
Kanawha River
Louisville
OHIO FALLS
Kentucky River
Evansville
Green River
KENTUCKY
Bowling Green
Barren River
Cumberland River
Nashville
Tennessee River
TENNESSEE
Florence
MUSCLE SHOALS
HUNTSVILLE
Chattanooga
MISSISSIPPI
ALABAMA
GEORGIA
MILES
25 0 50 100
Canals drawn under the supervision of ALVIN F. HARLOW
Cumberland Road drawn under the supervision of O.O. WINTHER

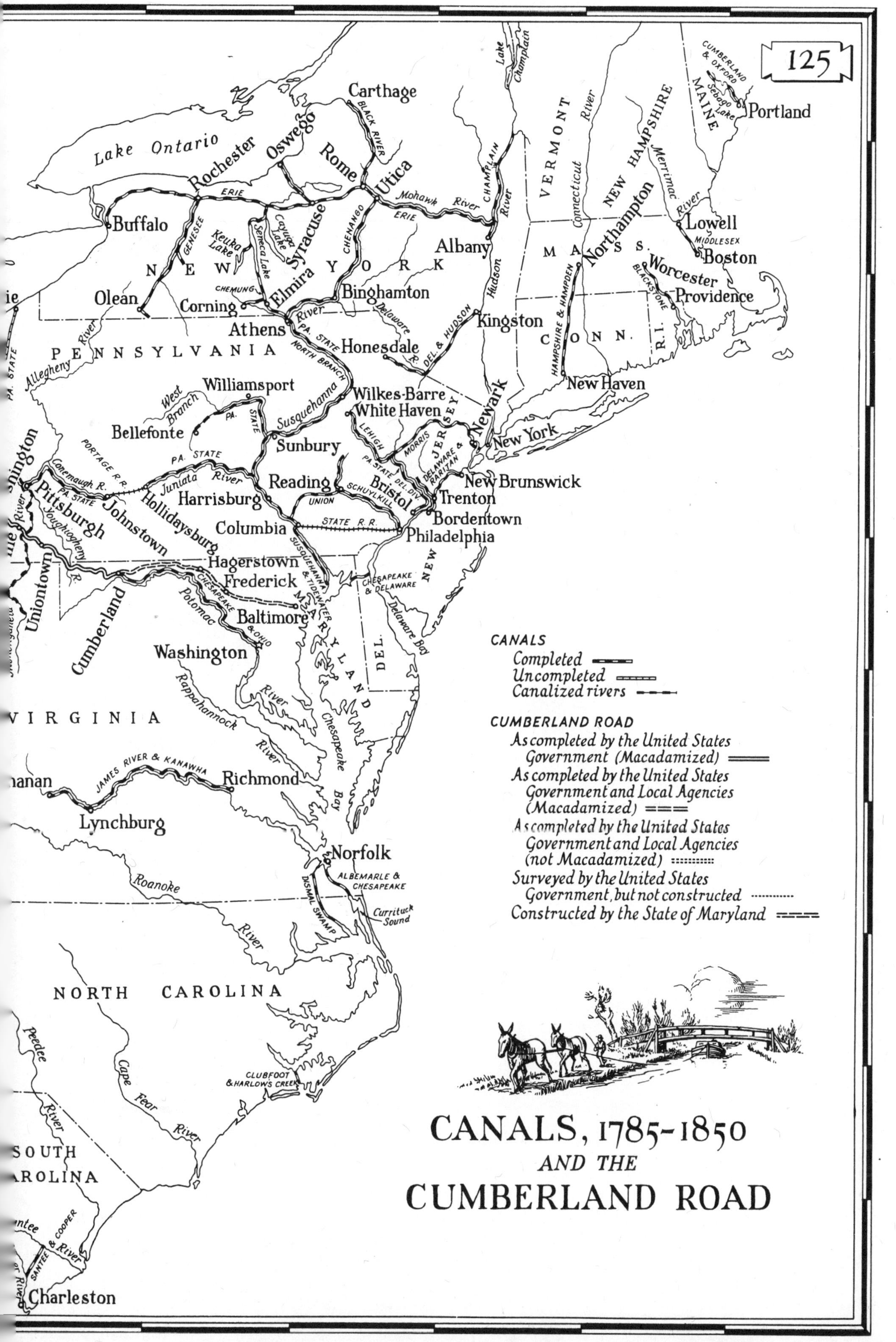

CANALS
Completed
Uncompleted
Canalized rivers
CUMBERLAND ROAD
As completed by the United States Government (Macadamized)
As completed by the United States Government and Local Agencies (Macadamized)
As completed by the United States Government and Local Agencies (not Macadamized)
Surveyed by the United States Government, but not constructed
Constructed by the State of Maryland
Lake Ontario
Lake Champlain
Carthage
BLACK RIVER
Rochester
Oswego
Rome
Utica
Buffalo
ERIE
Mohawk River
CHAMPLAIN
GENESEE
Keuka Lake
Seneca Lake
Cayuga Lake
Syracuse
CHENANGO
Albany
NEW YORK
Olean
Corning
CHEMUNG
Elmira
Binghamton
Athens
River
Delaware
Kingston
Honesdale
DEL. & HUDSON
PA. STATE
NORTH BRANCH
PENNSYLVANIA
Allegheny River
Williamsport
West Branch
Bellefonte
PA. STATE
Susquehanna
Wilkes-Barre
White Haven
LEHIGH
MORRIS
Sunbury
Reading
SCHUYLKILL
UNION
PORTAGE R.R.
PA. STATE
Juniata River
Conemaugh R.
Harrisburg
Pittsburgh
Johnstown
Hollidaysburg
Columbia
STATE R.R.
PA. STATE DEL. DIV.
Bristol
DELAWARE & RARITAN
NEW JERSEY
Newark
New York
New Brunswick
Trenton
Bordentown
Philadelphia
Youghiogheny R.
Uniontown
Hagerstown
Frederick
SUSQUEHANNA & TIDEWATER
CHESAPEAKE & DELAWARE
Cumberland
CHESAPEAKE & OHIO
Potomac
Baltimore
MARYLAND
Washington
DEL.
Delaware Bay
Rappahannock River
River
Chesapeake Bay
VIRGINIA
JAMES RIVER & KANAWHA
Richmond
Lynchburg
Norfolk
ALBEMARLE & CHESAPEAKE
DISMAL SWAMP
Currituck Sound
Roanoke River
NORTH CAROLINA
Peedee River
Cape Fear River
CLUBFOOT & HARLOWS CREEK
SOUTH CAROLINA
SANTEE & COOPER
Santee River
Charleston
VERMONT
Connecticut River
NEW HAMPSHIRE
Merrimac River
MAINE
CUMBERLAND & OXFORD
Sebago Lake
Portland
Lowell
MIDDLESEX
Boston
MASS.
Northampton
HAMPSHIRE & HAMPDEN
Worcester
BLACKSTONE
Providence
R.I.
CONN.
New Haven
Hudson River

CANALS, 1785-1850
AND THE
CUMBERLAND ROAD

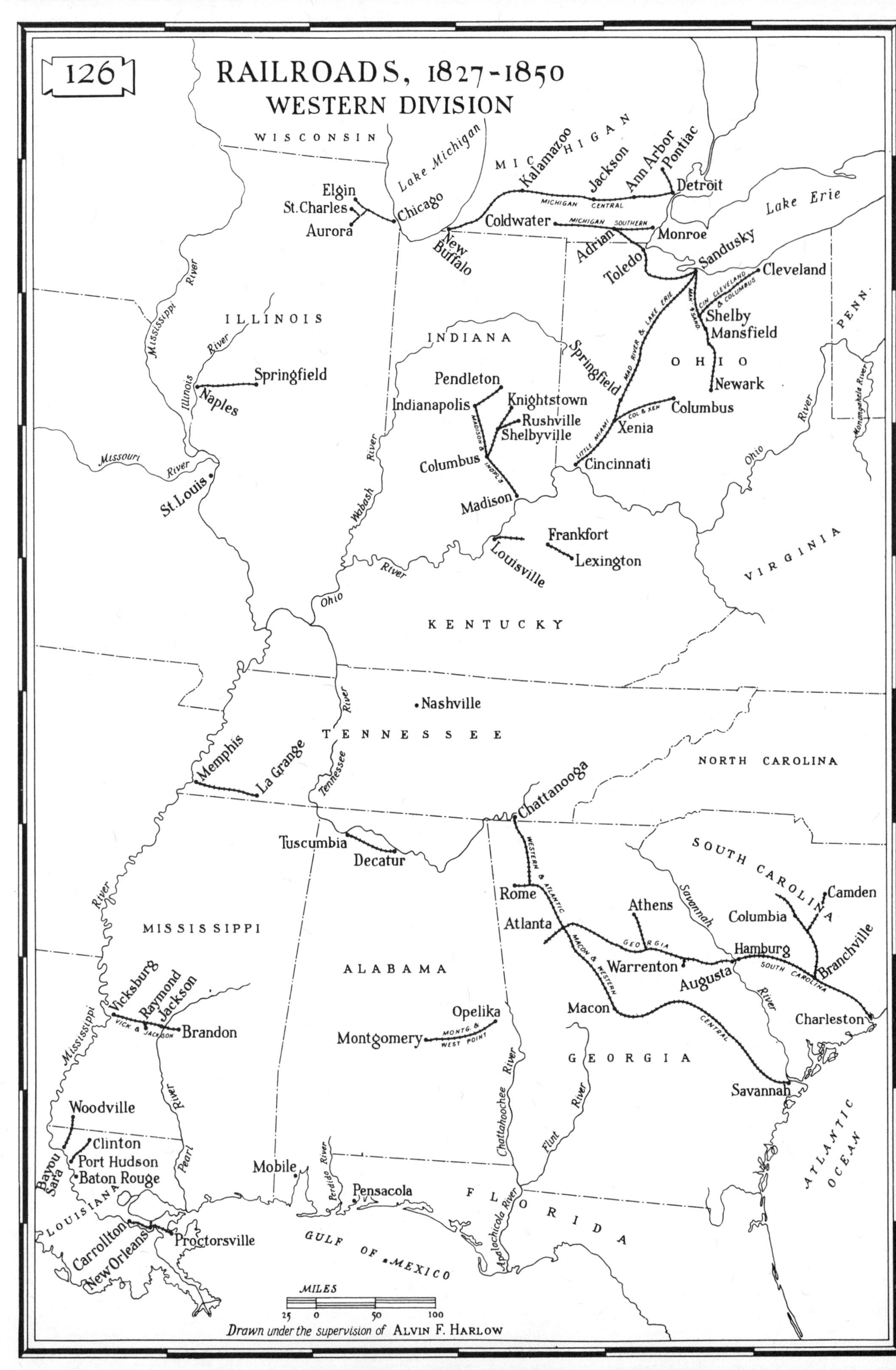
126
RAILROADS, 1827-1850
WESTERN DIVISION
WISCONSIN
MICHIGAN
Lake Michigan
Lake Erie
Elgin
St. Charles
Aurora
Chicago
New Buffalo
Kalamazoo
Jackson
Ann Arbor
Pontiac
Detroit
MICHIGAN CENTRAL
Coldwater
MICHIGAN SOUTHERN
Monroe
Adrian
Toledo
Sandusky
Cleveland
CIN. CLEVELAND & COLUMBUS
MAN. & SAND.
Shelby
Mansfield
PENN.
ILLINOIS
Mississippi River
Illinois River
Springfield
Naples
INDIANA
Pendleton
Indianapolis
Knightstown
Rushville
Shelbyville
MADISON & INDPLS
Columbus
Madison
Wabash River
Springfield
MAD RIVER & LAKE ERIE
OHIO
Newark
Columbus
COL & XEN
Xenia
LITTLE MIAMI
Cincinnati
Ohio River
Monongahela River
Missouri River
St. Louis
Frankfort
Lexington
Louisville
Ohio River
VIRGINIA
KENTUCKY
Nashville
TENNESSEE
Tennessee River
Memphis
La Grange
NORTH CAROLINA
Chattanooga
Tuscumbia
Decatur
WESTERN & ATLANTIC
Rome
SOUTH CAROLINA
Camden
Athens
Savannah
Columbia
Atlanta
GEORGIA
Hamburg
Branchville
Warrenton
Augusta
SOUTH CAROLINA
MACON & WESTERN
Macon
CENTRAL
Charleston
River
Savannah
MISSISSIPPI
Mississippi River
ALABAMA
Vicksburg
Raymond
Jackson
VICK & JACKSON
Brandon
Opelika
Montgomery
MONTG. & WEST POINT
GEORGIA
Chattahoochee River
Flint River
Pearl River
Woodville
Clinton
Port Hudson
Bayou Sara
Baton Rouge
Mobile
Perdido River
Pensacola
FLORIDA
Apalachicola River
ATLANTIC OCEAN
LOUISIANA
Carrollton
New Orleans
Proctorsville
GULF OF MEXICO
MILES
25 0 50 100
Drawn under the supervision of ALVIN F. HARLOW

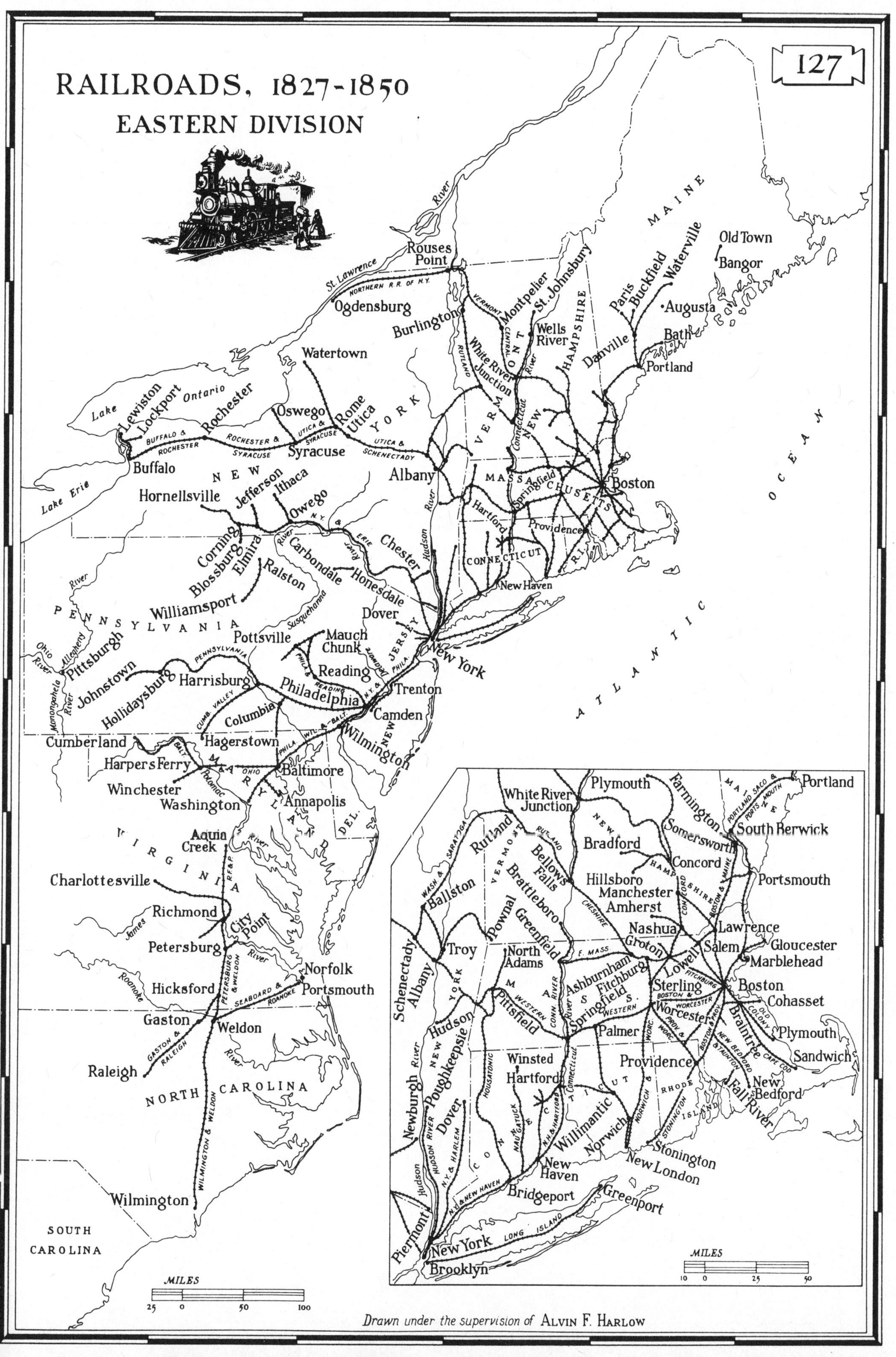
127
RAILROADS, 1827-1850
EASTERN DIVISION
Rouses Point
St. Lawrence
River
Northern R.R. of N.Y.
Ogdensburg
Burlington
Montpelier
St. Johnsbury
Wells River
Vermont Central
Rutland
White River Junction
Old Town
Bangor
Waterville
Buckfield
Paris
Augusta
Bath
Danville
Portland
Maine
New Hampshire
Watertown
Lake Ontario
Lewiston
Lockport
Rochester
Buffalo & Rochester
Rochester & Syracuse
Utica & Syracuse
Utica & Schenectady
Oswego
Rome
Utica
Syracuse
New York
Buffalo
Albany
Lake Erie
Hornellsville
Jefferson
Ithaca
Owego
N.Y. & Erie
Chester
Hudson River
Vermont
Massachusetts
Springfield
Boston
Hartford
Providence
Connecticut
R.I.
New Haven
Ocean
Atlantic
Corning
Blossburg
Elmira
Ralston
Carbondale
Honesdale
Williamsport
Pennsylvania
Susquehanna
Dover
Pottsville
Mauch Chunk
Ohio River
Allegheny
Pittsburgh
Johnstown
Hollidaysburg
Harrisburg
Pennsylvania
Reading
Phila. & Reading
Delaware
New Jersey
New York
Trenton
Phila.
N.Y. & Phila.
Philadelphia
Camden
Monongahela River
Cumb. Valley
Columbia
Wil. & Balt.
Wilmington
Cumberland
Hagerstown
Phila.
Balt. & Ohio
B. & O.
Harpers Ferry
Baltimore
Winchester
Potomac
Maryland
Annapolis
Washington
Del.
Aquia Creek
Virginia
R.F. & P.
Charlottesville
Richmond
James
City Point
Petersburg
Petersburg & Weldon
Norfolk
Portsmouth
Seaboard & Roanoke
Roanoke
Hicksford
Gaston
Weldon
Gaston & Raleigh
Raleigh
North Carolina
Wilmington & Weldon
Wilmington
South Carolina
Miles
25 0 50 100
Plymouth
White River Junction
Farmington
Portland
Portland, Saco & Portsmouth
Maine
Rutland
Vermont
New Hampshire
South Berwick
Somersworth
Bellows Falls
Bradford
Wash. & Saratoga
Brattleboro
Concord
Ballston
Hillsboro
Manchester
Portsmouth
Cheshire
Amherst
Boston & Maine
Pownal
Greenfield
Nashua
Lawrence
Troy
Groton
Lowell
Salem
Gloucester
North Adams
Fitchburg
Marblehead
Schenectady
Albany
Ashburnham
Sterling
Boston
Cohasset
Massachusetts
Western
Conn. River
Springfield
Boston & Worcester
Worcester
Hudson
Pittsfield
Palmer
Braintree
Old Colony
Plymouth
Sandwich
Cape Cod
New Bedford & Taunton
Winsted
Providence
New Bedford
Hartford
Housatonic
Rhode Island
Fall River
Newburgh
Poughkeepsie
Hudson River
Dover
N.Y. & Harlem
Naugatuck
N.H. & Hartford
Willimantic
Norwich
Norwich & Worc.
Stonington
Connecticut
New Haven
New London
Bridgeport
N.Y. & New Haven
Greenport
Long Island
Piermont
New York
Brooklyn
Miles
10 0 25 50
Drawn under the supervision of Alvin F. Harlow

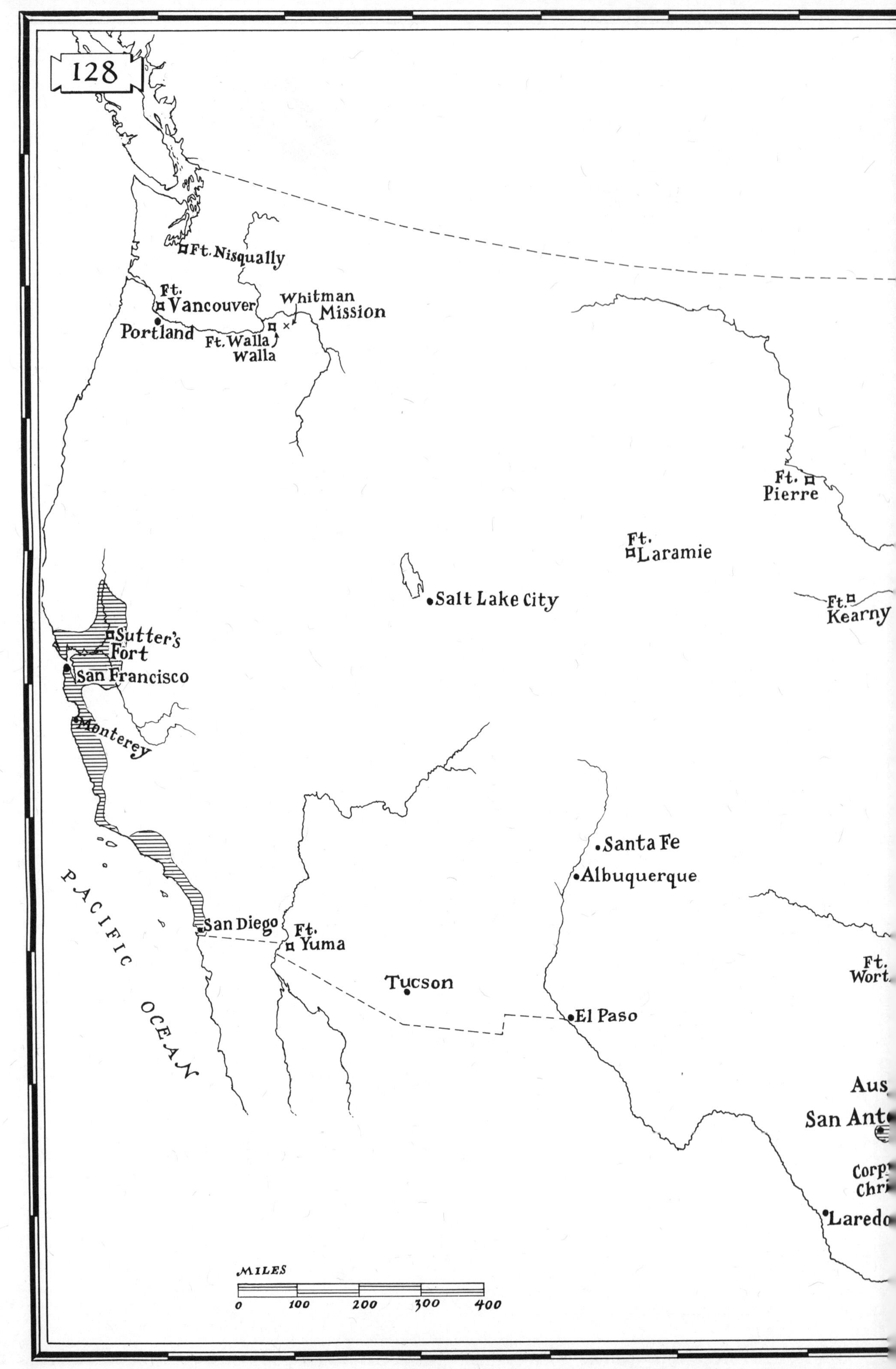
128
Ft. Nisqually
Ft. Vancouver
Whitman Mission
Portland
Ft. Walla Walla
Ft. Pierre
Ft. Laramie
Salt Lake City
Ft. Kearny
Sutter's Fort
San Francisco
Monterey
Santa Fe
Albuquerque
PACIFIC OCEAN
San Diego
Ft. Yuma
Tucson
El Paso
MILES
0
100
200
300
400

SETTLED AREAS 1850

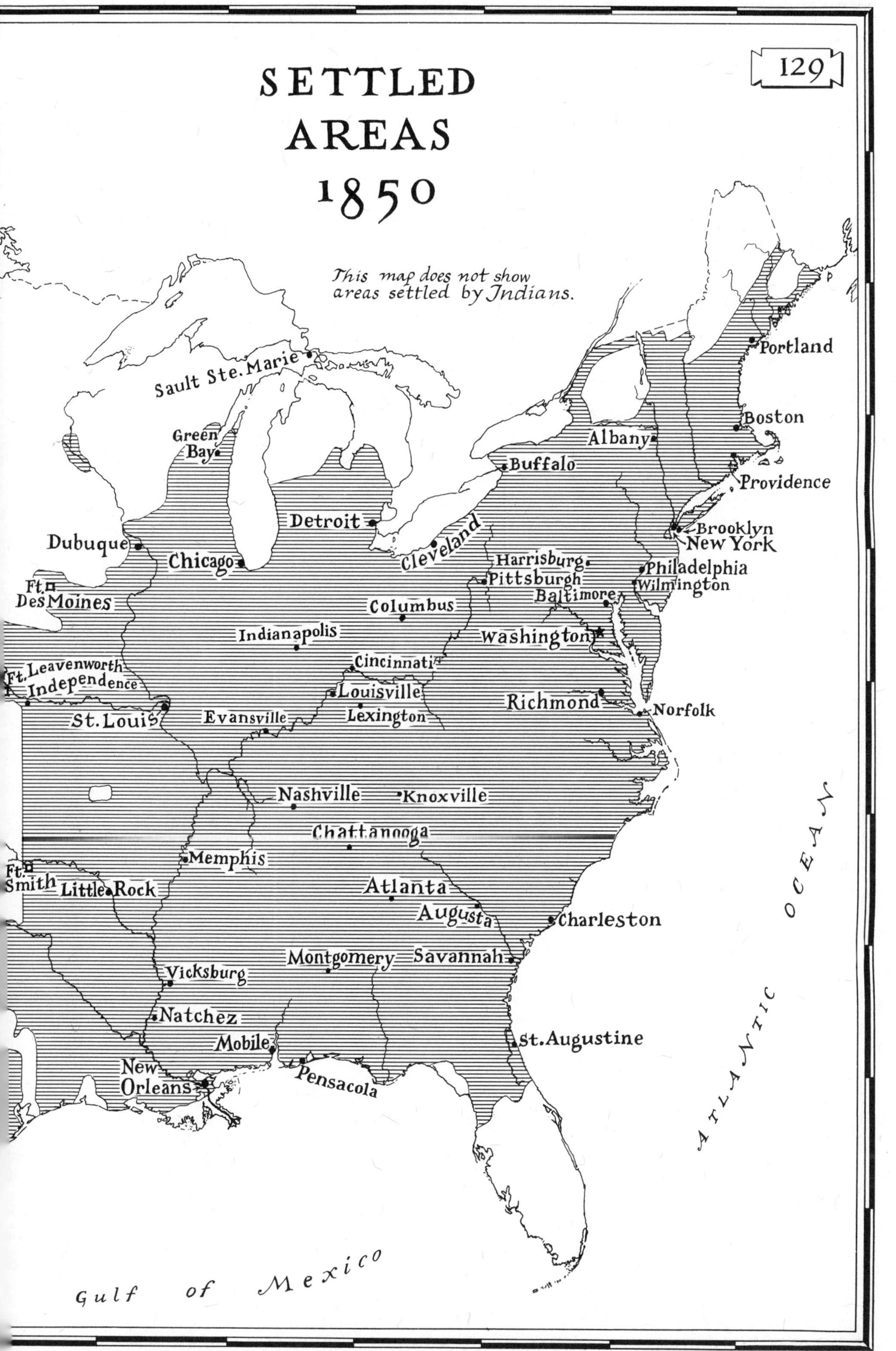
This map does not show areas settled by Indians.
Sault Ste. Marie
Green Bay
Portland
Boston
Albany
Buffalo
Providence
Detroit
Brooklyn
New York
Dubuque
Chicago
Cleveland
Harrisburg
Pittsburgh
Philadelphia
Wilmington
Ft. Des Moines
Baltimore
Columbus
Indianapolis
Washington
Cincinnati
Ft. Leavenworth
Independence
Louisville
Richmond
Norfolk
St. Louis
Evansville
Lexington
Nashville
Knoxville
Chattanooga
Memphis
Ft. Smith
Little Rock
Atlanta
Augusta
Charleston
Montgomery
Savannah
Vicksburg
Natchez
Mobile
St. Augustine
New Orleans
Pensacola
ATLANTIC OCEAN
Gulf of Mexico

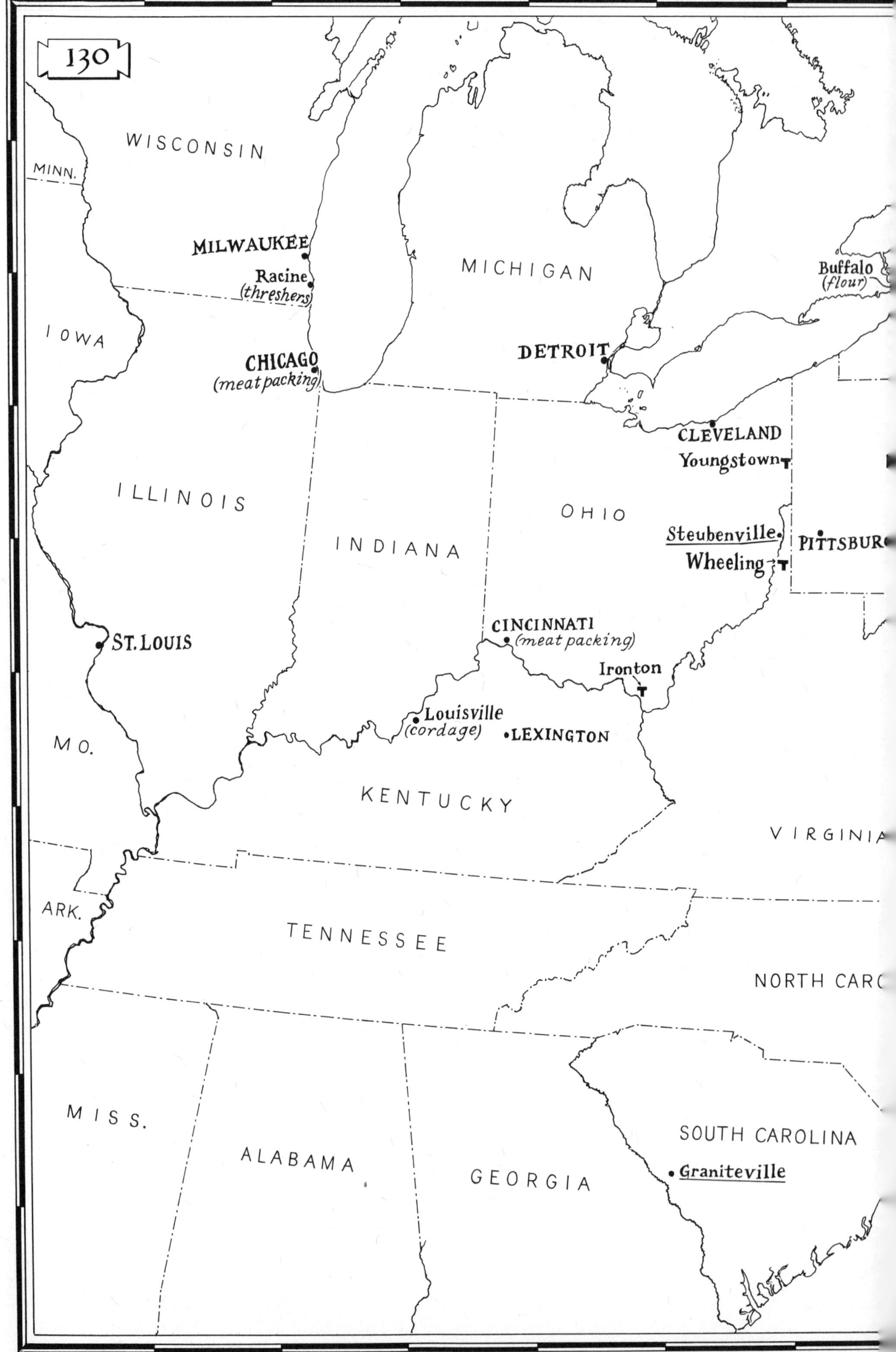
130
WISCONSIN
MINN.
MILWAUKEE
Racine
(threshers)
MICHIGAN
Buffalo
(flour)
IOWA
DETROIT
CHICAGO
(meat packing)
CLEVELAND
Youngstown
ILLINOIS
OHIO
INDIANA
Steubenville
Wheeling
PITTSBUR
CINCINNATI
(meat packing)
ST. LOUIS
Ironton
Louisville
(cordage)
LEXINGTON
MO.
KENTUCKY
VIRGINIA
ARK.
TENNESSEE
NORTH CARO
MISS.
SOUTH CAROLINA
ALABAMA
GEORGIA
Graniteville

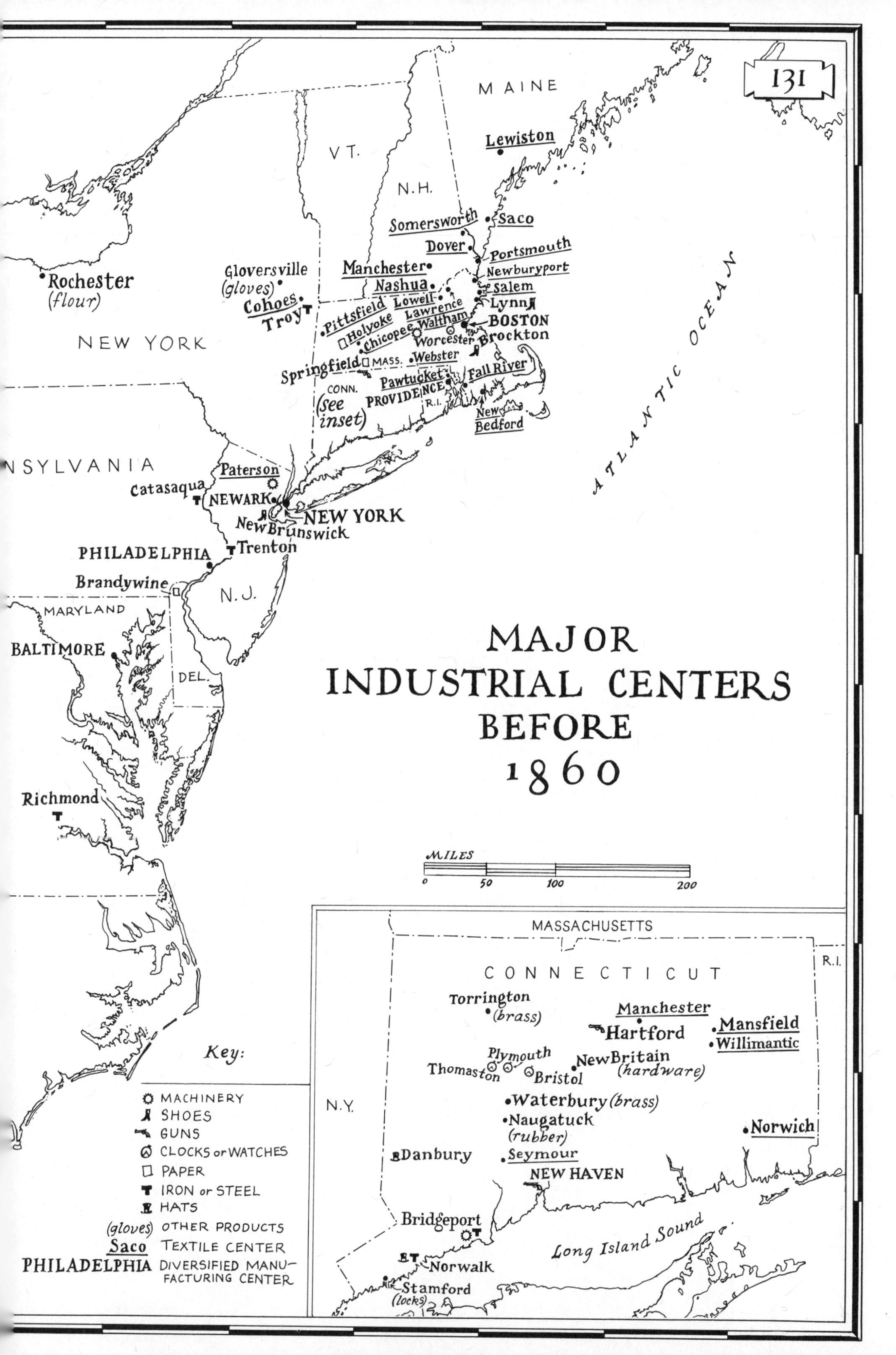
MAJOR INDUSTRIAL CENTERS BEFORE 1860
MAINE
Lewiston
VT.
N.H.
Somersworth
Saco
Dover
Portsmouth
Newburyport
Salem
Lynn
BOSTON
Brockton
Manchester
Nashua
Lowell
Lawrence
Waltham
Worcester
Webster
Pittsfield
Holyoke
Chicopee
Springfield
MASS.
Pawtucket
PROVIDENCE
R.I.
Fall River
New Bedford
CONN.
(see inset)
Gloversville
(gloves)
Cohoes
Troy
Rochester
(flour)
NEW YORK
ATLANTIC OCEAN
NSYLVANIA
Paterson
Catasaqua
NEWARK
NEW YORK
New Brunswick
Trenton
PHILADELPHIA
Brandywine
N.J.
MARYLAND
BALTIMORE
DEL.
Richmond
MILES
0
50
100
200
MASSACHUSETTS
CONNECTICUT
R.I.
Torrington
(brass)
Manchester
Hartford
Mansfield
Willimantic
Plymouth
Thomaston
Bristol
New Britain
(hardware)
Waterbury (brass)
Naugatuck
(rubber)
N.Y.
Norwich
Danbury
Seymour
NEW HAVEN
Bridgeport
Long Island Sound
Norwalk
Stamford
(locks)
Key:
MACHINERY
SHOES
GUNS
CLOCKS or WATCHES
PAPER
IRON or STEEL
HATS
(gloves) OTHER PRODUCTS
Saco TEXTILE CENTER
PHILADELPHIA DIVERSIFIED MANUFACTURING CENTER

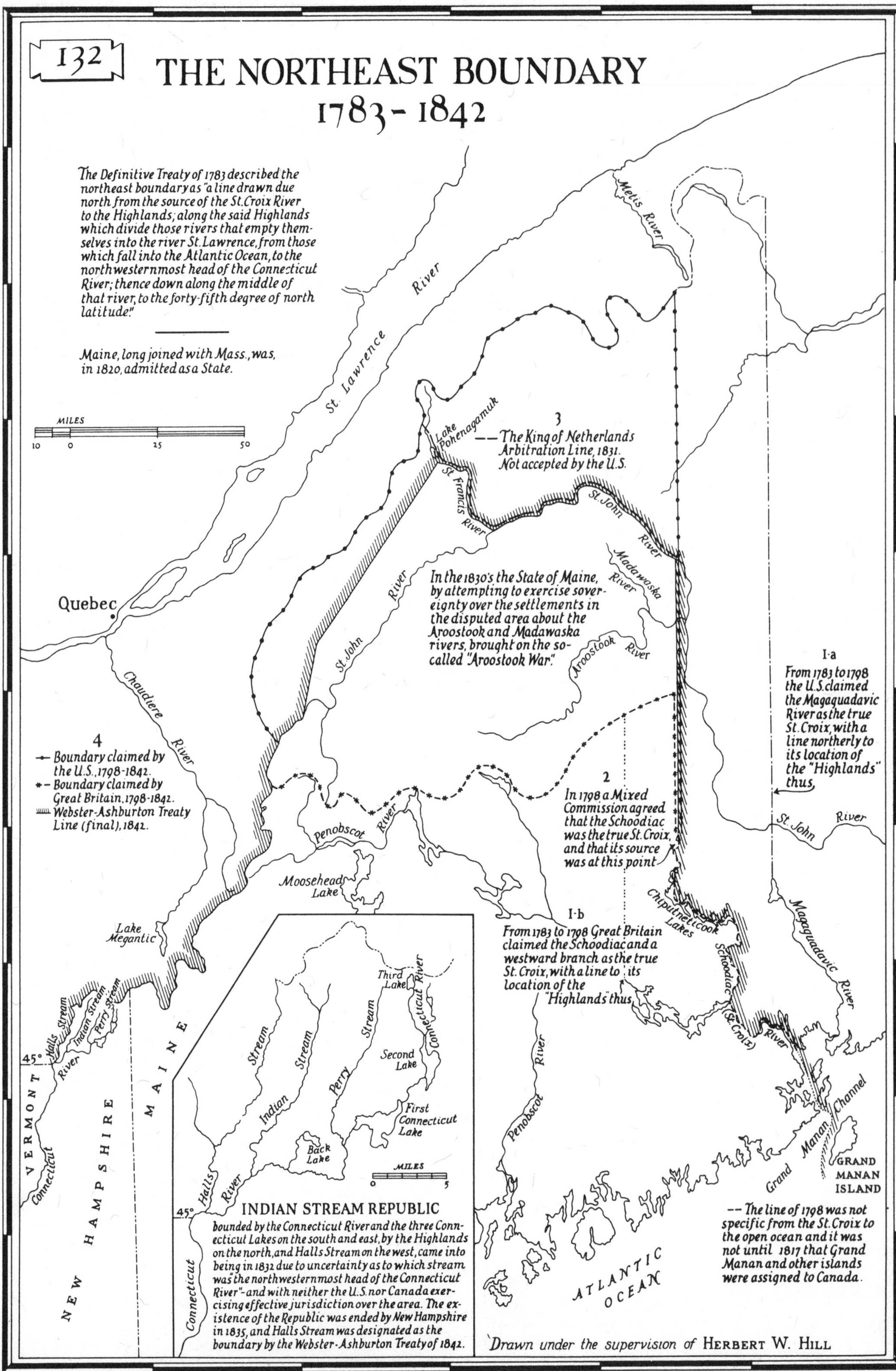
132
THE NORTHEAST BOUNDARY
1783-1842
The Definitive Treaty of 1783 described the northeast boundary as "a line drawn due north from the source of the St. Croix River to the Highlands; along the said Highlands which divide those rivers that empty themselves into the river St. Lawrence, from those which fall into the Atlantic Ocean, to the northwesternmost head of the Connecticut River; thence down along the middle of that river, to the forty-fifth degree of north latitude."
Maine, long joined with Mass., was, in 1820, admitted as a State.
MILES
10 0 25 50
St. Lawrence River
Metis River
Lake Pohenagamuk
3
The King of Netherlands Arbitration Line, 1831. Not accepted by the U.S.
St. Francis River
St. John River
Madawaska River
Quebec
In the 1830's the State of Maine, by attempting to exercise sovereignty over the settlements in the disputed area about the Aroostook and Madawaska rivers, brought on the so-called "Aroostook War."
Aroostook River
Chaudiere River
I-a
From 1783 to 1798 the U.S. claimed the Magaguadavic River as the true St. Croix, with a line northerly to its location of the "Highlands" thus.
4
Boundary claimed by the U.S., 1798-1842.
Boundary claimed by Great Britain, 1798-1842.
Webster-Ashburton Treaty Line (final), 1842.
2
In 1798 a Mixed Commission agreed that the Schoodiac was the true St. Croix, and that its source was at this point
Penobscot River
Moosehead Lake
I-b
From 1783 to 1798 Great Britain claimed the Schoodiac and a westward branch as the true St. Croix, with a line to its location of the "Highlands" thus.
Chiputneticook Lakes
Schoodiac (St. Croix) River
Magaguadavic River
Lake Megantic
Halls Stream
Indian Stream
Perry Stream
45°
River
VERMONT
Connecticut
NEW HAMPSHIRE
MAINE
Third Lake
Connecticut River
Stream
Indian Stream
Perry Stream
Second Lake
First Connecticut Lake
Back Lake
MILES
0 5
Halls River
45°
INDIAN STREAM REPUBLIC
bounded by the Connecticut River and the three Connecticut Lakes on the south and east, by the Highlands on the north, and Halls Stream on the west, came into being in 1832 due to uncertainty as to which stream was the northwesternmost head of the Connecticut River"-and with neither the U.S. nor Canada exercising effective jurisdiction over the area. The existence of the Republic was ended by New Hampshire in 1835, and Halls Stream was designated as the boundary by the Webster-Ashburton Treaty of 1842.
Connecticut
Penobscot River
ATLANTIC OCEAN
Grand Manan Channel
GRAND MANAN ISLAND
-- The line of 1798 was not specific from the St. Croix to the open ocean and it was not until 1817 that Grand Manan and other islands were assigned to Canada.
Drawn under the supervision of HERBERT W. HILL

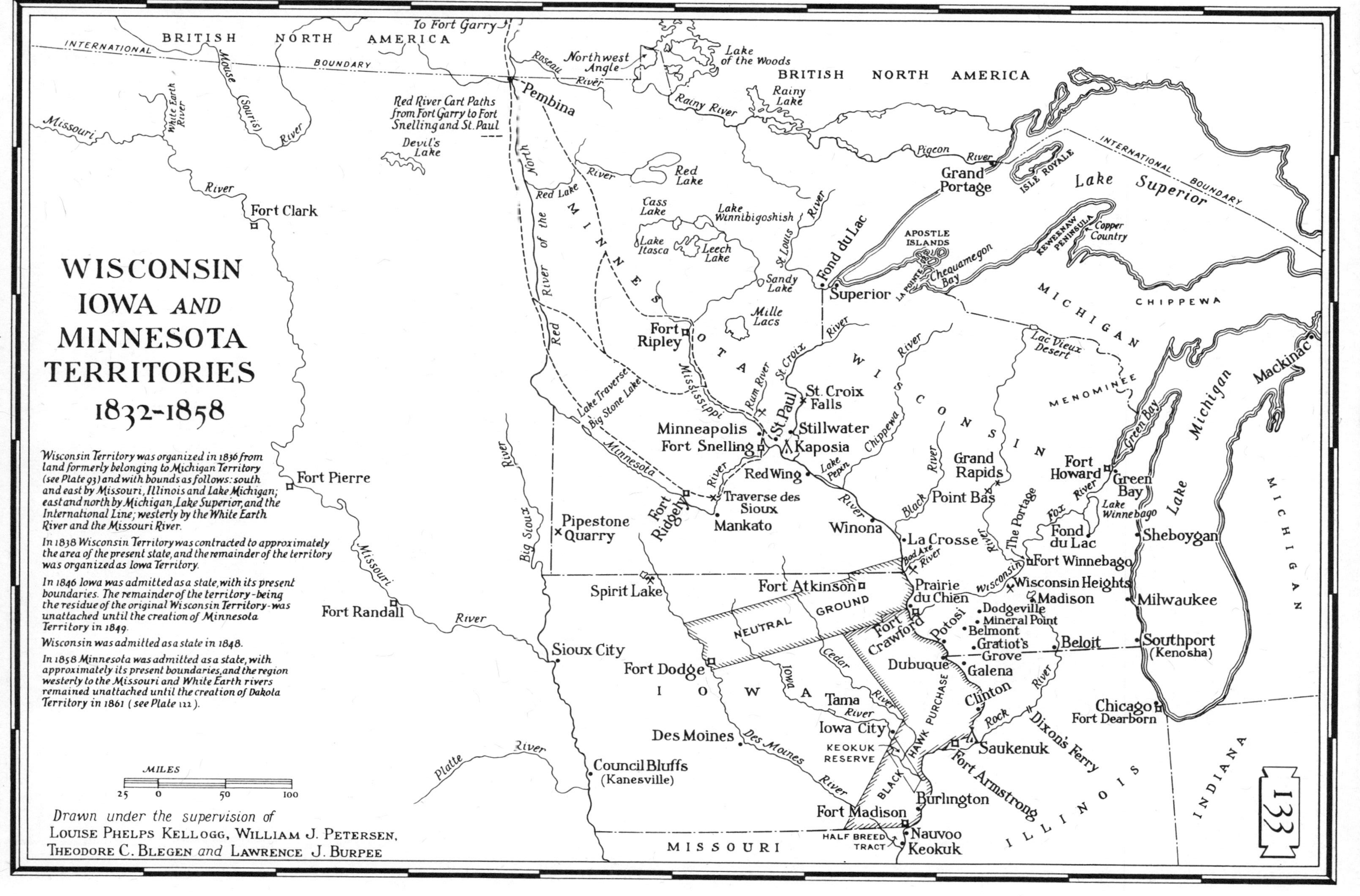
133
WISCONSIN
IOWA AND
MINNESOTA
TERRITORIES
1832-1858
Wisconsin Territory was organized in 1836 from land formerly belonging to Michigan Territory (see Plate 93) and with bounds as follows: south and east by Missouri, Illinois and Lake Michigan; east and north by Michigan, Lake Superior, and the International Line; westerly by the White Earth River and the Missouri River.
In 1838 Wisconsin Territory was contracted to approximately the area of the present state, and the remainder of the territory was organized as Iowa Territory.
In 1846 Iowa was admitted as a state, with its present boundaries. The remainder of the territory - being the residue of the original Wisconsin Territory - was unattached until the creation of Minnesota Territory in 1849.
Wisconsin was admitted as a state in 1848.
In 1858 Minnesota was admitted as a state, with approximately its present boundaries, and the region westerly to the Missouri and White Earth rivers remained unattached until the creation of Dakota Territory in 1861 (see Plate 122).
MILES
25 0 50 100
Drawn under the supervision of
Louise Phelps Kellogg, William J. Petersen,
Theodore C. Blegen and Lawrence J. Burpee
BRITISH NORTH AMERICA
INTERNATIONAL BOUNDARY
To Fort Garry
Mouse (Souris) River
White Earth River
Missouri
River
Fort Clark
Red River Cart Paths from Fort Garry to Fort Snelling and St. Paul
Devil's Lake
Pembina
Roseau River
Northwest Angle
Lake of the Woods
Rainy River
Rainy Lake
Pigeon River
Grand Portage
ISLE ROYALE
Lake Superior
KEWEENAW PENINSULA
Copper Country
APOSTLE ISLANDS
LA POINTE
Chequamegon Bay
CHIPPEWA
Fond du Lac
Superior
St. Louis River
Sandy Lake
Red Lake
Cass Lake
Lake Winnibigoshish
Lake Itasca
Leech Lake
Mille Lacs
North Red River of the
Red Lake River
MINNESOTA
Fort Ripley
Mississippi
Rum River
St. Croix River
St. Croix Falls
St. Paul
Stillwater
Kaposia
Minneapolis
Fort Snelling
Lake Traverse
Big Stone Lake
Minnesota River
Red Wing
Lake Pepin
Traverse des Sioux
Fort Ridgely
Mankato
Pipestone Quarry
Big Sioux River
Fort Pierre
Fort Randall
Missouri River
WISCONSIN
Chippewa River
Black River
Grand Rapids
Point Bas
Winona
La Crosse
Bad Axe River
The Portage
Wisconsin River
Fox River
MICHIGAN
Lac Vieux Desert
MENOMINEE
Fort Howard
Green Bay
Lake Winnebago
Fond du Lac
Fort Winnebago
Wisconsin Heights
Madison
Sheboygan
Milwaukee
Southport (Kenosha)
Lake Michigan
Mackinac
Prairie du Chien
Fort Crawford
Potosi
Dodgeville
Mineral Point
Belmont
Gratiot's Grove
Galena
Beloit
Dubuque
Spirit Lake
Fort Atkinson
NEUTRAL GROUND
Sioux City
Fort Dodge
IOWA
Iowa River
Cedar River
Tama
Iowa City
KEOKUK RESERVE
Des Moines
Des Moines River
HAWK PURCHASE
BLACK
Clinton
Rock River
Dixon's Ferry
Saukenuk
Fort Armstrong
Burlington
Fort Madison
HALF BREED TRACT
Nauvoo
Keokuk
Council Bluffs (Kanesville)
Platte River
MISSOURI
ILLINOIS
INDIANA
Chicago
Fort Dearborn

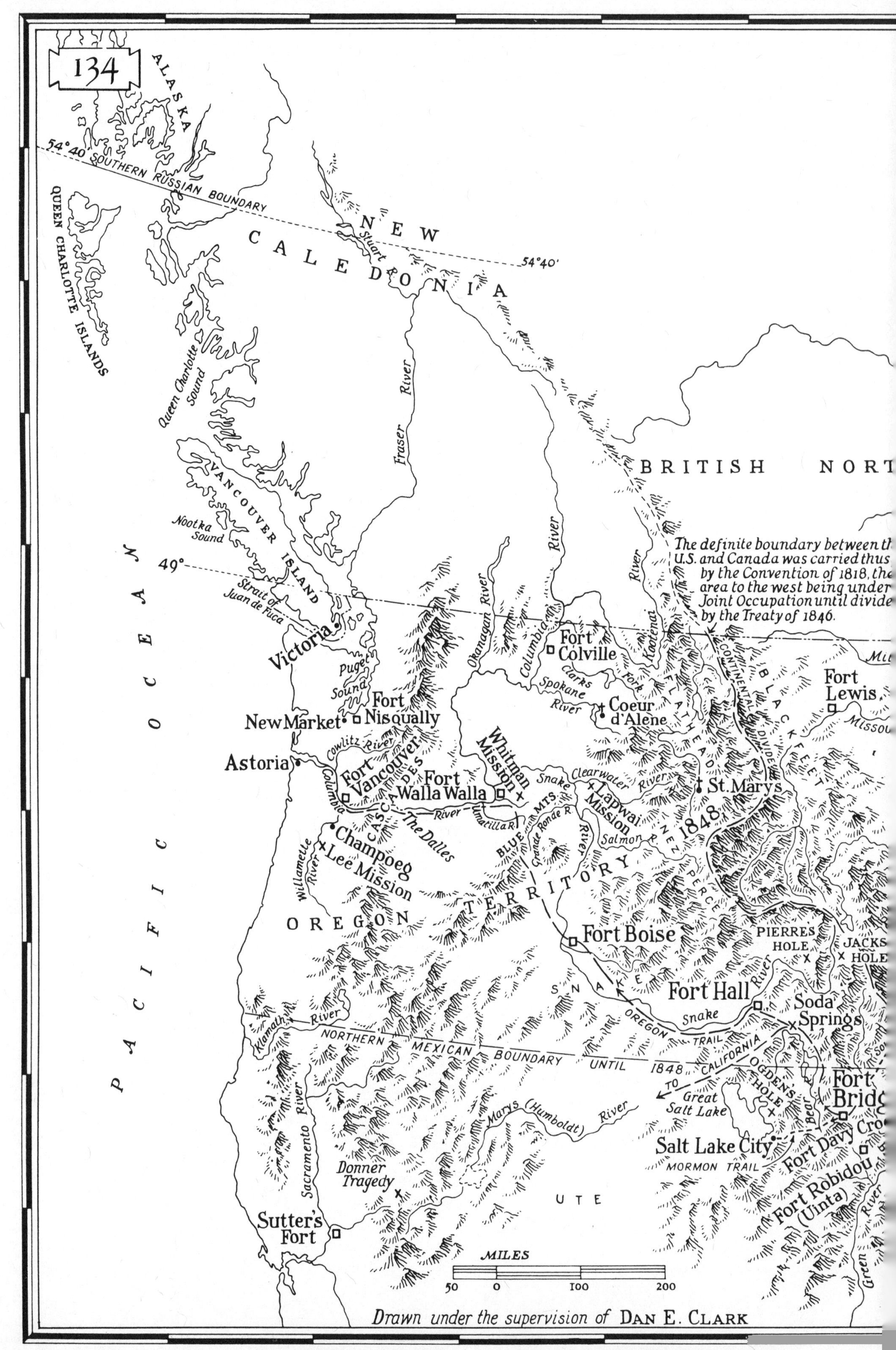

134
ALASKA
54°40' SOUTHERN RUSSIAN BOUNDARY
QUEEN CHARLOTTE ISLANDS
NEW CALEDONIA
Stuart
54°40'
Queen Charlotte Sound
Fraser River
VANCOUVER ISLAND
Nootka Sound
49°
Strait of Juan de Fuca
PACIFIC OCEAN
Victoria
Puget Sound
Fort Nisqually
New Market
Astoria
Cowlitz River
Fort Vancouver
Columbia
CASCADES
Fort Walla Walla
The Dalles
River
Champoeg
Lee Mission
Willamette River
OREGON TERRITORY
Okanagan River
Columbia River
Fort Colville
Clarks Fork
Spokane River
Coeur d'Alene
Whitman Mission
Snake
Clearwater River
Lapwai Mission
Umatilla R.
BLUE MTS.
Grande Ronde R.
Salmon R.
NEZ PERCE
1848
St. Marys
FLATHEAD
Kootenai River
BRITISH NORT
CONTINENTAL DIVIDE
BLACKFEET
The definite boundary between th U.S. and Canada was carried thus by the Convention of 1818, the area to the west being under Joint Occupation until divide by the Treaty of 1846.
Fort Lewis
Missou
Fort Boise
SNAKE
Fort Hall
River
PIERRES HOLE
JACKS HOLE
Soda Springs
Snake
OREGON TRAIL
CALIFORNIA
Klamath River
NORTHERN MEXICAN BOUNDARY UNTIL 1848
TO
Great Salt Lake
OGDEN'S HOLE
Fort Bridg
Bear
Marys (Humboldt) River
Salt Lake City
Fort Davy Cro
MORMON TRAIL
Fort Robidou (Uinta)
Green River
Sacramento River
Donner Tragedy
UTE
Sutter's Fort
MILES
50 0 100 200
Drawn under the supervision of DAN E. CLARK

THE UNORGANIZED TERRITORY AND OREGON COUNTRY 1836-1848

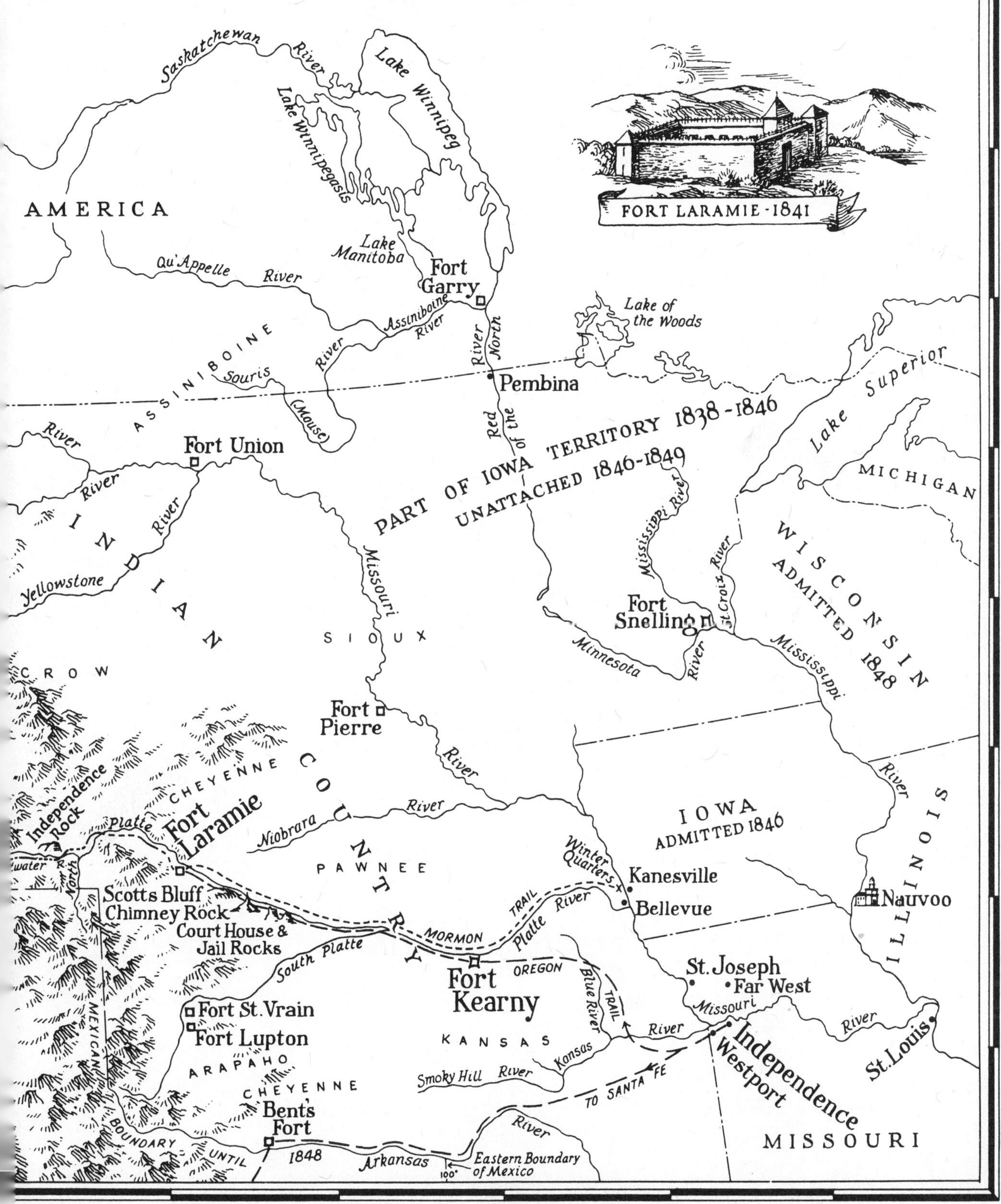
FORT LARAMIE-1841
AMERICA
Saskatchewan River
Lake Winnipeg
Lake Winnipegosis
Lake Manitoba
Fort Garry
Qu'Appelle River
Assiniboine River
Lake of the Woods
ASSINIBOINE
Souris River (Mouse)
Red River of the North
Pembina
Lake Superior
PART OF IOWA TERRITORY 1838-1846
UNATTACHED 1846-1849
Fort Union
Yellowstone River
MICHIGAN
WISCONSIN ADMITTED 1848
Mississippi River
St. Croix River
Fort Snelling
Minnesota River
Missouri
INDIAN COUNTRY
SIOUX
CROW
Fort Pierre
CHEYENNE
Independence Rock
Platte
Fort Laramie
Niobrara River
IOWA ADMITTED 1846
ILLINOIS
Winter Quarters
Kanesville
Bellevue
Nauvoo
PAWNEE
Scotts Bluff
Chimney Rock
Court House & Jail Rocks
MORMON TRAIL
Platte River
South Platte
Fort Kearny
OREGON TRAIL
Blue River
St. Joseph
Far West
Missouri River
Fort St. Vrain
Fort Lupton
KANSAS
Kansas
Independence
Westport
St. Louis
ARAPAHO
CHEYENNE
Smoky Hill River
TO SANTA FE
Bent's Fort
MEXICAN BOUNDARY UNTIL 1848
Arkansas River
Eastern Boundary of Mexico
100°
MISSOURI

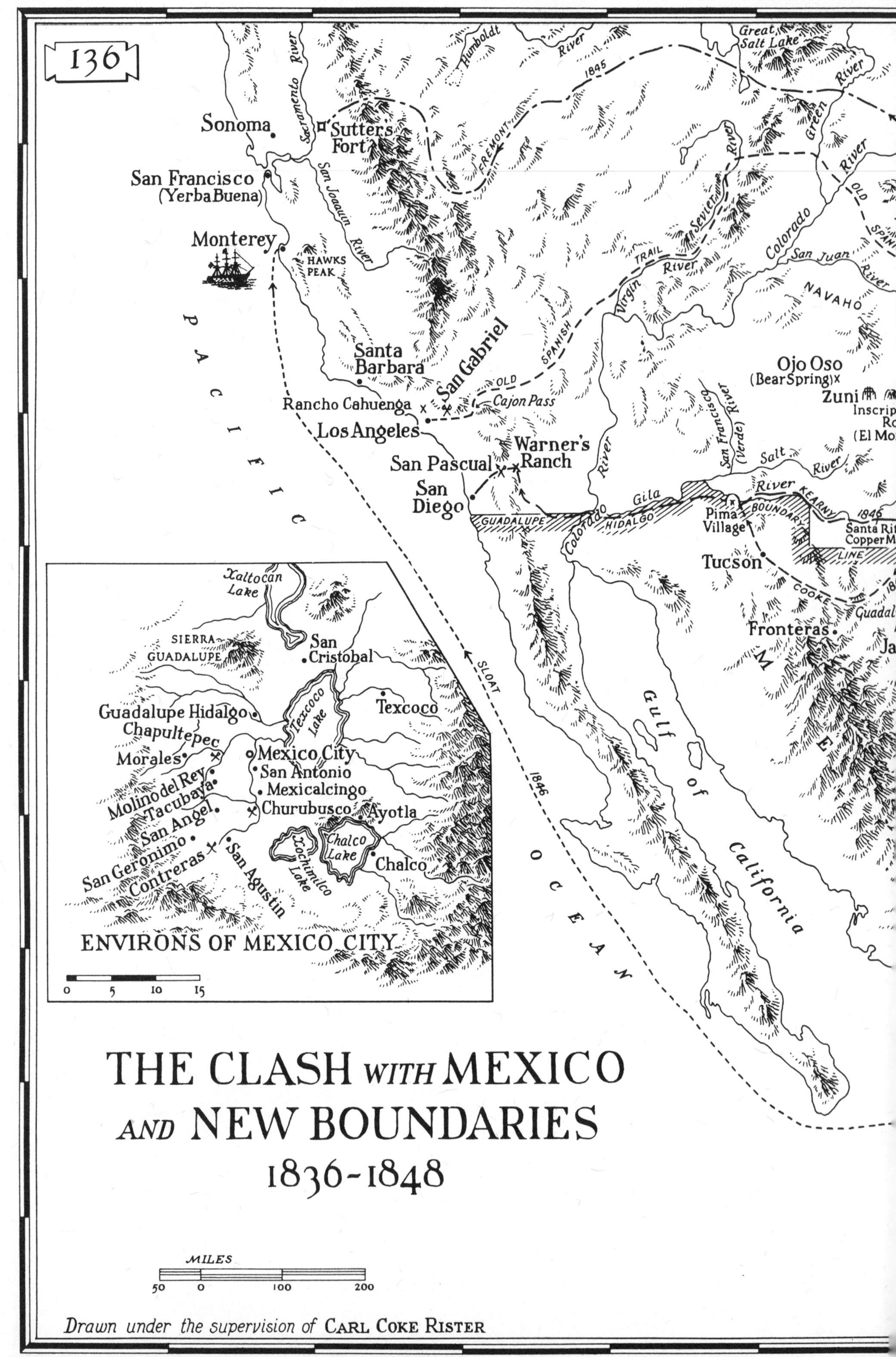

THE CLASH *WITH* MEXICO *AND* NEW BOUNDARIES 1836-1848

Drawn under the supervision of CARL COKE RISTER

Texas, subsequent to 1836, claimed the Rio Grande (Rio del Norte) and a line due north as its boundary. Mexico claimed the Nueces and a line easterly of the Staked Plains as shown below.
Fort Leavenworth
Westport
St. Louis
ILLINOIS
MISSOURI
KEARNY 1846
Bent's Fort
(SANTA FE TRAIL)
Arkansas
River
Pueblo
Cimarron
Taos
Santa Fe
Las Vegas
Canadian
Albuquerque
Peralta
Socorro
Valverde
Jornada del Muerto
ORGAN MTS.
Brazito
LLANO ESTACADO OR STAKED PLAINS
TEXAS ADMITTED 1845
TEXAS BOUNDARY BY MEXICO AS CLAIMED
Fort Gibson
Fort Smith
ARKANSAS
TENN.
MISSISSIPPI
LOUISIANA
Red
Pecos
Trinity
Sabine
Brazos
Colorado
Torrey's
Nacogdoches
Natchitoches
Fort Jesup
New Orleans
Austin
San Jacinto
San Antonio
GALVESTON ISLAND
Brazoria
Victoria
Goliad
Presidio del Norte
HIDALGO BOUNDARY LINE
Rio Grande
Conchos
Presidio de Rio Grande
Nueces
WOOL
Corpus Christi
Laredo
Chihuahua
DONIPHAN 1847
Monclova
Fort Brown
Mier
Matamoros
Saltillo
TAYLOR 1846-47
Parras
Buena Vista
Monterrey
Monte Morelos
QUITMAN 1846
Salado
Cedral
Victoria
PATTERSON 1847
SCOTT 1846
SCOTT 1847
Mazatlan
Panuco River
San Luis Potosi
Tampico
GULF OF MEXICO
Cerro Gordo
Perote
Jalapa
Vera Cruz
Mexico City
Puebla
Palo Alto
Point Isabel
Resaca de La Palma
Fort Brown
Rio Grande
Matamoros
Gulf of Mexico
PALO ALTO AND RESACA DE LA PALMA
0 5 10

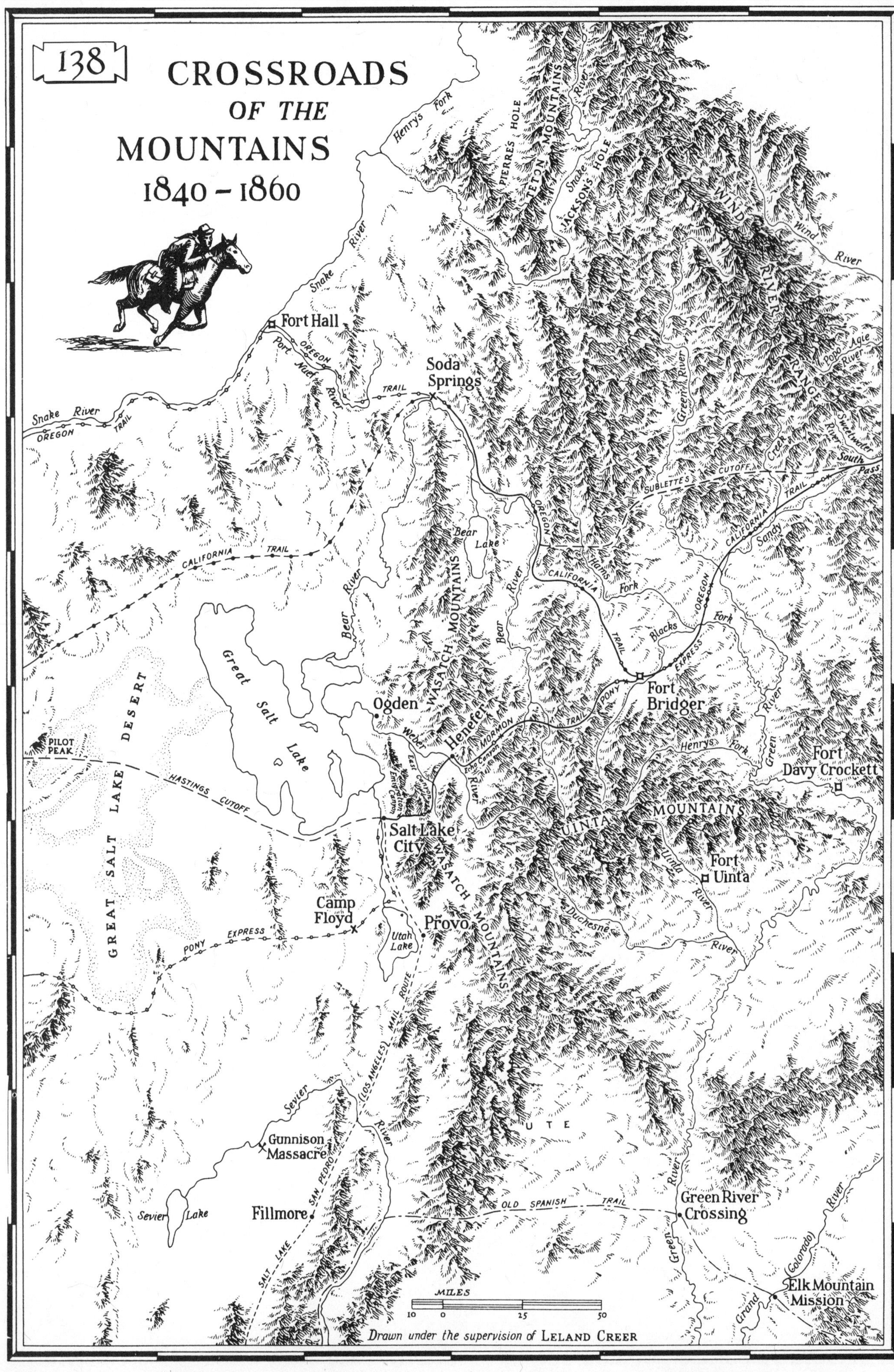
138
CROSSROADS
OF THE
MOUNTAINS
1840 – 1860
Henrys Fork
PIERRES HOLE
TETON MOUNTAINS
Snake River
JACKSONS HOLE
WIND RIVER RANGE
Wind River
Snake River
Fort Hall
Port Neuf River
OREGON TRAIL
Soda Springs
Snake River
OREGON TRAIL
Green River
Popo Agie River
Sweetwater River
Creek
South Pass
SUBLETTES CUTOFF
CALIFORNIA TRAIL
Sandy
OREGON
Bear Lake
CALIFORNIA TRAIL
Hams Fork
OREGON
Blacks Fork
Bear River
WASATCH MOUNTAINS
Bear River
Great Salt Lake
PONY EXPRESS
Fort Bridger
Ogden
Henefer
Weber
Echo Canyon
MORMON TRAIL
Henrys Fork
Green River
Fort Davy Crockett
GREAT SALT LAKE DESERT
PILOT PEAK
HASTINGS CUTOFF
East Canyon
Emigration Canyon
River
UINTA MOUNTAINS
Salt Lake City
WASATCH MOUNTAINS
Fort Uinta
Uinta River
Duchesne River
Camp Floyd
PONY EXPRESS
Utah Lake
Provo
MAIL ROUTE
(LOS ANGELES)
Sevier River
UTE
Gunnison Massacre
SAN PEDRO
Sevier Lake
Fillmore
OLD SPANISH TRAIL
Green River
Green River Crossing
Grand River
(Colorado)
River
SALT LAKE
Elk Mountain Mission
MILES
10 0 25 50
Drawn under the supervision of LELAND CREER

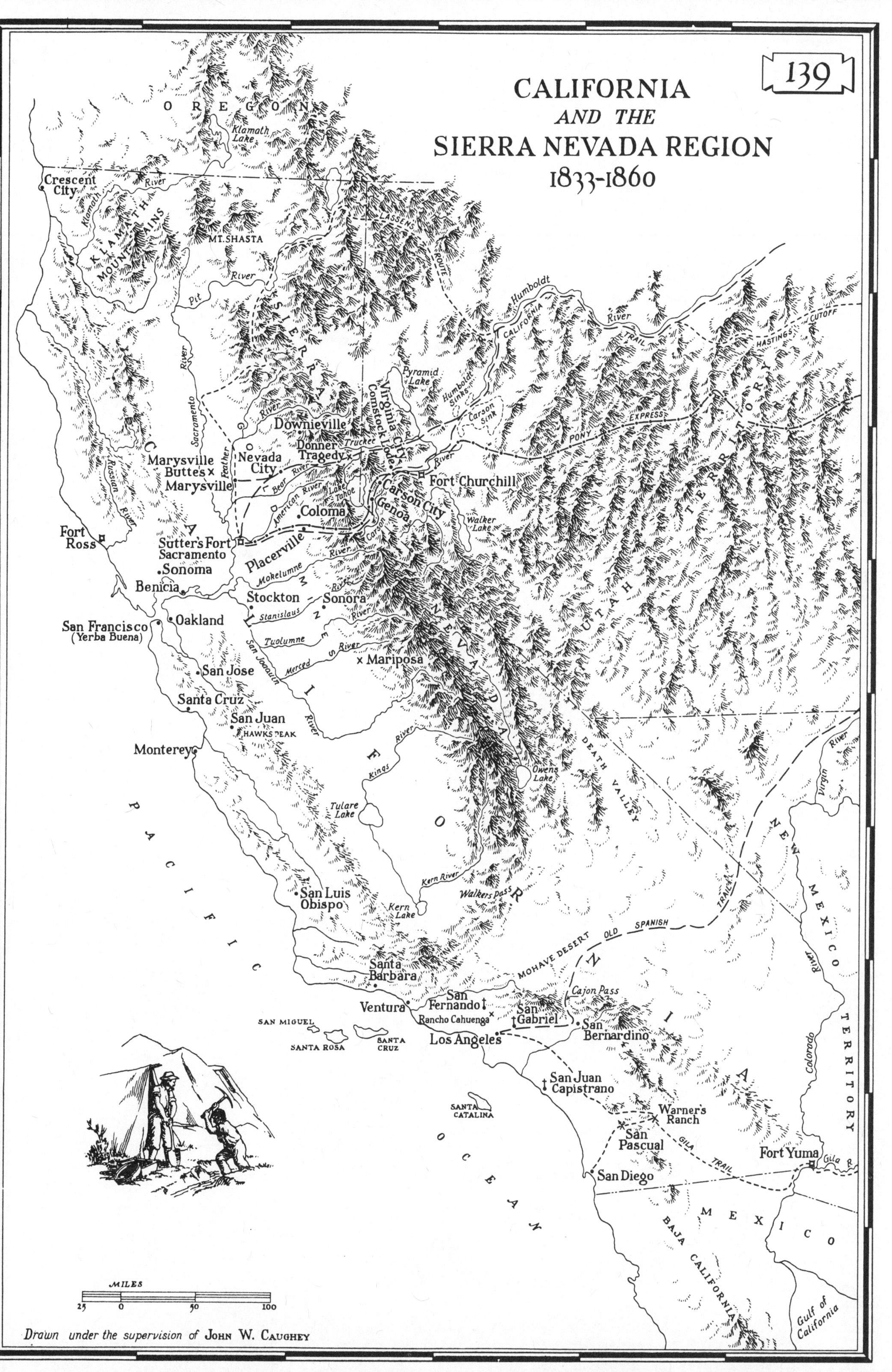
CALIFORNIA
AND THE
SIERRA NEVADA REGION
1833-1860
OREGON
Klamath Lake
Crescent City
KLAMATH MOUNTAINS
MT. SHASTA
Pit River
Sacramento River
LASSENS ROUTE
Humboldt River
CALIFORNIA TRAIL
HASTINGS CUTOFF
Pyramid Lake
Humboldt Sinks
Carson Sink
PONY EXPRESS
UTAH TERRITORY
Downieville
Virginia City
Comstock Lode
Donner Tragedy
Nevada City
Marysville Buttes
Marysville
Fort Churchill
Lake Tahoe
Carson City
Genoa
Coloma
Walker Lake
Fort Ross
Sutter's Fort
Sacramento
Placerville
Sonoma
Benicia
Stockton
Sonora
San Francisco
(Yerba Buena)
Oakland
Mariposa
San Jose
Santa Cruz
San Juan
HAWKS PEAK
Monterey
SIERRA NEVADA
DEATH VALLEY
Owens Lake
Tulare Lake
Kern River
Walkers Pass
San Luis Obispo
Kern Lake
OLD SPANISH TRAIL
MOHAVE DESERT
NEW MEXICO TERRITORY
PACIFIC OCEAN
Santa Barbara
Cajon Pass
Ventura
San Fernando
San Gabriel
Rancho Cahuenga
San Bernardino
Los Angeles
SAN MIGUEL
SANTA ROSA
SANTA CRUZ
San Juan Capistrano
SANTA CATALINA
Warner's Ranch
San Pascual
GILA TRAIL
Fort Yuma
Gila R.
San Diego
MEXICO
BAJA CALIFORNIA
Gulf of California
Colorado River
Virgin River
MILES
25 0 50 100
Drawn under the supervision of JOHN W. CAUGHEY

WESTWARD ADVANCE 1849–1860

Drawn under the supervision of LE ROY R. HAFEN *and* CARL COKE RISTER

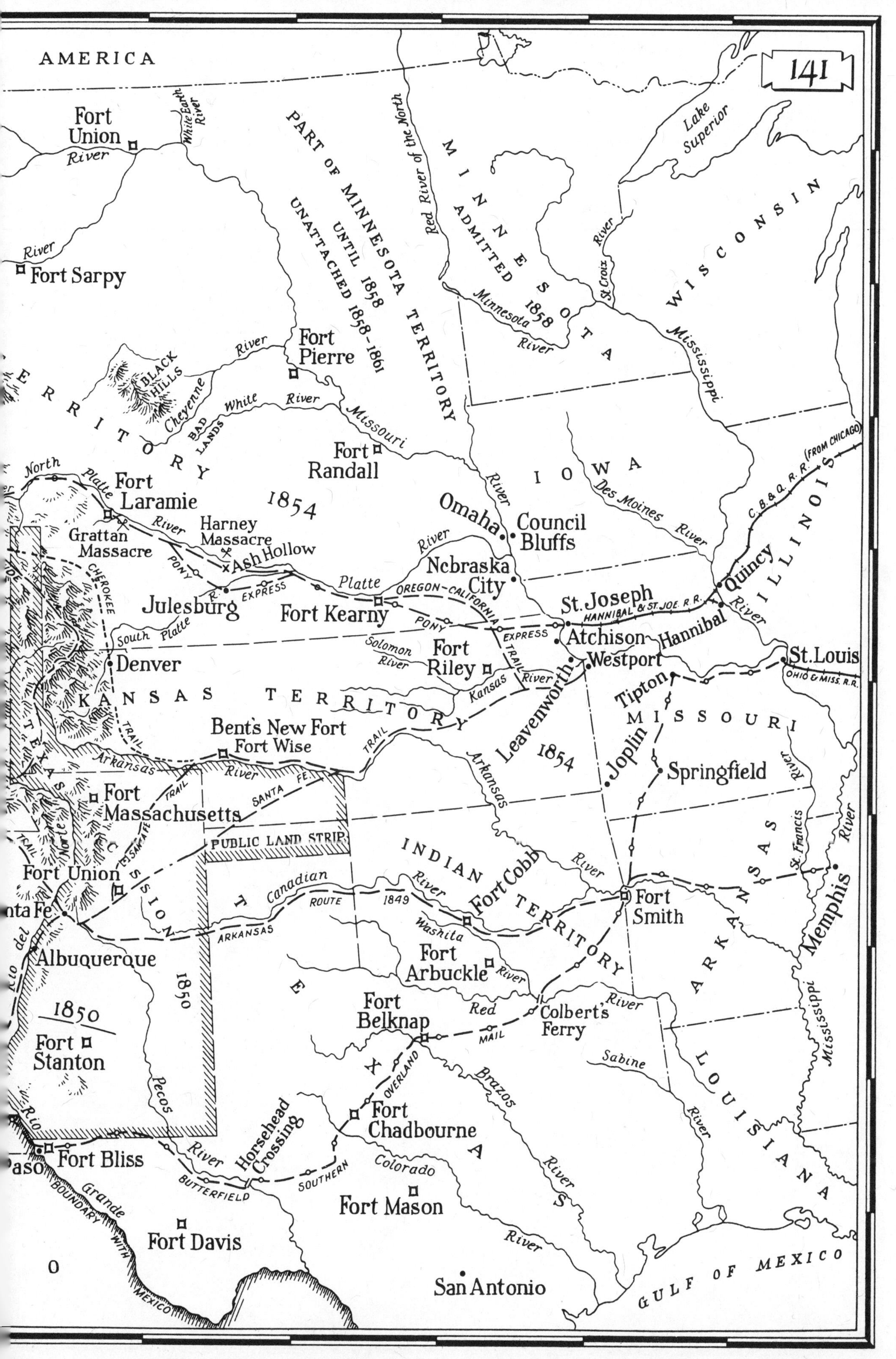
AMERICA
Fort Union
River
White Earth River
PART OF MINNESOTA TERRITORY
UNTIL 1858
UNATTACHED 1858-1861
Red River of the North
MINNESOTA
ADMITTED 1858
Lake Superior
WISCONSIN
St. Croix River
Minnesota River
Mississippi
River
Fort Sarpy
Fort Pierre
BLACK HILLS
Cheyenne
BAD LANDS
White River
Missouri
TERRITORY 1854
Fort Randall
IOWA
Des Moines River
North Platte
Fort Laramie
Grattan Massacre
Harney Massacre
Ash Hollow
Omaha
Council Bluffs
River
Nebraska City
C.B.&Q. R.R. (FROM CHICAGO)
ILLINOIS
Quincy
PONY
EXPRESS
Julesburg
Platte
Fort Kearny
OREGON-CALIFORNIA
TRAIL
St. Joseph
HANNIBAL & ST. JOE. R.R.
South Platte
Atchison
Hannibal
Solomon River
Fort Riley
Westport
St. Louis
OHIO & MISS. R.R.
Denver
CHEROKEE
KANSAS TERRITORY
Kansas River
Leavenworth
Tipton
MISSOURI
1854
Bent's New Fort
Fort Wise
Arkansas River
Joplin
Springfield
TEXAS
Fort Massachusetts
SANTA FE TRAIL
PUBLIC LAND STRIP
INDIAN TERRITORY
Fort Cobb
St. Francis
Fort Union
Canadian River
ROUTE 1849
ARKANSAS
Fort Smith
Memphis
Santa Fe
CESSION
Washita
Albuquerque
Fort Arbuckle
Rio del Norte
1850
Red River
Fort Belknap
Colbert's Ferry
MAIL
OVERLAND
Sabine
LOUISIANA
Fort Stanton
Pecos
Brazos
Fort Chadbourne
Horsehead Crossing
River
Paso
Fort Bliss
BUTTERFIELD
SOUTHERN
Colorado
Fort Mason
Rio Grande
BOUNDARY WITH MEXICO
Fort Davis
San Antonio
GULF OF MEXICO

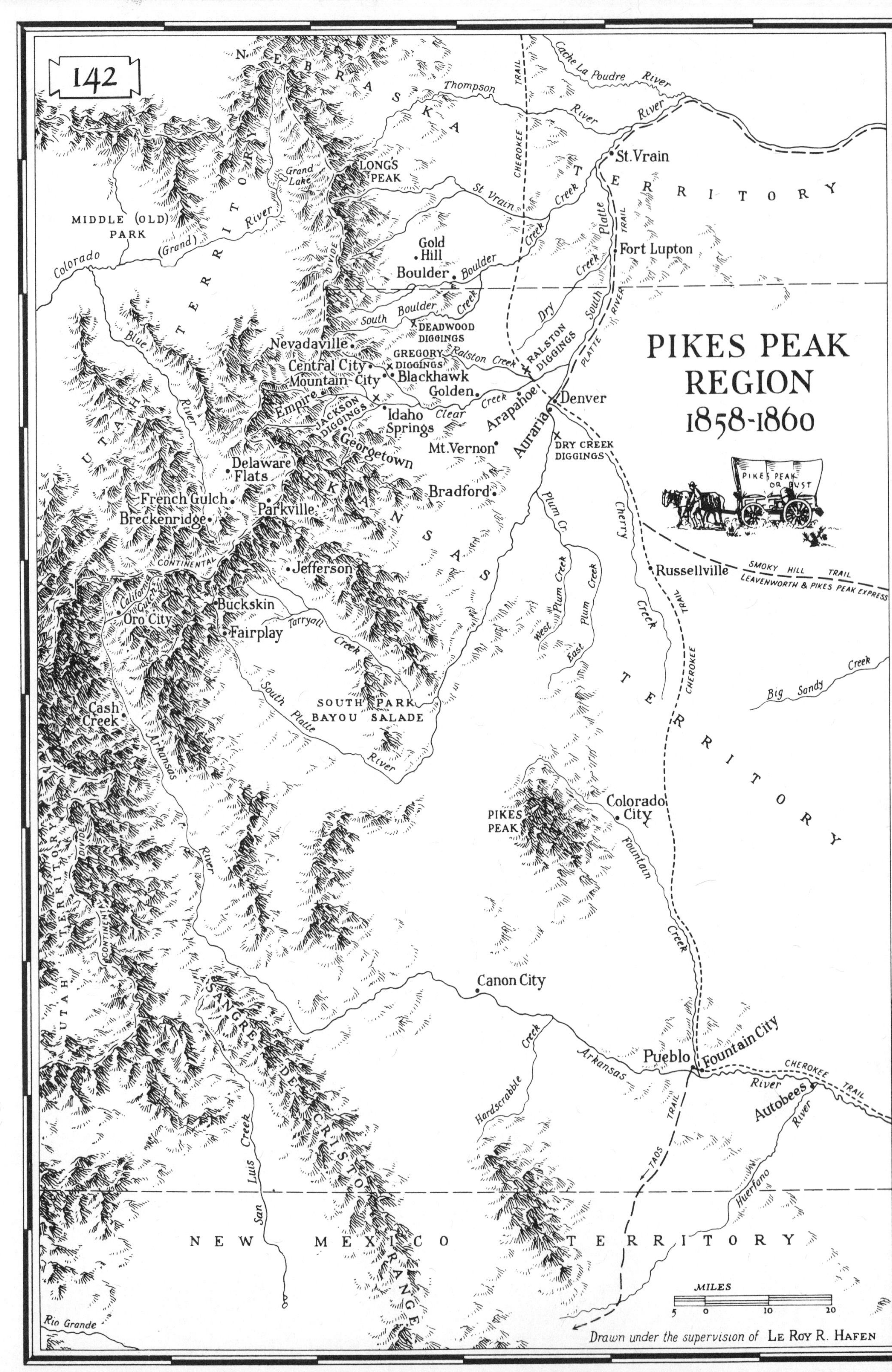
PIKES PEAK
REGION
1858-1860
PIKES PEAK OR BUST
NEBRASKA TERRITORY
KANSAS TERRITORY
UTAH TERRITORY
NEW MEXICO TERRITORY
Cache La Poudre River
Thompson River
CHEROKEE TRAIL
St. Vrain
St Vrain Creek
LONG'S PEAK
Grand Lake
MIDDLE (OLD) PARK
Colorado (Grand) River
DIVIDE
Gold Hill
Boulder
Boulder Creek
Fort Lupton
South Platte River
Dry Creek
South Boulder Creek
DEADWOOD DIGGINGS
Nevadaville
Central City
GREGORY DIGGINGS
Mountain City
Blackhawk
Ralston Creek
RALSTON DIGGINGS
Golden
Arapahoe
Denver
Auraria
Empire
JACKSON DIGGINGS
Idaho Springs
Clear Creek
Georgetown
Mt. Vernon
DRY CREEK DIGGINGS
Blue River
Delaware Flats
French Gulch
Breckenridge
Parkville
Bradford
Plum Cr.
Cherry Creek
CONTINENTAL
Jefferson
Russellville
SMOKY HILL TRAIL
LEAVENWORTH & PIKES PEAK EXPRESS
California Gulch
Oro City
Buckskin
Fairplay
Tarryall Creek
West Plum Creek
East Plum Creek
CHEROKEE TRAIL
Big Sandy Creek
SOUTH PARK
BAYOU SALADE
South Platte River
Cash Creek
Arkansas River
PIKES PEAK
Colorado City
Fountain Creek
CONTINENTAL DIVIDE
Canon City
SANGRE DE CRISTO RANGE
Creek
Arkansas River
Pueblo
Fountain City
CHEROKEE TRAIL
Autobees
Hardscrabble
Huerfano River
San Luis Creek
TAOS TRAIL
Rio Grande
MILES
5 0 10 20
Drawn under the supervision of LE ROY R. HAFEN

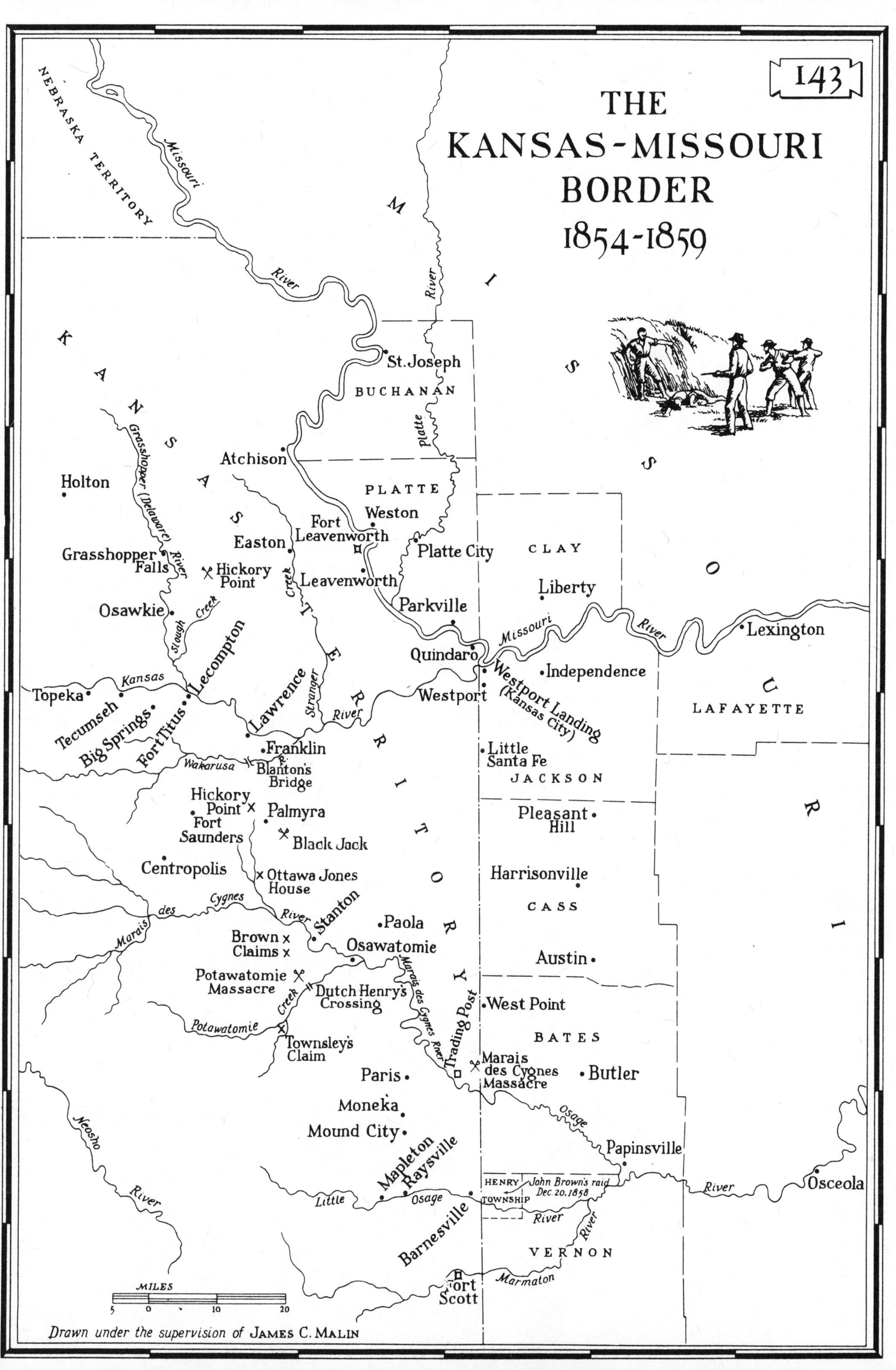
THE KANSAS-MISSOURI BORDER 1854-1859
NEBRASKA TERRITORY
KANSAS TERRITORY
MISSOURI
Missouri River
Missouri River
Missouri River
St. Joseph
BUCHANAN
Platte
Atchison
PLATTE
Weston
Fort Leavenworth
Platte City
CLAY
Liberty
Leavenworth
Parkville
Easton
Holton
Grasshopper (Delaware) River
Grasshopper Falls
Hickory Point
Osawkie
Slough Creek
Creek
Lecompton
Kansas
Topeka
Tecumseh
Big Springs
Fort Titus
Lawrence
Stranger
River
Quindaro
Westport
Westport Landing (Kansas City)
Independence
Lexington
LAFAYETTE
Franklin
Wakarusa
Blanton's Bridge
Little Santa Fe
JACKSON
Hickory Point
Fort Saunders
Palmyra
Black Jack
Pleasant Hill
Centropolis
Ottawa Jones House
Harrisonville
Marais des Cygnes River
Stanton
Paola
CASS
Brown Claims
Osawatomie
Austin
Potawatomie Massacre
Dutch Henry's Crossing
Marais des Cygnes River
Trading Post
West Point
Potawatomie Creek
Townsley's Claim
BATES
Marais des Cygnes Massacre
Butler
Paris
Moneka
Mound City
Osage
Papinsville
Neosho River
Mapleton
Raysville
HENRY TOWNSHIP
John Brown's raid Dec. 20, 1858
Little Osage River
River
Osceola
Barnesville
VERNON
Marmaton
Fort Scott
MILES
5 0 10 20
Drawn under the supervision of JAMES C. MALIN

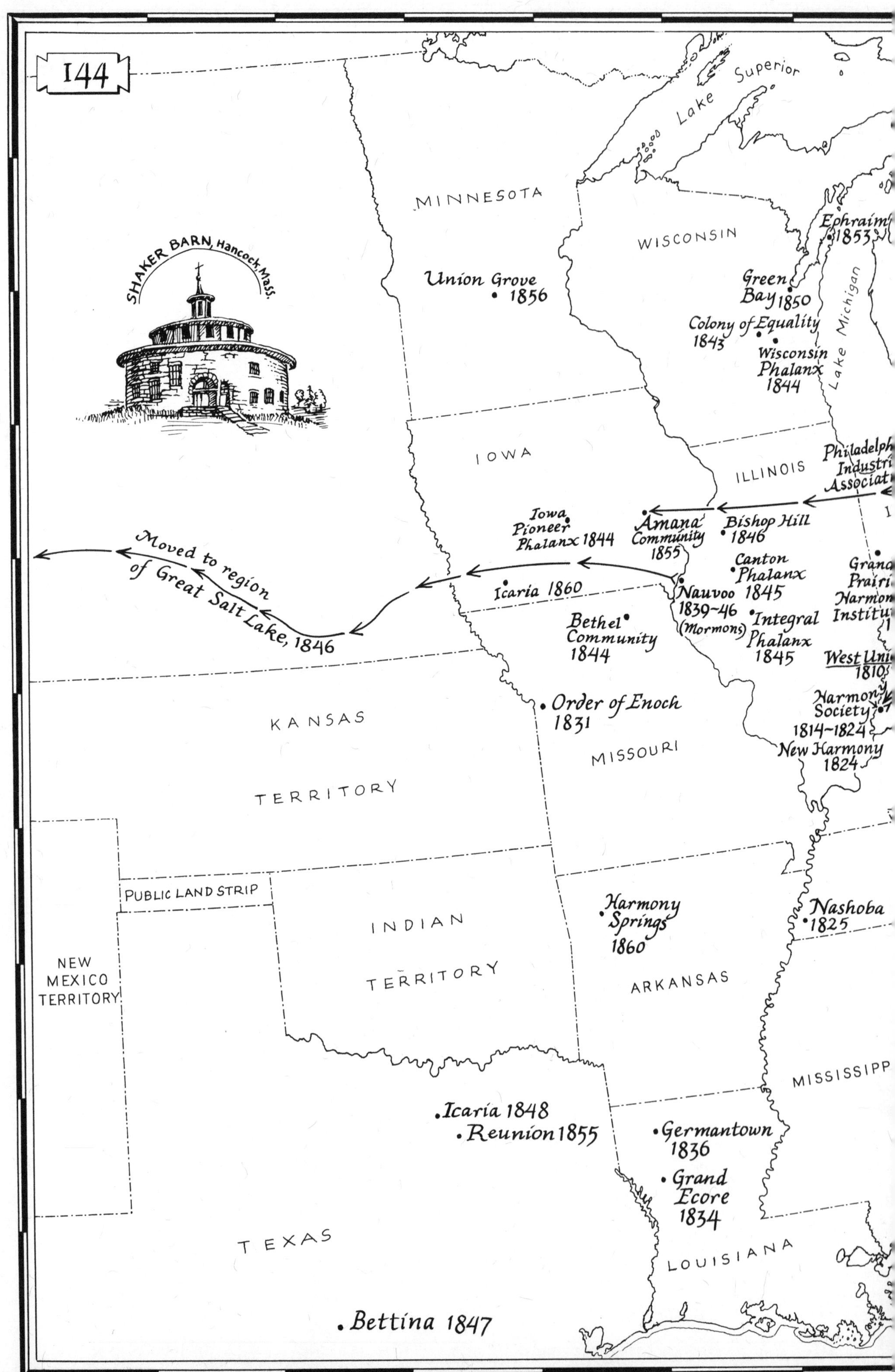

Lake Superior
MINNESOTA
WISCONSIN
SHAKER BARN, Hancock, Mass.
Union Grove 1856
Ephraim 1853
Green Bay 1850
Colony of Equality 1843
Wisconsin Phalanx 1844
Lake Michigan
IOWA
ILLINOIS
Iowa Pioneer Phalanx 1844
Amana Community 1855
Bishop Hill 1846
Canton Phalanx 1845
Moved to region of Great Salt Lake, 1846
Icaria 1860
Nauvoo 1839-46 (Mormons)
Integral Phalanx 1845
Bethel Community 1844
Harmony Society 1814-1824
New Harmony 1824
KANSAS TERRITORY
Order of Enoch 1831
MISSOURI
PUBLIC LAND STRIP
NEW MEXICO TERRITORY
INDIAN TERRITORY
Harmony Springs 1860
Nashoba 1825
ARKANSAS
MISSISSIPP
Icaria 1848
Reunion 1855
Germantown 1836
Grand Ecore 1834
TEXAS
LOUISIANA
Bettina 1847

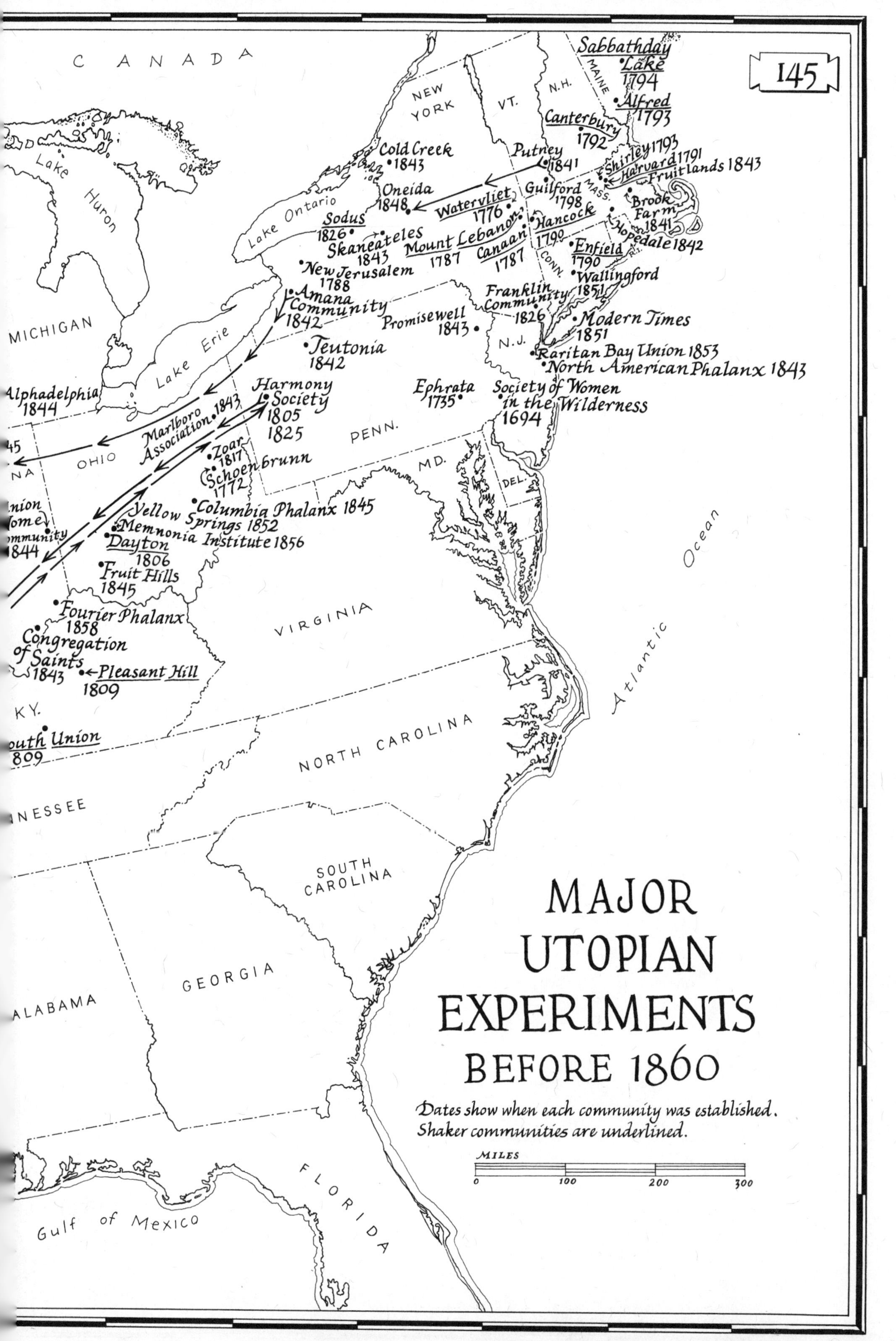

MAJOR UTOPIAN EXPERIMENTS BEFORE 1860

Dates show when each community was established. Shaker communities are underlined.

UNIVERSAL MALE SUFFRAGE 1789~1897

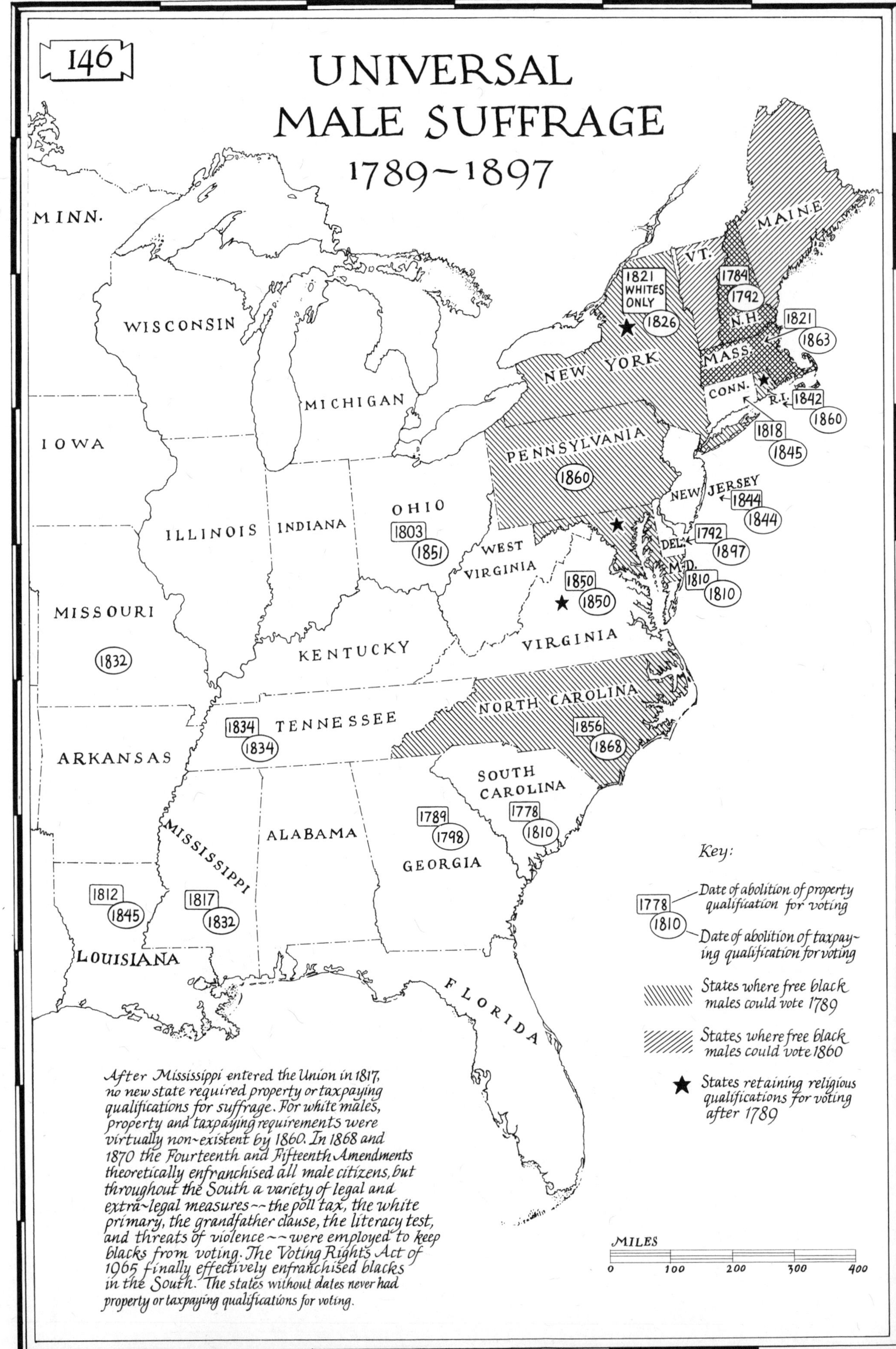

After Mississippi entered the Union in 1817, no new state required property or taxpaying qualifications for suffrage. For white males, property and taxpaying requirements were virtually non-existent by 1860. In 1868 and 1870 the Fourteenth and Fifteenth Amendments theoretically enfranchised all male citizens, but throughout the South a variety of legal and extra-legal measures -- the poll tax, the white primary, the grandfather clause, the literacy test, and threats of violence -- were employed to keep blacks from voting. The Voting Rights Act of 1965 finally effectively enfranchised blacks in the South. The states without dates never had property or taxpaying qualifications for voting.

VII THE CIVIL WAR AND RECONSTRUCTION

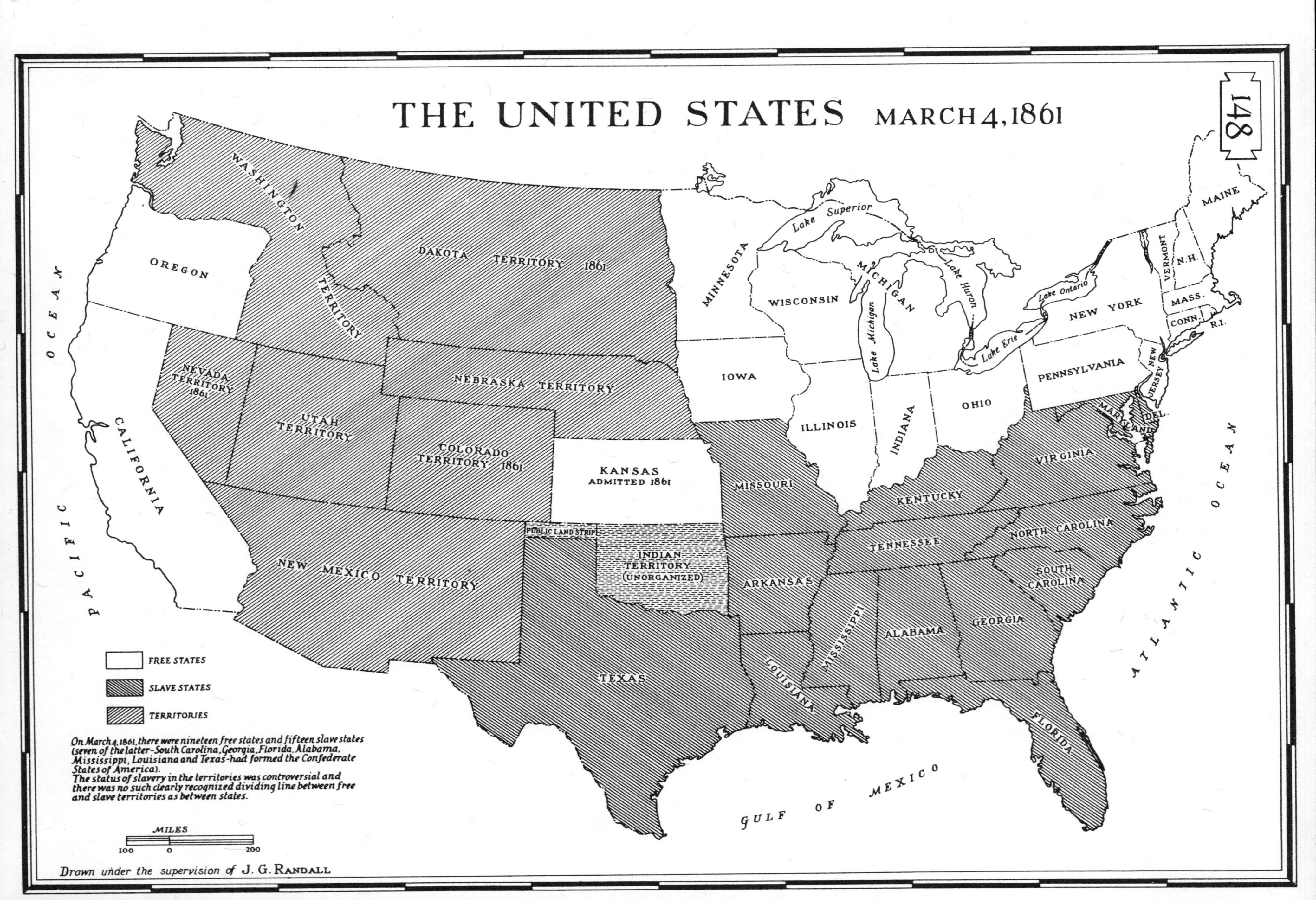
148
THE UNITED STATES MARCH 4, 1861
WASHINGTON TERRITORY
OREGON
DAKOTA TERRITORY 1861
MINNESOTA
Lake Superior
WISCONSIN
MICHIGAN
Lake Michigan
Lake Huron
Lake Ontario
Lake Erie
NEW YORK
VERMONT
N.H.
MAINE
MASS.
CONN.
R.I.
NEVADA TERRITORY 1861
UTAH TERRITORY
NEBRASKA TERRITORY
COLORADO TERRITORY 1861
KANSAS ADMITTED 1861
IOWA
ILLINOIS
INDIANA
OHIO
PENNSYLVANIA
NEW JERSEY
DEL.
MARYLAND
CALIFORNIA
VIRGINIA
MISSOURI
KENTUCKY
PUBLIC LAND STRIP
INDIAN TERRITORY (UNORGANIZED)
NEW MEXICO TERRITORY
ARKANSAS
TENNESSEE
NORTH CAROLINA
SOUTH CAROLINA
MISSISSIPPI
ALABAMA
GEORGIA
TEXAS
LOUISIANA
FLORIDA
PACIFIC OCEAN
ATLANTIC OCEAN
GULF OF MEXICO
FREE STATES
SLAVE STATES
TERRITORIES
On March 4, 1861, there were nineteen free states and fifteen slave states (seven of the latter-South Carolina, Georgia, Florida, Alabama, Mississippi, Louisiana and Texas-had formed the Confederate States of America).
The status of slavery in the territories was controversial and there was no such clearly recognized dividing line between free and slave territories as between states.
MILES
100
0
200
Drawn under the supervision of J. G. Randall

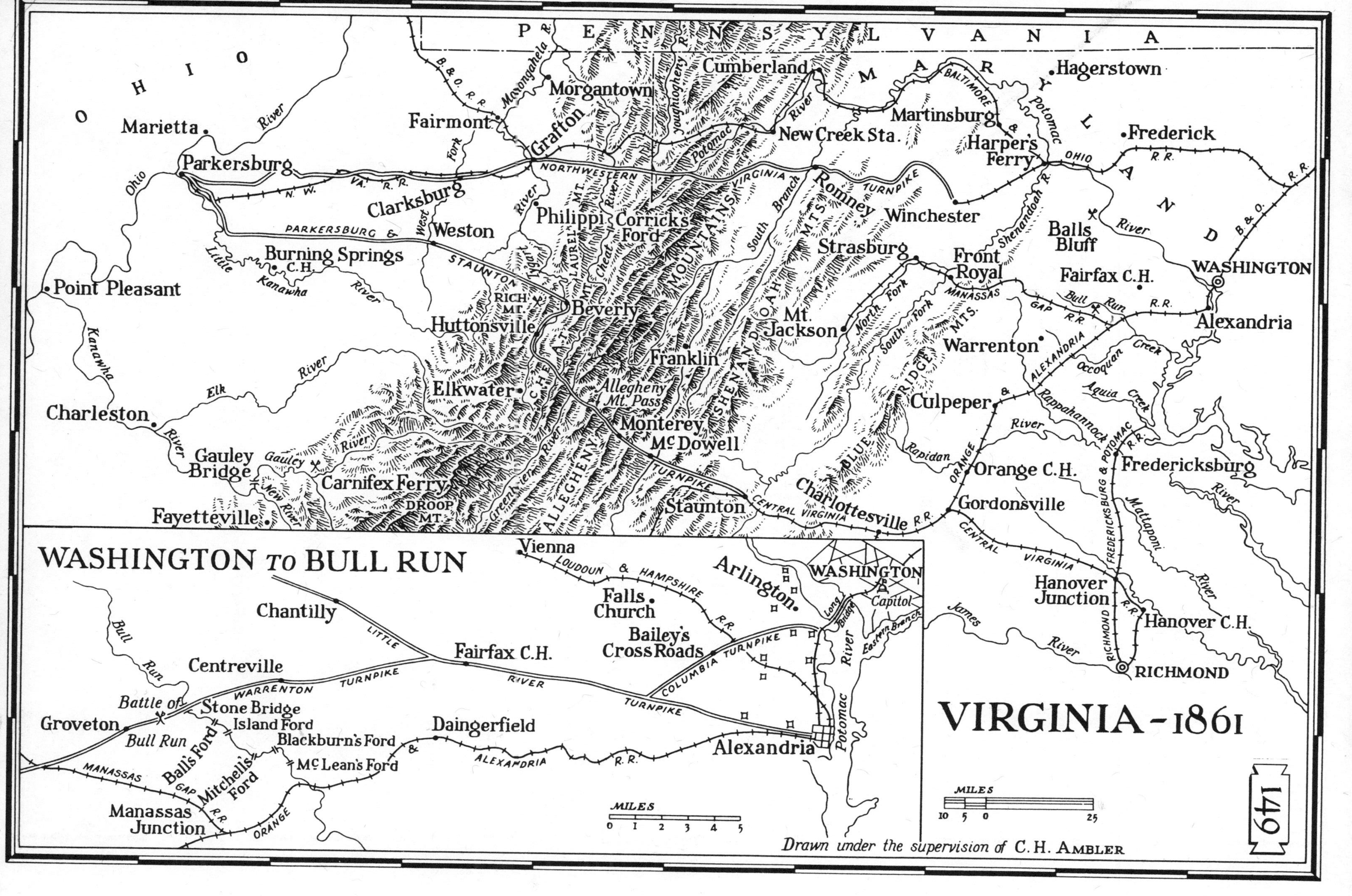
VIRGINIA-1861
WASHINGTON TO BULL RUN
149
PENNSYLVANIA
MARYLAND
OHIO
Marietta
Parkersburg
Point Pleasant
Charleston
Gauley Bridge
Fayetteville
Carnifex Ferry
Burning Springs C.H.
Clarksburg
Weston
Fairmont
Morgantown
Grafton
Philippi
Corricks Ford
Rich Mt.
Beverly
Huttonsville
Elkwater
Cheat Mt.
Allegheny Mt. Pass
Monterey
McDowell
Franklin
Staunton
Droop Mt.
Cumberland
New Creek Sta.
Romney
Martinsburg
Harper's Ferry
Hagerstown
Frederick
Winchester
Strasburg
Front Royal
Mt. Jackson
Warrenton
Culpeper
Orange C.H.
Gordonsville
Charlottesville
Balls Bluff
Fairfax C.H.
Washington
Alexandria
Fredericksburg
Hanover Junction
Hanover C.H.
Richmond
Allegheny
Mountains
Laurel Mt.
Shenandoah Mts.
Blue Ridge Mts.
Ohio River
Kanawha
Little Kanawha
Elk River
Gauley
New River
Greenbrier River
West Fork
Tygart
Cheat River
Monongahela
Youghiogheny
Potomac
South Branch
North Fork
South Fork
Shenandoah R.
Bull Run
Occoquan
Creek
Aquia Creek
Rappahannock
Rapidan
River
Mattaponi
James River
B. & O. R.R.
Baltimore & Ohio R.R.
Northwestern Virginia Turnpike
N.W. Va. R.R.
Parkersburg & Staunton Turnpike
Manassas Gap R.R.
Orange & Alexandria R.R.
Central Virginia R.R.
Richmond Fredericksburg & Potomac R.R.
Vienna
Loudoun & Hampshire R.R.
Falls Church
Arlington
Washington
Capitol
Long Bridge
Eastern Branch
Potomac River
Chantilly
Little River Turnpike
Fairfax C.H.
Bailey's Cross Roads
Columbia Turnpike
Centreville
Warrenton Turnpike
Battle of Bull Run
Groveton
Stone Bridge
Island Ford
Ball's Ford
Blackburn's Ford
Mitchell's Ford
McLean's Ford
Manassas Junction
Manassas Gap R.R.
Orange
Daingerfield
Alexandria & R.R.
Alexandria
Bull Run
MILES
0 1 2 3 4 5
MILES
10 5 0 25
Drawn under the supervision of C.H. Ambler

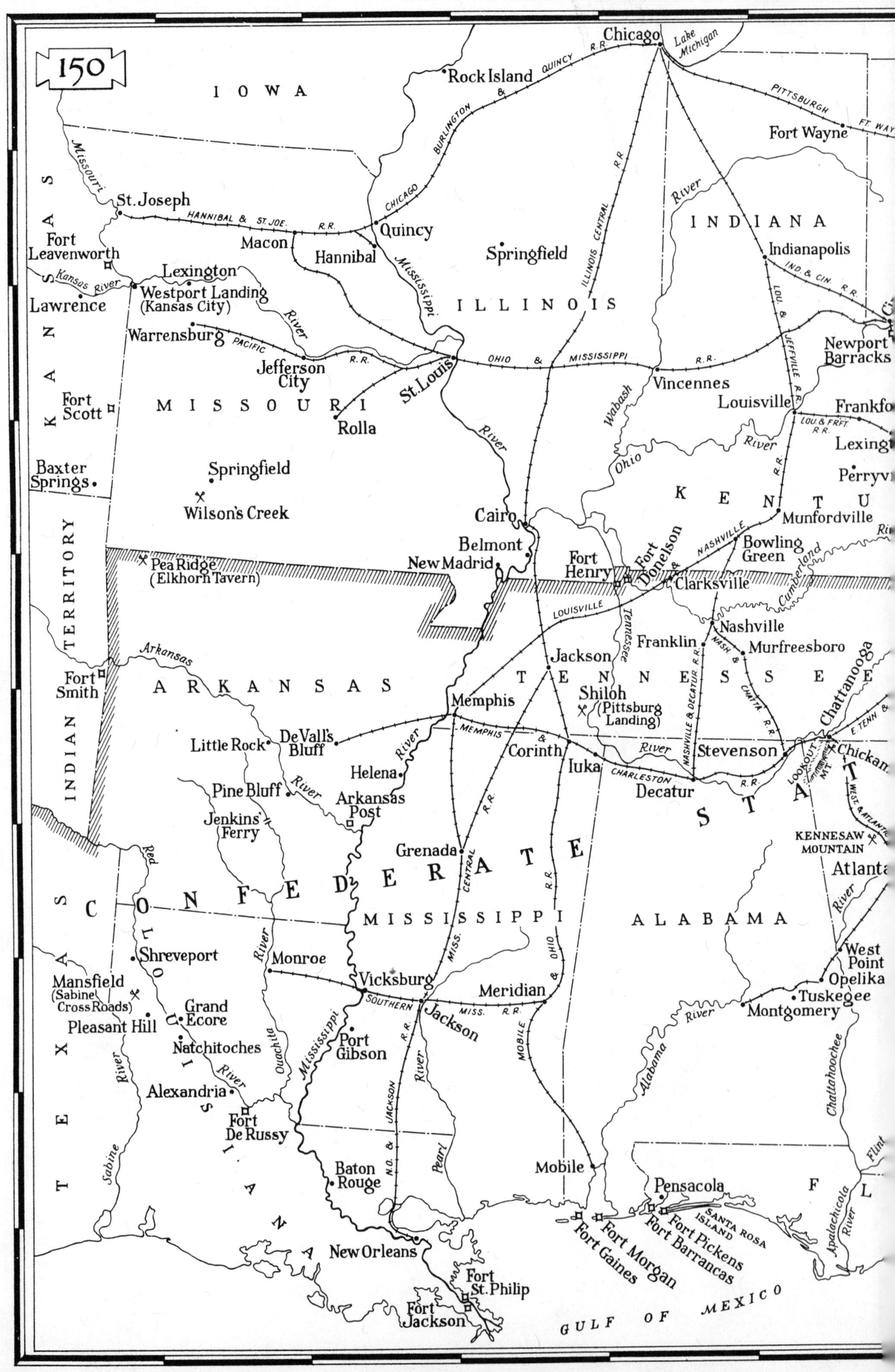
150
IOWA
Chicago
Lake Michigan
Rock Island
CHICAGO BURLINGTON & QUINCY R.R.
PITTSBURGH FT. WAYNE
Fort Wayne
Missouri
KANSAS
St. Joseph
HANNIBAL & ST. JOE. R.R.
Macon
Quincy
Hannibal
Fort Leavenworth
Mississippi
Springfield
ILLINOIS CENTRAL R.R.
River
INDIANA
Indianapolis
IND. & CIN. R.R.
Kansas River
Lexington
Westport Landing
(Kansas City)
Lawrence
River
ILLINOIS
LOU. & JEFFVILLE R.R.
Warrensburg
PACIFIC R.R.
Jefferson City
St. Louis
OHIO & MISSISSIPPI R.R.
Newport Barracks
Vincennes
Wabash
Louisville
Fort Scott
MISSOURI
Rolla
River
LOU. & FRFT. R.R.
River
Ohio
Baxter Springs
Springfield
Wilson's Creek
R.R.
KENTU
Cairo
Munfordville
INDIAN TERRITORY
Belmont
Bowling Green
NASHVILLE
Pea Ridge
(Elkhorn Tavern)
New Madrid
Fort Henry
Fort Donelson
Clarksville
Cumberland
LOUISVILLE
Tennessee
Nashville
Franklin
Murfreesboro
NASH & CHATTA R.R.
NASHVILLE & DECATUR R.R.
Arkansas
Jackson
Fort Smith
ARKANSAS
TENNESSEE
Chattanooga
Memphis
Shiloh
(Pittsburg Landing)
MEMPHIS & CHARLESTON R.R.
Little Rock
DeVall's Bluff
Corinth
Iuka
River
Stevenson
E. TENN
Helena
River
Decatur
LOOKOUT MT.
Pine Bluff
River
Arkansas Post
WEST. & ATLANTIC
Jenkins' Ferry
KENNESAW MOUNTAIN
Grenada
CONFEDERATE STAT
Atlanta
Red
MISS. CENTRAL R.R.
River
TEXAS
MISSISSIPPI
ALABAMA
LOUISIANA
Shreveport
River
Monroe
West Point
Mansfield
(Sabine Cross Roads)
Vicksburg
Opelika
Grand Ecore
SOUTHERN MISS. R.R.
Meridian
Tuskegee
Pleasant Hill
Jackson
MOBILE & OHIO R.R.
River
Montgomery
Natchitoches
Port Gibson
Ouachita
Mississippi
River
River
Alabama
Chattahoochee
Alexandria
River
N.O. & JACKSON R.R.
Fort De Russy
Sabine
Pearl
Flint
Baton Rouge
Mobile
Pensacola
FL
SANTA ROSA ISLAND
Fort Gaines
Fort Morgan
Fort Pickens
Fort Barrancas
Apalachicola River
New Orleans
Fort St. Philip
Fort Jackson
GULF OF MEXICO

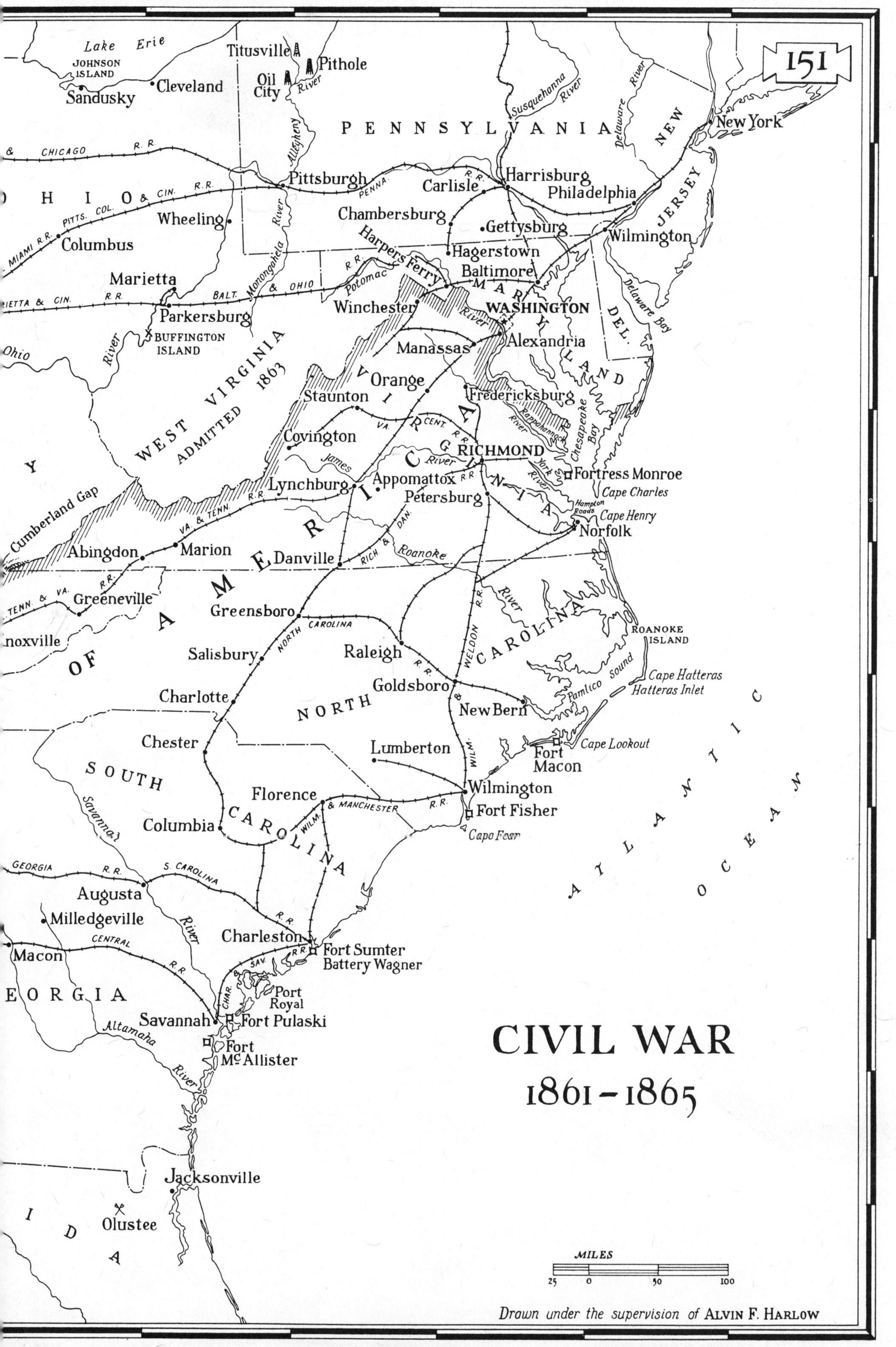

CIVIL WAR
1861–1865
Lake Erie
JOHNSON ISLAND
Sandusky
Cleveland
Titusville
Pithole
Oil City
River
Allegheny
PENNSYLVANIA
Susquehanna River
Delaware River
NEW
New York
& CHICAGO R. R.
Pittsburgh
PENNA.
R. R.
Carlisle
Harrisburg
Philadelphia
JERSEY
OHIO
PITTS. COL. & CIN. R. R.
MIAMI R. R.
Columbus
Wheeling
Monongahela River
Chambersburg
Gettysburg
Wilmington
Harpers Ferry
Hagerstown
Baltimore
Marietta
BALT. & OHIO
MARIETTA & CIN. R. R.
Potomac
Parkersburg
Winchester
MARYLAND
WASHINGTON
DEL.
Delaware Bay
BUFFINGTON ISLAND
Ohio
River
Alexandria
Manassas
WEST VIRGINIA ADMITTED 1863
VIRGINIA
Orange
Staunton
Fredericksburg
Rappahannock River
Chesapeake Bay
VA. CENT. R. R.
Covington
RICHMOND
James River
York River
Fortress Monroe
Cape Charles
Lynchburg
Appomattox
Petersburg
R. R.
Hampton Roads
Cape Henry
Norfolk
Cumberland Gap
VA. & TENN. R. R.
Abingdon
Marion
Danville
RICH. & DAN.
Roanoke
AMERICA
TENN. & VA. R. R.
Greeneville
Knoxville
OF
Greensboro
NORTH CAROLINA
River
ROANOKE ISLAND
Salisbury
Raleigh
R. R.
WELDON R. R.
CAROLINA
Goldsboro
Pamlico Sound
Cape Hatteras
Hatteras Inlet
Charlotte
NORTH
New Bern
WILM. &
Chester
Lumberton
Fort Macon
Cape Lookout
SOUTH
Savannah
Florence
Wilmington
Fort Fisher
WILM. & MANCHESTER R. R.
Columbia
CAROLINA
Cape Fear
ATLANTIC
OCEAN
GEORGIA R. R.
S. CAROLINA
Augusta
Milledgeville
River
CENTRAL R. R.
R. R.
Charleston
Fort Sumter
Battery Wagner
Macon
CHAR. & SAV.
GEORGIA
Port Royal
Savannah
Fort Pulaski
Altamaha River
Fort McAllister
Jacksonville
Olustee
IDA
MILES
25 0 50 100
Drawn under the supervision of ALVIN F. HARLOW

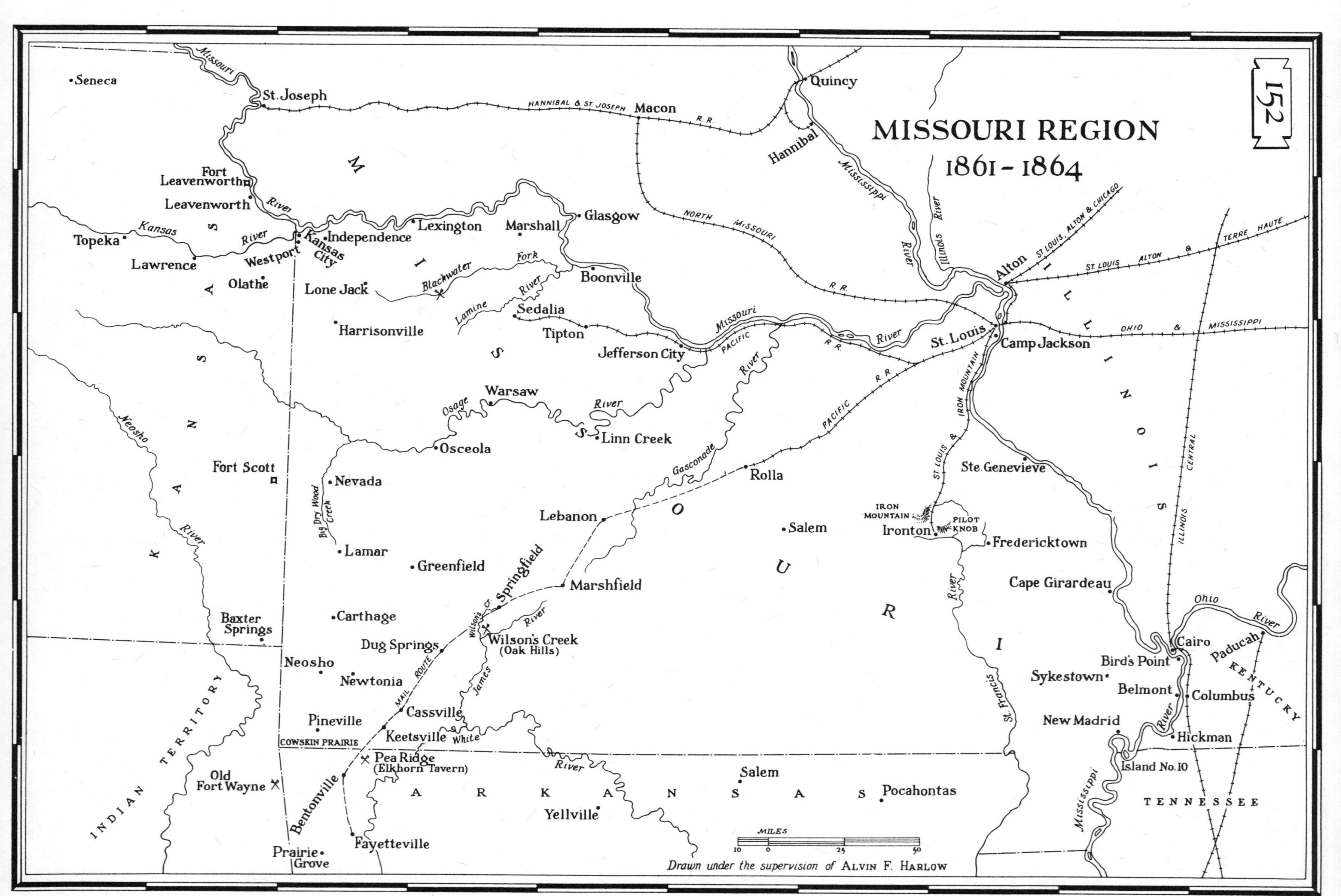
152
MISSOURI REGION
1861 - 1864
Drawn under the supervision of ALVIN F. HARLOW
MILES
10 0 25 50
Seneca
St. Joseph
Fort Leavenworth
Leavenworth
Topeka
Lawrence
Olathe
Westport
Kansas City
Independence
Lexington
Marshall
Glasgow
Boonville
Lone Jack
Harrisonville
Sedalia
Tipton
Jefferson City
Warsaw
Linn Creek
Osceola
Fort Scott
Nevada
Lamar
Greenfield
Carthage
Baxter Springs
Neosho
Newtonia
Dug Springs
Pineville
Cassville
Keetsville
COWSKIN PRAIRIE
Pea Ridge (Elkhorn Tavern)
Bentonville
Fayetteville
Prairie Grove
Old Fort Wayne
Yellville
Salem
Pocahontas
Springfield
Wilson's Creek (Oak Hills)
Marshfield
Lebanon
Rolla
Salem
Iron Mountain
Ironton
Pilot Knob
Fredericktown
Ste. Genevieve
Cape Girardeau
Cairo
Bird's Point
Sykestown
Belmont
Columbus
Paducah
New Madrid
Hickman
Island No. 10
St. Louis
Camp Jackson
Alton
Quincy
Hannibal
Macon
MISSOURI
KANSAS
ILLINOIS
KENTUCKY
TENNESSEE
ARKANSAS
INDIAN TERRITORY
HANNIBAL & ST. JOSEPH R.R.
NORTH MISSOURI R.R.
PACIFIC R.R.
ST. LOUIS & IRON MOUNTAIN
ST. LOUIS, ALTON & CHICAGO
ST. LOUIS ALTON & TERRE HAUTE
OHIO & MISSISSIPPI
ILLINOIS CENTRAL
MAIL ROUTE
Missouri River
Mississippi River
Illinois River
Kansas River
Neosho River
Osage River
Gasconade River
Blackwater Fork
Lamine River
Big Dry Wood Creek
Wilson's Cr.
James River
White River
St. Francis River
Ohio River

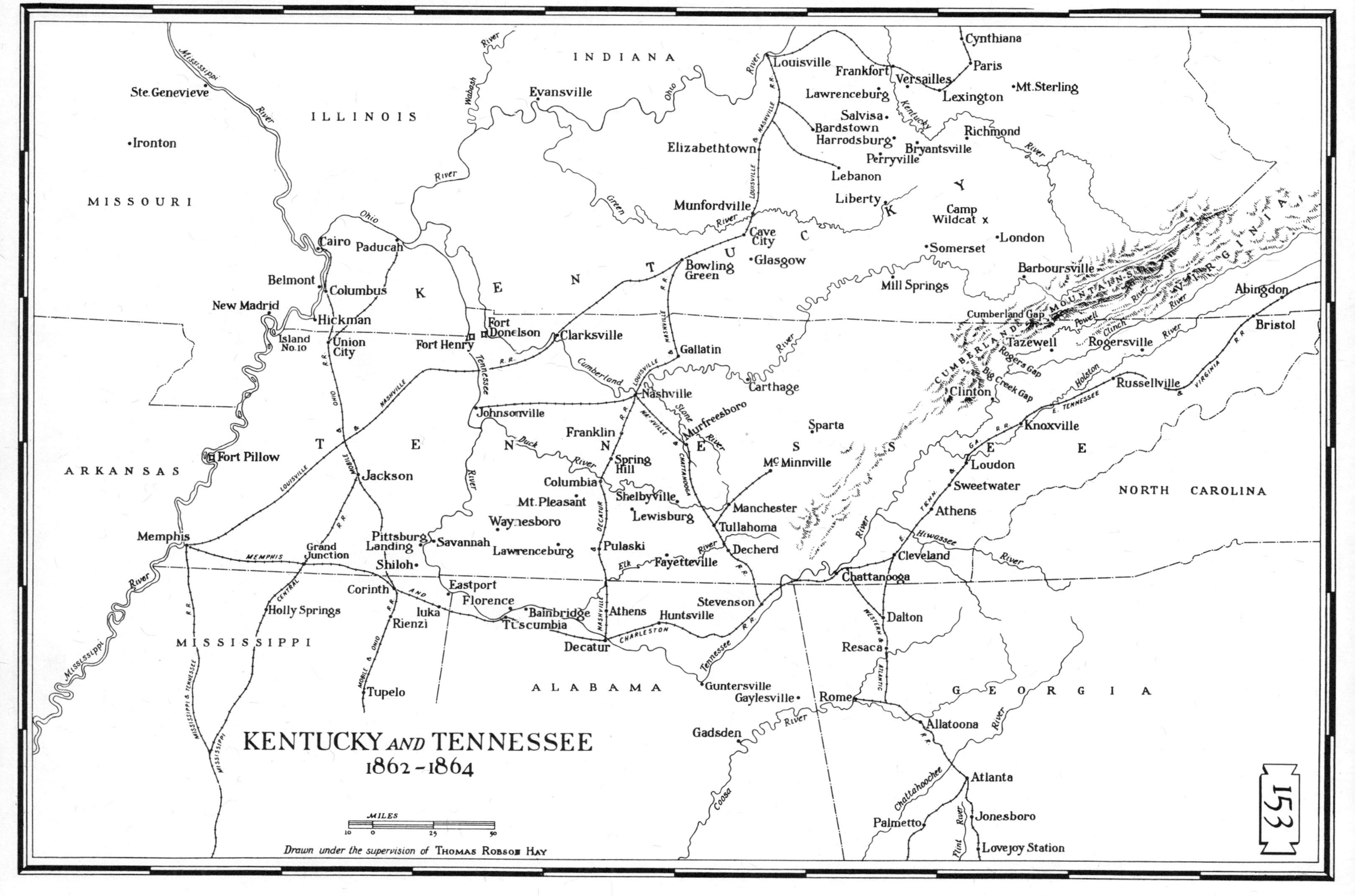
153
KENTUCKY AND TENNESSEE
1862-1864
MILES
10
0
25
50
Drawn under the supervision of Thomas Robson Hay
INDIANA
ILLINOIS
MISSOURI
ARKANSAS
MISSISSIPPI
ALABAMA
GEORGIA
NORTH CAROLINA
VIRGINIA
KENTUCKY
TENNESSEE
CUMBERLAND MOUNTAINS
Ste. Genevieve
Ironton
Evansville
Cairo
Paducah
Belmont
Columbus
New Madrid
Hickman
Island No. 10
Union City
Fort Henry
Fort Donelson
Clarksville
Fort Pillow
Jackson
Memphis
Grand Junction
Pittsburg Landing
Savannah
Shiloh
Corinth
Holly Springs
Iuka
Rienzi
Eastport
Florence
Bainbridge
Tuscumbia
Tupelo
Decatur
Athens
Huntsville
Stevenson
Guntersville
Gaylesville
Gadsden
Louisville
Frankfort
Versailles
Cynthiana
Paris
Lexington
Mt. Sterling
Lawrenceburg
Salvisa
Bardstown
Harrodsburg
Bryantsville
Perryville
Richmond
Elizabethtown
Lebanon
Liberty
Munfordville
Cave City
Glasgow
Bowling Green
Camp Wildcat
London
Somerset
Barboursville
Mill Springs
Cumberland Gap
Tazewell
Rogersville
Rogers Gap
Big Creek Gap
Clinton
Abingdon
Bristol
Russellville
Knoxville
Loudon
Sweetwater
Athens
Cleveland
Chattanooga
Dalton
Resaca
Rome
Allatoona
Atlanta
Jonesboro
Lovejoy Station
Palmetto
Gallatin
Carthage
Nashville
Murfreesboro
Sparta
McMinnville
Johnsonville
Franklin
Spring Hill
Columbia
Mt. Pleasant
Shelbyville
Lewisburg
Manchester
Tullahoma
Decherd
Waynesboro
Lawrenceburg
Pulaski
Fayetteville
Mississippi River
Ohio River
Wabash River
Green River
Kentucky River
Cumberland River
Tennessee River
Duck River
Stone River
Elk River
Powell River
Clinch River
Holston River
Hiwassee River
Coosa River
Chattahoochee River
Flint River
Louisville & Nashville R.R.
Mobile & Ohio R.R.
Memphis & Charleston R.R.
Mississippi Central R.R.
Mississippi & Tennessee R.R.
Nashville & Chattanooga R.R.
Nashville & Decatur R.R.
Western & Atlantic R.R.
E. Tennessee & Virginia R.R.
E. Tenn. & Ga. R.R.

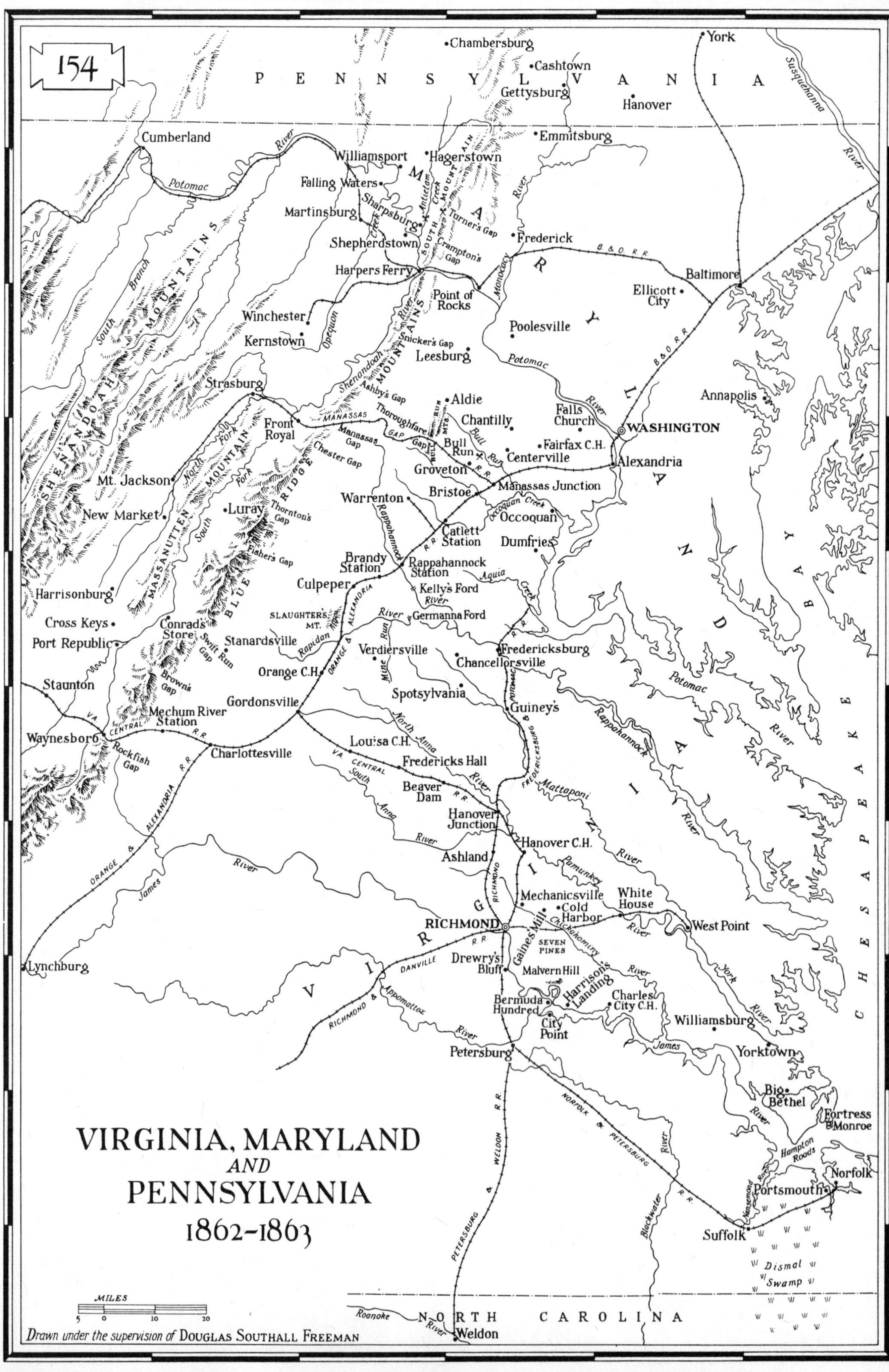

VIRGINIA, MARYLAND
AND
PENNSYLVANIA
1862–1863

Drawn under the supervision of DOUGLAS SOUTHALL FREEMAN

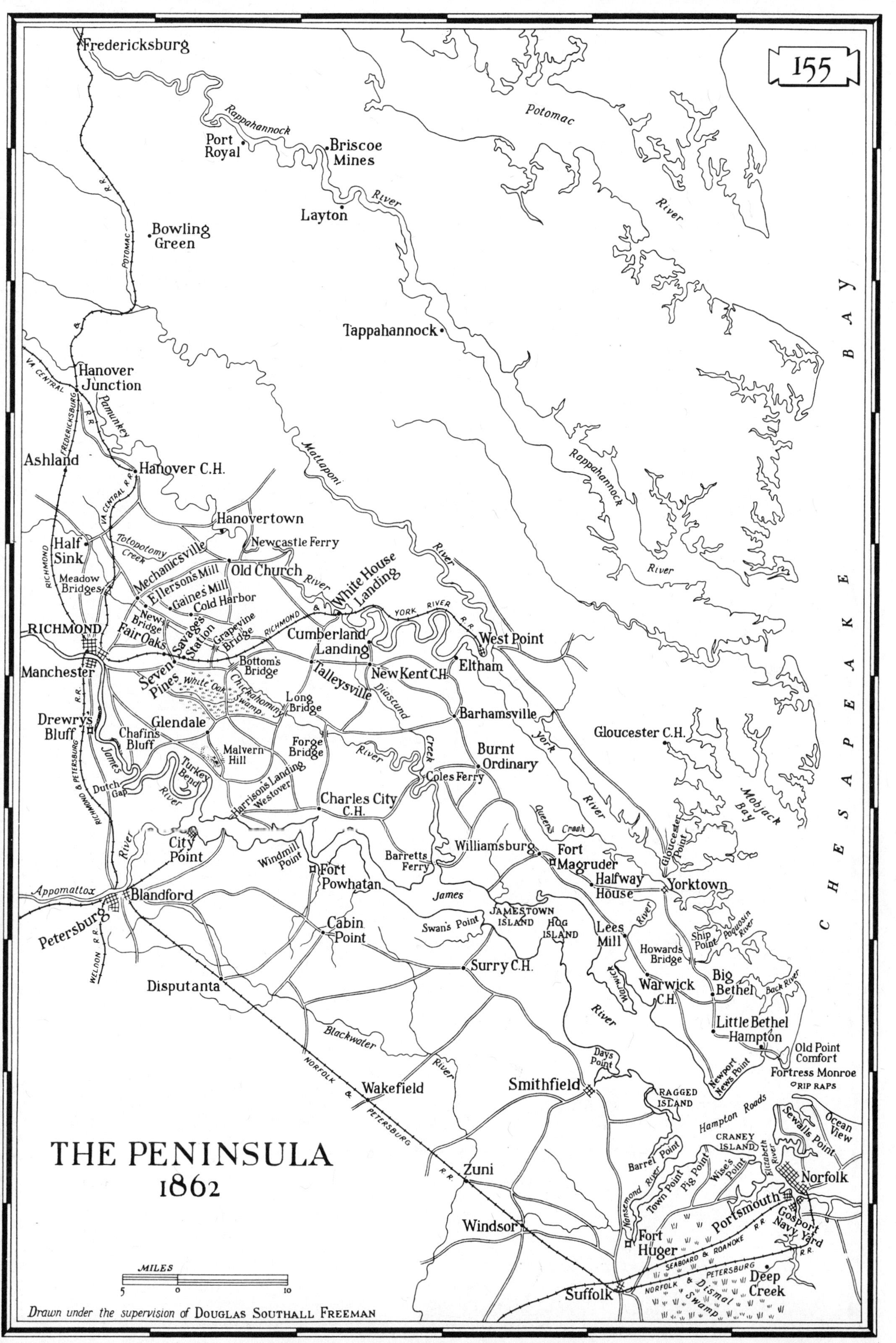
155
THE PENINSULA
1862
Fredericksburg
Rappahannock
River
Port Royal
Briscoe Mines
Layton
Bowling Green
Potomac
River
Tappahannock
Hanover Junction
Pamunkey
Ashland
Hanover C.H.
Hanovertown
Newcastle Ferry
Half Sink
Meadow Bridges
Totopotomy Creek
Mechanicsville
Ellerson's Mill
Gaine's Mill
Cold Harbor
Old Church
River
White House Landing
Mattaponi
River
Rappahannock
River
RICHMOND
Manchester
New Bridge
Fair Oaks
Savage's Station
Grapevine Bridge
Cumberland Landing
West Point
Eltham
Seven Pines
White Oak Swamp
Chickahominy
Bottom's Bridge
Talleysville
New Kent C.H.
Diascund Creek
Long Bridge
Barhamsville
Drewrys Bluff
Chafin's Bluff
Glendale
Malvern Hill
Forge Bridge
River
Burnt Ordinary
York
River
Gloucester C.H.
James
Turkey Bend
Dutch Gap
River
Harrisons Landing
Westover
Coles Ferry
Charles City C.H.
Queens Creek
Mobjack Bay
City Point
River
Windmill Point
Fort Powhatan
Barretts Ferry
Williamsburg
Fort Magruder
Halfway House
Gloucester Point
Yorktown
Appomattox
Petersburg
Blandford
James
JAMESTOWN ISLAND
HOG ISLAND
Swan's Point
Cabin Point
Lees Mill
River
Ship Point
Poquosin River
Howards Bridge
Surry C.H.
Disputanta
Warwick C.H.
Warwick
Big Bethel
Back River
River
Little Bethel
Hampton
Blackwater
River
Days Point
Newport News Point
Old Point Comfort
Fortress Monroe
RIP RAPS
Wakefield
Smithfield
RAGGED ISLAND
Hampton Roads
Ocean View
Sewalls Point
CRANEY ISLAND
Elizabeth River
Barrel Point
Nansemond River
Town Point
Pig Point
Wise's Point
Norfolk
Zuni
Portsmouth
Gosport Navy Yard
Windsor
Fort Huger
Suffolk
Deep Creek
Dismal Swamp
CHESAPEAKE BAY
VA CENTRAL R.R.
RICHMOND FREDERICKSBURG & POTOMAC R.R.
RICHMOND & YORK RIVER R.R.
RICHMOND & PETERSBURG R.R.
WELDON R.R.
NORFOLK & PETERSBURG R.R.
SEABOARD & ROANOKE R.R.
MILES
5 0 10
Drawn under the supervision of Douglas Southall Freeman

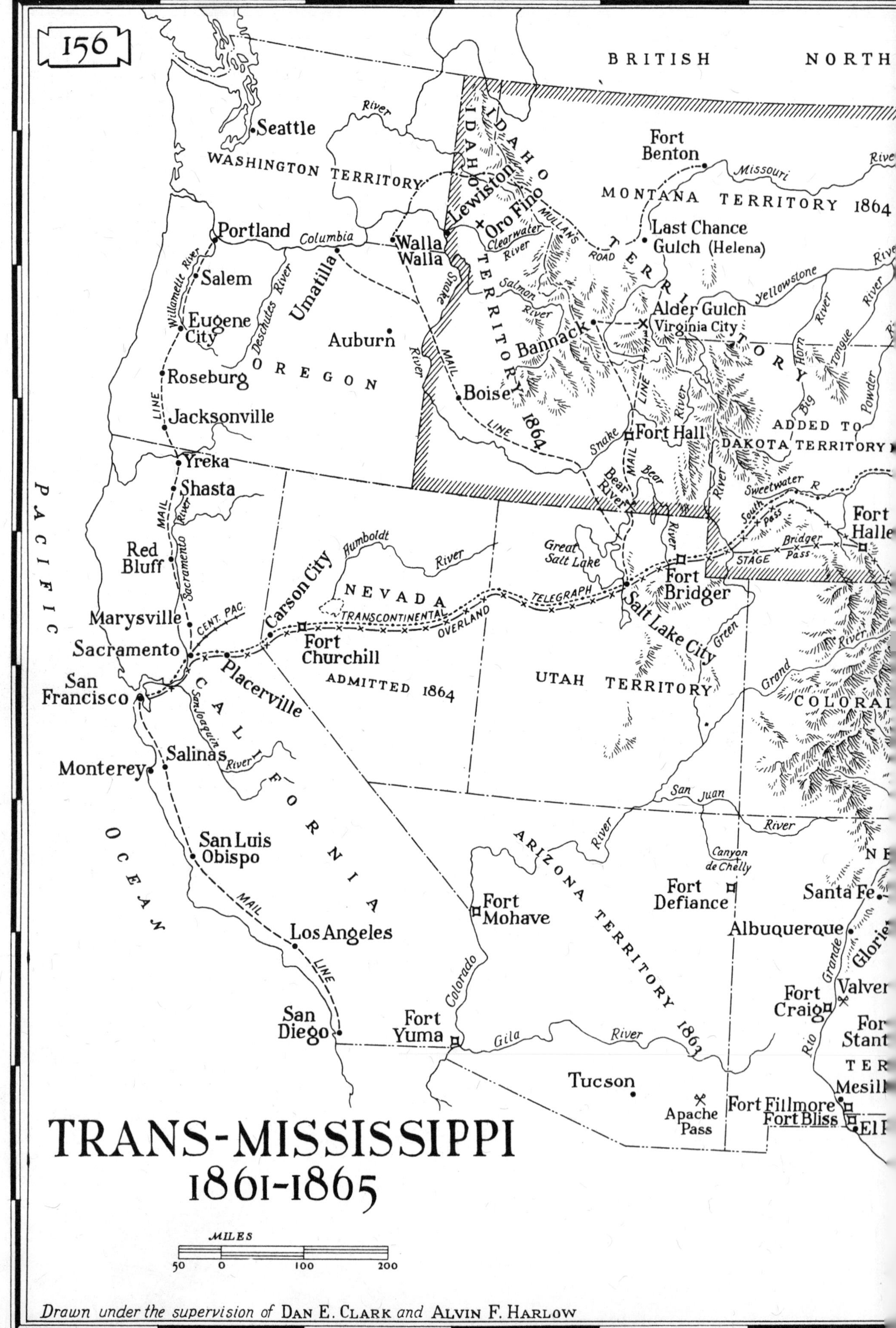

156
BRITISH NORTH
WASHINGTON TERRITORY
Seattle
River
IDAHO
IDAHO TERRITORY
Lewiston
Oro Fino
Clearwater River
MULLAN'S ROAD
Fort Benton
Missouri
River
MONTANA TERRITORY 1864
Last Chance Gulch (Helena)
Portland
Columbia
Walla Walla
Salem
Willamette River
Deschutes River
Unatilla
Snake
Salmon River
Eugene City
Auburn
OREGON
Alder Gulch
Virginia City
Bannack
Yellowstone
TERRITORY
Roseburg
River
MAIL LINE
Boise
1864
Horn River
Big Horn
Tongue River
Powder
Jacksonville
Snake
Fort Hall
ADDED TO DAKOTA TERRITORY
Yreka
Shasta
Bear River
Bear
Sweetwater R.
South Pass
Fort Halleck
PACIFIC
MAIL
Red Bluff
Sacramento River
Humboldt
River
Great Salt Lake
Bridger Pass
STAGE
Carson City
NEVADA
TELEGRAPH
Fort Bridger
Marysville
CENT. PAC.
TRANSCONTINENTAL
OVERLAND
Salt Lake City
Green
Sacramento
Fort Churchill
Placerville
River
San Francisco
CALIFORNIA
ADMITTED 1864
UTAH TERRITORY
Grand
COLORADO
San Joaquin River
Salinas
Monterey
San Juan
River
OCEAN
San Luis Obispo
ARIZONA TERRITORY 1863
Canyon de Chelly
Fort Defiance
Santa Fe
Fort Mohave
Albuquerque
MAIL LINE
Los Angeles
Glorieta
Colorado
Rio Grande
Valverde
Fort Craig
San Diego
Fort Yuma
Gila
River
Fort Stanton
TER
Tucson
Mesilla
Apache Pass
Fort Fillmore
Fort Bliss
El Paso
TRANS-MISSISSIPPI
1861-1865
MILES
50 0 100 200
Drawn under the supervision of DAN E. CLARK and ALVIN F. HARLOW

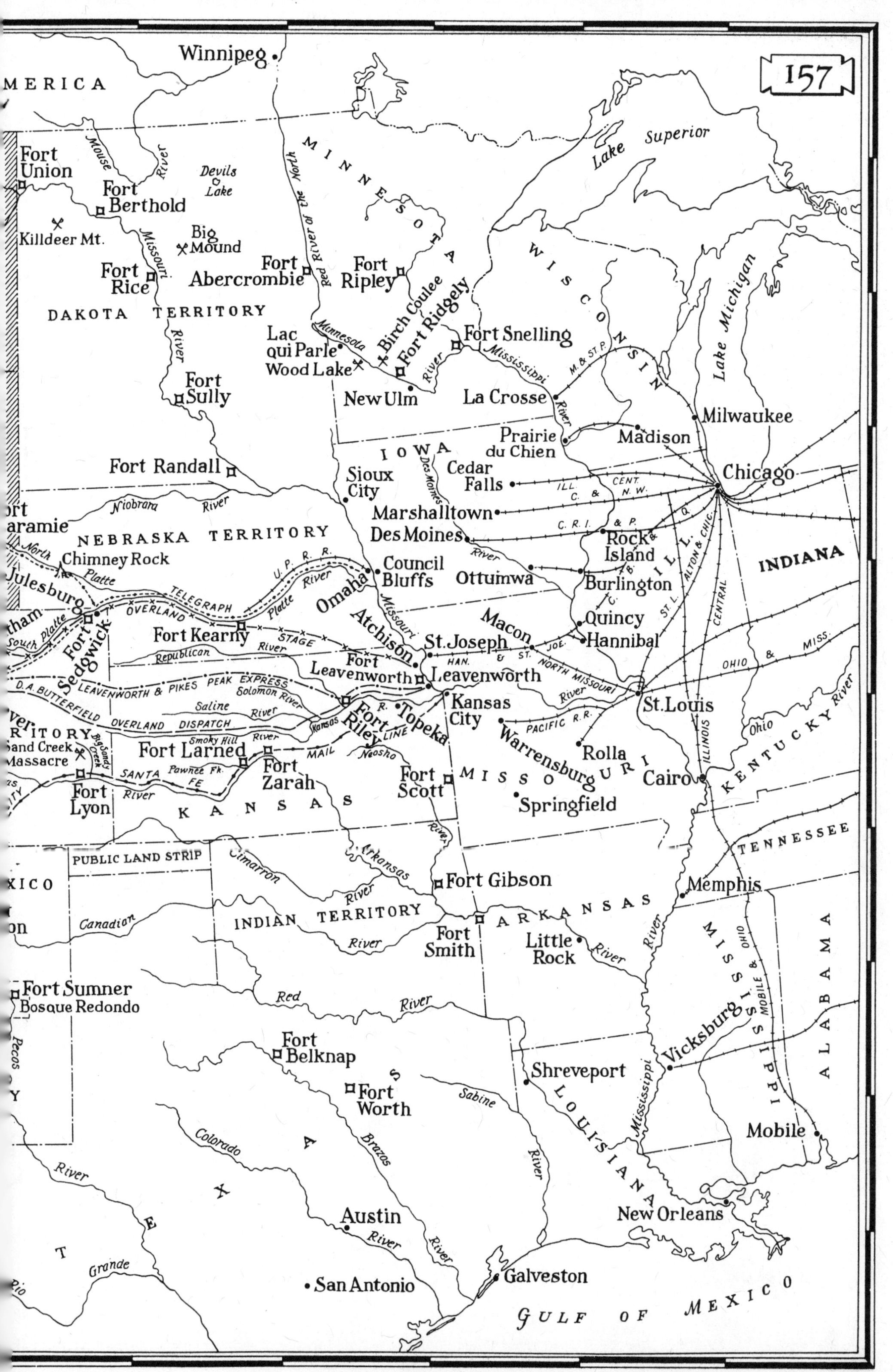

Winnipeg
MERICA
Lake Superior
Fort Union
Mouse
River
Devils Lake
Fort Berthold
MINNESOTA
Red River of the North
Killdeer Mt.
Big Mound
Missouri
WISCONSIN
Lake Michigan
Fort Rice
Fort Abercrombie
Fort Ripley
DAKOTA TERRITORY
Birch Coulee
Fort Ridgely
Fort Snelling
Lac qui Parle
Minnesota
Wood Lake
River
Mississippi
M. & ST. P.
Fort Sully
New Ulm
La Crosse
Milwaukee
Prairie du Chien
Madison
IOWA
Fort Randall
Sioux City
Cedar Falls
Des Moines
Chicago
Niobrara
River
ILL. C. & CENT. N.W.
Marshalltown
C. R. I. & P.
Des Moines
Rock Island
C. B. & Q.
ILL. ALTON & CHIC.
NEBRASKA TERRITORY
North Platte
Chimney Rock
Julesburg
U. P. R. R.
Council Bluffs
Ottumwa
Burlington
INDIANA
TELEGRAPH
OVERLAND
Platte River
Omaha
Missouri
Fort Sedgwick
South Platte
Fort Kearny
STAGE
Atchison
Macon
Quincy
Hannibal
ST. L.
CENTRAL
Republican River
Fort Leavenworth
Leavenworth
St. Joseph
HAN. & ST. JOE.
NORTH MISSOURI
OHIO & MISS.
LEAVENWORTH & PIKES PEAK EXPRESS
Solomon River
D. A. BUTTERFIELD OVERLAND DISPATCH
Saline River
Kansas
Fort Riley
Topeka
Kansas City
PACIFIC R.R.
St. Louis
ILLINOIS
Ohio
River
KENTUCKY
Sand Creek Massacre
Big Sandy Creek
Smoky Hill River
MAIL LINE
Neosho
Fort Larned
Warrensburg
Rolla
Cairo
SANTA FE
Pawnee Fk.
Fort Zarah
Fort Scott
MISSOURI
Springfield
Fort Lyon
River
KANSAS
River
PUBLIC LAND STRIP
Cimarron
Arkansas River
TENNESSEE
Fort Gibson
Memphis
Canadian
INDIAN TERRITORY
ARKANSAS
Fort Smith
Little Rock
River
River
MISSISSIPPI
MOBILE & OHIO
ALABAMA
Fort Sumner
Bosque Redondo
Red River
Pecos
Fort Belknap
Vicksburg
Shreveport
Mississippi
Fort Worth
Sabine
LOUISIANA
Colorado
Brazos
River
Mobile
TEXAS
River
New Orleans
Austin
River
Rivers
Grande
Galveston
San Antonio
GULF OF MEXICO

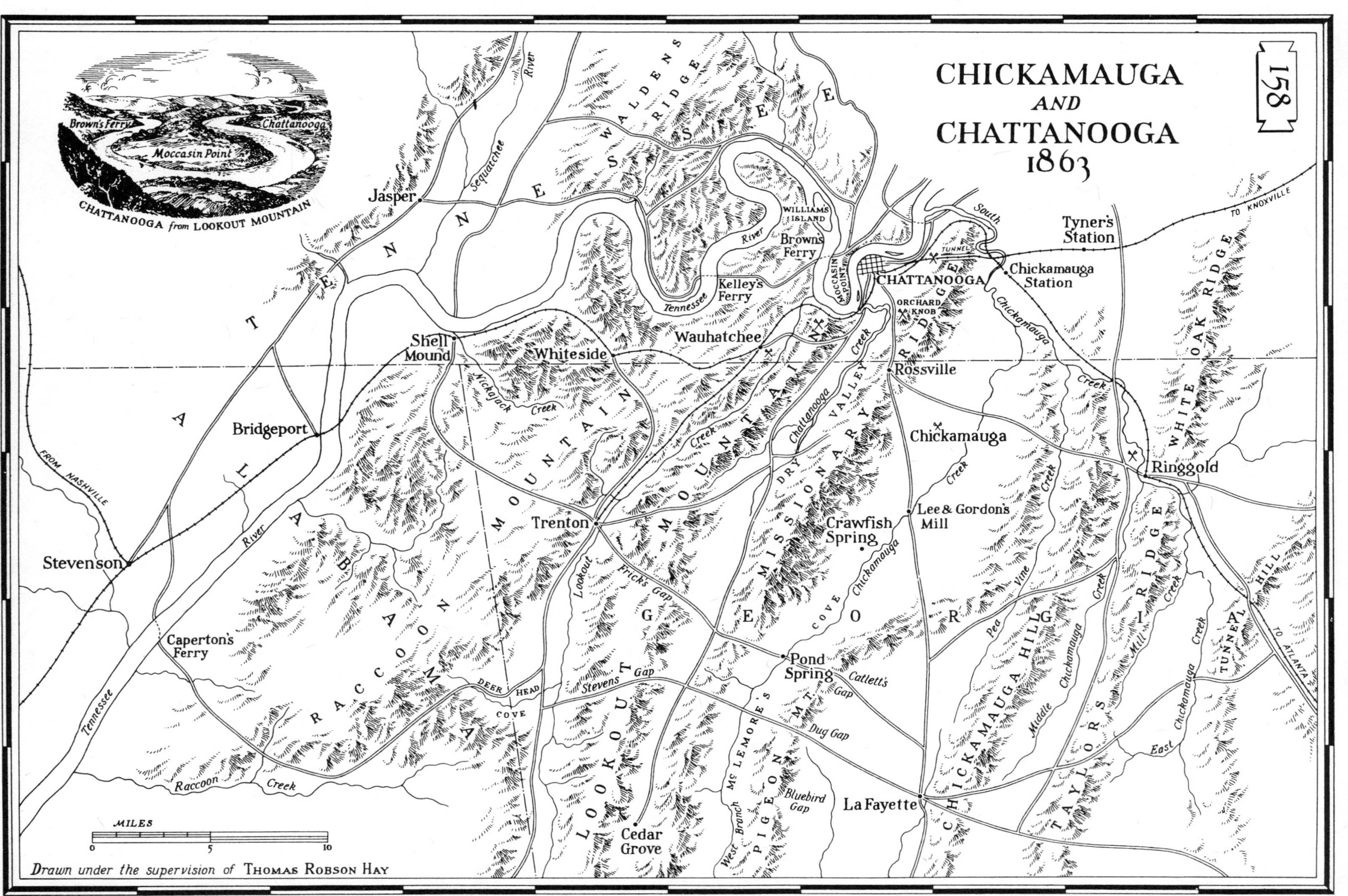
158
CHICKAMAUGA
AND
CHATTANOOGA
1863
Brown's Ferry
Chattanooga
Moccasin Point
CHATTANOOGA from LOOKOUT MOUNTAIN
TENNESSEE
ALABAMA
WALDENS RIDGE
Jasper
Sequatchee River
WILLIAMS ISLAND
Browns Ferry
Kelley's Ferry
Tennessee River
MOCCASIN POINT
CHATTANOOGA
TUNNEL
South
Tyner's Station
Chickamauga Station
TO KNOXVILLE
ORCHARD KNOB
MISSIONARY RIDGE
Shell Mound
Whiteside
Wauhatchee
Rossville
Nickajack Creek
Chattanooga Creek
Chickamauga Creek
Bridgeport
Chickamauga
Ringgold
WHITE OAK RIDGE
FROM NASHVILLE
LOOKOUT MOUNTAIN
RACCOON MOUNTAIN
Trenton
Lee & Gordon's Mill
Crawfish Spring
Stevenson
DRY VALLEY
Lookout Creek
Frick's Gap
Chickamauga
COVE
GEORGIA
Pea Vine Creek
CHICKAMAUGA HILL
Middle Chickamauga Creek
Mill Creek
TAYLORS RIDGE
TUNNEL HILL
TO ATLANTA
Caperton's Ferry
Pond Spring
Catlett's Gap
Stevens Gap
DEER HEAD COVE
Dug Gap
Mc LEMORE'S COVE
PIGEON MT
Bluebird Gap
East Chickamauga Creek
Raccoon Creek
La Fayette
Cedar Grove
West Branch
MILES
0
5
10
Drawn under the supervision of THOMAS ROBSON HAY

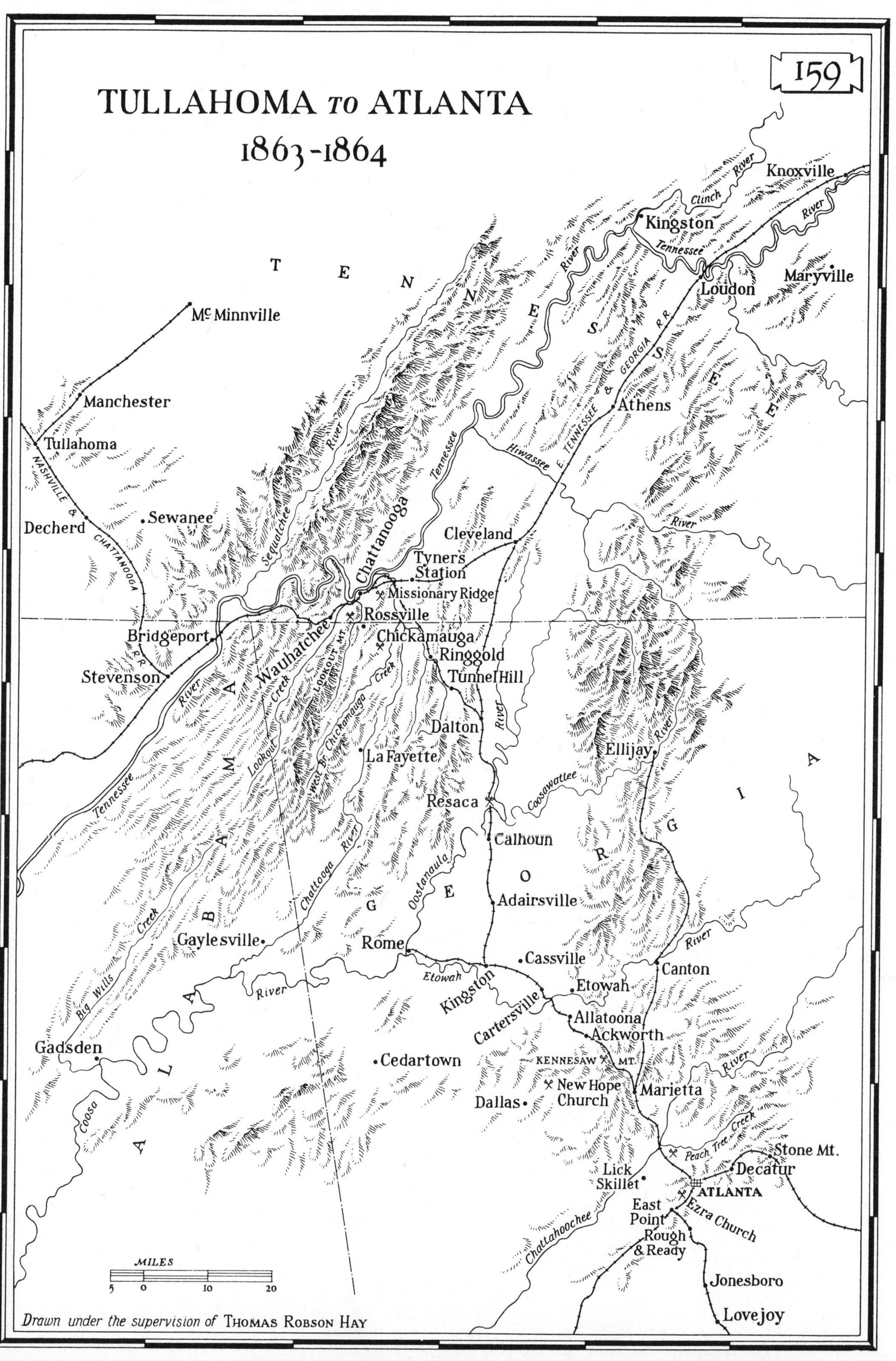
159
TULLAHOMA TO ATLANTA
1863-1864
TENNESSEE
ALABAMA
GEORGIA
Mc Minnville
Manchester
Tullahoma
NASHVILLE & CHATTANOOGA R.R.
Decherd
Sewanee
Bridgeport
Stevenson
Knoxville
Kingston
Loudon
Maryville
Clinch River
Tennessee River
Athens
E. TENNESSEE & GEORGIA R.R.
Hiwassee River
Cleveland
Tyners Station
Missionary Ridge
Chattanooga
Sequatchee River
Rossville
Chickamauga
Ringgold
Tunnel Hill
Wauhatchee
Lookout Creek
LOOKOUT MT.
Chickamauga Creek
West Br. Chickamauga
Dalton
La Fayette
Ellijay
Coosawattee
Resaca
Calhoun
Adairsville
Oostanaula
Chattooga River
Big Wills Creek
Gaylesville
Rome
Cassville
Etowah
Etowah River
Kingston
Cartersville
Allatoona
Ackworth
Canton
KENNESAW MT.
New Hope Church
Marietta
Dallas
Cedartown
Gadsden
Coosa
Peach Tree Creek
Stone Mt.
Decatur
Lick Skillet
ATLANTA
East Point
Ezra Church
Rough & Ready
Chattahoochee
Jonesboro
Lovejoy
MILES
5 0 10 20
Drawn under the supervision of Thomas Robson Hay

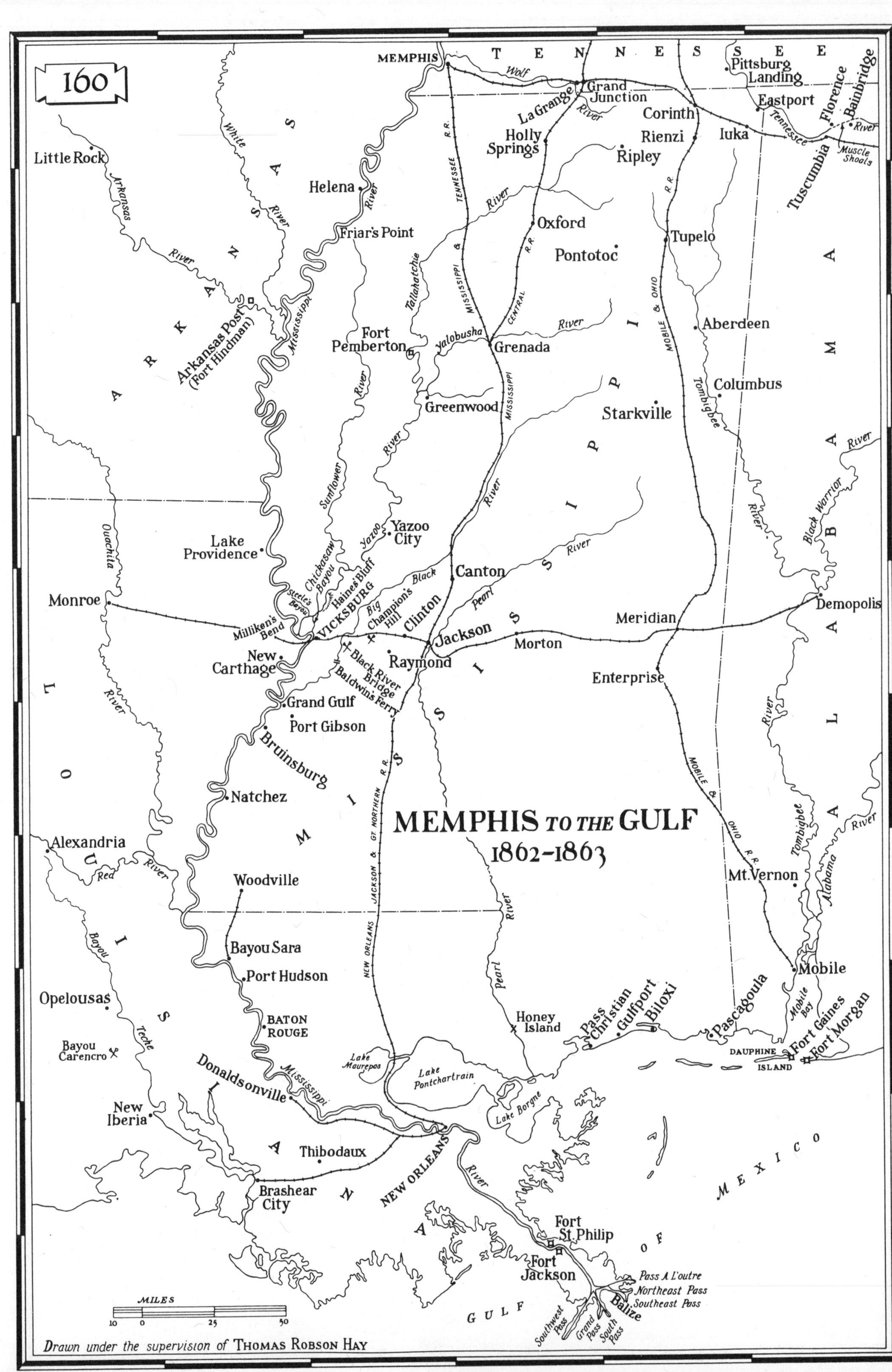
160
MEMPHIS TO THE GULF
1862-1863
MEMPHIS
TENNESSEE
ARKANSAS
MISSISSIPPI
ALABAMA
LOUISIANA
GULF OF MEXICO
Pittsburg Landing
Grand Junction
La Grange
Corinth
Eastport
Florence
Bainbridge
Holly Springs
Rienzi
Iuka
Ripley
Tuscumbia
Muscle Shoals
Little Rock
Helena
Friar's Point
Oxford
Pontotoc
Tupelo
Arkansas Post (Fort Hindman)
Fort Pemberton
Grenada
Aberdeen
Greenwood
Columbus
Starkville
Yazoo City
Lake Providence
Canton
Monroe
Milliken's Bend
VICKSBURG
Haines's Bluff
Steele's Bayou
Chickasaw Bayou
Champions Hill
Clinton
Jackson
Meridian
Morton
Demopolis
New Carthage
Raymond
Black River Bridge
Baldwins Ferry
Enterprise
Grand Gulf
Port Gibson
Bruinsburg
Natchez
Alexandria
Woodville
Mt. Vernon
Bayou Sara
Port Hudson
Mobile
Opelousas
BATON ROUGE
Honey Island
Pass Christian
Gulfport
Biloxi
Pascagoula
Mobile Bay
Fort Gaines
Fort Morgan
DAUPHINE ISLAND
Bayou Carencro
Lake Maurepas
Lake Pontchartrain
Lake Borgne
Donaldsonville
New Iberia
Thibodaux
NEW ORLEANS
Brashear City
Fort St. Philip
Fort Jackson
Pass A L'outre
Northeast Pass
Southeast Pass
Balize
Southwest Pass
Grand Pass
South Pass
Wolf River
White River
Arkansas River
Mississippi River
Tallahatchie
Yalobusha River
Sunflower River
Yazoo
Big Black
Pearl River
Ouachita
Red River
Bayou Teche
Tennessee River
Tombigbee River
Black Warrior River
Alabama River
MISSISSIPPI & TENNESSEE R.R.
MISSISSIPPI CENTRAL R.R.
MOBILE & OHIO R.R.
NEW ORLEANS JACKSON & GT NORTHERN R.R.
MILES
10 0 25 50
Drawn under the supervision of THOMAS ROBSON HAY

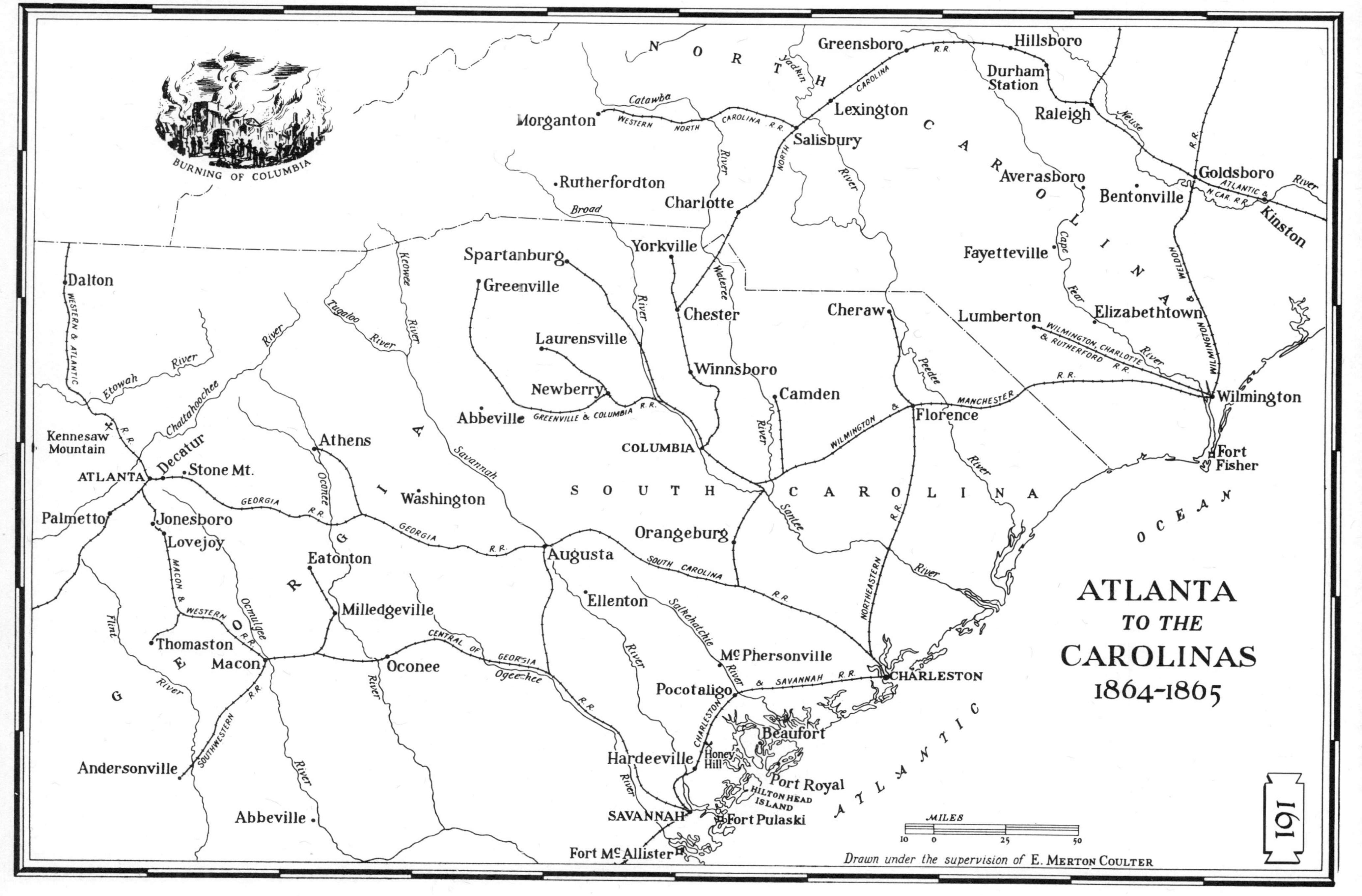
ATLANTA
TO THE
CAROLINAS
1864-1865
BURNING OF COLUMBIA
NORTH CAROLINA
SOUTH CAROLINA
GEORGIA
ATLANTIC OCEAN
Greensboro
Hillsboro
Durham Station
Raleigh
Lexington
Salisbury
Morganton
Rutherfordton
Charlotte
Goldsboro
Kinston
Averasboro
Bentonville
Fayetteville
Elizabethtown
Lumberton
Wilmington
Fort Fisher
Yorkville
Spartanburg
Greenville
Chester
Cheraw
Laurensville
Winnsboro
Newberry
Camden
Abbeville
Florence
COLUMBIA
Orangeburg
CHARLESTON
Mc Phersonville
Pocotaligo
Beaufort
Honey Hill
Port Royal
HILTON HEAD ISLAND
Fort Pulaski
Hardeeville
SAVANNAH
Fort Mc Allister
Ellenton
Augusta
Washington
Athens
Eatonton
Milledgeville
Oconee
Macon
Thomaston
Lovejoy
Jonesboro
Stone Mt.
Decatur
ATLANTA
Palmetto
Kennesaw Mountain
Dalton
Andersonville
Abbeville
Catawba
Yadkin
Neuse
Cape Fear River
Broad River
Wateree River
Peedee River
Santee
Keowee River
Tugaloo River
Savannah
Saluda River
Salkehatchie River
Ogeechee
Oconee River
Ocmulgee
Flint River
Etowah River
Chattahoochee River
WESTERN & ATLANTIC
GEORGIA R.R.
MACON & WESTERN R.R.
SOUTHWESTERN R.R.
CENTRAL OF GEORGIA R.R.
SOUTH CAROLINA R.R.
CHARLESTON & SAVANNAH R.R.
NORTHEASTERN R.R.
WILMINGTON & MANCHESTER R.R.
GREENVILLE & COLUMBIA R.R.
NORTH CAROLINA R.R.
WESTERN NORTH CAROLINA R.R.
WILMINGTON & WELDON R.R.
WILMINGTON, CHARLOTTE & RUTHERFORD R.R.
ATLANTIC & N. CAR. R.R.
MILES
10 0 25 50
Drawn under the supervision of E. Merton Coulter
161

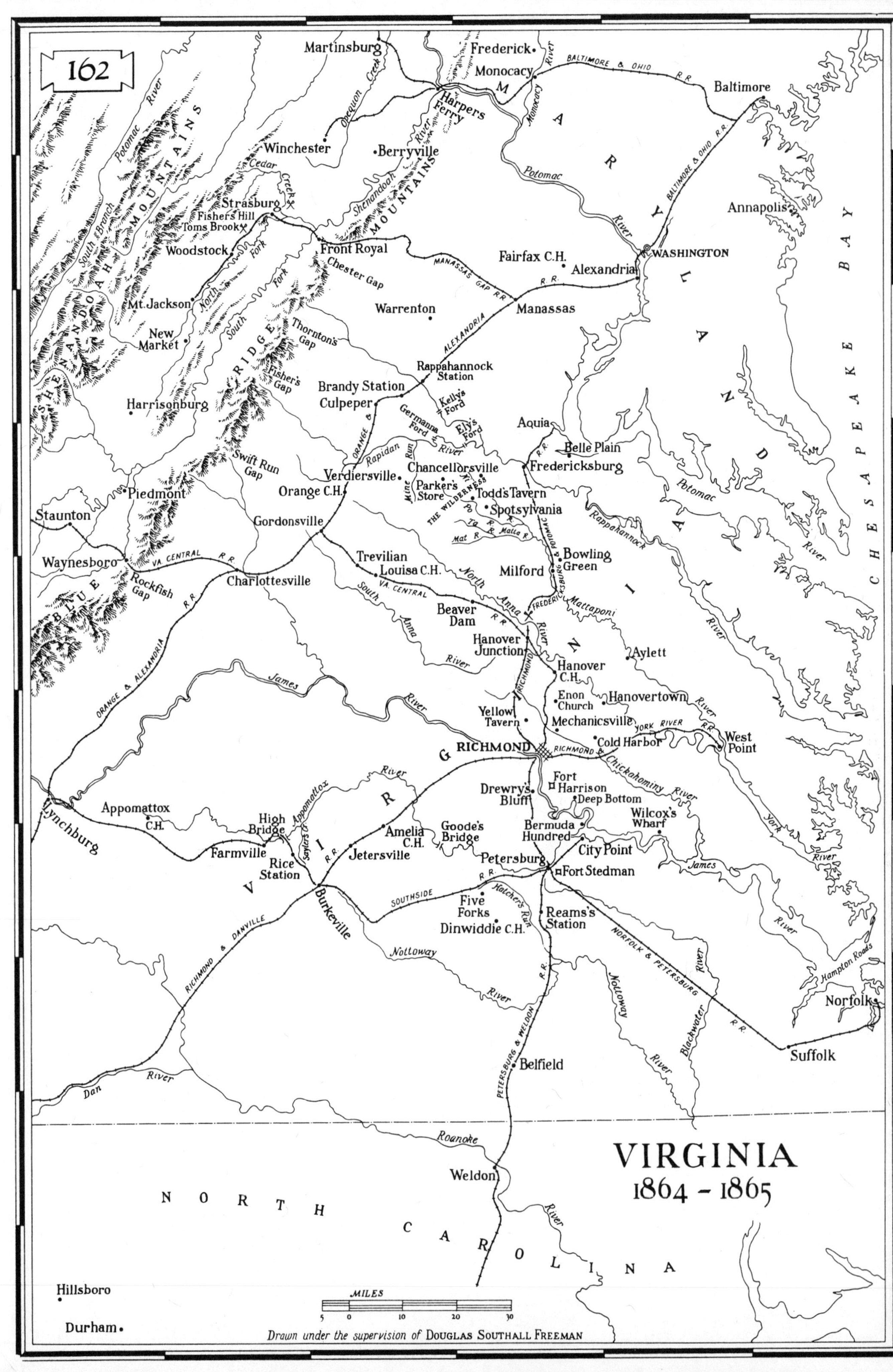
162
VIRGINIA
1864 - 1865
Martinsburg
Frederick
Monocacy
Harpers Ferry
Baltimore
Winchester
Berryville
Strasburg
Fishers Hill
Toms Brook
Woodstock
Front Royal
Chester Gap
Fairfax C.H.
Alexandria
WASHINGTON
Annapolis
Mt. Jackson
New Market
Warrenton
Manassas
Thornton's Gap
Rappahannock Station
Brandy Station
Culpeper
Fisher's Gap
Harrisonburg
Kelly's Ford
Germanna Ford
Ely's Ford
Aquia
Belle Plain
Fredericksburg
Swift Run Gap
Chancellorsville
Verdiersville
Parker's Store
Todd's Tavern
Spotsylvania
THE WILDERNESS
Orange C.H.
Piedmont
Staunton
Gordonsville
Waynesboro
Rockfish Gap
Charlottesville
Trevilian
Louisa C.H.
Milford
Bowling Green
Beaver Dam
Hanover Junction
Hanover C.H.
Aylett
Enon Church
Hanovertown
Yellow Tavern
Mechanicsville
Cold Harbor
West Point
RICHMOND
Fort Harrison
Drewry's Bluff
Deep Bottom
Wilcox's Wharf
Bermuda Hundred
City Point
Fort Stedman
Petersburg
Goode's Bridge
Amelia C.H.
Jetersville
Appomattox C.H.
High Bridge
Farmville
Rice Station
Lynchburg
Burkeville
Five Forks
Dinwiddie C.H.
Reams's Station
Norfolk
Suffolk
Hampton Roads
Belfield
Weldon
Hillsboro
Durham
SHENANDOAH MOUNTAINS
BLUE RIDGE
MARYLAND
VIRGINIA
NORTH CAROLINA
CHESAPEAKE BAY
BALTIMORE & OHIO R.R.
MANASSAS GAP R.R.
ORANGE & ALEXANDRIA R.R.
VA. CENTRAL R.R.
RICHMOND & FREDERICKSBURG & POTOMAC
RICHMOND & DANVILLE
SOUTHSIDE R.R.
NORFOLK & PETERSBURG R.R.
PETERSBURG & WELDON R.R.
YORK RIVER R.R.
Potomac River
Shenandoah River
Rapidan River
James River
Rappahannock River
York River
Nottoway River
Blackwater River
Dan River
Roanoke River
Chickahominy River
Mattaponi River
North Anna River
South Anna River
MILES
0 10 20 30
Drawn under the supervision of DOUGLAS SOUTHALL FREEMAN

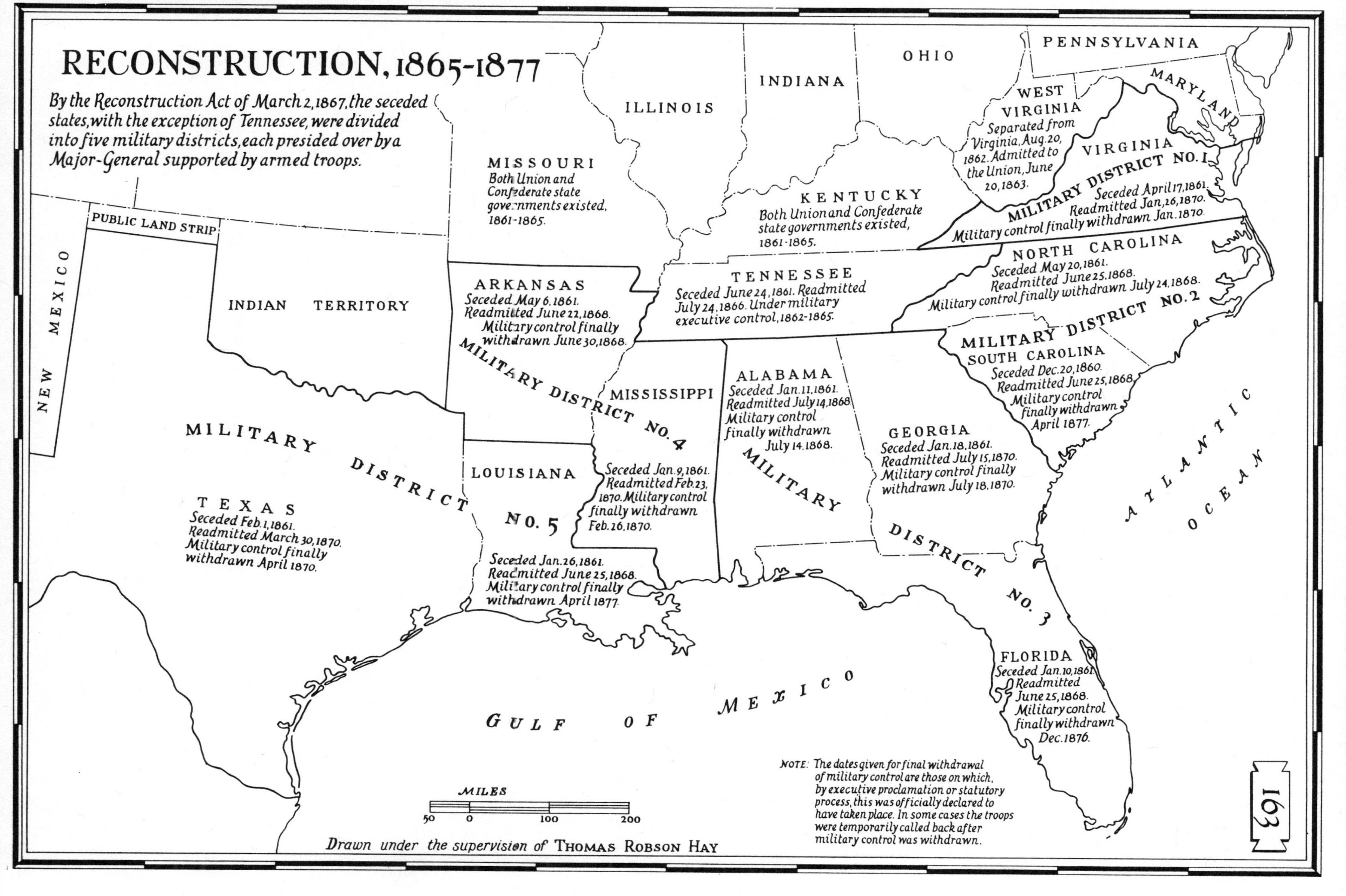

RECONSTRUCTION, 1865-1877
By the Reconstruction Act of March 2, 1867, the seceded states, with the exception of Tennessee, were divided into five military districts, each presided over by a Major-General supported by armed troops.
PENNSYLVANIA
OHIO
INDIANA
ILLINOIS
MISSOURI
Both Union and Confederate state governments existed, 1861-1865.
MARYLAND
WEST VIRGINIA
Separated from Virginia, Aug. 20, 1862. Admitted to the Union, June 20, 1863.
VIRGINIA
MILITARY DISTRICT NO. 1
Seceded April 17, 1861. Readmitted Jan. 26, 1870. Military control finally withdrawn Jan. 1870.
KENTUCKY
Both Union and Confederate state governments existed, 1861-1865.
NORTH CAROLINA
Seceded May 20, 1861. Readmitted June 25, 1868. Military control finally withdrawn July 24, 1868.
MILITARY DISTRICT NO. 2
SOUTH CAROLINA
Seceded Dec. 20, 1860. Readmitted June 25, 1868. Military control finally withdrawn April 1877.
TENNESSEE
Seceded June 24, 1861. Readmitted July 24, 1866. Under military executive control, 1862-1865.
NEW MEXICO
PUBLIC LAND STRIP
INDIAN TERRITORY
ARKANSAS
Seceded May 6, 1861. Readmitted June 22, 1868. Military control finally withdrawn June 30, 1868.
MILITARY DISTRICT NO. 4
MISSISSIPPI
Seceded Jan. 9, 1861. Readmitted Feb. 23, 1870. Military control finally withdrawn Feb. 26, 1870.
ALABAMA
Seceded Jan. 11, 1861. Readmitted July 14, 1868. Military control finally withdrawn July 14, 1868.
GEORGIA
Seceded Jan. 18, 1861. Readmitted July 15, 1870. Military control finally withdrawn July 18, 1870.
MILITARY DISTRICT NO. 3
FLORIDA
Seceded Jan. 10, 1861. Readmitted June 25, 1868. Military control finally withdrawn Dec. 1876.
MILITARY DISTRICT NO. 5
TEXAS
Seceded Feb. 1, 1861. Readmitted March 30, 1870. Military control finally withdrawn April 1870.
LOUISIANA
Seceded Jan. 26, 1861. Readmitted June 25, 1868. Military control finally withdrawn April 1877.
ATLANTIC OCEAN
GULF OF MEXICO
MILES
50 0 100 200
NOTE: The dates given for final withdrawal of military control are those on which, by executive proclamation or statutory process, this was officially declared to have taken place. In some cases the troops were temporarily called back after military control was withdrawn.
Drawn under the supervision of THOMAS ROBSON HAY
163

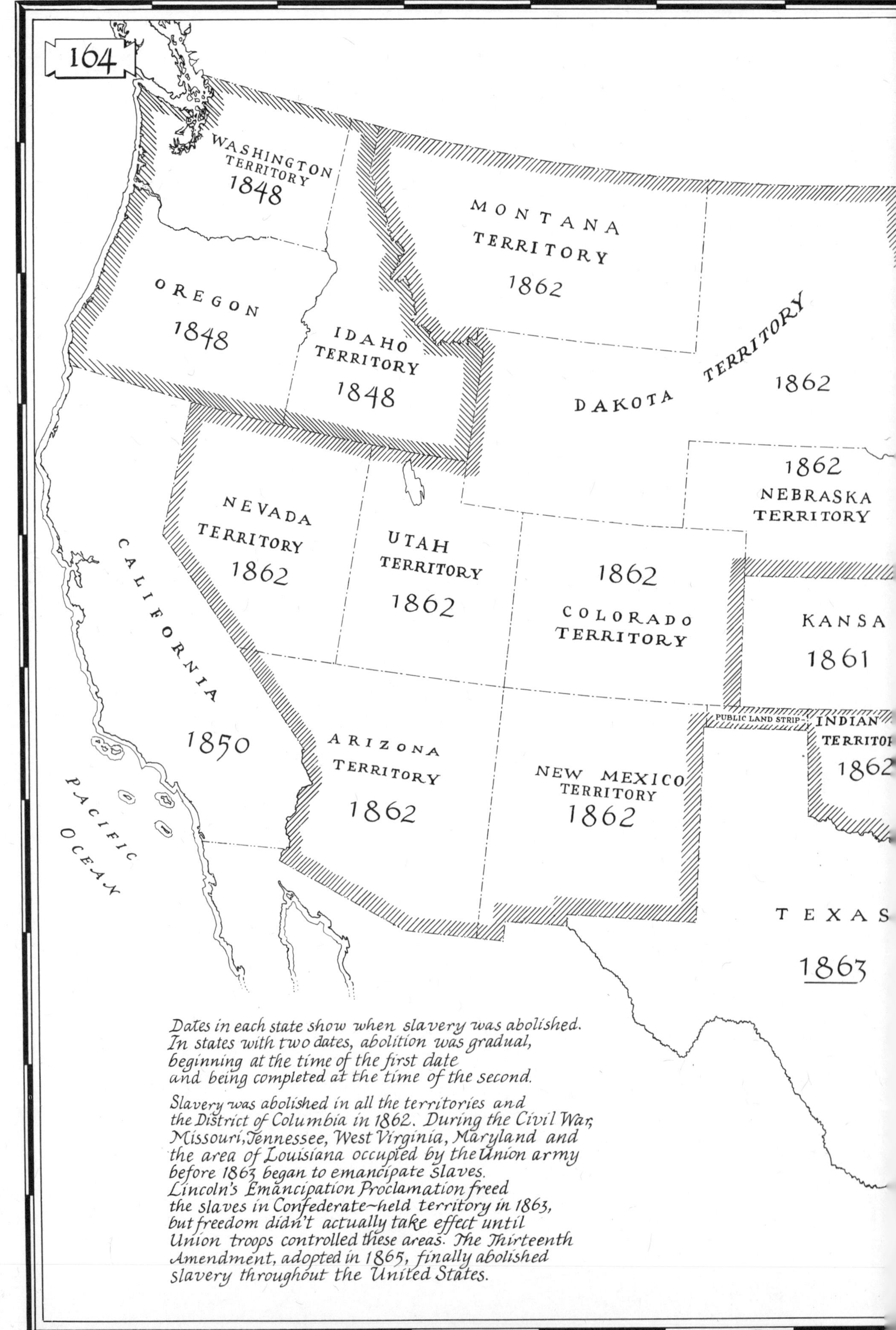

Dates in each state show when slavery was abolished. In states with two dates, abolition was gradual, beginning at the time of the first date and being completed at the time of the second.

Slavery was abolished in all the territories and the District of Columbia in 1862. During the Civil War, Missouri, Tennessee, West Virginia, Maryland and the area of Louisiana occupied by the Union army before 1863 began to emancipate slaves. Lincoln's Emancipation Proclamation freed the slaves in Confederate-held territory in 1863, but freedom didn't actually take effect until Union troops controlled these areas. The Thirteenth Amendment, adopted in 1865, finally abolished slavery throughout the United States.

THE ABOLITION OF SLAVERY
1777~1865
MINNESOTA
1820
WISCONSIN
1787
MICHIGAN
1787
IOWA
1820
ILLINOIS
1787
INDIANA
1787
OHIO
1787
PENNSYLVANIA
1780, 1850
NEW YORK
1799, 1827
VT.
1777
N.H.
1783
MAINE
1780
MASS.
1780
CONN.
1784 1848
R.I.
1784 1842
NEW JERSEY
1804, 1846
DEL. 1865
MD. 1865
WEST VIRGINIA
1865
VIRGINIA
1863
MISSOURI
1865
KENTUCKY
1865
TENNESSEE
1865
NORTH CAROLINA
1863
ARKANSAS
1863
SOUTH CAROLINA
1863
MISSISSIPPI
1863
ALABAMA
1863
GEORGIA
1863
LOUISIANA
1863
1865
FLORIDA
1863
ATLANTIC OCEAN
Key:
1863: Slaves freed by the Emancipation Proclamation
Slaves freed by the Oregon Act of 1848
Slaves freed by act of Congress, 1862
MILES
100
200
300
400

VIII THE END OF THE FRONTIER

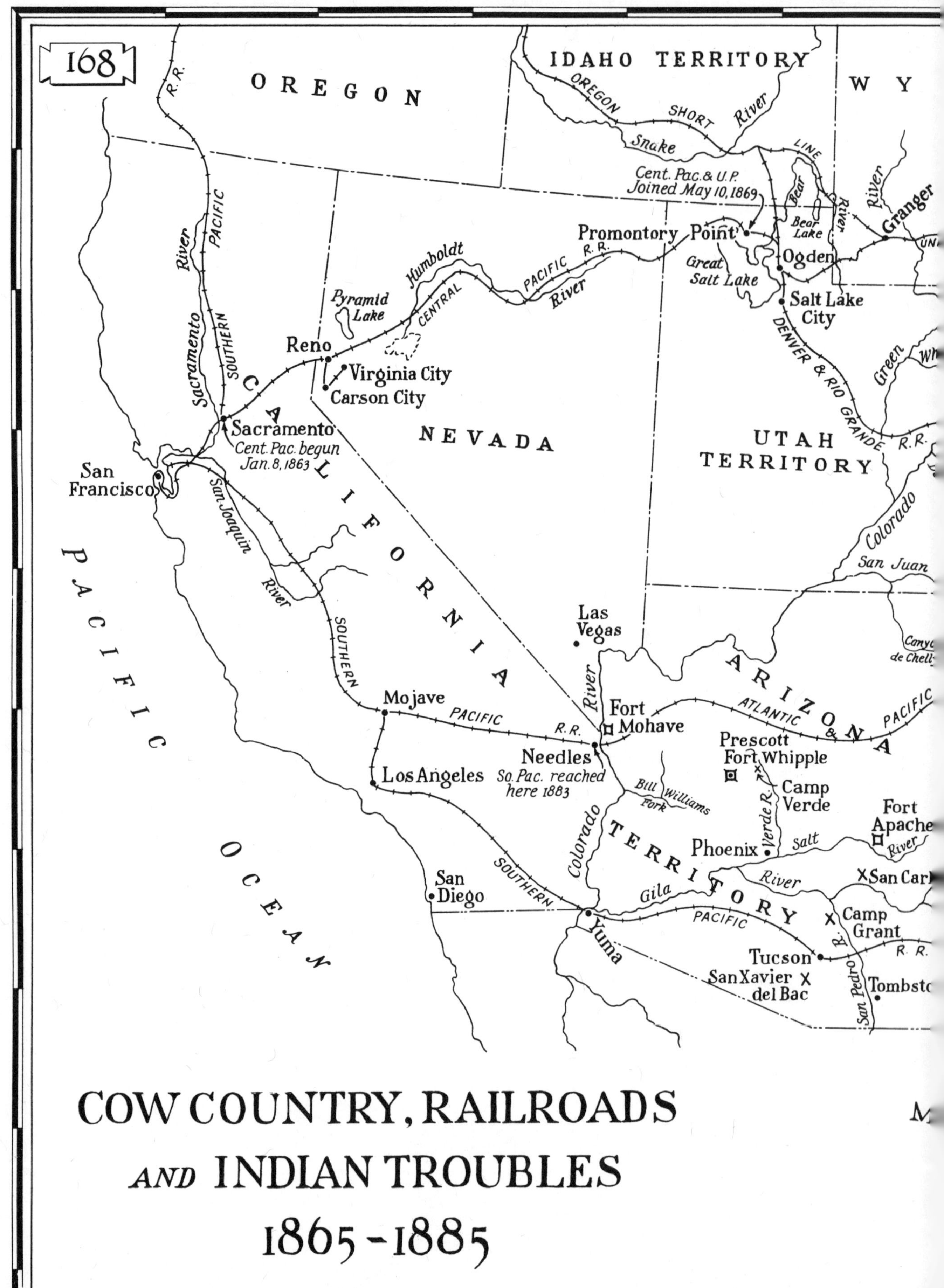
168
OREGON
IDAHO TERRITORY
W Y
OREGON SHORT LINE
Snake River
Cent. Pac. & U.P. Joined May 10, 1869
Promontory Point
Bear Lake
Ogden
Granger
Great Salt Lake
Salt Lake City
Pyramid Lake
Humboldt River
CENTRAL PACIFIC R.R.
Reno
Virginia City
Carson City
Sacramento River
SOUTHERN PACIFIC R.R.
Sacramento
Cent. Pac. begun Jan. 8, 1863
San Francisco
San Joaquin River
NEVADA
UTAH TERRITORY
DENVER & RIO GRANDE R.R.
Green
Colorado
San Juan
CALIFORNIA
PACIFIC OCEAN
Las Vegas
Canyon de Chelly
ARIZONA TERRITORY
Fort Mohave
ATLANTIC & PACIFIC
Mojave
PACIFIC R.R.
Needles
So. Pac. reached here 1883
Los Angeles
Prescott
Fort Whipple
Camp Verde
Bill Williams Fork
Verde R.
Fort Apache
Phoenix
Salt River
Gila River
San Carl
Camp Grant
San Diego
SOUTHERN PACIFIC R.R.
Yuma
Tucson
San Xavier del Bac
San Pedro R.
Tombsto
COW COUNTRY, RAILROADS AND INDIAN TROUBLES 1865-1885
MILES
50 0 100 200
Drawn under the supervision of ALVIN F. HARLOW and CARL COKE RISTER

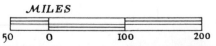

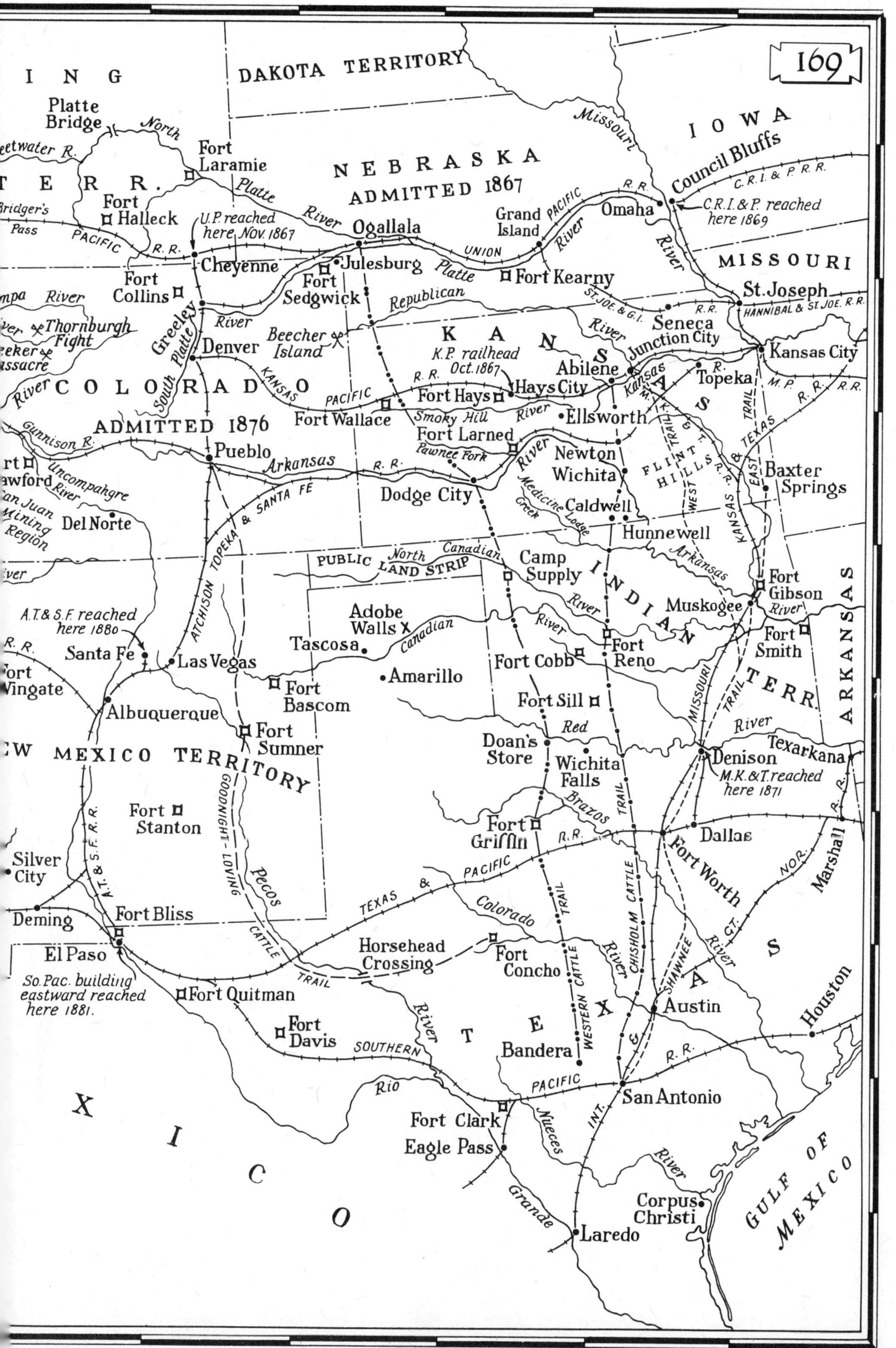
DAKOTA TERRITORY
I N G
Platte Bridge
North
eetwater R.
Fort Laramie
T E R R.
NEBRASKA
ADMITTED 1867
IOWA
Council Bluffs
C.R.I. & P. R.R.
C.R.I.&P. reached here 1869
Missouri
Fort Halleck
Bridger's Pass
PACIFIC R.R.
U.P. reached here Nov. 1867
Platte
River
Ogallala
Grand Island
PACIFIC
R.R.
Omaha
River
UNION
MISSOURI
Cheyenne
Julesburg
Platte
Fort Sedgwick
Fort Kearny
Fort Collins
mpa River
Republican
ST. JOE & G.I.
Seneca
R.R.
St. Joseph
HANNIBAL & ST. JOE. R.R.
Thornburgh Fight
eeker Massacre
Greeley
South Platte
River
Denver
Beecher Island
K A N S A S
River
Junction City
Kansas City
K.P. railhead Oct. 1867
Abilene
Topeka
River
COLORADO
ADMITTED 1876
KANSAS
PACIFIC
R.R.
Fort Hays
Hays City
Kansas
M.P. R.R.
R.R.
Fort Wallace
Smoky Hill
River
Ellsworth
Gunnison R.
Pueblo
Arkansas
R.R.
Fort Larned
Pawnee Fork
River
Newton
Wichita
FLINT HILLS
WEST TRAIL
M.K. & T. R.R.
KANSAS & TEXAS
EAST TRAIL
Baxter Springs
rt Crawford
Uncompahgre River
San Juan Mining Region
Del Norte
ATCHISON TOPEKA & SANTA FE
Dodge City
Medicine Lodge Creek
Caldwell
Hunnewell
PUBLIC LAND STRIP
North Canadian
Camp Supply
INDIAN TERR.
Arkansas
Fort Gibson
River
Muskogee
A.T.&S.F. reached here 1880
Adobe Walls
Canadian
River
Fort Smith
ARKANSAS
R.R.
Santa Fe
Las Vegas
Tascosa
Fort Cobb
Fort Reno
Fort Wingate
Fort Bascom
Amarillo
Albuquerque
Fort Sill
MISSOURI
TRAIL
Red
River
Fort Sumner
Doan's Store
Wichita Falls
Denison
Texarkana
NEW MEXICO TERRITORY
M.K.&T. reached here 1871
GOODNIGHT-LOVING
Fort Stanton
A.T.&S.F. R.R.
Brazos
TRAIL
Fort Griffin
R.R.
Dallas
Fort Worth
Marshall
R.R.
Silver City
Pecos
PACIFIC
TEXAS &
NOR.
Deming
Fort Bliss
Colorado
TRAIL
CHISHOLM CATTLE TRAIL
GT.
River
El Paso
CATTLE
Horsehead Crossing
Fort Concho
WESTERN CATTLE TRAIL
SHAWNEE
T E X A S
So. Pac. building eastward reached here 1881.
TRAIL
Fort Quitman
River
Austin
Houston
Fort Davis
SOUTHERN
Bandera
&
R.R.
PACIFIC
Rio
San Antonio
INT.
Fort Clark
Nueces
Eagle Pass
River
M E X I C O
GULF OF MEXICO
Grande
Corpus Christi
Laredo

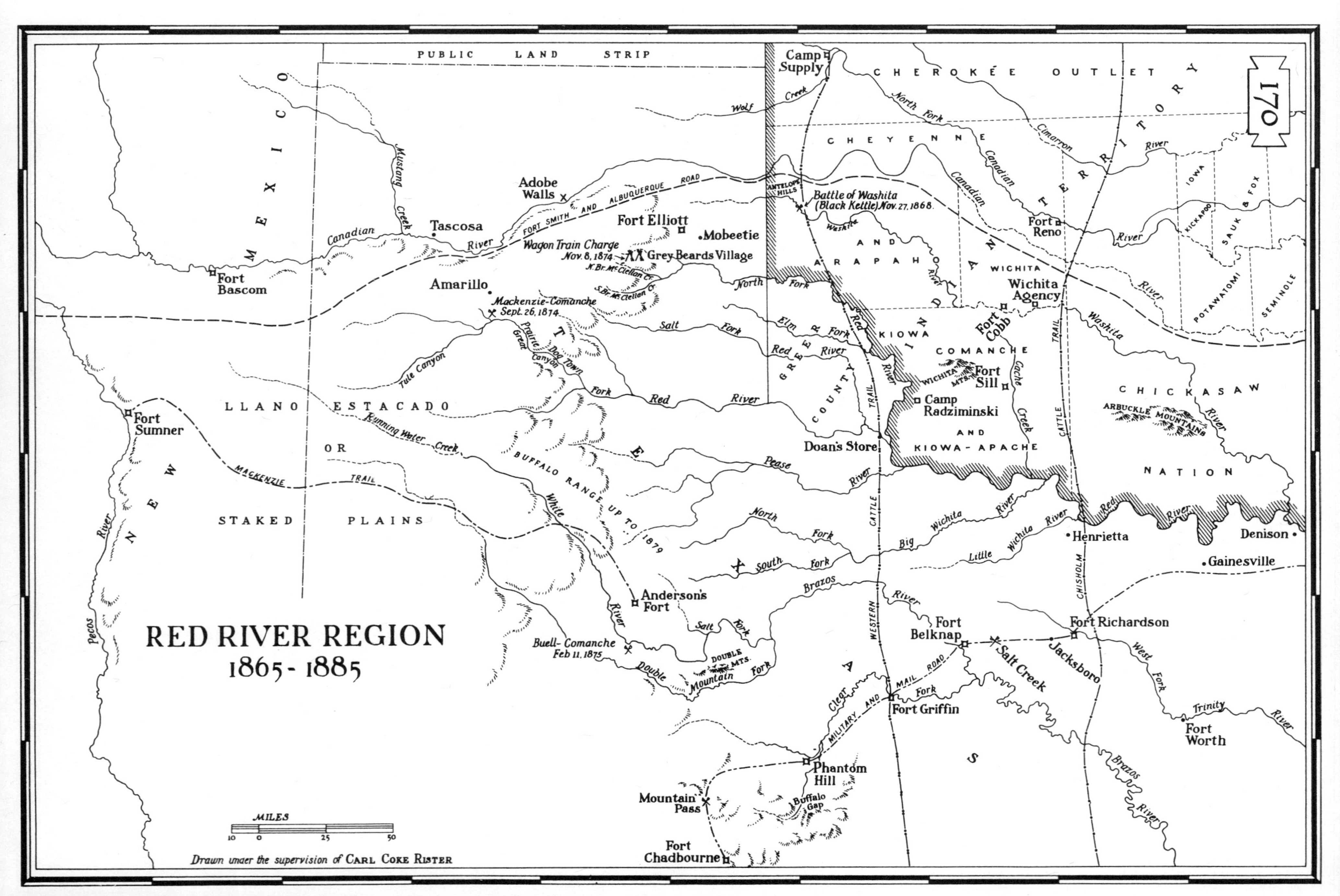

170
RED RIVER REGION
1865-1885
PUBLIC LAND STRIP
CHEROKÉE OUTLET
INDIAN TERRITORY
NEW MEXICO
TEXAS
CHEYENNE AND ARAPAHO
WICHITA
KIOWA COMANCHE AND KIOWA-APACHE
CHICKASAW NATION
IOWA
KICKAPOO
SAUK & FOX
POTAWATOMI
SEMINOLE
GREER COUNTY
LLANO ESTACADO OR STAKED PLAINS
Camp Supply
Adobe Walls
Tascosa
Fort Elliott
Mobeetie
Wagon Train Charge Nov. 8, 1874
Grey Beards Village
N. Br. McClellan Cr.
S. Br. McClellan Cr.
Amarillo
Mackenzie-Comanche Sept. 26, 1874
Fort Bascom
Fort Sumner
Battle of Washita (Black Kettle) Nov. 27, 1868
Antelope Hills
Fort Reno
Wichita Agency
Fort Cobb
Fort Sill
Wichita Mts.
Camp Radziminski
Arbuckle Mountains
Doan's Store
Henrietta
Denison
Gainesville
Fort Richardson
Jacksboro
Salt Creek
Fort Belknap
Fort Griffin
Phantom Hill
Buffalo Gap
Mountain Pass
Fort Chadbourne
Fort Worth
Anderson's Fort
Buell-Comanche Feb 11, 1875
Double Mts.
Fort Smith and Albuquerque Road
Buffalo Range up to 1879
Mackenzie Trail
Western Cattle Trail
Chisholm Cattle Trail
Military and Mail Road
Canadian River
North Fork Canadian
Cimarron River
Wolf Creek
Mustang Creek
Washita River
North Fork Red River
Salt Fork Red River
Elm Fork
Red River
Cache Creek
Pease River
Tule Canyon
Great Prairie Dog Town Fork
Running Water Creek
White River
North Fork
South Fork
Big Wichita River
Little Wichita River
Brazos River
Salt Fork
Double Mountain Fork
Clear Fork
West Fork
Trinity River
Pecos River
MILES
10 0 25 50
Drawn under the supervision of Carl Coke Rister

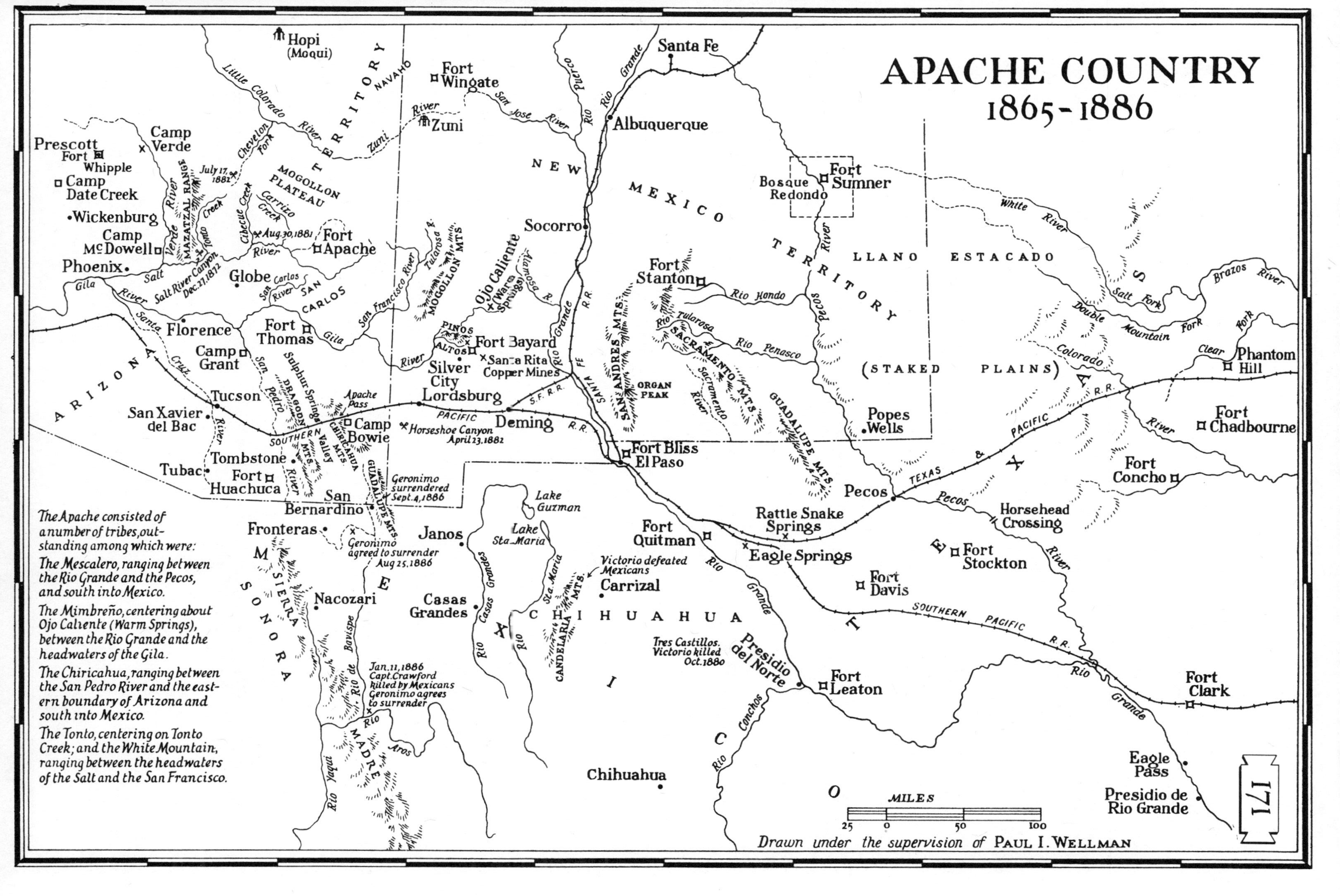

The Apache consisted of a number of tribes, outstanding among which were:

The Mescalero, ranging between the Rio Grande and the Pecos, and south into Mexico.

The Mimbreño, centering about Ojo Caliente (Warm Springs), between the Rio Grande and the headwaters of the Gila.

The Chiricahua, ranging between the San Pedro River and the eastern boundary of Arizona and south into Mexico.

The Tonto, centering on Tonto Creek; and the White Mountain, ranging between the headwaters of the Salt and the San Francisco.

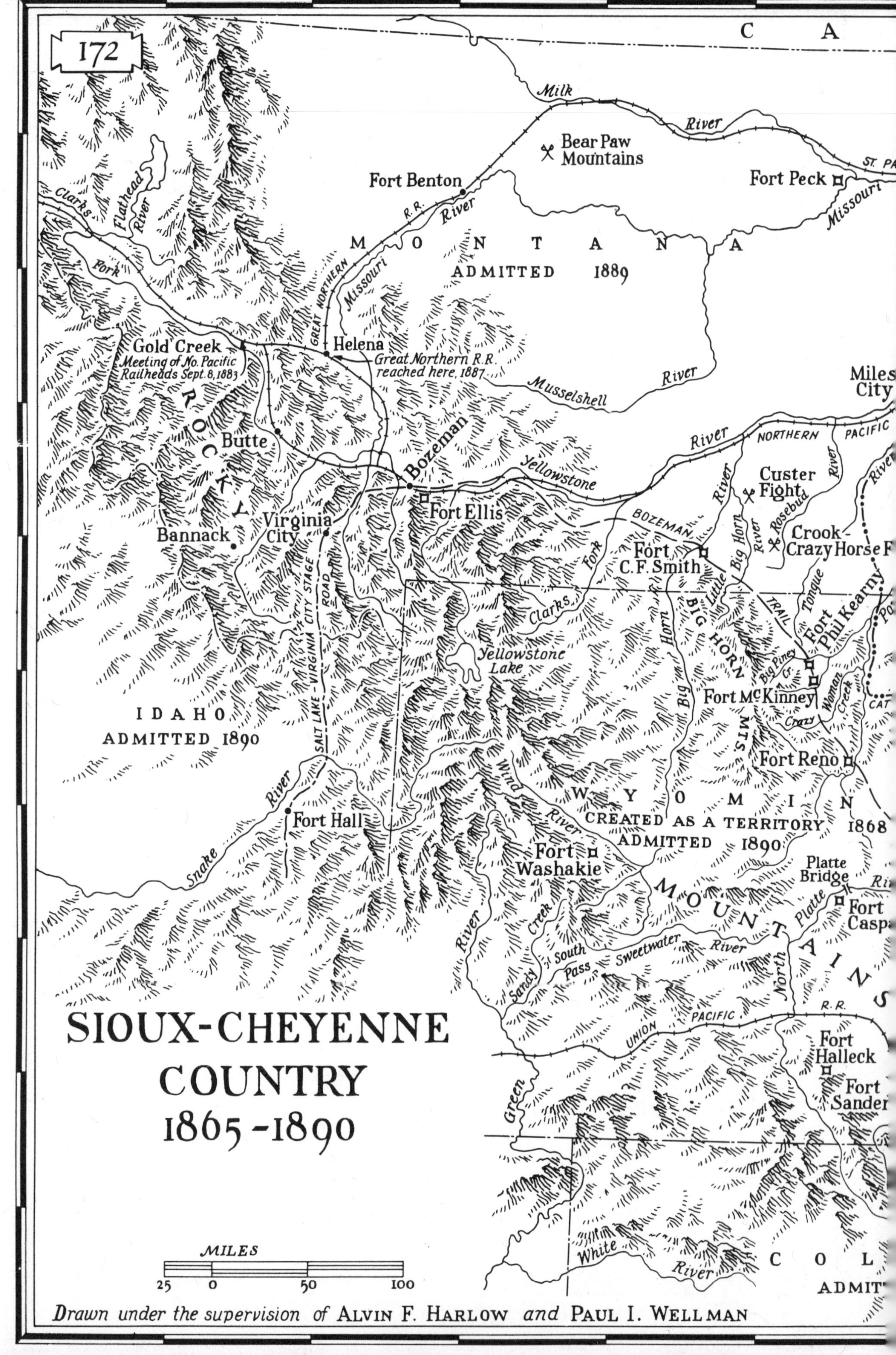

Drawn under the supervision of ALVIN F. HARLOW and PAUL I. WELLMAN

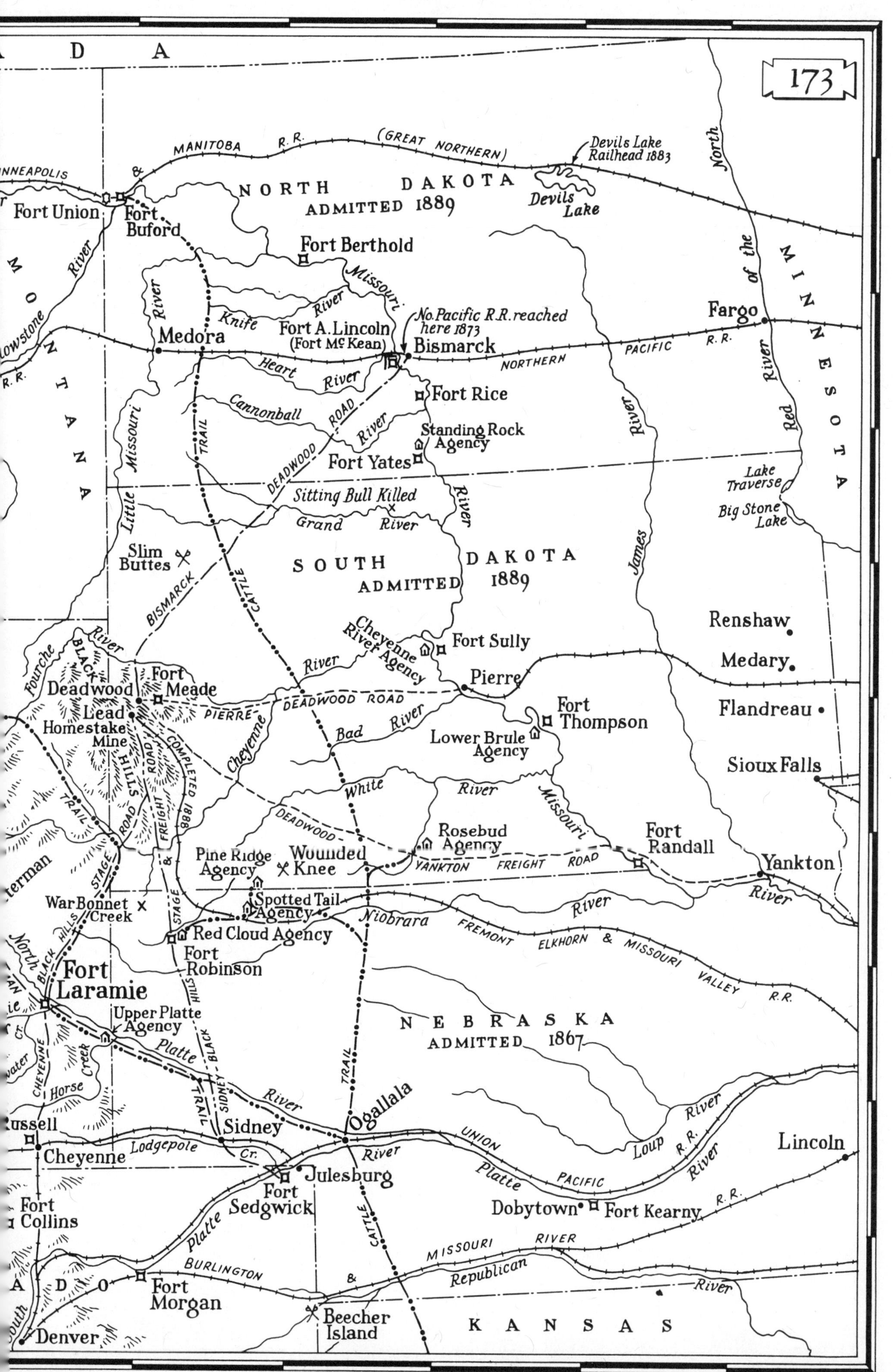
D A
MANITOBA R.R. (GREAT NORTHERN)
&
Devils Lake Railhead 1883
NORTH DAKOTA
ADMITTED 1889
Devils Lake
Fort Union
Fort Buford
Fort Berthold
Missouri River
Knife River
Little Missouri River
Yellowstone River
MONTANA
No. Pacific R.R. reached here 1873
Fargo
Medora
Fort A. Lincoln (Fort McKean)
Bismarck
NORTHERN PACIFIC R.R.
Heart River
Fort Rice
Cannonball River
Standing Rock Agency
Fort Yates
DEADWOOD ROAD
TRAIL
North of the Red River
MINNESOTA
Lake Traverse
Big Stone Lake
James River
Sitting Bull Killed
Grand River
Slim Buttes
SOUTH DAKOTA
ADMITTED 1889
BISMARCK
CATTLE
Renshaw
Medary
Flandreau
Sioux Falls
Cheyenne River Agency
Fort Sully
Pierre
Belle Fourche River
BLACK HILLS
Deadwood
Fort Meade
Lead
Homestake Mine
PIERRE DEADWOOD ROAD
Cheyenne River
Fort Thompson
Lower Brule Agency
Bad River
White River
COMPLETED 1888
FREIGHT ROAD
STAGE ROAD
TRAIL
Fetterman
DEADWOOD
Rosebud Agency
Fort Randall
Yankton
Pine Ridge Agency
Wounded Knee
YANKTON FREIGHT ROAD
War Bonnet Creek
Spotted Tail Agency
Red Cloud Agency
Niobrara River
FREMONT ELKHORN & MISSOURI VALLEY R.R.
Fort Robinson
North Platte
BLACK HILLS
Fort Laramie
Upper Platte Agency
NEBRASKA
ADMITTED 1867
CHEYENNE
Horse Creek
Platte River
SIDNEY - BLACK HILLS TRAIL
Ogallala
Loup River
Russell
Sidney
Cheyenne
Lodgepole Cr.
UNION PACIFIC R.R.
Platte River
Lincoln
Julesburg
Fort Sedgwick
CATTLE
Fort Collins
Dobytown
Fort Kearny
R.R.
MISSOURI RIVER
BURLINGTON &
Republican River
Fort Morgan
Beecher Island
KANSAS
Denver
South Platte

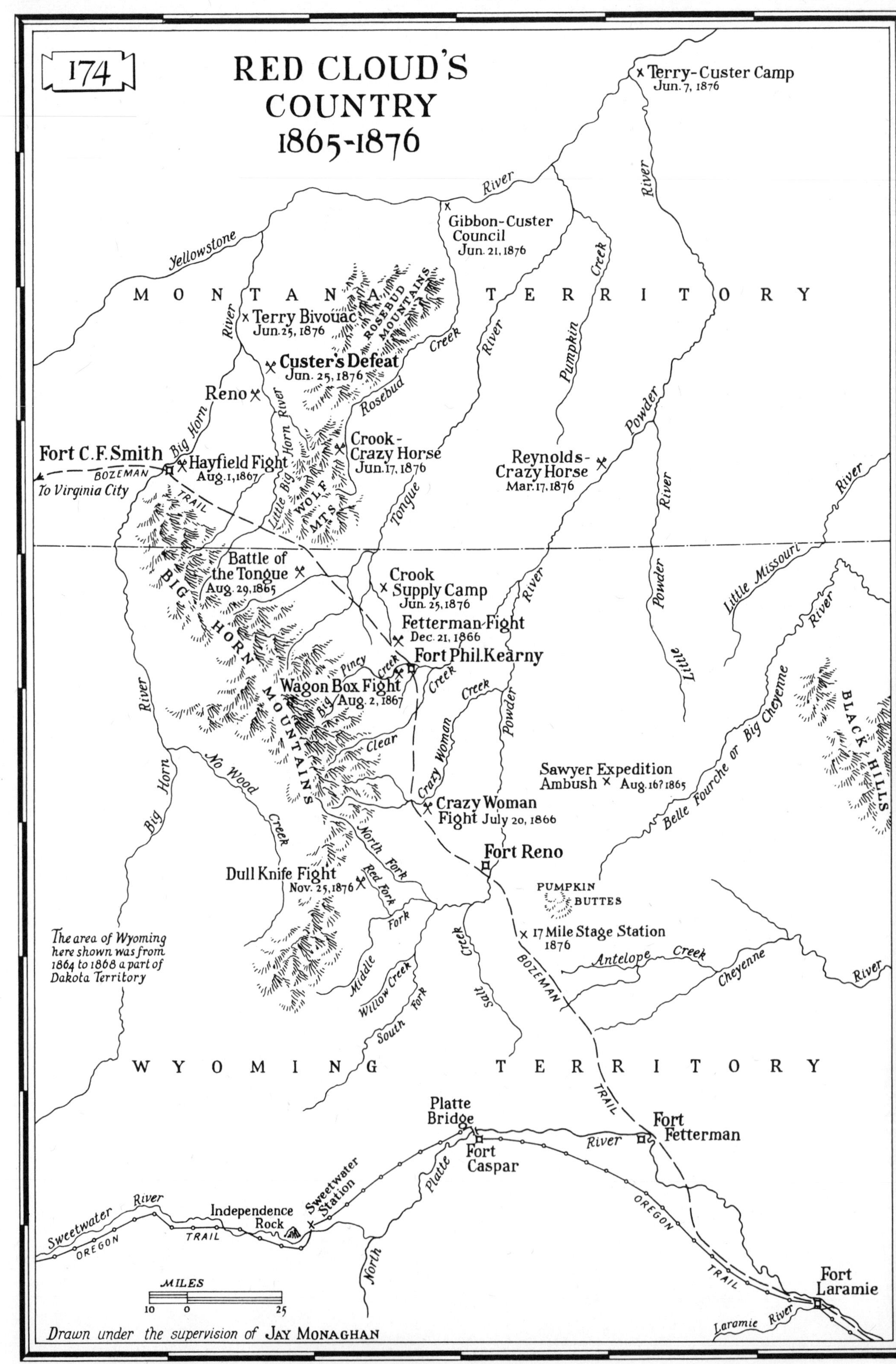

174
RED CLOUD'S COUNTRY 1865-1876
Terry-Custer Camp
Jun. 7, 1876
Gibbon-Custer Council
Jun. 21, 1876
Yellowstone
River
MONTANA TERRITORY
Terry Bivouac
Jun. 25, 1876
ROSEBUD MOUNTAINS
Custer's Defeat
Jun. 25, 1876
Reno
Rosebud
Creek
Pumpkin
Creek
Powder
River
Fort C.F. Smith
Hayfield Fight
Aug. 1, 1867
BOZEMAN
TRAIL
To Virginia City
Big Horn
Little Big Horn
WOLF MTS.
Crook-Crazy Horse
Jun. 17, 1876
Tongue
Reynolds-Crazy Horse
Mar. 17, 1876
Battle of the Tongue
Aug. 29, 1865
Crook Supply Camp
Jun. 25, 1876
Fetterman Fight
Dec. 21, 1866
Fort Phil. Kearny
Little Missouri
Little Powder
BIG HORN MOUNTAINS
Piney
Creek
Wagon Box Fight
Aug. 2, 1867
Big
Clear
Crazy Woman
BLACK HILLS
Belle Fourche or Big Cheyenne
No Wood Creek
Sawyer Expedition Ambush
Aug. 16? 1865
Crazy Woman Fight
July 20, 1866
Fort Reno
North Fork
Red Fork
Dull Knife Fight
Nov. 25, 1876
PUMPKIN BUTTES
17 Mile Stage Station
1876
Middle Fork
Willow Creek
South Fork
Salt Creek
Antelope Creek
Cheyenne River
The area of Wyoming here shown was from 1864 to 1868 a part of Dakota Territory
WYOMING TERRITORY
Platte Bridge
Fort Caspar
Fort Fetterman
River
Platte
North
Sweetwater River
Sweetwater Station
Independence Rock
OREGON TRAIL
MILES
10 0 25
Fort Laramie
Laramie River
Drawn under the supervision of JAY MONAGHAN

THE NORTHWEST 1865–1890

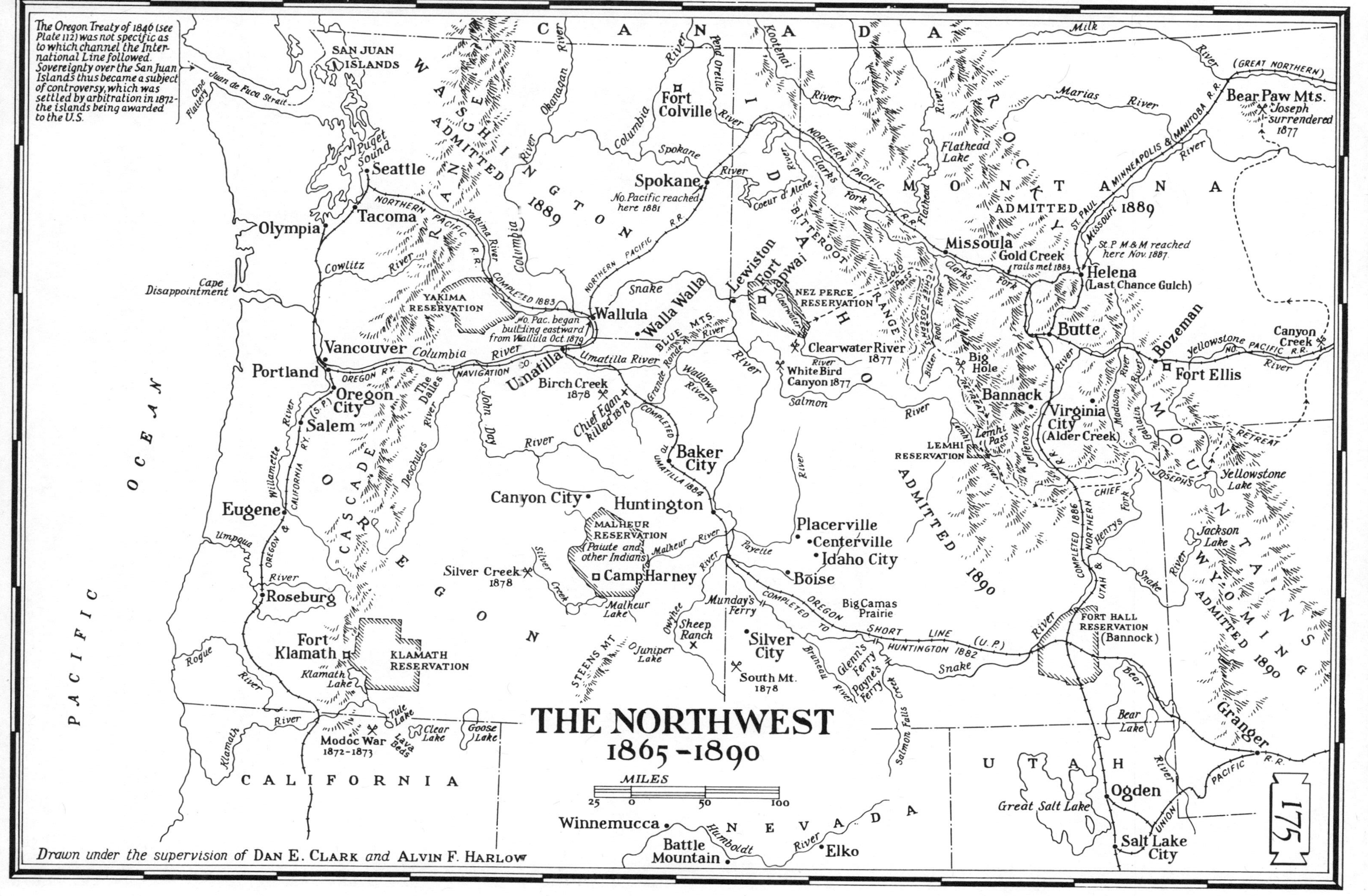

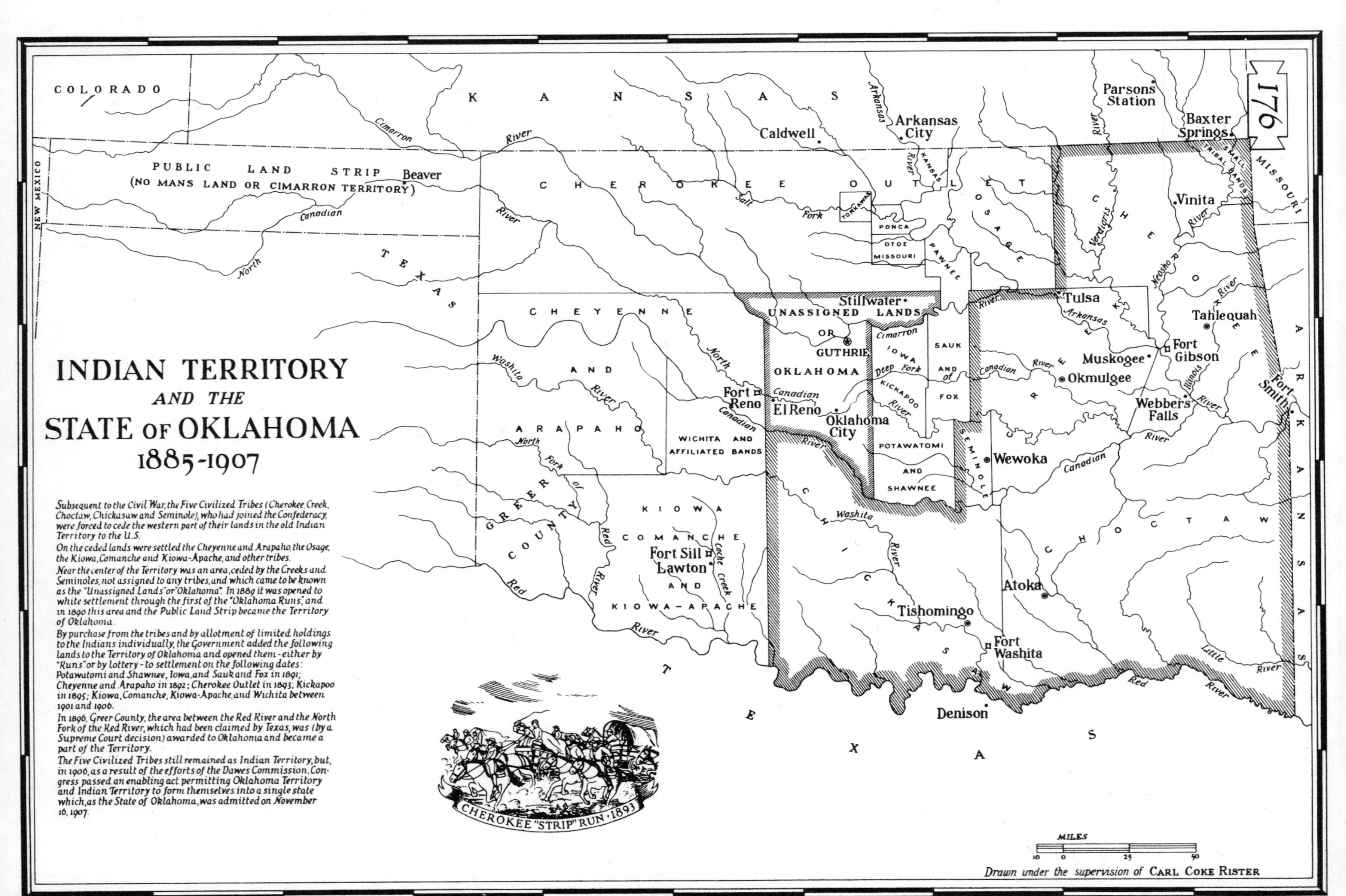

INDIAN TERRITORY
AND THE
STATE OF OKLAHOMA
1885-1907

Subsequent to the Civil War, the Five Civilized Tribes (Cherokee, Creek, Choctaw, Chickasaw and Seminole), who had joined the Confederacy, were forced to cede the western part of their lands in the old Indian Territory to the U.S.

On the ceded lands were settled the Cheyenne and Arapaho, the Osage, the Kiowa, Comanche and Kiowa-Apache, and other tribes.

Near the center of the Territory was an area, ceded by the Creeks and Seminoles, not assigned to any tribes, and which came to be known as the "Unassigned Lands" or "Oklahoma". In 1889 it was opened to white settlement through the first of the "Oklahoma Runs", and in 1890 this area and the Public Land Strip became the Territory of Oklahoma.

By purchase from the tribes and by allotment of limited holdings to the Indians individually, the Government added the following lands to the Territory of Oklahoma and opened them – either by "Runs" or by lottery – to settlement on the following dates: Potawatomi and Shawnee, Iowa, and Sauk and Fox in 1891; Cheyenne and Arapaho in 1892; Cherokee Outlet in 1893; Kickapoo in 1895; Kiowa, Comanche, Kiowa-Apache, and Wichita between 1901 and 1906.

In 1896, Greer County, the area between the Red River and the North Fork of the Red River, which had been claimed by Texas, was (by a Supreme Court decision) awarded to Oklahoma and became a part of the Territory.

The Five Civilized Tribes still remained as Indian Territory, but, in 1906, as a result of the efforts of the Dawes Commission, Congress passed an enabling act permitting Oklahoma Territory and Indian Territory to form themselves into a single state which, as the State of Oklahoma, was admitted on November 16, 1907.

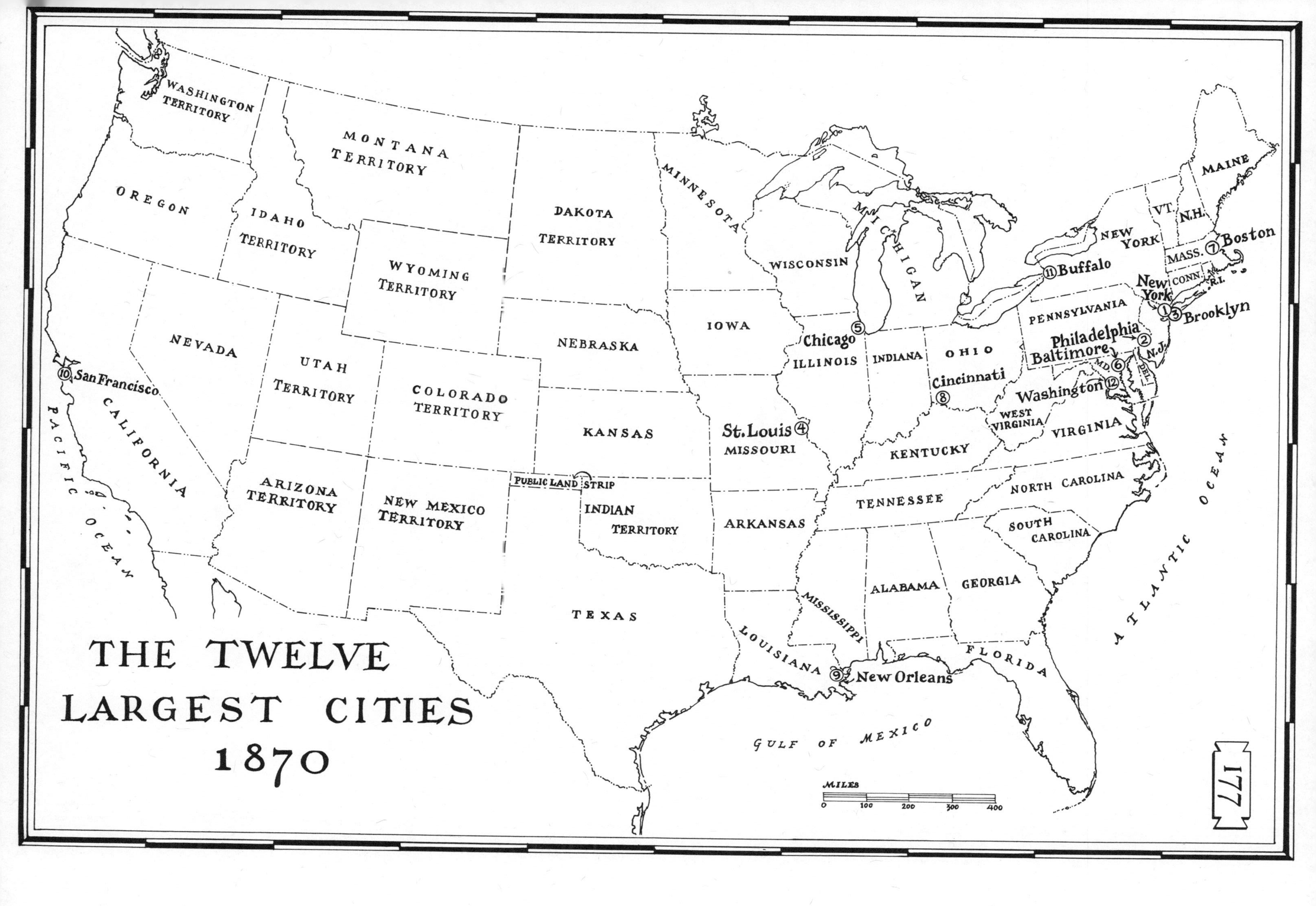

177
THE TWELVE
LARGEST CITIES
1870
WASHINGTON TERRITORY
OREGON
IDAHO TERRITORY
MONTANA TERRITORY
DAKOTA TERRITORY
MINNESOTA
WISCONSIN
MICHIGAN
WYOMING TERRITORY
NEVADA
UTAH TERRITORY
COLORADO TERRITORY
NEBRASKA
IOWA
KANSAS
CALIFORNIA
ARIZONA TERRITORY
NEW MEXICO TERRITORY
PUBLIC LAND STRIP
INDIAN TERRITORY
TEXAS
MISSOURI
ARKANSAS
LOUISIANA
MISSISSIPPI
ILLINOIS
INDIANA
OHIO
KENTUCKY
TENNESSEE
ALABAMA
GEORGIA
FLORIDA
SOUTH CAROLINA
NORTH CAROLINA
VIRGINIA
WEST VIRGINIA
MD.
DEL.
N.J.
PENNSYLVANIA
NEW YORK
VT.
N.H.
MAINE
MASS.
CONN.
R.I.
1 New York
2 Philadelphia
3 Brooklyn
4 St. Louis
5 Chicago
6 Baltimore
7 Boston
8 Cincinnati
9 New Orleans
10 San Francisco
11 Buffalo
12 Washington
PACIFIC OCEAN
ATLANTIC OCEAN
GULF OF MEXICO
MILES
0 100 200 300 400

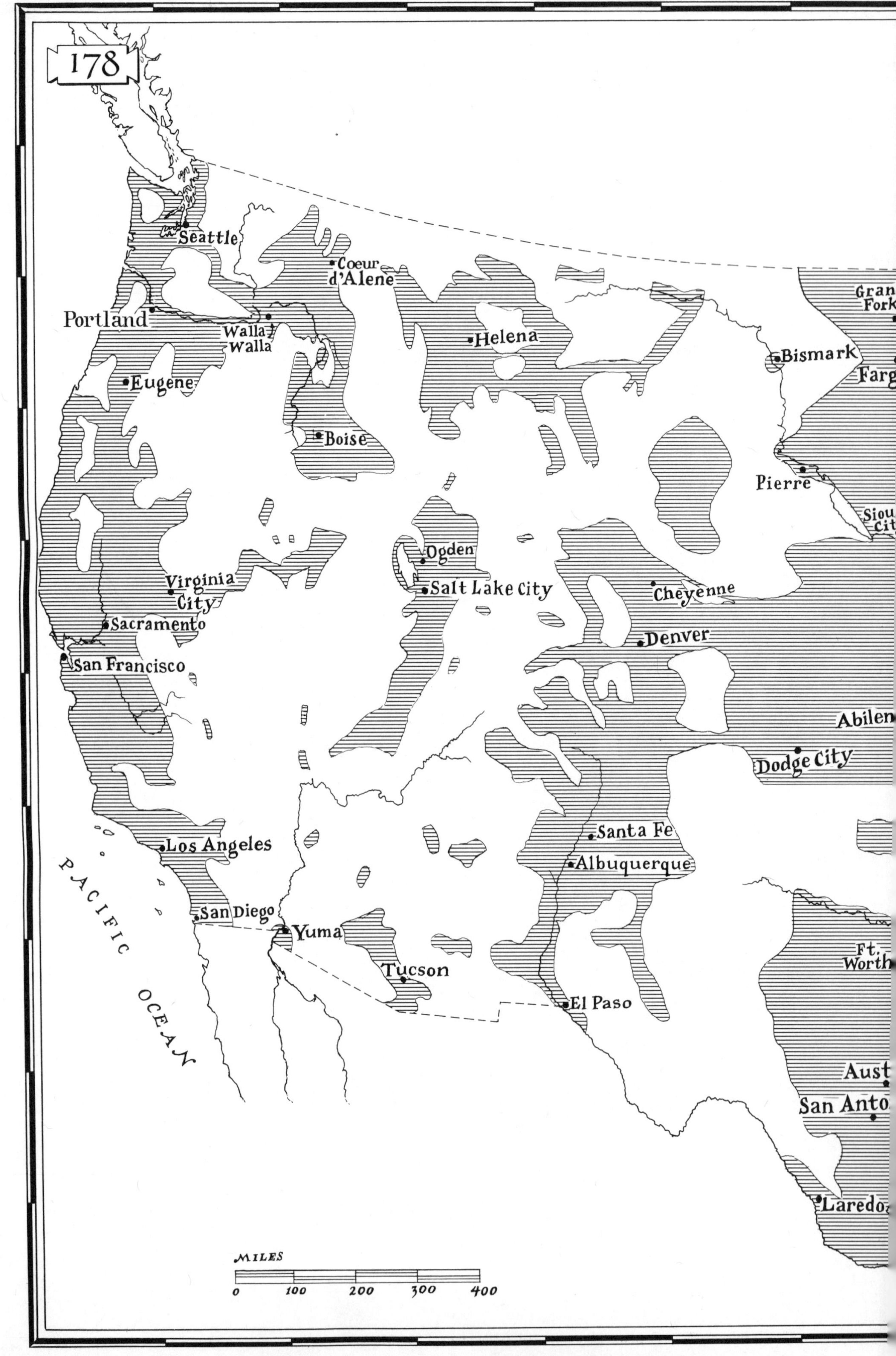
178
Seattle
Coeur d'Alene
Portland
Walla Walla
Helena
Bismark
Eugene
Boise
Pierre
Ogden
Salt Lake City
Virginia City
Cheyenne
Sacramento
Denver
San Francisco
Dodge City
Santa Fe
Los Angeles
Albuquerque
PACIFIC OCEAN
San Diego
Yuma
Tucson
El Paso
MILES
0
100
200
300
400

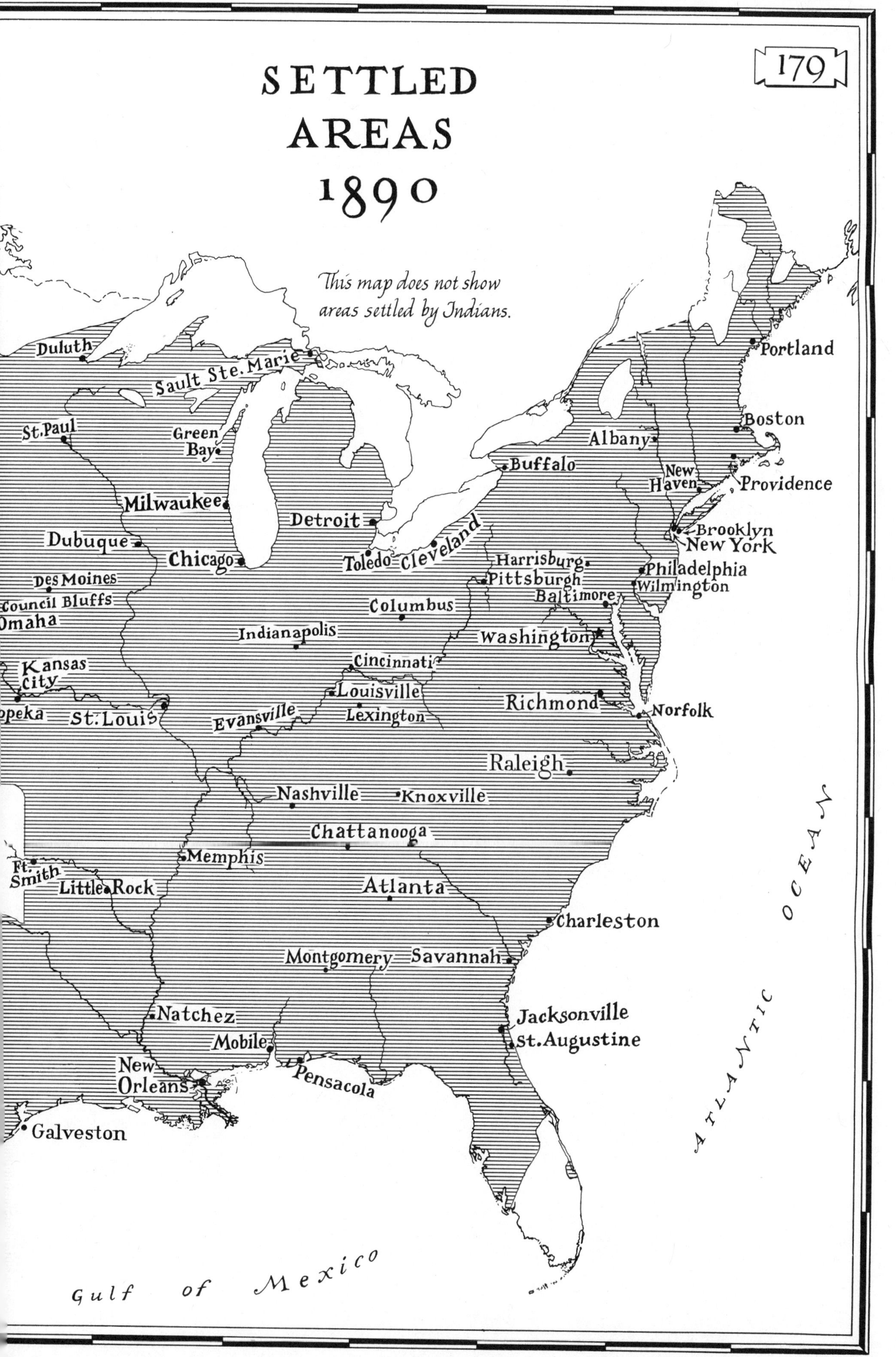
SETTLED AREAS 1890
This map does not show areas settled by Indians.
Duluth
Sault Ste. Marie
St. Paul
Green Bay
Milwaukee
Dubuque
Chicago
Des Moines
Council Bluffs
Omaha
Kansas City
Topeka
St. Louis
Detroit
Toledo
Cleveland
Buffalo
Columbus
Indianapolis
Cincinnati
Louisville
Lexington
Evansville
Harrisburg
Pittsburgh
Baltimore
Washington
Richmond
Norfolk
Raleigh
Portland
Boston
Albany
New Haven
Providence
Brooklyn
New York
Philadelphia
Wilmington
Nashville
Knoxville
Chattanooga
Memphis
Ft. Smith
Little Rock
Atlanta
Charleston
Montgomery
Savannah
Natchez
Mobile
New Orleans
Pensacola
Jacksonville
St. Augustine
Galveston
Gulf of Mexico
ATLANTIC OCEAN

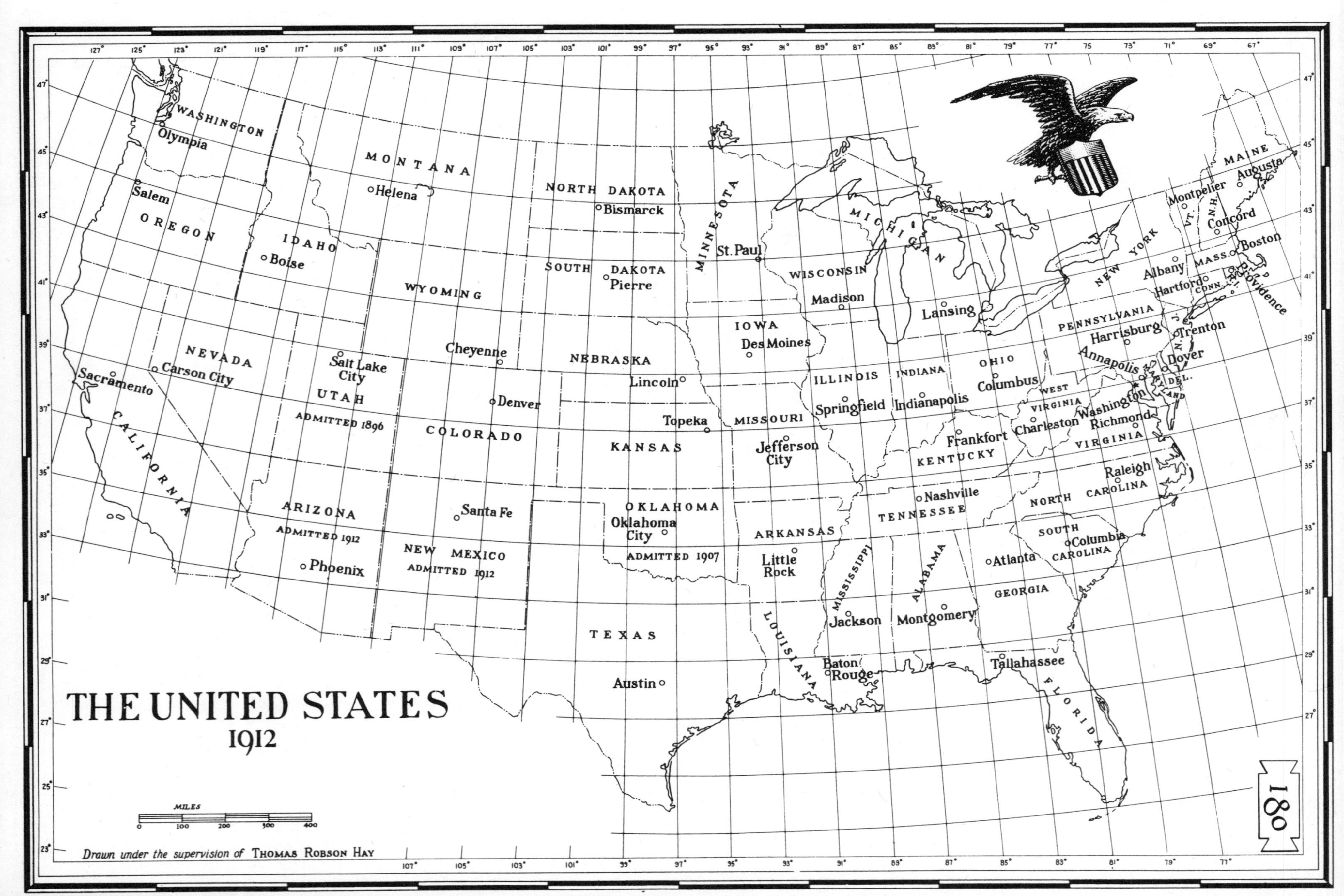

180
THE UNITED STATES
1912
Drawn under the supervision of THOMAS ROBSON HAY
MILES
0
100
200
300
400
WASHINGTON
Olympia
OREGON
Salem
CALIFORNIA
Sacramento
NEVADA
Carson City
IDAHO
Boise
MONTANA
Helena
WYOMING
Cheyenne
UTAH
Salt Lake City
ADMITTED 1896
COLORADO
Denver
ARIZONA
ADMITTED 1912
Phoenix
NEW MEXICO
ADMITTED 1912
Santa Fe
NORTH DAKOTA
Bismarck
SOUTH DAKOTA
Pierre
NEBRASKA
Lincoln
KANSAS
Topeka
OKLAHOMA
Oklahoma City
ADMITTED 1907
TEXAS
Austin
MINNESOTA
St. Paul
IOWA
Des Moines
MISSOURI
Jefferson City
ARKANSAS
Little Rock
LOUISIANA
Baton Rouge
WISCONSIN
Madison
ILLINOIS
Springfield
MICHIGAN
Lansing
INDIANA
Indianapolis
OHIO
Columbus
KENTUCKY
Frankfort
TENNESSEE
Nashville
MISSISSIPPI
Jackson
ALABAMA
Montgomery
GEORGIA
Atlanta
FLORIDA
Tallahassee
SOUTH CAROLINA
Columbia
NORTH CAROLINA
Raleigh
VIRGINIA
Richmond
WEST VIRGINIA
Charleston
Washington
MARYLAND
Annapolis
DEL.
Dover
N.J.
Trenton
PENNSYLVANIA
Harrisburg
NEW YORK
Albany
CONN.
Hartford
R.I.
Providence
MASS.
Boston
VT.
Montpelier
N.H.
Concord
MAINE
Augusta

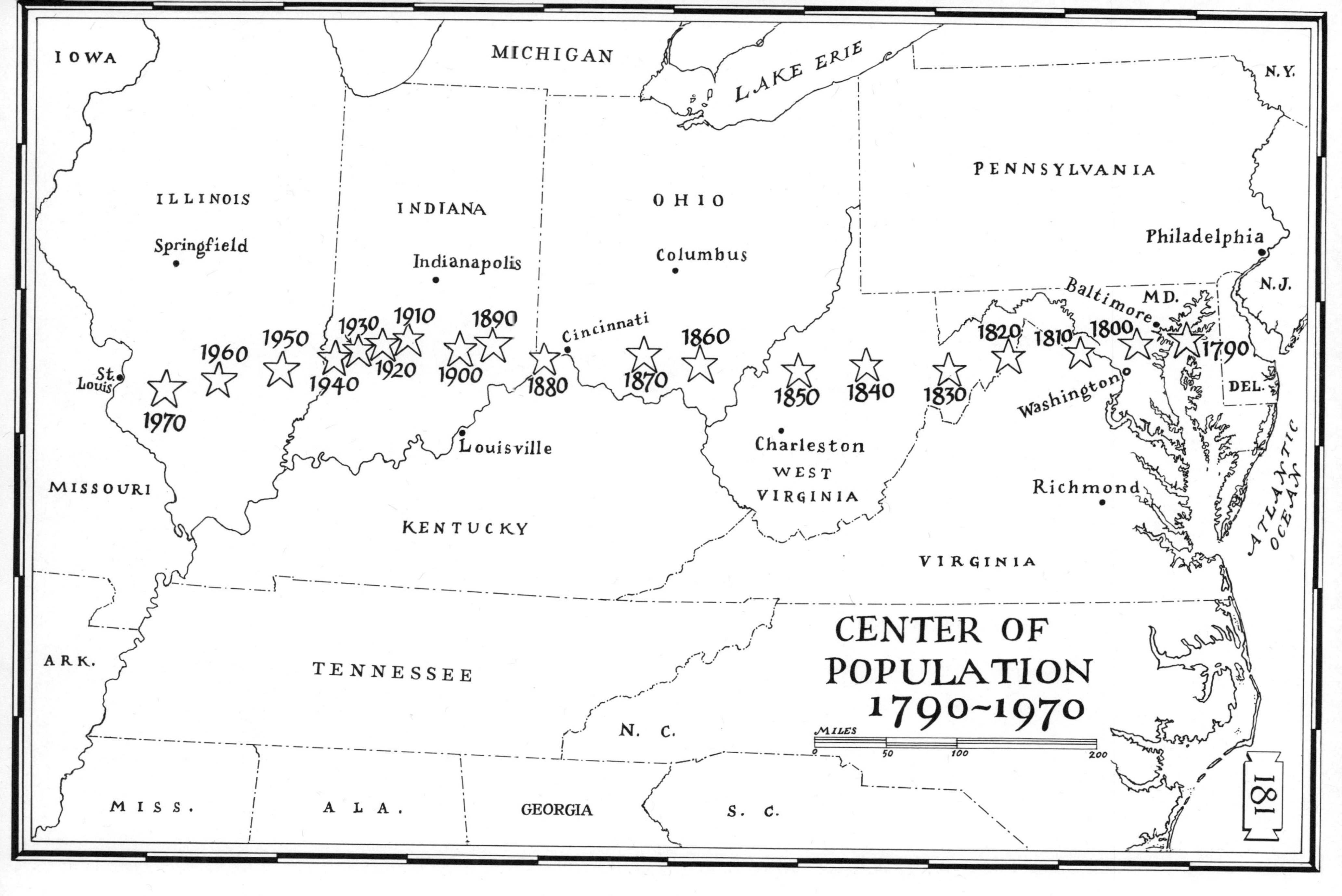
CENTER OF POPULATION 1790~1970
181
IOWA
MICHIGAN
LAKE ERIE
N.Y.
PENNSYLVANIA
Philadelphia
N.J.
MD.
Baltimore
DEL.
ILLINOIS
Springfield
INDIANA
Indianapolis
OHIO
Columbus
Cincinnati
St. Louis
Louisville
MISSOURI
KENTUCKY
Charleston
WEST VIRGINIA
VIRGINIA
Richmond
Washington
ATLANTIC OCEAN
ARK.
TENNESSEE
N. C.
MISS.
ALA.
GEORGIA
S. C.
1790
1800
1810
1820
1830
1840
1850
1860
1870
1880
1890
1900
1910
1920
1930
1940
1950
1960
1970
MILES
0
50
100
200

IX THE UNITED STATES AS A WORLD POWER, 1898–1977

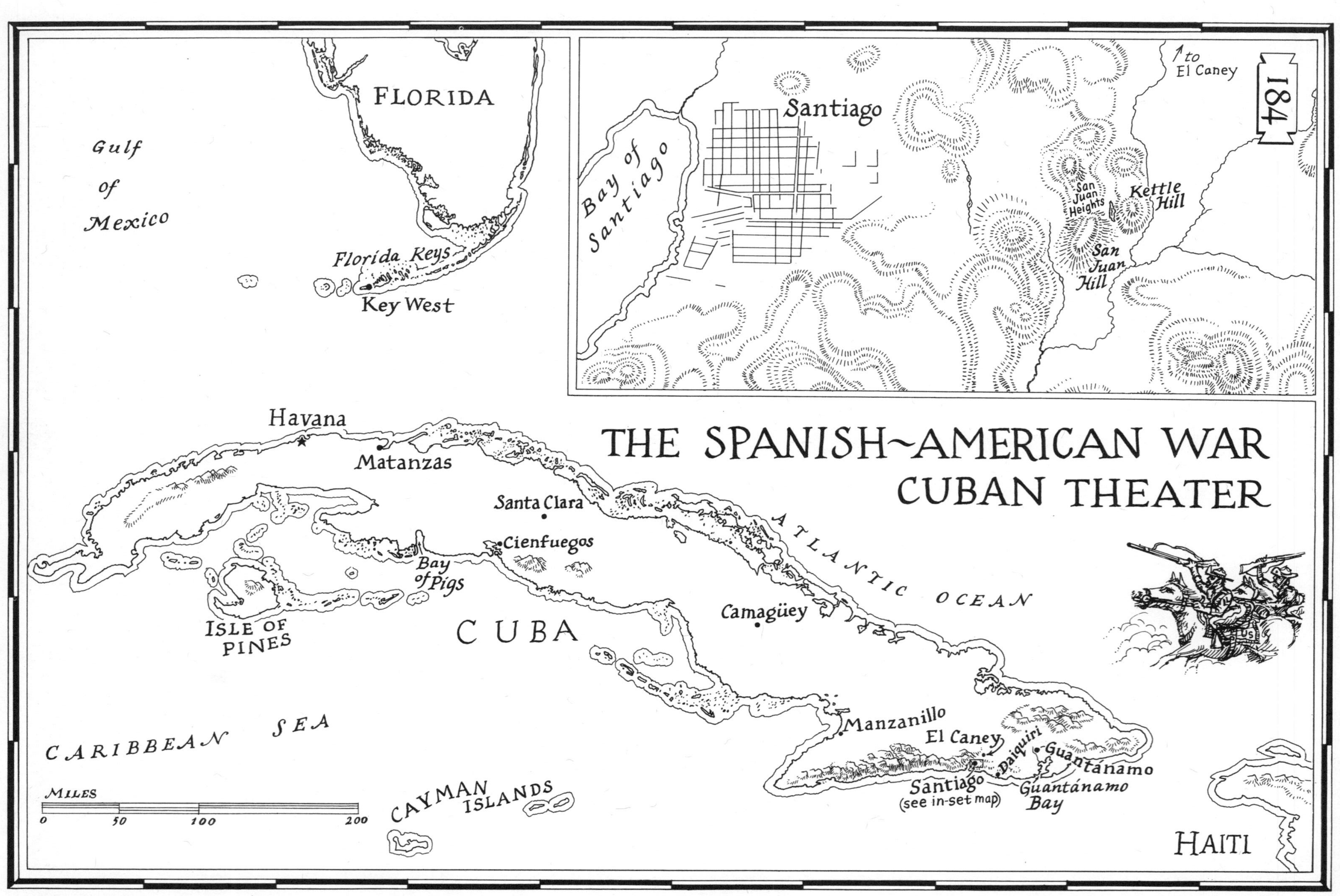
184
THE SPANISH~AMERICAN WAR
CUBAN THEATER
FLORIDA
Gulf of Mexico
Florida Keys
Key West
Santiago
Bay of Santiago
San Juan Heights
Kettle Hill
San Juan Hill
to El Caney
Havana
Matanzas
Santa Clara
Cienfuegos
Bay of Pigs
ISLE OF PINES
CUBA
Camagüey
ATLANTIC OCEAN
Manzanillo
El Caney
Daiquiri
Guantánamo
Santiago
(see in-set map)
Guantánamo Bay
CARIBBEAN SEA
CAYMAN ISLANDS
MILES
0 50 100 200
HAITI

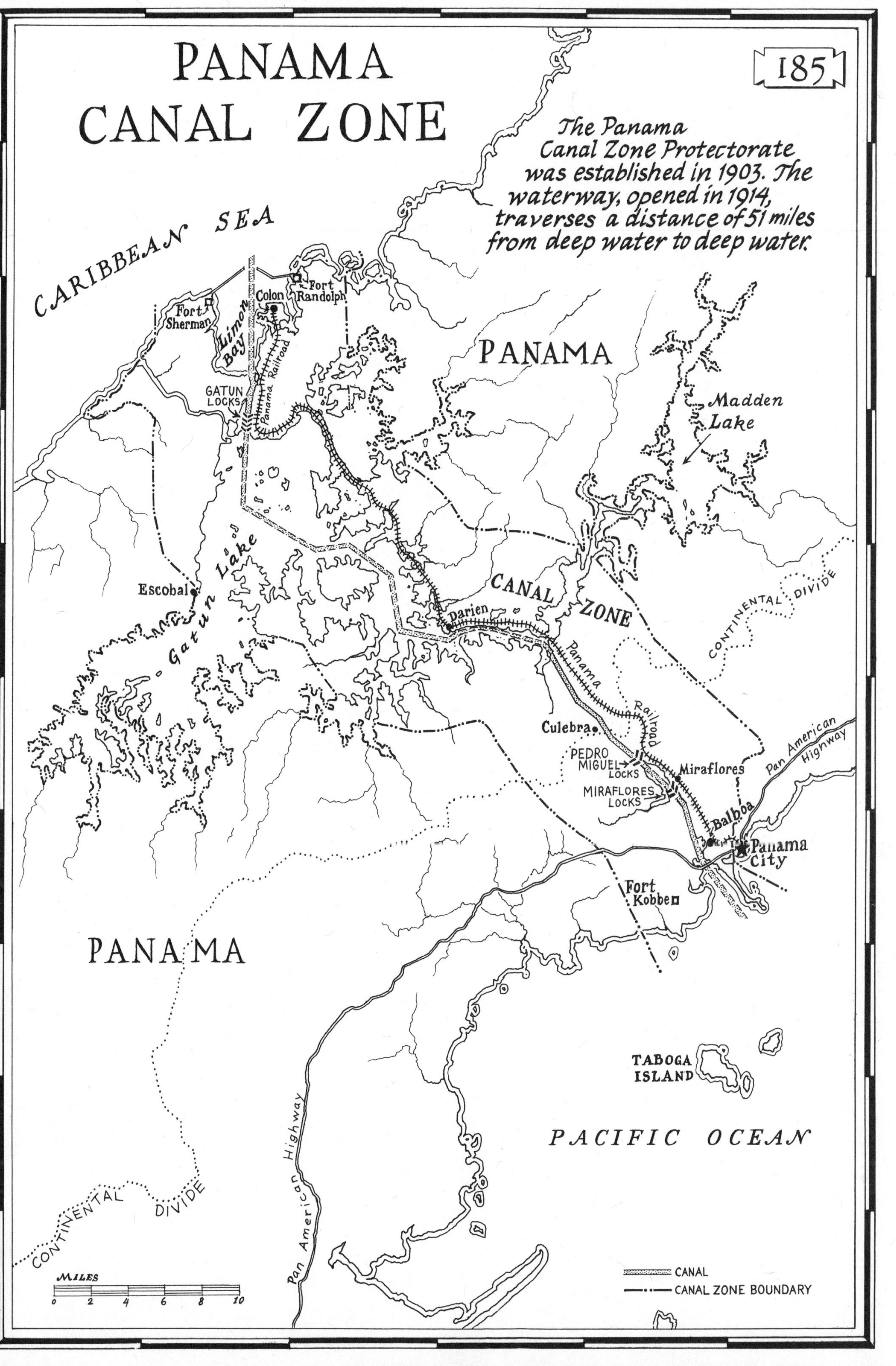

PANAMA CANAL ZONE
185
The Panama Canal Zone Protectorate was established in 1903. The waterway, opened in 1914, traverses a distance of 51 miles from deep water to deep water.
CARIBBEAN SEA
Fort Sherman
Limon Bay
Colon
Fort Randolph
Panama Railroad
GATUN LOCKS
PANAMA
Madden Lake
Escobal
Gatun Lake
CANAL ZONE
Darien
CONTINENTAL DIVIDE
Panama Railroad
Culebra
PEDRO MIGUEL LOCKS
Miraflores
MIRAFLORES LOCKS
Balboa
Pan American Highway
Panama City
Fort Kobbe
PANAMA
TABOGA ISLAND
PACIFIC OCEAN
Pan American Highway
CONTINENTAL DIVIDE
MILES
0 2 4 6 8 10
CANAL
CANAL ZONE BOUNDARY

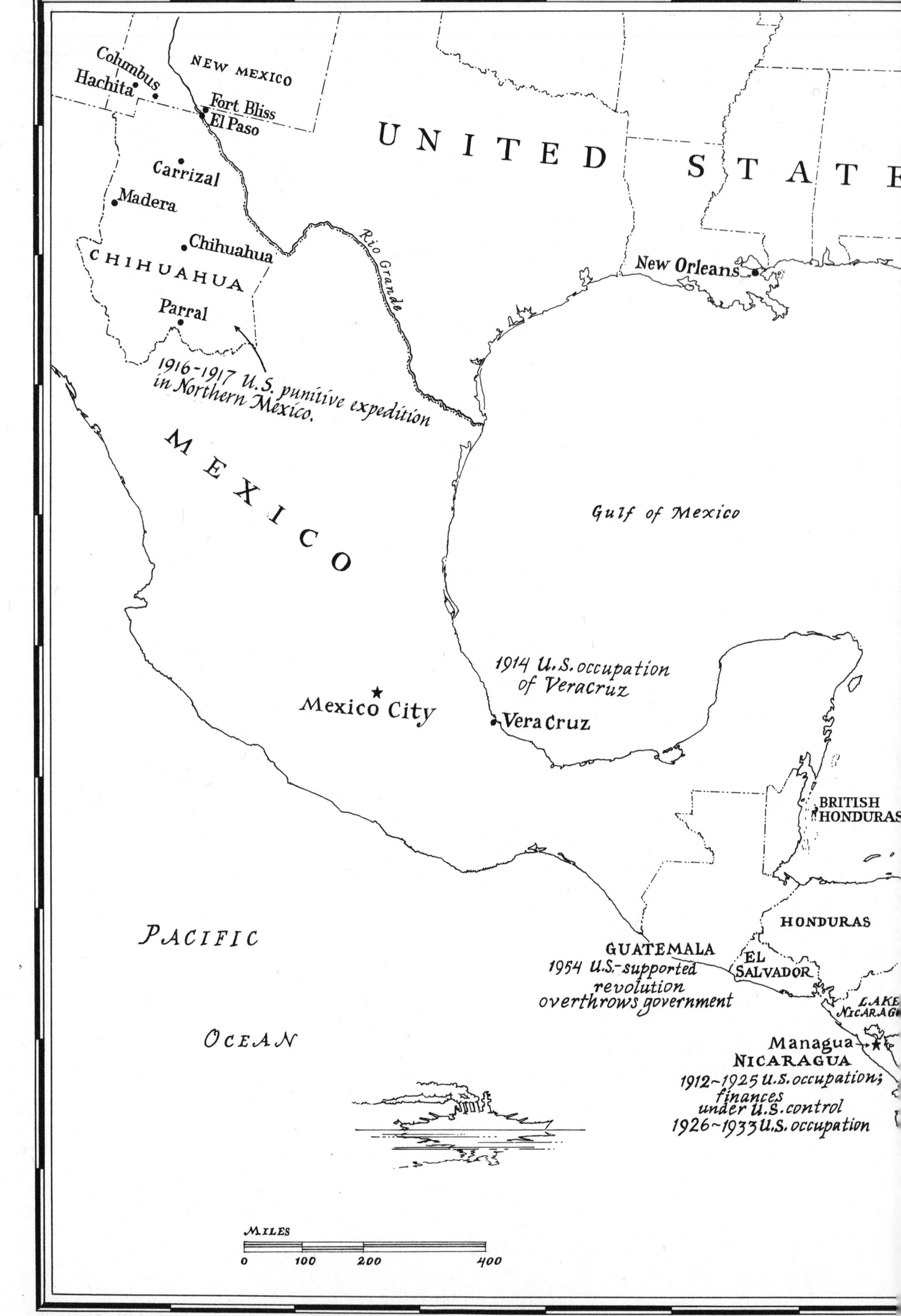

NEW MEXICO
Columbus
Hachita
Fort Bliss
El Paso
UNITED STATES
Carrizal
Madera
Chihuahua
CHIHUAHUA
Parral
Rio Grande
New Orleans
1916-1917 U.S. punitive expedition in Northern Mexico.
MEXICO
Gulf of Mexico
1914 U.S. occupation of Veracruz
Mexico City
Vera Cruz
BRITISH HONDURAS
HONDURAS
PACIFIC
OCEAN
GUATEMALA
1954 U.S.-supported revolution overthrows government
EL SALVADOR
LAKE NICARAGUA
Managua
NICARAGUA
1912~1925 U.S. occupation; finances under U.S. control
1926~1933 U.S. occupation
MILES
0
100
200
400

UNITED STATES INTERVENTIONS IN THE CARIBBEAN AND MIDDLE AMERICA 1898–1966
Tampa
Miami
Key West
Havana
ATLANTIC
OCEAN
CUBA
Bay of Pigs
Isle of Pines
1903–1925 Formally claimed by U.S.
CUBA
1898–1902 U.S. occupation
1902–1934 U.S. maintains right to intervene under Platt Amendment
1906–1909 U.S. occupation
1917 U.S. occupation
1961 Unsuccessful anti-Castro invasion, supported by the U.S.
1962 U.S. blockade
Caimanera
Guantánamo
JAMAICA
Port-au-Prince
HAITI
1915–1934
U.S. occupation
DOMINICAN REPUBLIC
Samaná Bay
1916–1924 U.S. occupation
1965–1966 U.S. occupation
PUERTO RICO
1898
Annexed
U.S. VIRGIN ISLANDS
1917
Purchased
CARIBBEAN SEA
PANAMA
1903 U.S. supported revolution against Colombia
1903 Control of Canal Zone granted to U.S.
COSTA RICA
CANAL ZONE
Colon
PANAMA
COLOMBIA
VENEZUELA

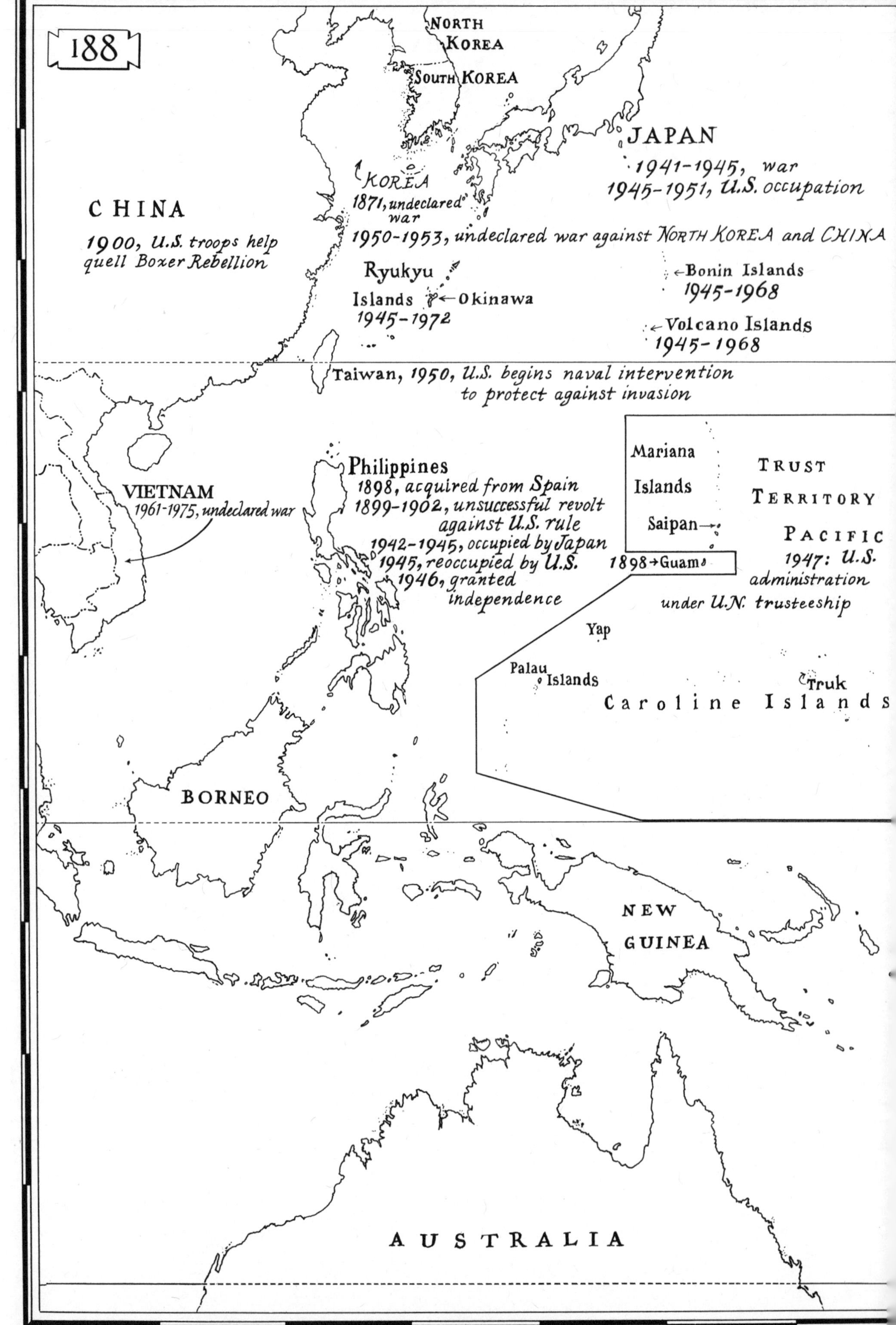

NORTH KOREA
SOUTH KOREA
JAPAN
1941-1945, war
1945-1951, U.S. occupation
CHINA
1900, U.S. troops help quell Boxer Rebellion
KOREA
1871, undeclared war
1950-1953, undeclared war against NORTH KOREA and CHINA
Ryukyu Islands
1945-1972
Okinawa
Bonin Islands
1945-1968
Volcano Islands
1945-1968
Taiwan, 1950, U.S. begins naval intervention to protect against invasion
Mariana Islands
Saipan
1898→Guam
TRUST TERRITORY PACIFIC
1947: U.S. administration under U.N. trusteeship
Philippines
1898, acquired from Spain
1899-1902, unsuccessful revolt against U.S. rule
1942-1945, occupied by Japan
1945, reoccupied by U.S.
1946, granted independence
VIETNAM
1961-1975, undeclared war
Yap
Palau Islands
Truk
Caroline Islands
BORNEO
NEW GUINEA
AUSTRALIA

THE UNITED STATES IN THE PACIFIC 1867 – 1975

Dates indicate the date of U.S. annexation or occupation

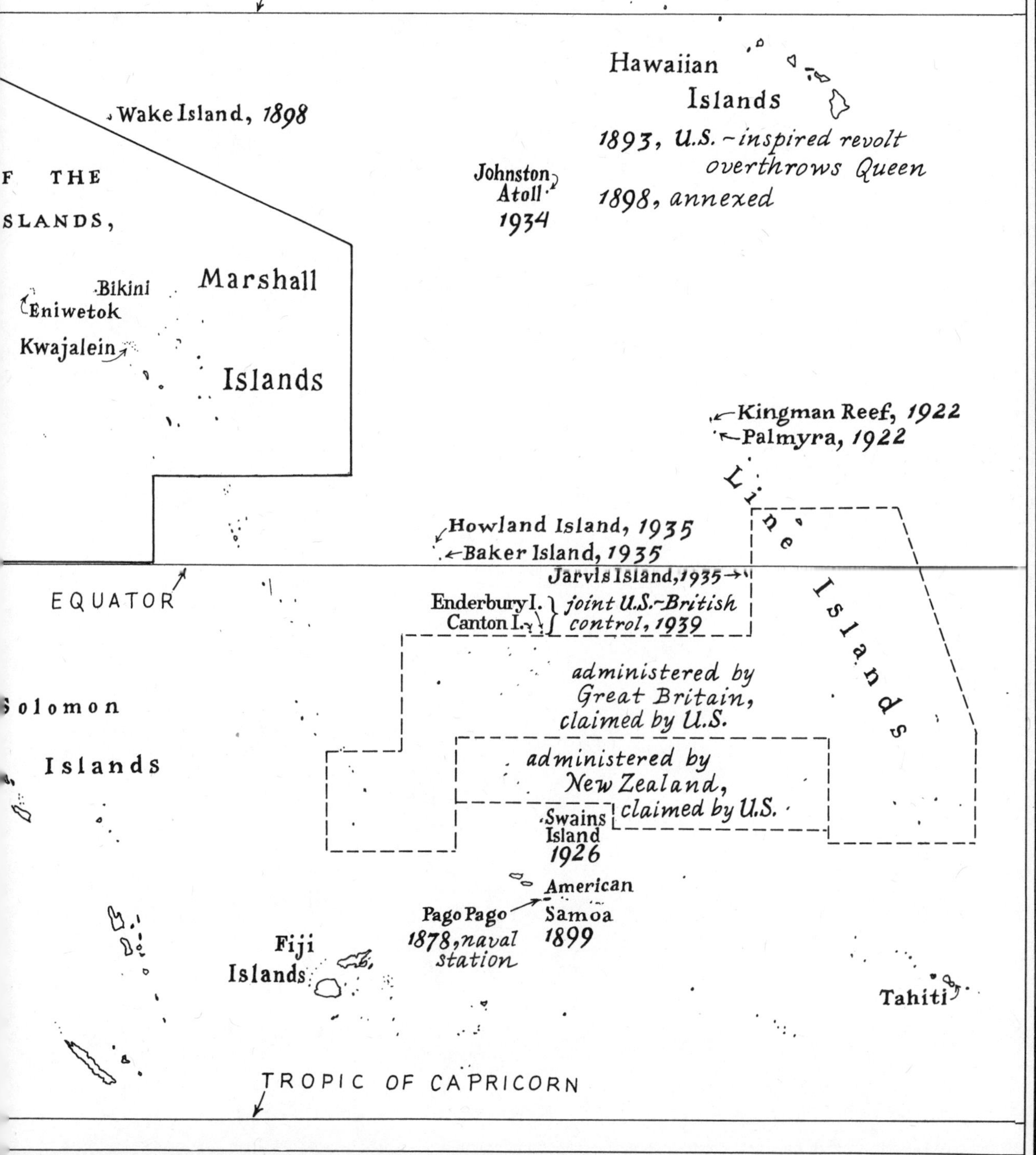

WORLD WAR I
THE WESTERN FRONT, 1917-1918

NETHERLANDS
Antwerp
Brussels
Liège
BELGIUM
Mons
Sambre R.
Meuse River
Rhine River
Coblenz
LUX-
EMBOURG
Moselle River
GERMANY
Quentin
Sedan
Argonne
Forest
Armistice Line
River
issons
Rheims
uresches
Verdun
Metz
LORRAINE
Marne
Château-
Thierry
Bar-
le-Duc
Saint-
Mihiel
Seicheprey
Pont-à-Mousson
Strasbourg
River
Meuse River
Moselle River
ALSACE
Rhine River
Chaumont
SWITZERLAND
MILES
0
50
100

WORLD WAR II
MEDITERRANEAN THEATER

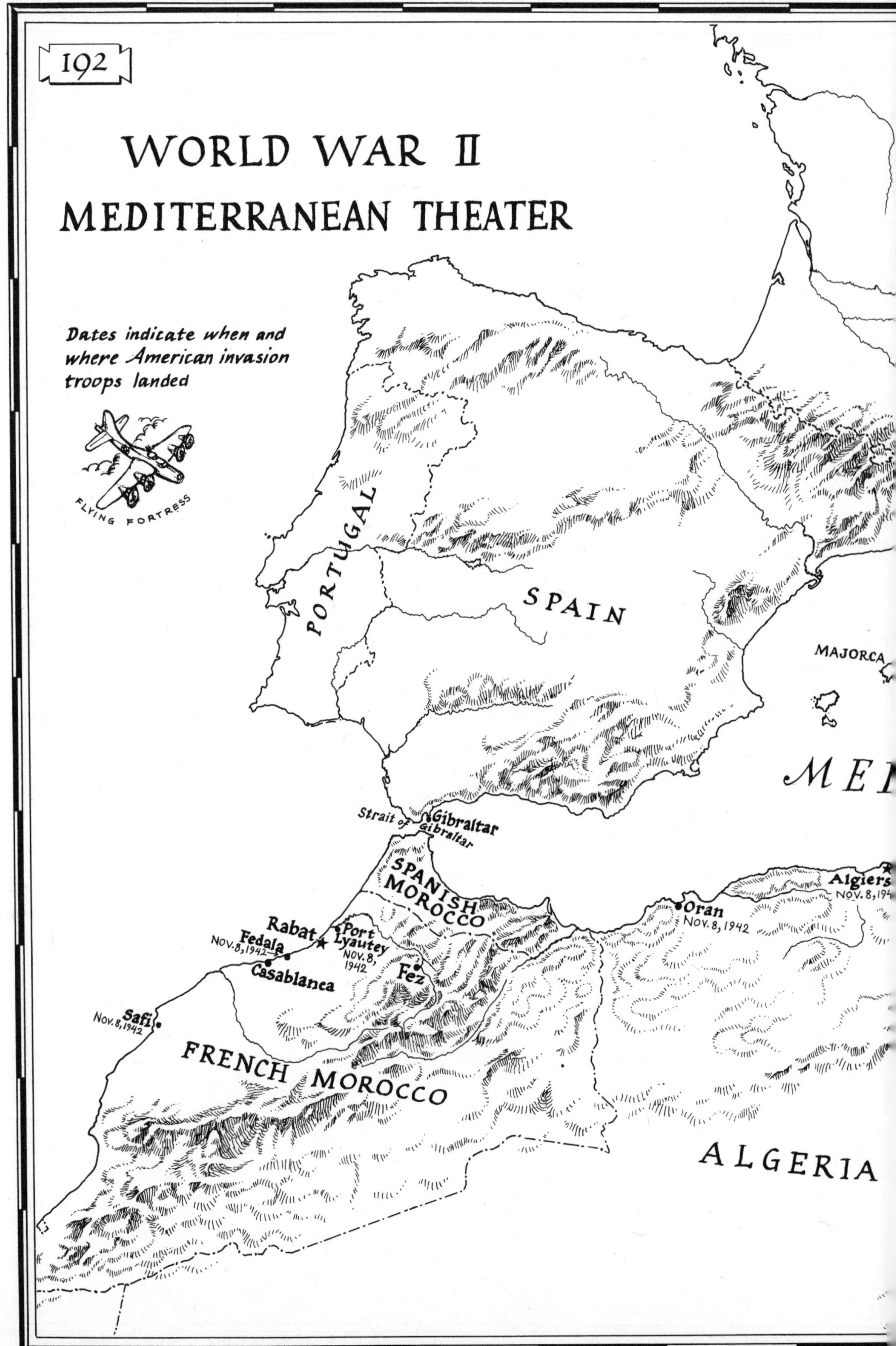

FRANCE
Po River
Ferrara
Bologna
Marseille
Pisa
Arno R.
Florence
Gothic Line
Ancona
St. Raphael
St. Maxime
St. Tropez
Cavalaire
Cap Negre
Toulon
ALL AUGUST 15, 1944
ELBA
CORSICA
SEPT. 13-30, 1943
ITALY
ADRIATIC SEA
Pescara
Gustav Line
Rome
Termoli
Anzio
Nettuno
JAN. 22, 1944
Monte Cassino
Foggia
MINORCA
SARDINIA
Naples
Bari
TYRRHENIAN SEA
Salerno
Amalfi
SEPT. 9, 1943
Paestum
SEPT. 9, 1943
Taranto
TERRANEAN SEA
Palermo
Messina
Marsala
Reggio di Calabria
Strait of Messina
Bougie
Bone
Bizerte
Cape Bon
SICILY
Catania
Licata
JULY 10, 1943
Gela
JULY 10, 1943
Syracuse
Tunis
Scoglitti
JULY 10, 1943
Enfidaville
MALTA
Sbeitla
Kasserine Pass
Gafsa
MEDITERRANEAN SEA
Mareth
TUNISIA
LIBYA
Miles
0
50
100
200

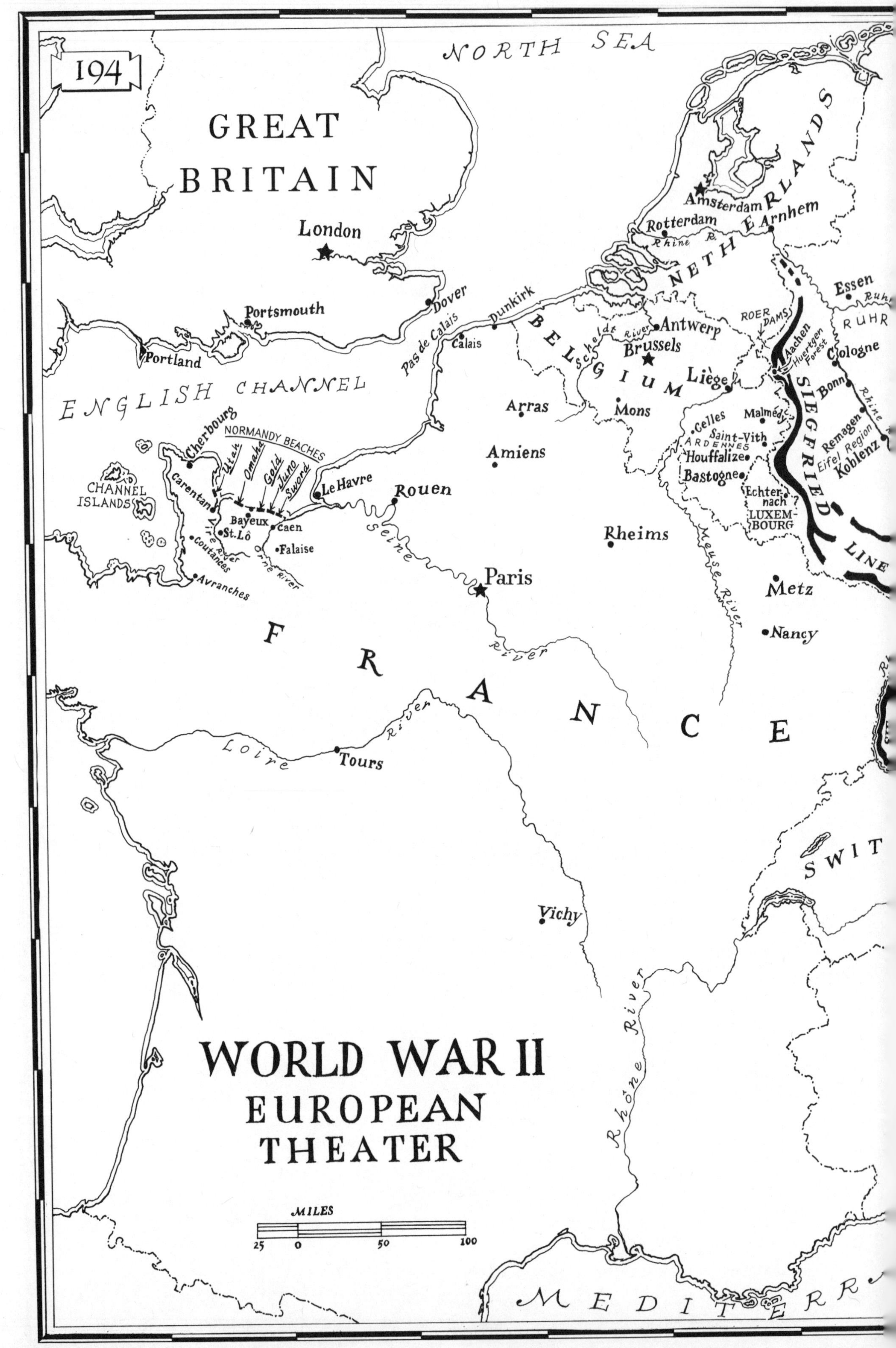
NORTH SEA
GREAT BRITAIN
London
Portsmouth
Dover
Portland
ENGLISH CHANNEL
Pas de Calais
Calais
Dunkirk
NORMANDY BEACHES
Utah
Omaha
Gold
Juno
Sword
Cherbourg
Carentan
CHANNEL ISLANDS
Bayeux
St. Lô
Caen
Falaise
Coutances
Vire River
Orne River
Avranches
Le Havre
Rouen
Seine
Amiens
Arras
Paris
Rheims
NETHERLANDS
Amsterdam
Rotterdam
Arnhem
Rhine R.
BELGIUM
Scheldt River
Antwerp
Brussels
Liège
Mons
ROER DAMS
Aachen
Huertgen Forest
Essen
Ruhr
RUHR
Cologne
Bonn
Rhine
Remagen
Eifel Region
Koblenz
Celles
Malmédy
Saint-Vith
ARDENNES
Houffalize
Bastogne
Echternach
LUXEMBOURG
SIEGFRIED LINE
Meuse River
Metz
Nancy
River
FRANCE
Loire River
Tours
Vichy
Rhône River
SWIT
MEDITERR
WORLD WAR II
EUROPEAN THEATER
MILES
25
0
50
100

Hamburg
U.S. ZONE
Bremen
Elbe River
Bergen-Belsen
Berlin
Potsdam
POLAND
Magdeburg
Paderborn
GERMANY
Torgau
Mulde River
Leipzig
Dresden
Buchenwald
Frankfurt
Prague
UNITED STATES ZONE OF OCCUPATION
CZECHOSLOVAKIA
Dachau
Munich
Linz
Mauthausen
Vienna
AUSTRIA
BRENNER PASS
HUNGARY
RLAND
ITALY
YUGOSLAVIA
ADRIATIC SEA
SEA

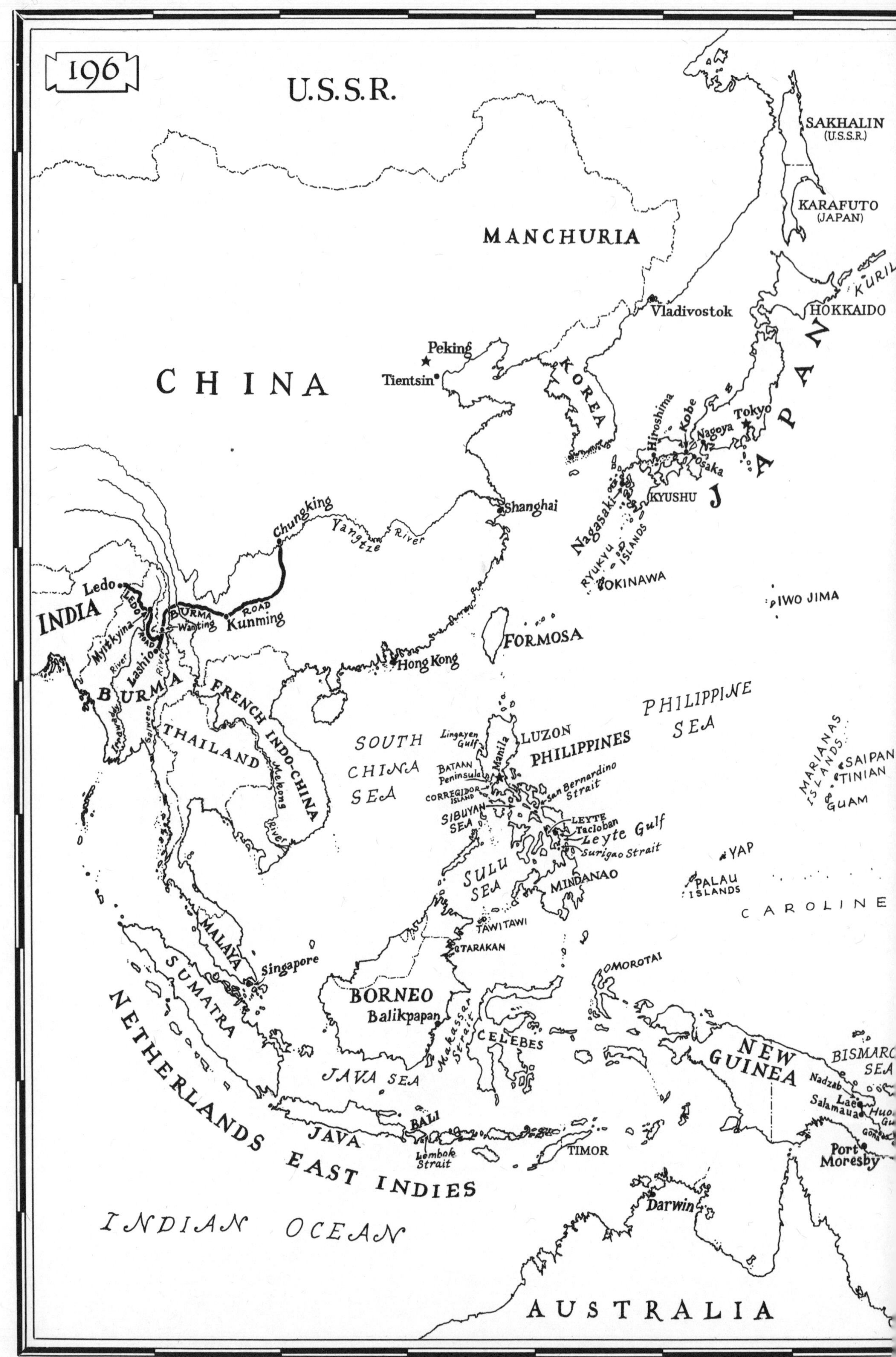
U.S.S.R.
SAKHALIN
(U.S.S.R.)
KARAFUTO
(JAPAN)
MANCHURIA
KURILE
HOKKAIDO
Vladivostok
Peking
Tientsin
CHINA
KOREA
JAPAN
Hiroshima
Kobe
Tokyo
Nagoya
Osaka
KYUSHU
Nagasaki
Shanghai
Chungking
Yangtze River
RYUKYU ISLANDS
OKINAWA
IWO JIMA
Ledo
LEDO ROAD
BURMA ROAD
Wanting
Kunming
INDIA
Myitkyina
Lashio
BURMA
Irrawaddy River
Salween River
FORMOSA
Hong Kong
FRENCH INDO-CHINA
THAILAND
Mekong River
SOUTH CHINA SEA
Lingayen Gulf
LUZON
Manila
PHILIPPINES
PHILIPPINE SEA
BATAAN Peninsula
CORREGIDOR ISLAND
San Bernardino Strait
SIBUYAN SEA
LEYTE
Tacloban
Leyte Gulf
Surigao Strait
MARIANAS ISLANDS
SAIPAN
TINIAN
GUAM
YAP
PALAU ISLANDS
SULU SEA
MINDANAO
CAROLINE
TAWITAWI
TARAKAN
MALAYA
Singapore
MOROTAI
SUMATRA
BORNEO
Balikpapan
Makassar Strait
CELEBES
NEW GUINEA
BISMARCK SEA
Nadzab
Lae
Salamaua
Port Moresby
JAVA SEA
BALI
JAVA
Lombok Strait
TIMOR
NETHERLANDS EAST INDIES
Darwin
INDIAN OCEAN
AUSTRALIA

WORLD WAR II
PACIFIC THEATER

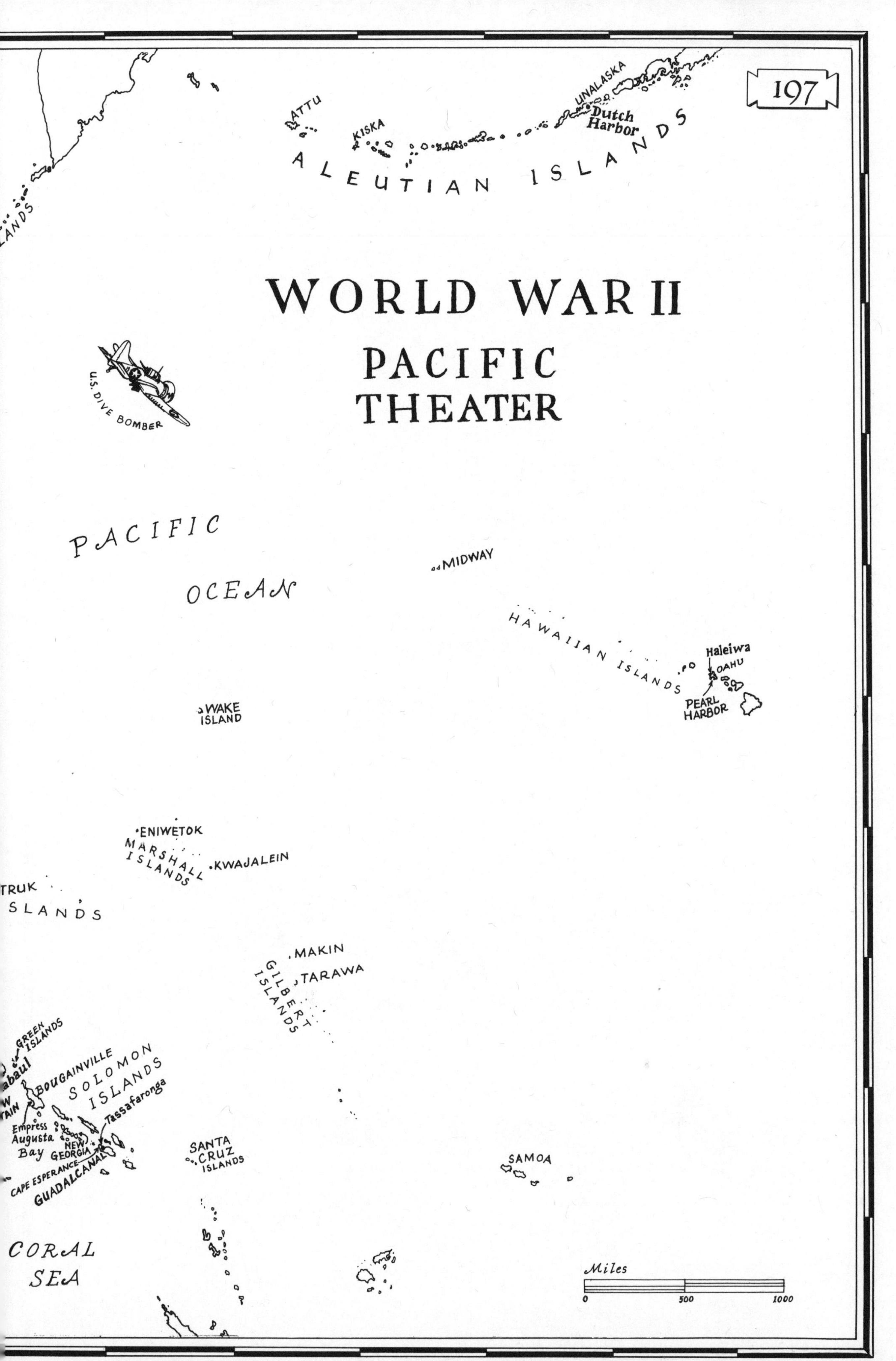

ATTU
KISKA
UNALASKA
Dutch Harbor
ALEUTIAN ISLANDS
U.S. DIVE BOMBER
PACIFIC
OCEAN
MIDWAY
HAWAIIAN ISLANDS
Haleiwa
OAHU
PEARL HARBOR
WAKE ISLAND
ENIWETOK
MARSHALL ISLANDS
KWAJALEIN
TRUK
SLANDS
MAKIN
TARAWA
GILBERT ISLANDS
GREEN ISLANDS
abaul
BOUGAINVILLE
SOLOMON ISLANDS
Tassafaronga
Empress Augusta Bay
NEW GEORGIA
CAPE ESPERANCE
GUADALCANAL
SANTA CRUZ ISLANDS
SAMOA
CORAL SEA
Miles
0
500
1000

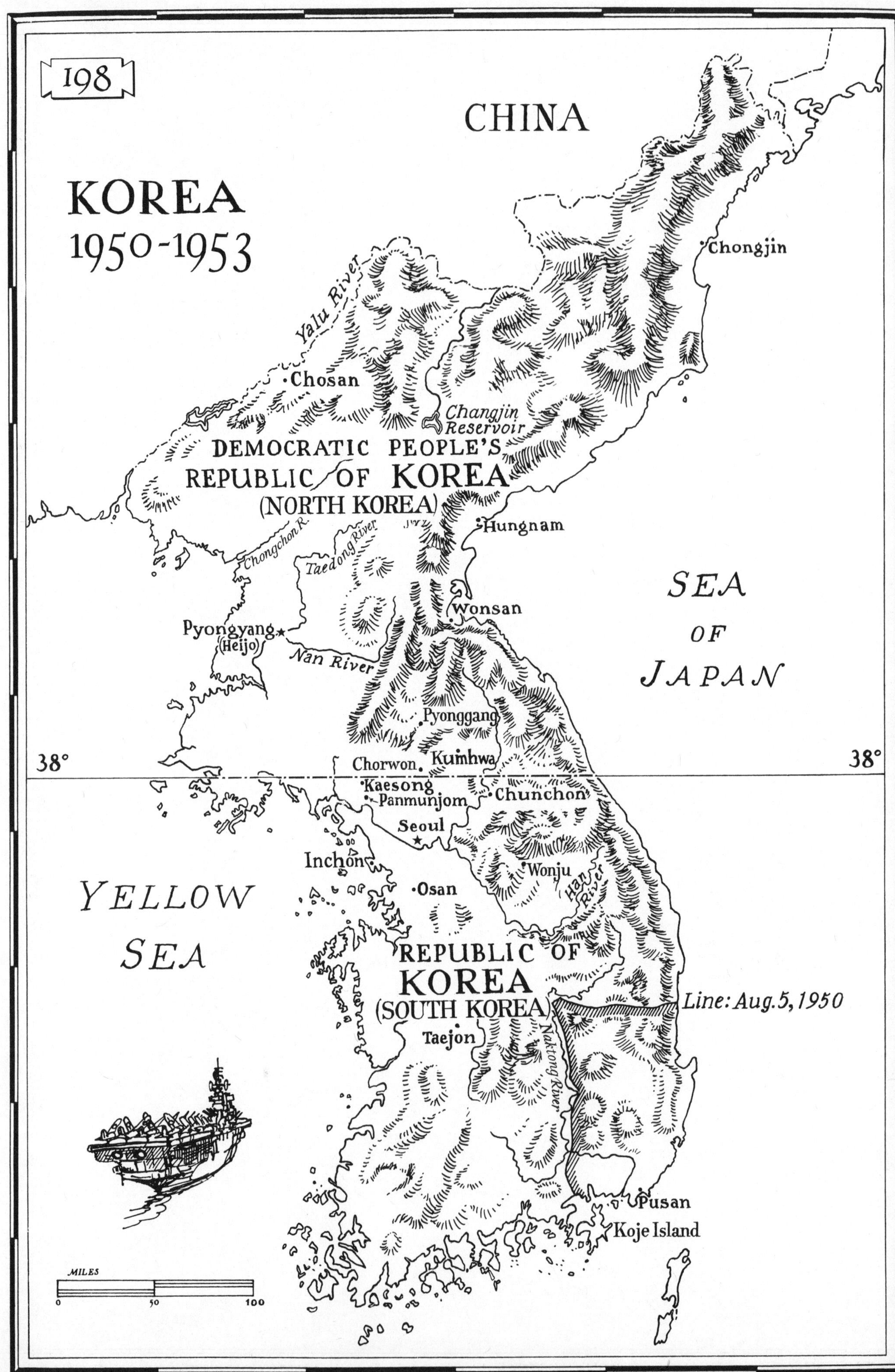

198
CHINA
KOREA
1950-1953
Chongjin
Yalu River
Chosan
Changjin Reservoir
DEMOCRATIC PEOPLE'S
REPUBLIC OF KOREA
(NORTH KOREA)
Hungnam
Chongchon R.
Taedong River
SEA
OF
JAPAN
Wonsan
Pyongyang
(Heijo)
Nan River
Pyonggang
38°
Chorwon
Kumhwa
38°
Kaesong
Panmunjom
Chunchon
Seoul
Inchon
Wonju
YELLOW
SEA
Osan
Han River
REPUBLIC OF
KOREA
(SOUTH KOREA)
Line: Aug. 5, 1950
Taejon
Naktong River
Pusan
Koje Island
MILES
0
50
100

CHINA
DEMOCRATIC REPUBLIC
OF
VIETNAM
(NORTH VIETNAM)
Hanoi
Dien Bien Phu
Haiphong
Mekong River
Mekong R.
GULF OF
TONKIN
Vientiane
LAOS
Mekong River
Ho Chi Minh Trail
Udon Thani (Udorn)
Demilitarized Zone
17°
Quang Tri
Khe Sanh
Hue
Da Nang
THAILAND
Chu Lai
VAN TUONG
PENINSULA
My Lai
Quang Ngai
Ubon Ratchathani
Nakhon Ratchasima
(Korat)
Dak To
Kontum
Pleiku
Nakhon Phanom
Bangkok
IA DRANG
VALLEY
Qui Nhon
CENTRAL
HIGHLANDS
CAMBODIA
Mekong River
REPUBLIC
OF
VIETNAM
(SOUTH VIETNAM)
Nha Trang
CAM RANH
BAY
GULF OF
SIAM
Phnom
Penh
An Loc
Tan Son Hut
Air
Base
Bien Hoa
Saigon
Sihanoukville
Long Xuyen
MEKONG
DELTA
SOUTH CHINA
SEA
VIETNAM
1961-1975
Phuoc Long
Miles
0
50
100
Air Force bases in Thailand

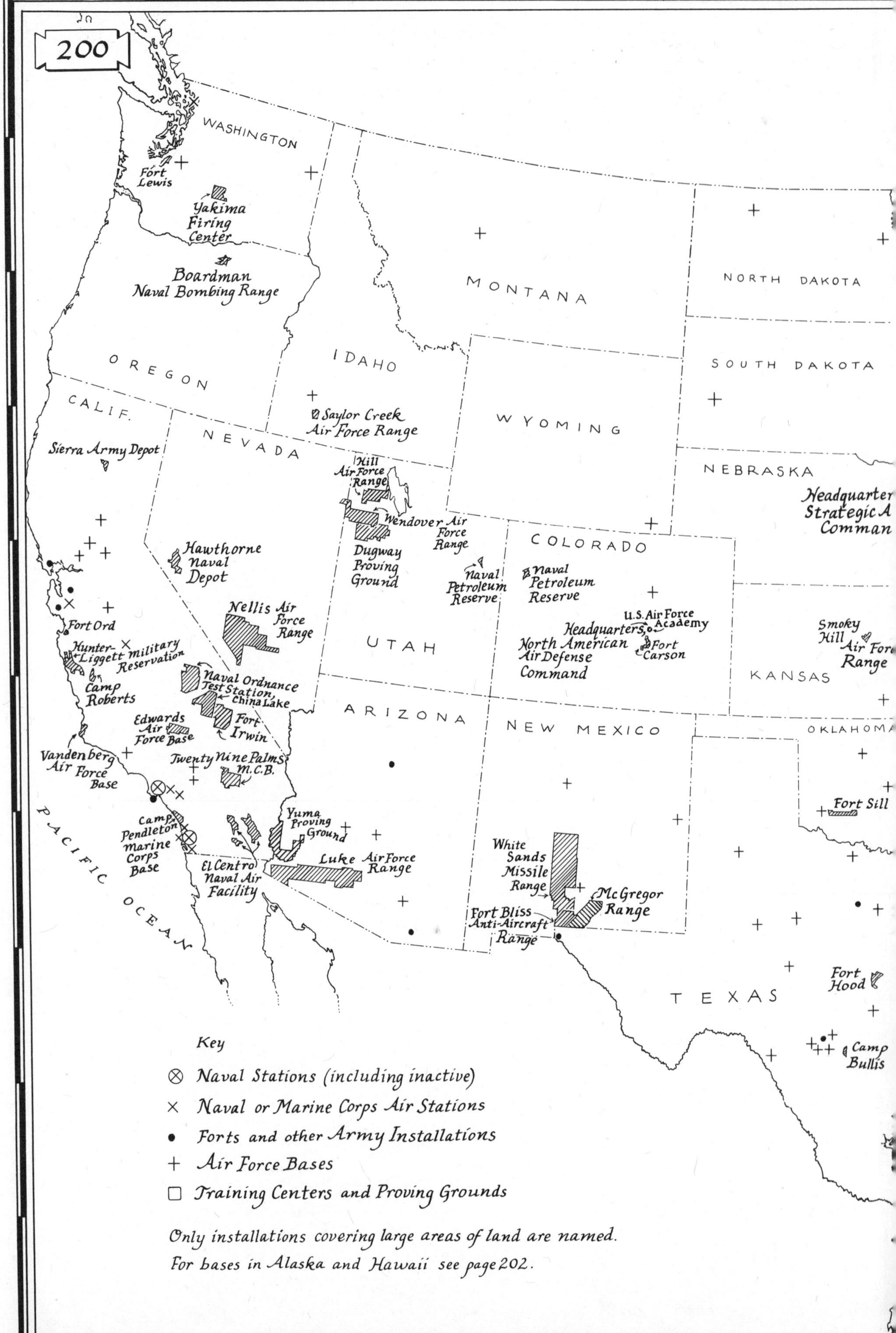

WASHINGTON
Fort Lewis
Yakima Firing Center
Boardman Naval Bombing Range
OREGON
IDAHO
MONTANA
NORTH DAKOTA
SOUTH DAKOTA
WYOMING
NEBRASKA
Headquarter Strategic A Comman
CALIF.
NEVADA
Saylor Creek Air Force Range
Sierra Army Depot
Hill Air Force Range
Wendover Air Force Range
Dugway Proving Ground
Hawthorne Naval Depot
Naval Petroleum Reserve
COLORADO
Naval Petroleum Reserve
U.S. Air Force Academy
Headquarters, North American Air Defense Command
Fort Carson
Nellis Air Force Range
UTAH
Fort Ord
Hunter-Liggett Military Reservation
Camp Roberts
Naval Ordnance Test Station, China Lake
Fort Irwin
Edwards Air Force Base
KANSAS
Smoky Hill Air Force Range
ARIZONA
NEW MEXICO
OKLAHOMA
Vandenberg Air Force Base
Twenty Nine Palms M.C.B.
Fort Sill
PACIFIC OCEAN
Camp Pendleton Marine Corps Base
Yuma Proving Ground
El Centro Naval Air Facility
Luke Air Force Range
White Sands Missile Range
McGregor Range
Fort Bliss Anti-Aircraft Range
TEXAS
Fort Hood
Camp Bullis
Key
Naval Stations (including inactive)
Naval or Marine Corps Air Stations
Forts and other Army Installations
Air Force Bases
Training Centers and Proving Grounds
Only installations covering large areas of land are named.
For bases in Alaska and Hawaii see page 202.

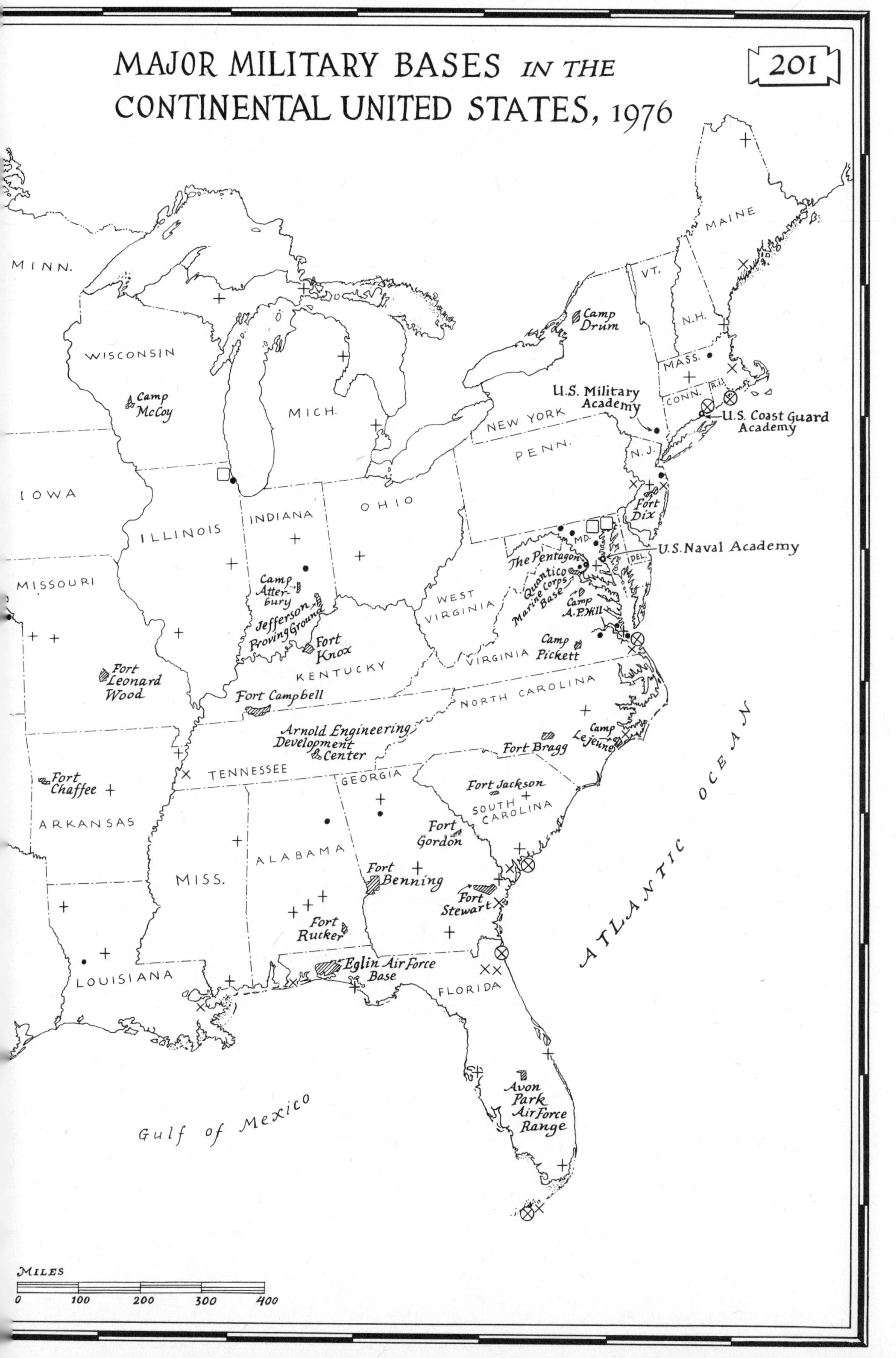

MAJOR MILITARY BASES IN THE CONTINENTAL UNITED STATES, 1976
201
MAINE
VT.
N.H.
MASS.
CONN.
R.I.
Camp Drum
U.S. Military Academy
U.S. Coast Guard Academy
NEW YORK
PENN.
N.J.
Fort Dix
MD.
DEL.
U.S. Naval Academy
The Pentagon
Quantico Marine Corps Base
Camp A.P. Hill
Camp Pickett
WEST VIRGINIA
VIRGINIA
NORTH CAROLINA
Camp Lejeune
Fort Bragg
SOUTH CAROLINA
Fort Jackson
GEORGIA
Fort Gordon
Fort Benning
Fort Stewart
FLORIDA
Avon Park Air Force Range
Eglin Air Force Base
ALABAMA
Fort Rucker
MISS.
LOUISIANA
ARKANSAS
Fort Chaffee
TENNESSEE
Arnold Engineering Development Center
KENTUCKY
Fort Campbell
Fort Knox
Jefferson Proving Ground
Camp Atterbury
INDIANA
OHIO
ILLINOIS
MISSOURI
Fort Leonard Wood
IOWA
MINN.
WISCONSIN
Camp McCoy
MICH.
ATLANTIC OCEAN
Gulf of Mexico
MILES
0 100 200 300 400

MAJOR AMERICAN MILITARY INSTALLATIONS ABROAD, 1977

Key

N: NAVY

A: ARMY

AF: AIR FORCE

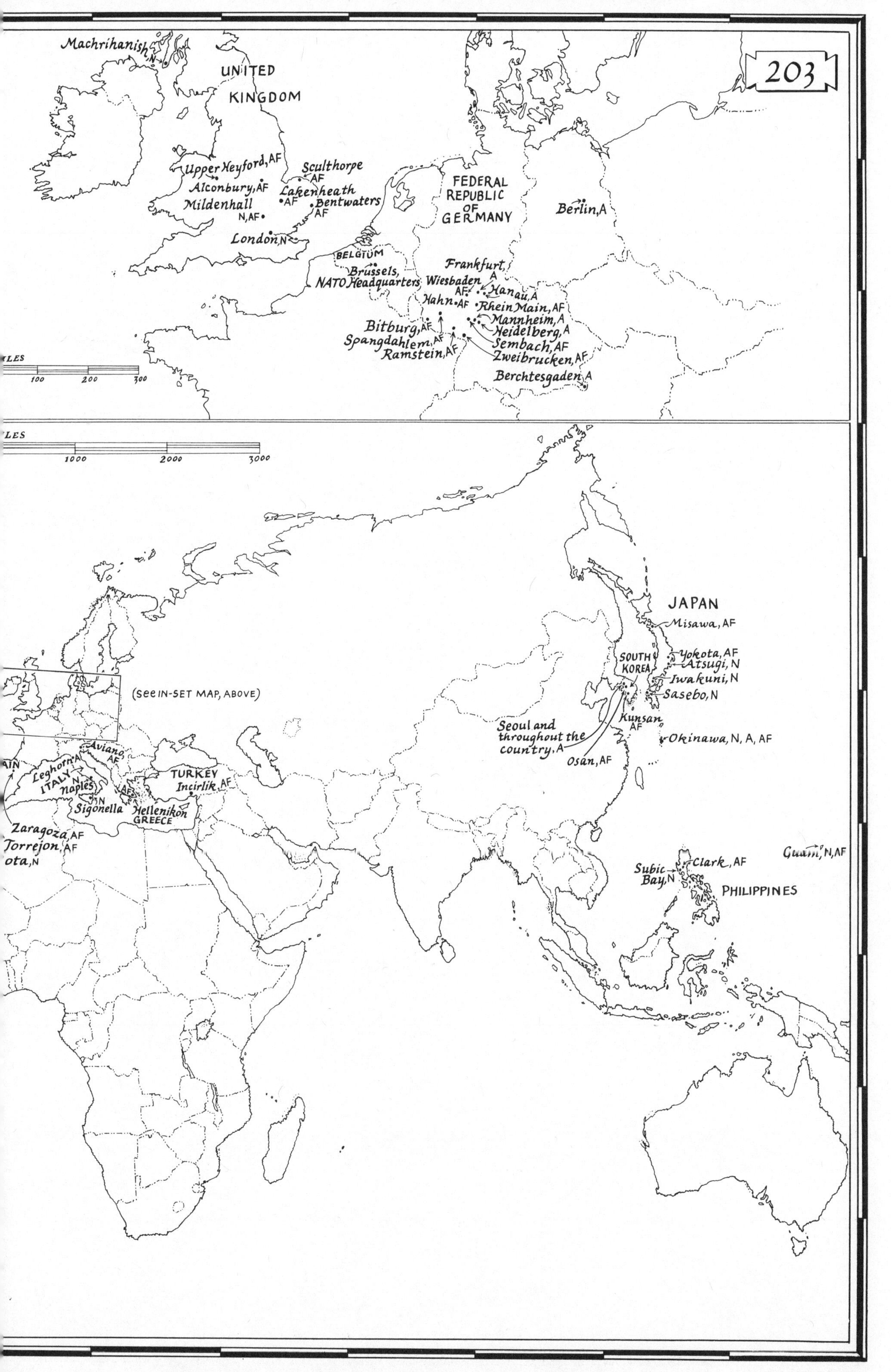
Machrihanish, N
UNITED KINGDOM
Upper Heyford, AF
Alconbury, AF
Mildenhall N, AF
Sculthorpe AF
Lakenheath AF
Bentwaters AF
London, N
BELGIUM
Brussels, NATO Headquarters
FEDERAL REPUBLIC OF GERMANY
Berlin, A
Frankfurt, A
Wiesbaden AF
Hanau, A
Hahn AF
Rhein Main, AF
Mannheim, A
Heidelberg, A
Bitburg, AF
Spangdahlem, AF
Ramstein, AF
Sembach, AF
Zweibrucken, AF
Berchtesgaden, A
MILES
100
200
300
MILES
1000
2000
3000
(SEE IN-SET MAP, ABOVE)
JAPAN
Misawa, AF
Yokota, AF
Atsugi, N
Iwakuni, N
Sasebo, N
SOUTH KOREA
Kunsan AF
Seoul and throughout the country, A
Osan, AF
Okinawa, N, A, AF
Aviano AF
Leghorn, A
ITALY
Naples N
Sigonella N
AF
TURKEY
Incirlik, AF
Hellenikon
GREECE
Zaragoza, AF
Torrejon, AF
Rota, N
Guam, N, AF
Subic Bay, N
Clark, AF
PHILIPPINES

X SOCIAL AND ECONOMIC DEVELOPMENTS

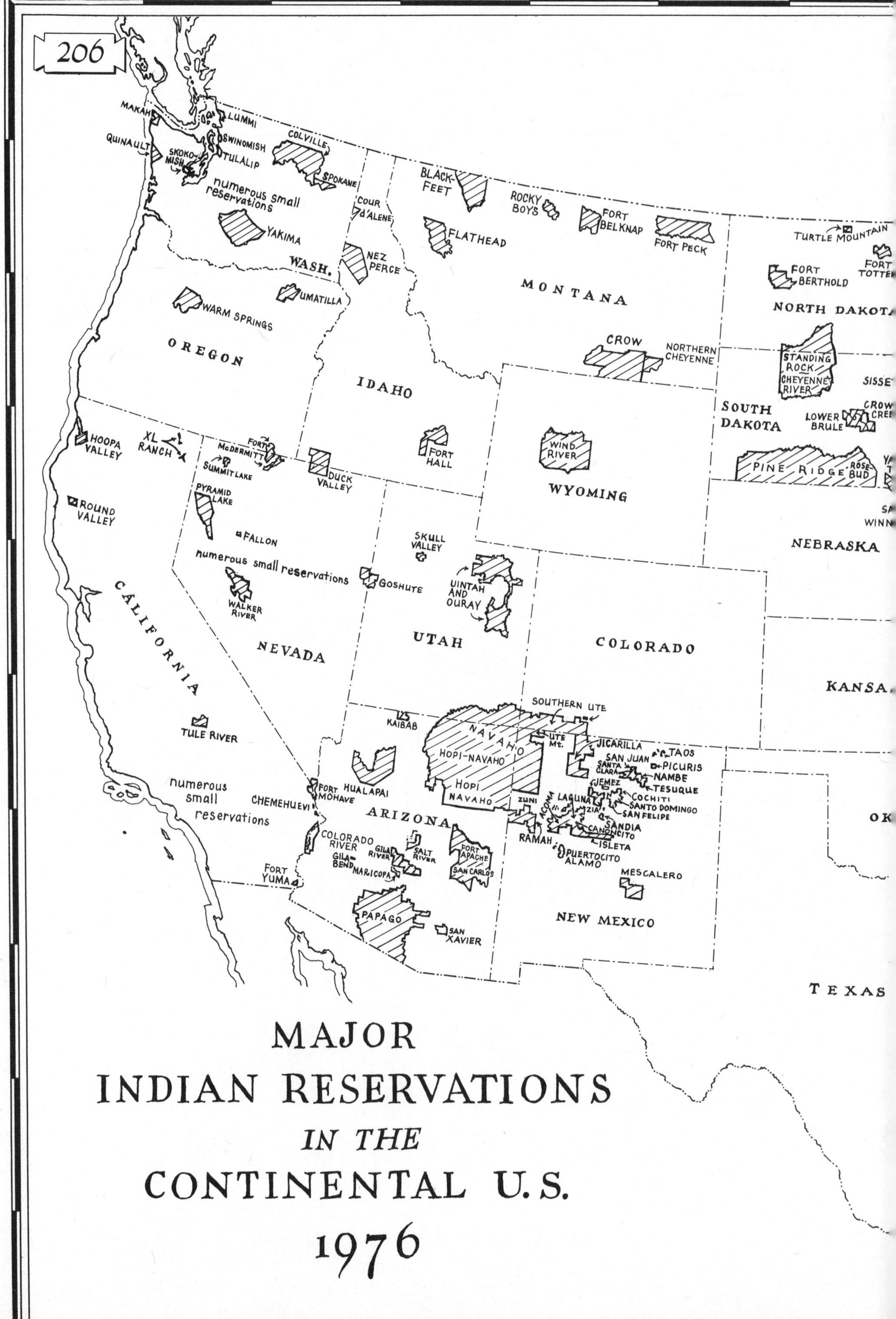
MAKAH
LUMMI
QUINAULT
SWINOMISH
SKOKO-MISH
TULALIP
COLVILLE
SPOKANE
numerous small reservations
YAKIMA
WASH.
COUR d'ALENE
NEZ PERCE
BLACK-FEET
ROCKY BOYS
FORT BELKNAP
FORT PECK
FLATHEAD
MONTANA
TURTLE MOUNTAIN
FORT BERTHOLD
NORTH DAKOTA
UMATILLA
WARM SPRINGS
OREGON
IDAHO
CROW
NORTHERN CHEYENNE
STANDING ROCK
CHEYENNE RIVER
SOUTH DAKOTA
LOWER BRULE
PINE RIDGE
ROSE-BUD
HOOPA VALLEY
XL RANCH
FORT McDERMITT
SUMMIT LAKE
DUCK VALLEY
FORT HALL
WIND RIVER
WYOMING
ROUND VALLEY
PYRAMID LAKE
FALLON
numerous small reservations
WALKER RIVER
NEVADA
SKULL VALLEY
GOSHUTE
UINTAH AND OURAY
UTAH
COLORADO
NEBRASKA
KANSAS
CALIFORNIA
TULE RIVER
SOUTHERN UTE
KAIBAB
NAVAHO
HOPI-NAVAHO
HOPI
NAVAHO
UTE Mt.
JICARILLA
TAOS
SAN JUAN
PICURIS
SANTA CLARA
NAMBE
TESUQUE
JEMEZ
COCHITI
SANTO DOMINGO
SAN FELIPE
ZUNI
ACOMA
LAGUNA
ZIA
SANDIA
CANONCITO
ISLETA
RAMAH
PUERTOCITO
ALAMO
MESCALERO
NEW MEXICO
HUALAPAI
FORT MOHAVE
numerous small reservations
CHEMEHUEVI
ARIZONA
COLORADO RIVER
GILA RIVER
SALT RIVER
GILA-BEND
MARICOPA
FORT APACHE
SAN CARLOS
FORT YUMA
PAPAGO
SAN XAVIER
TEXAS

MAJOR
INDIAN RESERVATIONS
IN THE
CONTINENTAL U.S.
1976

RED LAKE
NETT LAKE
DEER CREEK
GRAND PORTAGE
LEECH LAKE
WHITE EARTH
FOND du LAC
L'ANSE
BAD RIVER
LAC du FLAMBEAU
LAC COURT OREILLES
STOCKBRIDGE
ONEIDA
MICHIGAN
MINNESOTA
WISCONSIN
IOWA
OMAHA
SAC AND FOX
KICKAPOO
POTAWATOMI
MISSOURI
ILLINOIS
INDIANA
OHIO
KENTUCKY
OSAGE
OMA
ARKANSAS
TENNESSEE
MISSISSIPPI
CHOCTAW
ALABAMA
GEORGIA
LOUISIANA
FLORIDA
BRIGHTON
BIG CYPRESS
HOLLYWOOD
MICCOSUKEE
SOUTH CAROLINA
NORTH CAROLINA
CHEROKEE
VIRGINIA
WEST VIRGINIA
MD.
DEL.
N.J.
PENNSYLVANIA
NEW YORK
SAINT REGIS
ONONDAGA
TUSCARORA
TONAWANDA
CATTARAUGUS
OIL SPRINGS
ALLEGANY
VT.
N.H.
MAINE
MASS.
CONN.
R.I.

MILES
0 100 200 300 400

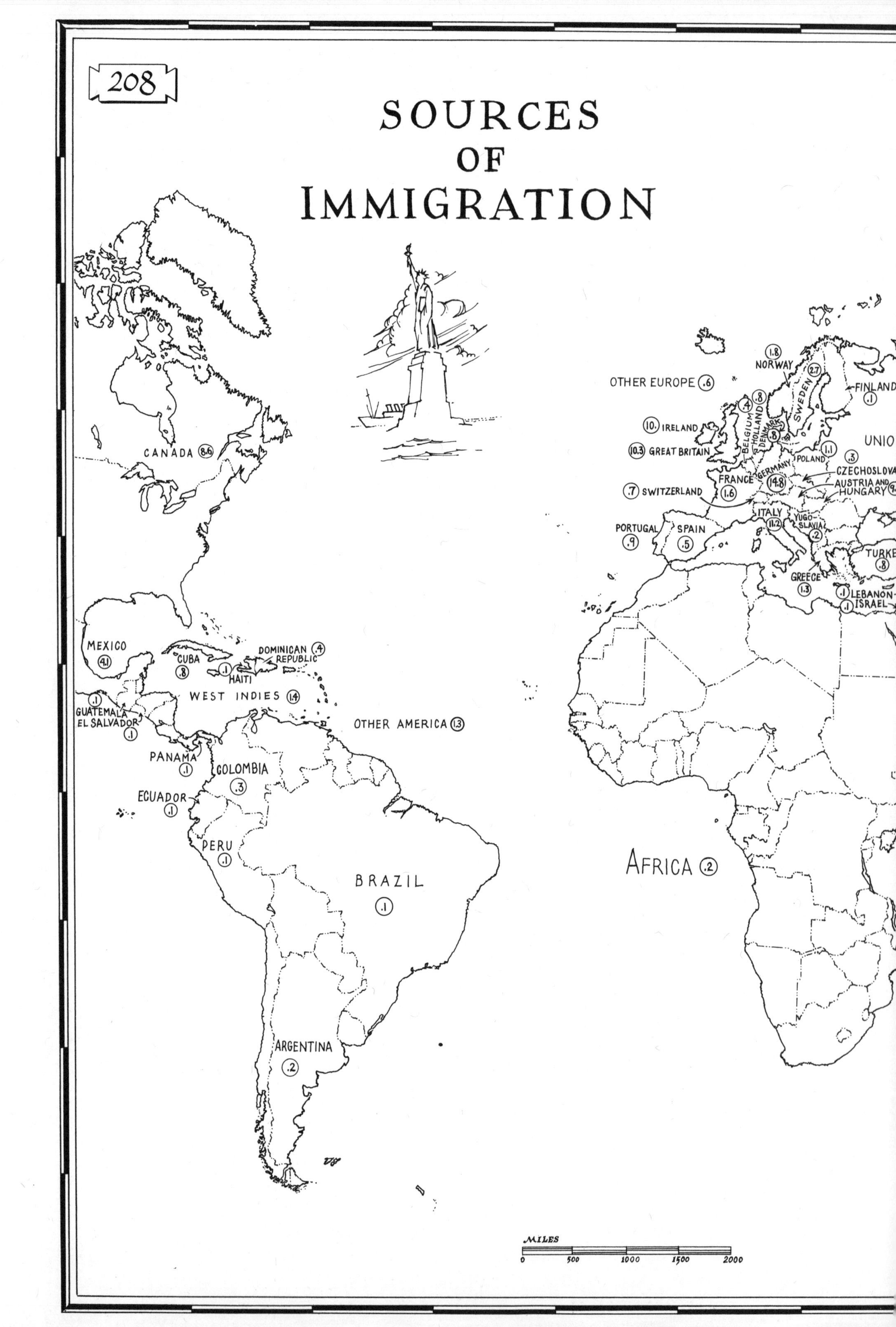

208
SOURCES OF IMMIGRATION
CANADA 8.6
MEXICO 4.1
CUBA .8
HAITI .1
DOMINICAN REPUBLIC .4
WEST INDIES 1.4
GUATEMALA .1
EL SALVADOR .1
PANAMA .1
OTHER AMERICA 1.3
COLOMBIA .3
ECUADOR .1
PERU .1
BRAZIL .1
ARGENTINA .2
OTHER EUROPE .6
NORWAY 1.8
SWEDEN 2.7
FINLAND .1
IRELAND 10.
GREAT BRITAIN 10.3
BELGIUM .4
HOLLAND .8
DENMARK .8
POLAND 1.1
GERMANY 14.8
FRANCE 1.6
AUSTRIA AND HUNGARY 9.2
SWITZERLAND .7
PORTUGAL .9
SPAIN .5
ITALY 11.2
YUGOSLAVIA .2
GREECE 1.3
TURKEY .8
LEBANON .1
ISRAEL .1
AFRICA .2
MILES
0
500
1000
1500
2000

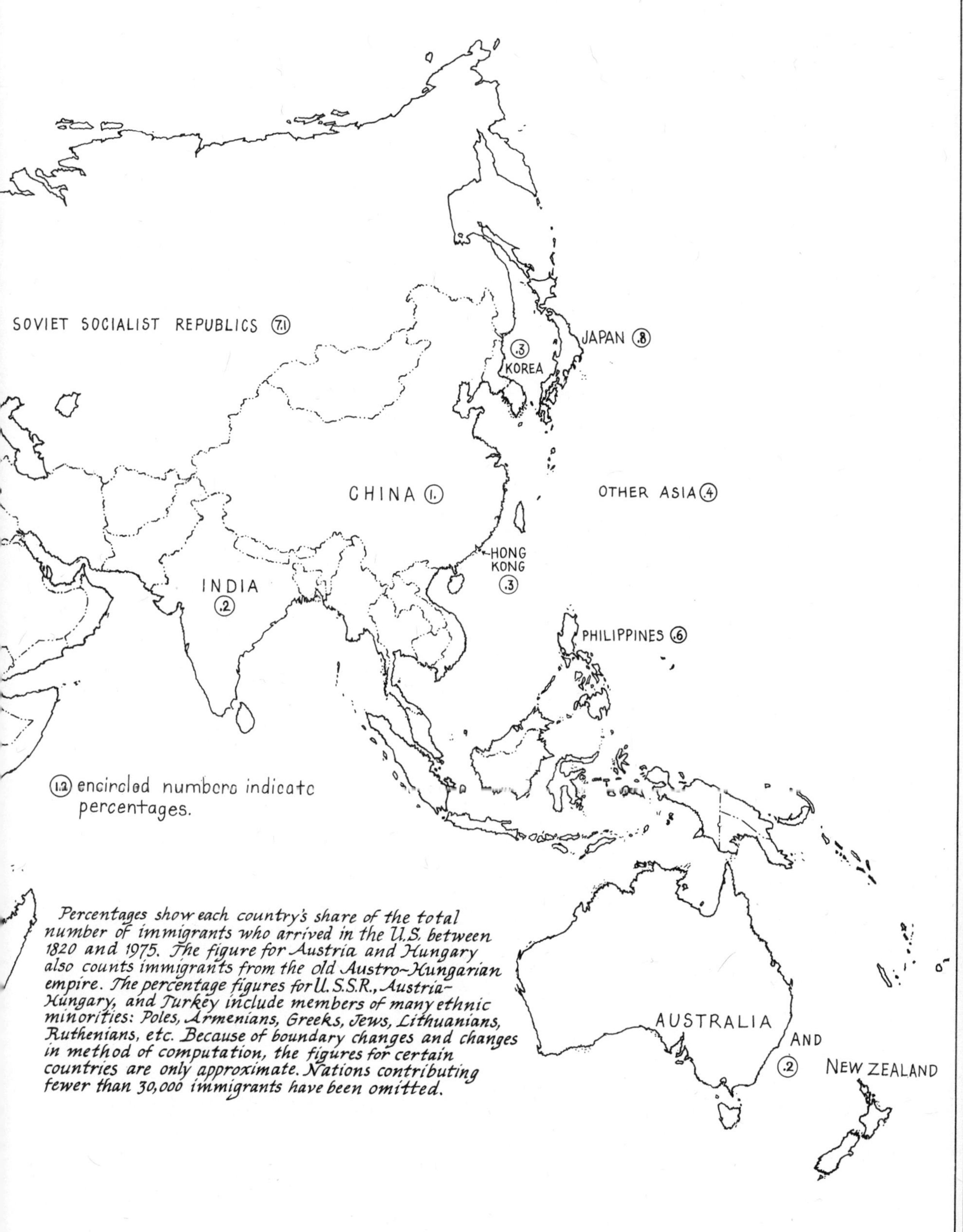

Percentages show each country's share of the total number of immigrants who arrived in the U.S. between 1820 and 1975. The figure for Austria and Hungary also counts immigrants from the old Austro-Hungarian empire. The percentage figures for U.S.S.R., Austria-Hungary, and Turkey include members of many ethnic minorities: Poles, Armenians, Greeks, Jews, Lithuanians, Ruthenians, etc. Because of boundary changes and changes in method of computation, the figures for certain countries are only approximate. Nations contributing fewer than 30,000 immigrants have been omitted.

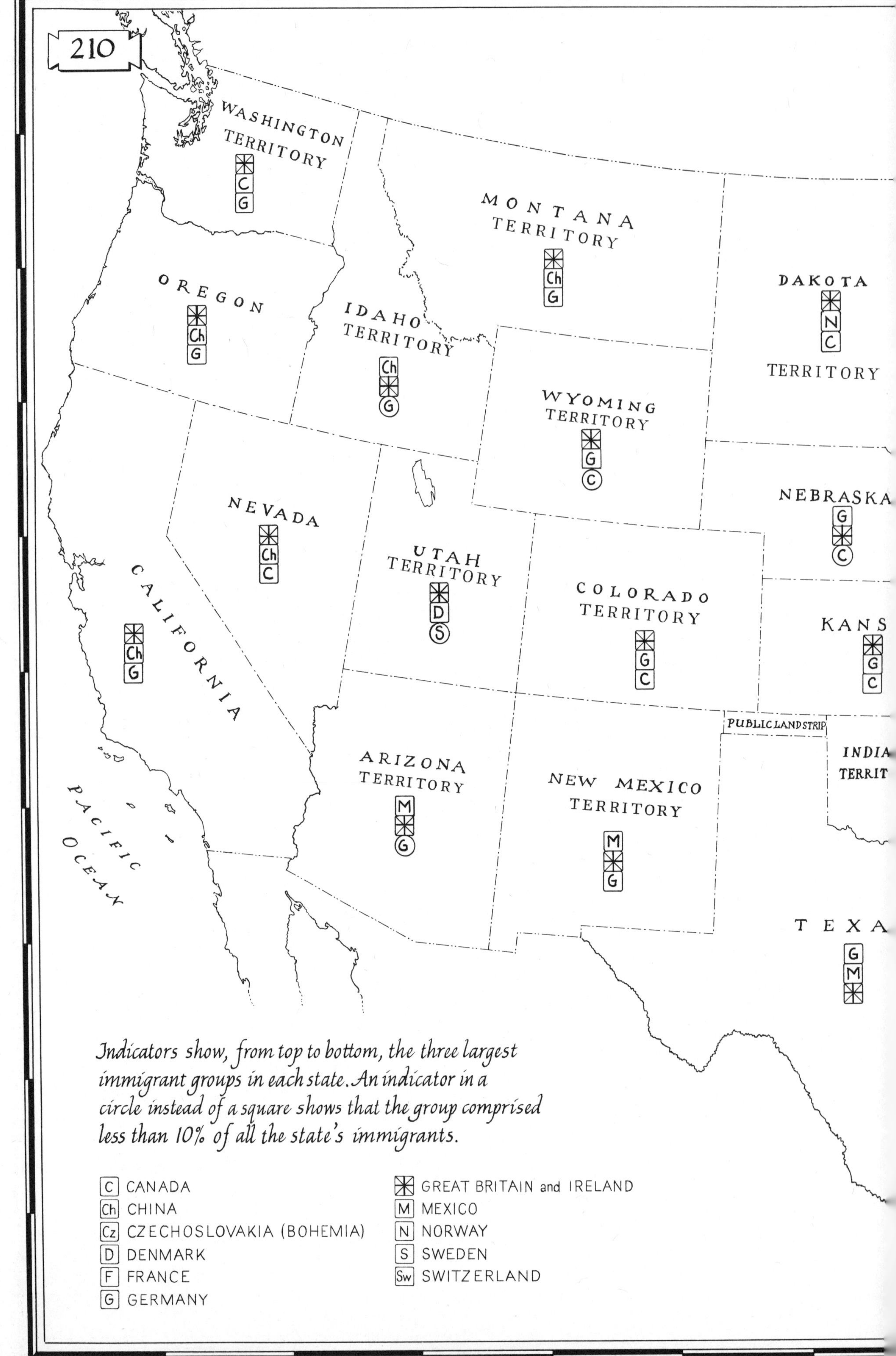

Indicators show, from top to bottom, the three largest immigrant groups in each state. An indicator in a circle instead of a square shows that the group comprised less than 10% of all the state's immigrants.

SOURCES OF IMMIGRATION 1870

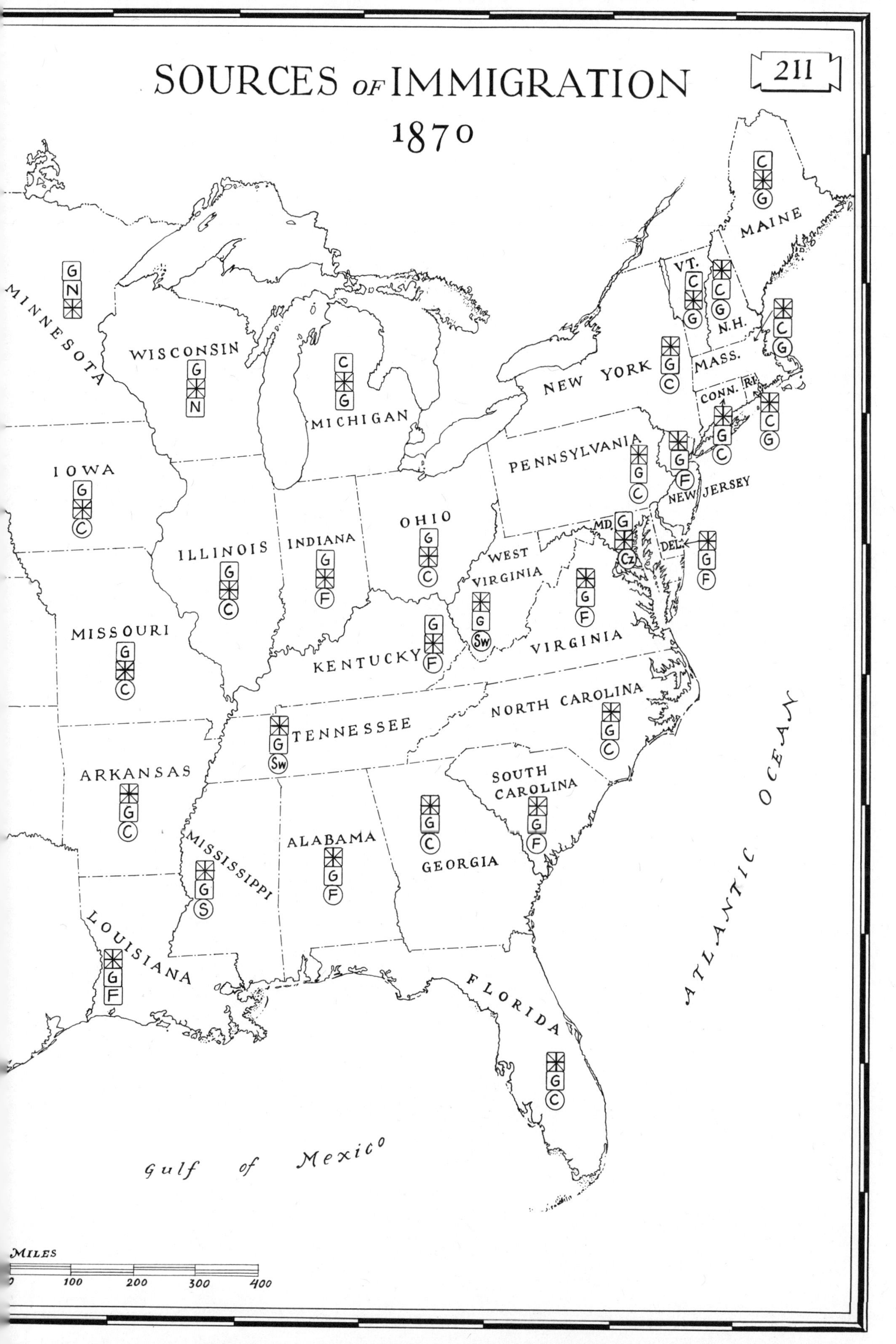

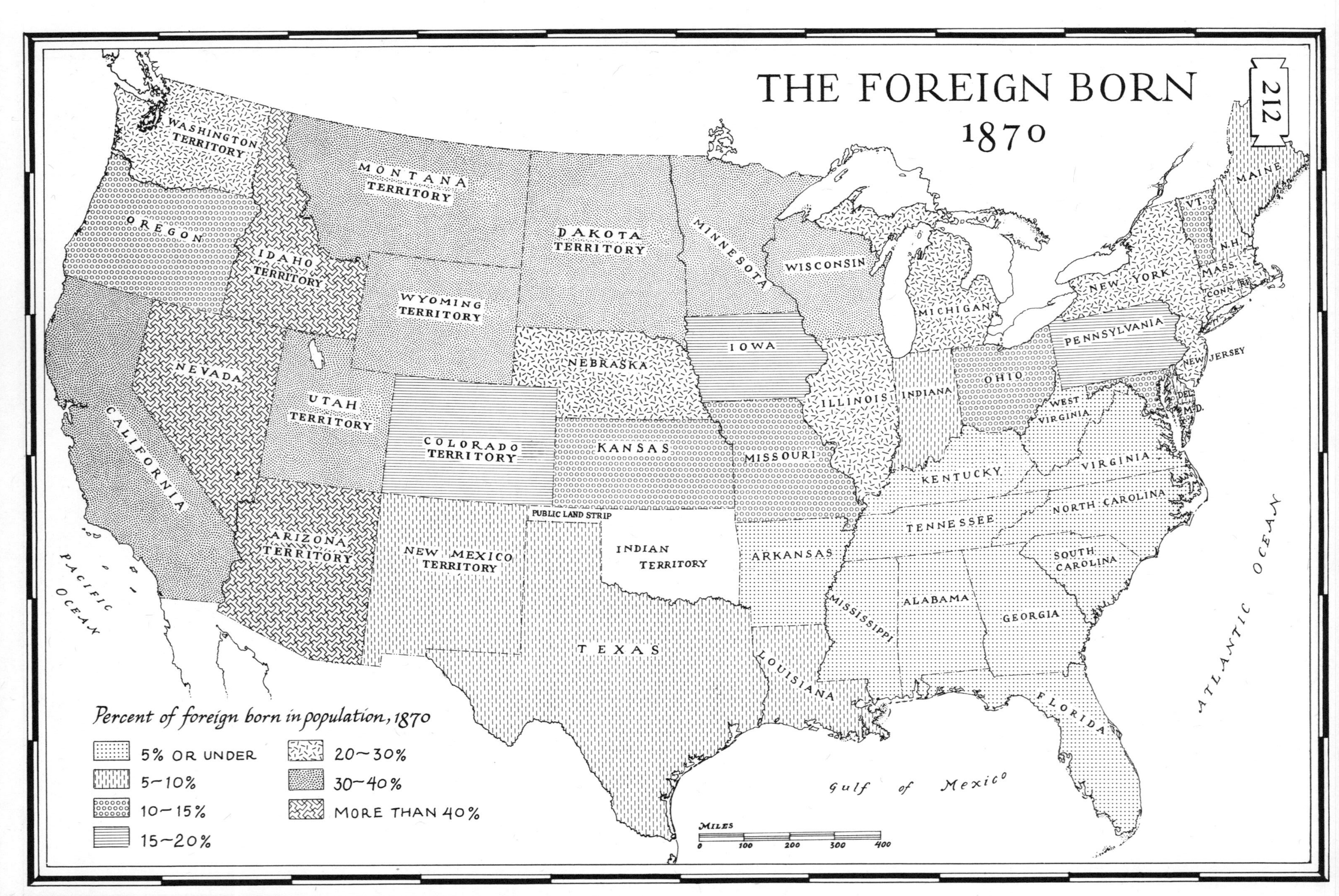
212
THE FOREIGN BORN
1870
WASHINGTON TERRITORY
OREGON
CALIFORNIA
NEVADA
IDAHO TERRITORY
MONTANA TERRITORY
WYOMING TERRITORY
UTAH TERRITORY
ARIZONA TERRITORY
COLORADO TERRITORY
NEW MEXICO TERRITORY
DAKOTA TERRITORY
NEBRASKA
KANSAS
PUBLIC LAND STRIP
INDIAN TERRITORY
TEXAS
MINNESOTA
IOWA
MISSOURI
ARKANSAS
LOUISIANA
WISCONSIN
ILLINOIS
MICHIGAN
INDIANA
OHIO
KENTUCKY
TENNESSEE
MISSISSIPPI
ALABAMA
GEORGIA
FLORIDA
SOUTH CAROLINA
NORTH CAROLINA
VIRGINIA
WEST VIRGINIA
PENNSYLVANIA
NEW YORK
NEW JERSEY
DEL.
MD.
VT.
N.H.
MAINE
MASS.
CONN.
R.I.
PACIFIC OCEAN
ATLANTIC OCEAN
Gulf of Mexico
MILES
0 100 200 300 400
Percent of foreign born in population, 1870
5% OR UNDER
5–10%
10–15%
15–20%
20–30%
30–40%
MORE THAN 40%

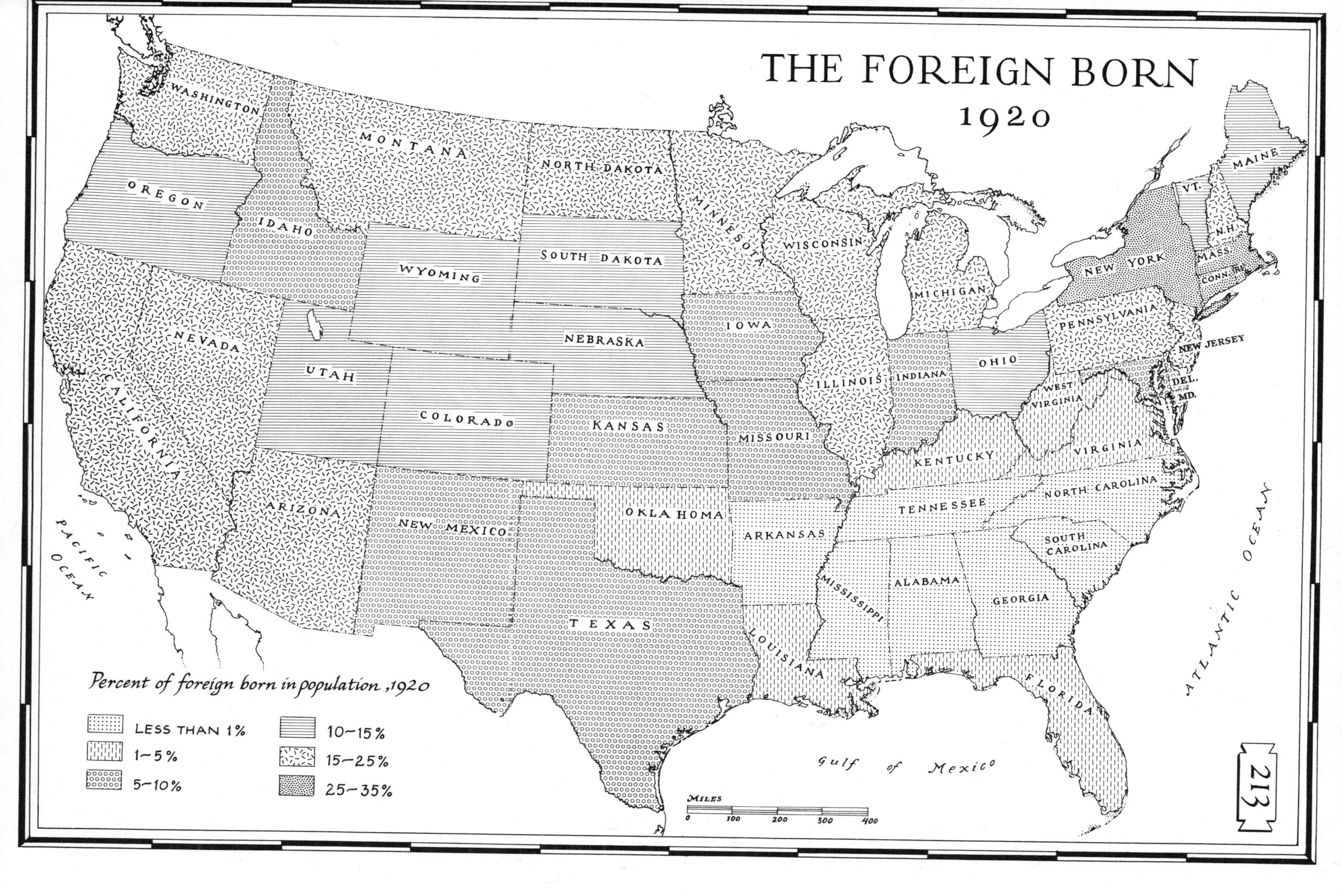

THE FOREIGN BORN
1920
213
WASHINGTON
OREGON
CALIFORNIA
NEVADA
IDAHO
MONTANA
WYOMING
UTAH
COLORADO
ARIZONA
NEW MEXICO
NORTH DAKOTA
SOUTH DAKOTA
NEBRASKA
KANSAS
OKLAHOMA
TEXAS
MINNESOTA
IOWA
MISSOURI
ARKANSAS
LOUISIANA
WISCONSIN
ILLINOIS
MICHIGAN
INDIANA
OHIO
KENTUCKY
TENNESSEE
MISSISSIPPI
ALABAMA
GEORGIA
FLORIDA
SOUTH CAROLINA
NORTH CAROLINA
VIRGINIA
WEST VIRGINIA
PENNSYLVANIA
NEW YORK
NEW JERSEY
DEL.
MD.
CONN.
R.I.
MASS.
VT.
N.H.
MAINE
PACIFIC OCEAN
ATLANTIC OCEAN
Gulf of Mexico
MILES
0 100 200 300 400
Percent of foreign born in population, 1920
LESS THAN 1%
1–5%
5–10%
10–15%
15–25%
25–35%

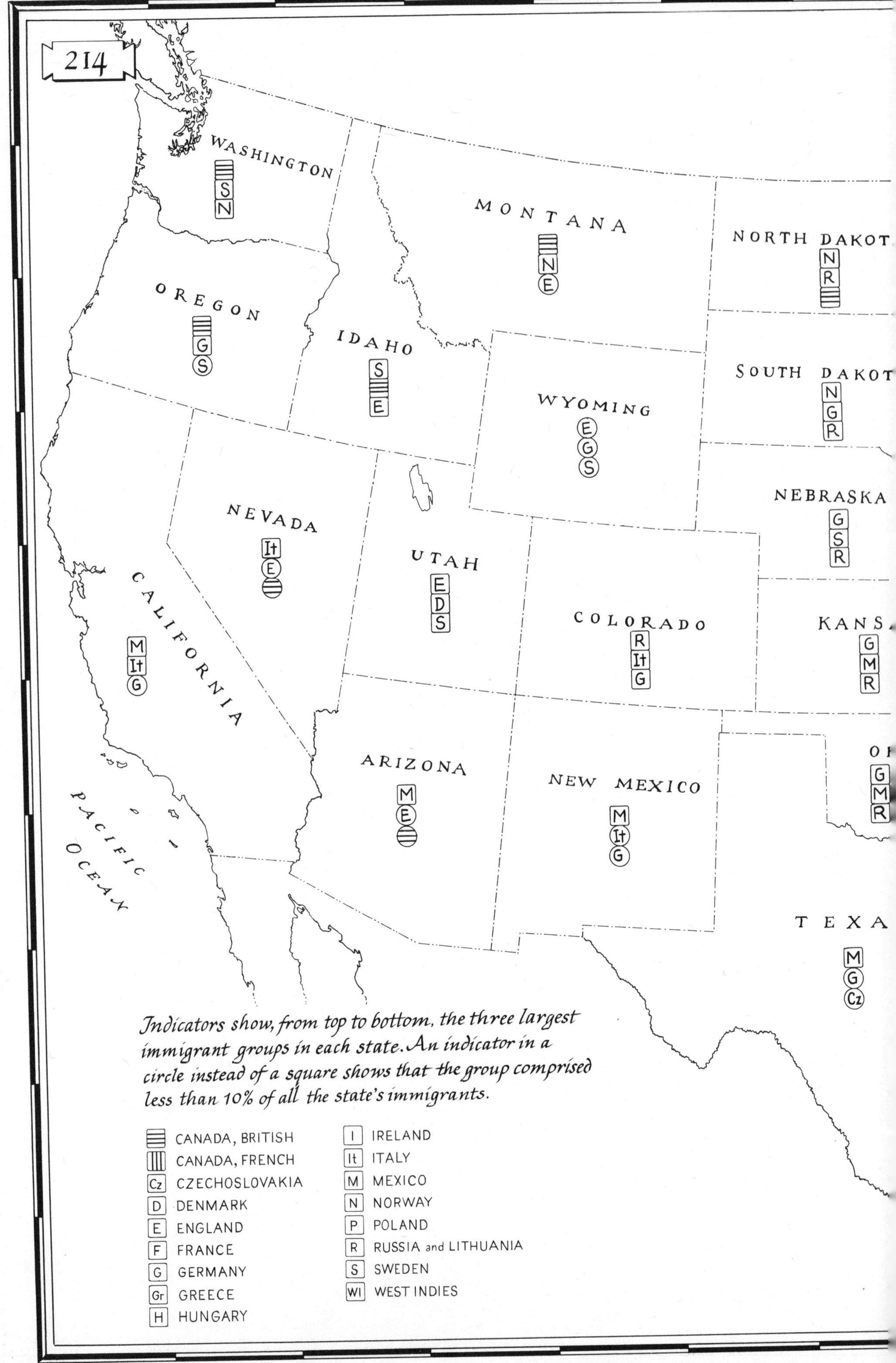

WASHINGTON
MONTANA
NORTH DAKOT
OREGON
IDAHO
SOUTH DAKOT
WYOMING
NEBRASKA
NEVADA
UTAH
CALIFORNIA
COLORADO
KANS
ARIZONA
NEW MEXICO
PACIFIC OCEAN
TEXA
Indicators show, from top to bottom, the three largest immigrant groups in each state. An indicator in a circle instead of a square shows that the group comprised less than 10% of all the state's immigrants.
CANADA, BRITISH
CANADA, FRENCH
Cz CZECHOSLOVAKIA
D DENMARK
E ENGLAND
F FRANCE
G GERMANY
Gr GREECE
H HUNGARY
I IRELAND
It ITALY
M MEXICO
N NORWAY
P POLAND
R RUSSIA and LITHUANIA
S SWEDEN
WI WEST INDIES

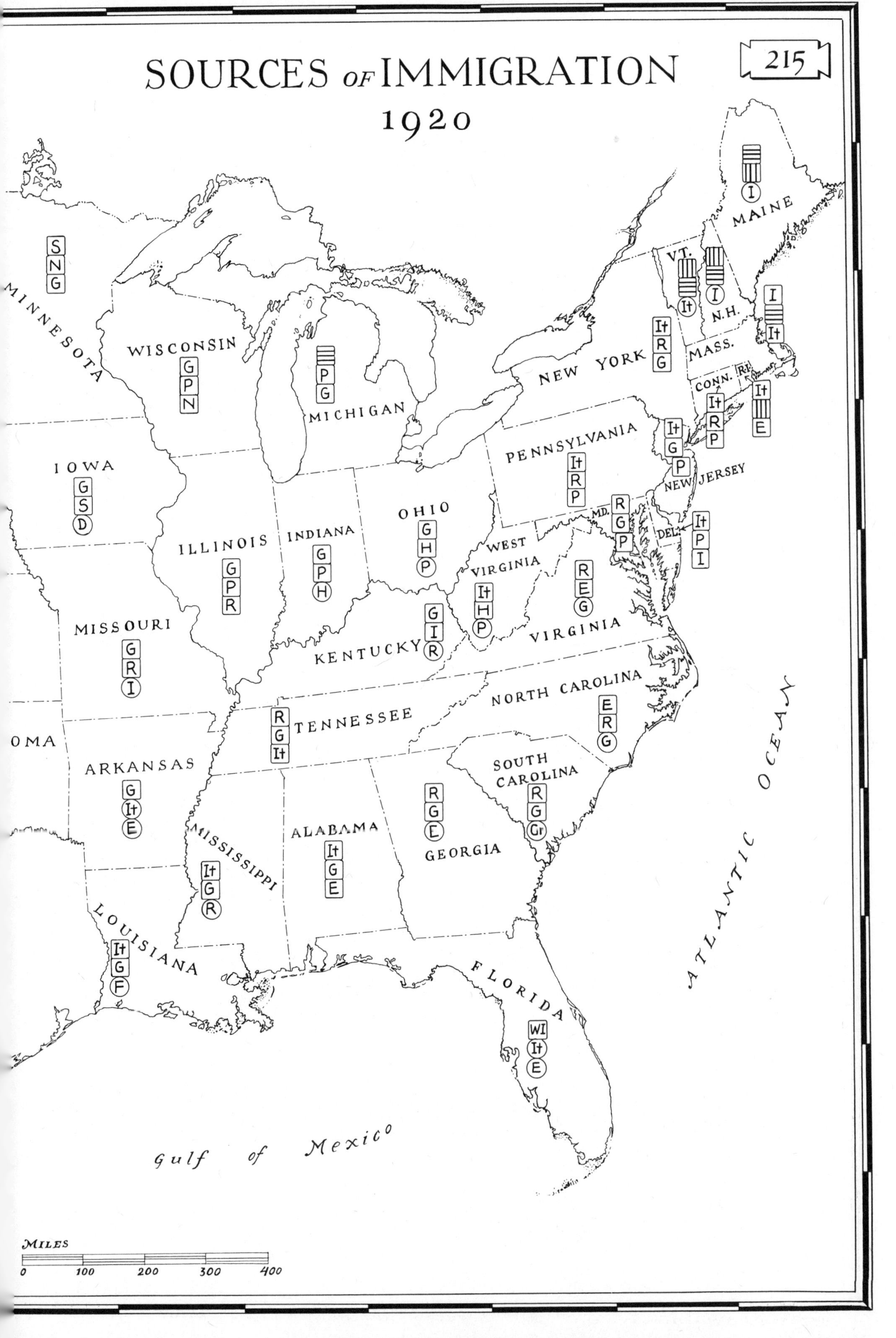
SOURCES OF IMMIGRATION
1920
MINNESOTA
WISCONSIN
MICHIGAN
IOWA
ILLINOIS
INDIANA
OHIO
MISSOURI
KENTUCKY
WEST VIRGINIA
VIRGINIA
PENNSYLVANIA
NEW YORK
NEW JERSEY
MD.
DEL.
VT.
N.H.
MAINE
MASS.
CONN.
R.I.
NORTH CAROLINA
SOUTH CAROLINA
TENNESSEE
ARKANSAS
OMA
MISSISSIPPI
ALABAMA
GEORGIA
LOUISIANA
FLORIDA
ATLANTIC OCEAN
Gulf of Mexico
MILES
0 100 200 300 400

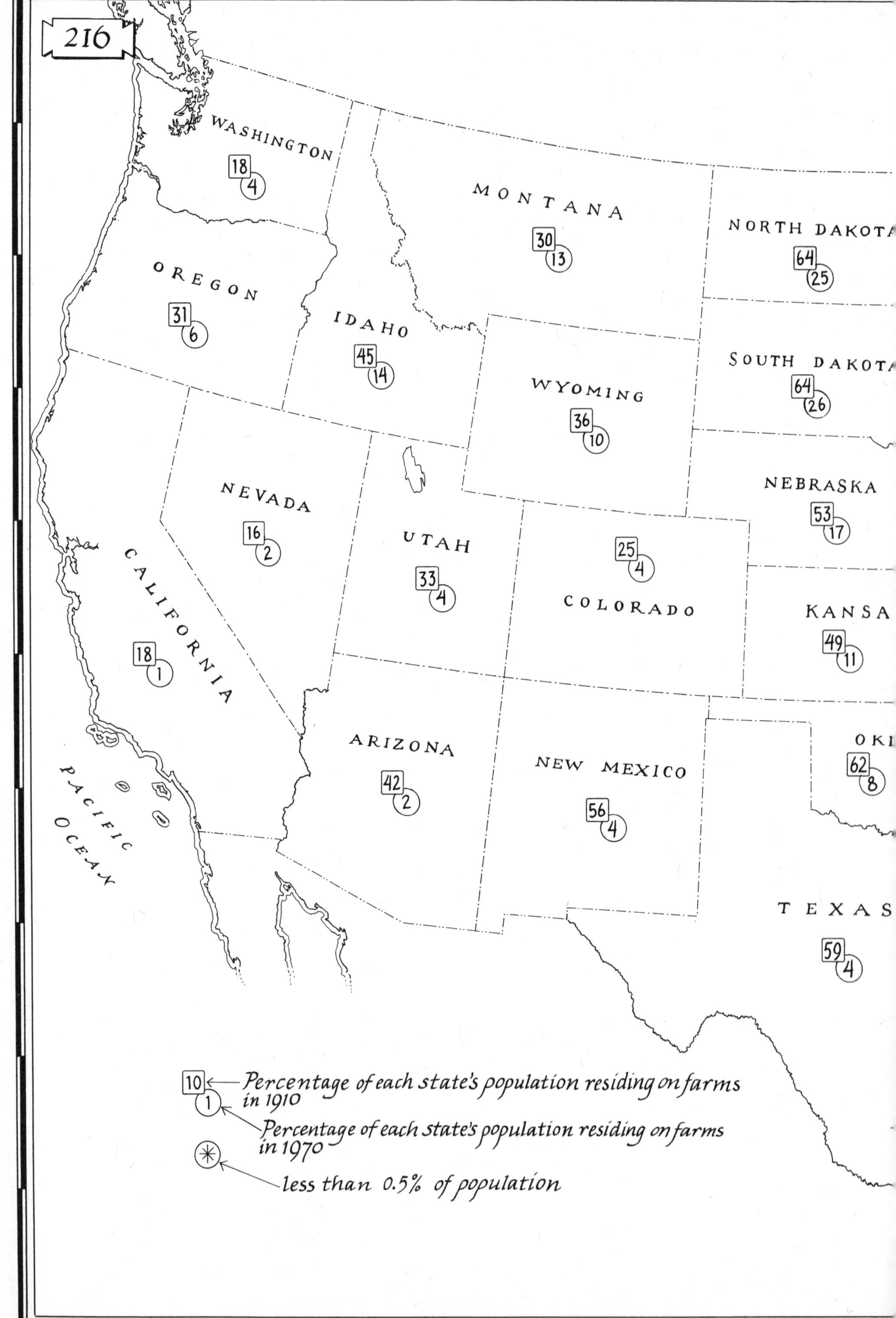
WASHINGTON
18
4
MONTANA
30
13
NORTH DAKOTA
64
25
OREGON
31
6
IDAHO
45
14
SOUTH DAKOTA
64
26
WYOMING
36
10
NEBRASKA
53
17
NEVADA
16
2
UTAH
33
4
25
4
COLORADO
KANSA
49
11
CALIFORNIA
18
1
ARIZONA
42
2
NEW MEXICO
56
4
OKL
62
8
PACIFIC OCEAN
TEXAS
59
4
10
1
Percentage of each state's population residing on farms in 1910
Percentage of each state's population residing on farms in 1970
less than 0.5% of population

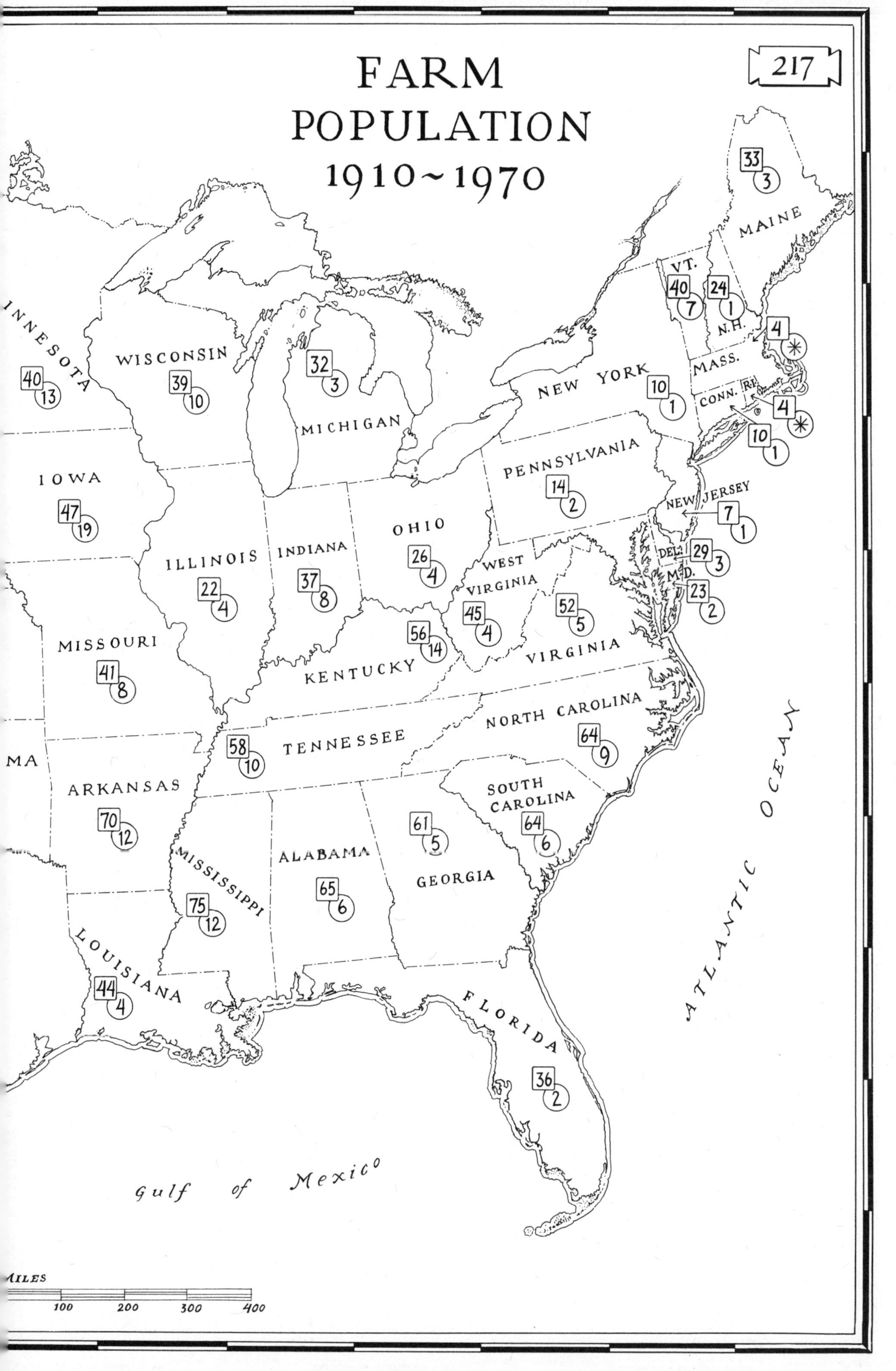
FARM
POPULATION
1910~1970
MAINE 33 3
VT. 40 7
N.H. 24 1
MASS. 4
R.I. 4
CONN. 10 1
NEW YORK 10 1
INNESOTA 40 13
WISCONSIN 39 10
MICHIGAN 32 3
PENNSYLVANIA 14 2
NEW JERSEY 7 1
IOWA 47 19
ILLINOIS 22 4
INDIANA 37 8
OHIO 26 4
WEST VIRGINIA 45 4
DEL. 29 3
MD. 23 2
VIRGINIA 52 5
MISSOURI 41 8
KENTUCKY 56 14
NORTH CAROLINA 64 9
TENNESSEE 58 10
MA
ARKANSAS 70 12
SOUTH CAROLINA 64 6
GEORGIA 61 5
ALABAMA 65 6
MISSISSIPPI 75 12
LOUISIANA 44 4
FLORIDA 36 2
ATLANTIC OCEAN
Gulf of Mexico
MILES
100
200
300
400

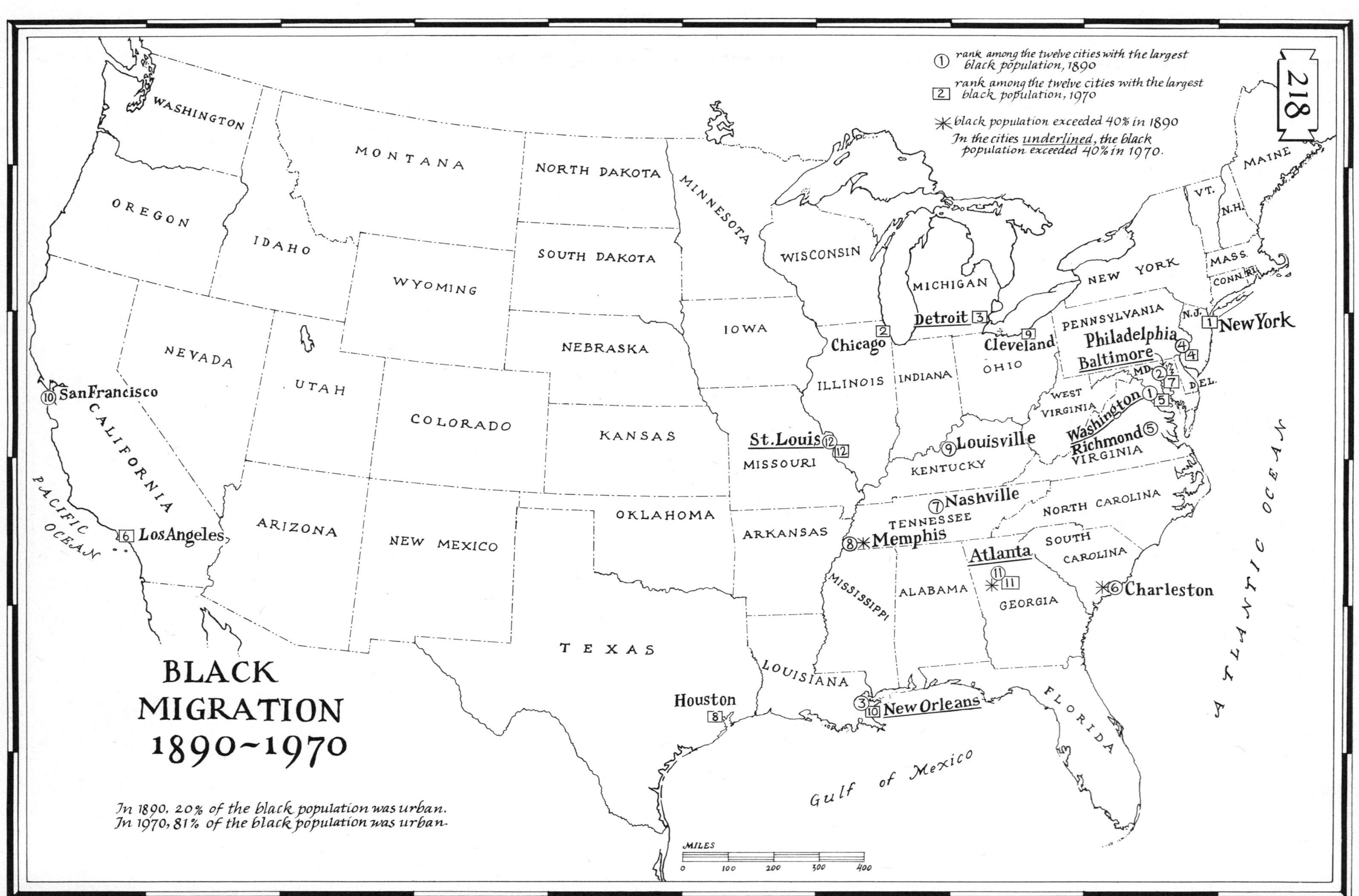
218
BLACK MIGRATION 1890~1970
① rank among the twelve cities with the largest black population, 1890
[2] rank among the twelve cities with the largest black population, 1970
✳ black population exceeded 40% in 1890
In the cities underlined, the black population exceeded 40% in 1970.
In 1890, 20% of the black population was urban.
In 1970, 81% of the black population was urban.
WASHINGTON
OREGON
CALIFORNIA
NEVADA
IDAHO
MONTANA
WYOMING
UTAH
ARIZONA
COLORADO
NEW MEXICO
NORTH DAKOTA
SOUTH DAKOTA
NEBRASKA
KANSAS
OKLAHOMA
TEXAS
MINNESOTA
IOWA
MISSOURI
ARKANSAS
LOUISIANA
WISCONSIN
ILLINOIS
MICHIGAN
INDIANA
OHIO
KENTUCKY
TENNESSEE
MISSISSIPPI
ALABAMA
GEORGIA
FLORIDA
SOUTH CAROLINA
NORTH CAROLINA
VIRGINIA
WEST VIRGINIA
PENNSYLVANIA
NEW YORK
MD.
DEL.
N.J.
CONN.
R.I.
MASS.
VT.
N.H.
MAINE
PACIFIC OCEAN
ATLANTIC OCEAN
Gulf of Mexico
⑩ San Francisco
[6] Los Angeles
Houston [8]
St. Louis ⑫ [12]
Chicago [2]
Detroit [3]
Cleveland [9]
⑨ Louisville
⑦ Nashville
⑧✳ Memphis
Atlanta ⑪ ✳ [11]
③ [10] New Orleans
✳⑥ Charleston
Washington ① [5]
Richmond ⑤
Baltimore ② [7]
Philadelphia ④ [4]
[1] New York
MILES
0 100 200 300 400

MAJOR RACE RIOTS 1865 – 1976

Except where indicated, riots involved hostilities between blacks and whites. Racial turmoil also occured in:
Brownsville, Texas, 1906
Houston, Texas, 1917
Omaha, Nebraska, 1919
Tulsa, Oklahoma, 1921
Los Angeles, California, 1965
San Francisco, California, 1877 (anti-Chinese riots)

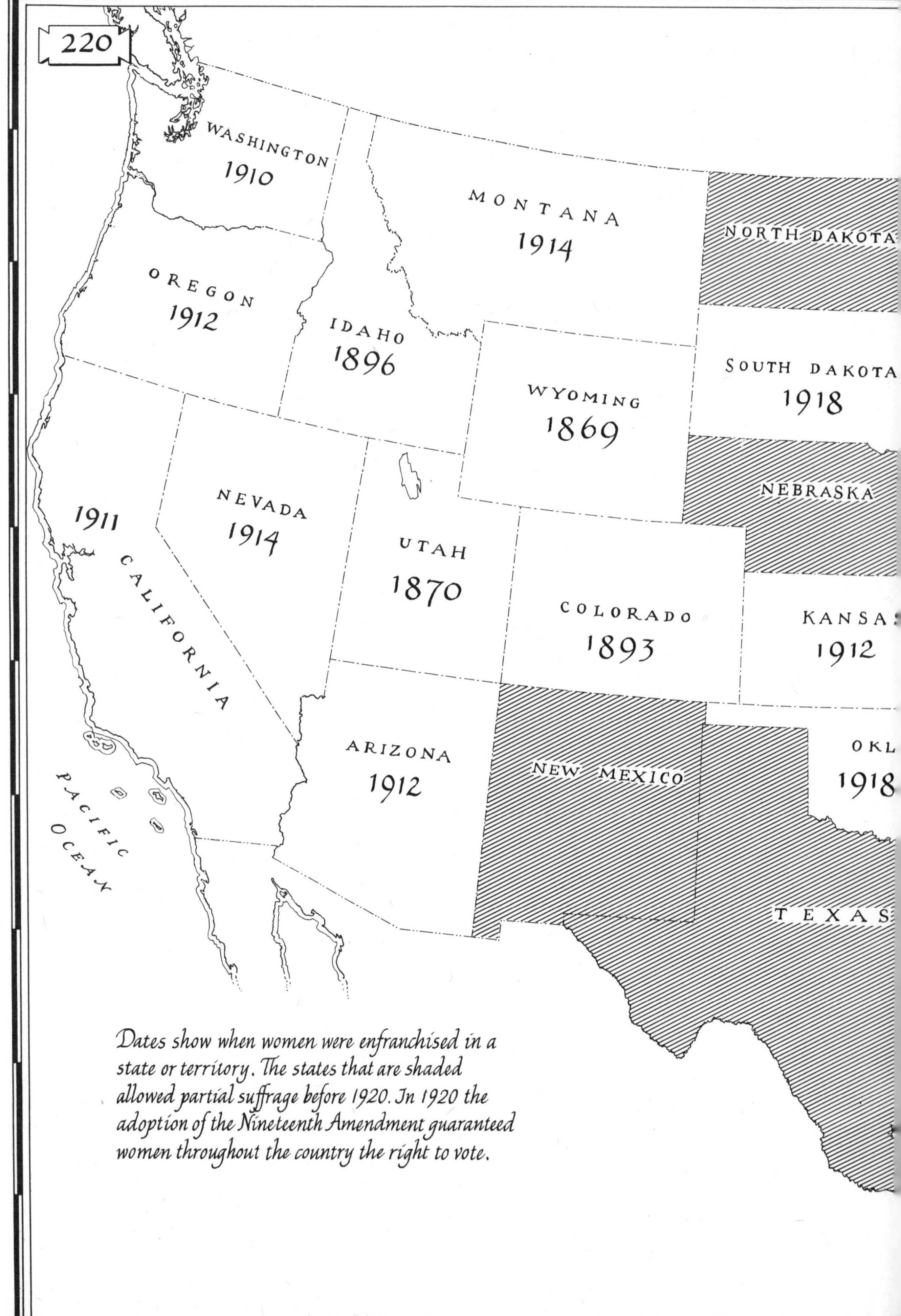

Dates show when women were enfranchised in a state or territory. The states that are shaded allowed partial suffrage before 1920. In 1920 the adoption of the Nineteenth Amendment guaranteed women throughout the country the right to vote.

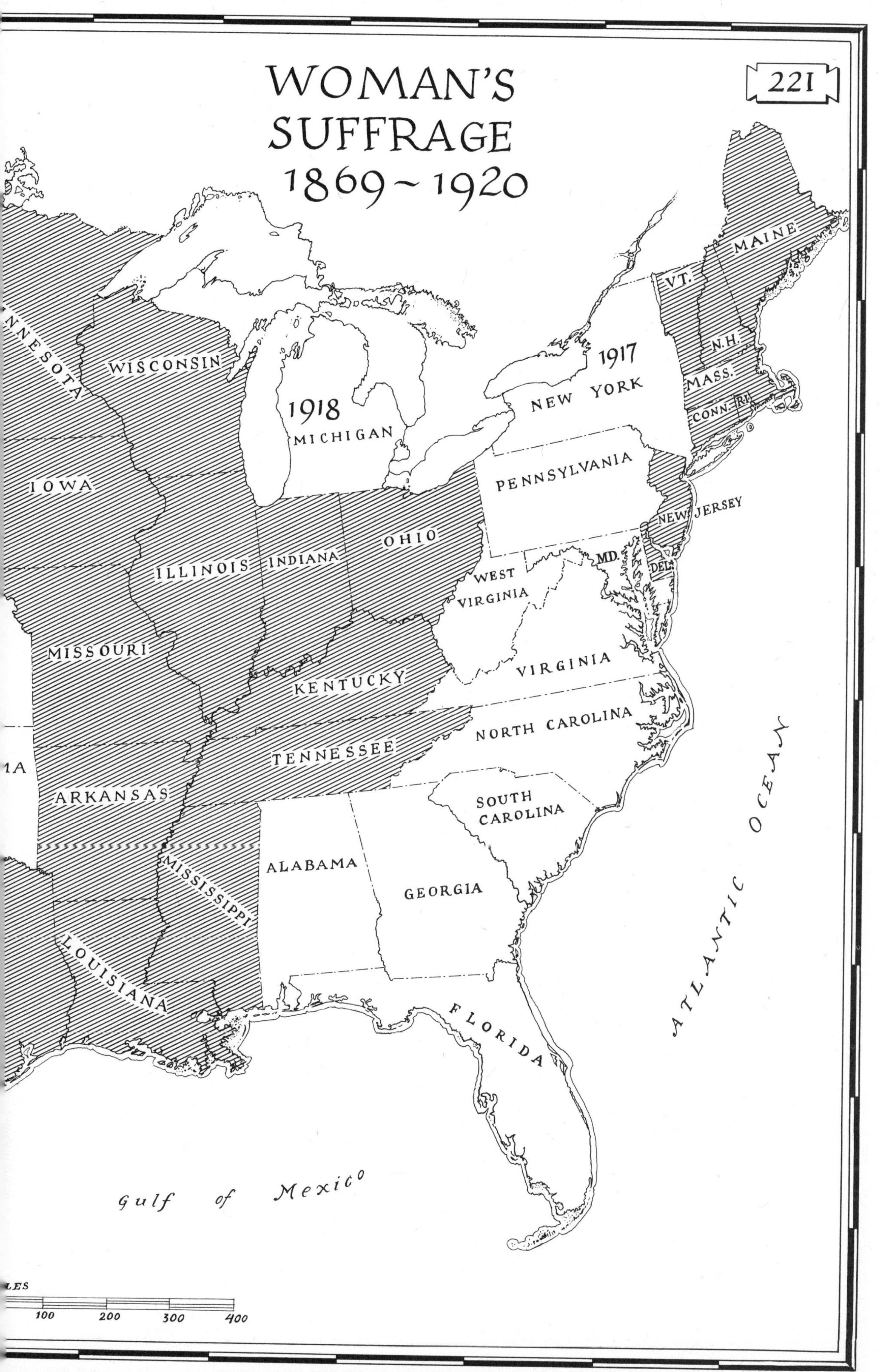

WOMAN'S SUFFRAGE 1869~1920
221
MAINE
VT.
N.H.
MASS.
CONN.
R.I.
NEW YORK
1917
1918
MICHIGAN
WISCONSIN
NNESOTA
IOWA
ILLINOIS
INDIANA
OHIO
PENNSYLVANIA
NEW JERSEY
MD.
DELA
WEST VIRGINIA
VIRGINIA
KENTUCKY
MISSOURI
TENNESSEE
NORTH CAROLINA
SOUTH CAROLINA
ARKANSAS
MISSISSIPPI
ALABAMA
GEORGIA
LOUISIANA
FLORIDA
MA
ATLANTIC OCEAN
Gulf of Mexico
LES
100
200
300
400

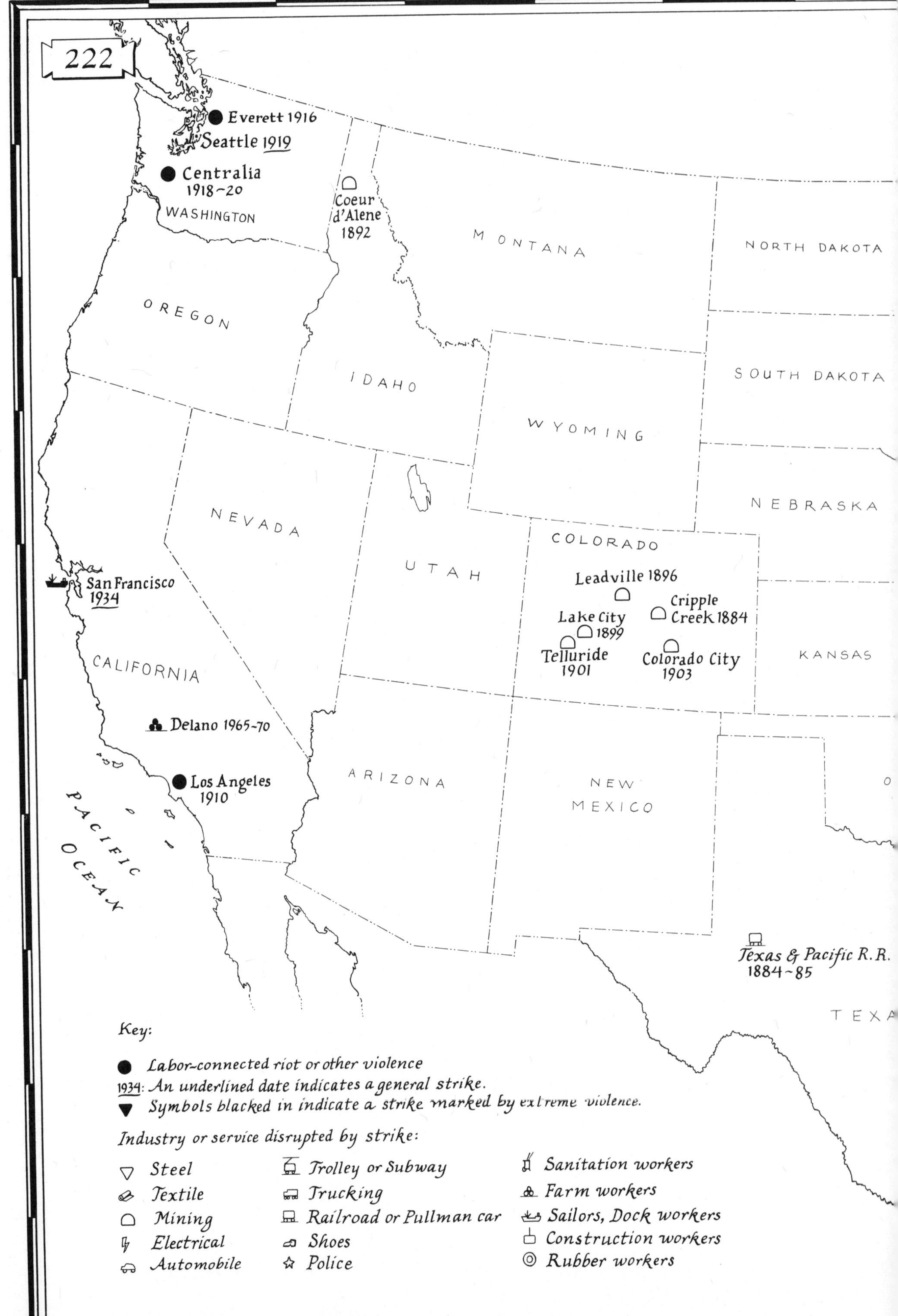
Everett 1916
Seattle 1919
Centralia 1918–20
WASHINGTON
Coeur d'Alene 1892
MONTANA
NORTH DAKOTA
OREGON
IDAHO
SOUTH DAKOTA
WYOMING
NEBRASKA
NEVADA
UTAH
COLORADO
Leadville 1896
Cripple Creek 1884
Lake City 1899
Telluride 1901
Colorado City 1903
KANSAS
San Francisco 1934
CALIFORNIA
Delano 1965–70
Los Angeles 1910
ARIZONA
NEW MEXICO
PACIFIC OCEAN
Texas & Pacific R.R. 1884–85
Key:
Labor-connected riot or other violence
1934: An underlined date indicates a general strike.
Symbols blacked in indicate a strike marked by extreme violence.
Industry or service disrupted by strike:
Steel
Textile
Mining
Electrical
Automobile
Trolley or Subway
Trucking
Railroad or Pullman car
Shoes
Police
Sanitation workers
Farm workers
Sailors, Dock workers
Construction workers
Rubber workers

LABOR STRIFE 1803–1970

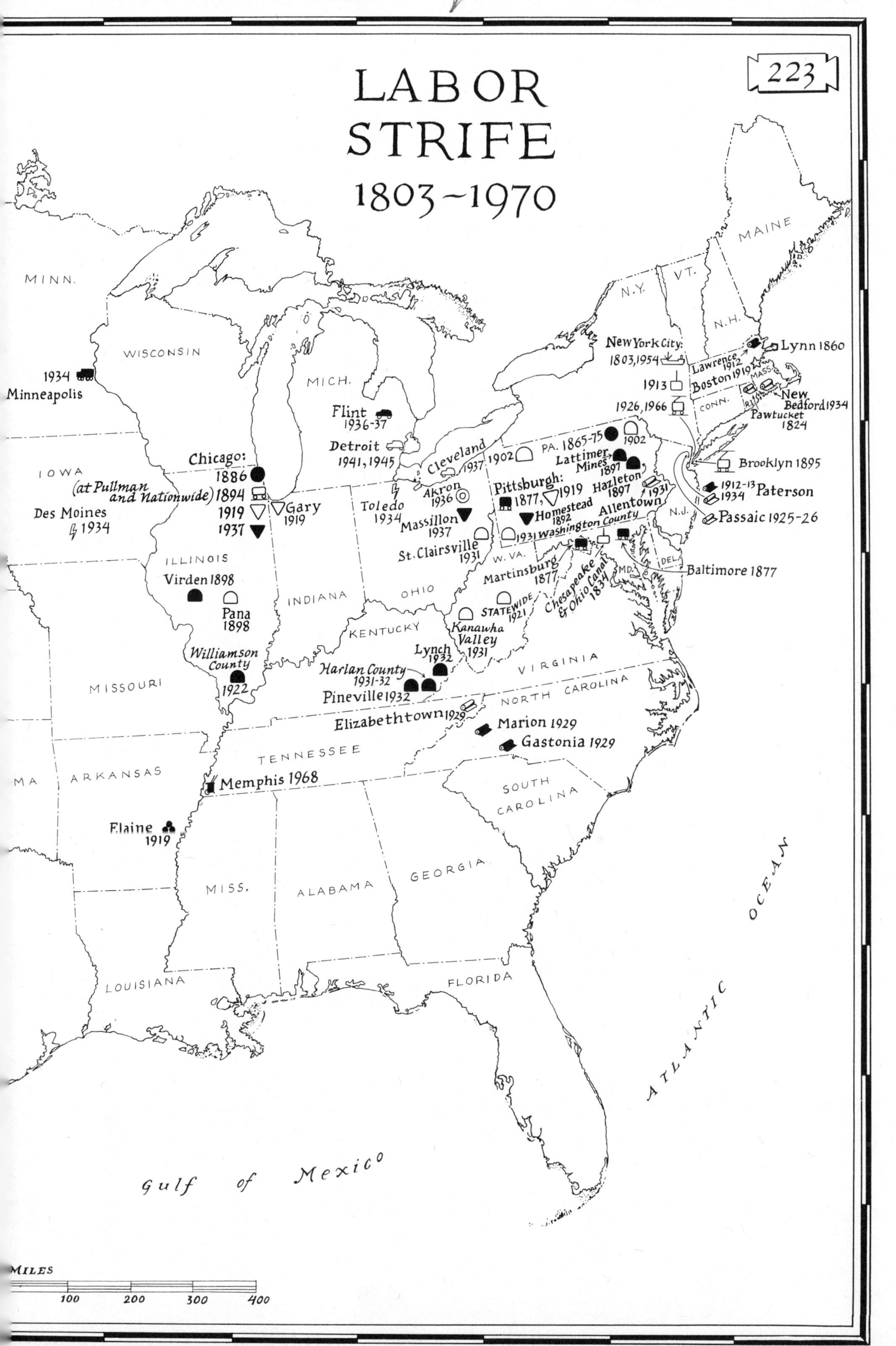

MINN.
WISCONSIN
MICH.
IOWA
ILLINOIS
INDIANA
OHIO
PA.
N.Y.
VT.
N.H.
MAINE
MASS.
CONN.
R.I.
N.J.
DEL.
MD.
W. VA.
KENTUCKY
VIRGINIA
NORTH CAROLINA
SOUTH CAROLINA
TENNESSEE
MISSOURI
ARKANSAS
MISS.
ALABAMA
GEORGIA
FLORIDA
LOUISIANA
1934 Minneapolis
Chicago: 1886
(at Pullman and Nationwide) 1894
1919
1937
Gary 1919
Des Moines 1934
Virden 1898
Pana 1898
Williamson County 1922
Flint 1936-37
Detroit 1941, 1945
Cleveland 1937
Toledo 1934
Akron 1936
Massillon 1937
St. Clairsville 1931
1902
1865-75
1902
Lattimer Mines 1897
Hazleton 1897
Pittsburgh: 1877, 1919
Homestead 1892
1931 Washington County
Allentown 1931
Martinsburg 1877
Chesapeake & Ohio Canal 1834
STATEWIDE 1921
Kanawha Valley 1931
Baltimore 1877
New York City: 1803, 1954
1913
1926, 1966
Brooklyn 1895
1912-13 1934 Paterson
Passaic 1925-26
Lawrence 1912
Boston 1919
Lynn 1860
New Bedford 1934
Pawtucket 1824
Lynch 1932
Harlan County 1931-32
Pineville 1932
Elizabethtown 1929
Marion 1929
Gastonia 1929
Memphis 1968
Elaine 1919
MA
Gulf of Mexico
ATLANTIC OCEAN
MILES
100
200
300
400

LEADING INDUSTRIAL STATES 1850~1973

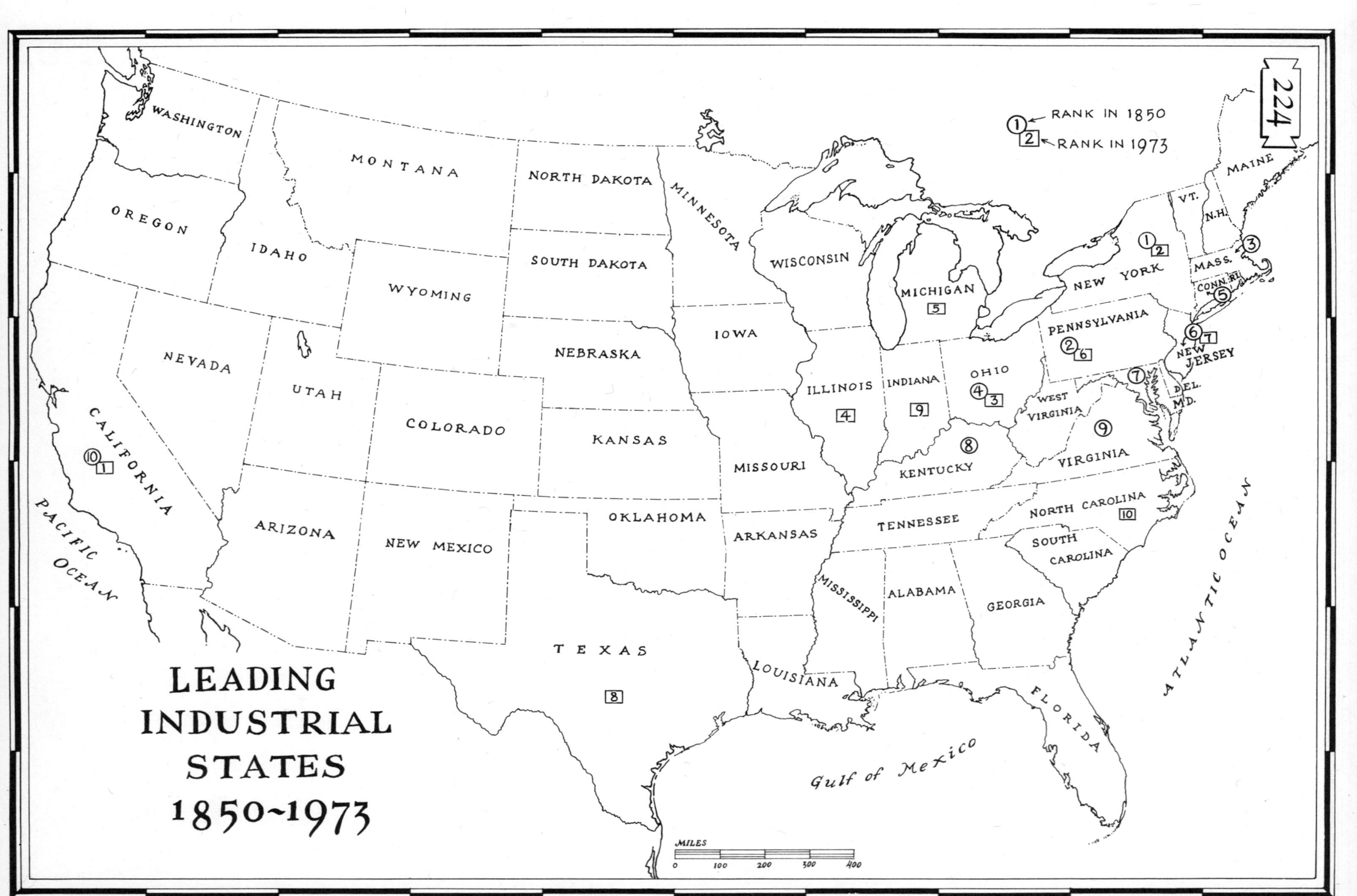

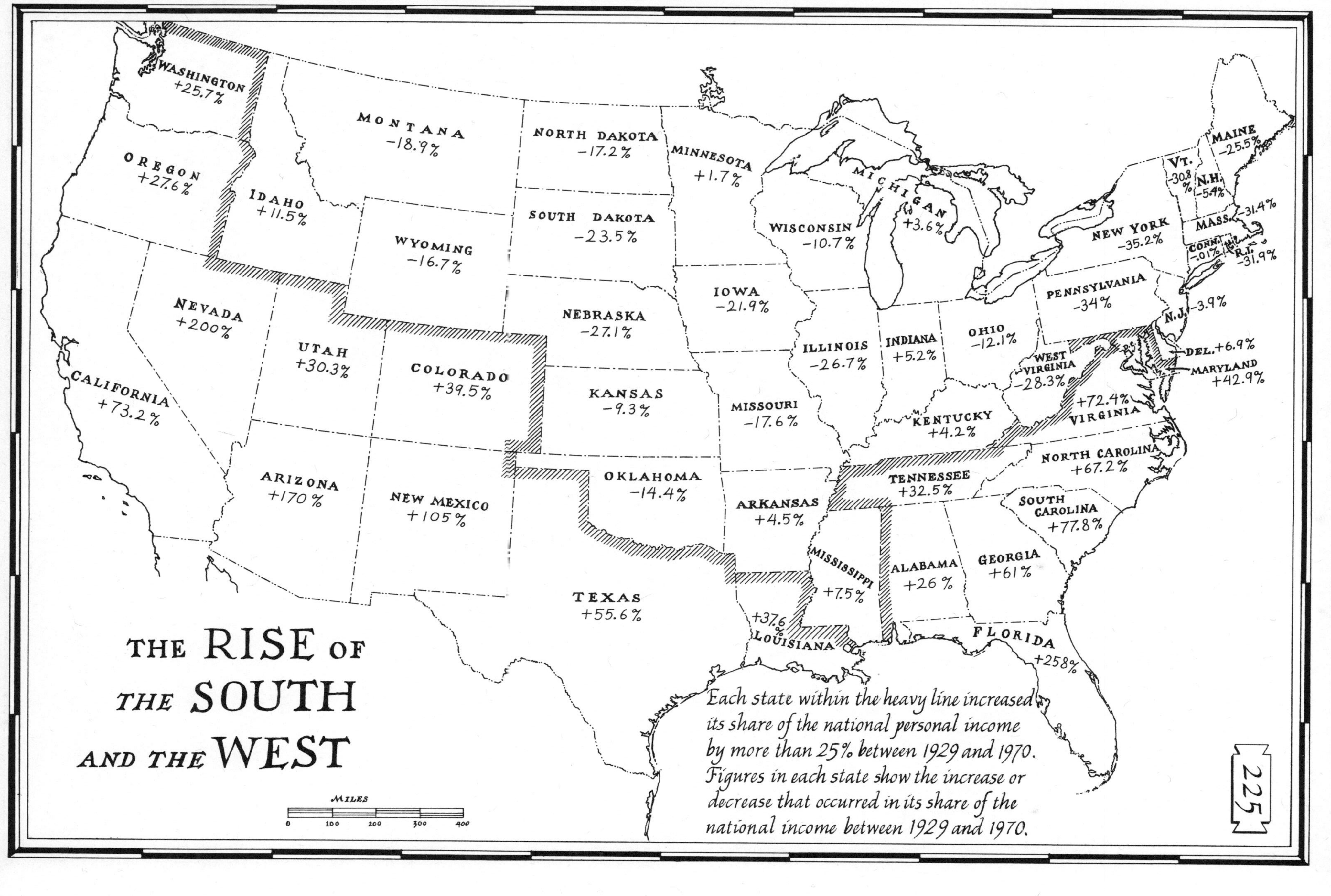
THE RISE OF THE SOUTH AND THE WEST
WASHINGTON +25.7%
OREGON +27.6%
CALIFORNIA +73.2%
IDAHO +11.5%
NEVADA +200%
MONTANA -18.9%
WYOMING -16.7%
UTAH +30.3%
ARIZONA +170%
COLORADO +39.5%
NEW MEXICO +105%
NORTH DAKOTA -17.2%
SOUTH DAKOTA -23.5%
NEBRASKA -27.1%
KANSAS -9.3%
OKLAHOMA -14.4%
TEXAS +55.6%
MINNESOTA +1.7%
IOWA -21.9%
MISSOURI -17.6%
ARKANSAS +4.5%
LOUISIANA +37.6%
WISCONSIN -10.7%
ILLINOIS -26.7%
MICHIGAN +3.6%
INDIANA +5.2%
OHIO -12.1%
KENTUCKY +4.2%
TENNESSEE +32.5%
MISSISSIPPI +7.5%
ALABAMA +26%
GEORGIA +61%
FLORIDA +258%
SOUTH CAROLINA +77.8%
NORTH CAROLINA +67.2%
VIRGINIA +72.4%
WEST VIRGINIA -28.3%
PENNSYLVANIA -34%
NEW YORK -35.2%
N.J. -3.9%
DEL. +6.9%
MARYLAND +42.9%
D.C.
CONN. -.01%
R.I. -31.9%
MASS. -31.4%
VT. -30.8%
N.H. -5.4%
MAINE -25.5%
MILES
0 100 200 300 400
Each state within the heavy line increased its share of the national personal income by more than 25% between 1929 and 1970. Figures in each state show the increase or decrease that occurred in its share of the national income between 1929 and 1970.

226
OREGON
CALIFORNIA
1900-1976
MAJOR IRRIGATED AREAS
OIL FIELDS
Redwood National Park
TULE LAKE RESERVOIR
Lassen Volcanic National Park
North Fork
Middle Fork
South Fork
Feather River
NEVADA
Reno
LAKE TAHOE
Sacramento
San Francisco
Berkeley
Oakland
San Jose
HETCH HETCHY RESERVOIR
Yosemite National Park
San Joaquin River
CALIFORNIA AQUEDUCT
SAN JOAQUIN VALLEY
Owens River
Kings Canyon Nat'l. Park
Sequoia Nat'l. Park
Fresno
Coalinga
LOS ANGELES AQUEDUCT
DEATH VALLEY
Las Vegas
HOOVER DAM
SEARLES LAKE (DRY SALT)
Bakersfield
LAKE MOJAVE
SAN ANDREAS FAULT
Mojave
Boron
DAVIS DAM
Needles
MOJAVE DESERT
PACIFIC OCEAN
Santa Barbara
Mount Wilson
Pasadena
LAKE HAVASU
Hollywood
Los Angeles
Riverside
COLORADO RIVER AQUEDUCT
Santa Monica
Watts
Whittier
Anaheim
Santa Ana
Wilmington
Long Beach
Huntington Beach
San Clemente
Mount Palomar
PARKER DAM
Colorado River
IMPERIAL VALLEY
IMPERIAL DAM
San Diego
MEXICO
MILES
25 0 50 100

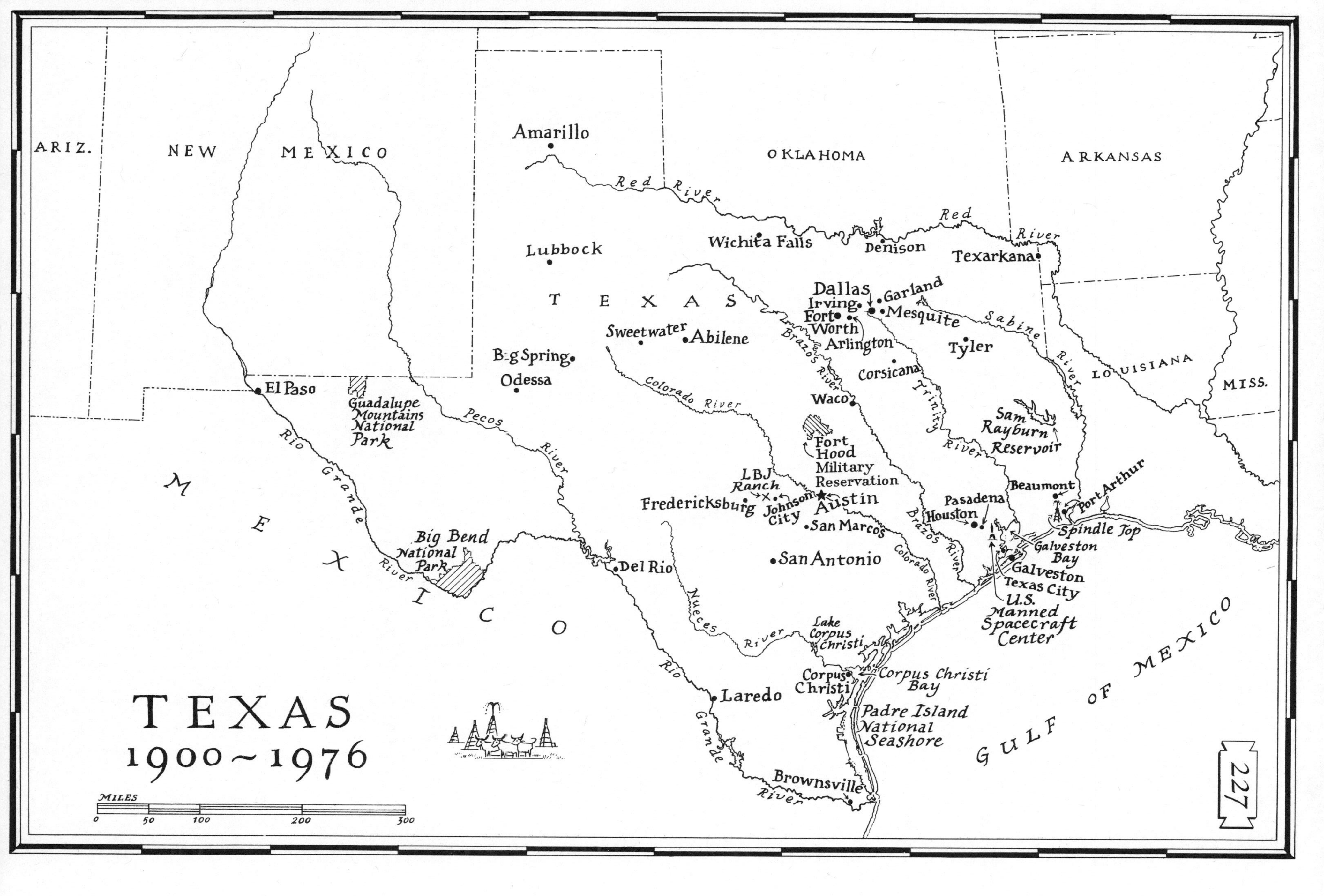
TEXAS
1900~1976
ARIZ.
NEW MEXICO
OKLAHOMA
ARKANSAS
LOUISIANA
MISS.
TEXAS
MEXICO
GULF OF MEXICO
Amarillo
Red River
Red River
Wichita Falls
Denison
Texarkana
Lubbock
Dallas
Garland
Irving
Mesquite
Fort Worth
Arlington
Sabine River
Tyler
Sweetwater
Abilene
Brazos River
Big Spring
Odessa
Corsicana
Trinity River
El Paso
Colorado River
Waco
Guadalupe Mountains National Park
Pecos River
Sam Rayburn Reservoir
Fort Hood Military Reservation
Rio Grande River
LBJ Ranch
Fredericksburg
Johnson City
Austin
Beaumont
Pasadena
Port Arthur
Houston
Spindle Top
San Marcos
Brazos River
Big Bend National Park
Galveston Bay
San Antonio
Colorado River
Galveston
Del Rio
Texas City
Nueces River
U.S. Manned Spacecraft Center
Lake Corpus Christi
Corpus Christi
Corpus Christi Bay
Laredo
Padre Island National Seashore
Rio Grande River
Brownsville
MILES
0
50
100
200
300

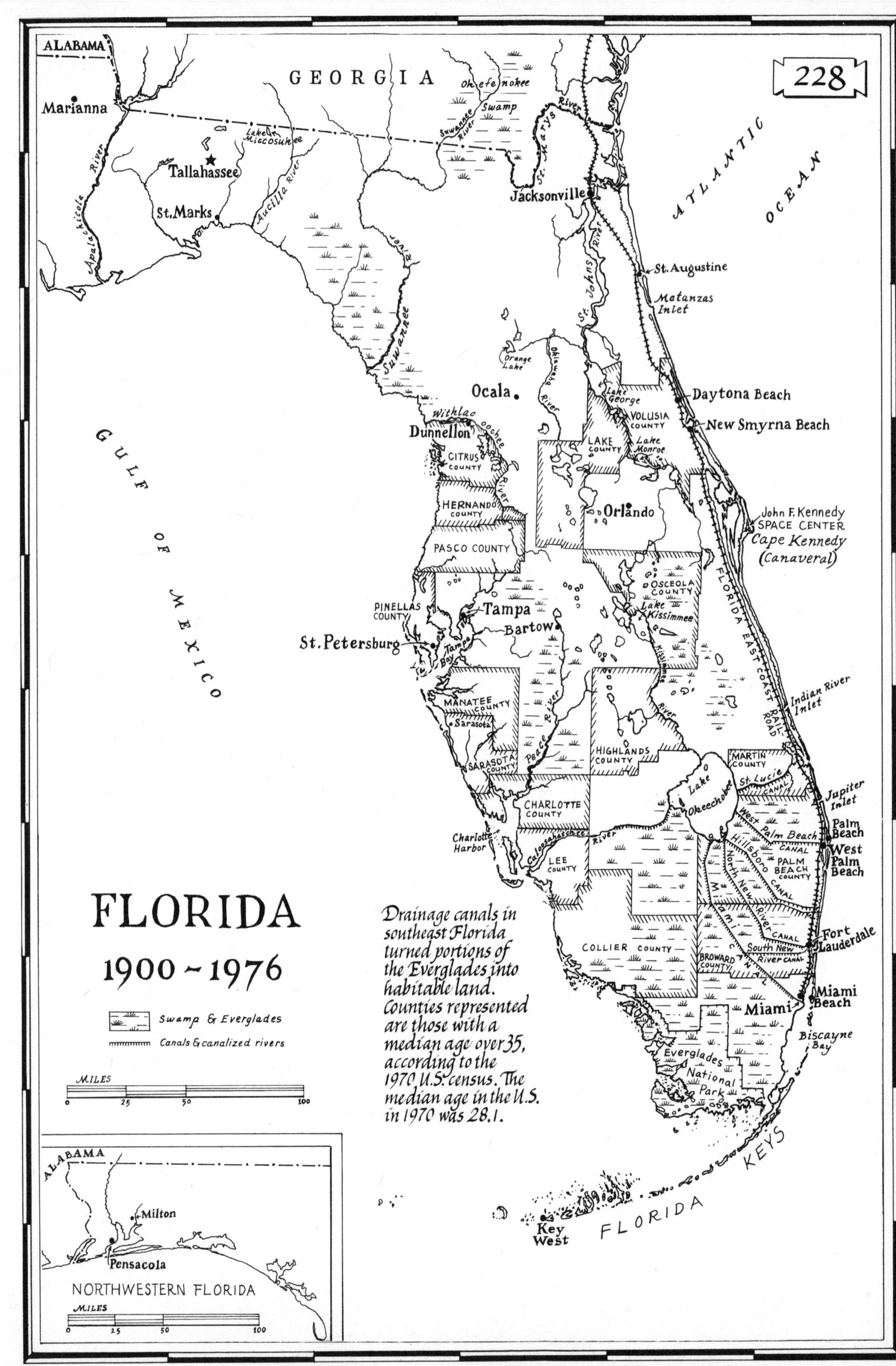

228
FLORIDA
1900 ~ 1976
Swamp & Everglades
Canals & canalized rivers
MILES
0
25
50
100
Drainage canals in southeast Florida turned portions of the Everglades into habitable land. Counties represented are those with a median age over 35, according to the 1970 U.S. census. The median age in the U.S. in 1970 was 28.1.
ALABAMA
GEORGIA
Marianna
Tallahassee
St. Marks
Apalachicola River
Aucilla River
Lake Miccosukee
Okefenokee Swamp
Swannee River
St. Marys River
Suwannee River
Jacksonville
ATLANTIC OCEAN
St. Johns River
St. Augustine
Matanzas Inlet
Orange Lake
Oklawaha River
Ocala
Withlacoochee River
Dunnellon
Lake George
VOLUSIA COUNTY
Daytona Beach
New Smyrna Beach
LAKE COUNTY
Lake Monroe
CITRUS COUNTY
HERNANDO COUNTY
Orlando
John F. Kennedy SPACE CENTER
Cape Kennedy (Canaveral)
PASCO COUNTY
GULF OF MEXICO
OSCEOLA COUNTY
Lake Kissimmee
PINELLAS COUNTY
Tampa
Bartow
St. Petersburg
Tampa Bay
Kissimmee River
FLORIDA EAST COAST RAIL ROAD
Indian River Inlet
MANATEE COUNTY
Sarasota
Peace River
HIGHLANDS COUNTY
SARASOTA COUNTY
MARTIN COUNTY
St. Lucie CANAL
Lake Okeechobee
Jupiter Inlet
CHARLOTTE COUNTY
Charlotte Harbor
Caloosahatchee River
West Palm Beach CANAL
Palm Beach
West Palm Beach
Hillsboro CANAL
PALM BEACH COUNTY
North New River CANAL
Miami CANAL
LEE COUNTY
COLLIER COUNTY
Fort Lauderdale
South New River CANAL
BROWARD COUNTY
Miami
Miami Beach
Biscayne Bay
Everglades National Park
FLORIDA KEYS
Key West
NORTHWESTERN FLORIDA
ALABAMA
Milton
Pensacola
MILES
0
25
50
100

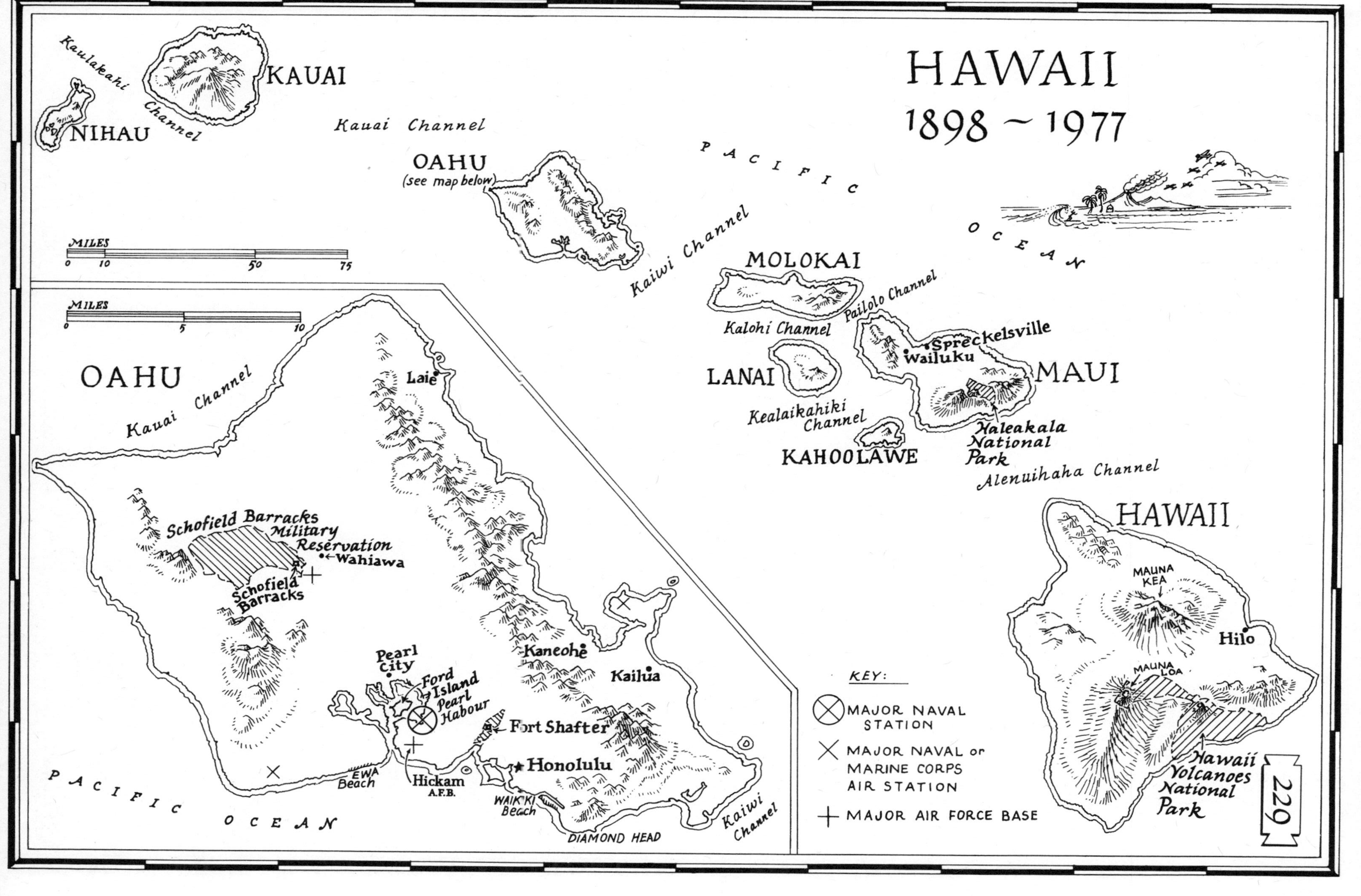
HAWAII
1898 ~ 1977
KAUAI
NIHAU
Kaulakahi Channel
Kauai Channel
OAHU
(see map below)
PACIFIC OCEAN
Kaiwi Channel
MOLOKAI
Pailolo Channel
Kalohi Channel
LANAI
Spreckelsville
Wailuku
MAUI
Kealaikahiki Channel
KAHOOLAWE
Haleakala National Park
Alenuihaha Channel
HAWAII
MAUNA KEA
MAUNA LOA
Hilo
Hawaii Volcanoes National Park
MILES
0 10 50 75
MILES
0 5 10
OAHU
Kauai Channel
Laie
Schofield Barracks Military Reservation
Wahiawa
Schofield Barracks
Pearl City
Ford Island
Pearl Habour
Kaneohe
Kailua
Fort Shafter
Honolulu
Hickam A.F.B.
EWA Beach
WAIKIKI Beach
DIAMOND HEAD
Kaiwi Channel
PACIFIC OCEAN
KEY:
MAJOR NAVAL STATION
MAJOR NAVAL or MARINE CORPS AIR STATION
MAJOR AIR FORCE BASE

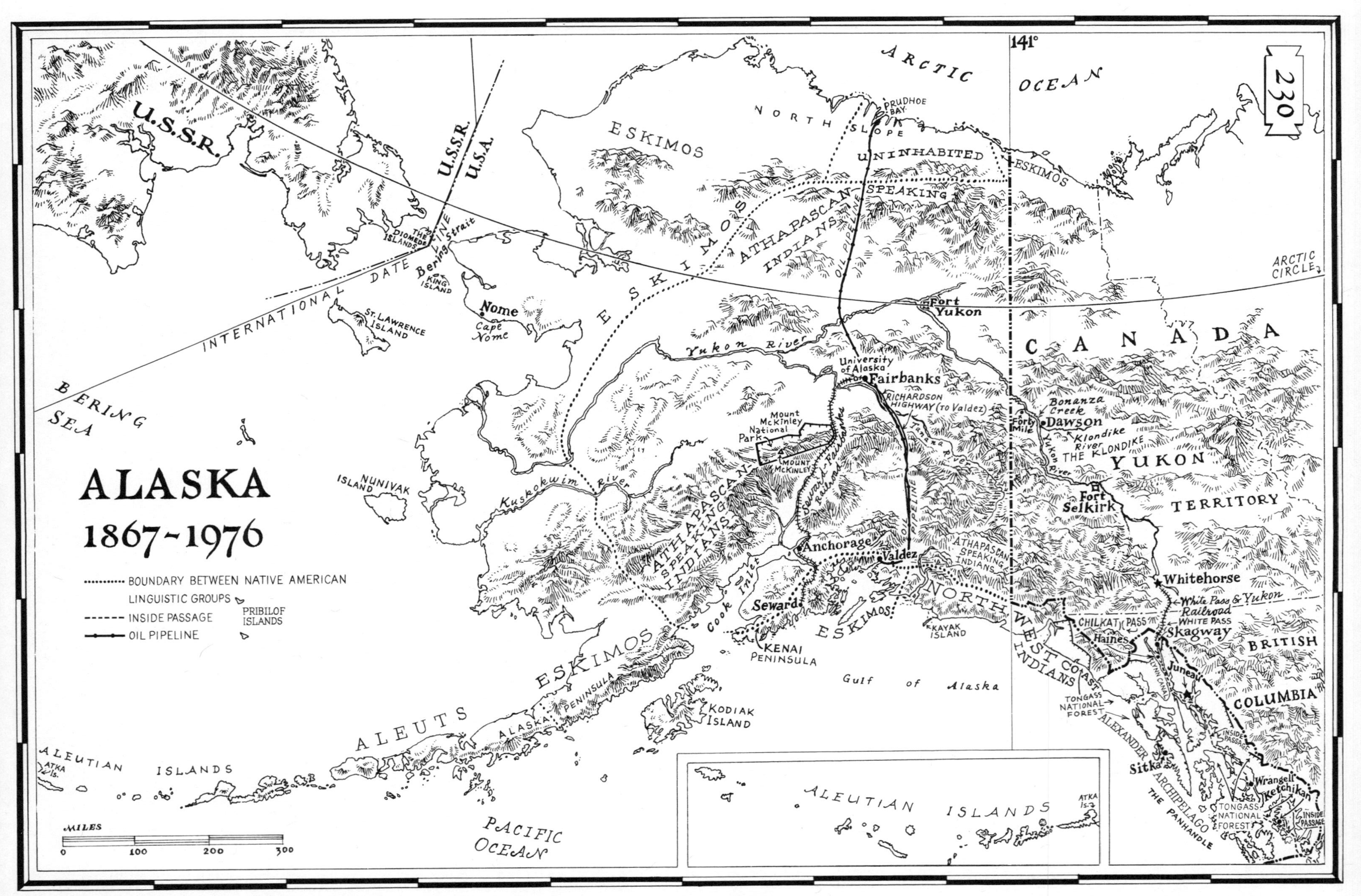

230
ALASKA
1867-1976
BOUNDARY BETWEEN NATIVE AMERICAN LINGUISTIC GROUPS
INSIDE PASSAGE
OIL PIPELINE
PRIBILOF ISLANDS
MILES
0
100
200
300
ARCTIC OCEAN
141°
ARCTIC CIRCLE
PRUDHOE BAY
NORTH SLOPE
ESKIMOS
UNINHABITED
ATHAPASCAN SPEAKING INDIANS
OIL PIPELINE
U.S.S.R.
U.S.A.
THE DIOMEDE ISLANDS
Bering Strait
INTERNATIONAL DATE LINE
KING ISLAND
ST. LAWRENCE ISLAND
Nome
Cape Nome
BERING SEA
NUNIVAK ISLAND
Yukon River
Fort Yukon
University of Alaska
Fairbanks
RICHARDSON HIGHWAY (TO Valdez)
Tanana River
Mount McKinley National Park
MOUNT McKINLEY
Seward-Fairbanks Railroad
Kuskokwim River
Anchorage
Valdez
Seward
Cook Inlet
KENAI PENINSULA
KAYAK ISLAND
Gulf of Alaska
KODIAK ISLAND
ALASKA PENINSULA
ALEUTS
ALEUTIAN ISLANDS
ATKA IS.
PACIFIC OCEAN
CANADA
Bonanza Creek
Forty Mile
Dawson
Klondike River
THE KLONDIKE
YUKON
Yukon River
Fort Selkirk
TERRITORY
Whitehorse
White Pass & Yukon Railroad
WHITE PASS
CHILKAT PASS
Haines
Skagway
BRITISH COLUMBIA
NORTHWEST COAST INDIANS
TONGASS NATIONAL FOREST
LYNN CANAL
Juneau
ALEXANDER ARCHIPELAGO
THE PANHANDLE
Sitka
INSIDE PASSAGE
Wrangell
Ketchikan

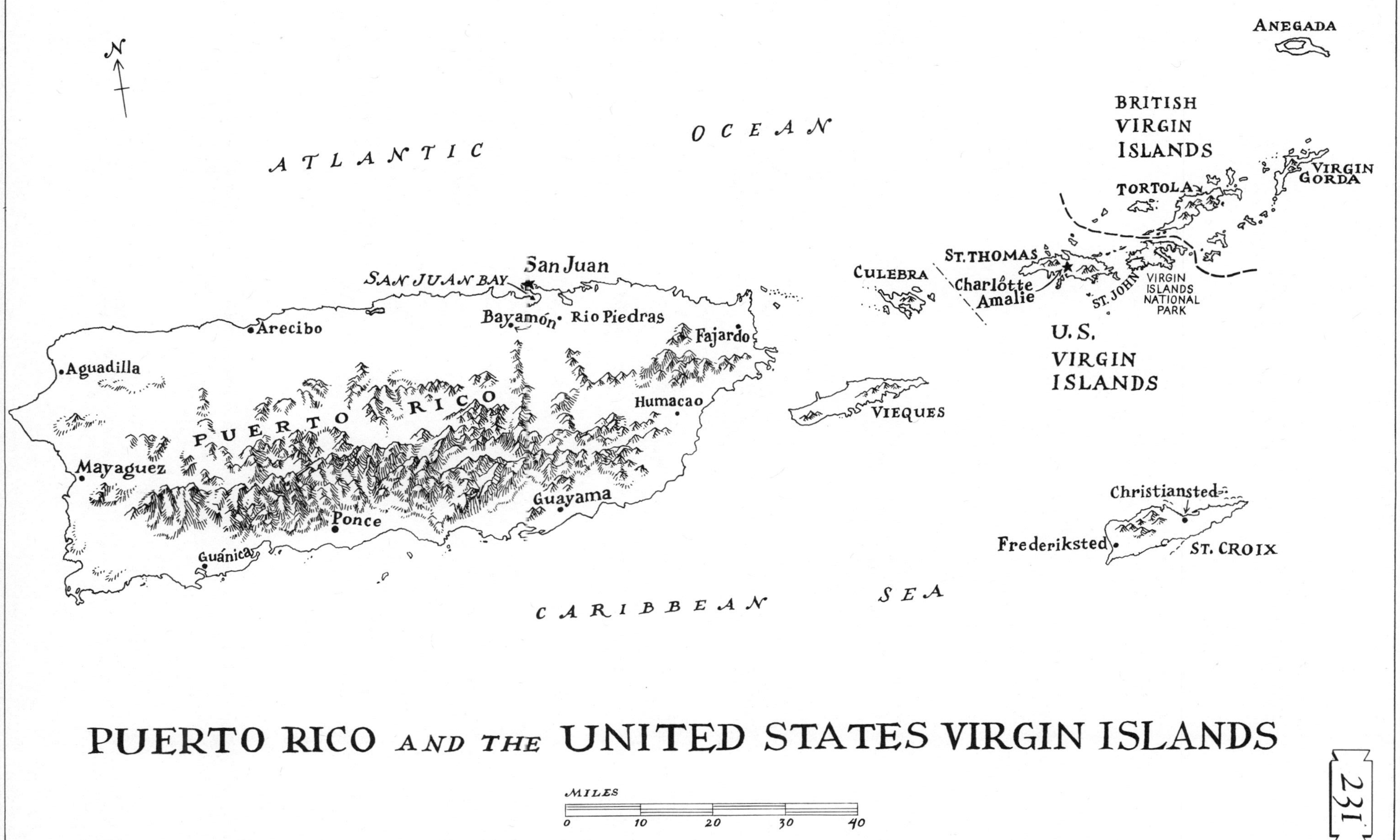

PUERTO RICO AND THE UNITED STATES VIRGIN ISLANDS

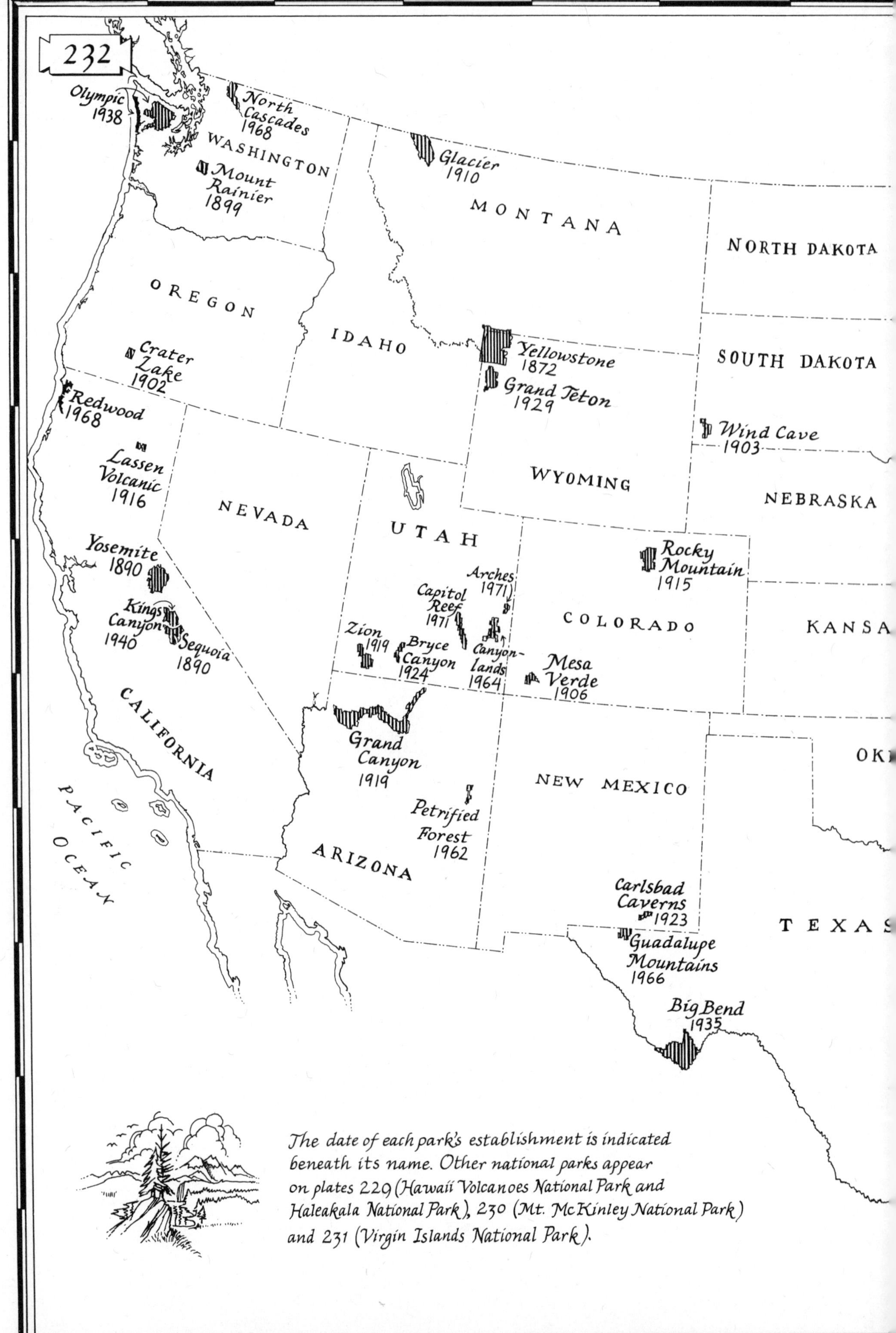

The date of each park's establishment is indicated beneath its name. Other national parks appear on plates 229 (Hawaii Volcanoes National Park and Haleakala National Park), 230 (Mt. McKinley National Park) and 231 (Virgin Islands National Park).

NATIONAL PARKS 1872~1976
Voyageurs 1971
Isle Royale 1931
Acadia 1919
Shenandoah 1926
Mammoth Cave 1926
Great Smoky Mountains 1926
Hot Springs 1921
att 1906
Everglades 1934
MAINE
VT.
N.H.
MASS.
R.I.
CONN.
NEW YORK
NEW JERSEY
PENNSYLVANIA
MD.
DEL.
WEST VIRGINIA
VIRGINIA
NORTH CAROLINA
SOUTH CAROLINA
GEORGIA
FLORIDA
ALABAMA
MISSISSIPPI
TENNESSEE
KENTUCKY
OHIO
INDIANA
ILLINOIS
MICHIGAN
WISCONSIN
INNESOTA
IOWA
MISSOURI
ARKANSAS
LOUISIANA
MA
ATLANTIC OCEAN
Gulf of Mexico
ILES
100
200
300
400

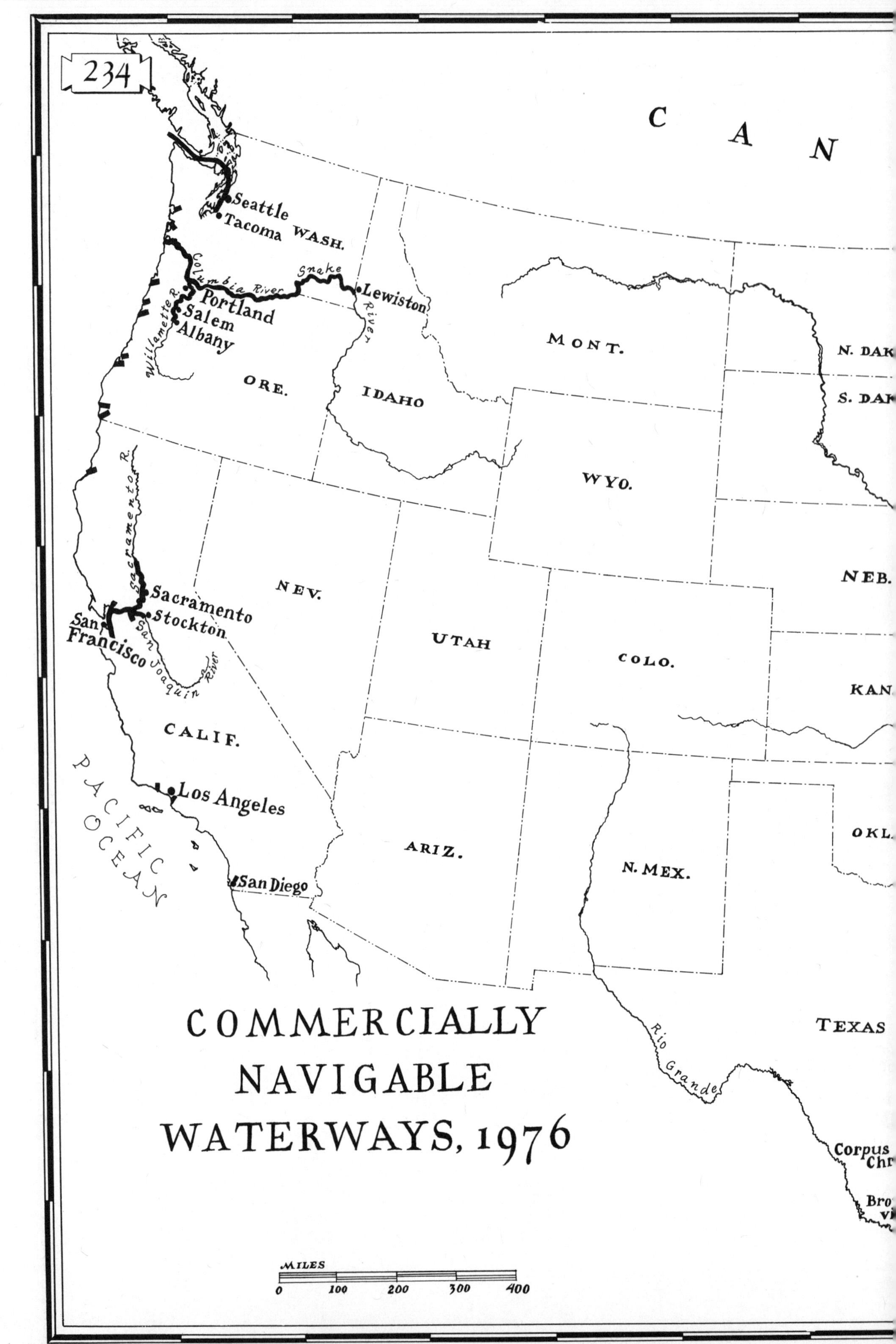

COMMERCIALLY NAVIGABLE WATERWAYS, 1976

ADA
LAKE SUPERIOR
Duluth
Sault Ste. Marie
MINN.
WIS.
Minneapolis
Green Bay
Appleton
Milwaukee
LAKE MICHIGAN
MICH.
LAKE HURON
Saginaw
Detroit
Chicago
Sioux City
IOWA
Missouri River
Mississippi River
Illinois River
ILL.
IND.
OHIO
Toledo
Cleveland
LAKE ERIE
Toronto
LAKE ONTARIO
Oswego
Syracuse
Buffalo
Albany
N.Y.
St. Lawrence River
Hudson R.
VT.
Connecticut R.
N.H.
MAINE
Penobscot R.
Kennebec R.
Bangor
Belfast
Bath
Augusta
Portsmouth
MASS.
Boston
CONN.
R.I.
Providence
New London
New York
PA.
Allegheny R.
Delaware R.
Pittsburgh
Philadelphia
Baltimore
N.J.
DEL.
MD.
Potomac R.
Washington D.C.
W.VA.
Cincinnati
Ohio River
Kanawha River
Charleston
Rappahannock R.
Richmond
York River
James River
Norfolk
Elizabeth City
VA.
Kansas City
St. Louis
MO.
Kentucky R.
Louisville
KY.
Bowling Green
Cumberland R.
Roanoke River
N.C.
Tulsa
Muskogee
Arkansas River
ARK.
Memphis
Nashville
TENN.
Tennessee R.
Knoxville
Fayetteville
Cape Fear R.
Wilmington
S.C.
Savannah R.
Little Rock
MISS.
Tombigbee River
Black Warrior R.
Birmingham
Augusta
Charleston
Camden
Ouachita River
Selma
Alabama R.
Chattahoochee River
Columbus
Savannah
ALA.
GA.
Pearl River
Baton Rouge
Atchafalaya R.
Apalachicola R.
Jacksonville
LA.
Mobile
New Orleans
St. Marks
FLA.
St. Johns River
Beaumont
Houston
Victoria
Tampa
ATLANTIC OCEAN
Gulf of Mexico
Caloosahatchee River
Miami
Navigable waterway

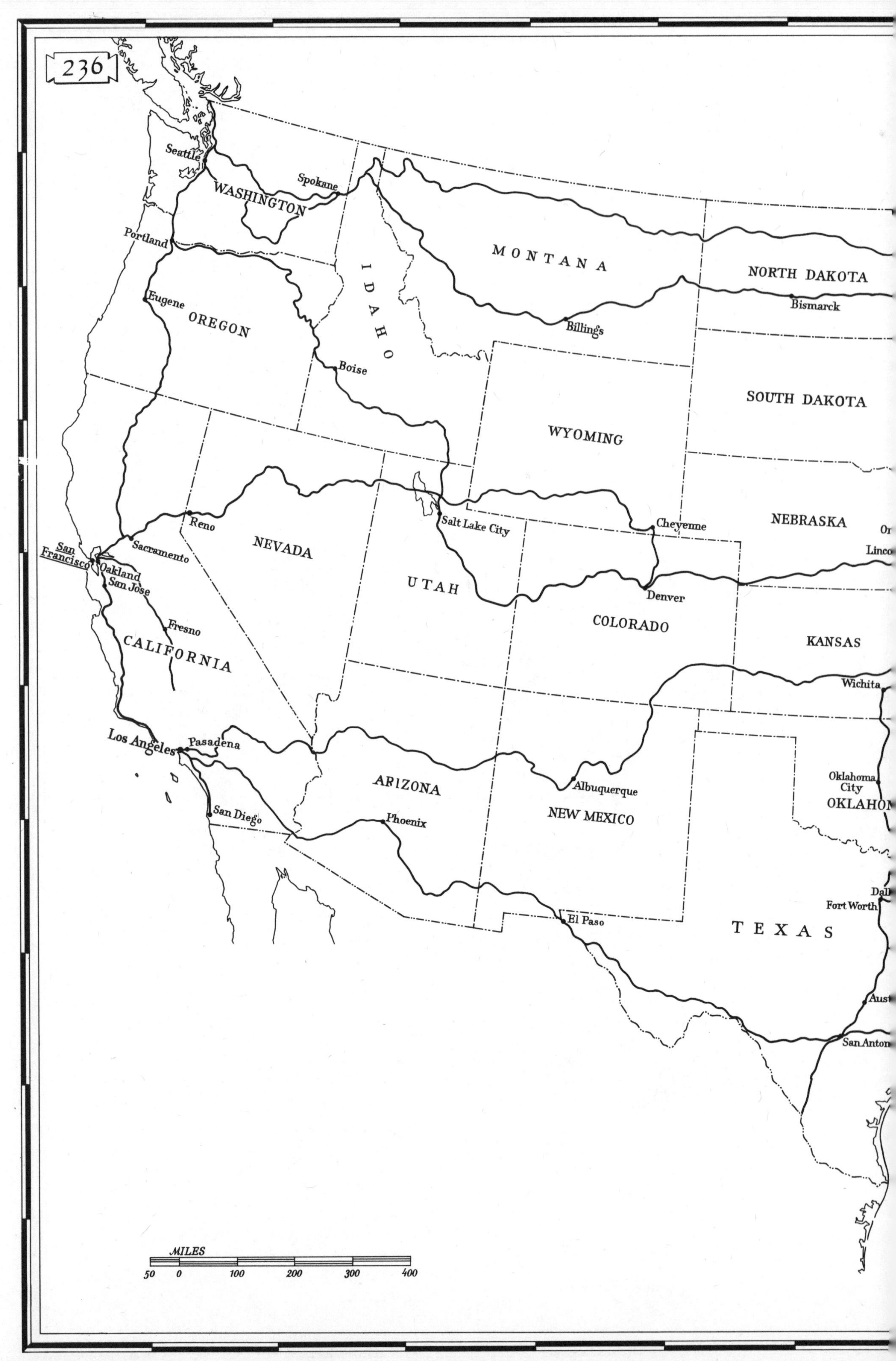
Seattle
Spokane
WASHINGTON
Portland
MONTANA
NORTH DAKOTA
IDAHO
Eugene
OREGON
Billings
Bismarck
Boise
SOUTH DAKOTA
WYOMING
NEBRASKA
Salt Lake City
Reno
Cheyenne
San Francisco
Sacramento
NEVADA
Oakland
San Jose
UTAH
Denver
Fresno
COLORADO
CALIFORNIA
KANSAS
Wichita
Los Angeles
Pasadena
ARIZONA
Albuquerque
Oklahoma City
San Diego
Phoenix
NEW MEXICO
Fort Worth
El Paso
TEXAS
San Anton
MILES
50 0 100 200 300 400

RAILROAD PASSENGER LINES 1977

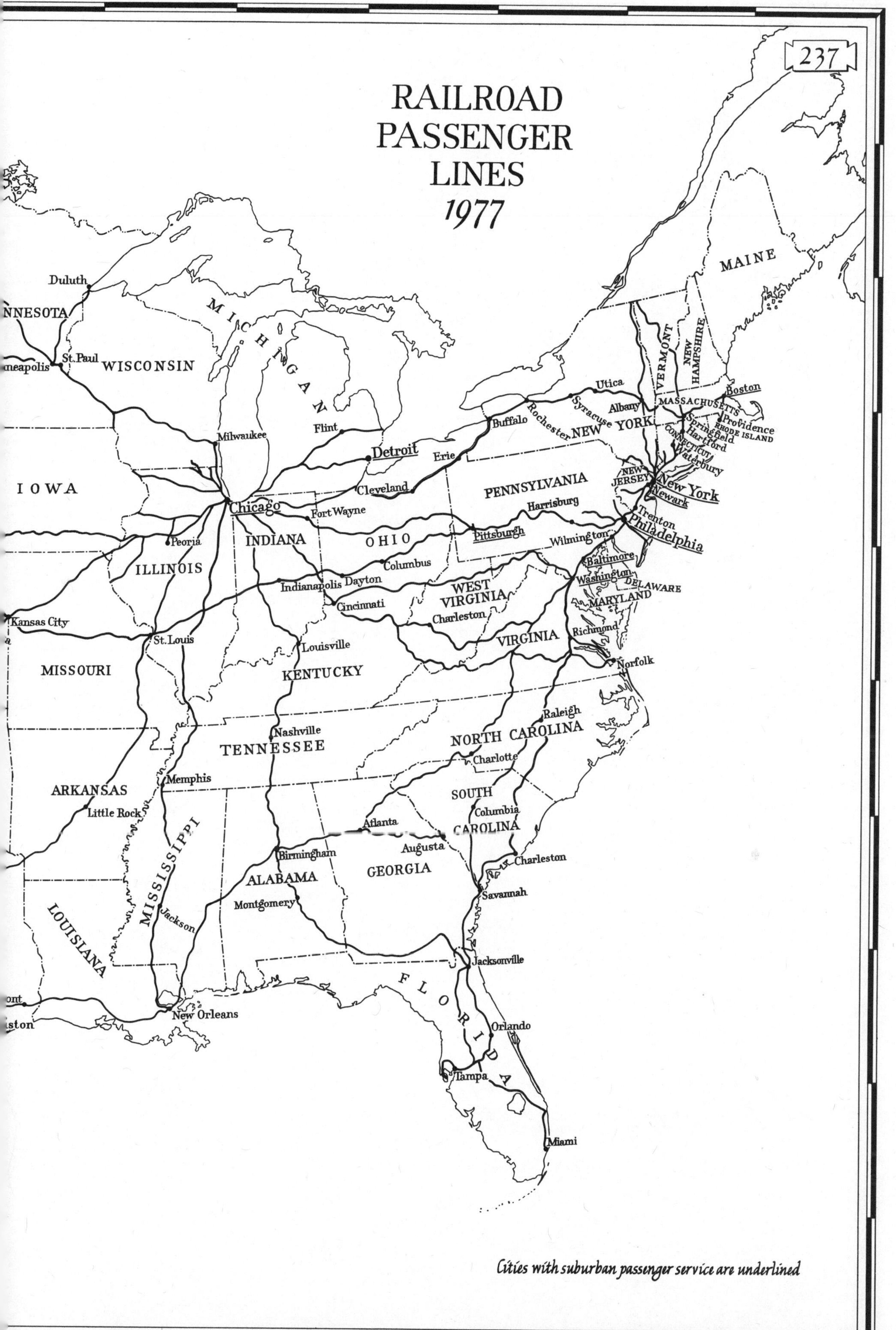

Cities with suburban passenger service are underlined

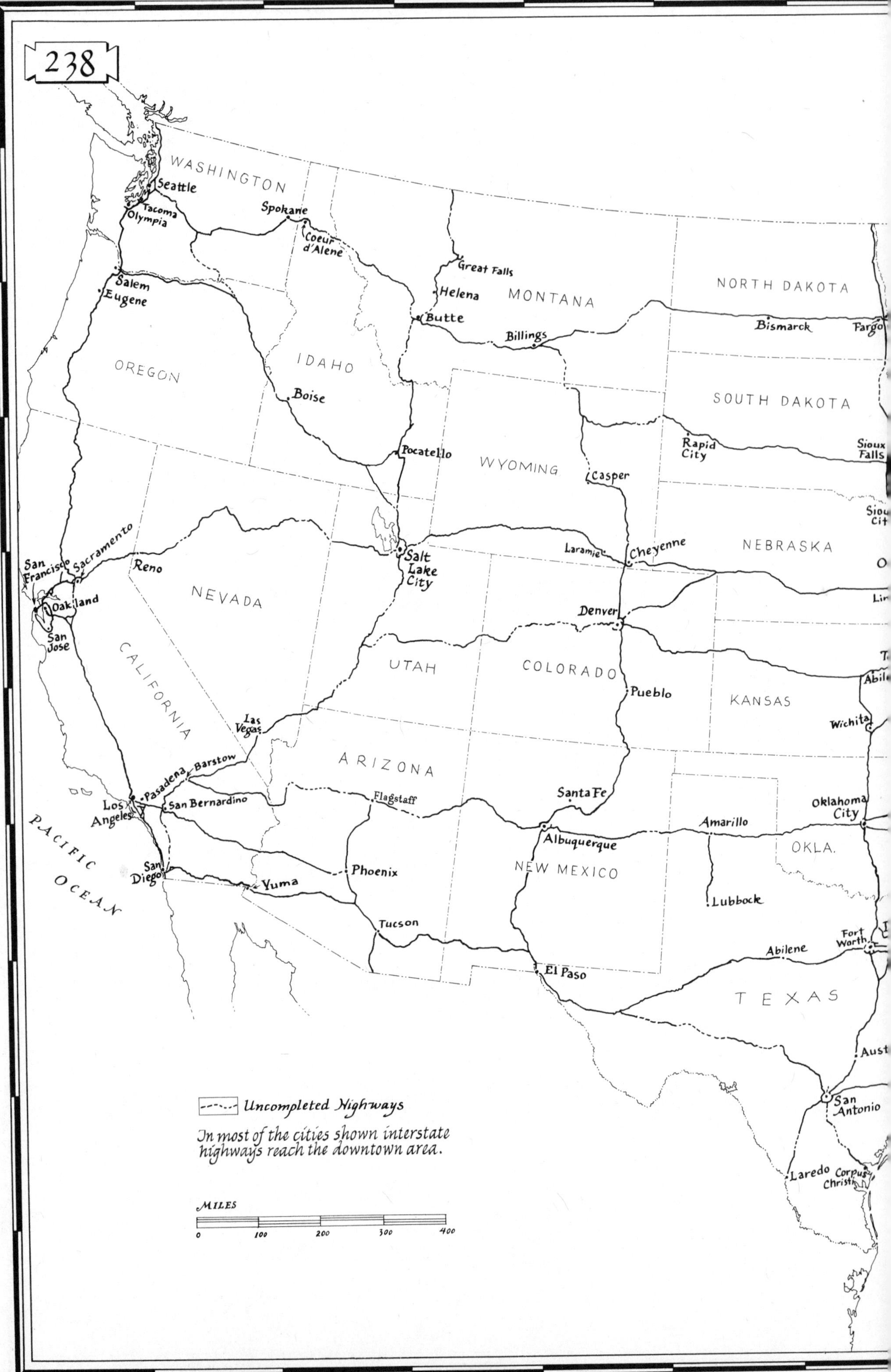
WASHINGTON
Seattle
Tacoma
Olympia
Spokane
Coeur d'Alene
Great Falls
Helena
MONTANA
Butte
Billings
NORTH DAKOTA
Bismarck
Fargo
Salem
Eugene
OREGON
IDAHO
Boise
SOUTH DAKOTA
Rapid City
Sioux Falls
Pocatello
WYOMING
Casper
NEBRASKA
Laramie
Cheyenne
San Francisco
Sacramento
Reno
Salt Lake City
Oakland
NEVADA
San Jose
Denver
UTAH
COLORADO
CALIFORNIA
Pueblo
KANSAS
Wichita
Las Vegas
ARIZONA
Barstow
Pasadena
San Bernardino
Los Angeles
Flagstaff
Santa Fe
Oklahoma City
Amarillo
Albuquerque
OKLA.
PACIFIC OCEAN
San Diego
Phoenix
Yuma
NEW MEXICO
Lubbock
Tucson
Fort Worth
Abilene
El Paso
TEXAS
San Antonio
Laredo
Corpus Christi
Uncompleted Highways
In most of the cities shown interstate highways reach the downtown area.
MILES
0
100
200
300
400

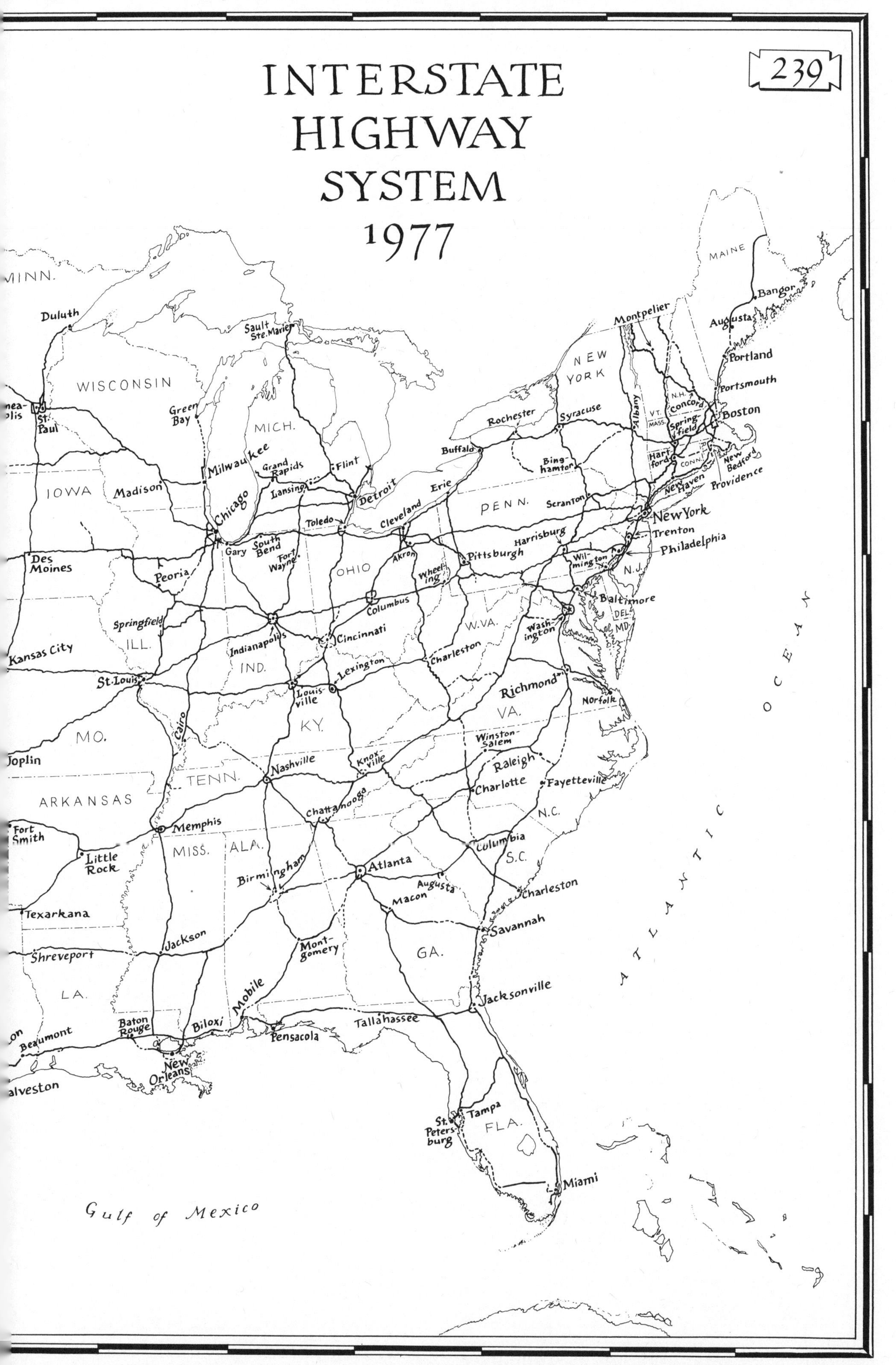
INTERSTATE HIGHWAY SYSTEM 1977
MINN.
Duluth
WISCONSIN
Sault Ste. Marie
Green Bay
MICH.
Milwaukee
Grand Rapids
Flint
Lansing
Detroit
Madison
IOWA
Chicago
Gary
South Bend
Fort Wayne
Toledo
Cleveland
Erie
Buffalo
Rochester
Syracuse
NEW YORK
Albany
Montpelier
MAINE
Bangor
Augusta
Portland
Portsmouth
N.H.
Concord
VT.
MASS.
Boston
Springfield
Hartford
CONN.
New Bedford
Providence
New Haven
Binghamton
Scranton
PENN.
New York
Trenton
Philadelphia
Harrisburg
Pittsburgh
Akron
Wheeling
Wilmington
N.J.
Baltimore
DEL.
MD.
Washington
W.VA.
OHIO
Columbus
Des Moines
Peoria
Springfield
ILL.
Indianapolis
Cincinnati
Kansas City
IND.
Charleston
St. Louis
Louisville
Lexington
Richmond
Norfolk
VA.
KY.
MO.
Cairo
Joplin
Winston-Salem
Raleigh
Nashville
Knoxville
TENN.
Charlotte
Fayetteville
ARKANSAS
N.C.
Chattanooga
Fort Smith
Memphis
Columbia
Little Rock
MISS.
ALA.
Atlanta
S.C.
Birmingham
Augusta
Charleston
Macon
Texarkana
Savannah
Jackson
Montgomery
GA.
Shreveport
LA.
Mobile
Jacksonville
Baton Rouge
Biloxi
Tallahassee
Beaumont
Pensacola
New Orleans
Galveston
Tampa
St. Petersburg
FLA.
Miami
Gulf of Mexico
ATLANTIC OCEAN

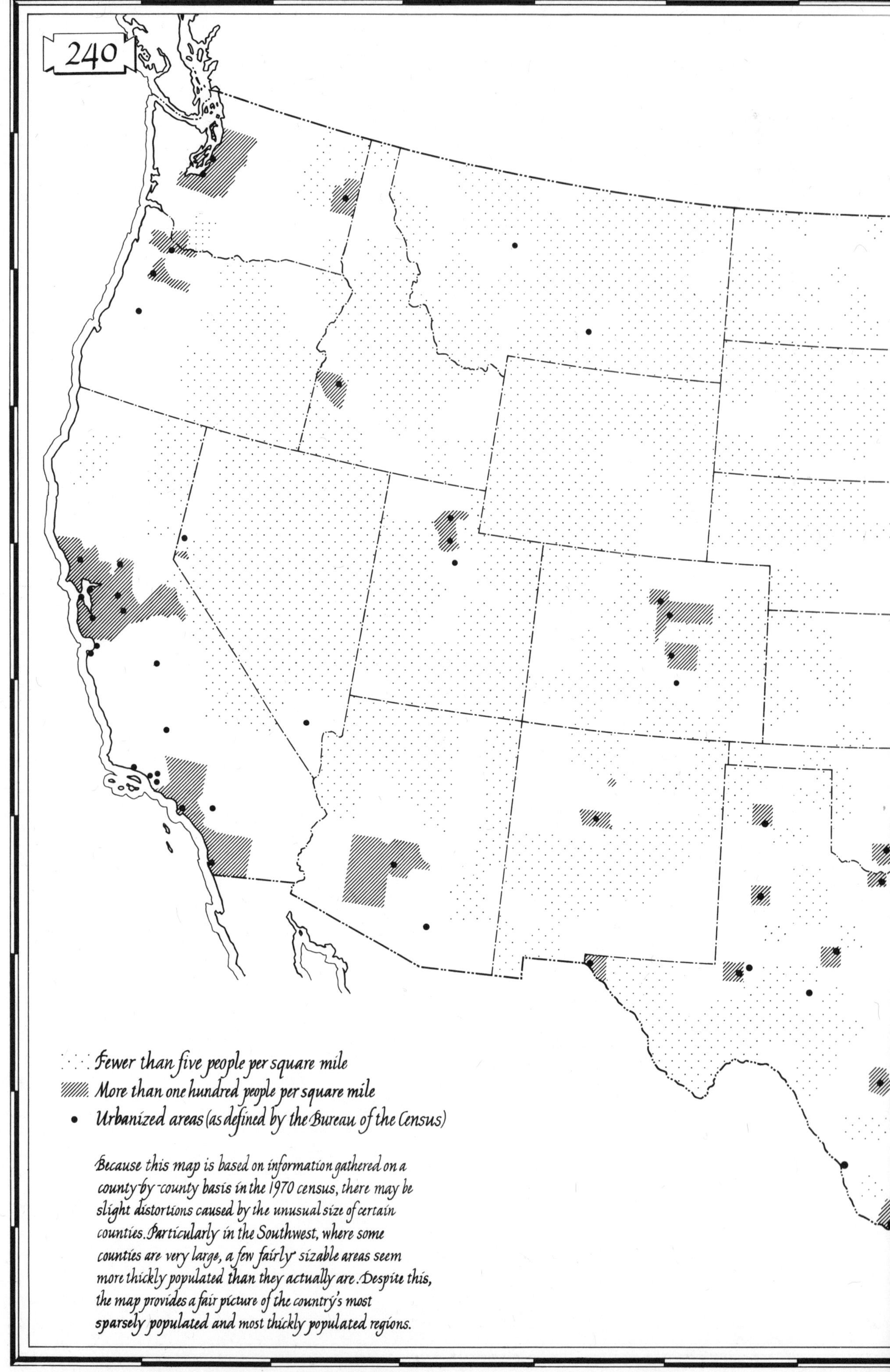

Fewer than five people per square mile
More than one hundred people per square mile
Urbanized areas (as defined by the Bureau of the Census)
Because this map is based on information gathered on a county-by-county basis in the 1970 census, there may be slight distortions caused by the unusual size of certain counties. Particularly in the Southwest, where some counties are very large, a few fairly sizable areas seem more thickly populated than they actually are. Despite this, the map provides a fair picture of the country's most sparsely populated and most thickly populated regions.

POPULATION DENSITY *IN THE* CONTINENTAL U.S., 1970

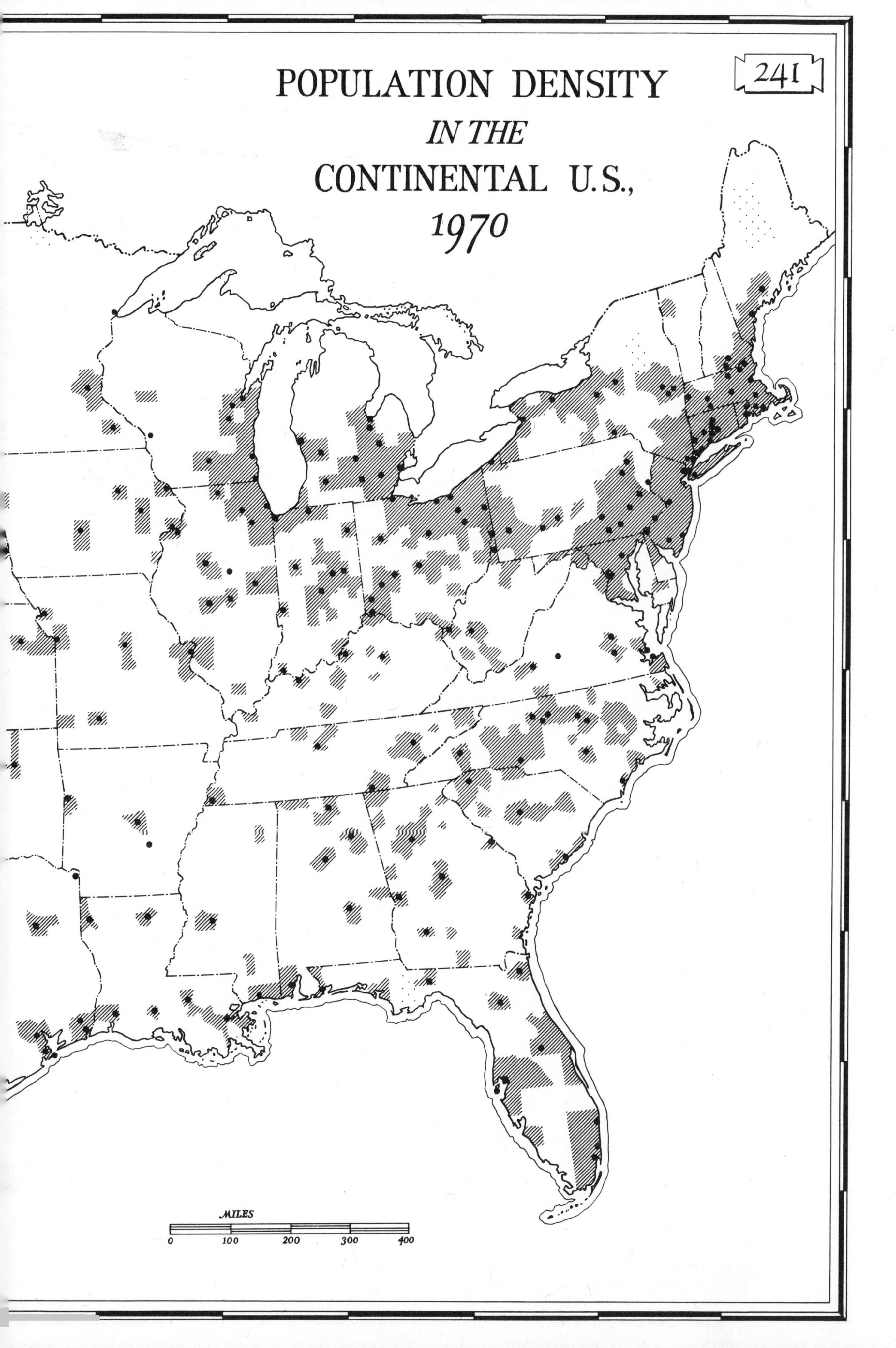

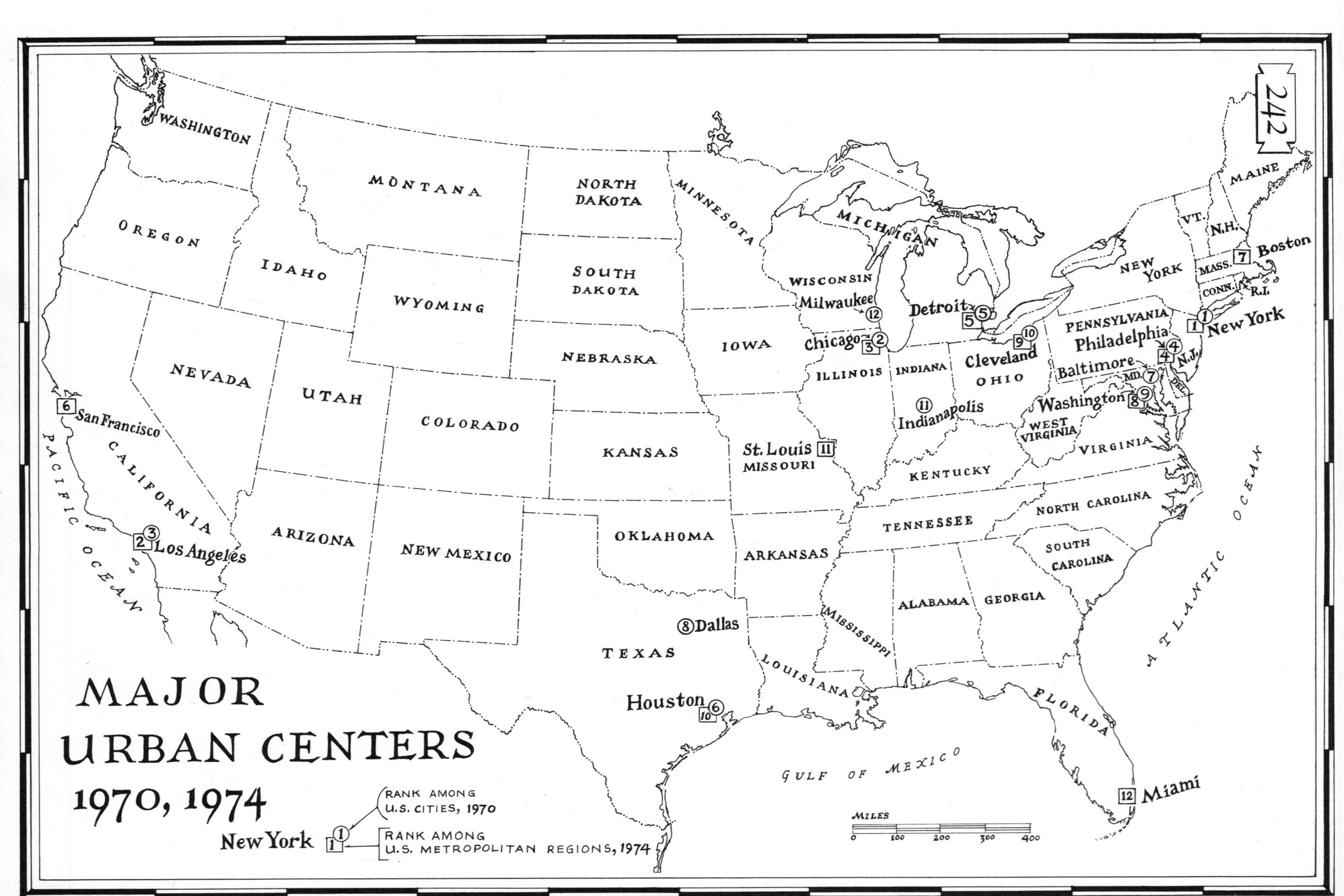
MAJOR URBAN CENTERS 1970, 1974
RANK AMONG U.S. CITIES, 1970
RANK AMONG U.S. METROPOLITAN REGIONS, 1974
New York 1 1
WASHINGTON
OREGON
CALIFORNIA
NEVADA
IDAHO
MONTANA
WYOMING
UTAH
ARIZONA
COLORADO
NEW MEXICO
NORTH DAKOTA
SOUTH DAKOTA
NEBRASKA
KANSAS
OKLAHOMA
TEXAS
MINNESOTA
IOWA
MISSOURI
ARKANSAS
LOUISIANA
WISCONSIN
ILLINOIS
MICHIGAN
INDIANA
OHIO
KENTUCKY
TENNESSEE
MISSISSIPPI
ALABAMA
GEORGIA
FLORIDA
SOUTH CAROLINA
NORTH CAROLINA
VIRGINIA
WEST VIRGINIA
PENNSYLVANIA
NEW YORK
MD.
DEL.
N.J.
CONN.
R.I.
MASS.
VT.
N.H.
MAINE
6 San Francisco
3 2 Los Angeles
8 Dallas
6 10 Houston
St. Louis 11
Milwaukee 12
Chicago 2 3
Detroit 5 5
Indianapolis 11
Cleveland 9 10
Philadelphia 4 4
Baltimore 7
Washington 9 8
1 1 New York
7 Boston
12 Miami
PACIFIC OCEAN
GULF OF MEXICO
ATLANTIC OCEAN
MILES
0 100 200 300 400

INDEX

This Index is designed to serve two main purposes. First, it enables the user of the *Atlas* to turn, quickly and definitely, to the map or maps on which a given location is shown.

Second, it serves as a cross reference, enabling the user of the work to follow, from map to map, the development of areas in succeeding periods of our history. Thus, the advance of the frontier may be visualized; or the evolution of a Territory, in its changing extents, may be followed through to the final creation of the State; or the migrations and removals of the various Indian tribes may be traced.

In the indexing of historical locations some inconsistencies are inevitable. An Indian village of the time of DeSoto can scarcely be listed as being in a present-day state. On the other hand, Harpers Ferry was important historically long before the existence of the state of West Virginia; Vincennes was a French frontier post sixty years before the Territory of Indiana was formed; yet, for the purposes of an index, it would be confusing to identify these places other than in their present states. Again, as between towns which have had a continuing existence and those which have disappeared or which are not direct descendants of existing towns of the same name, a distinction in the form of listing is desirable—although the basis for decision is often very slight indeed.

Also, there is the matter of spellings, accents and possessives. No uniformity existed, nor is it the province of an atlas of American history to establish uniformity, but rather, in each case, to follow the form most used over the greatest period of time, and, where distinct variations occur, to list those variations with a reference to the form used.

Thus, without departing too greatly from consistency, the editors, in compiling the following Index, have endeavored to so list each location that it may be readily found in the Index—from which the user will turn to the proper map, where the status of the place, during the period of the map, will be amply evident.

INDEX

ATLAS OF AMERICAN HISTORY
CSS